BRIEF CONTENTS

NEW Achieve FOR *MODERN PRINCIPLES:* MACROECONOMICS

Engage Every Student with Achieve

Achieve is a comprehensive set of interconnected teaching and assessment tools. It incorporates the most effective elements from Macmillan's market-leading solutions in a single, easy-to-use platform. Our resources were co-designed with instructors and students, using a foundation of learning research and rigorous testing.

MARGINAL REVOLUTION UNIVERSITY

Enhance Your Experience with Engaging Videos from Marginal Revolution University

The fifth edition of *Modern Principles* continues to feature the unique partnership between Macmillan Learning and Marginal Revolution University (MRU). Founded by Tyler Cowen and Alex Tabarrok as an instructional extension of their world-renowned Marginal Revolution blog, MRU features perhaps the most extensive series of economics education videos available. More than 150 of these videos have been deeply integrated into the text and pedagogy of *Modern Principles*, extending the authors' perspectives into the online learning space, and providing valuable tools for both instructors and students throughout the learning path.

This unprecedented system consists of three types of video:

MRU

mru.org/intro-econ

PRINCIPLES ECONOMICS

Meet Your Authors

▲ Students can watch these videos within the e-book itself or access them via short URLs found within the text.

1. **Engagement Videos**: Providing a succinct (5–7 minutes) overview of topics within the chapter, the authors themselves show just how economics impacts the daily lives of students.
   - Best assigned prior to class to help introduce new topics, each engagement video features a short, auto-graded quiz to help students recall the information for class time.

2. **Lecture Videos**: Designed to complement coverage in the text, these videos are slightly longer (7–10 minutes) than engagement videos, and feature straightforward exposition of topics by the authors.
   - Lecture Videos can be used as a remediation tool for students, helping fill knowledge gaps that may persist after class time and/or reading the book.
   - Lecture Videos are also ideal for online or distance learning courses. Instructors can assign these videos, along with the accompanying auto-graded quiz, to cover material in greater depth or explore topics outside of those covered during "class time."

3. **Office Hours Videos**: The direct result of feedback from both instructors and students since the launch of MRU, Office Hours videos feature a staff economist working through some of the more intricate problems and models found in the book—another great remediation tool that can make for more efficient student/instructor interactions.

At the conclusion of the end-of-chapter problems, you will find a complete list of the MRU videos for that chapter. Each video listing contains a shortened

URL to that video (live links within Achieve), as well as an inventory of the end-of-chapter problems that pertain to that particular video.

Here are just a few of our favorite videos available with *Modern Principles*. Enjoy!

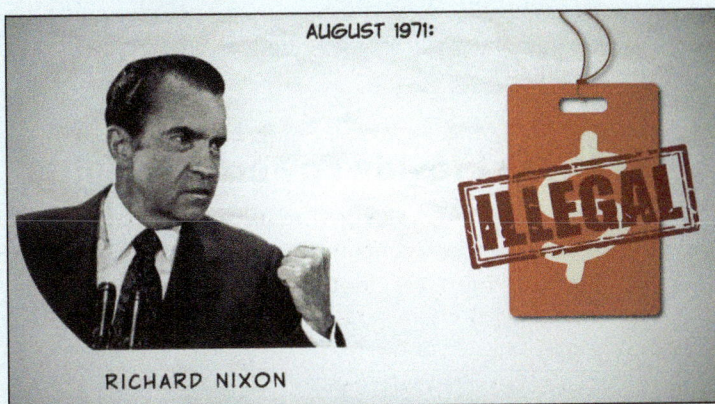

▲ See **Chapter 5** for **Price Ceilings: The U.S. Economy Flounders in the 1970s (mru.org/price-ceilings).**

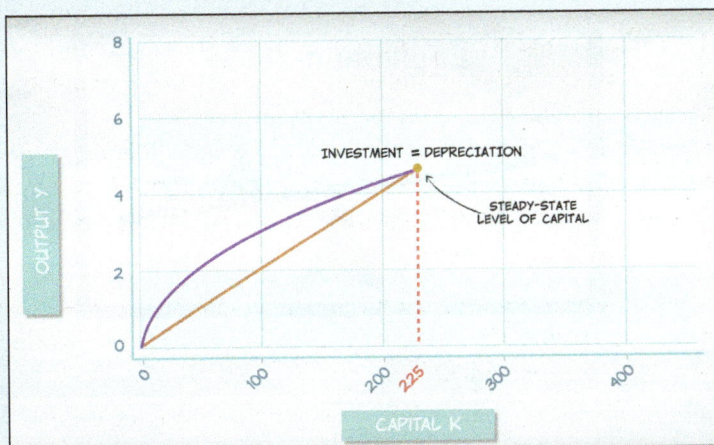

▲ See **Chapter 8** for **The Solow Model and the Steady State (mru.org/solow-steady-state).**

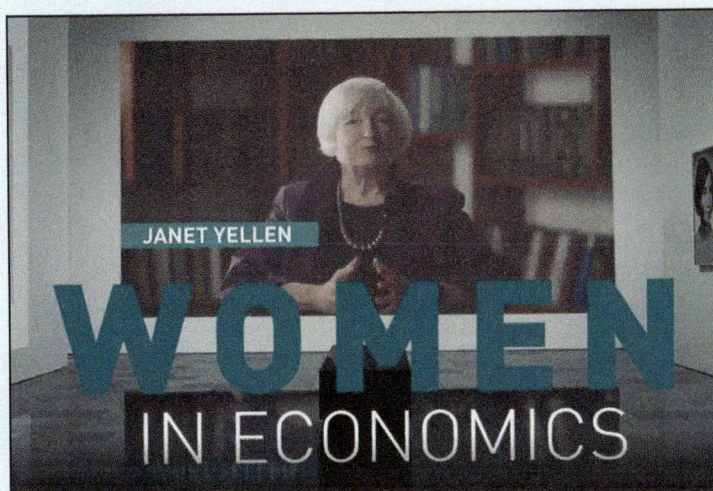

▲ See **Chapter 16** for a new video on **Women In Economics: Janet Yellen (mru.org/yellen).**

Achieve

Everything You Need in a Single Learning Path

Achieve is an online learning system that supports students and instructors at every step, from the first point of contact with new content to demonstrating mastery of concepts and skills. Powerful resources including an integrated e-book, robust homework, and a wealth of interactives create an extraordinary learning resource for students.

Learning Objectives Provide Powerful Insights

Every asset you can assign in Achieve is tagged to a learning objective. Insights and reporting help instructors and students understand how they are performing against objectives, enabling more efficient and effective interventions.

PRE-CLASS

▶ **Pre-Class Tutorials with Bridge Questions** Developed by two pioneers in active-learning methods—Eric Chiang, Florida Atlantic University, and José Vazquez, University of Illinois at Urbana-Champaign—pre-class tutorials foster basic understanding of core economic concepts before students ever set foot in class. Students watch pre-lecture videos and complete bridge questions that prepare them to engage in class. Instructors receive data about student comprehension that can inform the lecture preparation.

◀ **LearningCurve Adaptive Quizzing** With a game-like interface, this popular and effective quizzing engine offers students a low-stakes way to brush up on concepts and help identify knowledge gaps. Questions are linked to relevant e-book sections, providing both the incentive to read and a framework for an efficient reading experience.

◀ **Instructor Activity Guides** These guides provide instructors with a structured plan to facilitate an activity that encourages student engagement in both face-to-face and remote learning courses. Each guide is based on a single topic and allows students to participate through questions, group work, presentations, and/or simulations. The guide displays the activity type, estimated prep and class time, implementation

---

Class Discussion, Remote Learning Activity

Instructor Activity Guide: Experimental Derivation of a Demand Curve

Best For
Small Classes; Remote Instruction

🕐 **Class Time**
40 minutes

Implementation Effort
Moderate

△ **Bloom's Taxonomy**
Apply

Activity Summary

In this activity, the instructor conducts a live auction for two drinks. Student responses are recorded to create a demand schedule and demand curve. The class then discusses factors that may shift the demand curve.

For video conferencing lectures (synchronous learning):

1. Use iClicker Cloud to record answers in real time. Prior to the lecture, set up a series of questions in iClicker Cloud which emulates the same responses you would expect to receive from a face-to-face class. Go over the instructions for the game, and then have students respond using the iClicker app. Some games may be more interesting if you repeat them a few times to see how students change their answers as they learn how their peers respond.
2. Some games only work if student answers are hidden from the class so have students submit their answers via a private chat to you or email. Then, reveal to the class how everyone responded.

Resources for this Activity

🖥 Clicker Questions for Experimental Derivation of a Demand Curve
⤓ Download

Recommended Tools

🌐 iClicker Cloud

Two drinks (such as Coke or coffee)

---

instructions, suggestions for remote implementation where applicable, and Learning Objectives and Bloom's Level for ease of use. Our Instructor Activity Guides encourage engagement from a Pre-Class Reflection question to prime student interest and offer follow-up clicker questions to measure comprehension.

POST-CLASS

Interactive E-Book The Achieve e-book allows students to highlight and take notes; instructors can choose to assign sections of the e-book as part of their course assignments. The e-book includes embedded MRU videos as well as step-by-step graphs for complex figures.

Step-by-Step Graphs Available in the e-book, step-by-step graphs mirror how an instructor constructs graphs in the classroom. By breaking down the process into its components, these graphs create more manageable "chunks" for students to understand each step of the process.

▶ **Discovering Data**
These exercises require students to use the Federal Reserve Economic Database (FRED) related to the concepts discussed in the chapter. Students will get practical experience manipulating data by being asked, for example, to track the impact of a sales tax on tobacco sales. In working these problems, students will gain a greater understanding of core concepts while also working with an impressive data resource.

Supply and Demand — Ask FRED

The accompanying graph shows the global price of crude oil using several series over the 2006–2010 period. The 2008–2009 recession is shown by the shaded area.

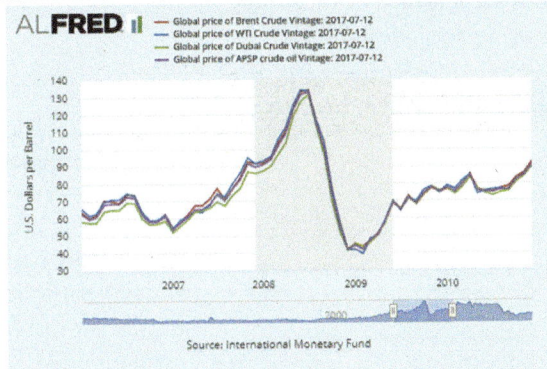

Source: International Monetary Fund

Which of the following likely caused demand to decrease for crude oil during the last recession?

○ The population decreased.
○ Consumer incomes decreased.
○ The price of oil complements increased.
○ The price of oil substitutes decreased.

◀ **Work It Out** These skill-building activities pair sample end-of-chapter problems with targeted feedback and video explanations to help students solve problems step by step. This approach allows students to work independently, tests their comprehension of concepts, and prepares them for class and exams.

▶ **End-of-Chapter Questions** Developed by economists active in the classroom, these multistep questions are adapted from problems found in the text. Each problem is paired with rich feedback for incorrect and correct responses that guide students through the process of problem solving. These questions also feature our user-friendly graphing tool, designed so students focus entirely on economics and not on how to use the application.

EconoFact Analysis Macmillan Learning has partnered with EconoFact to bring incisive and accessible analysis of current economic and policy trends into the economics classroom. The EconoFact Network provides even-handed and timely analysis of economic issues drawing on relevant data, historical experience, and well-regarded economic frameworks presented in the form of a short memo. In Achieve, instructors can access in-class activity guides to help integrate the memos into their own lectures. Instructors can also access and assign assessment on each memo that starts with basic reading comprehension and builds up to applying the analytical tools students have learned in their course to the economic or policy issue covered in the memo.

Homework Curated homework problems feature algorithmically generated variables and our user-friendly graphing tool. These problems are multistep with a variety of answer inputs—each with detailed and targeted feedback specific to that answer.

Practice Quizzes Designed to be used as a study tool, these quizzes feature questions from the Test Bank and allow for multiple attempts as students familiarize themselves with content.

Powerful Support for Instructors

Test Bank This comprehensive Test Bank contains multiple-choice and short-answer questions to help instructors assess students' comprehension, interpretation, and ability to synthesize.

Lecture Slides These brief, interactive, and visually interesting slides are designed to hold students' attention in class with graphics and animations demonstrating key concepts and real-world examples.

Clicker Slides These slides contain questions to incorporate active learning in the classroom. Students can participate by using the iClicker app on their smartphone or laptop.

Instructor's Resource Manual
The Instructor's Resource Manual offers instructors teaching materials and tips to enhance the classroom experience, along with chapter objectives, outlines, and a breakdown of the large library of MRU videos.

Solutions Manual The Solutions Manual contains detailed solutions to all end-of-chapter problems from the textbook.

Gradebook Assignment scores are collected into a comprehensive gradebook providing instructors reporting on individuals and overall course performance.

LMS Integration LMS Integration is included so that all students' scores in Achieve can easily integrate into a school's learning management system and that an instructor's gradebook and roster are always in sync.

iClicker Integration With Achieve's seamless integration with iClicker, you can help any student participate—in the classroom or virtually. iClicker's attendance feature gets students in class, then instructors can choose from flexible polling and quizzing options to engage, check understanding, and get feedback from students in real time. iClicker also allows students

to participate using laptops, mobile devices, or iClicker remotes—whichever each student prefers. Additionally, we offer Instructor Activity Guides and book-specific iClicker question slides within Achieve to make the most out of your class time. It's no surprise that over a decade after being founded by educators, iClicker still leads the market. And thousands of instructors continue to give every student a voice with our simple, award-winning student engagement solutions.

Customer Support Our Achieve Client Success Specialist Team—dedicated platform experts—provides collaboration, software expertise, and consulting to tailor each course to fit your instructional goals and student needs. Start with a demo at a time that works for you to learn more about how to set up your customized course. Talk to your sales representative or visit https://www.macmillanlearning.com/college/us/contact-us/training-and-demos for more information.

Pricing and bundling options are available at the Macmillan student store: store.macmillanlearning.com/

WHAT'S NEW IN THE FIFTH EDITION?

We take our title, *Modern Principles of Economics*, seriously. When it comes to new editions, we don't just add a box or two—we rewrite entire chapters with new examples and applications, and we cut older material to make way for the new.

Pandemics are not new to *Modern Principles*. In the very first edition, we included pandemics as a potential generator of negative real shock to long-run aggregate supply. We also warned in our chapter on trade that it was unwise to outsource the vaccine supply to other countries as there might not be enough to go around. We have updated these elements to acknowledge the COVID-19 pandemic.

Why Are There Fewer Working Age Men in the Labor Force?

In **Chapter 11, Unemployment and Labor Force Participation,** we have an extensive new section on this worrying trend, the decline of the labor force participation by working age men. It's a great question to examine because economists haven't reached a consensus on answers. Are high welfare payments to blame? Lower wages? Changing societal roles for men and women? We illustrate how an economist uses models like supply and demand to interpret the data and to suggest hypotheses to test. In *Modern Principles,* we try to illustrate the economic way of thinking rather than to present a fixed set of conclusions..

▶ See **Chapter 11** to see how supply and demand can help explain the decline in the male labor force participation rate.

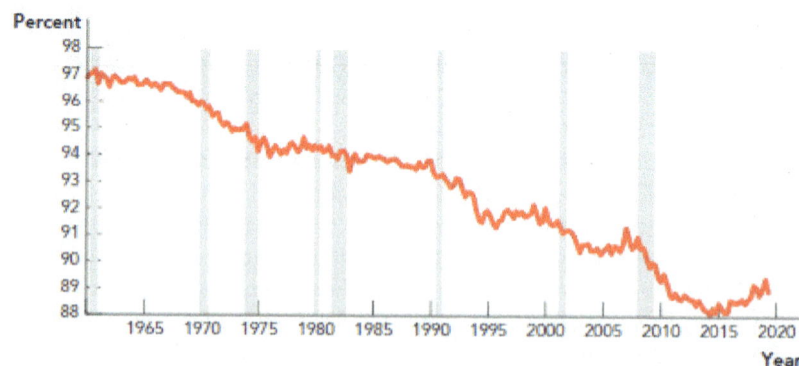

The Slowly but Steadily Declining Male Labor Force Rate

Data from: OECD, Main Economic Indicators—complete database, Main Economic Indicators (database), http://dx.doi.org/10.1787/data-00052-en; https://fred.stlouisfed.org/graph/?g=p5vm.

Supply Chains and Bottlenecks

During the COVID-19 pandemic in the United States, a lack of nasal swabs slowed the rollout of testing and many people feared that there wouldn't be enough glass vials to distribute a coronavirus vaccine to billions of people. Thus, the inability to quickly produce more of a single item created discoordination throughout the entire economy. Similarly, shocks to a single sector can ripple up and down supply chains creating effects far from their place of origination. We discuss these issues in **Chapter 14, Transmission and Amplification Mechanisms**. This unique chapter goes beyond Aggregate Demand and Aggregate Supply to present a more sophisticated and realistic view of how demand and supply shocks are transmitted and amplified throughout the economic network.

◀ Will a lack of glass vials delay a coronavirus vaccine? See **Chapter 14** to learn how the inability to quickly produce more of item creates discoordination.

The Trade War!

The recent increase in tariffs has prompted much discussion about international trade and economists have a comparative advantage in this discussion! This increase is unprecedented in the post–World War II era and has stimulated new research on the effects of tariffs and on free trade. We draw on new research on the tariffs and the preceding "China Shock" to rewrite **Chapter 19, International Trade**. In this chapter, we also cover how the shortage of masks has impacted trade and national security during the COVID-19 pandemic. We have the most relevant and timely chapter on international trade in the textbook business!

HUGH THRELFALL/ALAMY

◀ See **Chapter 19** to find out why Nintendo recently switched production from China to Vietnam.

Our goal in *Modern Principles* is to apply the principles of economics to important questions and these new changes illustrate that goal in action. These are just some of the major changes to *Modern Principles*. You will also find lots of changes to our chapter on the federal budget, due to the recent tax law changes; more material on political economy throughout and in our political economy chapter; and updated graphs and data throughout.

MODERN PRINCIPLES: MACROECONOMICS

Fifth Edition

Tyler Cowen
George Mason University

Alex Tabarrok
George Mason University

macmillan international
HIGHER EDUCATION

Senior Vice President, Content Strategy: Charles Linsmeier
Program Director: Shani Fisher
Senior Executive Program Manager: Carolyn Merrill
Senior Development Editor: Lukia Kliossis
Director of Media Editorial, Social Sciences: Noel Hohnstine
Senior Media Editor: Lindsay Neff
Assistant Editor: Amanda Gaglione
Marketing Manager: Clay Bolton
Marketing Assistant: Steven Huang
Media Project Manager: Andrew Vaccaro
Assessment Manager: Kristyn Brown
Senior Assessment Editor: Joshua Hill
Director of Content Management Enhancement: Tracey Kuehn
Senior Managing Editor: Lisa Kinne
Senior Content Project Manager: Edgar Doolan
Director of Design, Content Management: Diana Blume
Design Services Manager: Natasha A.S. Wolfe
Executive Permissions Editor: Robin Fadool
Permissions Project Manager: Richard Fox
Senior Workflow Project Manager: Paul Rohloff
Production Supervisor: Robert Cherry
Composition: Lumina Datamatics, Inc.
Printing and Binding: King Printing Co., Inc.

ISBN-13: 978-1-319-38400-5
ISBN-10: 1-319-38400-5

Printed in the United States of America
2 3 4 5 6   25 24 23 22 21

WORTH PUBLISHERS
One New York Plaza
Suite 4600
New York, NY 10004-1562
www.macmillanlearning.com

Economics is the study of how to get the most out of life.

Tyler and Alex

ABOUT THE AUTHORS

ALEX TABARROK

Tyler Cowen (left, in North Korea) is Holbert C. Harris Professor of Economics at George Mason University. His latest book is *Big Business.* With Alex Tabarrok, he writes an economics blog at MarginalRevolution.com. He has published in the *American Economic Review, Journal of Political Economy,* and many other economics journals. He also writes regularly for the popular press, including the *New York Times,* the *Washington Post, Forbes,* the *Wilson Quarterly, Money Magazine,* and many other outlets.

Alex Tabarrok (right, in South Korea) is Bartley J. Madden Chair in Economics at the Mercatus Center at George Mason University. His latest book is *Launching the Innovation Renaissance.* His research looks at bounty hunters, judicial incentives and elections, crime control, patent reform, methods to increase the supply of human organs for transplant, and the regulation of pharmaceuticals. He is the editor of the books *Entrepreneurial Economics: Bright Ideas from the Dismal Science* and *The Voluntary City: Choice, Community, and Civil Society,* among others. His papers have appeared in the *Journal of Law and Economics, Public Choice, Economic Inquiry,* the *Journal of Health Economics,* the *Journal of Theoretical Politics,* the *American Law and Economics Review,* and many others. Popular articles have appeared in the *New York Times,* the *Wall Street Journal, Forbes,* and many other magazines and newspapers.

PREFACE: TO THE INSTRUCTOR

> The prisoners were dying of scurvy, typhoid fever, and smallpox, but nothing was killing them more than bad incentives.

That is the opening from Chapter 1 of *Modern Principles*, and only an economist could write such a sentence. Only an economist could see that incentives are operating just about everywhere, shaping every aspect of our lives, whether it be how good a job you get, how much wealth an economy produces, and, yes, how a jail is run and how well the prisoners are treated. We are excited about this universal and powerful applicability of economics, and we have written this book to get you excited too.

In the first four editions, we wanted to accomplish several things. We wanted to show the power of economics for understanding our world. We wanted to create a book full of vivid writing and powerful stories. We wanted to present modern economics, not the musty doctrines or repetitive examples of a generation ago. We wanted to show—again and again—that incentives matter, whether discussing the tragedy of the commons, political economy, or what economics has to say about wise investing. Most generally, we wanted to make the invisible hand visible, namely to show that there is a hidden order behind the world that can be illuminated by economics.

Guiding Principles and Innovations: In a Nutshell

Modern Principles offers the following features and benefits:

1. We teach the economic way of thinking.
2. Less is more. This is a textbook of *principles*, not a survey or an encyclopedia. We use fewer yet more consistent and more comprehensive models.
3. No tools without applications. Real-world vivid applications are used to develop theory. Applications are not pushed aside into distracting boxes that students do not read.
4. Today's students live in a globalized economy. Events in China, India, Europe, and the Middle East affect their lives. *Modern Principles* features international examples and applications throughout, rather than just segregating all of the international topics in a single chapter.
5. *Modern Principles* has a more intuitive development of markets and their interconnectedness than does any other textbook. More than any other textbook, we teach students how the *price system* works.
6. *Modern Principles* helps students to see the invisible hand. We offer an intuitive proof of several "invisible hand theorems." For example, we show that through the operation of incentives and the price system, well-functioning markets will minimize the aggregate sum of the costs of production even though no one intends this result. Local knowledge creates a global benefit.
7. Other textbooks do not offer a balanced treatment of real business cycle theory and New Keynesian theory, instead favoring one theory and

relegating the other to a few pages that are poorly integrated with the overall macro model. In contrast, we believe that adequately explaining business fluctuations, unemployment, and both the potential and limits of monetary and fiscal policy requires a balanced but unified treatment that draws on ideas from both models.

8. Why are some nations rich and other nations poor? *Modern Principles* has more material on development and growth than any other principles textbook.

9. *Modern Principles* offers the most intuitive development of the Solow model of growth in any textbook, starting with Chapter 8 and continuing in the Chapter 14 appendix.

10. Financial panics and asset bubbles are covered—a topic of great interest in today's environment! In fact, we included substantial material on banking panics, bubbles, wealth shocks, and the importance of financial intermediation in the very first draft of *Modern Principles*. Our book incorporates these topics from the ground floor rather than squeezing the material into boxes or appended paragraphs. There are separate and comprehensive chapters on financial intermediation (Chapter 9) and on the stock market (Chapter 10).

11. *Modern Principles* explains how fiscal and monetary policy work differently, depending on whether the shock hitting the economy is a real shock or a nominal shock.

12. We look closely at unemployment, its nature and causes, including the unusually long duration of unemployment experienced in the United States after the financial crisis. We also look at labor force participation rates in the United States over time and around the world.

13. A modern text needs to place economics in real-world context. We don't just add boxes as we "update" our text. We write and rewrite entire chapters. In the fifth edition, for example, we rewrote large parts of the trade chapter (Chapter 19) to explain the economics and the politics of the Trump tariff. We also added to our material on pandemics (covered from the first edition!) to address COVID-19. We discuss, for example, the importance of supply chains and networks in new material in Chapter 14, Amplification and Transmission Mechanisms. We have also included brief discussions of the effects of the pandemic in our chapters on fiscal policy and the Federal budget. The pandemic is having huge effects on economies throughout the world and it may take decades before we get a true handle on all the effects but *Modern Principles* is committed to being relevant to students now.

Make the Invisible Hand Visible

One of the most remarkable discoveries of economic science is that under the right conditions the pursuit of self-interest can promote the social good. Nobel laureate Vernon Smith put it this way:

At the heart of economics is a scientific mystery . . . a scientific mystery as deep, fundamental and inspiring as that of the expanding universe or the forces that bind matter. . . . How is order produced from freedom of choice?

We want students to be inspired by this mystery and by how economists have begun to solve it. Thus, we will explain how markets generate cooperation from people across the world, how prices act as signals and coordinate appropriate responses to changes in economic conditions, and how profit maximization leads to the minimization of industry costs (even though no one intends such an end).

We strive to make the invisible hand visible, and we do so with the core idea of supply and demand as the organizing principle of economics. Thus, we start with supply and demand, including producer and consumer surplus and the two ways of reading the curves, and then we build equilibrium in its own chapter, then elasticity, then taxes and subsidies, then the price system, then price ceilings and floors, then international trade, and then externalities. All of this material is based on supply and demand so that students are continually gaining experience using the same tools to solve more and deeper problems as they proceed. The interaction of supply and demand generates market prices and quantities, which in turn lies behind the spread of information from one part of a market economy to another. Thus, we show how the invisible hand works through the *price system*.

Demonstrate the Power of Incentives

Our second goal in writing *Modern Principles of Economics* is to show—again and again—that incentives matter. In fact, incentives are the theme throughout *Modern Principles*, whether discussing the supply of oil, the effects of price controls, or the gains from international trade.

Present Modern Models and Vivid Applications

"Modern" is our third goal in writing *Modern Principles*. We knew that to reflect modern macroeconomics, we had to cover the Solow model and the economics of ideas, real business cycles, and New Keynesian economics. While most textbooks now cover the rudiments of economic growth, the importance of ideas as a driving factor is rarely even mentioned. Other textbooks do not offer a balanced treatment of real business cycle theory and New Keynesian theory, instead favoring one theory and relegating the other to a few pages that are poorly integrated with the overall macro model. In contrast, we believe that adequately explaining business fluctuations, unemployment, and both the potential and limits of monetary and fiscal policy requires a balanced but unified treatment that draws on ideas from both models.

We also knew that financial crises and bubbles are very real, and that fluctuations in output and employment are a social and economic issue around the world. In fact, we included substantial material on banking panics, bubbles, wealth shocks, and the importance of financial intermediation in the very first draft of *Modern Principles*. Our book incorporates these topics from the ground floor rather than attempting to squeeze such material into hastily added boxes or appended paragraphs.

Alternative Paths Through the Book

Modern Principles of Macroeconomics has been written with trade-offs in mind and it's easy to pick and choose from among the chapters when time constrains. We offer a few quick suggestions.

We spend more time on price controls than do other books because we don't confine ourselves to the usual shortage diagram. We illustrate the general equilibrium effects of price controls. We have also included a section of advanced material on the losses from random allocation that may be skipped in larger classes or if time constrains.

Instructors could cover only a portion of the Solow model in Chapter 8. We sometimes do this in our larger classes, so this will be a good choice for many. The chapter has been written so that the most intuitive and important aspects of the model are covered in the beginning, more difficult and detailed material in the middle may be skipped, and then important material on growth and ideas is covered toward the end of the chapter. The material in the middle may be skipped without loss of continuity. Instructors with smaller and more advanced classes can easily cover the full chapter.

One important point: It is **not** at all necessary to teach the Solow model to cover our chapters on business fluctuations. The supply side is dealt with by using a long-run aggregate supply curve, which is explained in those chapters without relying on the Solow model.

We have divided the chapters on macroeconomic policy and institutions so that an instructor can cover monetary policy without covering the details of the Federal Reserve system and open market operations, and one can cover fiscal policy without covering the details of the federal budget: taxes and spending. The details are important and these chapters place monetary and fiscal policy within an institutional context, so we do not necessarily recommend this limited approach, but when time is limited, more options are better than fewer.

Finally, one could skip international finance. To us, international economics means primarily that economics can help us to understand the world, not just one country and not just one time. As a result, we have included many international examples throughout *Modern Principles*. If time constrains, the details of tariffs, exchange rates, and trade deficits may be left to another course. Alas, we live in a finite world.

Most of all, we hope that *Modern Principles* helps you, the teacher, to have fun! We love economics and we have fun teaching economics. We have written this text for people not afraid to say the same. Don't hesitate to e-mail us with your questions, thoughts, and experiences, or just to say hello!

ACKNOWLEDGMENTS

We are most grateful to the following reviewers, both users and nonusers, for their careful chapter reviews used in the development of the fifth edition of *Modern Principles*.

Lane Boyte-Eckis
Troy State University, Dothan

Sarah Estelle
Hope College

Chris Fawson
Utah State University, Logan

David Gillette
Truman State University

Kevin Gomez
Creighton University

Jeremy Groves
Northern Illinois University, DeKalb

Joseph Guider
Caldwell College

Sheryl Hadley
Johnson City Community College

Rik Hafer
Lindenwood University, St. Charles

Timothy Harris
Illinois State University

Alexander Hill
Arizona State University

Russell Kashian
University of Wisconsin, Whitewater

Onur Kesten
Carnegie Mellon University

Elijah Kosse
South Dakota State University

Nakul Kumar
North Virginia Community College, Alexandria

David Lanzilla
College of Central Florida

Rob Lester
Colby College

Gary McDonnell
Northern Michigan University

Shelby Nickole Moore
Amarillo College

Eric Parsons
University of Missouri

John Robinson
James Madison University

Kyle Ross
Kansas State University

Jeff Sarbaum
University of North Carolina, Greensboro

James K. Self
Indiana University

Sara Sheikh
Calhoun Community College, Decatur

Ronald Shirley
Calhoun Community College, Huntsville

Stephen L. S. Smith
Hope College

Nathanael Snow
Ball State University

Michael Tasto
Southern New Hampshire University

Andrew Vassallo
Shippensburg University of Pennsylvania

Randall Waldron
John Brown University

Susan Watson
Texas Christian University

Michael Youngblood
Rock Valley College

And we would also like to acknowledge again the contributions of the following reviewers whose comments and suggestions helped to shape the first four editions of this text.

Rashid Al-Hmoud
Texas Tech University

Lian An
University of North Florida

Michael Applegate
Oklahoma State University

J. J. Arias
Georgia College and State University

Oz Aydemir
Broome Community College

Scott Baier
Clemson University

Justin Barnette
Kent State University

Jim Barbour
Elon University

David Beckworth
Texas State University

Robert Beekman
University of Tampa

Jodi Beggs
Northeastern University

Douglas Bice
Middle Georgia State University—Macon

James Bolchalk
Kent State University—Geauga Campus

Karla Borja
University of Tampa

Ryan Bosworth
North Carolina State University

Carter Braxton
University of Minnesota—Twin Cities

Jennifer Brown
Eastern Connecticut State University

Paul Byrne
Washburn University

Douglas Campbell
University of Memphis

Randall Campbell
Mississippi University

Michael Carew
Baruch College

Shawn Carter
Jacksonville State University

Suparna Chakraborty
Baruch College and Graduate Center, The City University of New York

Anoshua Chaudhuri
San Francisco State University

Susan Christoffersen
Philadelphia University

Philip Coelho
Ball State University

Gregory Colson
The University of Georgia

Jim Couch
North Alabama University

Scott Cunningham
University of Georgia

Manabendra Dasgupta
University of Alabama at Birmingham

Amlan Datta
Texas Tech University

John Dawson
Appalachian State University

John Deskins
West Virginia University

Timothy M. Diette
Washington and Lee University

Eva Dziadula
University of Notre Dame

Ann Eike
University of Kentucky

Harold Elder
University of Alabama

Carlos Elias
Radford University

Tisha Emerson
Baylor University

Molly Espey
Clemson University

Patricia Euzent
University of Central Florida

William Feipel
Illinois Central University

Paul Fisher
Henry Ford College

Amanda S. Freeman
Kansas State University

Gary Galles
Pepperdine University

Mallika Garg
University of Louisville

Neil Garston
California State University, Los Angeles

Pedro Gete
Georgetown University

Bill Gibson
The University of Vermont

Bob Gillette
University of Kentucky

Lynn G. Gillette
Sierra Nevada College

Gerhard Glomm
Indiana University

Christian Glupker
Grand Valley State University

Stephan F. Gohmann
University of Louisville

Michael Gootzeit
University of Memphis

Alan Grant
Baker University

Carole Green
University of South Florida

Paul Grimes
Mississippi State University

Philip J. Grossman
St. Cloud State University

Jeremy Groves
Northern Illinois University

Darrin Gulla
University of Kentucky

Mike Hammock
Middle Tennessee State University

Kyle Hampton
The Ohio State University

Andrew Hanssen
Clemson University

Darcy Hartman
The Ohio State University

Joe Haslag
University of Missouri—Columbia

Sarah Helms
University of Alabama—Birmingham

Matthew Henry
University of Georgia

Bradley Hobbs
Florida Gulf Coast University

Paul Holmes
Ashland University

John Hsu
Contra Costa College

Jeffrey Hummel
San Jose State University

Sarah Jackson
Indiana University of Pennsylvania

Dennis Jansen
Texas A&M University

Andres Jauregui
Columbus State University

Bruce Johnson
Centre College

Veronica Kalich
Baldwin Wallace College

Lillian Kamal
University of Hartford

John Keating
University of Kansas

Logan Kelly
Bryant University

Brian Kench
University of Tampa

Jongsung Kim
Bryant University

Mikhail Kouliavstev
Stephen F. Austin State University

Kate Krause
University of New Mexico

David Kreutzer
James Madison University

Robert Krol
California State University, Northridge

Daniel Kuo
Orange Coast College

Gary Lape
Liberty University

Rodolfo Ledesma
Marian College

Jim Lee
Texas A&M University —Corpus Christi

Susane Leguizamon
Western Kentucky University

Daniel Lin
American University

Solina Lindahl
California State Polytechnic University

Melody Lo
The University of Texas at San Antonio (UTSA)

Edward Lopez
San Jose State University

Hari Luitel
St. Cloud State University

Michael Mace
Sierra College

Douglas Mackenzie
State University of New York —Plattsburgh

Michael Makowsky
Towson University

John Marcis
Coastal Carolina University

Catherina Matraves
Michigan State University

Norman Maynard
The University of Oklahoma

John Mbaku
Weber State University

Neil Meredith
West Texas A&M University

Meghan Millea
Mississippi State University

Stephen Miller
University of Nevada, Las Vegas

Ida Mirzaie
The Ohio State University

David (Mitch) Mitchell
South Alabama University

Karl A. Mitchell
Queens College, The City University of New York

Chuck Moul
Miami University (Ohio)

Ranganath Murthy
Bucknell University

Todd Myers
Grossmont College

Andre Neveu
Skidmore College

Joan Nix
Queens College, The City University of New York

Lydia Ortega
San Jose State University

Alexandre Padilla
Metropolitan State College of Denver

Zuohong Pan
Western Connecticut State University

Eric Parsons
University of Missouri

Biru Paksha Paul
State University of New York —Cortland

John Perry
Centre College

Steven Peterson
The University of Idaho

Gina C. Pieters
University of Minnesota

Dennis Placone
Clemson University

Jennifer M. Platania
Elon University

Brennan Platt
Brigham Young University

William Polley
Western Illinois University

Benjamin Powell
Suffolk University

Margaret Ray
University of Mary Washington

Dan Rickman
Oklahoma State University

Antonio Rodriguez
Texas A&M International University

Duane Rosa
West Texas A&M University

Paul Roscelli
Canada College

Kyle Ross
Kansas State University

Jason C. Rudbeck
The University of Georgia

Fred Ruppel
Eastern Kentucky University

Mikael Sandberg
University of Florida

Scott Sandok
Hennepin Technical College

Nori Sasaki
McHenry County College

Jeff Sarbaum
University of North Carolina at Greensboro

Michael Scott
University of Oklahoma

Kurt Von Seekamm
Salem State University

Angela Seidel
Saint Francis University

James Self
Indiana University

Daniel M. Settlage
The University of Arkansas —Fort Smith

David Shideler
Murray State University

Mark Showalter
Brigham Young University

Randy Simmons
Utah State University

Senad Sinanovic
Clemson University

Jennifer Sobotka
Radford University

Martin Spechler
Indiana University—Purdue University, Indianapolis

David Spencer
Brigham Young University

Richard Stahl
Louisiana State University

Dean Stansel
Florida Gulf Coast University

Liliana V. Stern
Auburn University

Kay Strong
Bowling Green State University—Firelands

Jim Swofford
University of South Alabama

Timothy Terrell
Wofford College

Kawin Thamtanajit
University of Delaware

Edward Timmons
Saint Francis University

Sandra Trejos
Clarion University of Pennsylvania

Marie Truesdell
Marian College

Norman T. Van Cott
Ball State University

Kristin A. Van Gaasbeck
California State University—Sacramento

Michael Visser
Sonoma State University

Yoav Wachsman
Coastal Carolina University

Randall Waldron
John Brown University

Doug Walker
Georgia College and State University

Christopher Waller
Notre Dame University

Ashlie Warnick
Carroll Community College

Tyler Watts
Ball State University

Tara Westerhold
Western Illinois University

Robert Whaples
Wake Forest University

Mark Wheeler
Western Michigan University

Jonathan Wight
University of Richmond

Steven Yamarik
California State University, Long Beach

We would like to thank the following instructors who have aided us in the preparation and extensive review of the ancillary package. This list of contributors and reviewers is comprehensive of those who have contributed across editions at this time and will continue to grow as new resources are developed.

Michael Applegate
Oklahoma State University

Margaret Aproberts-Warren
University of California, Santa Cruz

Kevin Beckwith
Salem State University

Brett Block
University of Colorado —Boulder

Douglas Campbell
University of Memphis

John Dawson
Appalachian State University

Eli Dourado
George Mason University

Thomas Dunn
Jim Swofford
University of South Alabama

Pat Euzent
University of Central Florida

Paul Fisher
Henry Ford Community College

David Gillette
Truman State University

Jeremy Groves
Northern Illinois University

Kyle Hampton
University of Alaska, Anchorage

Alanna Holowinsky
Red River College

Garett Jones
George Mason University

David Kalist
Shippensburg University of Pennsylvania

Lillian Kamal
University of Hartford

Tori Knight
Carson-Newman University

Heather Leau
Vanderbilt University

Solina Lindahl
California Polytechnic State University

Ryan Oprea
University of California, Santa Cruz

Jennifer Platania
University of West Florida

Benjamin Powell
Suffolk University

Irina Pritchett
North Carolina State University

Angela Seidel
Saint Francis University

James Self
Indiana University

Kenneth Slaysman
York College of Pennsylvania

Bhavneet Walia
Western Illinois University

Anne Walker
Boise State University

James Watson
University of Colorado—Boulder

Tyler Watts
Ball State University

Mark Wheeler
Western Michigan University

Sheng Yang
Black Hills State University

David Youngberg
George Mason University

We were fortunate to have eagle-eyed readers of the proofs of the book during the production process: Paul Fisher, Henry Ford College. Our student Sarah Oh provided invaluable help in updating figures and tables. The Mercatus Center supplied an essential work environment. Teresa Hartnett has done a great job as our agent.

Most of all we are grateful to the team at Worth. The idea for this book was conceived by Paul Shensa, who has seen it through with wise advice from day one. Bruce Kaplan, our original development editor, is the George Martin of book production. We are very fortunate that Bruce has been succeeded by Lukia Kliossis, who has brought fresh eyes to the project and has pushed us to keep improving and innovating. Thanks as well to Carolyn Merrill, Senior Executive Program Manager, and Assistant Editor Amanda Gaglione, whose hard work throughout helped to keep things moving smoothly.

We are fortunate to have had such a talented production and design group for our book. Paul Rohloff and Edgar Doolan coordinated the entire production process with the help of Lisa Kinne. Natasha Wolfe and John Callahan managed the creation of the beautiful interior design and the cover. Robin Fadool went beyond the call of duty in tracking down sometimes obscure photos. It has been a delight to work with all of them.

Lindsay Neff put together the media team and ably brought the resources and media package to market.

Clay Bolton stands out in the marketing of this book. He has been energetic and relentless.

Most of all, we want to thank our families for their support and understanding. Tyler wishes to offer his personal thanks to Natasha and Yana. It is Alex's great fortune to be able to thank Monique, Connor, and Maxwell and his parents for years of support and encouragement.

Tyler Cowen
Alex Tabarrok

CONTENTS

1

The Big Ideas

The prisoners were dying of scurvy, typhoid fever, and small-pox, but nothing was killing them more than bad incentives. In 1787, the British government had hired sea captains to ship convicted felons to Australia. Conditions on board the ships were monstrous; some even said the conditions were worse than on slave ships. On one voyage, more than one-third of the men died, and the rest arrived beaten, starved, and sick. A first mate remarked cruelly of the convicts, "Let them die and be damned, the owners have [already] been paid for their passage."[1]

The British public had no love for the convicts, but it wasn't prepared to give them a death sentence either. Newspapers editorialized in favor of better conditions; clergy appealed to the captains' sense of humanity; and legislators passed regulations requiring better food and water, light and air, and proper medical care. Yet the death rate remained shockingly high. Nothing appeared to be working until an economist suggested something new. Can you guess what the economist suggested?

Instead of paying the captains for each prisoner placed on board the ship in Great Britain, the economist suggested paying for each prisoner that walked off the ship in Australia. In 1793, the new system was implemented and immediately the survival rate shot up to 99%. One astute observer explained what had happened: "Economy beat sentiment and benevolence."[2]

The story of the convict ships illustrates the first big lesson that runs throughout this book and throughout economics: *incentives matter.*

By **incentives**, we mean rewards and penalties that motivate behavior. Let's take a closer look at incentives and some of the other big ideas in economics. On first reading, some of these ideas may seem surprising or difficult to understand. Don't worry: We will be explaining everything in more detail.

We see the following list as the most important and fundamental contributions of economics to human understanding; we call these contributions *Big Ideas.* Some economists might arrange this list in a different manner or order, but these are generally accepted principles among good economists everywhere.

CHAPTER OUTLINE

Big Ideas in Economics

1. Incentives Matter

2. Good Institutions Align Self-Interest with the Social Interest

3. Trade-offs Are Everywhere

4. Think on the Margin

5. Trade Makes People Better Off

6. Wealth and Economic Growth Are Important

7. Institutions Matter

8. Economic Booms and Busts Cannot Be Avoided but Can Be Moderated

9. Inflation Is Caused by Increases in the Supply of Money

10. Central Banking Is a Hard Job

The Biggest Idea of All: Economics Is Fun

▶ MRU Video

• Meet Your Authors

Incentives are rewards and penalties that motivate behavior.

1

MRU

PRINCIPLES ECONOMICS

Meet Your Authors

Big Idea One: Incentives Matter

When the captains were paid for every prisoner who they took on board, they had little incentive to treat the prisoners well. In fact, the incentives were to treat the prisoners badly. Instead of feeding the prisoners, for example, some of the captains hoarded the prisoners' food, selling it in Australia for a tidy profit.

When the captains were paid for prisoners who survived the journey, however, their incentives changed. Whereas before, the captains had benefited from a prisoner's death, now the incentive system "secured to every poor man who died at least one sincere mourner."[3] The sincere mourner? The captain, who was at least sincere about mourning the money he would have earned had the poor man survived.

Incentives are everywhere. In the United States, we take it for granted that when we go to the supermarket, the shelves will be stocked with kiwi fruit from New Zealand, rice from India, and wine from Chile. Every day we rely on the work of millions of other people to provide us with food, clothing, and shelter. Why do so many people work for our benefit? In his 1776 classic, *The Wealth of Nations*, Adam Smith explained:

> It is not from the benevolence of the butcher, the brewer, or the baker, that we expect our dinner, but from their regard to their own interest.

Do economists think that everyone is self-interested all the time? Of course not. We love our spouses and children just like everyone else! But economists do think that people respond in predictable ways to incentives of all kinds. Fame, power, reputation, sex, and love are all important incentives. Economists even think that benevolence responds to incentives. It's not surprising to an economist, for example, that charities publicize the names of their donors. Some people do give anonymously, but how many buildings on your campus are named Anonymous Hall?

Big Idea Two: Good Institutions Align Self-Interest with the Social Interest

The story of the convict ships hints at a second lesson that runs throughout this book: When self-interest aligns with the broader public interest, we get good outcomes, but when self-interest and the social interest are at odds, we get bad outcomes, sometimes even cruel and inhumane outcomes. Paying the ship captains for every prisoner who walked off the ship was a good payment system because it created incentives for the ship captains to do the right thing, not just for themselves but also for the prisoners and for the government that was paying them.

It's a remarkable finding of economics that under the right conditions markets align self-interest with the social interest. You can see what we mean by thinking back to the supermarket example. The supermarket is stocked with products from around the world because markets channel and coordinate the self-interest of millions of people to achieve a social good. The farmer who woke at 5 AM to tend crops, the trucker who delivered the goods to the market, the entrepreneur who risked their capital to build the supermarket—all of these people acted in their own interest, but in so doing, they also acted in your interest.

In a striking metaphor, Adam Smith said that when markets work well, those who pursue their own interest end up promoting the social interest, as if led to do so by an "invisible hand." The idea that the pursuit of self-interest can be in the social interest—that at least sometimes, "greed is good"—was one of the most surprising discoveries of economic science, and after several hundred years this insight is still not always appreciated. Throughout this book, we emphasize ways in which individuals acting in their self-interest produce outcomes that were not part of their intention or design, but that nevertheless have desirable properties.

Not from benevolence but from self-interest

Markets, however, do not always align self-interest with the social interest. Sometimes the invisible hand is absent, not just invisible. Market incentives, for example, can be too strong. A firm that doesn't pay for the pollution that it emits into the air has too great an incentive to emit pollution. Fishermen sometimes have too strong an incentive to catch fish, thereby driving the stock of fish into collapse. In other cases, market incentives are too weak. Did you get your flu shot this year? The flu shot prevents you from getting the flu (usually), but it also reduces the chances that other people will get the flu. When deciding whether to get a flu shot, did you take into account the social interest or just your self-interest?

When markets don't properly align self-interest with the social interest, another important lesson of economics is that government can sometimes improve the situation by changing incentives with taxes, subsidies, or other regulations.

Big Idea Three: Trade-offs Are Everywhere

Vioxx users were outraged when Merck withdrew the arthritis drug from the market after a study showed that it could cause strokes and heart attacks. Vioxx had been on the market for five years and had been used by millions of people. Patients were angry at Merck and at the Food and Drug Administration (FDA). How could the FDA, which is charged with ensuring that new pharmaceuticals are safe and effective, have let Vioxx onto the market? Many people demanded more testing and safer pharmaceuticals. Economists worried that approved pharmaceuticals could become too safe.

Too safe! Is it possible to be too safe?! Yes, because trade-offs are everywhere. Researching, developing, and testing a new drug cost time and resources. On average, it takes about 12 years and $1 billion to bring a new drug to market. More testing means that approved drugs will have fewer side effects, but there are two important trade-offs: *drug lag* and *drug loss*.

Testing takes time so more testing means that good drugs are delayed, just like bad drugs. On average, new drugs work better than old drugs. So the longer it takes to bring new drugs to market, the more people are harmed who could have benefited if the new drugs had been approved earlier.[4] You can die because an unsafe drug is approved—you can also die because a safe drug has *not yet* been approved. This is *drug lag*.

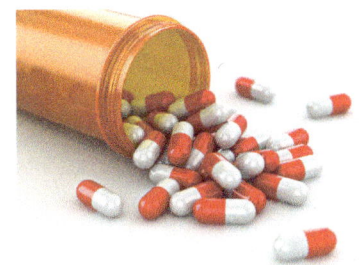

Are pharmaceuticals too safe?

Testing not only takes time, it is costly. The greater the costs of testing, the fewer new drugs there will be. The costs of testing are a hurdle that each potential drug must leap if it is to be developed. Higher costs mean a higher hurdle, fewer new drugs, and fewer lives saved. You can die because an unsafe drug is approved—you can also die because a safe drug is *never* developed. This is *drug loss*.

Thus, society faces a trade-off. More testing means the drugs that are (eventually) approved will be safer but it also means more drug lag and drug loss. When thinking about FDA policy, we need to look at both sides of the trade-off if we are to choose wisely.

The inevitability of trade-offs is the consequence of a big fact about the world, **scarcity**. We face trade-offs because we don't have enough resources to satisfy all of our wants—more of this means less of that. The **great economic problem** is how to arrange our scarce resources to satisfy as many of our wants as possible. So how do we solve this problem? One goal of this textbook is to explain the role of markets and prices in solving the great economic problem.

Trade-offs are closely related to another important idea in economics, opportunity cost.

Opportunity Cost

Every choice involves something gained and something lost. The **opportunity cost** of a choice is the value of the opportunities lost. Consider the choice to attend college. What is the cost of attending college? At first, you might calculate the cost by adding together the price of tuition, books, and room and board—that might be $22,000 or more a year. But that's not the opportunity cost of attending college. What opportunities are you losing when you attend college?

The main opportunity lost when you attend college is (probably) the opportunity to have a full-time job. Most of you reading this book could easily get a job earning $25,000 a year or maybe more. If you spend four years in college, that's $100,000 that you are giving up to get an education. The opportunity cost of college is probably higher than you thought. Perhaps you ought to ask more questions in class to get your money's worth! (But go back to the list of items we totaled earlier—tuition, books, and room and board—one of these items should *not* count as part of the opportunity cost of college. Which one? Answer: Room and board is not a cost of college if you would have to pay for it whether you go to college or not.)

The concept of opportunity cost is important for two reasons. First, if you don't understand the opportunities you are losing when you make a choice, you won't recognize the real trade-offs that you face. Recognizing trade-offs is the first step in making wise choices. Second, most of the time people do respond to changes in opportunity costs—*even when money costs have not changed*—so if you want to understand behavior, you need to understand opportunity cost.

What would you predict, for example, would happen to college enrollment during a recession? The price of tuition, books, and room and board doesn't fall during a recession but the opportunity cost of attending college does fall. Why? During a recession, the unemployment rate increases so it's harder to get a high-paying job. That means you lose less by attending college when the unemployment rate is high. We therefore predict that college enrollments increase when the unemployment rate increases; in opportunity costs terms, it

---

A resource is **scarce** when there isn't enough to satisfy all of our wants.

The **great economic problem** is how to arrange our scarce resources to satisfy as many of our wants as possible.

The **opportunity cost** of a choice is the value of the opportunities lost.

is cheaper to go to college. In 2009, as the unemployment rate soared, the college enrollment rate hit 70.1%, the highest rate ever.

Big Idea Four: Think on the Margin

Robert is cruising down Interstate 80 toward Des Moines, Iowa. Robert wants to get to his destination quickly and safely and he doesn't want to get a speeding ticket. The speed limit is 70 mph but he figures the risk of a ticket is low if he travels just a little bit faster, so Robert sets the cruise control to 72 mph. The road is straight and flat, and after 20 minutes he hasn't seen another car, so he thumbs it up a few clicks to 75. As he approaches Des Moines, Robert spots a police cruiser and thumbs it down to 70. After Des Moines it's nothing but quiet cornfields once again, so he thumbs it up to 72. Crossing the state line into Nebraska, Robert notices that the speed limit is 75, so he thumbs it up to 77 before thumbing it down again as he approaches Omaha.

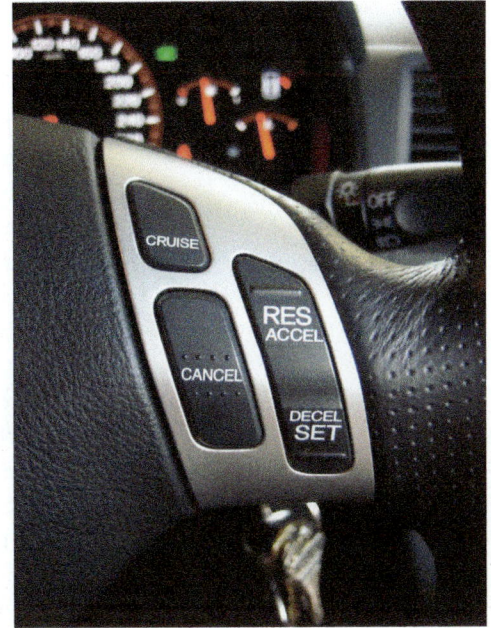

Thinking on the margin A little bit faster? Or a little bit slower?

Robert and his thumb illustrate what economists mean by thinking on the margin. As Robert drives, he constantly weighs benefits and costs and makes a decision: a little bit faster or a little bit slower?

Thinking on the margin is just making choices by thinking in terms of marginal benefits and marginal costs, the benefits and costs of a little bit more (or a little bit less). Most of our decisions in life involve a little bit more of something or a little bit less, and it turns out that thinking on the margin is also useful for understanding how consumers and producers make decisions. Should the consumer buy a few more apples or a few less? Should the oil well produce a few more barrels of oil or a few less?

In this book, you will find lots of talk about marginal choices, including marginal cost (the additional cost from producing a little bit more), marginal revenue (the additional revenue from producing a little bit more), and marginal tax rates (the tax rate on an additional dollar of income). This point about margins is really just a way of restating the importance of trade-offs. If you wish to understand human behavior, look at the trade-offs that people face. Those trade-offs usually involve choices about a little bit more or a little bit less.

The importance of thinking on the margin did not become commonplace in economics until 1871, when marginal thinking was simultaneously described by three economists: William Stanley Jevons, Carl Menger, and Leon Walras. Economists refer to the "marginal revolution" to explain this transformation in economic thought.

Big Idea Five: Trade Makes People Better Off

When Alex and Shruti trade, both of them are made better off. (Alex does regret buying a certain polka-dot sweater so take this as a general principle, not a mathematical certainty.) The principle is simple but important because exchange makes Alex and Shruti better off whether Alex and Shruti live in the same country and share the same language and religion or they live worlds apart geographically and culturally. The benefits of trade, however, go beyond those of exchange. The real power of trade is the power to increase production through specialization.

Few of us could survive if we had to produce our own food, clothing, and shelter (let alone our own cell phones and jet aircraft). Self-sufficiency is death. We survive and prosper only because specialization increases productivity. With specialization, the auto mechanic learns more about cars and the thoracic surgeon learns more about hearts than either could if each one of them needed to repair both cars and hearts. Through the division of knowledge, the sum total of knowledge increases and in this way so does productivity.

Trade also allows us to take advantage of economies of scale, the reduction in costs created when goods are mass-produced. No farmer could ever afford a combine harvester if he was growing wheat only for himself, but when a farmer grows wheat for thousands, a combine harvester reduces the cost of bread for all.

Martha Stewart may be the world's best ironer but she once sheepishly admitted that she doesn't always do her own ironing. Why not? Everyone can benefit from trade, even those who are not especially productive. The reason is that especially productive people can't do everything! Martha Stewart may be able to iron a blouse better than anyone else in the world, but she still hires people to do her ironing because for her an hour of ironing comes at the price of an hour spent running her business. Given the choice of spending an hour ironing or running her business, Martha Stewart is better off running her business. In other words, Martha Stewart's *opportunity cost* of ironing is very high.

The theory of comparative advantage says that when people or nations specialize in goods in which they have a low opportunity cost, they can trade to mutual advantage. Thus, Martha Stewart can benefit by buying ironing services even from people who are not as good at ironing as she is. Notice that the better Martha Stewart gets at running her business, the greater her cost of ironing. So when Martha becomes more productive, this increases her demand to trade. In a similar way, the greater the productivity of American business in producing jet aircraft or designing high-technology devices, the greater will be our demand to trade for textiles or steel.

Big Idea Six: Wealth and Economic Growth Are Important

Every year, several hundred million people contract malaria. In mild cases, malaria causes fever, chills, and nausea. In severe cases, malaria can cause kidney failure, coma, brain damage, and for about a million people a year—mostly children—death. Today, we think of malaria as a "tropical" disease, but malaria was once common in the United States. George Washington caught malaria, as did James Monroe, Andrew Jackson, Abraham Lincoln, Ulysses S. Grant, and James A. Garfield. Malaria was present in America until the late 1940s, when the last cases were wiped out by better drainage, removal of mosquito-breeding sites, and the spraying of insecticides. The lesson? Wealth—the ability to pay for the prevention of malaria—ended the disease in the United States. And wealth comes from economic growth. So the incidence of malaria is not just about geography; it's also about economics.

Malaria is far from the only problem that diminishes with wealth and economic growth. In the United States, one of the world's richest countries, 993 out of every 1,000 children born survive to the age of 5. In Liberia, one of the world's poorest countries, only about 765 children survive to age 5 (i.e., 235

FIGURE 1.1

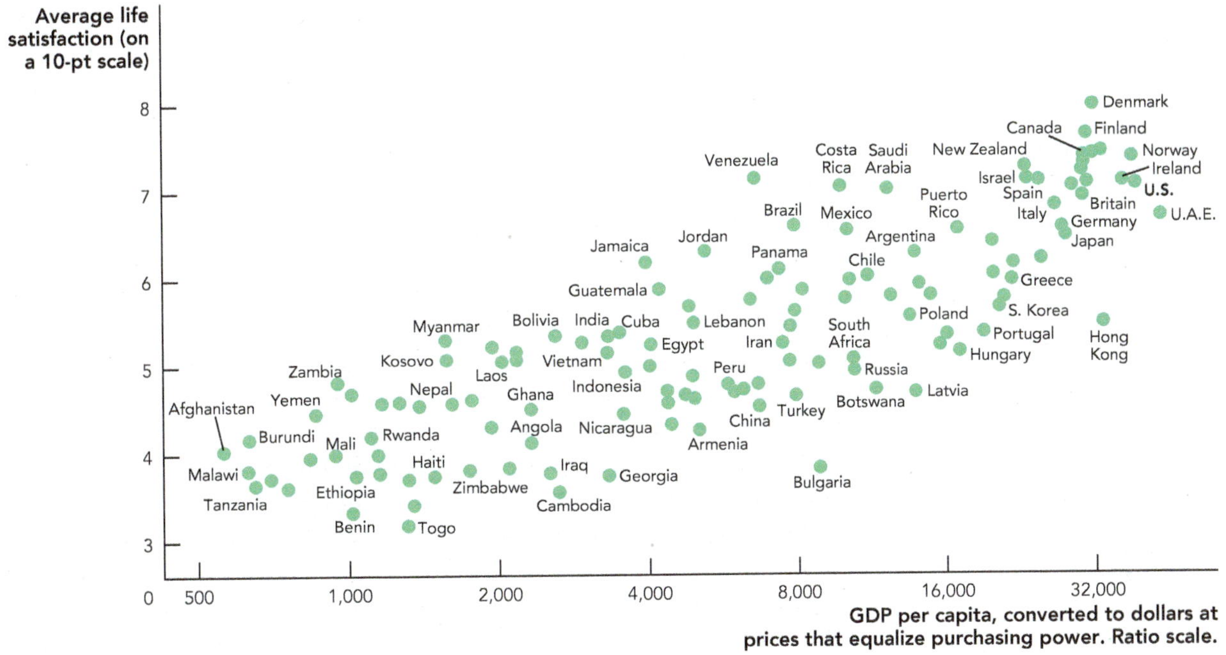

Money and Happiness Are Positively Correlated People in countries with higher GDP per capita tend to have happier, more satisfied lives. Within a country, people with higher incomes also tend to be a little bit happier.

Data from: Betsey Stevenson and Justin Wolfers, "Economic Growth and Subjective Well-Being: Reassessing the Easterlin Paradox," *Brookings Papers on Economic Activity,* Spring 2008.

of every 1,000 children die before seeing their fifth birthday). Overall, it's the wealthiest countries that have the highest rates of infant survival.

Indeed, if you look at most of the things that people care about, they are much easier to come by in wealthier economies. Wealth brings us flush toilets, antibiotics, higher education, the ability to choose the career we want, fun vacations, and, of course, a greater ability to protect our families against catastrophes. Wealth also brings women's rights and political liberty, at least in most (but not all) countries. Wealthier economies lead to richer and more fulfilled, even happier lives, as seen in Figure 1.1. In short, *wealth matters, and understanding economic growth is one of the most important tasks of economics.*

Big Idea Seven: Institutions Matter

If wealth is so important, what makes a country rich? The most proximate cause is that wealthy countries have lots of physical and human capital per worker and they produce things in a relatively efficient manner, using the latest technological knowledge. But why do some countries have more physical and human capital and why is it organized well using the latest technological knowledge? In a word, incentives, which of course takes us back to Big Idea One.

Entrepreneurs, investors, and savers need incentives to save and invest in physical capital, human capital, innovation, and efficient organization. Among the most powerful institutions for supporting good incentives are property rights, political stability, honest government, a dependable legal system, and competitive and open markets.

Consider South and North Korea. South Korea has a per capita income more than 10 times greater than its immediate neighbor, North Korea. South Korea is a modern, developed economy but in North Korea people still starve or can go for months without eating meat. And yet both countries were equally poor in 1950 and, of course, the two countries share the same language and cultural and historical background. What differs is their economic systems and the incentives at work.

Macroeconomists are especially interested in the incentives to produce new ideas. If the world never had any new ideas, the standard of living would eventually stagnate. But entrepreneurs draw on new ideas to create new products like iPhones, new pharmaceuticals, self-driving cars, and many other innovations. Just about any device you use in daily life is based on a multitude of ideas and discoveries, the lifeblood of economic growth. New ideas, of course, require incentives and that means an active scientific community and the freedom and incentive to put new ideas into action. Ideas also have peculiar properties. One apple feeds one person but one idea can feed the world. Ideas, in other words, aren't used up when they are used and that has tremendous implications for understanding the benefits of trade, the future of economic growth, and many other topics.

Big Idea Eight: Economic Booms and Busts Cannot Be Avoided but Can Be Moderated

We have seen that growth matters and that the right institutions foster growth. But no economy grows at a constant pace. Economies advance and recede, rise and fall, boom and bust. In a recession, wages fall and many people are thrown into miserable unemployment. Unfortunately, we cannot avoid all recessions. Booms and busts are part of the normal response of an economy to changing economic conditions. When the weather is bad in India, for example, crops fail and the economy grows more slowly or perhaps it grows not at all. The weather doesn't much affect the economy in the United States, but the U.S. economy is buffeted by other unavoidable shocks.

Although some booms and busts are part of the normal response of an economy to changing economic conditions, not all booms and busts are normal. The Great Depression (1929–1940) was not normal, but rather it was the most catastrophic economic event in the history of the United States. National output plummeted by 30%, unemployment rates exceeded 20%, and the stock market lost more than two-thirds of its value. Almost overnight the United States went from confidence to desperation. The Great Depression, however, didn't have to happen. Most economists today believe that if the government, especially the U.S. Federal Reserve, had acted more quickly and more appropriately, the Great Depression would have been shorter and less deep. At the time, however, the tools at the government's disposal—monetary and fiscal policy—were not well understood.

Today, the tools of monetary and fiscal policy are much better understood. When used appropriately, these tools can reduce swings in unemployment and GDP. Unemployment insurance can also reduce some of the misery that accompanies a recession. The tools of monetary and fiscal policy, however, are not all-powerful. At one time it was thought that these tools could end all recessions, but we know now that this is not the case. Furthermore, when used poorly, monetary and fiscal policy can make recessions worse and the economy more volatile.

A significant task of macroeconomic theory is to understand both the promise and the limits of monetary and fiscal policy in smoothing out the normal booms and busts of the macroeconomy.

Big Idea Nine: Inflation Is Caused by Increases in the Supply of Money

Yes, economic policy can be useful but sometimes policy goes awry, for instance, when **inflation** gets out of hand. Inflation, one of the most common problems in macroeconomics, refers to an increase in the general level of prices. Inflation makes people feel poorer but, perhaps more important, rising and especially volatile prices make it harder for people to figure out the real values of goods, services, and investments. For these and other reasons, most people (and economists) dislike inflation.

Inflation is an increase in the general level of prices.

But where does inflation come from? The answer is simple: Inflation is caused by a sustained increase in the supply of money. When people have more money, they spend it, and without an increase in the supply of goods, prices must rise. As Nobel laureate Milton Friedman once wrote: "Inflation is always and everywhere a monetary phenomenon."

The United States, like other advanced economies, has a central bank; in the United States that bank is called the Federal Reserve. The Federal Reserve has the power and the responsibility to regulate the supply of money in the American economy. This power can be used for good, such as when the Federal Reserve holds off or minimizes a recession. But the power also can be used for great harm if the Federal Reserve encourages too much growth in the supply of money. The result will be inflation and economic disruption.

In Zimbabwe, the government ran the printing presses at full speed for many years. By the end of 2007, prices were rising at an astonishing rate of 150,000% per year. The United States has never had a problem of this scope or anything close to it but inflation remains a common concern.

A billionaire in Zimbabwe

Amazingly, the inflation rate in Zimbabwe kept rising. In January of 2008, the government had to issue a 10-million-dollar bank note (worth about 4 U.S. dollars), and a year later they announced a 20-*trillion*-dollar note that bought about what 10 million dollars had a year earlier. In early 2009, the inflation rate leaped to billions of percent per month! Finally, in April of 2009, the government stopped issuing the Zimbabwean dollar altogether and permitted trade using foreign currencies such as the South African rand and U.S. dollar.

Big Idea Ten: Central Banking Is a Hard Job

The Federal Reserve ("the Fed") is often called on to combat recessions. But this is not always easy to do. Typically, there is a lag—often of many months—between when the Fed makes a decision and when the effects of that decision on the economy are known. In the meantime, economic conditions have changed so you should think of the Fed as shooting at a moving target. No one can foresee the future perfectly and so the Fed's decisions are not always the right ones.

As mentioned, too much money in the economy means that inflation will result. But not enough money in the economy is bad as well and can lead to a recession or a slowing of economic growth. These ideas are an important and extensive topic in macroeconomics, but the key problem is that a low or falling money supply forces people to cut their prices and wages and this adjustment doesn't always go smoothly.

The Fed is always trying to get it "just right," but some of the time it fails. Sometimes the failure is a mistake the Fed could have avoided, but other times it simply isn't possible to always make the right guess about where the world is headed. Thus, in some situations the Fed must accept a certain amount of either inflation or unemployment. Central banking relies on economic tools, but in the final analysis it is as much an art as a science.

Most economists think that the Fed does more good than harm. But if you are going to understand the Fed, you have to think of it as a highly fallible institution that faces a very difficult job.

The Biggest Idea of All: Economics Is Fun

When you put all these ideas and others together, you see that economics is both exciting and important. Economics teaches us how to make the world a better place. It's about the difference between wealth and poverty, work and unemployment, happiness and misery. Economics increases your understanding of the past, present, and future.

As you will see, the basic principles of economics hold everywhere, whether it is in a rice paddy in Vietnam or a stock market in São Paulo, Brazil. No matter what the topic, the principles of economics apply to all countries, not just to your own. Moreover, in today's globalized world, events in China and India influence the economy in the United States, and vice versa. For this reason, you will find that our book is truly international and full of examples and applications from Algeria to Zimbabwe.

But economics is also linked to everyday life. Economics can help you think about your quest for a job, how to manage your personal finances, and how to deal with debt, inflation, a recession, or a bursting stock market bubble. In short, economics is about understanding your world.

We are excited about economics and we hope that you will be too. Perhaps some of you will even become economics majors. If you are thinking about majoring, you might want to know that a bachelor's degree in economics is one of the best-paying degrees, with starting salaries just behind chemical and nuclear engineering. That reflects the value of an economics degree and the world's recognition of that value. But if your passion lies elsewhere, that's okay too; a course in the principles of economics will take you a long way toward understanding your world. With a good course, a good professor, and a good textbook, you'll never look at the world the same way again. So just remember: *See the Invisible Hand. Understand Your World.*

CHAPTER REVIEW

Go online to practice with more examples of these types of problems, including live links to videos, data sources, and feedback.

▶ Problems with this icon relate to optional MRU videos.

KEY CONCEPTS

incentives, p. 1

scarcity, p. 4

great economic problem, p. 4

opportunity cost, p. 4

inflation, p. 9

FACTS AND TOOLS

1. A headline[5] in the *New York Times* read: "Study Finds Enrollment Is Up at Colleges Despite Recession." How would you rewrite this headline now that you understand the idea of opportunity cost?

2. When bad weather in India destroys the crop, does this sound like a fall in the total "supply" of crops or a fall in people's "demand" for crops? Keep your answer in mind as you learn about economic booms and busts later on.

3. How much did national output fall during the Great Depression? According to the chapter, which government agency might have helped to avoid much of the Great Depression had it acted more quickly and appropriately?

4. The chapter lists four things that entrepreneurs save and invest in. Which of the four are actual objects, and which are more intangible, like concepts or ideas or plans? Feel free to use Wikipedia or some other reference source to get definitions of unfamiliar terms.

5. Who has a better incentive to work long hours in a laboratory researching new cures for diseases: a scientist who earns a percentage of the profits from any new medicine she might invent, or a scientist who will get a handshake and a thank you note from her boss if she invents a new medicine?

6. In the discussion of Big Idea Five, the chapter says that "self-sufficiency is death" because most of us would not be able to produce for ourselves the food and shelter that we need to survive.

In addition to *death*, however, one could also say that self-sufficiency is *boredom* or *ignorance*. How does specialization and trade help you to avoid boredom and ignorance?

THINKING AND PROBLEM SOLVING

▶ 7. In recent years, Zimbabwe has had hyperinflation, with prices tripling (or more!) every month. According to what you learned in this chapter, what do you think the government can do to end this hyperinflation?

8. Some people worry that machines will take jobs away from people, making people permanently unemployed. Only 150 years ago in the United States, most people were farmers. Now, machines do almost all of the farm work and fewer than 2% of Americans are farmers, yet that 2% produces enough food to feed the entire country while still exporting food overseas.

   a. What happened to all of those people who used to work on farms? Do you think most adult males in the United States are unemployed nowadays, now that farm work is gone?

   b. Some people say that it's okay for machines to take jobs because we'll get jobs fixing the machines. Just from looking around, do you think that most working Americans are earning a living by fixing farm equipment? If not, what do you think most working people are doing instead? (We'll give a full answer later in this book.)

9. Let's connect Big Ideas Six and Nine: Do you think that people in poor countries are poor because they don't have enough money? In other words, could a country get richer by printing more pieces of paper called "money" and handing those out to its citizens?

10. Nobel Prize winner Milton Friedman said that a bad central banker is like a "fool in the shower." In a shower, of course, when you turn the faucet, water won't show up in the showerhead for a

few seconds. So if a "fool in the shower" is always making big changes in the temperature based on how the water feels *right now*, the water is likely to swing back and forth between too hot and too cold. How does this apply to central banking?

11. According to the United Nations, there were roughly 300 million humans on the planet a thousand years ago. Essentially all of them were poor by modern standards: They lacked antibiotics, almost all lacked indoor plumbing, and none traveled faster than a horse or a river could carry them. Today, between 1 and 3 billion humans are poor out of about 7 billion total humans. So, over the last thousand years, what has happened to the *fraction* of humans who are poor: Did it rise, fall, or stay about the same? What happened to the total *number* of people living in deep poverty: rise, fall, or no change?

CHALLENGES

12. We claim that part of the reason the Great Depression was so destructive is because economists didn't understand how to use government policy very well in the 1930s. In your opinion, do you think that economists during the Great Depression would have agreed? In other words, if you had asked them why the Depression was

so bad, would they have said, "Because the government ignored our wise advice," or would they have said, "Because we don't have any good ideas about how to fix this"? What does your answer tell you about the confidence of economists and other experts?

13. Some problems that economists try to solve are easy *as economic problems* but hard *as political problems*. Medical doctors face similar kinds of situations: Preventing most deaths from obesity or lung cancer is easy *as a medical problem* (eat less, exercise more, don't smoke) but hard *as a self-control problem*. With this in mind, how is ending hyperinflation like losing 100 pounds?

14. As Nobel Prize winner and *New York Times* columnist Paul Krugman has noted, the field of economics is a lot like the field of medicine: They are fields where knowledge is limited (both are new as real scientific disciplines) and where many cures are quite painful (opportunity cost), but where regular people care deeply about the issues. What are some other ways that economics and medicine are alike?

15. Economics is sometimes called "the dismal science." Of the big ideas in this chapter, which sound dismal—like bad news?

MRU VIDEOS

Meet Your Authors
mru.org/intro-econ

Zimbabwe and Hyperinflation
mru.org/hyperinflation
Problem: **7**

2

The Power of Trade and Comparative Advantage

CHAPTER OUTLINE

Trade and Preferences

Specialization, Productivity, and the Division of Knowledge

Comparative Advantage

Trade and Globalization

Takeaway

▶ **MRU** Video

- How the Division of Knowledge Saved My Son's Life

Chaos, conflict, and war may dominate the news, but it's heartening to know that there is also an astounding amount of world *cooperation*. The next time you are in your local supermarket, stop and consider how many people cooperated to bring the fruits of the world to your table: kiwis from New Zealand, dried apricots from Turkey, dates from Egypt, mangoes from Mexico, bananas from Guatemala. How is it that farmers in New Zealand wake up at 5 AM to work hard tending their fields so that you, on the other side of the world, may enjoy a kiwi with your fruit salad?

This chapter is about a central feature of our world, trade. It's about how you eat reasonably well every day yet have little knowledge of farming, it's about how you cooperate with people whom you will never meet, and it's about how civilization is made possible.

We will focus on three of the benefits of trade:

1. Trade makes people better off when preferences differ.
2. Trade increases productivity through specialization and the division of knowledge.
3. Trade increases productivity through comparative advantage.

Trade and Preferences

In September 1995, Pierre Omidyar, a 28-year-old computer programmer, finished the code for what would soon become eBay. Searching around for a test item, Omidyar grabbed a broken laser pointer and posted it for sale with a starting price of $1. The laser pointer sold for $14.83. Astonished, Omidyar contacted the winning bidder to make sure he understood that the laser pointer was broken. "Oh yes," the bidder replied, "I am a collector of broken laser pointers." At that instant, Omidyar knew eBay was going to be a huge success. Within just a few years, he would become one of the richest men in the United States.

eBay profits by making buyers and sellers happy.

Today, eBay operates in more than 30 countries and earns billions of dollars in revenue. eBay's revenues, however, are a small share of the total value that is created for the hundreds of millions of buyers and sellers who trade everything on eBay from children's toys to the original Hollywood sign. Trade creates value by moving goods from people who value them less to people who value them more. Sam, for example, was going to trash the old Fisher Price garage that his kids no longer play with. Instead, Sam sells it on eBay to Jen who pays $65.50. What had been worth nothing is now worth at least $65.50. Value has been created. Trade makes Sam better off, Jen better off, and it makes eBay, the market maker who brought Sam and Jen together, better off. Trade makes people with different preferences better off.

Specialization, Productivity, and the Division of Knowledge

Simple trades of the kind found on eBay create value, but the true power of trade is discovered only when people take the next step, specialization. In a world without trade, no one can afford to specialize. People will specialize in the production of a single good only when they are confident that they will be able to trade that good for the many other goods that they want and need. Thus, as trade develops, so does specialization, and specialization turns out to vastly increase productivity.

How long could you survive if you had to grow your own food? Probably not very long. Yet most of us can earn enough money in a single day spent doing something other than farming to buy more food than we could grow in a year. Why can we get so much more food through trade than through personal production? The reason is that specialization greatly increases productivity. Farmers, for example, have two immense advantages in producing food compared with economics professors or students: Because they specialize, they know more about farming than other people, and because they sell large quantities, they can afford to buy large-scale farming machines. What is true for farming is true for just about every field of production—specialization increases productivity. Without specialization and trade, we would each have to produce our own food as well as other goods, and the result would be mass starvation and the collapse of civilization.

The human brain is limited and there is much to know. Thus, it makes sense to divide knowledge across many brains and then trade. In a primitive agricultural economy in which each person or household farms for themselves, each person has about the same knowledge as the person next door. In this case, the combined knowledge of a society of 1 million people barely exceeds that of a single person.[1] A society run with the knowledge of one brain is a poor and miserable society.

In a modern economy, many millions of times more knowledge is used than could exist in a single brain. In the United States, for example, we don't just have doctors—we have neurologists, cardiologists, gastroenterologists, gynecologists, and urologists, to name just a few of the many specializations in medicine.

Contra episode 56, even Spock's brain could not run a modern economy; the work needed to do that would have to be spread across millions of brains. For this reason, some economists consider "Spock's Brain" to be the worst *Star Trek* episode ever.

Knowledge increases productivity so specialization increases total output. All of this knowledge is possible, however, only because each person can specialize in the production of one good and then trade for all other desired goods. Without trade, specialization is impossible.

The extent of specialization in a modern economy explains why no one knows the full details of how even the simplest product is produced. A Valentine's Day rose may have been grown in Kenya, flown through Amsterdam to the United States on a refrigerated airplane, and trucked to Topeka by drivers staying awake with Colombian coffee. Each person in this process knows only a small part of the whole, but with trade and market coordination, they each do their part and the rose is delivered without anyone needing to understand the whole process.

The extent of specialization in modern society is remarkable. We have already mentioned the many specializations in medicine. We also have dog walkers, closet organizers, and manicurists. It's common to dismiss the latter jobs as frivolous, but trade connects all markets. It's the dog walkers, closet organizers, and manicurists who give the otolaryngologists—specialists in the nose, ear, and throat—the time they need to perfect their skills.

The division of knowledge increases with specialization and trade. Economic growth in the modern era is primarily due to the creation of new knowledge. Thus, one of the most momentous turning points in the division of knowledge happens when trade is extensive enough to support large numbers of scientists, engineers, and entrepreneurs, all of whom specialize in producing new knowledge.

Every increase in world trade is an opportunity to increase the division of knowledge and extend the power of the human mind. During the Communist era, for example, China was like an island cut off from the world economy: 1 billion people who neither traded many goods nor many ideas with the rest of the world. After the fall of the Berlin Wall, Eastern Europe, Russia, and later China and India joined the world economy adding to the world stock of scientists and engineers. Billions of minds were added to the division of knowledge and cooperation was extended further around the world than ever before.

Consider the many ideas and innovations that make life better, from antibiotics, to high-yield, disease-resistant wheat, to the semiconductor. Insofar as those goods have originated in one place and then been spread around the world, improving the lives of millions or billions, it is because of trade.

mru.org/division-knowledge

How The Division of Knowledge Saved My Son's Life

Reducing trade barriers, Berlin 1989

STRINGER/REUTERS/Newscom

Comparative Advantage

A third reason to trade is to take advantage of differences. Brazil, for example, has a climate ideally suited to growing sugar cane, China has an abundance of low-skill workers, and the United States has one of the best educated workforces in the world. Taking advantage of these differences suggests that world production can be maximized when Brazil produces sugar, China assembles iPads, and the United States devotes its efforts to designing the next generation of electronic devices.

Comparative advantage: It's a good thing. Martha Stewart may be the world's best ironer but she has admitted that she doesn't always do her own ironing. That's smart! Every hour Martha spends ironing is an hour less she has to run her billion-dollar business. The cost of ironing is too high for Martha Stewart, even if she is the world's best. Martha can be most productive if she does what she does most best.

Absolute advantage is the ability to produce the same good using fewer inputs than another producer.

A **production possibilities frontier** shows all the combinations of goods that a country can produce given its productivity and supply of inputs.

Taking advantage of differences is even more powerful than it looks. We say that a country has an **absolute advantage** in production if it can produce the same good using fewer inputs than another country. But to benefit from trade, a country need not have an absolute advantage. For example, even if the United States did have the world's best climate for growing sugar, it might still make sense for Brazil to grow sugar and for the United States to design iPads, if the United States had a bigger advantage in designing iPads than it did in growing sugar.

Here's another example of what economists call comparative advantage. Martha Stewart doesn't do her own ironing. Why not? Martha Stewart may, in fact, be the world's best ironer but she is also good at running her business. If Martha spent more time ironing and less time running her business, her blouses might be pressed more precisely but that would be a small gain compared with the loss from having someone else run her business. It's better for Martha if she specializes in running her business and then trades some of her income for other goods, such as ironing services, and of course many other goods and services as well.

The Production Possibility Frontier

The idea of comparative advantage is subtle but important. In order to give a precise definition, let's explore comparative advantage using a simple model. Suppose that there are just two goods, computers and shirts, and one input, labor. Assume that in Mexico, it takes 12 units of labor to make one computer and 2 units of labor to produce one shirt, and suppose that Mexico has 24 units of labor. Mexico, therefore, can produce 2 computers and 0 shirts or 0 computers and 12 shirts, or they can have any combination of computers and shirts along the line in the left panel of Figure 2.1 labeled Mexico's PPF. Mexico's PPF, short for Mexico's **production possibilities frontier**, shows all the combinations of computers and shirts that Mexico can produce given its productivity and supply of inputs. Mexico cannot produce outside of its PPF.

Similarly, assume that there are 24 units of labor in the United States but that in the United States it takes 1 unit of labor to produce either good. The United States therefore can produce 24 computers and 0 shirts, or 0 computers and 24 shirts, or any combination along the U.S. PPF shown in the right panel of Figure 2.1.

A PPF illustrates trade-offs. If Mexico wants to produce more shirts, it must produce fewer computers, and vice versa: It moves along its PPF. That's just another way of restating the fundamental principles of scarcity and opportunity cost.

Opportunity Costs and Comparative Advantage

In fact, there is a close connection between opportunity costs and the PPF. Remember, the opportunity cost of a choice is the value of the opportunities lost. Now look at the U.S. PPF in the right panel of Figure 2.1, notice that the slope, the rise over the run, is $-24/24 = -1$. In other words, for every additional shirt the United States produces, it must produce one fewer computer. One shirt has an opportunity cost of one computer and vice versa.

FIGURE 2.1

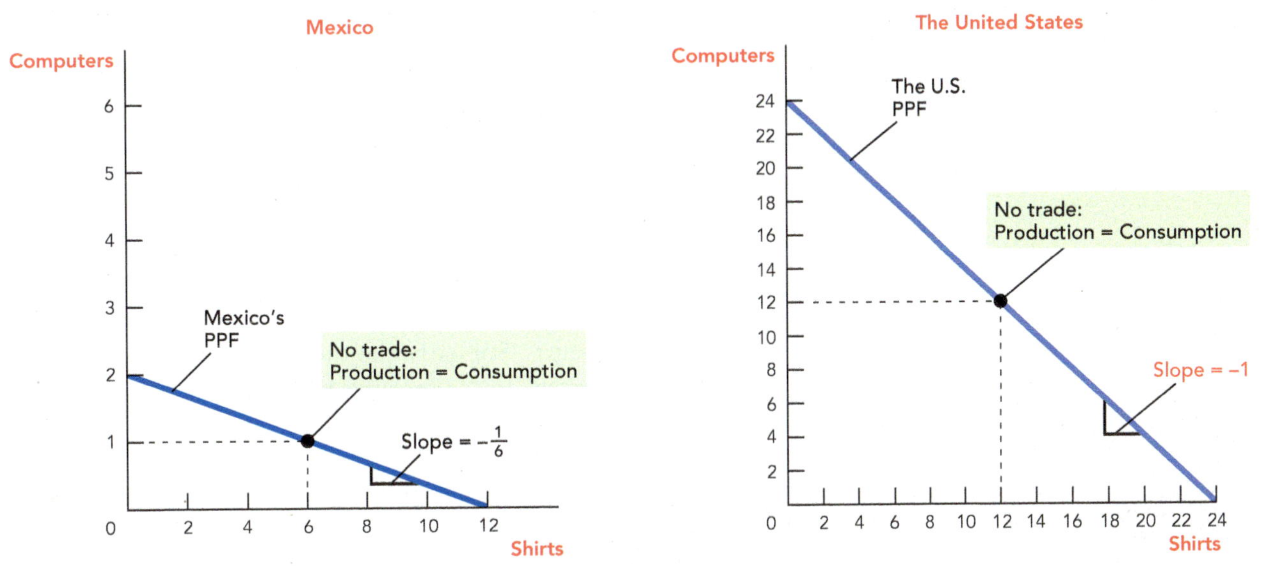

Production and Consumption in Mexico and the United States Without Trade

Now consider Mexico's PPF. The rise over the run is $-2/12 = -1/6$. In other words, for every additional shirt that Mexico produces, it must produce 1/6th less of a computer. Once again, the slope of the PPF tells us the opportunity cost. In Mexico, 1 shirt costs 1/6th of a computer, or 1 computer costs 6 shirts. We summarize the opportunity costs in Table 2.1.

Now here is the key. The (opportunity) cost of a shirt in the United States is one computer but the (opportunity) cost of a shirt in Mexico is just one-sixth of a computer. Thus, even though Mexico is less productive than the United States, Mexico has a lower cost of producing shirts! Since Mexico has the lower opportunity cost of producing shirts, we say that Mexico has a **comparative advantage** in producing shirts.

A country has a **comparative advantage** in producing goods for which it has the lower opportunity cost.

TABLE 2.1 OPPORTUNITY COSTS

Country	Opportunity Cost of 1 Computer	Opportunity Cost of 1 Shirt
Mexico	6 shirts	1/6 of a computer
United States	1 shirt	1 computer

Mexico is the low-cost producer of shirts.

The United States is the low-cost producer of computers.

Now let's look at the opportunity cost of producing computers. Again, the trade-off for the United States is easy to see: It can produce one additional computer by giving up one shirt so the cost of one computer is one shirt. But to produce one additional computer in Mexico requires giving up six shirts! Thus, the United States has the lower cost of producing computers or, economists say, it has a comparative advantage in producing computers.

We now know that the United States has a high cost of producing shirts and a low cost of producing computers. For Mexico, it's the reverse: Mexico has a low cost of producing shirts and a high cost of producing computers.

The theory of comparative advantage says that to increase its wealth, a country should produce the goods it can make at low cost and buy the goods that it can make only at high cost. Thus, the theory says the United States should make computers and buy shirts. Similarly, the theory says that Mexico should make shirts and buy computers. Let's use some numbers and some pictures to see whether the theory holds up in our example.

Suppose that Mexico and the United States each devote 12 units of labor to producing computers and 12 units to producing shirts. We can see from the PPFs that Mexico will produce one computer and six shirts and the United States will produce 12 computers and 12 shirts. At first, there is no trade, so production in each country is equal to consumption. We show the production–consumption point of each country with a black dot in Figure 2.1. Now, can Mexico and the United States make themselves better off through trade? Yes.

Imagine that Mexico moves 12 units of its labor out of computer production and into shirt production. Thus, Mexico specializes completely by allocating all 24 units of its labor to shirt production, thereby producing 12 shirts. Similarly, suppose that the United States moves 2 units of its labor out of shirt production and into computers—thus producing 14 computers and 10 shirts. Production in Mexico and the United States is now shown by the green points in Figure 2.2.

So, to finish the story, can you now see a way in which both Mexico and the United States can be made better off? Sure! Imagine that the United States trades one computer to Mexico in return for three shirts. Mexico is now able to consume one computer and nine shirts (three more shirts than before trade), while the United States is able to consume 13 computers (one more than before trade) and 13 shirts (one more than before trade).

Amazingly, both Mexico and the United States can now consume outside of their PPFs. In other words, before trade, Mexico could not have consumed one computer and nine shirts because this was outside their PPF. Similarly, before trade, the United States could not have consumed 13 computers and 13 shirts. But with trade, countries are able to increase their consumption beyond the range that was possible without trade.

Thus, when each country produces according to its comparative advantage and then trades, total production and consumption increase. Importantly, both Mexico and the United States gain from trade even though the United States is more productive than Mexico at producing *both* computers and shirts.

The theory of comparative advantage not only explains trade patterns it also tells us something remarkable: A country (or a person) will *always* be the low-cost seller of some good. The reason is clear: The greater the advantage a country has in producing A, the greater the cost to it of producing B. If you are a great pianist, the cost to you of doing anything else is very high. Thus, the greater your advantages in being a pianist, the greater the incentive you have to

FIGURE 2.2

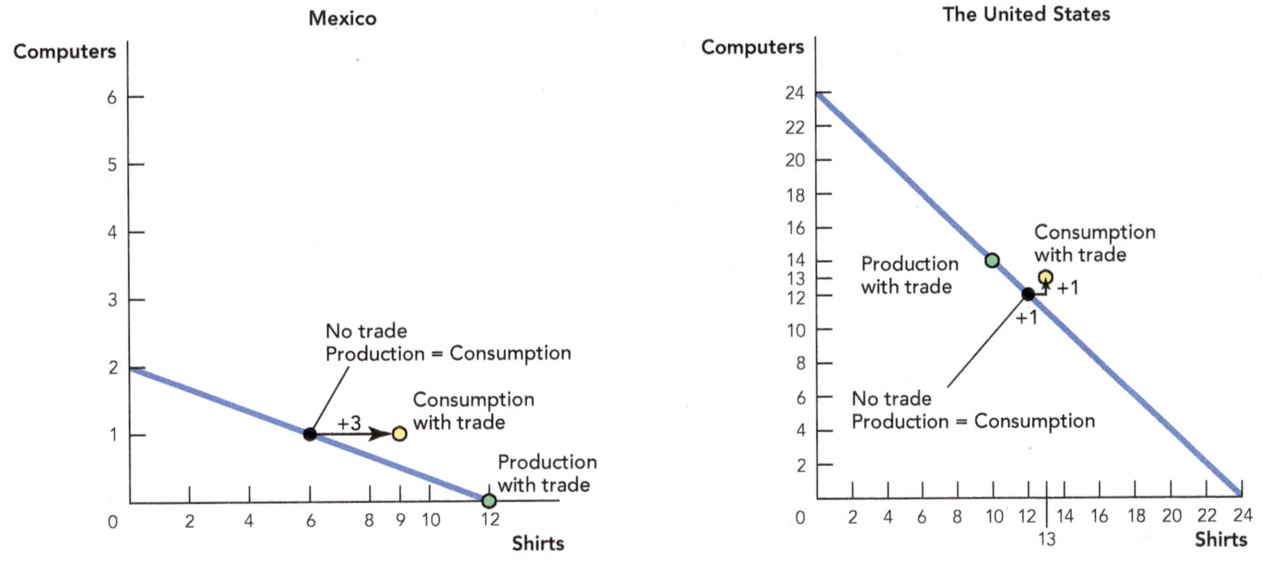

Production and Consumption in Mexico and the United States with Trade With no trade, Mexico produces and consumes one computer and six shirts and the United States produces and consumes 12 computers and 12 shirts. With specialization, Mexico produces zero computers and 12 shirts and the United States produces 14 computers and 10 shirts. By trading three shirts for one computer, Mexico increases its consumption (compared with the no-trade situation) by three shirts and the United States increases its consumption by one computer and one shirt.

trade with other people for other goods. It's the same for countries. The more productive the United States is at producing computers, the greater its demand will be to trade for shirts. Thus, countries with high productivity can always benefit by trading with lower-productivity countries, and countries with lower productivity need never fear that higher-productivity countries will outcompete them in the production of all goods.

When people fear that a country can be outcompeted in everything, they are making a common mistake, namely confusing absolute advantage with comparative advantage. A producer has an absolute advantage over another producer if it can produce more output from the same input. But what makes trade profitable is differences in comparative advantage, and a country will always have some comparative advantage.

Thus, everyone can benefit from trade. From the world's greatest genius down to the person of below-average ability, no individuals or countries are so productive or so unproductive that they cannot benefit from inclusion in the worldwide division of labor. The theory of comparative advantage tells us something vital about world trade and about world peace. Trade unites humanity.

Comparative Advantage and Wages

Comparative advantage is a difficult story to grasp. Most of the world hasn't got it yet so don't be too surprised if it takes you some time as well. You may at first be bothered by the fact that we did not explicitly discuss wages. Won't a country like the United States be uncompetitive in trade with low-wage countries like Mexico?

TABLE 2.2 CONSUMPTION IN MEXICO AND THE UNITED STATES (NO SPECIALIZATION OR TRADE)

Country Labor Allocation (Computers, Shirts)	Computers	Shirts
Mexico (12, 12)	1	6
United States (12, 12)	12	12
Total consumption	13	18

TABLE 2.3 CONSUMPTION IN MEXICO AND THE UNITED STATES (SPECIALIZATION AND TRADE)

Country	Computers	Shirts
Mexico	1	9 = 6 + 3
United States	13 = 12 + 1	13 = 12 + 1
Total consumption	14	22

In fact, wages are in our model, we just need to bring them to the surface. Doing so will provide another perspective on comparative advantage.

In our model, there is only one type of labor. In a free market, all workers of the same type will earn the same wage.* So, in this model there is just one wage in Mexico and one wage in the United States. We can calculate the wage in Mexico by summing up the total value of *consumption* in Mexico and dividing by the number of workers.† We can perform a similar calculation for the United States. To do this, we need only a price for computers and a price for shirts. Let's suppose that computers sell for $300 and shirts for $100 (this is consistent with trading one computer for three shirts as we did earlier). Let's look first at the situation with no trade (see Table 2.2). The value of Mexican consumption is $1 \times \$300$ plus $6 \times \$100$ for a total of $900. Since there are 24 workers, the average wage is $37.50. The value of U.S. consumption is $12 \times \$300 + 12 \times \$100 = \$4,800$ so the U.S. wage is $200.

Now consider the situation with trade (see Table 2.3). The value of Mexican consumption is now $1 \times \$300 + 9 \times \$100 = \$1,200$ for a wage of $50, while the U.S. wage is now $216.67 (check it!). Wages in both countries have gone up, just as expected.

But notice that the wage in Mexico is lower than the wage in the United States, both before and after trade. The reason is that the productivity of labor is lower in Mexico. Ultimately, it's the productivity of labor that determines the wage rate. Specialization and trade let workers make the most of what they have—it raises wages as high as possible given productivity—but trade does not directly increase productivity.‡ Trade makes both Einstein and his less clever accountant better off, but it doesn't make the accountant a skilled scientist like Einstein.

In summary, workers in the United States often fear trade because they think that they cannot compete with low-wage workers in other countries. Meanwhile, workers in low-wage countries fear trade because they think that they cannot compete with high-productivity countries like the United States! But differences in wages reflect differences in productivity. High-productivity countries have high wages; low-productivity countries have low wages. Trade means that workers in both countries can raise their wages to the highest levels allowed by their respective productivities.

---

* In a free market, the same good will tend to sell for the same price everywhere. Imagine that the wages in computer manufacturing exceed the wages in shirt manufacturing. Everyone wants a higher wage, so workers in the shirt industry will try to move to the computer industry. As the supply of workers in computer manufacturing increases, however, wages in the computer sector will fall. And, as the supply of workers in shirt manufacturing decreases, wages in that sector will increase. Only when workers of the same type are paid the same wage is there no incentive for workers to move.
† We calculate the value of consumption because at the end of the day workers care about what they consume, not what they produce.
‡ Trade can increase productivity by improving the division of knowledge and by diffusing information about advanced production techniques. These advantages of trade are important but the logic of comparative advantage does not require an increase in productivity.

Adam Smith on Trade

Notice that we have so far talked about trade without distinguishing it much from "international trade." Adam Smith had an elegant summary connecting the argument for trade to that for international trade:

> It is the maxim of every prudent master of a family never to attempt to make at home what it will cost him more to make than to buy. The tailor does not attempt to make his own shoes, but buys them of the shoemaker. The shoemaker does not attempt to make his own clothes, but employs a tailor. What is prudence in the conduct of every private family can scarce be folly in that of a great kingdom. If a foreign country can supply us with a commodity cheaper than we ourselves can make it, better buy it of them with some part of the produce of our own industry employed in a way in which we have some advantage.[2]

Adam Smith (1723–1790), author of *The Wealth of Nations* and one of the greatest economists of all time. When Smith could not finish teaching one semester, he told his students he would refund their tuition. When the students refused the refund saying they had learned so much already, Smith wept. We, however, will not refund the purchase price of this book even if you read only half of it. We are not as good economists as Adam Smith was.

Trade and Globalization

Does everyone always benefit from increased trade? No. In our simple model, workers within a country can easily switch between the shirt and computer sectors. In the real world, workers in the sector with increased demand (computers in the United States, shirts in Mexico) will see their wages rise while workers in the sector with decreased demand (shirts in the United States, computers in Mexico) will see their wages fall. Workers in sectors with falling wages will move to sectors with rising wages until wages in the sectors equalize, but the transition isn't always easy or quick. We will take another look at the gains and losses from trade in the chapter on international trade. Overall, however, greater trade increases total wealth. That typically brings benefits to a great many people in all parts of the trading world. We can see this theme throughout history.

Decreases in transportation costs, integration of world markets, and increased speed of communication have made the world a smaller place. But globalization is not new; rather, it has been a theme in human history since at least the Roman Empire, which knit together different parts of the world in a common economic and political area. When these trade networks later fell apart, the subsequent era was named "The Dark Ages."

Later, the European Renaissance arose from revitalized trade routes, the rebirth of commercially based cities, and the spread of science from China, India, and the Middle East. Periods of increased trade and the spread of ideas have been among the best for human progress. As economist Donald Boudreaux puts it: "Globalization is the advance of human cooperation across national boundaries."[3]

Takeaway

Simple trade makes people better off when preferences differ, but the true power of trade occurs when trade leads to specialization. Specialization creates enormous increases in productivity. Without trade, the knowledge used by an entire economy is approximately equal to the knowledge used by one brain. With specialization and trade, the total sum of knowledge used in an economy increases tremendously and far exceeds that of any one brain.

International trade is trade across political borders. The theory of comparative advantage explains how a country, just like a person, can increase its standard of living by specializing in what it can make at low (opportunity) cost and trading for

> ### CHECK YOURSELF
> - What does specialization do to productivity? Why?
> - How does trade let us benefit from the advantages of specialization?
> - Usain Bolt is the world's fastest human. Usain could probably mow his lawn very quickly, much more quickly and at least as well as Harry, who mows lawns for a living. Why would Usain Bolt pay Harry to mow his lawn rather than do it himself?

what it can make only at high cost. When we apply the logic of opportunity cost to trade, we discover that everyone has a comparative advantage in something, so everyone can benefit from inclusion in the world market.

CHAPTER REVIEW

Go online to practice with more examples of these types of problems, including live links to videos, data sources, and feedback.

▶ Problems with this icon relate to optional MRU videos.

KEY CONCEPTS

absolute advantage, p. 16

production possibilities frontier, p. 16

comparative advantage, p. 17

FACTS AND TOOLS

▶ 1. Use the idea of the "division of knowledge" to answer the following questions:

   a. Which country has more knowledge: Utopia, where in the words of Karl Marx, each person knows just enough about hunting, fishing, and cattle raising to "hunt in the morning, fish in the afternoon, [and] rear cattle in the evening," or Drudgia, where one-third of the population learns only about hunting, one-third only about fishing, and one-third only about cattle raising?

   b. Which planet has more knowledge: Xeroxia, each of whose 1 million inhabitants knows the same list of 1 million facts, or Differentia, whose 1 million inhabitants each know a different set of 1 million facts? How many facts are known in Xeroxia? How many facts are known in Differentia?

▶ 2. In *The Wealth of Nations*, Adam Smith said that one reason specialization makes someone more productive is because "a man commonly saunters a little in turning his hand from one sort of employment to another." How can you use this observation to improve your pattern of studying for your four or five college courses this semester?

▶ 3. Opportunity cost is one of the tougher ideas in economics. Let's make it easier by starting with some simple examples. In the following examples, find the opportunity cost. Your answer should be a *rate*, as in "1.5 widgets per year" or "6 lectures per month." Ignoring Adam Smith's insight from the previous question, assume that these relationships are simple linear ones, so that if you put in twice the time, you get twice the output, and half the time yields half the output.

   a. Erin has a choice between two activities: She can repair one transmission per hour or she can repair two fuel injectors per hour. What is the opportunity cost of repairing one transmission?

   b. Ruby works at a customer service center and every hour she has a choice between two activities: answering 200 telephone calls per hour or responding to 400 emails per hour. What is the opportunity cost of responding to 400 emails?

   c. Deirdre has a choice between writing one more book this year or five more articles this year. What is the opportunity cost of writing half a book this year, in terms of articles?

▶ 4. a. American workers are commonly paid much more than Chinese workers. *True or false:* This is largely because American workers are typically more productive than Chinese workers.

   b. Julia Child, an American chef (and World War II spy) who reintroduced French cooking to Americans in the 1960s, was paid much more than most American chefs. *True or false:* This was largely because Julia Child was much more productive than most American chefs.

▶ 5. According to the *Wall Street Journal* (August 30, 2007, "In the Balance"), it takes about 30 hours to assemble a vehicle in the United States. Let's use that fact plus a few invented numbers to sum up the global division of labor in auto manufacturing. In international economics, "North" is shorthand for the high-tech developed countries of East Asia, North America, and Western Europe, while "South" is shorthand for the rest of the world. Let's use that shorthand here.

a. Consider the following productivity table: Which region has an absolute advantage at making high-quality cars? Low-quality cars?

	Number of Hours to Make One High-Quality Car	Number of Hours to Make One Low-Quality Car
North	30	20
South	60	30

b. Using the information in the productivity table, estimate the opportunity cost of making high- or low-quality cars in the North and in the South. Which region has a comparative advantage (i.e., lowest opportunity cost) for manufacturing high-quality cars? For low-quality cars?

	Opportunity Cost of Making One High-Quality Car	Opportunity Cost of Making One Low-Quality Car
North	__ low-quality cars	__ high-quality cars
South	__ low-quality cars	__ high-quality cars

c. One million hours of labor are available for making cars in the North, and another 1 million hours of labor are available for making cars in the South. In a no-trade world, let's assume that two-thirds of the auto industry labor in each region is used to make high-quality cars and one-third is used to make low-quality cars. Solve for how many of each kind of car will be produced in the North and South, and add up to determine the total global output of each type of car. (Why will both kinds of cars be made? Because the low-quality cars will be less expensive.)

	Output of High-Quality Cars	Output of Low-Quality Cars
North		
South		
Global output		

d. Now allow specialization. If each region completely specializes in the type of car in which it holds the comparative advantage, what will the global output of high-quality cars be? Of low-quality cars? In the following table, report your answers. Is global output in each kind of car higher than before? (We'll solve a problem with the final step of trade in the Work It Out problem.)

	Output of High-Quality Cars	Output of Low-Quality Cars
North		
South		
Global output		

6. It has been reported that John Lennon was once asked whether Ringo was the best drummer in the world, and he quipped, "He's not even the best drummer in the Beatles!" (Paul also drummed on some of the White Album.) Assuming that this story is true and that Lennon was correct, explain, using economics, why it could still make sense to have Ringo on drums.

THINKING AND PROBLEM SOLVING

7. Fit each of the following examples into one of these reasons for trade division of knowledge or comparative advantage.

a. Two recently abandoned cats, Bingo and Tuppy, need to quickly learn how to catch mice in order to survive. If they also remain well groomed, they stand a better chance of surviving: Good grooming reduces the risk of disease and parasites. Each cat could go it alone, focusing almost exclusively on learning to catch mice. The alternative would be for Bingo to specialize in learning how to groom well and for Tuppy to specialize in learning how to catch mice well.

b. Supreme Court Chief Justice John Roberts hires attorneys who are less skilled than himself to do his taxes and routine legal work.

8. Nobel laureate Paul Samuelson said that comparative advantage is one of the few ideas in economics that is both "true and not obvious." Since it's not obvious, we should practice with it a bit. In each of the cases, determine the opportunity cost of each worker. Who has the absolute advantage at each task, and who has the comparative advantage?

a. In 30 minutes, Kana can either make miso soup or she can clean the kitchen. In 15 minutes, Mitchell can make miso soup; it takes Mitchell an hour to clean the kitchen.

b. In one hour, Ethan can bake 20 cookies or hang the drywall for two rooms. In one hour, Sienna can bake 100 cookies or hang the drywall for three rooms.

c. Kara can build two glass sculptures per day or she can design two full-page newspaper advertisements per day. Sara can build one glass sculpture per day or design four full-page newspaper ads per day.

d. Commander Data can write 12 excellent poems per day or solve 100 difficult physics problems per day. Riker can write one excellent poem per day or solve 0.5 difficult physics problems per day.

9. The federal education reform law known as No Child Left Behind requires every state to create standardized tests that measure whether students have mastered key subjects. Since the same test is given to all students in the same grade in the state, this encourages all schools within a state to cover the same material. According to the division of knowledge model, what are the costs of this approach?

10. In this chapter, we've often emphasized how specialization and exchange can create more *output*. But sometimes the output from voluntary exchange is difficult to measure and doesn't show up in GDP statistics. In each of the following cases, explain how the two parties involved might be able to make themselves *both* better off just by making a voluntary exchange.

a. Dana received two copies of *Gears of War 5* as birthday gifts. Evan received two copies of *Halo Infinite* as birthday gifts.

b. Jeb has a free subscription to *Field and Stream* but isn't interested in hunting. George has a free subscription to the *Miami Herald* but isn't all that interested in Florida news.

c. Pat has a lot of love to give, but it is worthless unless received by another. Terry is in the same sad situation.

11. Many people talk about manufacturing jobs leaving the United States and going to other places, like China. Why isn't it possible for all jobs to leave the United States and go overseas (as some people fear)?

12. Suppose the following table shows the number of labor hours needed to produce airplanes and automobiles in the United States and South Korea, but one of the numbers is unknown.

	Number of Hours to Produce One Airplane	Number of Hours to Produce One Auto
South Korea	2,000	?
United States	800	5

a. Without knowing the number of labor hours required to produce an auto in South Korea, you can't figure out which country has the comparative advantage in which good. Can you give an example of a number for the empty cell of the table that would give the United States the comparative advantage in the production of airplanes? What about South Korea?

b. Who has the absolute advantage in the production of airplanes? What about autos?

c. What exact number would you have to place in the empty cell of the table for it to be impossible that trade between the United States and South Korea could benefit both nations?

13. In the chapter, you saw how to create a production possibilities frontier for the United States and Mexico. Let's take a look at how to combine these PPFs to make one PPF for the U.S.–Mexico trade alliance. You'll use the same set of axes that was used in the chapter: computers on the vertical axis and shirts on the horizontal axis. Refer to Figure 2.1 and Table 2.1 as needed.

a. First, you need to plot the endpoints of the PPF by figuring out the maximum numbers of computers and shirts. If both the United States and Mexico produced only computers, how many would they produce? What if they only produced shirts? Plot these two points and label them as A (all computers) and Z (all shirts). The PPF for the U.S.–Mexico trade alliance is going to look a little different from the PPFs for the individual countries, so we don't want to simply connect the two points with a straight line. We need to figure out the rate at which the U.S.–Mexico trade alliance gives up computers to get shirts (or vice versa).

b. Starting at point A, if citizens of the United States or Mexico decided they wanted more shirts, where would those shirts be produced? Why? What do you think the PPF should look like as the U.S.–Mexico trade alliance initially moves away from point A?

c. Starting at point Z, if citizens of the United States or Mexico decided they wanted more computers, where would those computers be produced? Why? What do you think the PPF should look like as the U.S.–Mexico trade alliance initially moves away from point Z?

d. Plot the point at which each country is completely specializing in the good for which it has the comparative advantage. Label this point B. Connect points A, B, and Z. This is the PPF for the U.S.–Mexico trade alliance. Can you describe how this PPF is a combination of the two nations' separate PPFs?

e. Suppose now that a third nation, Haiti, enters the trade alliance. In Haiti, the opportunity cost of a computer is 12 shirts, and Haiti has the labor necessary to produce 1 computer (or 12 shirts). Can you draw a new PPF for the U.S.–Mexico–Haiti trade alliance?

f. Okay, what will happen to the PPF as more and more countries join the trade alliance? What would it look like with an infinite number of countries?

CHALLENGES

14. In the computers and shirts example from the chapter, the United States traded one computer to Mexico in exchange for three shirts. This is not just an arbitrary ratio of shirts to computers, however. Let's explore the *terms of trade* a little bit more.

a. Why is trading away a computer for three shirts a good trade for the United States? Why is it also a good deal for Mexico?

b. What if, instead, the agreed-upon terms of trade were one computer for eight shirts. Would this trade still benefit both the United States and Mexico?

c. What is the maximum (and minimum) number of shirts that a computer can trade for if the United States and Mexico are both to benefit from the trade?

15. Go to *www.Ted.com* and search for Thomas Thwaites's talk, "How I Built a Toaster—from Scratch." How much money and time do you think Thwaites spent building his toaster? How long do you think it would have taken Thwaites to earn enough money in, say, a minimum wage job to buy a toaster? Comment on the division of labor and the importance of specialization in increasing productivity.

WORK IT OUT

For interactive, step-by-step help in solving the following problem, go online.

Here's another specialization and exchange problem. This problem is wholly made-up, so that you won't be able to use your intuition about the names of countries or the products to figure out the answer.

a. Consider the following productivity table: Which country has an absolute advantage at making rotids? At making taurons?

	Number of Hours to Make One Rotid	Number of Hours to Make One Tauron
Mandovia	50	100
Ducennia	150	200

b. Using the information in the productivity table, estimate the opportunity cost of making rotids and taurons in Mandovia and Ducennia.

Which country has a comparative advantage at manufacturing rotids? At making taurons?

	Opportunity Cost of Making One Rotid	Opportunity Cost of Making One Tauron
Mandovia	— taurons	— rotids
Ducennia	— taurons	— rotids

c. One billion hours of labor are available for making products in Mandovia, and 2 billion hours of labor are available for making products in Ducennia. In a no-trade world, let's assume that half the labor in each country gets used to make each product. (In a semester-long international trade course, you'd build a bigger model that would determine just how the workers are divided up according to the forces of supply and demand.) Fill in the table.

	Output of Rotids	Output of Taurons
Mandovia		
Ducennia		
Total output		

d. Now allow specialization. If each country completely specializes in the product in which it holds the comparative advantage, what will the total output of rotids be? Of taurons? Is the total output of each product higher than before?

	Output of Rotids	Output of Taurons
Mandovia		
Ducennia		
Total output		

e. Finally, let's open up trade. Trade has to make both sides better off (or at least no worse off), and in this problem as in most negotiations, there's more than one price that can do so (just think about haggling over the price of a car or a house). Let's pick out a case that makes one side better off and leaves the other side just as well off as in a no-trade world. The price both sides agree to is three rotids for two taurons. Ship 5 million taurons in one direction, and 7.5 million rotids in the other direction (you'll have to figure out on your own which way the trade flows). In the following table, calculate the amount that each country gets to consume. Which country is better off under this set of prices? Which one is exactly as well off as before?

	Consumption of Rotids	Consumption of Taurons
Mandovia		
Ducennia		
Total consumption		

f. This time, the trade negotiations turn out differently: It's two rotids for one tauron. Have the correct country ship 10 million rotids, have the other send 5 million taurons, and fill out the table. One way to make sure you haven't made a mistake is to make sure that "total consumption" is equal to "total output" from part d: We can't create rotids and taurons out of thin air! Are both countries better off than if there were no trade? Which country likes this trade deal better than the deal from part e?

	Consumption of Rotids	Consumption of Taurons
Mandovia		
Ducennia		
Total consumption		

▶ MRU VIDEOS

The Big Ideas of Trade
mru.org/trade-ideas

Problems: **2, 6, 7, 9, 10**

Comparative Advantage
mru.org/comp-advantage

Problems: **1, 2, 7, 9, 10**

Another Look at Comparative Advantage
mru.org/comp-advantage-2

Problems: **1–6, 7, 8, 10, 12**

Comparative Advantage Homework
mru.org/comp-advantage-hw

Problems: **5, 9, 10, 14**

How the Division of Knowledge Saved My Son's Life
mru.org/division-labor

3

Supply and Demand

The world runs on oil. Every day about 82 *million* barrels of "black gold" flow from the earth and the sea to fuel the world's demand. Changes in the demand for and supply of oil can plunge one economy into recession while igniting a boom in another. In capitals from Washington to Riyadh, politicians carefully monitor the price of oil and so do ordinary consumers. Gasoline is made from oil so when world events like war in the Middle East disrupt the oil supply, prices at the corner gas station rise. The oil market is arguably the single most important market in the world.

The most important tools in economics are supply, demand, and the idea of equilibrium. Even if you understand little else, you may rightly claim yourself economically literate if you understand these tools. Fail to understand these tools and you will understand little else. In this chapter, we use the supply and demand for oil to explain the concepts of supply and demand. In the next chapter, we use supply, demand, and the idea of equilibrium to explain how prices are determined. So pay attention: This chapter and the next one are important. Really important.

The Demand Curve for Oil

How much oil would be demanded if the price of oil were $5 per barrel? What quantity would be demanded if the price were $20? What quantity would be demanded if the price were $55? A demand curve answers these questions. A **demand curve** is a function that shows the quantity demanded at different prices.

In Figure 3.1 on the next page, we show a hypothetical demand curve for oil and a table illustrating how a demand curve can be constructed from information on prices and quantities demanded. The demand curve tells us, for example, that at a price of $55 per barrel buyers are willing and able to buy 5 million barrels of oil a day or, more simply, at a price of $55 the **quantity demanded** is 5 million barrels a day (MBD).

Demand curves can be read in two ways. Read "horizontally," we can see from Figure 3.2 that at a price of $20 per barrel demanders are willing and able to buy 25 million barrels of oil per day. Read "vertically," we can see that the maximum price that demanders are willing to pay for 25 million barrels of oil a day is $20 per barrel. Thus, demand curves tell us the quantity demanded at

A **demand curve** is a function that shows the quantity demanded at different prices.

The **quantity demanded** is the quantity that buyers are willing and able to buy at a particular price.

FIGURE 3.1

Price	Quantity Demanded
$55	5
$20	25
$5	50

The Demand Curve for Oil Is a Function Showing the Quantity of Oil Demanded at Different Prices If the price of oil was $55 per barrel, the quantity demanded would be 5 million barrels of oil per day. If the price was $20 per barrel, what would the quantity demanded be?

any price or the maximum willingness to pay (per unit) for any quantity. Some applications are easier to understand with one reading than with the other so you should be familiar with both.

Ok, a demand curve is a function that shows the quantity that demanders are willing to buy at different prices. But what does the demand curve *mean*?

FIGURE 3.2

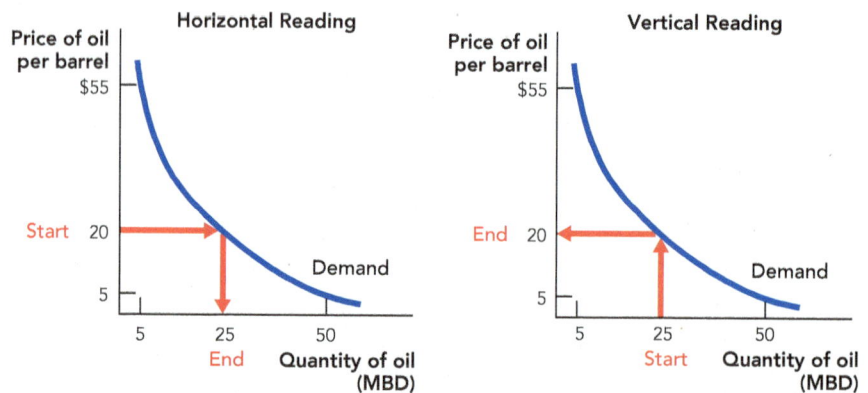

Reading a Demand Curve in Two Different Ways
Horizontal Reading: At a price of $20 per barrel, buyers are willing to buy 25 million barrels of oil per day.
Vertical Reading: The maximum price that demanders are willing to pay to purchase 25 million barrels of oil per day is $20 per barrel.

And why is the demand curve negatively sloped; that is, why is a greater quantity of oil demanded when the price is low?

Oil has many uses. A barrel of oil contains 42 gallons, and a little over half of that is used to produce gasoline (19.5 gallons) and jet fuel (4 gallons). The remaining 18.5 gallons are used for heating and energy generation and to make products such as lubricants, kerosene, asphalt, plastics, tires, and even rubber duckies (which are actually made not from rubber but from vinyl plastic).

Oil, however, is not equally valuable in all of its uses. Oil is more valuable for producing gasoline and jet fuel than it is for producing heating or rubber duckies. Oil is very valuable for transportation because in that use oil has few substitutes. There is no reasonable substitute for oil as jet fuel, for example, and although some hybrids like the Prius are moderately successful, pure electric cars like a Tesla remain costly. There are more substitutes for oil in heating and energy generation. In these fields, oil competes directly or indirectly against natural gas, coal, and electricity. Within each of these fields there are also more and less valuable uses. It's more valuable, for example, to raise the temperature in your house on a winter's day from 40 degrees to 65 degrees than it is to raise the temperature from 65 degrees to 70 degrees. Vinyl has high value as wire wrapping because it is fire-retardant, but we can probably substitute wooden toy boats for rubber duckies.

The fact that oil is not equally valuable in all of its uses explains why the demand curve for oil has a negative slope. When the price of oil is high, consumers will choose to use oil *only* in its most valuable uses (e.g., gasoline and jet fuel). As the price of oil falls, consumers will choose to also use oil in its less and less valued uses (heating and rubber duckies). Thus, a demand curve summarizes how millions of consumers choose to use oil given their preferences and the possibilities for substitution. Figure 3.3 illustrates these ideas with a demand curve for oil.

MRU

mru.org/demand

Why Does the Demand Curve Slope Down and Why Is This Important?

FIGURE 3.3

The Demand for Oil Depends on the Value of Oil in Different Uses When the price of oil is high, oil will be used only in its higher-valued uses. As the price of oil falls, oil will also be used in lower-valued uses.

(Top: ssuaphotos/Shutterstock)
(Bottom: Lew Robertson/Corbis)

In summary, a demand curve is a function that shows the quantity that demanders are willing and able to buy at different prices. The lower the price, the greater the quantity demanded—this is often called the "law of demand."

Consumer Surplus

If a consumer, say, the president of the United States, is willing to pay $80 per barrel to fuel his jet plane but the price of oil is only $20 per barrel, then the president earns a consumer surplus of $60 per barrel. If Joanne is willing to pay $25 and the price of oil is $20 per barrel, then Joanne earns a consumer surplus of $5 per barrel. For most of the products that you buy, you would probably be willing to pay more than the price, if you had to. The difference between what you are willing to pay and what you must pay (the price) is consumer surplus. **Consumer surplus** is the consumer's gain from exchange. Adding up consumer surplus for each consumer and for each unit, we can find **total consumer surplus**. On a graph, *total consumer surplus is the shaded area beneath the demand curve and above the price* (see Figure 3.4).

It's often convenient to approximate demand and supply curves with straight lines—this makes it easy to calculate areas like consumer surplus. The right panel of Figure 3.4 simplifies the left panel. Now we can calculate consumer surplus using a little high school geometry. Recall that the area of a triangle is $\frac{\text{Base} \times \text{Height}}{2}$. The base of the consumer surplus triangle is 90 million barrels and the height is $60 = $80 − $20, so consumer surplus equals $2,700 million ($\frac{1}{2} \times$ 90 million $\times$ $60).

Consumer surplus is the consumer's gain from exchange, or the difference between the maximum price a consumer is willing to pay for a certain quantity and the market price.

Total consumer surplus is measured by the area beneath the demand curve and above the price.

FIGURE 3.4

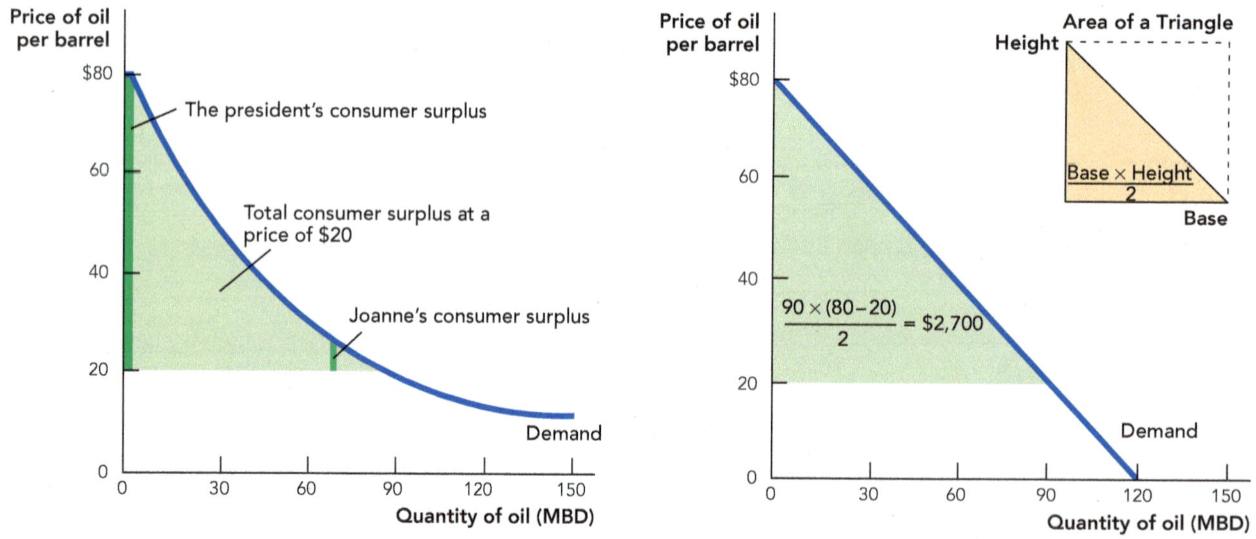

Total Consumer Surplus Is the Area Beneath the Demand Curve and Above the Price Total consumer surplus is the sum of consumer surplus of all buyers, the area beneath the demand curve and above the price. In the right panel, we show that consumer surplus is easy to calculate with a linear demand curve.

What Shifts the Demand Curve?

The demand curve for oil tells us the quantity of oil that people are willing to buy at a given price. Assume, for example, that at a price of $25 per barrel, the world demand for oil is 70 million barrels per day. An increase in demand means that at a price of $25, the quantity demanded increases to, say, 80 million barrels per day. Or, equivalently, it means that the maximum willingness to pay for 70 million barrels increases to say $50 per barrel. The left panel of Figure 3.5 shows an increase in demand. *An increase in demand shifts the demand curve outward, up and to the right.*

The right panel of Figure 3.5 shows a decrease in demand. *A decrease in demand shifts the demand curve inward, down and to the left.*

What kinds of things will increase or decrease demand? Unfortunately for economics students, a lot of things! Here is a list of some important demand shifters:

Important Demand Shifters

- Income
- Population
- Price of substitutes
- Price of complements
- Expectations
- Tastes

If you must, memorize the list. But keep in mind the question, "What would make people willing to buy a greater quantity at the same price?" Or equivalently, "What would make people willing to pay more for the same quantity?" With these questions in mind, you should always be able to come up with a fairly good list on your own.

FIGURE 3.5

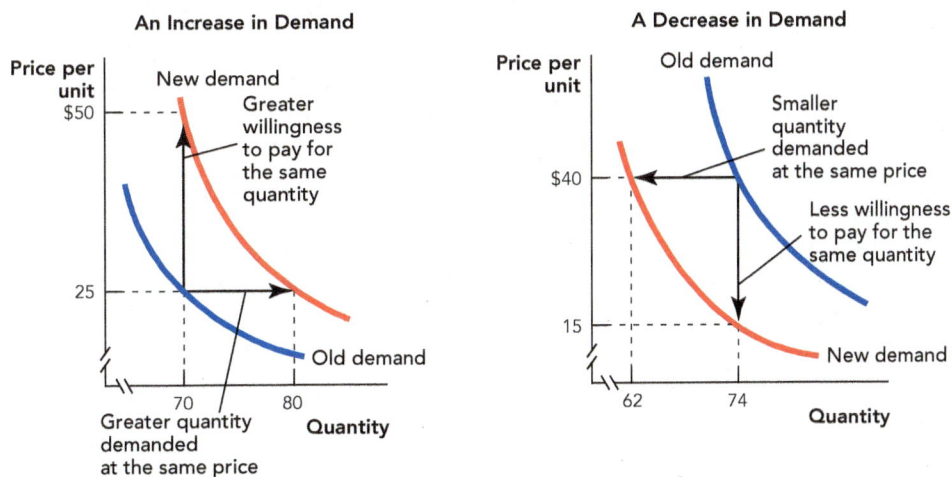

Shifting the Demand Curve An increase in demand shifts the demand curve outward, up and to the right. A decrease in demand shifts the demand curve inward, down and to the left.

Here are some examples of demand shifters in action.

Income When people get richer, they buy more stuff. In the United States, people buy bigger cars when their income increases and big cars increase the demand for oil. When income increases in China or India, many people buy their first car and that too increases the demand for oil. Thus, an increase in income will increase the demand for oil exactly as shown in the left panel of Figure 3.5.

When an *increase* in income *increases* the demand for a good, we say the good is a **normal good**. Most goods are normal; for example, cars, electronics, and restaurant meals are normal goods. Can you think of some goods for which an increase in income will *decrease* the demand? When we were young economics students, we didn't have a lot of money to go to expensive restaurants. For 50 cents and some boiling water, however, we could get a nice bowl of instant Ramen noodles. Ah, good times. When our income increased, however, our demand for Ramen noodles decreased—we don't buy Ramen noodles anymore! A good like Ramen noodles for which an *increase* in income *decreases* the demand is called an **inferior good**. What goods are you consuming now that you probably wouldn't consume if you were rich? Economic growth is rapidly increasing the incomes of millions of poor people in China and India. What goods do poor people consume in these countries today that they will consume less of 20 years from now?

Population More people, more demand. That's simple enough. Things get more interesting when some subpopulations increase more than others. The United States, for example, is aging. Today the 65-year-old and older crowd makes up about 14.5% of the population. By 2030, 19.4% of the population will be 65 years or older. In fact, demographers estimate that by 2030, 18.2 million people in the United States will be over 85 years of age![1] What sorts of goods and services will increase in demand with this increase in population? Which will decrease in demand? Entrepreneurs want to know the answers to these questions because big profits will flow to those who can anticipate new and expanded markets.

The Price of Substitutes and Complements Every good has substitutes and complements. Natural gas is a substitute for oil in some uses such as heating. Suppose that the price of natural gas goes down. What will happen to the demand for oil? When the price of natural gas goes down, some people will switch from oil furnaces to natural gas, so the demand for oil will decrease— the demand curve shifts down and to the left. Figure 3.6 illustrates.

More generally, a decrease in the price of a **substitute** will decrease demand for the other good. A decrease in the price of Pepsi, for example, will decrease the demand for Coca-Cola. Naturally, an increase in the price of a substitute will increase demand for the other good.

Complements are things that go well together such as ground beef and hamburger buns, sugar and tea, iPhones and iPhone apps. Demand for a good increases when the price of a complementary good decreases (and vice-versa).

It sounds complicated, so just remember that ground beef and hamburger buns are complements. Suppose the price of beef goes down. What happens to the demand for hamburger buns? If the price of beef goes down, people buy more ground beef and they also increase their demand for hamburger buns; that is, the demand curve for hamburger buns shifts up and to the right. A supermarket having a sale on ground beef, for example, will also want to stock up on hamburger buns.

In explaining the basics of lobbying and regulation, the Nobel Prize–winning economist George Stigler said, "the butter producers wish to suppress margarine and encourage the production of bread."[2] More generally, firms want the

A **normal good** is a good for which demand increases when income increases.

An **inferior good** is a good for which demand decreases when income increases.

Demographics and demand The number of old people in the United States is increasing. How will this increase in the elderly population shift the demand curve for different goods?

If two goods are **substitutes**, a decrease in the price of one good leads to a decrease in demand for the other good.

If two goods are **complements**, a decrease in the price of one good leads to an increase in the demand for the other good.

FIGURE 3.6

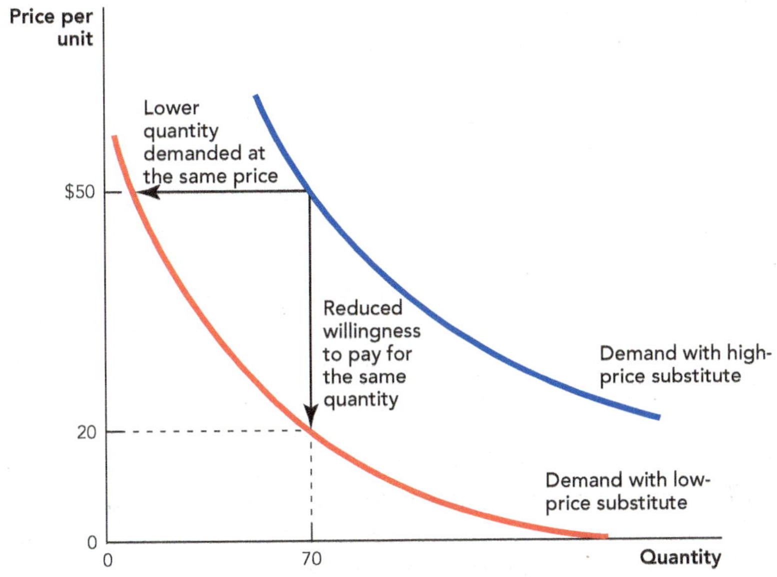

A Decrease in the Price of a Substitute (e.g., Natural Gas) Reduces the Demand for Oil When the price of a substitute falls, more people will want to buy the substitute so the demand for the substituted good falls.

CHECK YOURSELF

- Google makes its Android operating system for smartphones available for free under an open source license. Why?

substitutes for their products to be expensive and the complements to be cheap. So let's consider the last item in our list of complements, iPhones and iPhone apps. Does Apple want cheap apps or expensive apps? Apple wants cheap apps so we can predict that Apple will make it easy to write iPhone apps and that it will promote a competitive marketplace in apps.

Expectations In July 2019, oil prices spiked upward after Iran seized two British oil tankers in the Strait of Hormuz. Is a single oil tanker or even two so critical to the world supply of oil? No. But Iran, Iraq, and Saudi Arabia shipped 21 million barrels of oil through the strait every *day* and demanders of oil feared that the Iranian seizures might have been the start of a large-scale disruption. Fear of future disruptions encouraged businesses and governments to buy more oil now and increase emergency stockpiles. In other words, *the expectation of a reduction in the future oil supply increased the demand for oil today.*

You have probably responded to expectations about future events in a similar way. When the weather forecaster predicts a big storm, many people rush to the stores to stock up on storm supplies. In the week before Hurricane Sandy hit New Jersey, for example, sales of flashlights and batteries skyrocketed.

Expectations are powerful—they can be as powerful in affecting demand (and supply) as events themselves.

Tastes Tastes are always changing. The keto diet increased the demand for beef and helped to make steakhouses such as Outback Steakhouse and the Brazilian-inspired Fogo De Chão popular. But in recent years, the "ethical eating" trend has increased the demand for less processed foods and more plant-based foods, including new plant-based meat substitutes such as the Impossible™ Burger. You can now even buy an Impossible™ Burger at Burger King.

LeBron James's three NBA championships, four Most Valuable Player awards, and two Olympic gold medals have made him one of the most sought after

CHECK YOURSELF

- Economic growth in India is raising the income of Indian workers. What do you predict will happen to the demand for automobiles? What about the demand for charcoal bricks for home heating?
- As the price of oil rises, what do you predict will happen to the demand for mopeds?

athletes in the world for product endorsements. Nike pays LeBron millions of dollars. Why? Because LeBron's endorsement increases the demand for Nike shoes. Changes in tastes caused by fads, fashions, and advertising can all increase or decrease demand.

Can tastes change something like the demand for oil? Sure. The environmental movement has made people more aware of global climate change and how the consumption of oil adds carbon dioxide to the atmosphere. As a result, the demand for hybrid cars has increased, more people are recycling things like plastic bags, and more people are considering installing solar power cells on their rooftops as an alternative source of energy. All of these changes can be understood as a change in tastes or preferences.

The bottom line is that while many factors can shape market demand, most of these factors should make intuitive sense. After all, you are, on a daily basis, part of market demand.

The Supply Curve for Oil

The **supply curve** is a function that shows the quantity supplied at different prices.

The **quantity supplied** is the amount of a good that sellers are willing and able to sell at a particular price.

How much oil would oil producers supply to the world market if the price of oil were $5 per barrel? What quantity would be supplied if the price were $20? What quantity if the price were $55? A supply curve for oil answers these questions.

The **supply curve** for oil is a function showing the quantity of oil that suppliers would be willing and able to sell at different prices, or, more simply, the supply curve shows the **quantity supplied** at different prices. Figure 3.7 shows a hypothetical supply curve for oil. The price is on the vertical axis and

FIGURE 3.7

Price	Quantity Supplied
$55	50
$20	30
$5	10

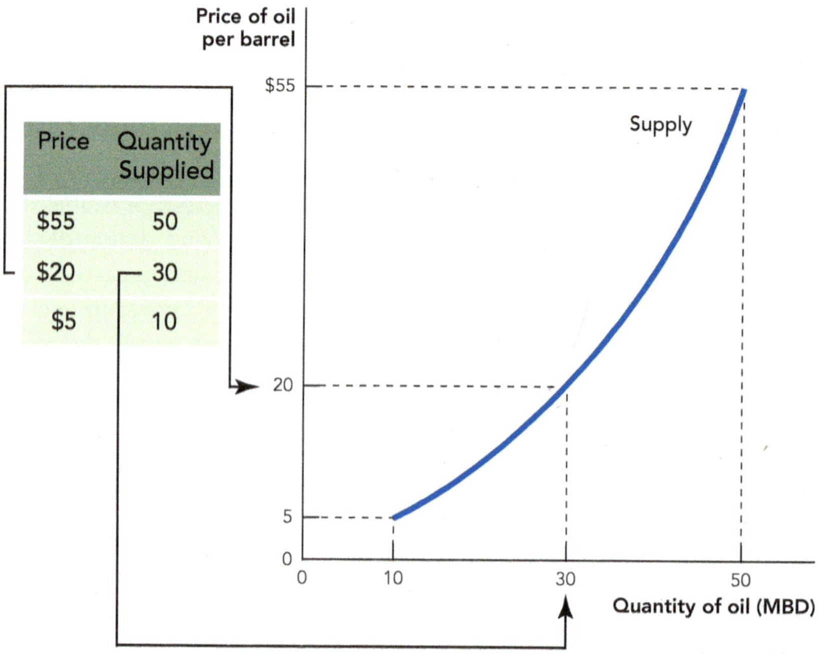

The Supply Curve for Oil Is a Function Showing the Quantity of Oil Supplied at Different Prices If the price of oil was $20 per barrel, the quantity of oil supplied would be 30 million barrels of oil per day. How much oil would suppliers be willing and able to sell at $55?

the quantity of oil is on the horizontal axis. The table beside the graph shows how a supply curve can be constructed from a table of prices and quantities supplied.

The supply curve tells us, for example, that at a price of $20 the quantity supplied is 30 million barrels of oil a day.

As with demand curves, supply curves can be read in two ways. Read "horizontally," Figure 3.8 shows that at a price of $20 per barrel suppliers are willing to sell 30 million barrels of oil per day. Read "vertically," the supply curve tells us that to produce 30 million barrels of oil a day, suppliers must be paid at least $20 per barrel. Thus, the supply curve tells us the maximum quantity that suppliers will supply at different prices or the minimum price at which suppliers will sell different quantities. The two ways of reading a supply curve are equivalent, but some applications are easier to understand with one reading and some with the other so you should be familiar with both.

Our hypothetical supply curve is not realistic because we just made up the numbers. But now that we know the technical meaning of a supply curve—*a function that shows the quantity that suppliers would be willing and able to sell at different prices*—we can easily explain its economic meaning.

Saudi Arabia, the world's largest oil producer, produces about 10 million barrels of oil per day. Surprisingly, the United States is not far behind, producing nearly 9 million barrels per day. But there is one big difference between Saudi oil and U.S. oil: U.S. oil costs much more to produce. The United States has been producing major quantities of oil since 1901 when, after drilling to a depth of 1,020 feet, mud started to bubble out of an oil well dug in Spindletop, Texas. Minutes later the drill bit exploded into the air and a fountain of oil leapt 150 feet into the sky. It took nine days to cap the well, and in the process a million barrels of oil were spilt. No one had ever seen so much oil. Within months the price of oil dropped from $2 per barrel to just 3 cents per barrel.[3]

It's safe to say that the United States will never see another gusher like Spindletop. Today the typical new well in the United States is drilled to a depth of

FIGURE 3.8

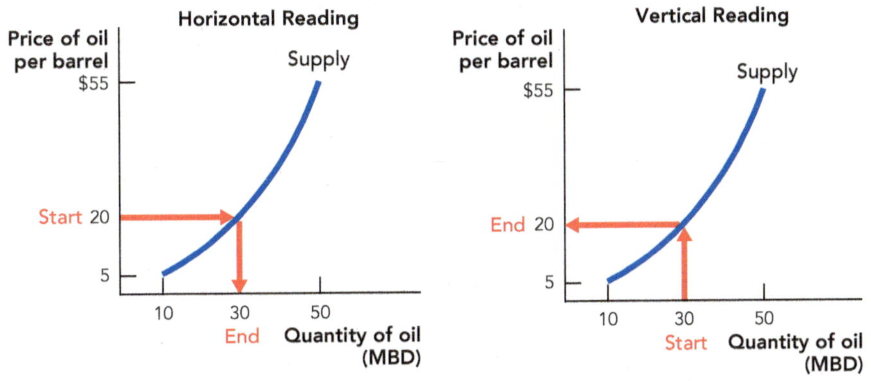

Reading a Supply Curve in Two Different Ways
Horizontal Reading: At a price of $20 per barrel, suppliers are willing to sell 30 million barrels of oil per day.
Vertical Reading: To produce 30 million barrels of oil a day, suppliers must be paid at least $20 per barrel.

more than 1 mile. Instead of gushing, most of the wells must be pumped or flooded with water to push the oil to the surface.[4] All this makes oil production in the United States much more expensive than it used to be and much more expensive than in Saudi Arabia, where oil is more plentiful than anywhere else in the world.

In Saudi Arabia, lifting a barrel of oil to the surface costs about $2. Costs in Iran and Iraq are only slightly higher. Nigerian and Russian oil can be extracted at a cost of around $5 and $7 per barrel, respectively. Alaskan oil costs around $10 to extract. Oil from Britain's North Sea costs about $12 to extract. There is more oil in Canada's tar sands than in all of Iran, but it costs about $22.50 per barrel to get the oil out of the sand.[5] In the continental United States, one of the oldest and most developed oil regions in the world, lifting costs are about $27.50. At a price of $40 per barrel, it becomes profitable to "sweat" oil out of Oklahoma oil shale.

Putting all of this together, we can construct a simple supply curve for oil. At a price of $2 per barrel, the only oil that would be profitable to produce would be oil from the lowest-cost wells in places like Saudi Arabia. As the price of oil rises, oil from Iran and Iraq become profitable. When the price reaches $5, Nigerian and then Russian producers begin to just break even. As the price rises yet further toward $10, Alaskan oil starts to break even and then become profitable. North Sea, Canadian, and then Texan oil fields come online and increase production as the price rises further. At higher prices, it becomes profitable to extract oil using even more exotic technologies or deeper wells in more inhospitable parts of the world. Figure 3.9 illustrates.

FIGURE 3.9

The Supply Curve for Oil As the price of oil rises, it becomes profitable to extract oil from more costly sources. Thus, as the price of oil rises, the quantity of oil supplied increases.

(Top: 24Novembers/Shutterstock*)*
(Bottom: Bettmann/Getty Images*)*

What's important to understand about Figure 3.9 is that as the price of oil rises, it becomes profitable to produce oil using methods and in regions of the world with higher costs of production. The higher the price of oil, the deeper the wells.

In summary, a supply curve is a function that shows the quantity that suppliers would be willing and able to sell at different prices. The higher the price, the greater the quantity supplied—this is often called the "law of supply."

Producer Surplus

Figure 3.9 suggests two other concepts of importance. If the price of oil is $40 per barrel and Saudi Arabia can produce oil at $2 per barrel, then we say that Saudi Arabia earns a **producer surplus** of $38 per barrel. Similarly, if the price of oil is $40 per barrel and Nigeria can produce at $5 a barrel, Nigeria earns a producer surplus of $35 per barrel. More generally, the difference between the lowest price that a producer is willing to sell a good for and the actual price is the producer's surplus, the producer's gain from exchange. Adding the producer surplus for each producer for each unit, we can find total producer surplus. Fortunately, this is easy to do on a diagram. *Total producer surplus is the area above the supply curve and below the price* (see Figure 3.10).

Consumer surplus measures the consumer's benefit from trade, and producer surplus measures the producer's benefit from trade. If we add the two surpluses together, we get a measure of the total gains from trade to market participants. All else equal, more benefits are better so throughout this text, we will be using consumer plus producer surplus as a measure of welfare to compare different institutions and policies such as markets, monopolies, price controls, quotas, taxes and subsidies. Which of these institutions maximizes total benefits and under what conditions? Of course, sometimes not all else is equal, and when we study externalities and ethics, we will look at situations where it's important to add to our measure of benefits (and costs) to take into account the effect of trade on bystanders and on broader social interests.

Producer surplus is the producer's gain from exchange, or the difference between the market price and the minimum price at which a producer would be willing to sell a particular quantity.

Total producer surplus is measured by the area above the supply curve and below the price.

FIGURE 3.10

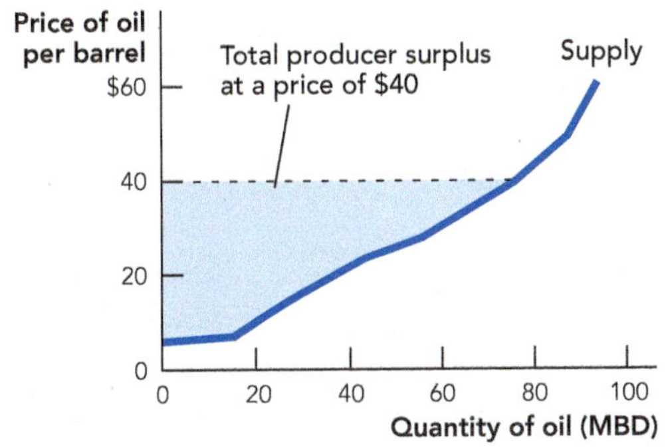

Total Producer Surplus Is the Area Above the Supply Curve and Below the Price Total producer surplus is the sum of the producer surplus of each seller, the area above the supply curve and below the price.

What Shifts the Supply Curve?

The second important concept suggested by Figure 3.9 is the connection between the supply curve and costs. What happens to the supply curve when the cost of producing oil falls? Suppose, for example, that a technological innovation in oil drilling such as sidewise drilling allows more oil to be produced at the same cost. What happens to the supply curve? The supply curve tells us how much suppliers are willing to sell at a particular price. The new technology makes some oil fields profitable that were previously unprofitable, so *at any price* suppliers are now willing to supply a greater quantity. Equivalently, the new technology lowers costs, so suppliers will be willing to sell any given quantity at a lower price. Either way, economists say that a decrease in costs increases supply. In terms of the diagram, *a decrease in costs means that the supply curve shifts down and to the right*, which the left panel of Figure 3.11 illustrates. Of course, *higher costs mean that the supply curve shifts in the opposite direction, up and to the left* as illustrated in the right panel of Figure 3.11.

Once you know that a decrease in costs shifts the supply curve down and to the right and an increase in costs shifts the supply curve up and to the left, then you really know everything there is to know about supply shifts. It can take a little practice, however, to identify the many factors that can change costs. Here are some important supply shifters:

Important Supply Shifters

- Technological innovations and changes in the price of inputs
- Taxes and subsidies
- Expectations
- Entry or exit of producers
- Changes in opportunity costs

FIGURE 3.11

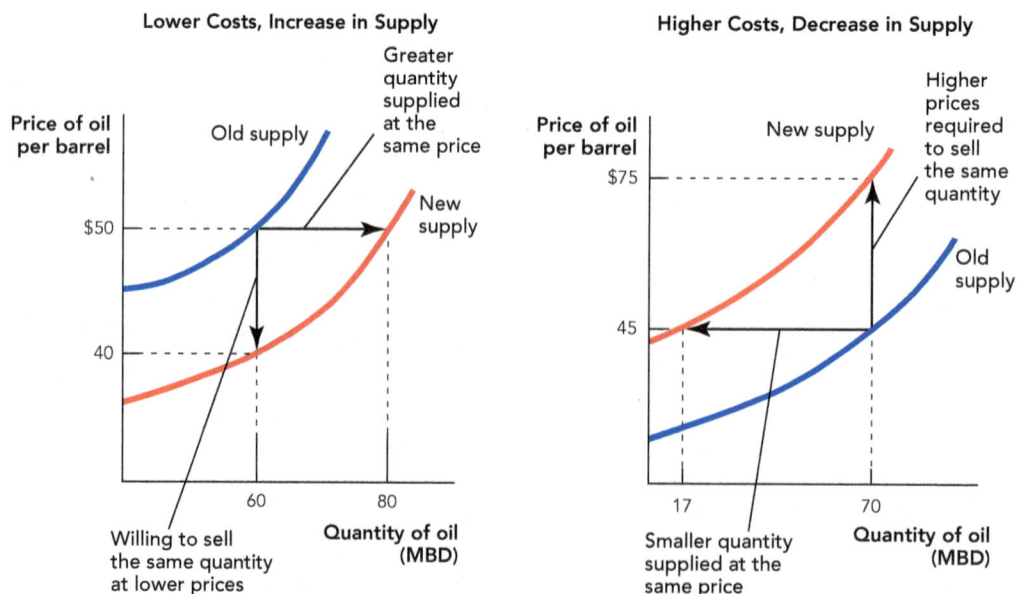

Lower Costs, Increase in Supply

Higher Costs, Decrease in Supply

Shifting the Supply Curve A decrease in costs increases supply, shifting the supply curve down and to the right. An increase in costs decreases supply, shifting the supply curve up and to the left.

It can also help in analyzing supply shifters to know that sometimes it's easier to think of cost changes as shifting the supply curve right or left, and other times it's a little easier to think of cost changes as shifting the supply curve up or down. These two methods of thinking about supply shifts are equivalent and correspond to the two methods of reading a supply curve, the horizontal and vertical readings, respectively. We will give examples of each method as we examine some cost shifters in action.

Technological Innovations and Changes in the Price of Inputs
We have already given an example of how improvements in technology can reduce costs, thus increasing supply. A reduction in input prices also reduces costs and thus has a similar effect. A fall in the wages of oil rig workers, for example, will reduce the cost of producing oil, shifting the supply curve down and to the right as in the left panel of Figure 3.11. Alternatively, an increase in the wages of oil rig workers will increase the cost of producing oil, shifting the supply curve up and to the left as in the right panel of Figure 3.11.

Taxes and Subsidies
We can get some practice using up or down shifts to analyze a cost change by examining the effect of a $10 oil tax on the supply curve for oil. As far as firms are concerned, a tax on output is the same as an increase in costs. If the government taxes oil producers $10 per barrel, this is exactly the same to producers as an increase in their costs of production of $10 per barrel.

In Figure 3.12, notice that before the tax, firms require $40 per barrel to sell 60 million barrels of oil per day (point a). How much will firms require to sell the same quantity of oil when there is a tax of $10 per barrel? Correct, $50. What firms care about is the take-home price. If firms require $40 per barrel to sell 60 million barrels of oil, that's what they require regardless of the tax. When the government takes $10 per barrel, firms must charge $50 to keep their take-home price at $40. Thus, in Figure 3.12, notice that the $10 tax shifts the supply curve up by exactly $10 at *every point* along the curve.

It's important to avoid one possible confusion. All we have said so far is that a $10 tax shifts the supply curve for oil up by $10. We haven't said anything about the effect of a tax on the *price* of oil—that's because we have not yet analyzed how market prices are formed. We are saving that topic for Chapter 4.

FIGURE 3.12

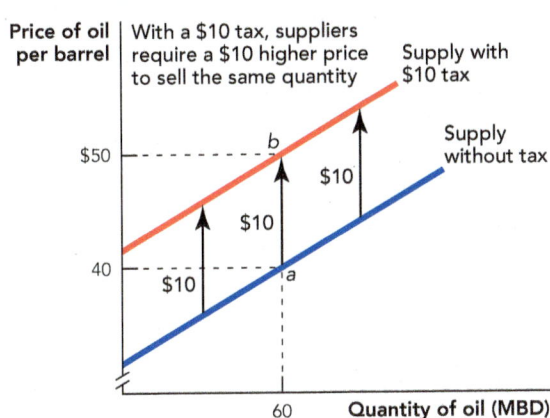

A Tax on Industry Output Shifts the Supply Curve Up by the Amount of the Tax When suppliers pay no tax, they are willing to supply 60 million barrels a day (MBD) of oil for a price of $40 per barrel. If they must pay a tax of $10 per barrel, they will be willing to supply 60 MBD for $10 more, or $50 a barrel. Thus, a tax shifts the supply curve up by the amount of the tax.

How does a subsidy, a tax-benefit, or write-off shift the supply curve? We will save that analysis for the end-of-chapter problems but here's a hint: A subsidy is the same as a negative or "reverse" tax.

Expectations Suppliers who expect that prices will increase in the future have an incentive to sell less today so that they can store goods for future sale. Thus, the expectation of a future price increase shifts today's supply curve to the left as illustrated in Figure 3.13. The shifting of supply in response to price expectations is the essence of *speculation*, the attempt to profit from future price changes.

Entry or Exit of Producers When the United States signed the North American Free Trade Agreement (NAFTA), reducing barriers to trade among the United States, Mexico, and Canada, Canadian producers of lumber entered the U.S. market and increased the supply of lumber. We can most easily think about this as a shift to the right of the supply curve.

In Figure 3.14, the domestic supply curve is the supply curve for lumber before NAFTA. The curve labeled domestic supply plus Canadian imports is the supply curve for lumber after NAFTA allowed Canadian firms to sell in the United States with fewer restrictions. The entry of more firms meant that

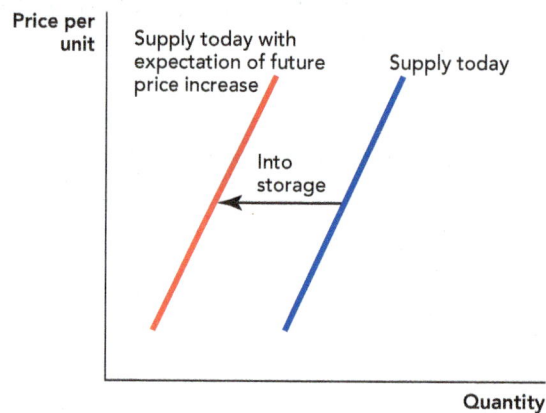

FIGURE 3.13

Expectations Can Shift the Supply Curve If sellers expect a higher price in the future, today's supply curve will shift to the left as producers store some of the good for future sale.

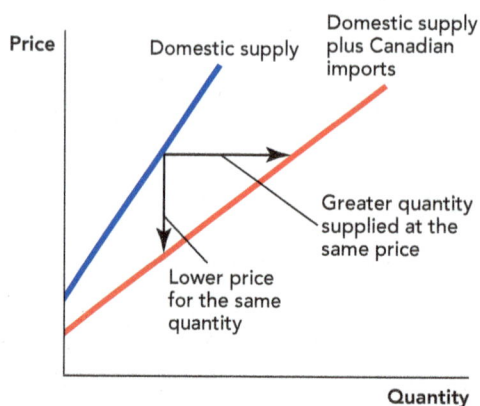

FIGURE 3.14

Entry Increases Supply The entry of lower-cost producers increases supply, thus shifting the supply curve to the right and down.

at any price a greater quantity of lumber was available; that is, the supply curve shifted to the right.*

In a later chapter, we discuss the effects of foreign trade at greater length.

Changes in Opportunity Costs The last important supply shifter, changes in opportunity costs, is the trickiest to understand. Recall from Chapter 1 that when the unemployment rates increase, more people tend to go to college. If you can't get a job, you aren't giving up many good opportunities by going to college. Thus, when the unemployment rate increases, the (opportunity) cost of college falls and so more people attend college. Notice that to understand how people behave, you must understand their opportunity costs.

Now suppose that a farmer is currently growing soybeans but that his land could also be used to grow wheat. If the price of *wheat* increases, then the farmer's opportunity cost of growing soybeans increases and the farmer will want to shift land from soybean production into the more profitable alternative of wheat production. As land is taken out of soybean production, the supply curve for soybeans shifts up and to the left.

In Figure 3.15, notice that before the increase in the price of wheat, farmers would be willing to supply 2,800 million bushels of soybeans at a price of $5 per bushel (point *a*). But when the price of wheat increases, farmers are willing to supply only 2,000 million bushels of soybeans at a price of $5 per bushel because an alternative use of the land (growing wheat) is now more valuable. Equivalently, before the increase in the price of wheat, farmers were

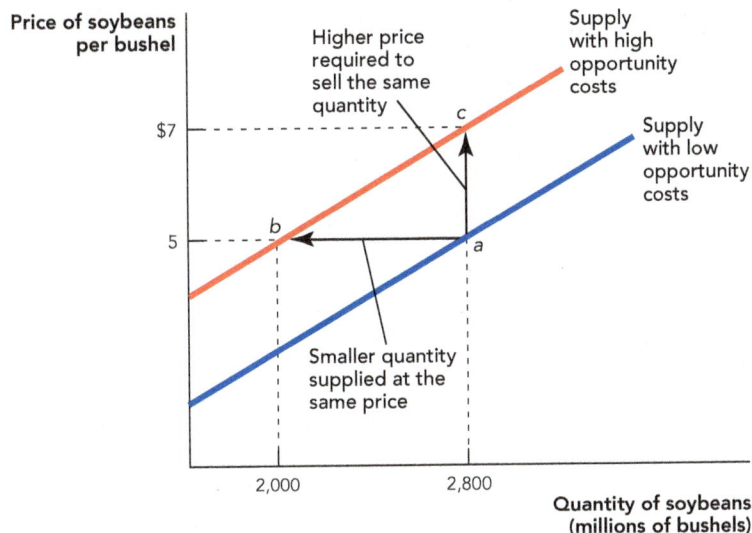

FIGURE 3.15

Higher (Opportunity) Costs Reduce Supply An increase in the price of wheat increases the opportunity cost of growing soybeans, which shifts the supply curve of soybeans up and to the left.

---

* It is equally correct to think of new entrants as shifting the supply curve down. Remember, it's ultimately costs that shift supply, and what increases supply is entry of *lower-cost* producers. Industry costs fell when Canadian producers entered the market because many Canadian producers had lower costs than some U.S. producers. As lower-cost Canadian producers entered the industry, higher-cost U.S. producers exited the industry, and industry costs decreased, thus shifting the supply curve down.

willing to sell 2,800 million bushels of soybeans for $5 per bushel, but after their opportunity costs increase, farmers require $7 per bushel to sell the same quantity (point *c*).

Similarly, a decrease in opportunity costs shifts the supply curve down and to the right. If the price of wheat falls, for example, the opportunity cost of growing soybeans falls and the supply curve for soybeans will shift down and to the right. It's just another example of a running theme throughout this chapter, namely that both supply and demand respond to incentives.

Takeaway

In this chapter, we have presented the fundamentals of the demand curve and the supply curve. The next chapter and much of the rest of this book build on these fundamentals. We thus give you fair warning. If you do not understand this chapter and the next, you will be lost!

A key point to know is that a demand curve is a function showing the quantity demanded at different prices. In other words, a demand curve shows how customers respond to higher prices by buying less and to lower prices by buying more. Another key point is that, similarly, a supply curve is a function showing the quantity supplied at different prices. In other words, a supply curve shows how producers respond to higher prices by producing more and to lower prices by producing less.

The difference between the maximum price a consumer is willing to pay for a product and the market price is the consumer's gain from exchange or consumer surplus. The difference between the market price and the minimum price at which a producer is willing to sell a product is the producer's gain from exchange or producer surplus. You should be able to identify total consumer and producer surplus, the total gain from exchange, on a diagram. In future chapters, we will be using total consumer plus total producer surplus to evaluate different institutions and policies.

When it comes to what shifts the supply and demand curves, we have listed some factors in this chapter. Yes, you should know these lists but more fundamentally you should know that an increase in demand *means* that buyers want a greater quantity at the same price or, equivalently, they are willing to pay a higher price for the same quantity. Thus, anything that causes buyers to want more at the same price or be willing to pay more for the same quantity increases demand. In a pinch, just think about some of the factors that would cause you to want more of a good at the same price or that would make you willing to pay more for the same quantity.

Similarly, an increase in supply *means* that sellers are willing to sell a greater quantity at the same price or, equivalently, they are willing to sell a given quantity at a lower price. Again, what would make you willing to sell more of a good for the same price or sell the same quantity for a lower price? (Here's a hint—you might be willing to do this if your costs had fallen.) Supply and demand curves are not just abstract constructs, they also shape your life.

In the next chapter, we will use supply curves and demand curves to answer one of the most crucial questions in economics: How is the price of a good determined?

CHAPTER REVIEW

Go online to practice with more examples of these types of problems, including live links to videos, data sources, and feedback.

▶ Problems with this icon relate to optional MRU videos.

KEY CONCEPTS

demand curve, p. 29

quantity demanded, p. 29

consumer surplus, p. 32

total consumer surplus, p. 32

normal good, p. 34

inferior good, p. 34

substitutes, p. 34

complements, p. 34

supply curve, p. 36

quantity supplied, p. 36

producer surplus, p. 39

total producer surplus, p. 39

FACTS AND TOOLS

1. When the price of a good increases, the quantity demanded _____. When the price of a good decreases, the quantity demanded _____.

2. When will people search harder for substitutes for oil: When the price of oil is high or when the price of oil is low?

3. Your roommate just bought a TomTom Spark GPS fitness watch for $130. She would have been willing to pay $250 for a device that could improve her morning runs by measuring the speed, distance, and duration of the runs, and calculating the calories she burns. How much consumer surplus does your roommate enjoy from the Nike+ Sportwatch?

4. What are three things that you'll buy less of once you graduate from college and get a good job? What kinds of goods are these called?

5. When the price of Apple MacBooks goes down, what probably happens to the demand for laptops featuring Microsoft Windows?

6. a. When the price of olive oil goes up, what probably happens to the demand for corn oil?

   b. When the price of petroleum goes up, what probably happens to the demand for natural gas? To the demand for coal? To the demand for solar power?

7. a. If everyone thinks that the price of tomatoes will go up next week, what is likely to happen to demand for tomatoes today?

   b. If everyone thinks that the price of gasoline will go up next week, what is likely to happen to the demand for gasoline today? (*Note:* Is this change in demand caused by consumers or by gas station owners?)

8. Along a supply curve, if the price of oil falls, what will happen to the quantity of oil supplied? Why?

9. If the price of cars falls, are carmakers likely to make more or fewer cars, according to the supply curve? (Notice that the "person on the street" often thinks the opposite is true!)

10. When is a pharmaceutical business more likely to hire highly educated, cutting-edge workers and use new, experimental research methods: When the business expects the price of its new drug to be low or when it expects the price to be high?

11. Imagine that a technological innovation reduces the costs of producing high-quality steel. What happens to the supply curve for steel?

12. When oil companies expect the price of oil to be higher next year, what happens to the supply of oil today?

13. Do taxes usually increase the supply of a good or reduce the supply?

THINKING AND PROBLEM SOLVING

▶ **14.** Consider the following supply curve for oil. Note that MBD stands for "millions of barrels per day," the usual way people talk about the supply of oil:

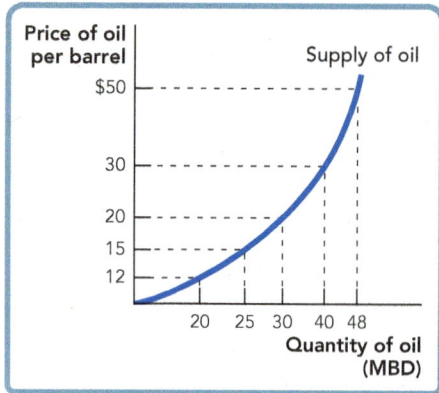

a. Based on this supply curve, fill in the table:

Price	Quantity Supplied
$12	
	40

b. If the price for a barrel of oil was $15, how much oil would oil suppliers be willing to supply?

c. What is the lowest price at which suppliers of oil would be willing to supply 20 MBD?

▶ **15.** From the following table of prices per 100 pencils and quantities supplied (in hundreds of pencils), draw the supply curve for pencils:

Price	Quantity Supplied
$5	20
$15	40
$25	50
$35	55

▶ **16.** Suppose LightBright and Bulbs4You were the only two suppliers of lightbulbs in Springfield. Draw the supply curve for the lightbulb industry in Springfield from the following table for the two companies. To create this "lightbulb industry supply curve," note that you'll add up the *total* number of bulbs that the industry will supply at a price of $1 (15 bulbs), and then do the same for the prices of $5, $7, and $10.

Price	Bulbs Supplied by LightBright	Bulbs Supplied by Bulbs4You
$1	10	5
$5	15	7
$7	25	15
$10	35	20

▶ **17.** Using the following diagram, identify and calculate total producer surplus if the price of oil is $50 per barrel. Recall that for a triangle, Area = (1/2) × Base × Height. (You never thought you'd use that equation unless you became an engineer, did you?)

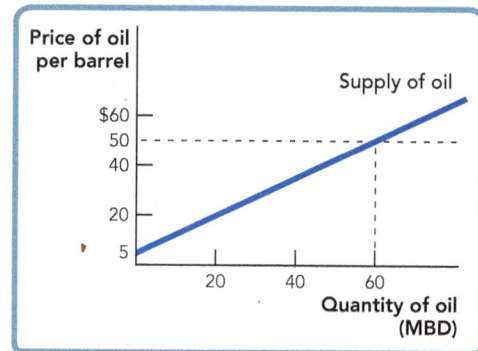

▶ **18.** In Sucrosia, the supply curve for sugar is as follows:

Price (per 100-pound bag)	Quantity
$30	10,000
$50	15,000
$70	20,000

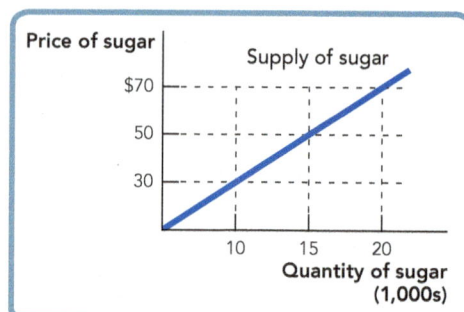

Under pressure from nutrition activists, the government decides to tax sugar producers with a $5 tax per 100-pound bag. Using the figure above, draw the new supply curve. After the tax is enacted, what price will bring forth quantities of 10,000? 15,000? 20,000? Give your answers in the table:

Price (per 100-pound bag)	Quantity
	10,000
	15,000
	20,000

19. Consider the farmers talked about in the chapter who have land that is suitable for growing both wheat and soybeans. Suppose all farmers are currently farming wheat but the price of soybeans rises dramatically.

  a. Does the opportunity cost of producing wheat rise or fall?

  b. Does this shift the supply curve for wheat (as in one of the panels of Figure 3.11), or is it a movement along a fixed supply curve?

  What direction is this shift or movement? Illustrate your answer in the following figure:

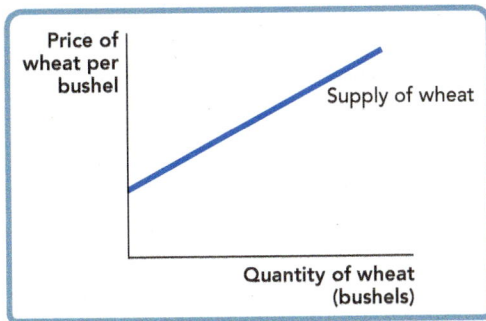

20. Consider the following demand curve for oil:

  a. Using this demand curve, fill in the following table:

Price	Quantity Demanded
	55
$25	

  b. If the price was $10, how much oil would be demanded?

  c. What is the maximum price (per barrel) that demanders will pay for 20 million barrels of oil?

21. From the following chart, draw the demand curve for pencils (in hundreds):

Price	Quantity Demanded (100s)
$5	60
$15	45
$25	35
$35	20

22. If the price of glass dramatically increases, what are we likely to see a lot less of: glass windows or glass bottles? Why?

23. Let's think about the demand for LED TVs.

  a. If the price for a 60-inch LED TV is $500, and Newhart would be willing to pay $3,000, what is Newhart's consumer surplus?

  b. Consider the following figure for the total demand for LED TVs. At $500 per TV, 1,200 TVs were demanded. What would be the total consumer surplus? Calculate the total, and identify it on the diagram.

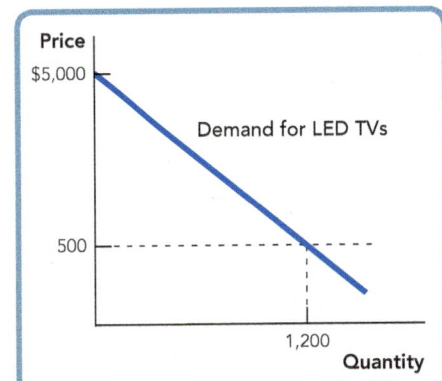

  c. Where is Newhart in the figure?

24. If income increases and the demand for good X shifts as shown in the figure, then is good X a normal or inferior good? Give an example of a good like good X.

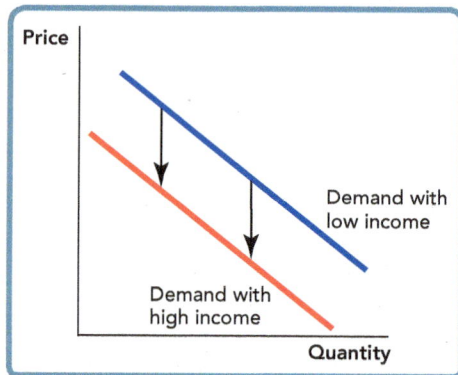

25. Assume that butter and margarine are substitutes. What will happen to the demand curve for butter if the price of margarine increases? Why?

26. Cars and gasoline are complements. What will happen to the demand curve for gasoline if the price of cars decreases? Why? (*Hint:* What happens to the quantity demanded of cars?)

27. Suppose that the supply curve for solar panels is as shown in the diagram:

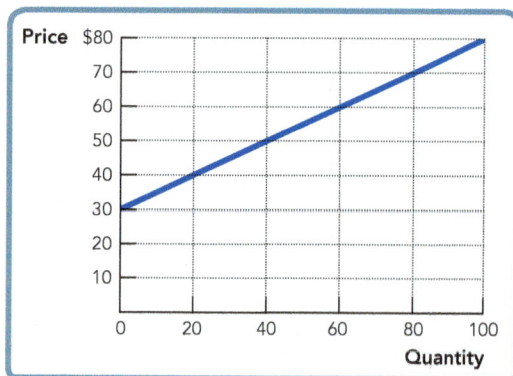

The government decides that it would like to increase the quantity of solar panels in use, so it offers a $20 subsidy per panel to producers. Draw the new supply curve. (*Hint:* Remember our analysis of how a tax affects supply, as shown in Figure 3.12, and bear in mind that a subsidy can be thought of as a "negative tax.")

CHALLENGES

28. Jessica is an economist. She loves being an economist so much that she would do it for a living even if she only earned $30,000 per year. Instead, she earns $103,000 per year. (*Note:* This is the average salary of new economists with a PhD degree.) How much producer surplus does Jessica enjoy?

29. The economist Bryan Caplan recently found a pair of $10 arch supports that saved him from the pain of major foot surgery. As he stated on his blog (econlog.econlib.org), he would have been willing to pay $100,000 to fix his foot problem, but instead he paid only a few dollars.

   a. How much consumer surplus did Bryan enjoy from this purchase?

   b. If the sales tax was 5% on this product, how much revenue did the government raise when Bryan bought his arch supports?

   c. If the government could have taxed Bryan based on his *willingness to pay* rather than on how much he *actually* paid, how much sales tax would Bryan have had to pay?

30. For most young people, working full time and going to school are substitutes: You tend to do one or the other. When it's tough to find a job, does that raise the opportunity cost of going to college or does it lower it? When it's tough to find a job, does the demand for college rise or fall?

31. What should happen to the "demand for speed" (measured by the average speed on highways) once airbags are included on cars?

32. The industrial areas in northeast Washington, D.C., were relatively dangerous in the 1980s. Over the last two decades, the area has become a safer place to work (although there are still several times more violent crimes per person in these areas compared with another D.C. neighborhood, Georgetown). When an area becomes a safer place to work, what probably happens to the "supply of labor" in that area?

Discovering DATA ⁛

33. The Federal Reserve Economic Data (FRED) database is available at https://fred.stlouisfed .org/. Go to FRED and search for data on crude oil prices. You will find several series; click on one of them such as the Global price of WTI Crude. Adjust the dates to focus in on the 2006–2010 period. The 2008–2009 recession is shown by the shaded area.

a. Print the graph.

b. What happened to crude oil prices during the recession, especially as the recession continued?

c. Do you think the change in price was driven more by a shift to demand or to supply? Using the lists of important demand and supply shifters from Chapter 3, what was the major factor shifting demand or supply?

d. FRED has several series for the oil price. Why doesn't it matter which one we use?

e. Optional: Using what you learn in the next chapter, draw a demand and supply diagram. Label the initial price the "pre-recession price." Show the new demand or supply curve. Label the new price the "recession price."

WORK IT OUT

For interactive, step-by-step help in solving the following problem, go online.

The supply curve for rice is as follows:

Price (per 100-pound bag)	Quantity
$40	10,000
$60	15,000
$80	20,000

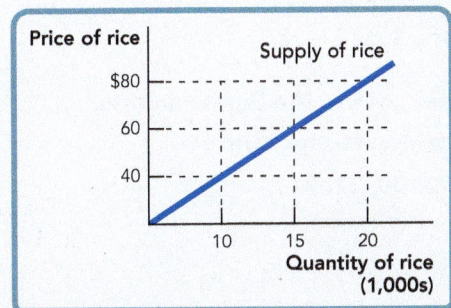

Under pressure from nutrition activists, the government decides to tax rice producers with a $5 tax per 100-pound bag. Using the preceding figure, draw the new supply curve. After the tax is enacted, what price will bring forth quantities of 10,000? 15,000? 20,000? Give your answers in the table:

Price (per 100-pound bag)	Quantity
	10,000
	15,000
	20,000

▶ MRU VIDEOS

Why Does the Demand Curve Slope Down and Why Is This Important?

mru.org/demand

Problem: **1**

Why Do (Most) Supply Curves Slope Up and Why Is This Important?

mru.org/supply

Problems: **1–5, 14–18**

A Deeper Look at the Demand Curve

mru.org/deeper-look-demand

Problems: **20, 21, 23**

The Demand Curve Shifts

mru.org/demand-shifts

Problems: **2–7, 10, 20–26, 28-30**

A Deeper Look at the Supply Curve

mru.org/deeper-look-supply

Problems: **14–17**

The Supply Curve Shifts

mru.org/supply-shifts

Problems: **11, 13, 18, 19, 31, 32**

4

Equilibrium

How Supply and Demand Determine Prices

In Chapter 3, we introduced the supply curve and the demand curve. In that chapter, we wrote things like "if the price is $20 per barrel, the quantity supplied will be 50 million barrels per day (MBD)" and "if the price is $50, the quantity demanded will be 120 MBD." But how is price determined?

We are now ready for the big event: equilibrium. Figure 4.1 puts the supply curve and demand curve for oil together in one diagram. Notice the one point where the curves meet. The price at the meeting point is called the equilibrium price and the quantity at the meeting point is called the equilibrium quantity.

The equilibrium price is $30 and the equilibrium quantity is 65 MBD. What do we mean by equilibrium? We say that $30 and 65 are the equilibrium price and quantity because at any other price and quantity, economic forces are put in play that push prices and quantities toward these values. The equilibrium price and quantity are the only price and quantity that in a free market are stable. The sketch at right gives an intuitive feel for what we mean by equilibrium—the force of gravity pulls the ball down the side of the bowl until it comes to a state of rest. We will now explain the economic forces that push and pull prices toward their equilibrium values.

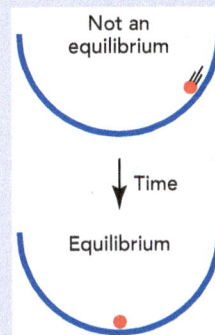

Thinking About Equilibrium

Equilibrium and the Adjustment Process

Imagine that demand and supply were as in Figure 4.1, but the price was above the equilibrium price of $30, say at $50—we would then have the situation depicted in the left panel of Figure 4.2.

At a price of $50, suppliers want to supply 100, but at that price the quantity demanded by buyers is just 32, which creates an excess supply, or **surplus**, of 68. What will suppliers do if they cannot sell all of their output at a price of $50? Hold a sale! Each seller will reason that by pricing just a little bit below their competitors, they will be able to sell much more. *Competition will push prices down whenever there is a surplus.* As competition pushes prices down, the quantity demanded will increase and the quantity supplied will decrease.

FIGURE 4.1

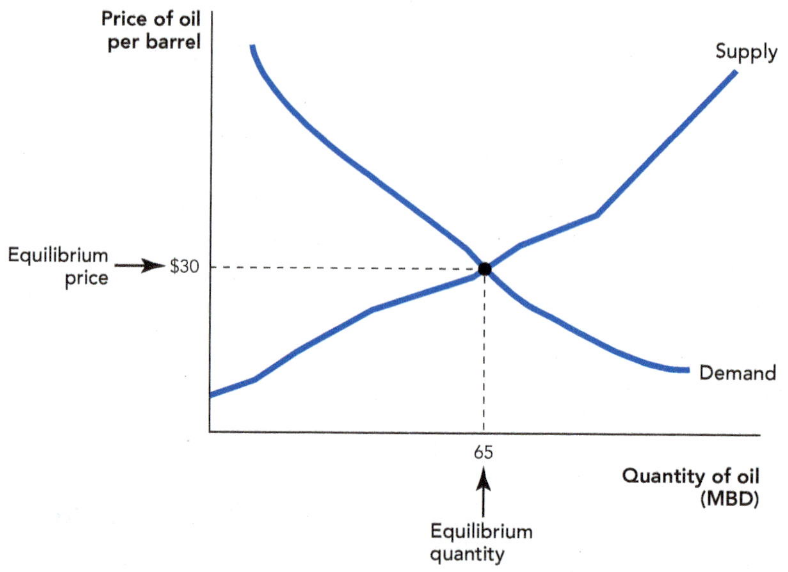

Price Is Determined by Supply and Demand Equilibrium occurs when the quantity demanded equals the quantity supplied. The quantity demanded equals the quantity supplied only when the price is $30 and the quantity exchanged is 65; hence, $30 is the equilibrium price and 65 the equilibrium quantity.

A **surplus** is a situation in which the quantity supplied is greater than the quantity demanded.

A **shortage** is a situation in which the quantity demanded is greater than the quantity supplied.

The **equilibrium price** is the price at which the quantity demanded is equal to the quantity supplied.

The **equilibrium quantity** is the quantity at which the quantity demanded is equal to the quantity supplied.

Only at a price of $30 will equilibrium be restored because only at that price does the quantity demanded (65) equal the quantity supplied (65).

What if price is below the equilibrium price? The right panel of Figure 4.2 shows that at a price of $15 demanders want 95 but suppliers are only willing to sell 24, which creates an excess demand, or **shortage**, of 71. What will sellers do if they discover that at a price of $15, they can easily sell all of their output and still have buyers asking for more? Raise prices! Buyers also have an incentive to offer higher prices when there is a shortage because when they can't buy as much as they want at the going price, they will try to outbid other buyers by offering sellers a higher price. *Competition will push prices up whenever there is a shortage.* As prices are pushed up, the quantity supplied increases and the quantity demanded decreases until at a price of $30 there is no longer an incentive for prices to rise and equilibrium is restored.

If competition pushes the price down whenever it is above the **equilibrium price** and it pushes the price up whenever it is below the equilibrium price, what happens at the equilibrium price? *The equilibrium price is stable because at the equilibrium price the quantity demanded is exactly equal to the quantity supplied.* Because every buyer can buy as much as they want at the equilibrium price, buyers don't have an incentive to push prices up. Since every seller can sell as much as they want at the equilibrium price, sellers don't have an incentive to push prices down. Of course, buyers would like lower prices, but any buyer who offers sellers a lower price will be scorned. Similarly, sellers would like higher prices, but any seller who tries to raise their asking price will quickly lose customers.

Finally, at the equilibrium price the quantity demanded is equal to the quantity supplied and that quantity is called the **equilibrium quantity**.

FIGURE 4.2

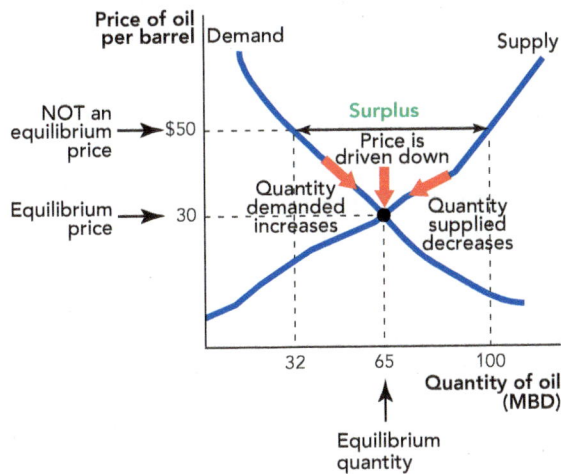

A Surplus Drives Prices Down At a price of $50 there is a surplus of oil. When there is a surplus, sellers have an incentive to decrease their price and buyers have an incentive to offer lower prices. The price decreases until at $30 the quantity demanded equals the quantity supplied and there is no longer an incentive for price to fall.

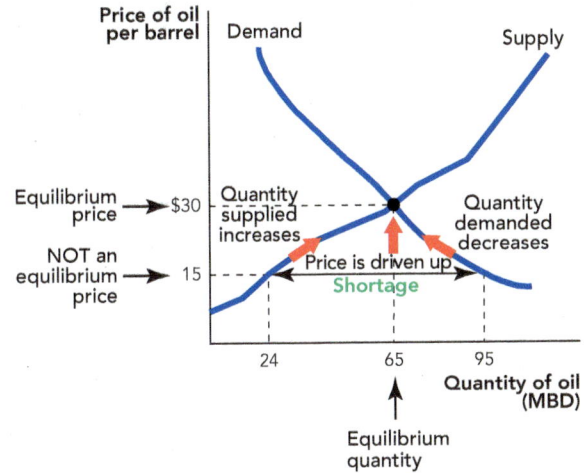

A Shortage Drives Prices Up At a price of $15 there is a shortage of oil. When there is a shortage, sellers have an incentive to increase the price and buyers have an incentive to offer higher prices. The price increases until at $30 the quantity supplied equals the quantity demanded and there is no longer an incentive for the price to rise.

Who Competes with Whom?

Sellers want higher prices and buyers want lower prices so the person in the street often thinks that sellers compete *against* buyers.

But economists understand that regardless of what sellers want, what they do when they compete is lower prices. *Sellers compete with other sellers.* Similarly, buyers may want lower prices but what they do when they compete is raise prices. *Buyers compete with other buyers.*

If the price of a good that you want is high, should you blame the seller? Not if the market is competitive. Instead, you should "blame" other buyers for outbidding you.

A Free Market Maximizes Producer Plus Consumer Surplus (the Gains from Trade)

Figure 4.3 provides another perspective on the market equilibrium. Consider panel A. At a price of $15 suppliers will voluntarily produce 24 MBD. But notice that this is only enough oil to satisfy some of the buyers' wants. Which ones? The buyers will allocate what oil they have to their highest-valued wants. In panel A of Figure 4.3, the 24 MBD of oil will be used to satisfy the wants labeled "Satisfied wants." All other wants will remain unsatisfied. Now suppose that suppliers could be induced to sell just one more barrel of oil. How much would buyers be willing to pay for this barrel of oil? We can read the value of this additional barrel of oil by the height of the demand curve at

FIGURE 4.3

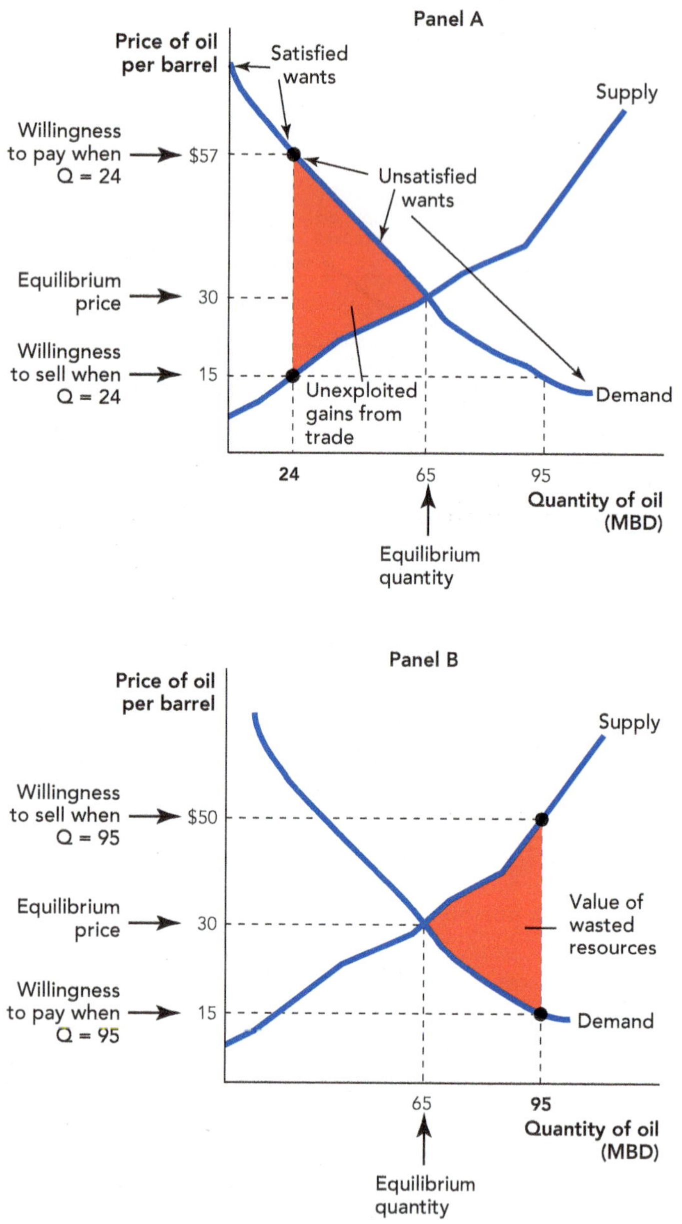

Panel A

Price of oil per barrel

Satisfied wants

Willingness to pay when → $57
Q = 24

Unsatisfied wants

Supply

Equilibrium price → 30

Willingness to sell when → 15
Q = 24

Unexploited gains from trade

Demand

24   65   95

Quantity of oil (MBD)

Equilibrium quantity

Panel B

Price of oil per barrel

Supply

Willingness to sell when → $50
Q = 95

Equilibrium price → 30

Value of wasted resources

Willingness to pay when → 15
Q = 95

Demand

65   95

Quantity of oil (MBD)

Equilibrium quantity

At the Equilibrium Quantity There Are No Unexploited Gains from Trade or Any Wasteful Trades

Panel A: Unexploited gains from trade exist when quantity is below the equilibrium quantity. Buyers are willing to pay as much as $57 for the 24th unit and sellers are willing to sell the 24th unit for as little as $15, so not trading the 24th unit leaves $42 in unexploited gain from trade. Only at the equilibrium quantity are there no unexploited gains from trade.

Panel B: Resources are wasted at quantities greater than the equilibrium quantity. Sellers want at least $50 for the 95th unit, but buyers are willing to pay only $15 so selling the 95th unit wastes $35 in resources. Only at the equilibrium quantity are there no wasted resources.

24 MBD. Buyers would be willing to pay up to $57 (or $56.99 if you want to be very precise), the value of the first unsatisfied want for an additional barrel of oil when 24 MBD are currently being bought. How much would sellers be willing to accept for one additional barrel of oil? We can read the lowest price at which sellers are willing to sell an additional barrel of oil by the height of the supply curve at 24 MBD. (Since sellers will be just willing to sell an additional barrel of oil when it covers their additional costs, we can also read this as the cost of producing an additional barrel of oil when 24 MBD are currently being produced.) Sellers would be willing to sell an additional barrel of oil for as little as $15.

Buyers are willing to pay $57 for an additional barrel of oil, and sellers are willing to sell an additional barrel for as little as $15. Trade at any price between $57 and $15 can make both buyers and sellers better off. There are potential gains from trade so long as buyers are willing to pay more than sellers are willing to accept. Now notice that *there are unexploited gains from trade at any quantity less than the* equilibrium quantity. Economists believe that in a free market unexploited gains from trade won't last for long. We expect, therefore, that in a free market the quantity bought and sold will increase until the equilibrium quantity of 65 is reached.

We have shown that gains from trade push the quantity toward the equilibrium quantity. What about a push for trade coming from the other direction? In a free market, why won't the quantity bought and sold *exceed* the equilibrium quantity?

Now consider panel B of Figure 4.3. Suppose that for some reason suppliers produce a quantity of 95. At that quantity it costs suppliers $50 to produce the last barrel of oil (say, by squeezing it out of the Athabasca tar sands). How much is that barrel of oil worth to buyers? Again, we can read this from the height of the demand curve at 95 MBD. It's only $15 (they get a few extra rubber duckies). So if quantity supplied exceeds the equilibrium quantity, it costs the sellers more to produce a barrel of oil than that barrel of oil is worth to buyers.

In a free market, suppliers won't spend $50 to produce something they can sell for at most $15—that's a recipe for bankruptcy.* We expect, therefore, that in a free market, the quantity bought and sold will decrease until the equilibrium quantity of 65 MBD is reached.

Suppliers won't try to drive themselves into bankruptcy, but if they did, would this be a good thing? Even at the equilibrium quantity, buyers have unsatisfied wants. Wouldn't it be a good idea to satisfy even more wants? No. The reason is that resources are wasted if the quantity exceeds the equilibrium quantity.

Imagine once again that suppliers were producing 95 units and thus were producing many barrels of oil whose cost exceeded their worth. This would be a loss not just to the suppliers but also to society. Producing oil takes resources—labor, trucks, pipes, and so forth. Those resources, or the value of those resources, could be used to produce something people really are willing to pay for—economics textbooks, for example, or iPads. If we waste resources producing barrels of oil for $50 that are worth only $15, we have fewer resources to produce goods that cost only $32 but that people value at $75. We have only a limited number of resources and getting the most out of those resources means producing neither too little of a good (as in panel A of Figure 4.3) nor too much of a good (as in panel B). Markets can help us to achieve this goal.

Figure 4.3 shows why in a free market there tends not to be unexploited gains from trade—at least not for long—or wasteful trades. Put these two things together and we have a remarkable result. *A free market maximizes the gains from trade.* The gains from trade can be broken down into producer surplus and consumer surplus, so we can also say that *a free market maximizes producer plus consumer surplus.*

Figure 4.4 illustrates how the gains from trade—producer plus consumer surplus—are maximized at the equilibrium price and quantity. Maximizing the gains from trade, however, requires more than just producing at the equilibrium price and quantity. In addition, goods must be produced at the lowest possible cost and they must be used to satisfy the highest value demands. In Figure 4.4, for example, notice that every seller has lower costs than every nonseller. Also, every buyer has a higher willingness to pay for the good than every nonbuyer.

Imagine if this claim were not true; suppose, for example, that Joe is willing to pay $50 for the good and there are two sellers: Alice with costs of $40 and Barbara with costs of $20. It's possible that Joe and Alice could make a deal, splitting the gains from trade of $10. But this trade would not maximize the gains from trade because if Joe and Barbara trade, the gains from trade are much higher, $30. Over time, both Joe and Barbara will figure this out, so in equilibrium, we expect Joe to trade with Barbara, not Alice. Thus, when we say that a free market maximizes the gains from trade, we mean three closely related things:

1. The goods are bought by the buyers with the highest willingness to pay.

2. The goods are sold by the sellers with the lowest costs.

3. There are no unexploited gains from trade and no wasteful trades.

MRU

mru.org/equilibrium

Equilibrium and the Gains from Trade

---

* Can you think of when suppliers might do this? What about if they were being subsidized by the government? In that case, the buyers might value the good less than the cost to sellers, but so long as the government makes up the difference, the sellers will be happy to sell a large quantity.

FIGURE 4.4

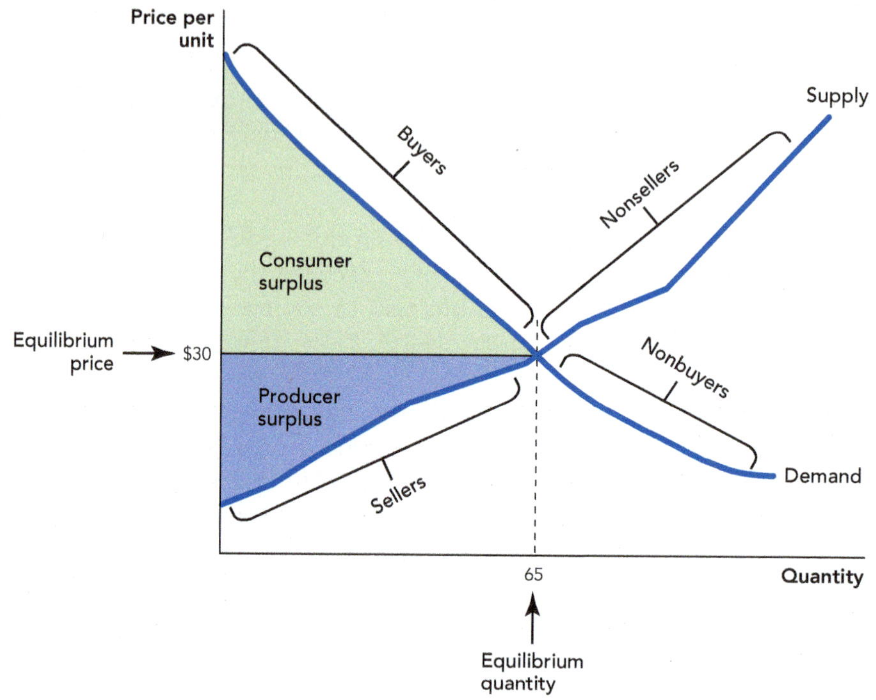

A Free Market Maximizes Producer Plus Consumer Surplus (the Gains from Trade)
A free market maximizes the gains from trade because (1) buyers are willing to pay more for the good than nonbuyers, (2) sellers are willing to sell the good at a lower price than nonsellers, and (3) there are no unexploited gains from trade and no wasteful trades.

CHECK YOURSELF

- As the price of cars goes up, which marketplace wants will be the first to go unsatisfied? Give an example.
- In the late 1990s, telecommunication firms laid a greater quantity of fiber-optic cable than the market equilibrium quantity (as proved by later events). Describe the nature of the losses from too much investment in fiber-optic cable. What market incentives exist to avoid these losses?
- Suppose that Kiran values a good at $50. Store A is willing to sell the good for $45, and store B is willing to sell the same good for $35. In a free market, what will be the total consumer surplus? Now suppose that store B is prevented from selling. What happens to the total consumer surplus?

Together, these three conditions imply that the gains from trade are maximized.

One of the remarkable lessons of economics is that under the right conditions, the pursuit of self-interest leads not to chaos but to a beneficial order. The maximization of consumer plus producer surplus in markets populated solely by self-interested individuals is one application of this central idea.

Does the Model Work? Evidence from the Laboratory

It's easy to see the equilibrium price and quantity when we draw textbook supply and demand curves, but in a real market the demanders and sellers do not know the true curves. Moreover, the conditions required to maximize the gains from trade are quite sophisticated. So how do we know whether the model really works?

In 1956, Vernon Smith launched a revolution in economics by testing the supply and demand model in the lab. Smith's early experiments were simple. He took a group of undergraduate students and broke them into two groups, buyers and sellers. Buyers were given a card that indicated their maximum willingness to pay. Sellers were given a card that indicated their cost, the minimum price at which they would be willing to sell. The buyers and sellers were then instructed to call out bids and offers ("I will sell for $3.00" or "I will pay $1.50"). Each student could earn a profit by the difference between their willingness to pay or sell and the contract price. For example, if you were a buyer and your card said $3.00 and you were able to make a deal with a seller to buy for $2.00, then you would have made a $1.00 profit.

The students knew only their own willingness to pay or to sell, but Vernon Smith knew the actual shape of the supply and demand curves. Smith knew the curves because he knew exactly what cards he had handed out. Data from one of Smith's first experiments are shown in Figure 4.5. Smith handed out 11 cards to sellers and 11 to buyers. The lowest-cost seller had costs of 75 cents, the next lowest-cost seller had costs of $1.00. Thus, at any price below 75 cents the quantity supplied on the market supply curve was zero; between 75 cents and $1, the quantity supplied was 1 unit; between $1.00 and $1.25, the next highest cost, 2 units; and so forth. Looking at the figure can you see how many units demanders were willing to buy at a price of $2.65? At a price of $2.65, the quantity demanded is 3 units. (To test yourself, identify, by their willingness to pay, exactly which three buyers are willing to buy at a price of $2.65.)

Smith knew from the graph that the equilibrium price and quantity as predicted by the supply and demand model were $2.00 and 6 units, respectively. But what would happen in the real world? Smith ran his experiment for 5 periods, each period about 5 minutes long. The right side of the figure shows the price for each completed trade in each period. The prices quickly converged toward the expected equilibrium price and quantity so that in the last period the average price was $2.03 and the quantity exchanged was 6 units.

Smith's market converged rapidly to the equilibrium price and quantity exactly as predicted by the supply and demand model. But recall that the model

FIGURE 4.5

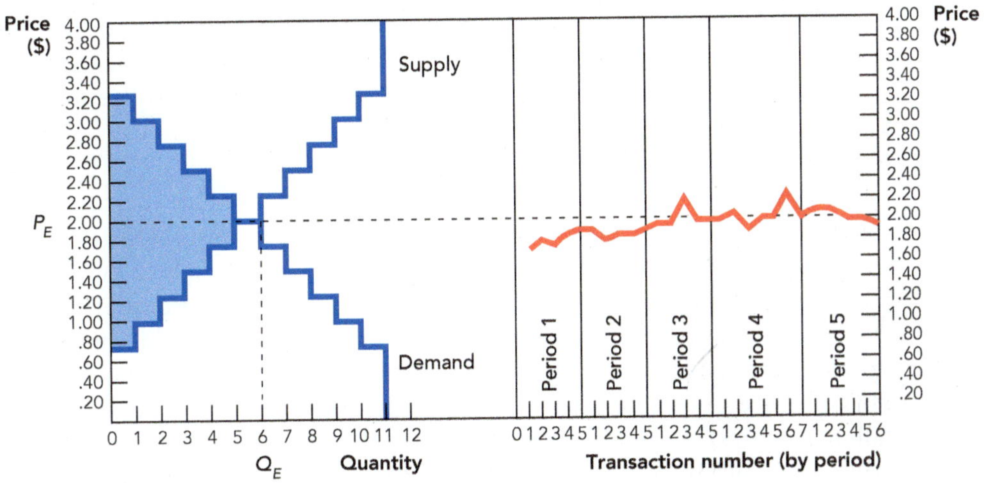

Economics as an Experimental Science Vernon Smith knew the true demand and supply curves, pictured on the left. On the right are the results from the actual market trades. Prices, quantities, and the gains from trade all converged quickly to those predicted by economic theory.

Data from: Smith, Vernon. 1962. An experimental study of competitive market behavior. Journal of Political Economy 70 (2): 111–137.

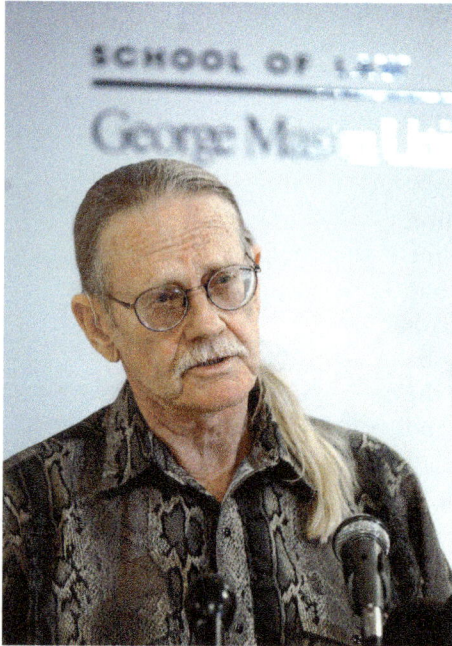

The idea of economics as an experimental science came to Vernon Smith in a fit of insomnia in 1956. Nearly 50 years later, Smith was awarded the 2002 Nobel Prize in Economics.

also predicts that a free market will maximize the gains from trade. Remember our conditions for efficiency, which in this context are that the supply of goods must be bought by the demanders with the highest willingness to pay, the supply of goods must be sold by the suppliers with the lowest costs, and the quantity traded should be equal to 6 units, neither more nor less.

So what happened in Smith's test of the market model? In the final period, 6 units were bought and sold and the buyers had the six highest valuations and the sellers the six lowest costs—exactly as predicted by the supply and demand model. Producer plus consumer surplus or total surplus was maximized. In fact, in the entire experiment only once was a seller with a cost greater than equilibrium price able to sell and only once was a buyer with a willingness to pay less than the equilibrium price able to buy—so total surplus was very close to being maximized throughout the experiment.

Vernon Smith began his experiments thinking that they would prove the supply and demand model was wrong. Decades later he wrote:

I am still recovering from the shock of the experimental results. The outcome was unbelievably consistent with competitive price theory. . . . But the results *can't* be believed, I thought. It must be an accident, so I must take another class and do a new experiment with different supply and demand schedules.[1]

Many thousands of experiments later, the supply and demand model remains of enduring value. In 2002, Vernon Smith was awarded the Nobel Prize in Economics for establishing laboratory experiments as an important tool in economic science.

Shifting Demand and Supply Curves

Another way of testing the supply and demand model is to examine the model's predictions about what happens to equilibrium price and quantity when the supply or demand curves shift. Even if the model doesn't give us precise predictions (outside the lab), we can still ask whether the model helps us to understand the world.

Imagine, for example, that technological innovations reduce the costs of producing a good. As we know from Chapter 3, a fall in costs shifts the supply curve down and to the right as shown in Figure 4.6. The result of lower costs is a lower price and an increase in quantity. Begin at the Old Equilibrium Price and Quantity at point *a*. Now a decrease in costs shifts the Old Supply curve down and to the right out to the New Supply curve. Notice at the Old Equilibrium Price there is now a surplus—in other words, now that their costs have fallen, suppliers are willing to sell more at the old price than demanders are willing to buy. The excess supply, however, is temporary. Competition between sellers pushes prices down, and as prices fall, the quantity demanded increases. Prices fall and quantity demanded increases until the New Equilibrium Price and Quantity are established at point *b*. At the new equilibrium, the quantity demanded equals the quantity supplied.

We can see this process at work throughout the economy. As technological innovations reduce the price of computer chips, for example, prices fall and

FIGURE 4.6

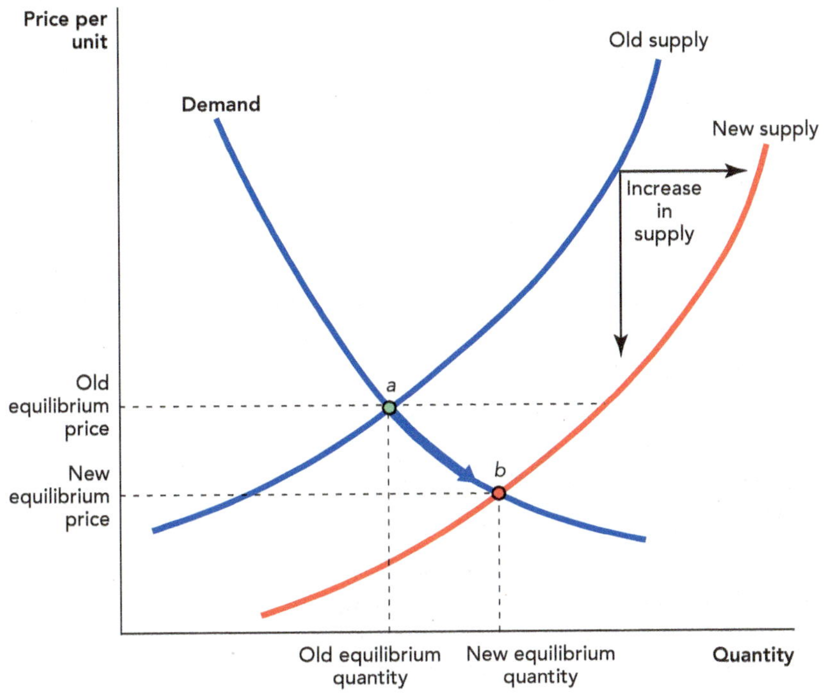

An Increase in Supply Reduces Price and Increases Quantity When costs fall, the supply curve shifts down and to the right, moving the equilibrium price and quantity from point *a* to point *b*, a reduction in price and an increase in quantity.

the quantity of chips—used in everything from computers to cell phones to toys—increases.

What about a decrease in supply? A decrease in supply will raise the market price and reduce the market quantity, exactly the opposite effects to an increase in supply. But don't take our word for it. Draw the diagram. The key to learning demand and supply is not to try to memorize everything that can happen. Instead, focus on learning how to use the tools. If you know how to use the tools, then simply by drawing a few pictures, you can deduce what happens to price and quantity for any configuration of demand and supply and for any set of shifts.

Figure 4.7 shows the same process for an increase in demand. Begin with the Old Equilibrium Price and Quantity at point *a*. Now suppose that demand increases to New Demand. As a result, the price and quantity are driven up to the New Equilibrium Price and Quantity at point *b*. Notice this time we omitted discussion of the temporary transition. So here's a good test of your knowledge. Can you explain *why* the price and quantity demanded increased with an increase in demand? (*Hint:* What happens at the Old Equilibrium Price after Demand has increased to New Demand?)

Of course, if we can analyze an increase in demand, then a decrease in demand is just the opposite: A decrease in demand will tend to decrease price and quantity. Once again, draw the diagram!

FIGURE 4.7

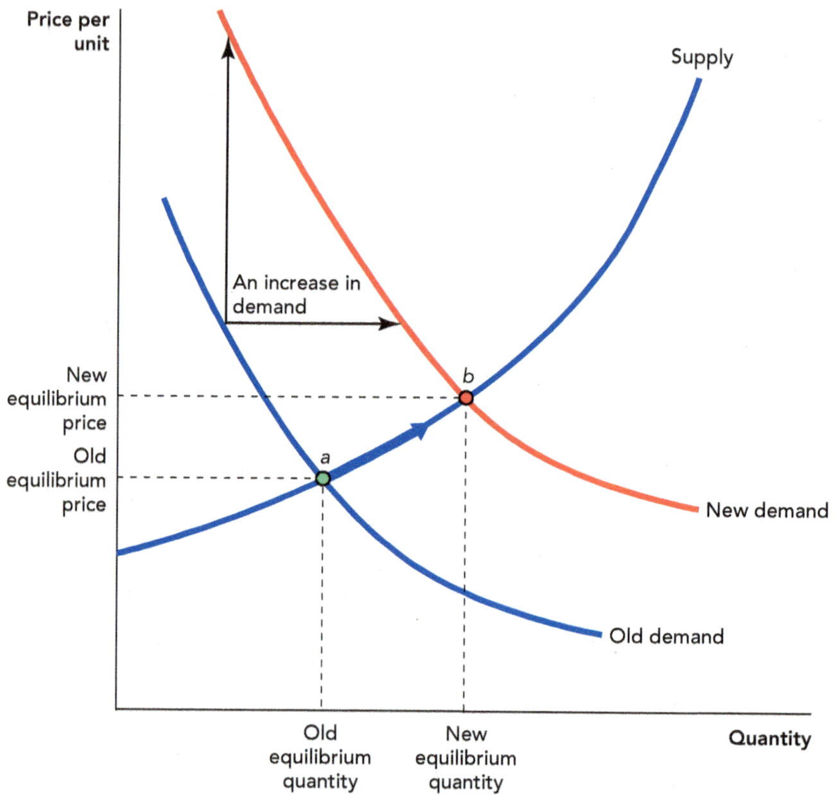

An Increase in Demand Increases Price and Quantity An increase in demand shifts the demand curve up and to the right, moving the equilibrium from point *a* to point *b*, an increase in price and quantity.

CHECK YOURSELF

- Flooding in Iowa destroys some of the corn and soybean crop. What will happen to the price and quantity for each of these crops?
- Resveratrol, which is found in the plant Japanese knotweed (and is also a component of red wine), has recently been shown to increase life expectancy in worms and fish. What are your predictions about the price and quantity of Japanese knotweed?
- Draw a graph showing the supply and demand for hybrid cars before and after an increase in the price of gasoline. What do you predict will happen to the price of hybrids as the price of gasoline rises?

Do you recall the list of demand and supply shifters that we presented in Chapter 3? We can now put all that knowledge to good use. With demand, supply, and the idea of equilibrium, we have powerful tools for analyzing how changes in income, population, expectations, technologies, input prices, taxes and subsidies, alternative uses of industry inputs, and other factors will change market prices and quantities. In fact, with our tools of demand, supply, and equilibrium, we can analyze and understand *any* change in *any* competitive market.

Terminology: Demand Compared with Quantity Demanded and Supply Compared with Quantity Supplied

Sometimes economists use very similar words for quite different things. (We're sorry but unfortunately it's too late to change terms.) In particular, there is a big difference between *demand* and *quantity demanded*. For example, an increase in the quantity demanded is a movement *along* a fixed demand curve.

An increase in demand is a *shift* of the entire demand curve (up and to the right).

Don't worry: You are *already* familiar with these differences; we just need to point them out to you and explain the associated differences in terminology. Panel A of Figure 4.8 is a repeat of Figure 4.6, showing that an increase in supply reduces the equilibrium price and increases the equilibrium quantity. But now we emphasize something a little different—the increase in supply pushes the price down, thereby causing an increase in the *quantity demanded* from 70 units to 90 units. Notice that the increase in the quantity demanded is a

FIGURE 4.8

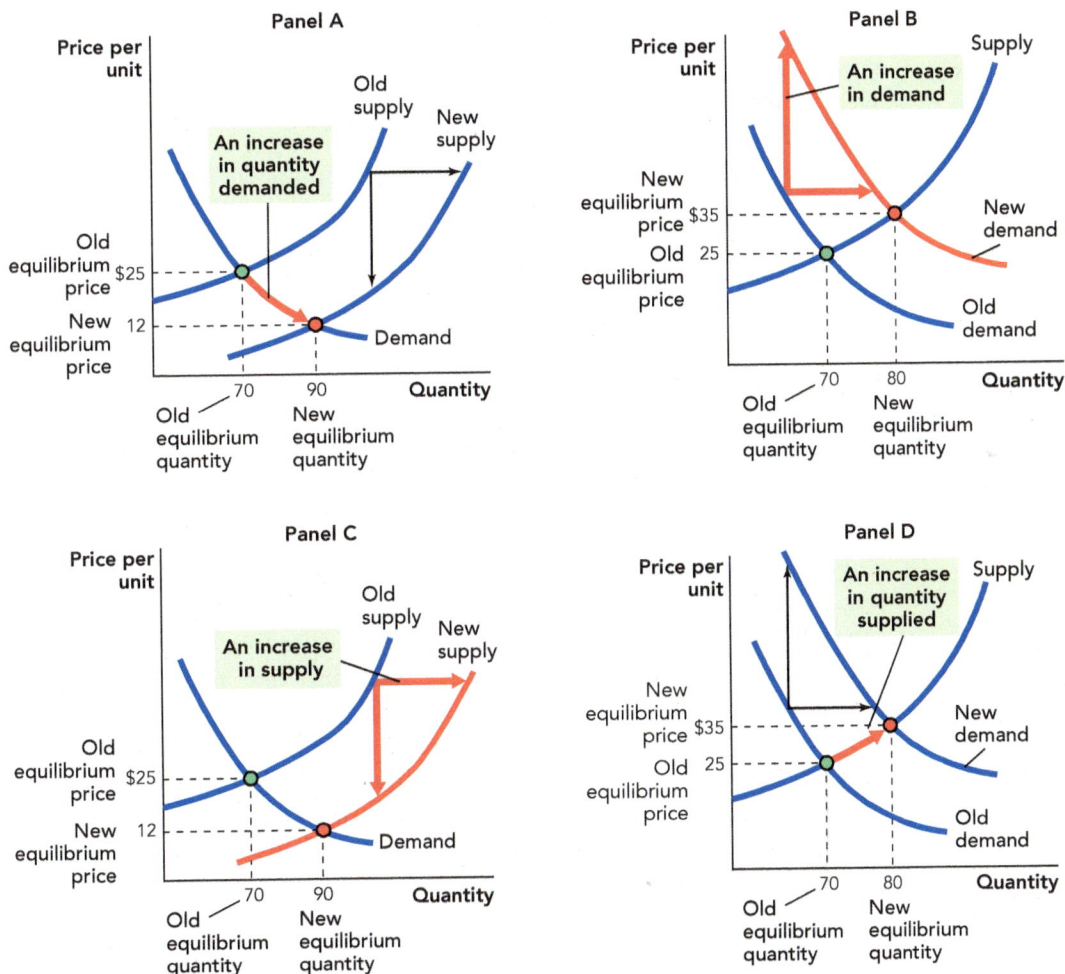

An Increase in Quantity Demanded Compared with an Increase in Demand, and an Increase in Supply Compared with an Increase in Quantity Supplied

Panel A: An increase in quantity demanded is a movement along a fixed demand curve caused by a shift in the supply curve.

Panel B: An increase in demand is a shift in the demand curve up and to the right.

Panel C: An increase in supply is a shift in the supply curve down and to the right.

Panel D: An increase in quantity supplied is a movement along a fixed supply curve caused by a shift in the demand curve.

movement along the demand curve. In panel A, the demand has not changed, only the quantity demanded.

Panel B is a repeat of Figure 4.7 and it shows an *increase in demand*. Notice that an increase in demand is a shift in the entire demand curve up and to the right. Indeed, we can also think about an increase in demand as the creation of a new demand curve, appropriately labeled New Demand.

Similarly, an increase in supply is a *shift* of the entire supply curve, whereas an increase in quantity supplied is a movement *along* a fixed supply curve. If you look closely at panels A and B, you will see that we have already shown you a shift in supply and a change in quantity supplied! But to make things clear, we repeat the analysis for supply in panels C and D: The graphs are the same but now we emphasize different things.

Panel C shows an increase in supply, a shift in the entire supply curve down and to the right. Panel D shows an increase in quantity supplied, namely a movement from 70 to 80 units along a fixed supply curve.

By comparing panels A and C, we can see that shifts in the supply curve create changes in quantity demanded. And by comparing panels B and D, we can see that shifts in the demand curve create changes in the quantity supplied.

A simple rule of thumb which will help everything fall into place is that what changes the equilibrium price and quantity are shifts in demand and supply, and *that's it*. So whenever you are asked, "Why did the price rise?" or "Why did the quantity fall?" always start with a shift in demand or supply. Everything else follows.

Understanding the Price of Oil

We can use the supply and demand model to understand some of the major events that have determined the price of oil over the past half century. Figure 4.9 shows the *real price* of oil in 2016 dollars between 1960 and 2016. (The real price corrects prices for inflation.)

From the early twentieth century to the 1970s, the demand for oil increased steadily, but major discoveries and improved production techniques meant that the supply of oil increased at an even faster pace, leading to modest declines in price. Contrary to popular belief, slightly declining prices over time are common for minerals and other natural resources supplied under competitive conditions.

Although the streets of Baghdad were paved with tar as early as the eighth century, the discovery and development of the modern oil industry in the Middle East were made primarily by U.S., Dutch, and British firms much later. For many decades, these firms controlled oil in the Middle East, giving local governments just a small cut of their proceeds. It's hard to take your oil well and leave the country, however, so the major firms were vulnerable to taxes and nationalization.

The Iranian government nationalized the British oil industry in Iran in 1951.[*] The Egyptians nationalized the Suez Canal, the main route through which oil flowed to the West, in 1956, leading to the Suez Crisis—a brief war that pitted Egypt against an alliance of the United Kingdom, France, and Israel. Further nationalizations and increased government control of the oil industry occurred throughout the 1960s and early 1970s.

---

[*] The nationalization was reversed in 1953 when the government of Mohammad Mosaddeq was toppled by a CIA-backed coup that brought the king, Mohammad Reza Pahlavi, back to power. The coup would have repercussions a quarter century later with the coming of the Iranian Revolution, when the American-backed government was overthrown by Islamic radicals.

FIGURE 4.9

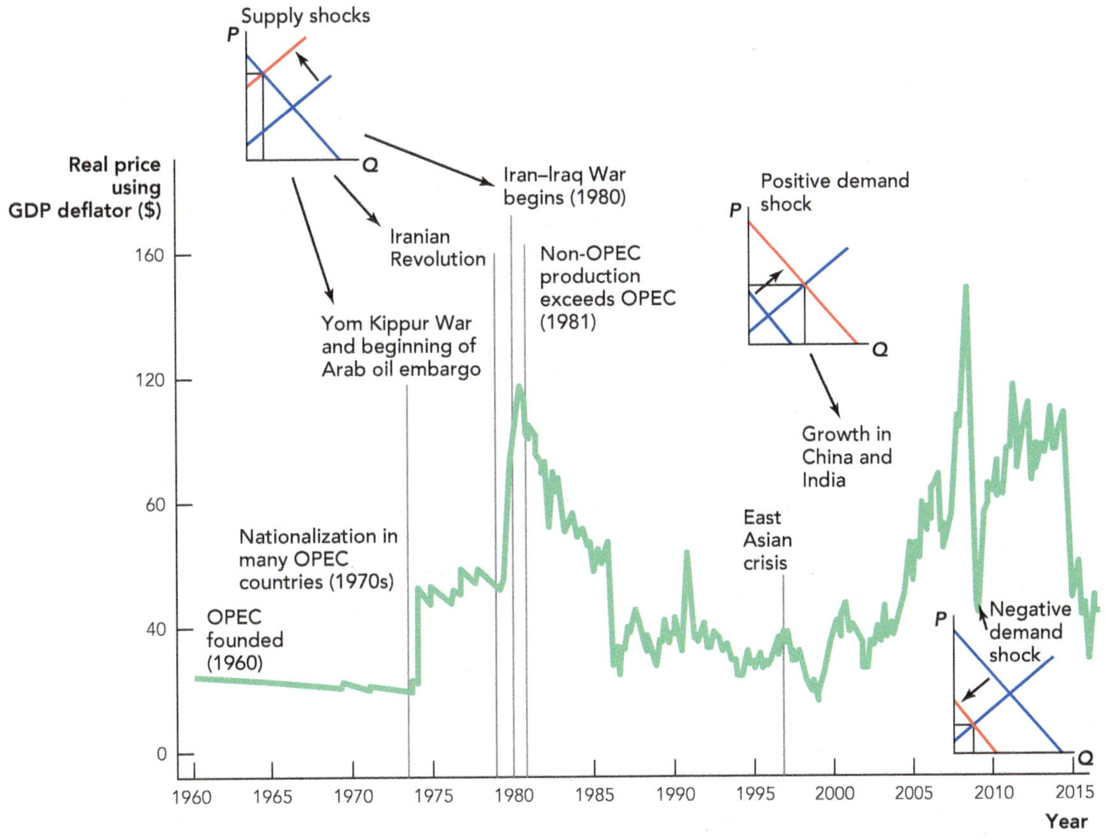

The Real Price of Oil

Data from: St. Louis Federal Reserve Economic Database. Corrected for inflation using CPI. Real price in 2016 dollars. https:// fred.stlouisfed.org/graph/?g=pLyg

OPEC, the Organization of the Petroleum Exporting Countries, was formed in 1960.* Initially, OPEC restricted itself to bargaining with the foreign nationals for a larger share of their oil revenues. By the early 1970s, however, further nationalizations in the OPEC countries made it possible for OPEC countries to act together to reduce supply and raise prices.

A triggering event for OPEC was the Yom Kippur War. Egypt and Syria attacked Israel in 1973 in an effort to regain the Sinai Peninsula and the Golan Heights, which Israel had captured in 1967. In an effort to punish Western countries that had supported Israel, a number of Arab exporting nations cut oil production. Supply had been increasing by about 7.5% per year in the previous decade, but between 1973 and 1974 production was dead flat. Prices tripled in just one year. The large increase in price from a small decline in supply (relative

* OPEC was founded by Iran, Iraq, Kuwait, Saudi Arabia, and Venezuela, later joined by Qatar (1961), Indonesia (1962–2009, 2016), Libya (1962), the United Arab Emirates (1967), Algeria (1969), Nigeria (1971), Ecuador (1973–1992), Gabon (1975–1994), and Angola (2007). Ecuador rejoined OPEC in 2007 and Gabon rejoined in 2016.

to what it would have been without the cut in production) demonstrated how much the world depended on oil.

Prices stabilized, albeit at a much higher level, after 1974, but political unrest in Iran in 1978, followed by revolution in 1979, cut Iranian oil production. This time the reduction in supply was accidental rather than deliberate, but the result was the same—sharply higher prices. When Iraq attacked Iran in 1980, production in both countries diminished yet again, pushing prices to their highest level in the twentieth century—$75.31 in 2005 dollars. Prices might have been driven even higher if demand had not been reduced by a recession in the United States.

Higher prices attract entry. In 1972, the United Kingdom produced 2,000 barrels of oil per day. By 1978, with the opening of the North Sea wells, the United Kingdom was producing 1 million barrels per day. In the same period, Norway increased production from 33,000 to 287,000 barrels per day and Mexico doubled its production from 506,000 barrels per day to a little more than 1 million barrels per day. By 1982, non-OPEC production exceeded OPEC production for the first time since OPEC was founded. Iranian production also began to recover, increasing by 1 million barrels per day in 1982. Prices began to fall during the 1980s and 1990s.

Prices can also fluctuate with shifts in demand. A sharp fall in the price of oil came in 2009 when the United States and many of the major economies in the world were in the trough of a deep recession. Incomes fell, reducing the demand for oil and reducing the price. As the United States slowly recovered, however, the demand for oil increased, driving up the price.

The economies of China and India have surged in the early twenty-first century to the point where millions of people are for the first time in the history of their country able to afford an automobile. In 1949, the Communists confiscated all the private cars in China. As late as 2000, there were just 6 million cars in all of China, but by 2010 more vehicles were bought in China than in the United States, almost 18 million in that one year alone. Total highway miles quadrupled between 2000 and 2010.[2] This increased demand for oil pushed prices up to levels not seen since the 1970s.[*] Moreover, unlike temporary events such as the Iranian Revolution and the Iran–Iraq War, the increase in demand in China and in other newly developing nations will not reverse soon. In the United States, there's nearly one car for every two people. China has a population of 1.3 billion people, so there is plenty of room for growth in the number of cars and thus the demand for oil. On the other hand, new discoveries and techniques such as fracking are increasing the supply of oil. Electric cars may also reduce the demand for oil. As you can see from the graph, oil prices are difficult to predict; the reason is that the social, technological and geopolitical factors that shift the demand and supply curves are difficult to predict. Nevertheless, demand and supply analysis is extremely useful in understanding how shifts in these factors influence the price of oil.

Takeaway

Now that you have finished reading this chapter, you should read it again. Really. Understanding supply and demand is critical to understanding economics, and in this chapter we have covered the most important aspects

CHECK YOURSELF

- In Figure 4.9, you will notice a jump in oil prices around 1991. What happened in this year to increase price? Was it a supply shock or a demand shock?
- In Figure 4.9, during what period would you include a small figure for positive supply shocks (increases in supply)? Explain the causes behind the positive supply shocks and the effect of these shocks on the price of oil.

---

[*] Improved technology is continually lowering the cost of discovering and producing oil (shifting the supply curve down and to the right), so what has happened in recent years is not simply an increase in demand but an increase in demand that has outstripped the increase in supply.

of the supply and demand model, namely how supply and demand together determine equilibrium price and quantity. You should understand, among other ideas, the following:

1. Market competition brings about an equilibrium in which the quantity supplied is equal to the quantity demanded.

2. Only one price/quantity combination is a market equilibrium and you should be able to identify this equilibrium in a diagram.

3. You should understand and be able to explain the incentives that enforce the market equilibrium. What happens when the price is above the equilibrium price? Why? What happens when the price is below the equilibrium price? Why?

4. The sum of consumer and producer surplus (the gains from trade) is maximized at the equilibrium price and quantity, and no other price/quantity combination maximizes consumer plus producer surplus.

5. You should know from Chapter 3 the major factors that shift demand and supply curves and from this chapter be able to explain and predict the effect of any such shift on the equilibrium price and quantity.

6. A "change in demand [the demand curve]" is not the same thing as "a change in quantity demanded"; a "change in supply [the supply curve]" is not the same thing as "a change in quantity supplied."

Most important, you should be able to work with supply and demand to answer questions about the world.

CHAPTER REVIEW

Go online to practice with more examples of these types of problems, including live links to videos, data sources, and feedback.

▶ Problems with this icon relate to optional MRU videos.

KEY CONCEPTS

surplus, p. 51

shortage, p. 52

equilibrium price, p. 52

equilibrium quantity, p. 52

FACTS AND TOOLS

▶ 1. If the price in a market is above the equilibrium price, does this create a surplus or a shortage?

▶ 2. When the price is above the equilibrium price, does greed (in other words, self-interest) tend to push the price down or up?

▶ 3. Robin is on eBay, bidding for a first edition of the influential Frank Miller graphic novel *Batman: The Dark Knight Returns*. In this market, who is Robin competing with: the seller of the graphic novel or the other bidders?

▶ 4. Now, Robin is in Japan, trying to get a job as a full-time translator; he wants to translate English TV shows into Japanese and vice versa. Robin notices that the wage for translators is very low. Who is the "competition" pushing the wage down: Does the competition come from businesses who hire the translators or from the other translators?

▶ 5. Jules wants to purchase a Royale with cheese from Vincent. Vincent is willing to offer this tasty burger for $3. The most Jules is willing to pay for the tasty burger is $8 (after all, his girlfriend is a vegetarian, so he doesn't get many opportunities for tasty burgers).

a. How large are the potential gains from trade if Jules and Vincent agree to make this trade? In other words, what is the sum of producer and consumer surplus if the trade happens?

b. If the trade takes place at $4, how much producer surplus goes to Vincent? How much consumer surplus goes to Jules?

c. If the trade takes place at $7, how much producer surplus goes to Vincent? How much consumer surplus goes to Jules?

6. What happened in Vernon Smith's lab? Choose the right answer:

a. The price and quantity were close to equilibrium but gains from trade were far from the maximum.

b. The price and quantity were far from equilibrium and gains from trade were far from the maximum.

c. The price and quantity were far from equilibrium but gains from trade were close to the maximum.

d. The price and quantity were close to equilibrium and gains from trade were close to the maximum.

7. When supply falls, what happens to quantity demanded in equilibrium? (This should get you to notice that both suppliers and demanders change their behavior when one curve shifts.)

8. a. When demand increases, what happens to price and quantity in equilibrium?

b. When supply increases, what happens to price and quantity in equilibrium?

c. When supply decreases, what happens to price and quantity in equilibrium?

d. When demand decreases, what happens to price and quantity in equilibrium?

9. a. When demand increases, what happens to price and quantity in equilibrium?

b. When supply increases, what happens to price and quantity in equilibrium?

c. When supply decreases, what happens to price and quantity in equilibrium?

d. When demand decreases, what happens to price and quantity in equilibrium?

No, this is not a mistake. Yes, it is that important.

10. What's the best way to think about the rise in oil prices in the 1970s, when wars and oil embargoes wracked the Middle East? Was it a rise in demand, a fall in demand, a rise in supply, or a fall in supply?

11. What's the best way to think about the rise in oil prices in the past 10 years, as China and India have become richer: Was it a rise in demand, a fall in demand, a rise in supply, or a fall in supply?

THINKING AND PROBLEM SOLVING

12. Suppose the market for batteries looks as follows:

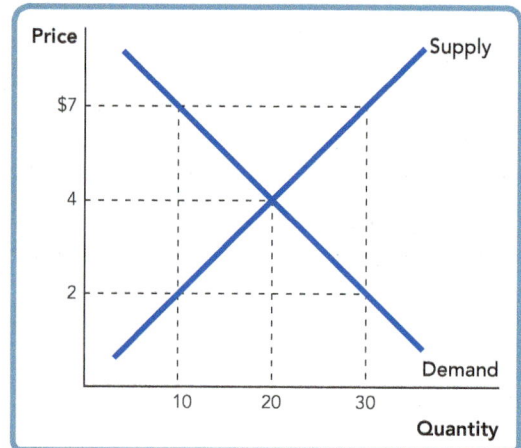

What are the equilibrium price and quantity?

13. Consider the following supply and demand tables for bread. Draw the supply and demand curves for this market. What are the equilibrium price and quantity?

Price of One Loaf	Quantity Supplied	Quantity Demanded
$0.50	10	75
$1	20	55
$2	35	35
$3	50	25
$5	60	10

14. If the price of a one-bedroom apartment in Washington, D.C., is currently $2,000 per month, but the supply and demand curves look as follows, then is there a shortage or surplus of apartments? What would we expect to happen to prices? Why?

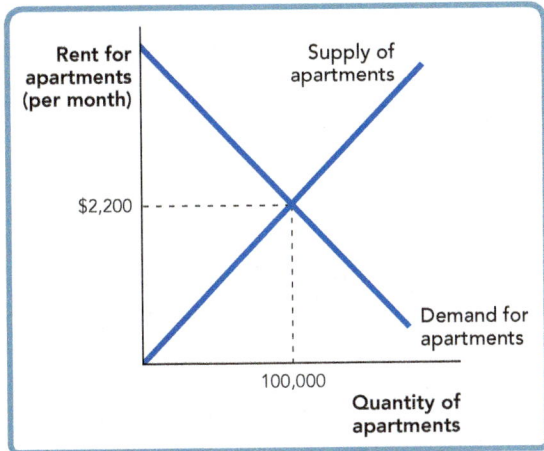

15. Determine the equilibrium quantity and price of Good X without drawing a graph.

Price of Good X	Quantity Supplied	Quantity Demanded
$22	100	225
$25	115	200
$30	130	175
$32	150	150
$40	170	110

16. In the following figure, how many pounds of sugar are sellers willing to sell at a price of $20? How much is demanded at this price? What is the buyer's willingness to pay when the quantity is 20 pounds? Is this combination of $20 per pound and a quantity of 20 pounds an equilibrium? If not, identify the unexploited gains from trade.

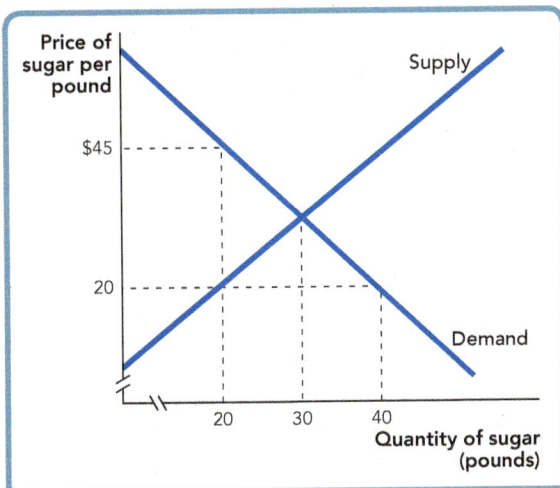

17. The market for marbles is represented in the following graph. What is the total producer surplus? The total consumer surplus? What are the total gains from trade?

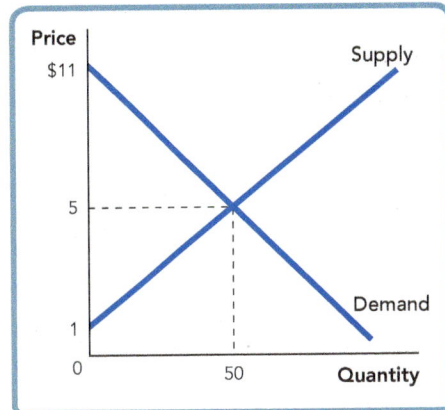

18. Suppose you decided to follow in Vernon Smith's footsteps and conducted your own experiment with your friends. You give out 10 cards: 5 cards to buyers with the figures for willingness to pay of $1, $2, $3, $4, and $5, and 5 cards to sellers with the amounts for costs of $1, $2, $3, $4, and $5. The rules are the same as Vernon Smith implemented.

　　a. Draw the supply and demand curves for this market. At a price of $3.50, how many units are demanded? And supplied?

　　b. Assuming the market works as predicted, and the market moves to equilibrium, will the buyer who values the good at $1 be able to purchase? Why or why not?

19. If the price of margarine decreases, what happens to the demand for butter? What happens to the equilibrium quantity and price for butter? What would happen if butter and margarine were not substitutes? Use a supply and demand diagram to support your answer.

20. The market for sugar is diagrammed:

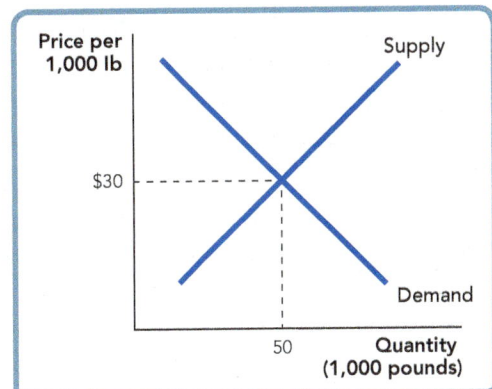

a. What would happen to the equilibrium quantity and price if the wages of sugar cane harvesters increased?

b. What if a new study was published that emphasized the negative health effects of consuming sugar?

21. If a snowstorm was forecast for the next day, what would happen to the demand for snow shovels? Is this a change in quantity demanded or a change in demand? This shift in the demand curve would affect the price: Would this cause a change in quantity supplied or a change in supply?

22. In recent years, the Paleo diet, which emphasizes eating more meat and fewer grains, has become very popular. What do you suppose that has done to the price and quantity of bread? Use supply and demand analysis to support your answer.

23. In recent years, there have been news reports that toys made in China are unsafe. When those news reports show up on CNN and Fox News, what probably happens to the demand for toys made in China? What probably happens to the equilibrium price and quantity of toys made in China? Are Chinese toymakers probably better or worse off when such news comes out?

24. Here's a quick problem to test whether you really understand what producer surplus and consumer surplus mean, rather than just relying on the geometry of demand and supply. For each of the two diagrams that follow, calculate producer surplus, consumer surplus, and total surplus. Assume the curves are perfectly vertical and perfectly horizontal.

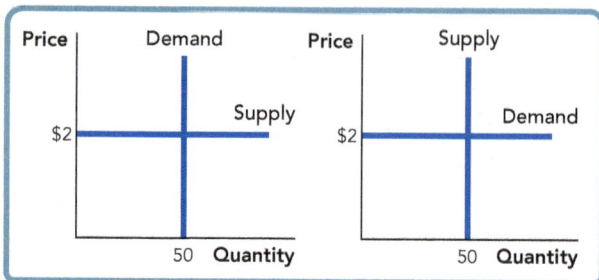

25. The diagram that follows shows the market for agricultural products. The shift from the old supply curve to the new supply curve is the result of technological and scientific advances in farming, including the production of more resilient and productive seeds. Calculate the change in consumer surplus and the change in producer surplus caused by these technological advances. Are buyers better or worse off as a result of these advancements? What about sellers? (Note that you cannot calculate consumer surplus directly with the information given in the diagram, but you don't need that information to calculate the *change* in consumer surplus.)

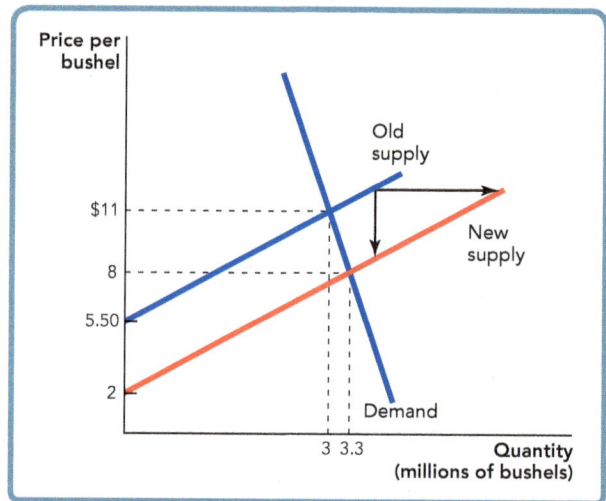

26. Now that you've mastered interpreting shifts in demand and supply, it's time to add another wrinkle: simultaneous shifts in both demand and supply. Most of the time, when we explore simultaneous shifts of demand and supply, we can determine the impact on either equilibrium price *or* equilibrium quantity, but not both. Fill in the missing cells in the following table to see why. Because two curves can shift in two directions, there are four cases to consider. The first column is done for you as an example.

	Case 1	Case 2	Case 3	Case 4
Change in demand	Increase	Increase	Decrease	Decrease
How demand change affects price	↑			
How demand change affects quantity	↑			
Change in supply	Increase	Decrease	Increase	Decrease
How supply change affects price	↓			
How supply change affects quantity	↑			
Combined effect of demand and supply on price	?			
Combined effect of demand and supply on quantity	↑			

27. In the last problem, you saw how simultaneous shifts in demand and supply can leave us with uncertainty about the impact on price or on quantity. An increase in both demand and supply will increase equilibrium quantity but have an ambiguous effect on equilibrium price. However, if we knew that there was a *significant* increase in demand and only a *small* increase in supply, we could conclude that the price would probably rise overall, albeit not by as much as would have been the case if supply had not increased slightly.

In each of the following examples, there are a *major* event and a *minor* event. Determine whether each change relates to demand or to supply, and then figure out the impact on price and quantity; be sure to say something about the relative magnitudes of the price and quantity changes.

a. *Market:* Rock salt

Major event: A bitterly cold and unusually snowy winter season has significantly depleted the amount of available rock salt.

Minor event: There is another snowstorm, and roads and sidewalks need to be salted.

b. *Market:* Smartphones

Major event: The proliferation of fast, reliable, affordable (or free) Wi-Fi and cellular signals increases the usability of smartphones.

Minor event: The production of smartphones is marked by modest technological advances.

c. *Market:* Canned tomatoes

Major event: A large canned tomato manufacturer begins to use cheap imported tomatoes from Mexico rather than domestic tomatoes.

Minor event: This causes a public relations fiasco, resulting in an organized effort to boycott canned tomatoes.

CHALLENGES

28. For many years, it was illegal to color margarine yellow (margarine is naturally white). In some states, margarine manufacturers were even required to color margarine pink! Who do you think supported these laws? Why? (*Hint:* Your analysis in question 8 from the previous section is relevant!)

29. Think about two products: "safe cars" (a heavy car such as a BMW 530xi with infrared night vision, four-wheel antilock brakes, and electronic stability control) and "dangerous cars" (a lightweight car such as _____ [name removed for legal reasons, but you can fill in as you wish]).

a. Are these two products substitutes or complements?

b. If new research makes it easier to produce safe cars, what happens to the supply of safe cars? What will happen to the equilibrium price of safe cars?

c. Now that the price of safe cars has changed, how does this impact the demand for dangerous cars?

d. Now let's tie all these links into one simple sentence:

In a free market, as engineers and scientists discover new ways to make cars safer, the number of dangerous cars sold will tend to _____.

30. Many clothing stores often have clearance sales at the end of each season. Using the tools you learned in this chapter, can you think of an explanation why?

31. a. If oil executives read in the newspaper that massive new oil supplies have been discovered under the Pacific Ocean but will likely only be useful in 10 years, what is likely to happen to the supply of oil *today*? What is the likely equilibrium impact on the price and quantity of oil *today*?

   b. If oil executives read in the newspaper that new solar-power technologies have been discovered but will likely only become useful in 10 years, what is likely to happen to the supply of oil *today*? What is the likely equilibrium impact on the price and quantity of oil *today*?

   c. What's the short version of these scenarios? Fill in the blank: If we learn *today* about promising *future* energy sources, today's price of energy will _____ and today's quantity of energy will _____.

32. Economists often say that prices are a "rationing mechanism." If the supply of a good falls, how do prices "ration" these now-scarce goods in a competitive market?

33. When the crime rate falls in the area around a factory, what probably happens to wages at that factory?

34. Let's take the idea from the previous question and use it to explain why businesses sometimes try to make their employees happy. If a business can make a job seem fun (by offering inexpensive pizza lunches) or at least safe (by nagging the city government to put police patrols around the factory), what probably happens to the supply of labor? What happens to the equilibrium wage if a factory or office or laboratory becomes a great place where people "really want to work"? How does this explain why the hourly wage for the median radio or television announcer is only $14.88 per hour, lower than almost any other job in the entertainment or broadcasting industry?

WORK IT OUT

For interactive, step-by-step help in solving the following problem, go online.

Consider the following supply and demand tables for milk. Draw the supply and demand curves for this market. What are the equilibrium price and quantity?

Price of One Gallon	Quantity Supplied	Quantity Demanded
$1	20	150
$2	40	110
$4	70	70
$6	100	50
$10	120	20

MRU VIDEOS

The Equilibrium Price

mru.org/equilibrium

Problems: **1, 7, 8, 30**

Equilibrium and the Gains from Trade

mru.org/explore-equilibrium

Problems: **1–5, 12–17, 24**

Does the Equilibrium Model Work?

mru.org/equilibrium-model

Problems: **6–11, 18–23, 25, 28–29**

Supply and Demand Terminology

mru.org/basic-terminology

Problems: **25–27, 30, 32**

5

Price Ceilings and Floors

On a quiet Sunday in August of 1971, President Richard Nixon shocked the nation by freezing all prices and wages in the United States. It was now illegal to raise prices—even if both buyers and sellers voluntarily agreed to the change. Nixon's order, one of the most significant peacetime interventions into the U.S. economy ever to occur, applied to almost all goods, and even though it was supposed to be in effect for only 90 days, it would have lasting effects for more than a decade.

A price is "a signal wrapped up in an incentive"; that is, prices signal information and create incentives to economize and seek out substitutes. Markets are also linked geographically, across different products, and through time. In this chapter, we show how price controls—laws making it illegal for prices to move above a maximum price (price ceilings) or below a minimum price (price floors)—interfere with all of these processes. We begin by explaining how a price control affects a single market, and then we turn to how price controls delink some markets and link others in ways that are counterproductive.

Price Ceilings

Nixon's price controls didn't have much effect immediately because prices were frozen near market levels. But the economy is in constant flux and market prices soon shifted. At the time of the freeze, prices were rising because of inflation, so the typical situation came to resemble that in Figure 5.1, with the controlled price below the uncontrolled or market equilibrium price.

When the maximum price that can be legally charged is below the market price, we say that there is a **price ceiling**. Economists call it a price ceiling because prices cannot legally go higher than the ceiling. Price ceilings create five important effects:

1. Shortages
2. Reductions in product quality
3. Wasteful lines and other search costs
4. A loss of gains from trade
5. A misallocation of resources

A **price ceiling** is a maximum price allowed by law.

FIGURE 5.1

Price Ceilings Create Shortages At the controlled price, the quantity demanded exceeds the quantity supplied, creating a shortage.

A shortage of vinyl in 1973 forced Capitol Records to melt down slow sellers so they could keep pressing Beatles' albums.

Shortages

When prices are held below the market price, the quantity demanded exceeds the quantity supplied. Economists call this a shortage. Figure 5.1 shows that the shortage is measured by the difference between the quantity demanded at the controlled price and the quantity supplied at the controlled price. Notice also that the lower the controlled price is relative to the market equilibrium price, the larger the shortage.

In some sectors of the economy, shortages appeared soon after prices were controlled in 1971. Increased demand in the construction industry, for example, meant that price controls hit that sector especially hard. Ordinarily, increased demand for steel bars, for example, would increase the price of steel bars, encouraging more production. But with a price ceiling in place, demanders could not signal their need to suppliers nor could they provide suppliers with an incentive to produce more. As a result, shortages of steel bars, lumber, toilets (for new homes), and other construction inputs were common. By 1973, there were shortages of wool, copper, aluminum, vinyl, denim, paper, plastic bottles, and more.

Reductions in Quality

At the controlled price, demanders find that there is a shortage of goods—they cannot buy as much of the good as they would like. Equivalently, at the controlled price, sellers find that there is an excess of demand or, in other words, *sellers have more customers than they have goods*. Ordinarily, this would be an opportunity to profit by raising prices, but when prices are controlled, sellers can't raise prices without violating the law. Is there another way that sellers can increase profits? Yes. It's much easier to evade the law by cutting quality than by raising price, so when prices are held below market levels, quality declines.

Thus, even when shortages were not apparent, quality was reduced. Books were printed on lower-quality paper, $2'' \times 4''$ lumber shrank to $1\frac{5}{8}'' \times 3\frac{5}{8}''$, and new automobiles were painted with fewer coats of paint. To help deal with the shortage of paper, some newspapers even switched to a smaller font size.[1]

Another way quality can fall is with reductions in service. Ordinarily, sellers have an incentive to please their customers, but when prices are held below market levels, sellers have more customers than they need or *want*. Customers without potential for profit are just a pain so when prices cannot rise, we can expect service quality to fall. The full-service gasoline station, for example, disappeared with price controls in 1973, and instead of staying open for 24 hours, gasoline stations would close whenever the owner wanted a lunch break.

The Great Matzo Ball Debate In 1972, AFL-CIO boss George Meany complained that the number of matzo balls in his favorite soup had sunk from four to three, in effect raising the price.

C. Jackson Grayson, chairman of the U.S. Price Commission, was worried about the bad publicity, so on *Face the Nation* he triumphantly held aloft a can of Mrs. Adler's Soup, claiming that his staff had opened many cans and concluded there were still four balls per can.

Whoever was right about the soup, Meany was certainly the better economist: Price ceilings reduce quality.

Wasteful Lines and Other Search Costs

The most serious shortage during the 1970s was for oil. The OPEC embargo in 1973 and the reduction in supply caused by the Iranian Revolution in 1979 increased the world price of oil, as we saw in Chapter 4. In the United States, however, price controls on domestically produced oil had not been lifted and the United States thus faced intense shortages of oil and long lines to purchase gasoline.

The long lines were not an accident. Figure 5.2 on the next page shows that wasteful lines are caused by price ceilings.

At the controlled price of $1, sellers supply Q_s units of the good. How much are demanders willing to pay (per unit) for these Q_s units? Recall that the demand curve shows the willingness to pay, so follow a line from Q_s up to the demand curve to find that demanders are willing to pay $3 per unit for Q_s units. The price controls, however, make it illegal for demanders to offer sellers a price of $3, but there are other ways of paying for gas.

Knowing that there is a shortage, some buyers might bribe station owners (or attendants) to fill up their tanks. Suppose that the average tank holds 20 gallons. Buyers would then be willing to pay $60 for a fill-up, the legal price of $20 plus a $40 under-the-table bribe. Thus, if bribes are common, the total price of gasoline—the legal price plus the bribe price—will rise to $3 per gallon ($60/20 gallons).

Corruption and bribes can be common, especially when price controls are long-lasting, but they were not a major problem during the gasoline shortages of the 1970s. Nevertheless, the total price of gasoline did rise well above the controlled price. Instead of competing by paying bribes, buyers competed by their willingness to wait in line. Remember that at the controlled price the quantity of gasoline demanded is greater than the quantity supplied, so some buyers are going to be disappointed—they are going to get less gasoline than they want and some buyers may get no gasoline at all. Buyers will compete to avoid being left with nothing. Let's assume that all gasoline station owners refuse bribes. Unfortunately, honesty does not eliminate the shortage.

mru.org/price-ceilings

Price Ceilings

FIGURE 5.2

Price Ceilings Create Wasteful Lines At the controlled price, the quantity of gasoline supplied is Q_s and buyers are willing to pay as much as $3 for a gallon of gasoline. But the maximum price that sellers can charge is $1. The difference between what buyers are willing to pay and what sellers can charge encourages buyers to line up to buy gasoline. Buyers will line up until the total price of gasoline, the out-of-pocket price plus the time cost, increases to $3 per gallon. Time spent waiting in line is wasted time. The total value of wasted time is given by the time cost per gallon multiplied by the quantity of gallons bought.

A first-come/first-served system is honest, but buyers who get to the gasoline station early will get the gas, leaving the latecomers with nothing. In this situation, how long will the lineups get?

Suppose that buyers value their time at $10 an hour and, as before, the average fuel tank holds 20 gallons. Eager to obtain gas during the shortage, a buyer arrives at the station early, perhaps even before it opens, and must wait in line for an hour before he is served. His total price of gas is $30: $1 per gallon for 20 gallons in out-of-pocket cost plus $10 in time cost. Since the total value of the gas is $60, that's still a good deal. But if it's a good deal for him, it's probably a good deal for other buyers, too, so the next time he wants to fill up, he is likely to discover that others have preceded him and now he has to wait longer. How much longer? Following the logic to its conclusion, we can see that the line will lengthen until the total cost for 20 gallons of gasoline is $60: $20 in cash paid to the station owner plus $40 in time costs (4 hours' worth of waiting). The price per gallon, therefore, rises to $3 ($60/20 gallons)—exactly as occurred with bribes!

Price controls do not eliminate competition. They merely change the form of competition. Is there a difference between paying in bribes and paying in time? Yes. Paying in time is much more wasteful. When a buyer bribes a gasoline station owner $40, at least the gasoline station owner gets the bribe. But when a buyer spends $40 worth of time or four hours waiting in line, the gasoline station owner doesn't get to add four hours

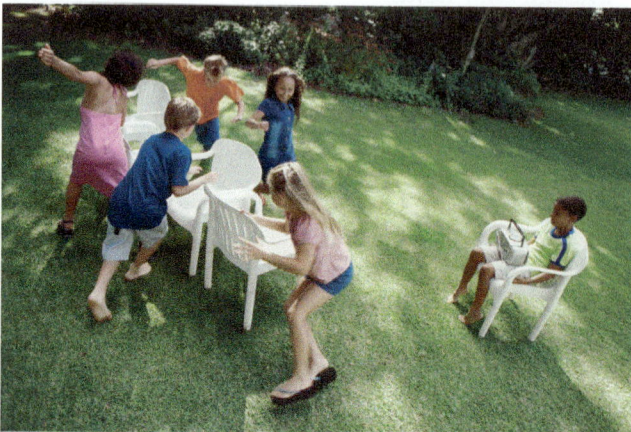

When the quantity demanded exceeds the quantity supplied, someone is going to be disappointed.

to his life. The bribe is transferred from the buyer to the seller, but the time spent waiting in line is simply lost. Figure 5.2 shows that when the quantity supplied is Q_s, the total price of gasoline will tend to rise to $3: a $1 money price plus a time-price of $2 per gallon. The total amount of waste from waiting in line is given by the shaded area, the per gallon time price ($2) multiplied by the number of gallons bought (Q_s).*

Lost Gains from Trade (Deadweight Loss)

Price controls also reduce the gains from trade. In Figure 5.3, at the quantity supplied Q_s, how much would demanders pay for one *additional* gallon of gasoline? The willingness to pay for a gallon of gas at Q_s is $3, so demanders would be willing to pay just a little bit less, say, $2.95, for an additional gallon. How much would suppliers require to sell an additional gallon? Supplier cost is read off the supply curve, so reading up from the quantity Q_s to the supply curve, we find that the willingness to sell at Q_s is $1; suppliers would be willing to supply an additional unit for just a little bit more, say, $1.05.

Demanders are willing to pay $2.95 for an additional gallon of gas, suppliers are willing to sell an additional gallon for $1.05, and so there is $1.90 of

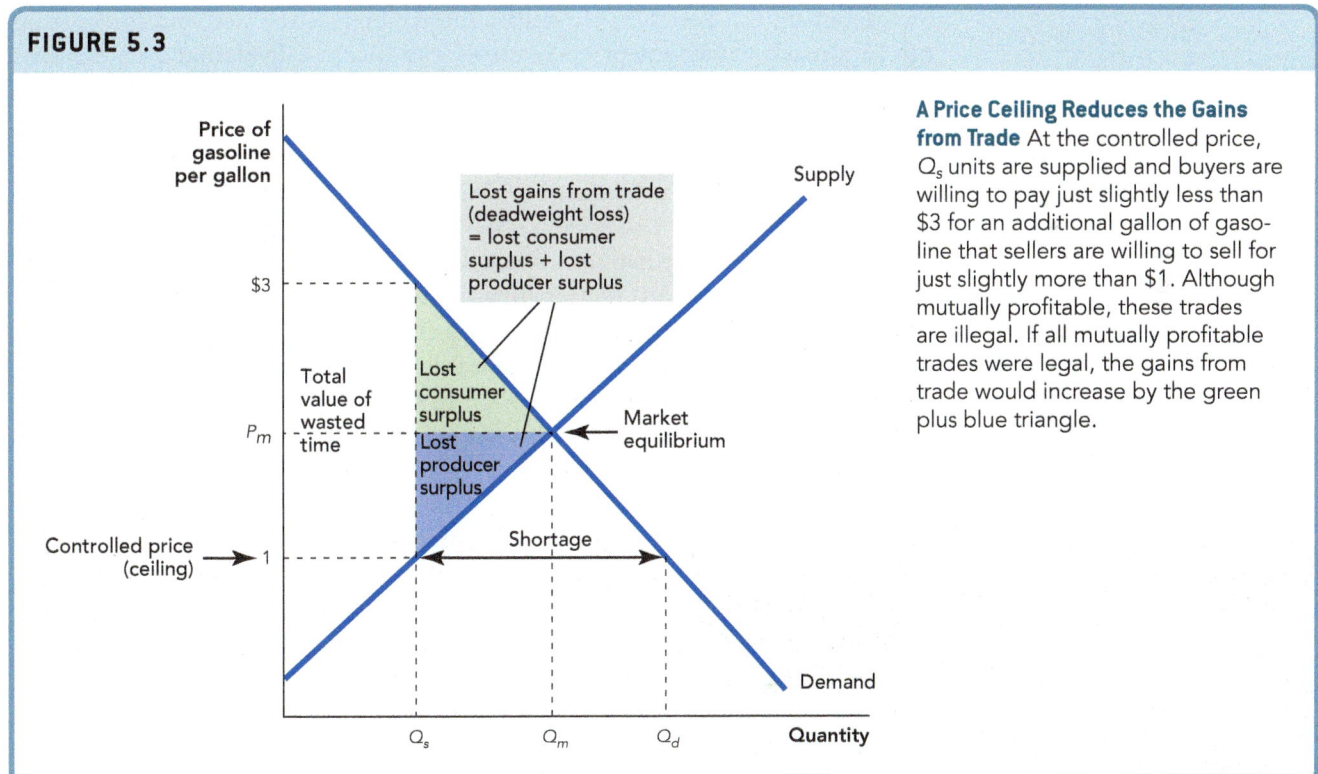

FIGURE 5.3

A Price Ceiling Reduces the Gains from Trade At the controlled price, Q_s units are supplied and buyers are willing to pay just slightly less than $3 for an additional gallon of gasoline that sellers are willing to sell for just slightly more than $1. Although mutually profitable, these trades are illegal. If all mutually profitable trades were legal, the gains from trade would increase by the green plus blue triangle.

* We need to qualify this slightly. If *every* buyer has a time value of $10 per hour, then the total time wasted will be the area as shaded in the diagram. If some buyers have a time value lower than $10, say, $5 per hour, they will wait in line for four hours, paying $20 in out-of-pocket costs but only $20 in time costs. If these buyers value the gasoline as highly as does the marginal buyer, at $60 for 20 gallons, they will earn what economists call a "rent" of $20; thus, not all of the rectangle would be wasted. Regardless of whether all of the rectangle or just some of the rectangle is wasted, it's important to see that (1) price ceilings generate shortages and lineups, (2) the lineups mean that the total price of the controlled good is higher than the controlled price (and perhaps even higher than the uncontrolled price), and (3) the time spent waiting in line is wasted.

potential gains from trade to split between them. But it's illegal for suppliers to sell gasoline at any price higher than $1. Buyers and sellers want to trade, but they are prevented from doing so by the threat of jail. If the price ceiling were lifted and trade were allowed, the quantity traded would expand from Q_s to Q_m and buyers would be better off by the green triangle labeled "Lost consumer surplus," while sellers would be better off by the blue triangle labeled "Lost producer surplus." But with a price ceiling in place, the quantity supplied is Q_s and together the lost consumer and producer surplus are lost gains from trade (economists also call this a **deadweight loss**).

A **deadweight loss** is the reduction in total surplus caused by a market distortion or inefficiency.

Recall from Chapter 4 that we said that in a free market the quantity of goods sold maximizes the sum of consumer and producer surplus. We can now see that in a market with a price ceiling, the sum of consumer and producer surplus is not maximized because the price control prevents mutually profitable gains from trade from being exploited.

In addition to these losses, price controls cause a misallocation of scarce resources; let's see how that works in more detail.

Misallocation of Resources

A price is a signal wrapped up in an incentive. Price controls distort signals and eliminate incentives. Imagine that it's sunny on the West Coast of the United States, but on the East Coast a cold winter increases the demand for heating oil. In a market without price controls, the increase in demand in the East pushes up prices in the East. Eager for profit, entrepreneurs buy oil in the West, where the oil is not much needed and the price is low, and they move it to the East, where people are cold and the price of oil is high. In this way, the price increase in the East is moderated and supplies of oil move to where they are needed most.

Now consider what happens when it is illegal to buy or sell oil at a price above a price ceiling. No matter how cold it gets in the East, the demanders of heating oil are prevented from bidding up the price of oil, so there's *no signal* and *no incentive* to ship oil to where it is needed most. Price controls mean that oil is misallocated. Swimming pools in California are heated, while homes in New Jersey are cold. In fact, this was exactly what happened in the United States, especially in the harsh winter of 1972–1973.

Once again recall from Chapter 4 that we said that in a free market the supply of goods is bought by the demanders who have the highest willingness to pay. We can now see that in a market with a price ceiling, demanders with the highest willingness to pay have no easy way to signal their demands nor do suppliers have an incentive to supply their demands. As a result, in a controlled market goods are misallocated.

Price controls cause resources to be misallocated not just geographically, but also across different uses of oil. Recall from Chapter 3 that the demand curve for oil shows the uses of oil from the highest-valued to the lowest-valued uses. In case you forgot, Figure 5.4 shows the key idea: High-valued uses are at the top of the curve and low-valued uses at the bottom. Without market prices, however, we have no guarantee that oil will flow to its

Ingram Publishing/Getty Images

Distorted signals cause resources to be misallocated.

highest-valued uses. As we have just seen, in a situation with price controls, it's possible to have plenty of oil to heat swimming pools in California (hello, rubber ducky!) and not enough oil for heating cold homes in New Jersey. Similarly, in 1974 *Business Week* reported, "While drivers wait in three-hour lines in one state, consumers in other states are breezing in and out of gas stations."[2]

Figure 5.5 illustrates the problem more generally. As we know, at the controlled price, the quantity demanded Q_d exceeds the quantity supplied Q_s and there is a shortage. Ideally, we would like to allocate the quantity of oil supplied Q_s, to its highest-valued uses; these are illustrated at the top of the demand curve by the thick line. But the potential consumers of the oil with the highest-valued uses are legally prevented from signaling their high value by offering to pay oil suppliers more than the controlled price. Oil suppliers, therefore, have no incentive to supply oil to just the highest-valued uses. Instead, oil suppliers will give the oil to any user who is willing to pay the controlled price—but most of these users of oil have lower-valued uses. Like the lines at the

FIGURE 5.4

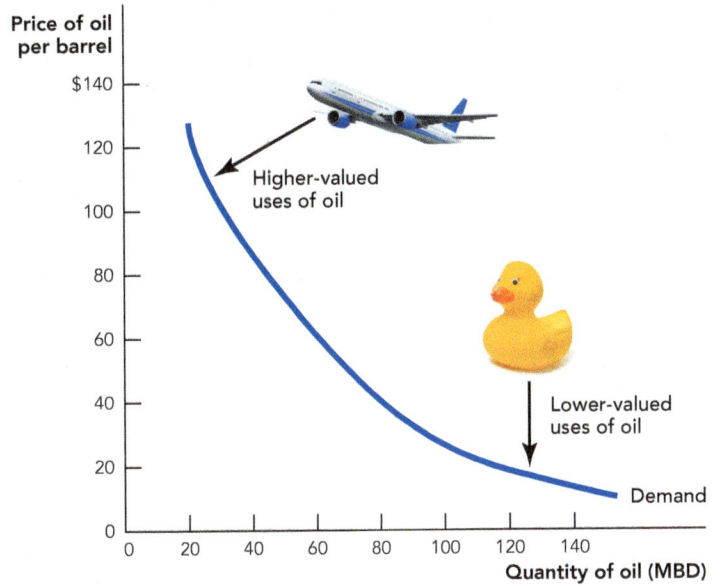

The Demand for Oil Depends on the Value of Oil in Different Uses When the price of oil is high, oil will only be used in the higher-valued uses. As the price falls, oil will also be used in lower-valued uses.

(Top: ssuaphotos/Shutterstock)
(Bottom: Lew Robertson/Corbis)

FIGURE 5.5

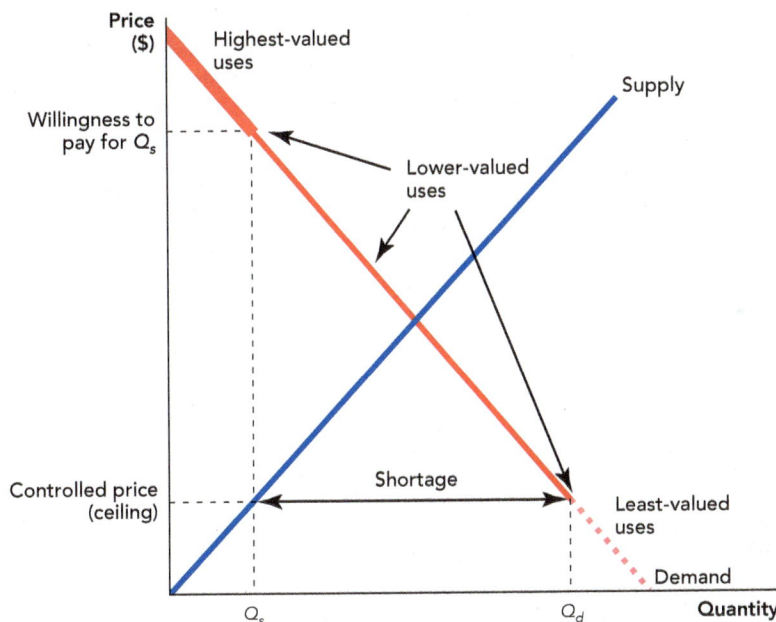

When Prices Are Controlled, Resources Do Not Flow to Their Highest-Valued Uses Gains from trades are maximized when goods flow to their highest-valued uses. A price control prevents the highest-valued uses from outbidding lower-valued uses, so some oil flows to lowered-value uses, even though it would be more valuable if used elsewhere.

gas station, it's first come/first served. In fact, the only uses of oil that definitely will not be satisfied are the least-valued uses. (Why not? The users with the least-valued uses are not even willing to pay the controlled price.)

When a crisis in the Middle East reduces the supply of oil, the price system rationally responds by reallocating oil from lower-valued uses to the highest-valued uses. In contrast, when the supply of oil is reduced and there are price ceilings, oil is allocated according to random and often trivial factors. The shortage of heating oil in 1971, for example, was exacerbated by the fact that President Nixon happened to impose price controls in *August* when the price of heating oil was near its seasonal low.[3] Since the price of heating oil was controlled at a low price, while gasoline was controlled at a slightly higher price, it was more profitable to turn crude oil into gasoline than into heating oil. As winter approached, the price of heating oil would normally have risen and refiners would have turned away from gasoline production to the production of heating oil, but price controls removed the incentive to respond rationally.

Advanced Material: The Loss from Random Allocation If there were no misallocation, then under a price control, consumer surplus would be the area between the demand curve and the price up to the quantity supplied, the green area in Figure 5.6. (Of course, some of this surplus will likely be eaten up by bribes, time spent waiting in line, and so forth as explained earlier.)

Under a price control, however, the good is not necessarily allocated to the highest-valued uses. As a result, consumer surplus will be less than the green area—but how much less? The worst-case scenario would occur if all the goods were allocated to the lower-valued uses, but that seems unlikely. A more realistic assumption is that under price controls, goods are allocated randomly so that a high-valued use is as likely as a low-valued use to be satisfied.

FIGURE 5.6

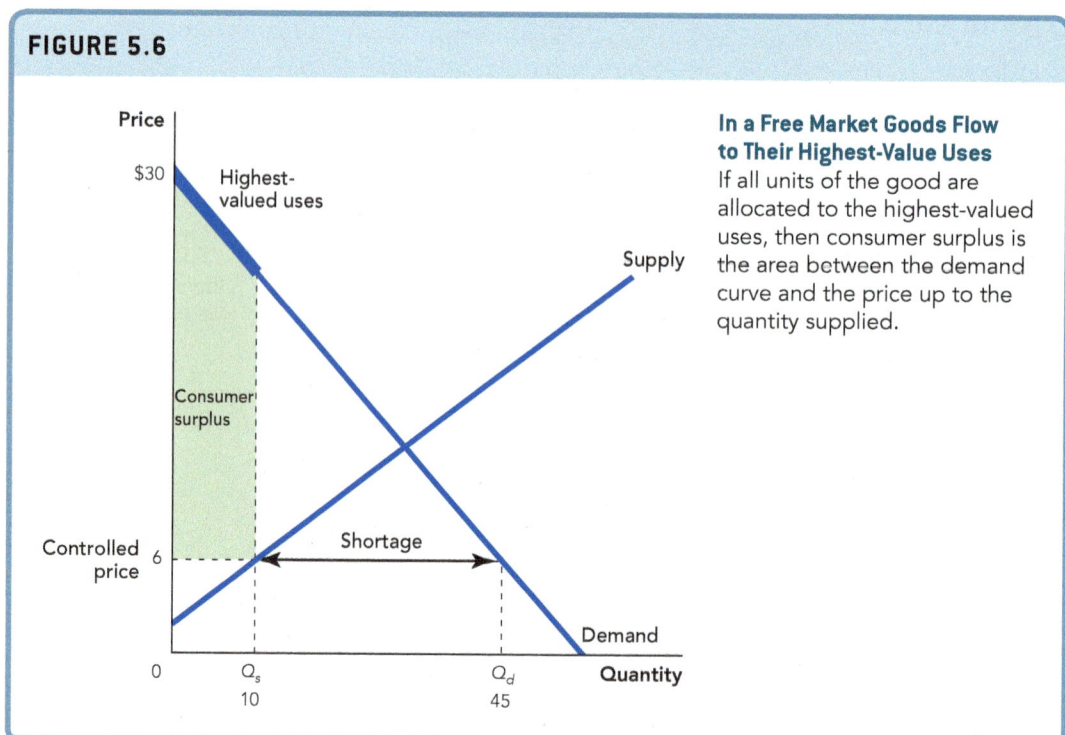

In a Free Market Goods Flow to Their Highest-Value Uses

If all units of the good are allocated to the highest-valued uses, then consumer surplus is the area between the demand curve and the price up to the quantity supplied.

FIGURE 5.7

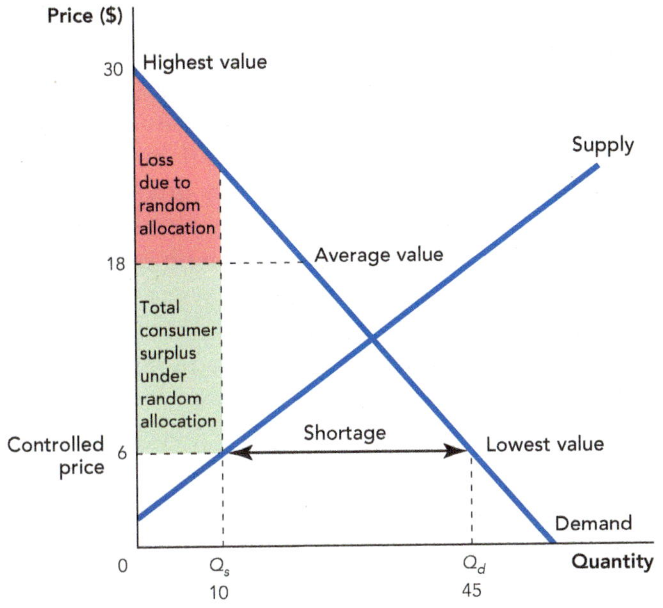

Consumer Surplus Falls Under Random Allocation When there is a price control, the buyers with the highest-valued uses cannot outbid other buyers, so goods will flow to any buyer willing to pay more than the controlled price of $6. If goods are allocated randomly to buyers with values between $30 and $6, the average value will be $18. Consumer surplus under random allocation is the green area. If goods were allocated to the highest-valued uses, consumer surplus would be larger, the red plus green areas. Thus, a price control misallocates resources, reducing consumer surplus.

In Figure 5.7 we show two uses. The highest-valued use has a value of $30 and the lowest-valued use has a value of $6. Now imagine that one unit of the good is allocated randomly between these two uses. Thus, with a probability of $\frac{1}{2}$, it will be allocated to the use with a value of 30, and with a probability of $\frac{1}{2}$, it will be allocated to the use with a value of 6. On average, how much value will this unit create? The average value will be

$$\text{Average value} = \frac{1}{2} \times \$30 + \frac{1}{2} \times \$6 = \$18$$

Extending this logic, it can be shown that if every use between the highest-valued use and the lowest-valued use is *equally* likely to be satisfied, then the average value is $18. Thus on average, a randomly allocated unit of the good will create a value of $18. If there are, say, 10 units allocated, then the total value of those units will be $10 \times \$18 = \$180$. Since the average value is $18 and the controlled price is $6, consumer surplus is the green area in Figure 5.7 labeled total consumer surplus under random allocation. But notice that the green area in Figure 5.7, consumer surplus under random allocation, is much less than the green area in Figure 5.6, consumer surplus under allocation to the highest-valued uses. The difference is the red area in Figure 5.7, the loss due to random allocation.

Misallocation and Production Chaos Shortages in one market create breakdowns and shortages in other markets, so the chaos of price controls expands even into markets without price controls. In ordinary times, we take it for granted that products will be available when we want them, but in an economy with many price controls, shortages of key inputs can appear at any time. In 1973, for example, million-dollar construction projects were delayed because a few thousand dollars' worth of steel bar was unavailable.[4]

Perhaps the height of misallocation occurred when shortages of steel drilling equipment made it difficult to expand oil production; this mistake took place even as the United States was undergoing the worst energy crisis in its history.[5]

As the shortages and misallocations grew worse, schools, factories, and offices were forced to close, and the government stepped in to allocate oil by command. President Nixon ordered gasoline stations to close between 9 PM Saturday and 12:01 AM Monday.[6] The idea was to prevent "wasteful" Sunday driving, but the ban simply encouraged people to fill their tanks earlier. Daylight savings time and a national 55-mph speed limit were put into place (the latter not to be repealed until 1995). Some industries, such as agriculture, were given priority treatment for fuel allocation, while others were forced to endure cutbacks. Fuel for noncommercial aircraft, for example, was cut by 42.5% in November of 1973, sending the local economy of Wichita, Kansas, where aircraft producers Cessna, Beech, and Lear were located, into a tailspin.[7]

The Everett Collection

President Nixon said no to commercial holiday lights during the Christmas of 1973.

Some of these ideas for conserving fuel were probably sensible while others were not, but without market prices, it's hard to tell which is which. The subtlety of the market process in allocating oil and taking advantage of links between markets is difficult, even impossible, to duplicate. C. Jackson Grayson was chairman of President Nixon's Price Commission, but after seeing how controls worked in practice, he said:

> Our economic understanding and models are simply not powerful enough to handle such a large and complex economic system better than the marketplace.[8]

The End of Price Ceilings

Price controls for most goods were lifted by April 1974, but controls on oil remained in place. Over the next seven years, controls on oil would be eased but at the price of substantial increases in complexity and bureaucracy. In September 1973, for example, price controls were lifted on new oil. "New oil" was defined as oil produced on a particular property in excess of the amount that had been produced in 1972. Decontrol of new oil was a good idea because it increased the incentive to develop new deposits. The two-tier system, however, also created wasteful gaming as firms shut down some oil wells only to drill "new" wells right next door.[9] The battle between entrepreneurs and regulators was met with increasingly complex rules. Thus, the two-tier program was extended to three tiers, then five, then eight, then eleven.

Price controls on oil ended as abruptly as they had begun when on the morning of January 20, 1981, Ronald Reagan was inaugurated as president, and before lunch with Congress, he performed his first act as president—eliminating all controls on oil and gasoline. As expected, the price of oil in the United States rose a little but the shortage ended overnight. Within a year, prices began to fall as supply increased and within a few years they were well below the levels of 1979. Fluctuations in the price of oil have continued to occur, of course, but since the ending of controls, there has been no shortage of oil in the United States.

Does Uber Price Gouge?

Price controls continue to be debated. Consider the ride-sharing service Uber. Uber brings together demanders and suppliers of car rides.

In setting the price for each ride, Uber considers local information about supply and demand. If a big concert has just ended or if it's raining, then demand may be especially high and Uber will often charge a higher price—called the surge price. Because Uber drivers get a share of the price, higher prices incentivize drivers to drive where and when demand has increased—where the big concert is getting out or when it's raining, for example. After a spike in demand following an Ariana Grande concert at Madison Square Garden, for example, Uber prices surged and the number of Uber drivers in that area increased by more than 75%.[10] Similarly, when it's raining in New York City, it's been estimated that the number of Uber rides goes up by about 25%. In contrast, taxis, which are fixed in number and do not have surge pricing, increase their number of rides by only 4% when it's raining.[11]

The higher price also reduces the number of people who want a ride. The higher the price, the more likely you will just walk, take your bike, or go an hour later when overall demand is lower. You could even try another ride-sharing service or call a cab. A recent study estimated that if the Uber price goes up by 10%, the quantity demanded falls by about 5.1%, for an implied price elasticity of −0.51 (i.e., −5.1%/10%).[12] The net result of Uber adjusting prices is that the quantity supplied and the quantity demanded are equalized. Even in busy times, anyone can get a ride fairly quickly so long as they are willing to pay the price.

Not everyone, however, likes surge pricing. Laws to restrict surge pricing have been proposed and have even passed in some places such as New Delhi, India. The problem with restricting surge pricing is that when users need rides the most, the price would be kept low by the law, and the quantity demanded would exceed the quantity supplied, as in Figure 5.1. The shortage would mean a long wait before you can get a ride. Indeed, the reason Uber introduced surge pricing was precisely to reduce the shortages and long waits that had often occurred when the demand for service increased with bad weather or when popular events concluded.

By the way, the same study showed that if consumers spend a dollar on Uber, they receive about an extra $1.60 in consumer surplus, and that is with surge pricing. Indeed, that is in part *because* surge pricing allocates rides to the high demanders. A price control would mean that the people with the highest demand for a ride would no longer have a way to signal that demand and rides would be allocated randomly instead of to those who value them the most. The net result would be a loss due to misallocation, as was shown in Figure 5.7.

The older, traditional system of hailing cabs in the street also had price controls, although not in such a visible manner. When the cab picks you up, by law the cabbie typically has to

Surge pricing means the number of Uber rides increases when it's raining.

svetikd/E+/Getty Images

A **rent control** is a price ceiling on rental housing.

charge you the regular price, even if it is raining or a cab is hard to come by. In Manhattan, sometimes it is very difficult to find a cab at rush hour and these hidden price controls are one of the reasons why (the supply of taxis is also limited by law). In the late 1980s in Tokyo when asset prices were booming, cab seekers would bid extra for cab rides. For instance, if it were raining, an eager cab seeker might hold up two fingers when trying to hail the cab. That is a sign the rider is willing to pay twice the normal fare, and of course cabs are more likely to stop for such high bidders. Holding up three fingers would signal a willingness to triple the price. That was an earlier form of surge pricing, just with a more primitive technology, and it evolved spontaneously through market competition for taxis.

Rent Controls

A **rent control** is a price ceiling on rental housing, such as apartments, so everything we have learned about price ceilings also applies to rent controls. Rent controls create shortages, reduce quality, create wasteful lines and increase the costs of search, cause a loss of gains from trade, and misallocate resources.

Shortages

Rent controls usually begin with a "rent freeze," which prohibits landlords from raising rents. Since rent controls are often put into place when rents are rising, the situation quickly comes to look like Figure 5.8, with the controlled rent below the market equilibrium rent.

Apartments are long-lasting goods that cannot be moved, so when rent controls are first imposed, owners of apartment buildings have few alternatives but to absorb the lower price. In other words, the short-run supply curve for

FIGURE 5.8

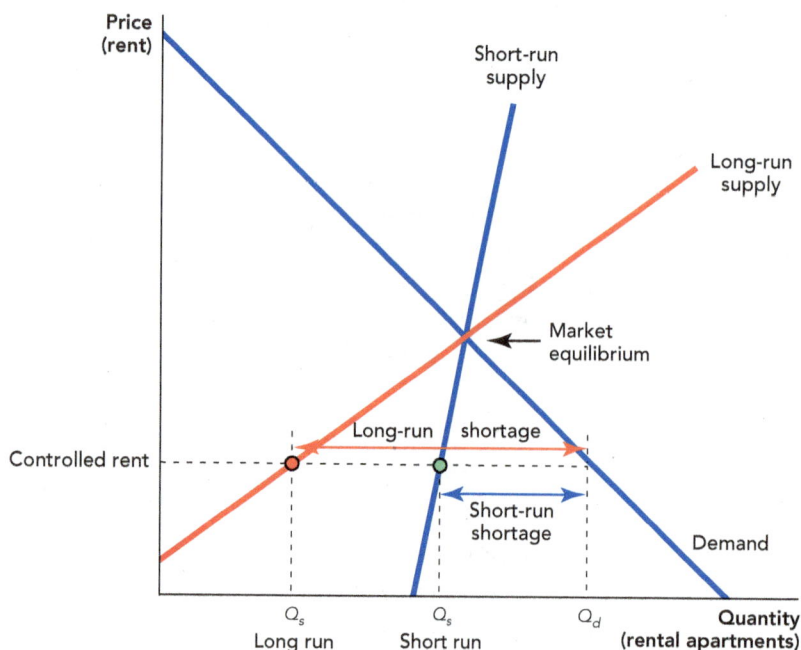

Rent Control Creates Larger Shortages in the Long Run Than in the Short Run
A rent control below the equilibrium price generates a shortage. The short-run shortage is small since the apartment units are already built. In the long run, fewer new units are built and old apartments are torn down or turned into condominiums so the long-run shortage is much greater.

apartments is inelastic. Thus, Figure 5.8 shows that even though the rent freeze may result in rents well below the market equilibrium level, there is only a small reduction in the quantity supplied in the short run.

In the long run, however, fewer new apartment units are built and older units are turned into condominiums or torn down to make way for parking garages or other higher-paying ventures. Rent controls introduced into San Francisco in 1994 encouraged landlords to reduce the stock of rental housing by 15%. Renters who had an apartment in 1994 benefited but at the expense not just of landlords but of future renters who had to pay higher prices in the market sector.[13] Thus, the long-run supply curve is much more elastic than the short-run supply curve, and the shortage grows over time from the short-run shortage to the long-run shortage.

Although old apartment buildings can't disappear overnight, future apartment buildings can. Developers look for profits over a 30-year or longer time frame, so even a modest rent control can sharply reduce the value

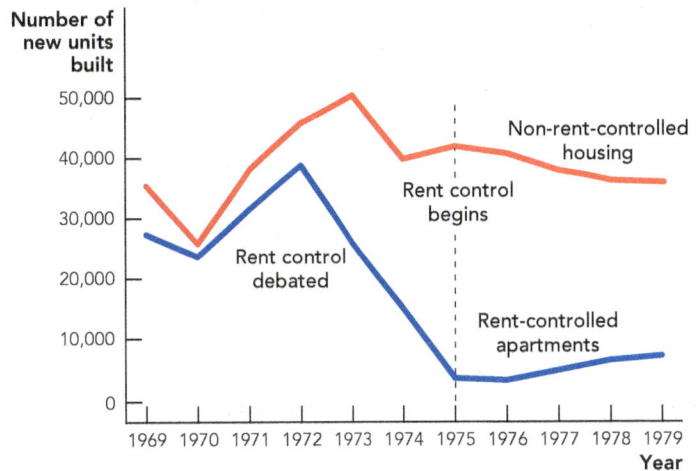

FIGURE 5.9

Rent Control Reduces the Building of New Apartments As rent control began to be debated in Ontario, the construction of new apartments plummeted. After rent control was put into place, fewer apartments were built than non-rent-controlled homes.

Data from: Smith, Lawrence B. 1988. An economic assessment of rent controls: The Ontario experience. *Journal of Real Estate Finance and Economics* 1: 217–231. *Note:* These figures are for private, unsubsidized housing.

of new apartment construction. Developers who fear that rent controls are likely will immediately end their plans to build. In the early 1970s, for example, rent control was debated in Ontario, Canada, and put into place in 1975. In the five years before controls were put into place, developers built an average of 27,999 new apartments per year. In the five years after controls were put into place, developers built only 5,512 apartments per year. Figure 5.9 graphs the number of new apartment starts and the number of new house starts per year from 1969 to 1979. The sharp drop in new apartment construction in the years when rent controls first started to be debated is obvious. But perhaps the drop was due to other factors like the state of the economy. To test for this possibility, we also graph the number of new houses that were built annually during this time. The demand for houses and the demand for apartments respond similarly to the economy, but price controls on houses were never debated or imposed. We can see from Figure 5.9 that prior to 1972 the number of new apartment starts was similar to the number of new house starts. But when rent control became a possibility, apartment construction fell but the construction of houses did not. Thus, it's likely that rent control and not the general state of the economy (which would also have affected house starts) was responsible for the sharp drop in the number of new apartments built.

Reductions in Product Quality

Rent controls also reduce housing quality, especially the quality of low-end apartments. When the price of apartments is forced down, owners attempt to stave off losses by cutting their costs. With rent controls, for example, owners mow the lawns less often, replace lightbulbs more slowly, and don't fix the elevators so quickly. When the controls are strong, cheap but serviceable apartment buildings turn into slums and then slums turn into abandoned and hollowed-out apartment blocks. In Manhattan, for example, 18% of the rent-controlled housing is "dilapidated or deteriorating," a much higher percentage than in the uncontrolled sector.[14] Rent controls in European countries have tended to be more restrictive than in the United States, leading the economist Assar Lindbeck to remark, "Rent control is the most effective method we know for destroying a city, except for bombing it."[15] Lindbeck, however, was wrong, at least according to Vietnam's foreign minister who in 1989 said, "The Americans couldn't destroy Hanoi, but we have destroyed our city by very low rents."[16]

Wasteful Lines, Search Costs, and Lost Gains from Trade

Lines for apartments are not as obvious as for gasoline, but finding an apartment in a city with extensive rent controls usually involves a costly search. New Yorkers have developed a number of tricks to help them, as the character played by Billy Crystal explained in the movie *When Harry Met Sally:*

> What you do is, you read the obituary column. Yeah, you find out who died, and go to the building and then you tip the doorman. What they can do to make it easier is to combine the obituaries with the real estate section. Say, then you'd have "Mr. Klein died today leaving a wife, two children, and a spacious three-bedroom apartment with a wood-burning fireplace."

The search can be especially costly for people who landlords think are not "ideal renters." At the controlled price, landlords have more customers than they have apartments, so they can pick and choose among prospective renters. Landlords prefer to rent to people who are seen as being more likely to pay the rent on time and not cause trouble for other tenants, for example, older, richer couples without children or dogs. Landlords might also discriminate on racial or other grounds. Indeed, a landlord who doesn't like your looks can turn you down and immediately rent to the next person in line. Landlords can discriminate even if there are no rent controls, but without rent controls, the vacancy rate will be higher because the quantity of apartments will be larger and turnover will be more common, so landlords who turn down prospective renters will lose money as they wait for their ideal renter. Rent controls reduce the price of discrimination, so remember the law of demand: When the price of discrimination falls, the quantity of discrimination demanded will increase.

Bribing the landlord or apartment manager to get a rent-controlled apartment is also common. Bribes are illegal but they can be disguised. An apartment might rent for $500 a month but come with $5,000 worth of "furniture." Renters refer to these kinds of tie-in sales as paying "key money," as in the rent is $500 a month but the key costs extra. Nora Ephron, the screenwriter for *When Harry Met Sally*, lived for many years in a five-bedroom luxury apartment that thanks

A rent-controlled apartment—furnished

to rent control cost her just $1,500 a month. She did, however, have to pay $24,000 in key money to get the previous renter to move out!

The analysis of lost gains from trade from rent controls is exactly the same as we showed in Figure 5.3 for price controls on gasoline. At the quantity supplied under rent control, demanders are willing to pay more for an apartment than sellers would require to rent the apartment. If buyers and sellers were free to trade, they could both be better off, but under rent control, these mutually profitable trades are illegal and the benefits do not occur.

Misallocation of Resources

As with gasoline, apartments under rent control are allocated haphazardly—some people with a high willingness to pay can't buy as much housing as they want, even as others with a low willingness to pay consume more housing than they would purchase at the market rate. The classic example is the older couple who stay in their large rent-controlled apartment even after their children have moved out. It's a great deal for the older couple, but not so good for the young couple with children who as a result are stuck in a cramped apartment with nowhere to go.

Economists can estimate the amount of misallocation by comparing the types of apartments that renters choose in cities like New York, which has had rent controls since they were imposed as a "temporary" measure in World War II, with the types of apartments that people choose in cities like Chicago, which has a free market in rental housing. In one study of this kind, Edward Glaeser and Erzo Luttmer found that as many as 21% of the renters in New York City live in an apartment that has more or fewer rooms than they would choose if they lived in a city without rent controls.[17] This misallocation of resources creates significant waste and hardship.

Rent Regulation

In the 1990s, many American cities with rent control changed policy and began to eliminate or ease rent controls. Some economists refer to these new policies not as rent control but as "rent regulation." A typical rent regulation limits price increases without limiting prices. Price increases, for example, might be limited to, say, 10% per year. Thus, rent regulations can protect tenants from sharp increases in rent, while still allowing prices to rise or fall over several years in response to market forces. Rent regulation laws usually also allow landlords to pass along cost increases so the incentive to cut back on maintenance is reduced. Economists are almost universally opposed to rent controls but some economists think that moderate rent regulation could have some benefits.[18]

Arguments for Price Ceilings

Without price controls on oil in 1973, some people might not have been able to afford to heat their homes. Without rent controls, some people may not be able to afford appropriate housing. It's not obvious that the poor are better off with shortages than with high prices. Nevertheless, *if* price controls were the *only* way to help the poor, then this would be an argument in favor of price controls.

Price controls, however, are never the only way to help the poor and they are rarely the best way. If affordable housing is a concern, for example, then

CHECK YOURSELF
- If landlords under rent control have an incentive to do only the minimum upkeep, what inevitably must accompany rent control? Think of a tenant with a dripping faucet: How does it get fixed?
- New York City has had rent control for decades. Assume you have been appointed to the mayor's housing commission and convince your commission members that rent control has been a bad thing for New York. How would you get rid of rent control, considering the vested interests?

a better policy than rent controls is for the government to provide housing vouchers. Housing vouchers, which are used extensively in the United States, give qualifying consumers a voucher worth, say, $500 a month that can be applied to any unit of housing.[19] Unlike rent controls, which create shortages, vouchers *increase* the supply of housing. Vouchers can also be targeted to consumers who need them, whereas rent controls in New York City have subsidized millionaires.

There are a few other sound arguments for price controls. The best case for price controls is to discipline monopolies. Alas, this explanation does not fit price controls on gasoline, apartments, bread, or almost all of the goods that price controls are routinely placed on.

One of the primary reasons for price controls may be that the public, unlike economists, does not see the consequences of price controls. People who have not been trained in economics rarely connect lineups with price controls. During the gasoline shortages of the 1970s, probably not one American in ten understood the connection between the controls and the shortage—most consumers blamed big oil companies and rich Arab sheiks.

Universal Price Controls

We have seen that price controls in the United States caused shortages, lineups, delays, quality reductions, misallocations, bureaucracy, and corruption. And the U.S. experience with extensive price controls was short, just a few months for most goods, and a few years for oil and a handful of other goods. What would happen if price controls on all goods remained in place for a lengthy period of time? An economy with permanent, universal price controls is in essence a "command economy," much as existed in the Communist countries prior to the fall of the Berlin Wall. In *The Russians*, Hedrick Smith described what it was like for consumers living in the Soviet Union in 1976:[20]

The list of scarce items is practically endless. They are not permanently out of stock, but their appearance is unpredictable. . . . Leningrad can be overstocked with cross-country skis and yet go several months without soap for washing dishes. In the Armenian capital of Yerevan, I found an ample supply of accordions but local people complained that they had gone for weeks without ordinary kitchen spoons or tea samovars. I knew a Moscow family that spent a frantic month hunting for a child's potty while radios were a glut on the market. . . .

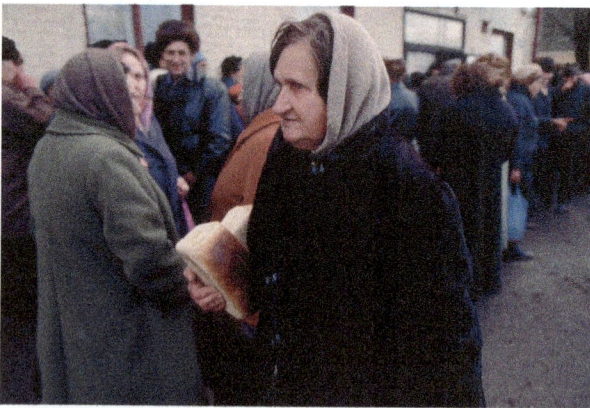

In the former Soviet Union, never-ending shortages meant that lining up for hours to get bread, shoes, or other goods was normal.

Peter Turnley/Getty Images

The accepted norm is that the Soviet woman daily spends two hours in line, seven days a week. . . . I have known of people who stood in line 90 minutes to buy four pineapples . . . three and a half hours to buy three large heads of cabbage only to find the cabbages were gone as they approached the front of the line, 18 hours to sign up to purchase a rug at some later date, all through a freezing December night to register on a list for buying a car, and then waiting 18 months for actual delivery, and terribly lucky at that.

The never-ending shortage of goods in the former Soviet Union suggests another reason why price controls are not eliminated even when doing so would make most people better off. Shortages were beneficial to the very same party elite who controlled prices. With all goods in permanent shortage, how did anyone in the Soviet Union obtain goods? By using *blat*. *Blat* is a Russian word meaning one has connections that can be used to get favors. As Hedrick Smith put it:

> In an economy of chronic shortages and carefully parceled-out privileges, blat is an essential lubricant of life. The more rank and power one has, the more blat one normally has . . . each has access to things or services that are hard to get and that other people want or need.

Consider the manager of a small factory that produces radios. Music may be the food that feeds people's souls but the manager would also like some beef. Shortages mean that the manager's salary is almost useless in helping him to obtain beef but what does he have of value? He has access to radios. If the manager can find a worker in a beef factory who loves music, he will have *blat*, a connection and something to trade. Even if he can't find someone with the exact opposite wants as he has, access to radios gives the manager power because people will want to do favors for him. But notice that the manager of the radio factory has *blat* only because of a shortage of radios. If radios were easily available at the market price, then the manager's access would no longer be of special value. The manager of the radio factory wants low prices because then he can legally buy radios at the official price and use them to obtain goods that he wants. Ironically, the managers and producers of beef, purses, and televisions all want shortages of their own good even though all would benefit if the shortages of all goods were eliminated.

Blat is a Russian word but it's a worldwide phenomena. Even in the United States, where by world standards corruption is low, *blat* happens. During the 1973–1974 oil crisis, for example, when the Federal Energy Office controlled the allocation of oil, it quickly became obvious that the way to get more oil was to use *blat*. Firms began to hire former politicians and bureaucrats who used their connections to help the firms get more oil. Today, the *blat* economy is much larger—about half of all federal politicians who leave office for the private sector become lobbyists.

Price Floors

When governments control prices, it is usually with a price ceiling designed to keep prices below market levels, but occasionally the government intervenes to keep prices above market levels. Can you think of an example? Here's a hint. Buyers usually outnumber sellers, so it's probably no accident that governments intervene to keep prices below market levels more often than they intervene to keep prices above market levels. The most common example of a price being controlled above market levels is the exception that proves the rule because it involves a good for which sellers outnumber buyers. Here's another hint. You own this good.

The good is labor, and the most common example of a price that is controlled above the market level is the minimum wage.

CHECK YOURSELF

- In the 1984 movie *Moscow on the Hudson*, a Soviet musician defects to the United States. Living in New York, he cannot believe the availability of goods and finds that he cannot break away from previous Soviet habits. In one memorable scene, he buys packages and packages of toilet paper. Why? Using the concepts from this chapter, explain why hoarding occurs under price controls and why it is wasteful.
- Shortages in the former Soviet Union were very common, but why were there also surpluses of some goods at some times?

A **price floor** is a minimum price allowed by law.

When the minimum price that can be legally charged is above the market price, we say that there is a **price floor**. Economists call it a price floor because prices cannot legally go below the floor. Price floors create four important effects:

1. Surpluses
2. Lost gains from trade (deadweight loss)
3. Wasteful increases in quality
4. A misallocation of resources

Surpluses

Figure 5.10 graphs the demand and supply of labor and shows how a price held above the market price creates a surplus, a situation in which the quantity of labor supplied exceeds the quantity demanded. We have a special word for a surplus of labor: unemployment.

The idea that a minimum wage creates unemployment should not be surprising. If the minimum wage did not create unemployment, the solution to poverty would be easy—raise minimum wages to $10, $20, or even $100 an hour! But at a high enough wage, none of us would be worth employing.

Can a more moderate minimum wage also create unemployment? Yes. A minimum wage of $7.25 an hour, the federal minimum in 2017, won't affect most workers who, because of their productivity, already earn more than $7.25 an hour. In the United States, for example, more than 95% of all workers paid by the hour already earn more than the minimum wage. A minimum wage, however, will decrease employment among low-skilled workers. The more employers have to pay for low-skilled workers, the fewer low-skilled workers they will hire.

Young people, for example, often lack substantial skills and are more likely to be made unemployed by the minimum wage. About a quarter of all workers

FIGURE 5.10

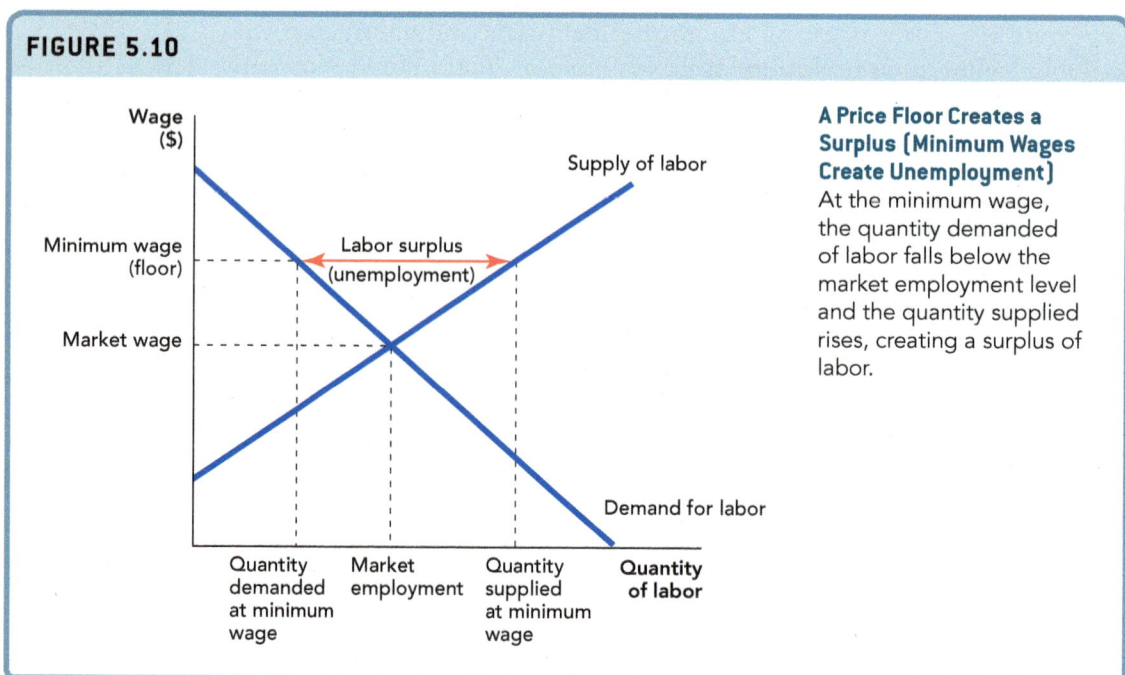

A Price Floor Creates a Surplus (Minimum Wages Create Unemployment) At the minimum wage, the quantity demanded of labor falls below the market employment level and the quantity supplied rises, creating a surplus of labor.

earning the minimum wage are teenagers (ages 16–19) and about half are less than 25 years of age.[21] Studies of the minimum wage verify that the unemployment effect is concentrated among teenagers.[22]

In addition to creating surpluses, a price floor, just like a price ceiling, reduces the gains from trade.

Lost Gains from Trade (Deadweight Loss)

Notice in Figure 5.11 that at the minimum wage employers are willing to hire Q_d workers. Employers would hire more workers if they could offer lower wages and, importantly, workers would be willing to work at lower wages if they were allowed to do so. If employers and workers could bargain freely, the wage would fall and the quantity of labor traded would increase to the level of market employment. Notice that at the market employment level, the gains from trade increase by the green and blue triangles. The green triangle is the increase in consumer surplus (remember that in this example it is the employers who are the consumers of labor) and the blue triangle is the increase in producer (worker) surplus. Since the minimum wage prevents employment from reaching the market employment level, there is a loss of consumer and producer surplus.

Although the minimum wage creates some unemployment and reduces the gains from trade, the influence of the minimum wage in the American economy is very small. Even for the young, the minimum wage is not very important because although most workers earning the minimum wage are young, most young workers earn more than the minimum wage. As noted, a majority of workers earning the minimum wage are younger than 25 years old but 88% of workers younger than 25 earn more than the minimum wage.[23]

FIGURE 5.11

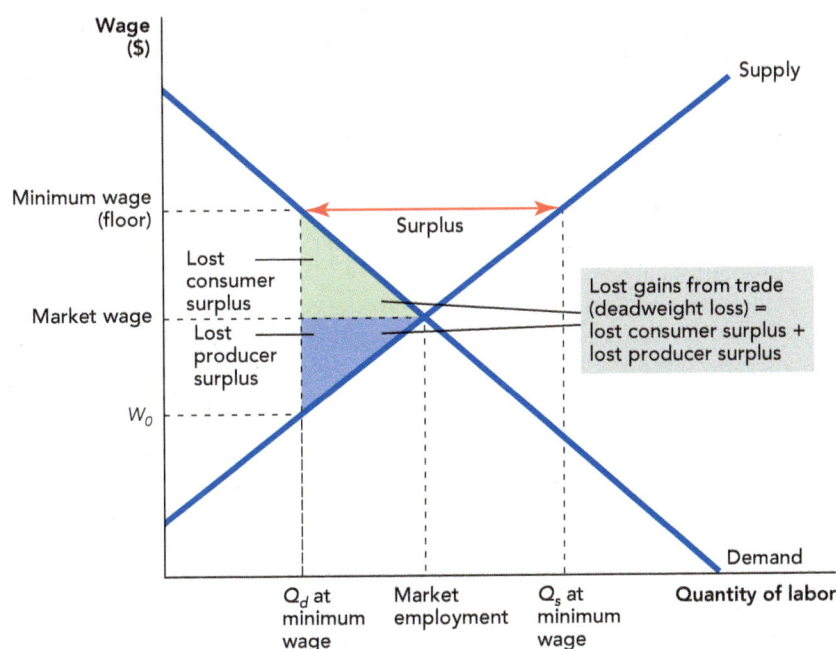

A Price Floor Reduces the Gains from Trade At the minimum wage, employers are willing to hire more workers at just less than the minimum wage and workers are willing to work additional hours for just more than W_0. Although mutually profitable, these trades are illegal. If all mutually profitable trades were legal, the gains from trade would increase by the green plus blue triangles.

Should the minimum wage be called the "Robot Employment Act"?

These facts may surprise you. The minimum wage is hotly debated in the United States. Democrats often argue that the minimum wage must be raised to help working families. Republicans respond that a higher minimum wage will create unemployment and raise prices as firms pass on higher costs to customers. Neither position is realistic. At best, the minimum wage will raise the wages of some teenagers and young workers whose wages would increase anyway as they improve their education and become more skilled. At worst, the minimum wage will raise the price of a hamburger and create unemployment among teenagers, many of whom will simply choose to stay in school longer (not necessarily a bad thing). The minimum wage debate is more about rhetoric than reality.

Even though small increases in the U.S. minimum wage won't change much, large increases would cause serious unemployment.

Keep in mind that there are substitutes for minimum wage workers. Higher minimum wages, for example, increase the incentive to move production to other cities, states, or countries where wages are lower. The United States imports lots of fruits and vegetables because it is cheaper to produce these abroad and ship them to the United States than it is to produce them here. Many minimum wage jobs are service jobs that cannot be moved abroad but firms can substitute capital—in the form of machines—for labor. If the minimum wage were to increase substantially, we might even see robots flipping burgers.

To explain the other important effects of price floors—wasteful increases in quality and a misallocation of resources—we turn from minimum wages to airline regulation.

Wasteful Increases in Quality

Many years ago, flying on an airplane was pleasurable; seats were wide, service was attentive, flights weren't packed, and the food was good. So airplane travel in the United States must have gotten worse, right? No, it has gotten better. Let's explain.

The Civil Aeronautics Board (CAB) extensively regulated airlines in the United States from 1938 to 1978. No firm could enter or exit the market, change prices, or alter routes without permission from the CAB. The CAB kept prices well above market levels, sometimes even denying requests by firms to lower prices!

We know that prices were kept above market levels because the CAB only had the right to control airlines operating *between* states. In-state airlines were largely unregulated. Using data from large states like Texas and California, it was possible to compare prices on unregulated flights to prices on regulated flights of the same distance. Prices on flights between San Francisco and Los Angeles, for example, were half the price of similar-length flights between Boston and Washington, D.C.

In Figure 5.12, firms are earning the CAB-regulated fare on flights that they would be willing to sell at the much lower price labeled "Willingness to sell."

FIGURE 5.12

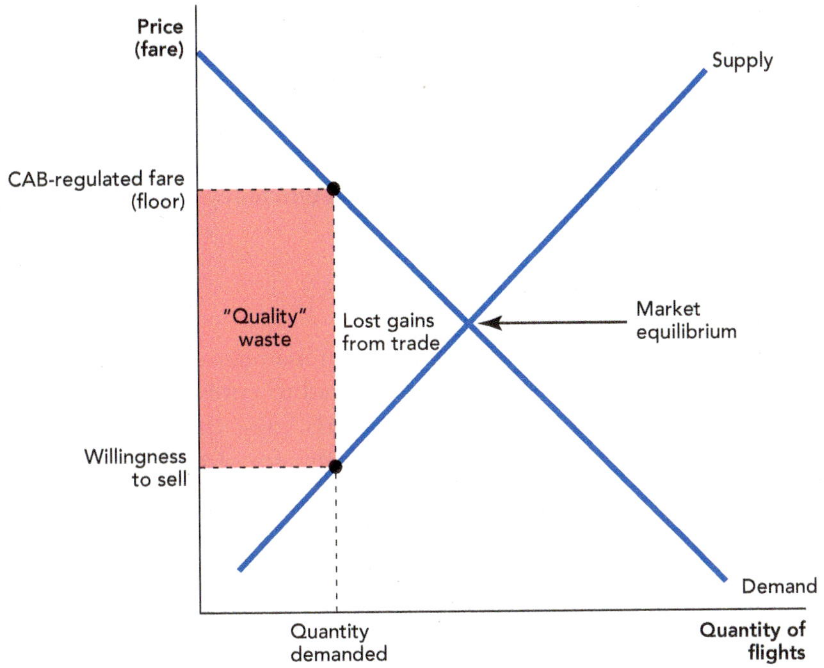

A Price Floor Creates Quality Waste
At the CAB-regulated fare, price is well above a seller's willingness to sell. Sellers cannot compete by offering lower prices so they compete by offering higher quality. Higher quality raises costs and reduces seller profit. Buyers enjoy the higher quality, but would prefer less quality at a lower price. Thus, the price floor encourages sellers to waste resources by producing more quality than buyers are willing to pay for.

Initially, therefore, regulation was a great deal for the airlines, who took home the red area as producer surplus.

A price floor means that prices are held *above* market levels, so firms want more customers. The price floor, however, makes it illegal to compete for more customers by lowering prices. So how do firms compete when they cannot lower prices? Price floors cause firms to compete by offering customers higher quality.

When airlines were regulated, for example, they competed by offering their customers bone china, fancy meals, wide seats, and frequent flights. Sounds good, right? Yes, but don't forget that the increase in quality came at a price. Would you rather have a fine meal on your flight to Paris or a modest meal and more money to spend at a real Parisian restaurant?

If consumers were willing to pay for fine meals on an airplane, airlines would offer that service. But if you have flown recently, you know that consumers would rather have a lower price. An increase in quality that consumers are not willing to pay for is a wasteful increase in quality. Thus, as firms competed by offering higher quality, the initial producer surplus was wasted away in frills that consumers liked but would not be willing to pay for—hence, the red area in Figure 5.12 is labeled "'Quality' waste."

Airline costs increased over time for another reason. The producer surplus initially earned by the airlines was a tempting target for unions who threatened to strike unless they got their share of the proceeds. The airlines didn't put up

Despite being more efficient than its rivals, airline regulation prevented Southwest from entering the national market until deregulation in 1978. Today, Southwest Airlines is one of the largest airlines in the world.

Jon Lord Photography/Alamy Stock Photo

too much of a fight because, when their costs rose, they could apply to the CAB for an increase in fares, thus passing along the higher costs to consumers. Many of the problems that older airlines have faced in recent times are due to generous pension and health benefits they are paying out, benefits that were granted when prices of flights were regulated above market levels.

By 1978, costs had increased so much that the airlines were no longer benefiting from regulation and were willing to accede to deregulation.[24] Deregulation lowered prices, increased quantity, and reduced wasteful quality competition.[25] Deregulation also reduced waste and increased efficiency in another way—by improving the allocation of resources.

The Misallocation of Resources

Regulation of airline fares could not have been maintained for 40 years if the CAB had not also regulated entry. Firms wanted to enter the airline industry because the CAB kept prices high, but the CAB knew that if entry occurred, prices would be pushed down. So under the influence of the older airlines, the CAB routinely prevented new competitors from entering. In 1938, for example, there were 16 major airlines; by 1974, there were just 10 despite 79 requests to enter the industry.

Restrictions on entry misallocated resources because low-cost airlines were kept out of the industry. Southwest Airlines, for example, began as a Texas-only airline because it could not get a license from the CAB to operate between states. (Lawsuits from competitors also nearly prevented Southwest from operating in Texas.) Southwest was able to enter the national market only after deregulation in 1978.

The entry of Southwest was not just a case of increasing supply. One of the virtues of the market process is that it is open to new ideas, innovations, and experiments. Southwest, for example, pioneered consistent use of the same aircraft to lower maintenance costs, greater use of smaller airports like Chicago's Midway, and long-term hedging of fuel costs. Southwest's innovations have made it one of the most profitable and largest airlines in the United States. Southwest's innovations have spread, in turn, to other firms such as JetBlue Airways, easyJet (Europe), and WestJet (Canada). Regulation of entry didn't just increase prices; it increased costs and reduced innovation. Deregulation improved the allocation of resources by allowing low-cost, innovative firms to expand nationally. Deregulation is the major reason why, today, flying is an ordinary event for most American families, rather than the province of the wealthy.

Takeaway

Price ceilings have several important effects: They create shortages, reductions in quality, wasteful lines and other search costs, a loss of gains from trade, and a misallocation of resources.

After reading this chapter, you should be able to explain all of these effects to your uncle. Also, to do well on the exam, you should be able to draw a diagram showing the price ceiling and correctly labeling the shortage. On the same diagram, can you locate the wasteful losses from waiting in line and the lost gains from trade? Review Figures 5.2 and 5.3 if you are having trouble with these questions. You should also understand why a price ceiling reduces product quality and how

CHECK YOURSELF

- The European Union guarantees its farmers that the price of butter will stay above a floor. The floor price is often above the market equilibrium price. What do you think has been the result of this?

- The United States has set a price floor for milk above the equilibrium price. Has this led to shortages or surpluses? How do you think the U.S. government has dealt with this? (*Hint:* Remember the cartons of milk you had in elementary school and high school? What was their price?)

price ceilings misallocate resources, not just in the market with the price ceiling but potentially throughout the economy.

Price floors create surpluses, a loss of gains from trade, wasteful increases in quality, and a misallocation of resources.

After reading this chapter, you should be able to explain all of these effects to your aunt. Can you show, using the tools of supply and demand, why a price floor creates a surplus, a deadweight loss, and a wasteful increase in quality? You should be able to label these areas on a diagram. You should also be able to explain how price floors cause resources to be misallocated.

CHAPTER REVIEW

Go online to practice with more examples of these types of problems, including live links to videos, data sources, and feedback.

▶ Problems with this icon relate to optional MRU videos.

KEY CONCEPTS

price ceiling, p. 71

deadweight loss, p. 76

rent control, p. 82

price floor, p. 88

FACTS AND TOOLS

▶ **1.** How does a free market eliminate a shortage?

▶ **2.** When a price ceiling is in place keeping the price below the market price, what's larger: quantity demanded or quantity supplied? How does this explain the long lines and wasteful searches we see in price-controlled markets?

▶ **3.** Suppose that the quantity demanded and quantity supplied in the market for milk is as follows:

Price per Gallon	Quantity Demanded	Quantity Supplied
$5	1,000	5,000
$4	2,000	4,500
$3	3,500	3,500
$2	4,100	2,000
$1	6,000	1,000

a. What is the equilibrium price and quantity of milk?

b. If the government places a price ceiling of $2 on milk, will there be a shortage or surplus of milk? How large will it be? How many gallons of milk will be sold?

▶ **4.** If a government decides to make health insurance affordable by requiring all health insurance companies to cut their prices by 30%, what will probably happen to the number of people covered by health insurance?

▶ **5.** The Canadian government has wage controls for medical doctors. To keep things simple, let's assume that they set one wage for all doctors: $100,000 per year. It takes about 6 years to become a general practitioner or a pediatrician, but it takes about 8 or 9 years to become a specialist like a gynecologist, surgeon, or ophthalmologist. What kind of doctor would you want to become under this system? (*Note:* The actual Canadian system does allow specialists to earn a bit more than general practitioners, but the difference isn't big enough to matter.)

▶ **6.** Between 2000 and 2008, the price of oil increased from $30 per barrel to $140 per barrel, and the price of gasoline in the United States rose from about $1.50 per gallon to more than $4.00 per gallon. Unlike in the 1970s when oil prices spiked, there were no long lines outside gas stations. Why?

7. Price controls distribute resources in many unintended ways. In the following cases, who will probably spend more time waiting in line to get scarce, price-controlled goods? Choose one from each pair:

    a. Working people or retired people?

    b. Lawyers who charge $800 per hour or fast-food employees who earn $8 per hour?

    c. People with desk jobs or people who can disappear for a couple of hours during the day?

8. In the chapter, we discussed how price ceilings can put goods in the wrong *place*, as when too little heating oil wound up in New Jersey during a harsh winter in the 1970s. Price controls can also put goods in the wrong *time* as well. If there are price controls on gasoline, can you think of some periods during which the shortage will get worse? (*Hint:* Gas prices typically rise during the busy Memorial Day and Labor Day weekends.)

9. a. Consider Figure 5.8. In a price-controlled market like this one, when will consumer surplus be larger: in the short run or in the long run?

    b. In this market, supply is more elastic, more flexible, in the long run. In other words, in the longer term, landlords and homebuilders can find something else to do for a living. In light of this and in light of the geometry of producer surplus in this figure, do rent controls hurt landlords and homebuilders more in the short run or in the long run?

10. Business leaders often say that there is a "shortage" of skilled workers, and so they argue that immigrants need to be brought in to do these jobs. For example, an AP article was entitled "New York farmers fear a shortage of skilled workers," and went on to point out that a special U.S. visa program, the H-2A program, "allows employers to hire foreign workers temporarily if they show that they were not able to find U.S. workers for the jobs."(*Source:* Thompson, Carolyn. May 13, 2008. N.Y. farmers fear a shortage of skilled workers. *Associated Press.*)

    a. How do unregulated markets cure a "labor shortage" when there are no immigrants to boost the labor supply?

    b. Why are businesses reluctant to let unregulated markets cure the shortage?

11. a. If the government forced all bread manufacturers to sell their products at a "fair price" that was half the current, free-market price, what would happen to the quantity supplied of bread?

    b. To keep it simple, assume that people must wait in line to get bread at the controlled price. Would consumer surplus rise, fall, or can't you tell with the information given?

    c. With these price controls on bread, would you expect bread *quality* to rise or fall?

12. A review of the jargon: Is the minimum wage a "price ceiling" or a "price floor"? What about rent control?

13. How do U.S. business owners change their behavior when the minimum wage rises? How does this impact teenagers?

14. The basic idea of deadweight loss is that a willing buyer and a willing seller can't find a way to make an exchange. In the case of the minimum wage law, the reason they can't make an exchange is because it's illegal for the buyer (the firm) to hire the seller (the worker) at any wage below the legal minimum. But how can this really be a "loss" from the worker's point of view? It's obvious why business owners would love to hire workers for less than the minimum wage, but if all companies obey the minimum wage law, why are some workers still willing to work for less than that?

Discovering DATA ⁞⁞

15. Go the FRED economic database (https://fred.stlouisfed.org/) and search for "percent hourly paid minimum wage."

    a. In 2015, what percent of hourly workers were paid the minimum wage or less?

    b. Hourly wage workers are about three-fifths of total workers (the remainder work on salary). Almost all salaried workers earn above the minimum wage. So what percentage of all workers earn the minimum wage or less?

THINKING AND PROBLEM SOLVING

▶ **16.** In rich countries, governments almost always set the fares for taxi rides. The prices for taxi rides are the same in safe neighborhoods and in dangerous neighborhoods. Where is it easier to find a cab? Why? If these taxi price controls were ended, what would probably happen to the price and quantity of cab rides in dangerous neighborhoods? (Aside: How do you think ride-sharing apps like Uber and Lyft have affected this problem?)

▶ **17.** When the United States had price controls on oil and gasoline, some parts of the United States had a lot of heating oil, while other states had long lines. As in the chapter, let's assume that winter oil demand is higher in New Jersey than in California. If there had been no price controls, what would have happened to the prices of heating oil in New Jersey and in California and how would "greedy businesspeople" have responded to these price differences?

▶ **18.** On January 31, 1990, the first McDonald's opened in Moscow, capital of the then Soviet Union. Economists often described the Soviet Union as a "permanent shortage economy," where the government kept prices permanently low in order to appear "fair."

An American journalist on the scene reported the customers seemed most amazed at the 'simple sight of polite shop workers . . . in this nation of commercial boorishness.'

  a. Why were most Soviet shop workers "boorish" when the McDonald's workers in Moscow were "polite"?

  b. What does your answer to the previous question tell you about the power of economic incentives to change human behavior? In other words, how entrenched is "culture"?

▶ **19.** Let's calculate the value of lost gains from trade in a regulated market. The government decides it wants to make basic bicycles more affordable, so it passes a law requiring that all one-speed bicycles sell for $30, well below the market price. Use the following data to calculate the lost gains from trade, just as in Figure 5.3. Supply and demand are straight lines.

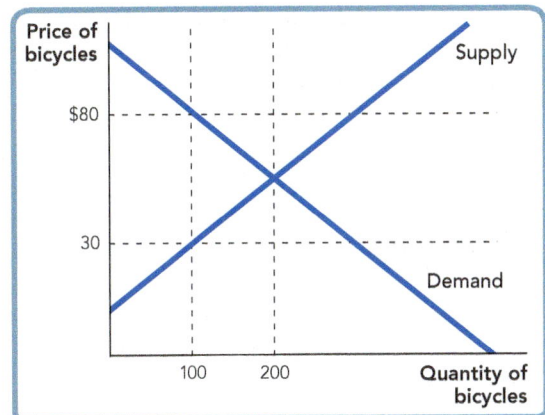

  a. What is the total value of wasted time in the price-controlled market?

  b. What is the value of the lost gains from trade?

  c. Note that we haven't given you the original market price of simple bicycles—why don't you need to know it? (*Hint:* The answer is a mix of geometry and economics.)

▶ **20.** During a crisis such as Hurricane Dorian governments often make it illegal to raise the price of emergency items like flashlights and bottled water. In practice, this means that these items get sold on a first-come/first-served basis.

  a. If a person has a flashlight that she values at $5, but its price on the black market is $40, what gains from trade are lost if the government shuts down the black market?

  b. Why might a person want to sell a flashlight for $40 during an emergency?

  c. Why might a person be willing to pay $40 for a flashlight during an emergency?

  d. When will entrepreneurs be more likely to fill up their pickup trucks with flashlights and drive into a disaster area: when they can sell their flashlights for $5 each or when they can sell them for $40 each?

▶ **21.** A "black market" is a place where people make illegal trades in goods and services. For instance, during the Soviet era, it was common for American tourists to take a few extra pairs of Levi's jeans when visiting the Soviet Union: They would sell the extra pairs at high prices on the illegal black market.

Consider the following claim: "Price-controlled markets tend to create black markets." Let's illustrate with the following figure. If there is a price ceiling in the market for cancer medication of $50 per pill, what is the *widest* price range within which you can *definitely* find both a buyer and a seller who would be willing to illegally exchange a pill for money? (There is only one correct answer.)

▶ **22.** So, knowing what you know now about price controls, are you in favor of setting a $2 per gallon price ceiling on gasoline? Create a pro–price control and an anti–price control answer.

▶ **23. a.** As we noted, Assar Lindbeck once said that short of aerial bombardment, rent control is the best way to destroy a city. What do you think Lindbeck might mean by this?

b. How does paying "key money" to a landlord reduce the severity of Lindbeck's "bombardment"?

24. In the town of Freedonia, the government declares that all street parking must be free: There can be no parking meters. In an almost identical town of Meterville, parking costs $5 per hour (or $1.25 per 15 minutes).

a. Where will it be easier to find parking: in Freedonia or Meterville?

b. One town will tend to attract shoppers who hate driving around looking for parking. Which one?

c. Why will the town from part b also attract shoppers with higher incomes?

▶ **25.** In the late 1990s, the town of Santa Monica, California, made it illegal for banks to charge people ATM fees. As you probably know, it's almost always free to use your own bank's ATMs, but there's usually a fee charged when you use another bank's ATM. (*Source:* The war on ATM fees, *Time*, November 29, 1999.) As soon as Santa Monica passed this law, Bank of America stopped allowing customers from other banks to use their ATMs: In bank jargon, B of A banned "out-of-network" ATM usage.

In fact, this ban lasted for only a few days, after which a judge allowed banks to continue to charge fees while awaiting a full court hearing on the issue. Eventually, the court declared the fee ban illegal under federal law. But let's imagine the effect of a full ban on out-of-network fees.

a. In the figure, indicate the new price per out-of-network ATM transaction after the fee ban. Also clearly label the shortage.

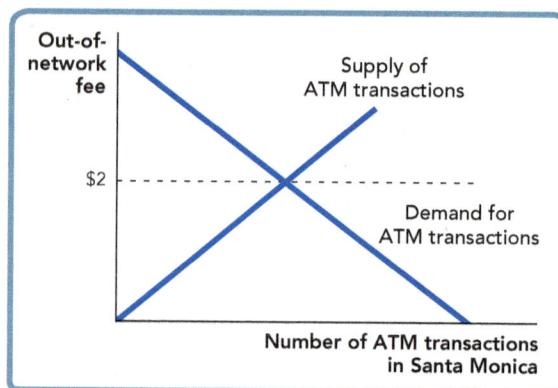

b. Calculate the exact amount of producer and consumer surplus in the out-of-network ATM market in Santa Monica after the ban. How large is producer surplus? How large is consumer surplus?

▶ **26.** Consider Figure 5.9. Your classmate looks at that chart and says, "Apartment construction slowed down years before rent control was passed, and after rent control was passed, more apartments were built. Rent control didn't cut the number of new apartments, it raised it. This proves that rent control works." What is wrong with this argument?

▶ **27.** Rent control creates a shortage of housing, which makes it hard to find a place to live. In a price-controlled market, people have to waste a lot of time trying to find these scarce, artificially cheap products. Yet Congressman Charles B. Rangel, the chairman of the powerful House Ways and Means Committee, lived in *four* rent-stabilized apartments in Harlem. Why are powerful individuals often able to "find" price-controlled goods much more often than the nonpowerful? What does this tell us about the political side effects of price controls?

(*Source:* Republicans question Rangel's tax break support, *New York Times,* November 25, 2008.)

28. In the 1970s, AirCal and Pacific Southwest Airlines flew only within California. As we mentioned, the federal price floors didn't apply to flights within just one state. A major route for these airlines was flying from San Francisco to Los Angeles, a distance of 350 miles. This is about the same distance as from Chicago, Illinois, to Cleveland, Ohio. Do you think AirCal flights had nicer meals than flights from Chicago to Cleveland? Why or why not?

29. President Jimmy Carter didn't just deregulate airline prices. He also deregulated much of the trucking industry as well. Trucks carry almost all of the consumer goods that you purchase, so almost every time you purchase something, you're paying money to a trucking company.

   a. Based on what happened in the airline industry after prices were deregulated, what do you think happened in the trucking industry after deregulation? You can find some answers here: http://www.econlib.org/Library/Enc1/TruckingDeregulation.html. For another look that is critical of trucking deregulation, but comes to basically the same answers, see Michael Belzer, 2000. *Sweatshops on Wheels: Winners and Losers in Trucking Deregulation.* Thousand Oaks, CA: Sage.

   b. Who do you think asked Congress and the president to keep price floors for trucking: consumer groups, retail shops like Walmart, or the trucking companies?

30. Suppose you're doing some history research on shoe production in ancient Rome, during the reign of the famous Emperor Diocletian. Your documents tell you how many shoes were produced each year in the Roman Empire, but they don't tell you the price of shoes. You find a document stating that in the year 301, Emperor Diocletian issued an "edict on prices," but you don't know whether he imposed price *ceilings* or price *floors*—your Latin is a little rusty. However, you can clearly tell from the documents that the number of shoes actually exchanged in markets fell dramatically, and that both potential shoe sellers and potential shoe buyers were unhappy with the edict. With the information given, can you tell whether Diocletian imposed a ceiling or a floor? If so, which is it? (Yes, there really was an edict of Diocletian, and Wikipedia has excellent coverage of ancient Roman history.)

Emperor Diocletian issued an Edict on Maximum Prices in the year 301 in an effort to control inflation. As usual, the edict created shortages, disruptions in trade, and a black market. Copia et demanda legi parendum.

31. In the market depicted in the figure, there is either a price ceiling or a price floor—surprisingly, it doesn't matter which one it is: Whether it's an $80 price floor or a $30 price ceiling, the chart looks the same.

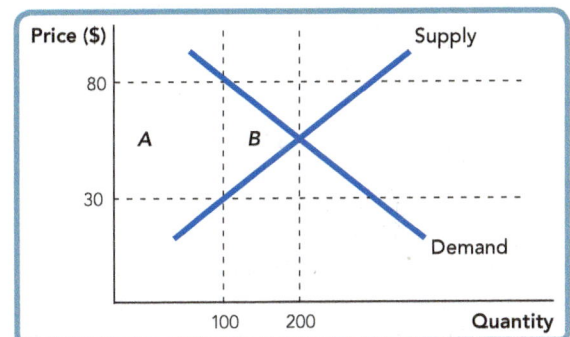

   In the chart, there's a rectangle and a triangle. One represents the value lost from "deals that don't get made" and one represents the value wasted in "deals that do get made." Which is which?

32. We noted that in the 1970s price floors on airline tickets caused wasteful increases in the quality of airline trips. Does the minimum wage cause wasteful increases in the quality of workers? If so, how? In other words, how are minimum-wage workers like airplane trips?

33. The city of Mumbai in India imposed rent controls on apartments in 1947. Despite inflation and changes in land value, allowable rents have hardly increased since that time! Use what you know about rent controls to speculate about the quality of rent-controlled buildings in Mumbai.

34. If a government decided to impose price controls on gasoline, what could it do to avoid the time wasted waiting in lines? There is surely more than one solution to this problem.

Bettmann/Getty Images

35. In New York City, some apartments are under strict rent control, while others are not. This is a theme in many novels and movies about New York, including *Bonfire of the Vanities* and *When Harry Met Sally*. One predictable side effect of rent control is the creation of a black market. Let's think about whether it's a good idea to allow this black market to exist.

   a. Harry is lucky enough to get a rent-controlled apartment for $300 per month. The market rent on such an apartment is $3,000 per month. Harry himself values the apartment at $2,000 per month, and he'd be quite happy with a regular $2,000 per month New York apartment. If he stays in the apartment, how much consumer surplus does he enjoy?

   b. If he illegally subleases his apartment to Sally on the black market for $2,500 per month and instead rents a $2,000 apartment, is he better off or worse off than if he obeyed the law?

36. Let's measure consumer surplus if the government imposes price controls and goods ended up being randomly allocated among those consumers willing to pay the controlled price. If the demand and supply curves are as in the figure, then:

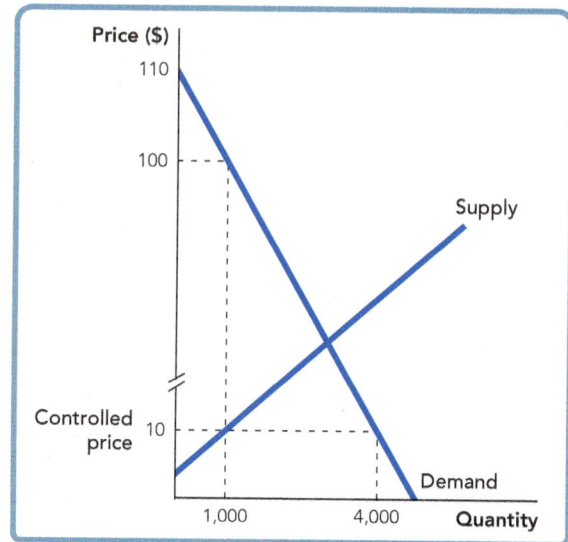

   a. What is consumer surplus under the price control?

   b. What would consumer surplus be if the quantity supplied were 1,000 but the goods were allocated to the highest-value users?

37. Antibiotics are often given to people with colds (even though they are not useful for that purpose), but they are also used to treat life-threatening infections. If there was a price control on antibiotics, what do you think would happen to the allocation of antibiotics across these two uses?

38. In a command economy such as the old Soviet Union, there were no prices for almost all goods. Instead, goods were allocated by a "central planner." Suppose that a good like oil becomes more scarce. What problems would a central planner face in reallocating oil to maximize consumer plus producer surplus?

39. Labor unions are some of the strongest proponents of the minimum wage. Yet in 2008, the median full-time union member earned $886 per week, an average of more than $22 per hour (http://www.bls.gov/news.release/union2 .nr0.htm). Therefore, a rise in the minimum wage doesn't directly raise the wage of many union workers. So why do unions support minimum wage laws? Surely, there's more than one reason why this is so, but let's see if economic theory can shed some light on the subject.

a. Skilled and unskilled labor are substitutes: For example, imagine that you can hire four low-skilled workers to move dirt with shovels at $5 an hour, or you can hire one skilled worker at $24 an hour to move the same amount of dirt with a skid loader. Using the tools developed in Chapter 3, what will happen to the demand for skilled labor if the price of unskilled labor increases to $6.50 per hour?

b. If the minimum wage rises, will that increase or decrease the demand for the average union worker's labor? Why?

c. Now, let's put the pieces together: Why might high-wage labor unions support an increase in the minimum wage?

40. In our Uber example, we said that after a spike in demand around Madison Square Garden, the number of Uber rides increased by more than 75% in the surrounding area, but when it starts to rain, Uber rides increase by the still substantial but lesser amount of 25%. Can you suggest one reason why the supply response is different in the two situations? (*Hint:* Think about elasticities of supply.)

WORK IT OUT

For interactive, step-by-step help in solving this problem, go online.

Suppose that the market for coats can be described as follows:

Price	Quantity Demanded (millions)	Quantity Supplied (millions)
$120	16	20
$100	18	18
$80	20	16
$60	22	14

a. What are the equilibrium price and quantity of coats?

b. Suppose the government sets a price ceiling of $80. Will there be a shortage, and if so, how large will it be?

c. Given that the government sets a price ceiling of $80, how much will demanders be willing to pay per unit of the good (i.e., what is the true price)? Suppose that people line up to get this good and that they value their time at $10 an hour. For how long will people wait in line to obtain a coat?

MRU VIDEOS

Price Ceilings: The US Economy Flounders in the 1970s
mru.org/price-ceilings
Problems: **1–3, 8–10, 28, 34, 38**

Price Ceilings: Shortages and Quality Reduction
mru.org/shortages-and-quality
Problems: **2–4, 9, 11, 16**

Price Ceilings: Lines and Search Costs
mru.org/lines-search-costs
Problems: **5–7, 19**

Price Ceilings: Deadweight Loss
mru.org/deadweight-loss
Problems: **14, 31**

Price Ceilings: Misallocation of Resources
mru.org/resources
Problems: **1, 8, 10, 20, 21**

Price Ceilings: Rent Controls
mru.org/rent-controls
Problems: **9, 12, 23, 25–28, 35–37**

Price Floors: The Minimum Wage
mru.org/min-wage
Problems: **12, 13, 32, 39**

Price Floors: Airline Fares
mru.org/airlines
Problems: **16–18, 28, 29**

Why Do Governments Enact Price Controls?
mru.org/price-controls
Problems: **22, 34**

Price Controls and Communism
mru.org/controls-and-communism
Problem: **38**

6

GDP and the Measurement of Progress

A visitor to India is immediately struck by the contrast between extreme poverty and rapid economic growth. Squalor in India is obvious; throughout India, you will see many people living in slums without easy access to steady electricity, piped water, or toilets. But India's growing wealth is also obvious: Cell phones are everywhere, new stores are opening, access to clean water is increasing, literacy is rising, and people are better fed. In the cities, there are more restaurants, more clothing shops, more factories, and more cars. Moreover, the rate of truly abject poverty, which the World Bank defines as living on less than $1.90 a day, approximately halved between 2000 and 2010 from a little more than 40% to a little more than 20%.

As a rough way of summarizing these changes in economic output and the standard of living, economists look to a country's gross domestic product (GDP) and its GDP per capita, two statistics designed to measure the value of economic production.

Figure 6.1 on the next page shows India's real GDP per capita—or GDP per person—between 1950 and 2017. Since a series of liberalization reforms were put in place in the late 1980s and early 1990s, India's real GDP per capita has been growing rapidly. In the 10 years between 2000 and 2010, for example, real GDP per capita grew at approximately 7% per year, leading to a doubling of real GDP per capita! As we will discuss, real GDP per capita is a rough measure of a country's standard of living. Thus, the standard of living in India roughly doubled in just 10 years. That is a notable improvement over India's previous growth performance and it represents the growing wealth and falling poverty of many Indians.

Table 6.1 lists GDP and GDP per capita for the 10 largest economies in 2017 (converted into U.S. dollars using PPP corrections). In the United States, where GDP was $18.22 trillion and the population was 324 million, GDP per capita was $56,153. Although China is the world's largest economy with a 2017 GDP of $18.4 trillion, it has a population of 1.4 billion people, so per capita GDP is only $13,051, a little bit less than Brazil ($14,109) and a little bit more than Indonesia ($10,842). Similarly, India has the third largest economy but, after China, it has the world's second largest population, so GDP per capita in India is only $6,282.

FIGURE 6.1

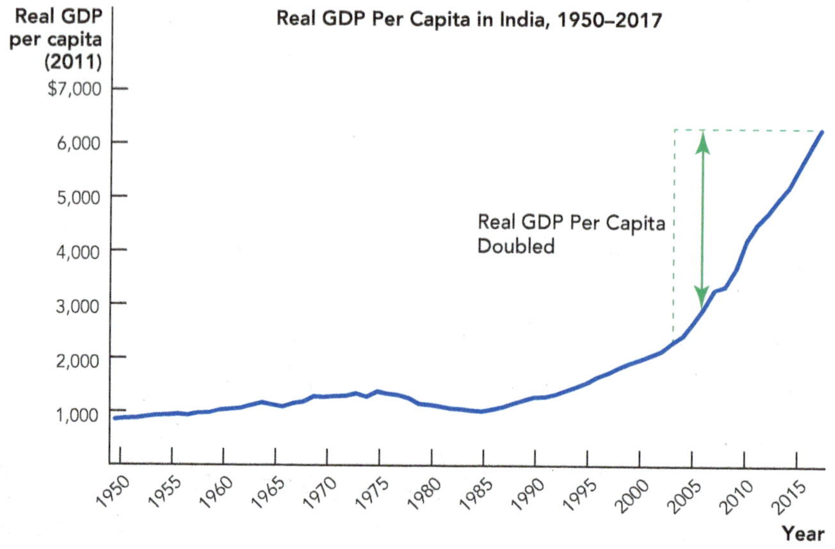

Real GDP Per Capita in India, 1950–2017

Real GDP per Capita in India, 1950–2017

Data from: Penn World Table 9.1.

Okay, we can see that GDP per capita gives us a rough guide to a country's standard of living, but what is GDP actually measuring? In this chapter, we will explain:

■ What the GDP statistic means and how it is measured

■ The difference between the level of GDP and the growth rate of GDP

TABLE 6.1 THE 10 LARGEST COUNTRIES RANKED BY GDP (2017)

	GDP (billions of U.S. dollars)	GDP per Capita (U.S. dollars)	Population (millions)
China	$18,396	$13,051	1,410
United States	$18,220	$56,153	324
India	$8,412	$6,282	1,339
Japan	$5,107	$40,064	127
Germany	$4,035	$49,141	82
Russia	$3,395	$23,579	144
Brazil	$2,953	$14,109	209
Indonesia	$2,862	$10,842	264
United Kingdom	$2,789	$42,138	66
France	$2,755	$40,975	67

Data from: Penn World Table 9.1 (2011 dollars, Real GDP at Constant National Prices, Population)

- The difference between nominal GDP and real GDP
- How growth in real GDP per capita is a standard measure of economic progress
- The use of GDP in business cycle measurement
- Problems with GDP as a measure of output and welfare

What Is GDP?

Gross domestic product (GDP) is the market value of all finished goods and services produced within a country in a year. **GDP per capita** is GDP divided by a country's population.

Let's take each part of the definition of GDP in turn.

GDP Is the Market Value ...

GDP measures an economy's total output, which includes millions of different goods and services. But some goods are obviously more valuable than others: A Ford Mustang is worth more than an iPad. To measure total output, therefore, it doesn't make sense to simply add up quantities. Instead, GDP uses market values to determine how much each good or service is worth and then sums the total.

For example, in 2016 the U.S. economy produced approximately 12 million cars and light vehicles and 8.6 billion chickens.[1] If the average price of a car was $28,000 and the average price of a chicken was $5, the market value of the production of cars was $336 billion ($28,000 × 12 million) and the market value of chicken production was $43 billion ($5 × 8.6 billion). Using prices in the calculations gives greater weight to goods and services that are more highly valued in the marketplace. Applying this procedure to all finished goods and services yields a figure for GDP. In Table 6.2, we show the addition to GDP created by the production of cars and chickens.

... of All Finished ...

What is a *finished* good or service? Some goods and services are sold to firms and then bundled or processed with other goods or services for sale at a later stage. These are called intermediate goods and services. We distinguish these from finished goods and services, which are sold to final users and then consumed or held in personal inventories.

Gross domestic product (GDP) is the market value of all finished goods and services produced within a country in a year.

GDP per capita is GDP divided by population.

🟢 **MRU**

mru.org/gdp

What Is Gross Domestic Product?

TABLE 6.2 GDP IS CALCULATED BY MULTIPLYING THE PRICE OF FINISHED GOODS AND SERVICES BY THEIR QUANTITIES AND ADDING THE MARKET VALUES

Finished Good	Price	×	Quantity	=	Market Value
Cars	$28,000	×	12 million	=	$336 billion
Chickens	$5	×	8.6 billion	=	$43 billion
					$379 billion ← Added to GDP

A computer chip is one example of an intermediate good. If an Intel chip were counted in GDP when it was sold to Dell, and then counted again when a consumer buys the Dell computer, the value of the computer chip would be counted twice. To avoid double counting, only the computer—the finished good—is included in the calculation of GDP.

We do, however, count the production of machinery and equipment used to produce other goods as part of GDP. A tractor, for example, may help to produce soybeans, but the tractor is not part of the finished product of soybeans. Thus, both tractor production and soybean production add to GDP, even though the computer chip does not.

... Goods and Services ...

The output of an economy includes both goods and services. Services provide a benefit to individuals without the production of tangible output. For example, paying a consultant to fix a software problem on a computer is a service and its market value is included in GDP. Other services include haircuts, transportation, entertainment, and spending on medical care.

Since 1950, the portion of U.S. GDP created by the production of services has increased from just under 50% to almost 70% (see Figure 6.2). Much of this increase is attributable to spending on medical services and recreational activities, which have both increased to more than 10 times their levels in 1950.[2]

Since U.S. GDP is about $21.4 trillion (2019), we can tell from Figure 6.2 that the value of finished services is about $14.5 trillion (0.68 × 18) and the value of finished goods about $6.8 trillion.

... Produced ...

GDP is meant to measure *production*, so sales of used goods, such as a used car, are not included in GDP.

CHECK YOURSELF

- The text says that the value of finished goods is about $6.8 trillion. Where does this number come from?

FIGURE 6.2

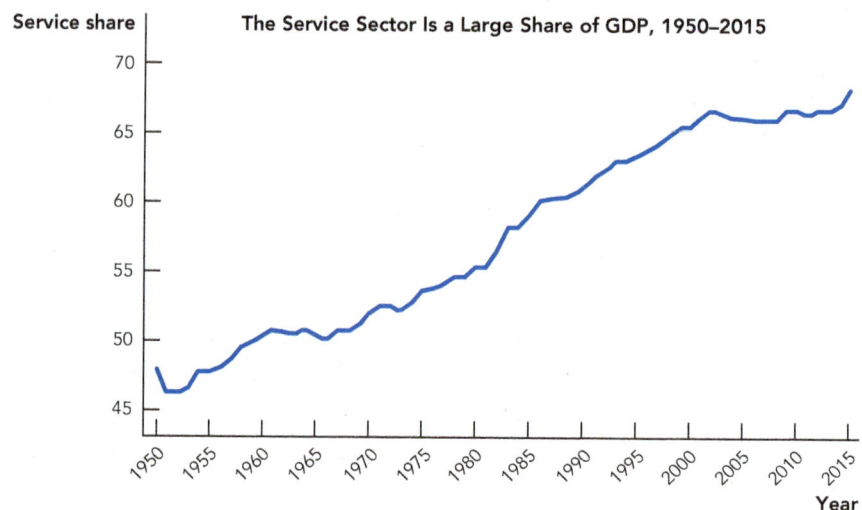

Service share

The Service Sector Is a Large Share of GDP, 1950–2015

Year

Services Are Increasing as a Share of U.S. GDP

Similarly, sales of old houses and sales of financial securities like stocks and bonds are not included in the calculation of GDP. The sale of an old house does not add to GDP because the house was not produced in the year in which it sold. Sales of newly built houses, however, are counted in GDP. Stocks and bonds are claims to financial assets—they are not themselves produced goods or services—so sales of stocks and bonds and other financial assets are not counted in GDP.

Even though the sales of old houses, used goods, and financial assets do not add to GDP, the services of real estate agents, used-car salespeople, and brokers do add to GDP because the services provided by these agents are produced in the year in which they are sold.

...within a Country...

U.S. GDP is the market value of the finished goods and services produced by labor and capital *located* in the United States, regardless of the nationality of the workers or the property owners. A citizen of Mexico who works temporarily in the United States adds to U.S. GDP. By the same reasoning, an American who works temporarily in Mexico contributes to Mexican GDP, not to U.S. GDP.

Gross national product (GNP) is very similar to GDP but GNP measures what is produced by the labor and property supplied by U.S. residents wherever in the world that labor or capital is located, rather than what is produced within the U.S. border. For a large nation like the United States, GDP and GNP are very similar but GDP has evolved into the more commonly used concept.

Gross national product (GNP) is the market value of all finished goods and services produced by a country's residents, wherever located, in a year.

...in a Year

GDP tells us how much the nation produced in a year, not how much the nation has accumulated in its entire history. You can think of GDP as being analogous to annual wages. Wages are not the same thing as wealth. Some retired people are wealthy even though their wages are low and some people with high wages have very little wealth (perhaps because they are at the beginning of their career or perhaps because they spend everything they earn and never save).

National wealth refers to the value of a nation's entire stock of assets. A tractor built in 2005 and still operating today is part of U.S. wealth but not part of today's GDP. One very crude estimate places U.S. national wealth at $100.4 trillion,[3] which is several times larger than its 2019 GDP of about $21.4 trillion.

Although we typically think of GDP on a yearly basis, it is also calculated every quarter of the year. The calculations are done by the Bureau of Economic Analysis (BEA), which is part of the Department of Commerce and based in Washington, D.C. If you want to see whether you understand what the bureau is up to, try testing yourself with the questions at right.

Growth Rates

To compute the growth rate of GDP from 2017 to 2018, for example, you need only two numbers: the GDP at the end of 2017 and the GDP at the end of 2018. Compute the percentage change as

$$\frac{GDP_{2018} - GDP_{2017}}{GDP_{2017}} \times 100 = \text{GDP growth rate for 2018}$$

Using actual figures (in billions), we get

$$\frac{\$20,580 - \$19,519}{\$19,519} \times 100 = 5.4\%$$

Thus, the growth rate for U.S. GDP for 2018 was 5.4%. An annual growth rate of 5.4% sounds pretty good but what we have just calculated is the growth rate of nominal GDP and if we are interested in the standard of living what we want to know is the growth rate of real GDP.

Nominal vs. Real GDP

Nominal variables, such as **nominal GDP,** have not been adjusted for changes in prices.

Nominal GDP is calculated using prices at the time of sale. Thus, GDP in 2018 is calculated using 2018 prices and GDP in 2017 is calculated using 2017 prices. What this means is that when we compare GDP in two different years we are seeing both the change in output and the change in prices. What we would like to know is whether the increase in GDP between 2017 and 2018 was due mostly to greater production—more cars and more chickens—or mostly due to increases in prices between 2017 and 2018. Economists usually are more interested in increases in production than increases in prices because only increases in production are true increases in the standard of living. But how can we measure increases in production while controlling for increases in prices? Here is what we know so far:

2018 nominal GDP = 2018 prices × 2018 quantities = $20.58 trillion

2017 nominal GDP = 2017 prices × 2017 quantities = $19.52 trillion

Can you see how to compare the increase in production from 2017 to 2018? Suppose we calculate GDP in 2017 using 2018 prices instead of 2017 prices. The U.S. Bureau of Economic Analysis (BEA) does just this and finds the following:

2018 GDP in 2018 dollars = 2018 prices × 2018 quantities
= $20.58 trillion

2017 GDP in 2018 dollars = 2018 prices × 2017 quantities
= $19.99 trillion

What this tells us is that if prices in 2017 were the same as in 2018, then GDP in 2017 would have been measured as $19.99 trillion. Economists also say that 2017 GDP in 2018 dollars is real GDP in 2018 dollars. Since 2018 GDP is already in 2018 dollars, it's also real GDP in 2018 dollars.

Now that we have real GDP in 2017 and real GDP in 2018, we can find the increase in real GDP. Between 2017 and 2018, the growth rate of real GDP was (20.58 − 19.99)/19.99 = 0.0295 × 100 = 2.95%. Thus in 2018 the economy produced 2.95% more goods and services than in 2017. That's about average performance but notice that the growth rate of real GDP was quite a bit lower than the growth rate of nominal GDP that we calculated earlier—5.4%.

If we want to compare GDP over time, we should always compare real GDP, that is, GDP calculated using the *same prices in all years*. Interestingly, it doesn't matter much what prices we use to calculate real GDP, so long as we use the same prices in all years.

Real GDP calculations become trickier the longer the period we compare. In 1925, for example, what was the price of a computer? Economists and statisticians involved in calculating real GDP must worry about the value of new goods and changes in the quality of goods. The more years that pass, the more difficult it is to determine how to adjust for those quality changes.

The real versus nominal distinction is an important one in economics and it will recur throughout this book. A **real variable** is one that corrects for inflation, namely a general increase in prices over time. In later chapters, we will discuss the real price of housing, real wages, and the real interest rate and we will show in more detail how to convert nominal data into real data.

Real variables, such as **real GDP**, have been adjusted for changes in prices by using the same set of prices in all time periods.

The GDP Deflator

The GDP deflator is a price index that can be used to measure inflation. We will be discussing price indexes and inflation at greater length in Chapter 12. The GDP deflator, however, is very easy to calculate once we know nominal and real GDP for a given year. The GDP deflator is simply the ratio of nominal to real GDP (multiplied by 100).

$$\text{GDP deflator} = \frac{\text{Nominal GDP}}{\text{Real GDP}} \times 100$$

For example, let's calculate the GDP deflator for 2016. We can easily find 2016 nominal GDP and 2016 real GDP (using 2009 dollars) from the U.S. Bureau of Economic Analysis. Here are the numbers:

$$\textbf{2016 nominal GDP} = \textbf{2016 prices} \times \textbf{2016 quantities}$$
$$= \$18.57 \text{ trillion}$$

$$\textbf{2016 real GDP (in 2009 dollars)} = \textbf{2009 prices} \times \textbf{2016 quantities}$$
$$= \$16.66 \text{ trillion}$$

$$\textbf{GDP deflator} = \frac{\textbf{2016 prices} \times \textbf{2016 quantities}}{\textbf{2009 prices} \times \textbf{2016 quantities}}$$
$$= \frac{18.57 \text{ trillion}}{16.66 \text{ trillion}} = \frac{2016 \text{ prices}}{2009 \text{ prices}}$$
$$= 1.1145 \times 100 = 111.45$$

To see why the GDP deflator can be used to measure inflation, notice that the deflator is a ratio of prices. What the deflator tells us is that 2016 prices were about 11.45% higher (111.45 − 100) than 2009 prices.

Real GDP Growth

If pressed to choose a single indicator of *current* economic performance, most economists would probably choose real GDP growth. Figure 6.3 shows the annual percentage changes in real GDP for the United States from 1948 to 2018. U.S. real GDP growth was high during the 1960s, but the 1973 and 1979 oil price shocks slowed growth in the 1970s and early 1980s. Growth was more solid after the 1982 recession until the mid-2000s but still somewhat slower than in the 1960s. The severe recession of 2009 and slow recovery since then is also evident in the figure. Note that the long-term (since 1948) average growth rate of real U.S. GDP has been about 3.2% per year. You can use these figures as benchmarks to gauge current growth rates.

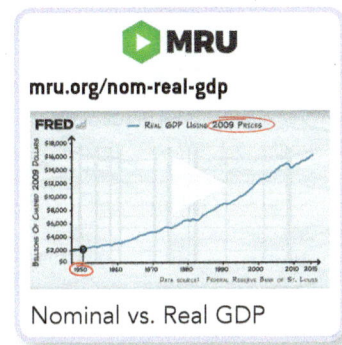

mru.org/nom-real-gdp

Nominal vs. Real GDP

FIGURE 6.3

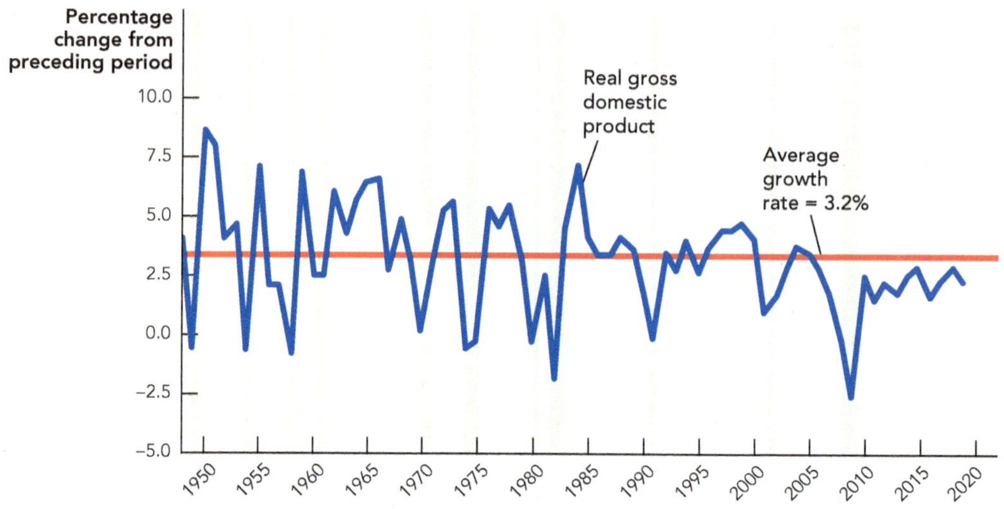

The Growth Rate of Real GDP (United States, 1948–2018)

Data from: Bureau of Economic Analysis, https://fred.stlouisfed.org/graph/?g=q6ZE

Real GDP Growth per Capita

Growth in real GDP per capita is usually the best reflection of changing living standards. Growth in real GDP typically gives the same broad idea of how economic conditions are changing as does growth in real GDP per capita, but there can be big differences for countries with rapidly growing populations. For instance, between 1993 and 2003, Guatemala experienced real GDP growth of about 3.6% a year. That might sound good but over that same period population grew at 2.8% a year, so real GDP per capita in Guatemala grew at just 0.8% a year. In comparison, real GDP per capita in the United States typically grows by about 2.1% a year. Thus, not only is the United States richer than Guatemala, people in the United States are getting richer faster.

Nigeria is a tragic example of a growth disaster. In 1960, when Nigeria gained its independence from Great Britain, vast deposits of oil were discovered and the future looked bright. But a vicious civil war, dictatorship, and massive corruption meant that the oil wealth disappeared in arms purchases and secret Swiss bank accounts. Incredibly for an economy in the modern era, real GDP per capita in Nigeria was a little bit lower in 2000 than it had been in 1960.

Although it seems shocking that a country could be no richer in 2000 than in 1960, it's important to remember that throughout most of human history, a failure to grow is *normal*. In the next chapter, we will begin to explain not only why some nations are poor but the truly mysterious question: Why are any nations rich?

Cyclical and Short-Run Changes in GDP

So far we have focused on GDP as a way to compare economic output across countries and over long periods. GDP is also used to measure short-run fluctuations in an economy, namely the ups and downs in economic growth that

CHECK YOURSELF

- Name a country with a high GDP but a low GDP per capita.
- Name a country with a low GDP but a high GDP per capita.
- Why do we often convert nominal variables into real variables?

occur within the space of a few years. As we saw in Figure 6.3, U.S. growth rates varied considerably from 1948 to 2018. In some years, such as 2009, the growth rate was negative. **Recessions**—significant, widespread declines in real GDP and employment—are of special concern to policymakers and the public.

A **recession** is a significant, widespread decline in real GDP and employment.

The National Bureau of Economic Research (NBER), a research organization based in Cambridge, Massachusetts, is considered the most authoritative source on identifying U.S. recessions. The official NBER definition of a recession is as follows:

> A recession is a significant decline in economic activity spread across the economy, lasting more than a few months, normally visible in real GDP, real income, employment, industrial production, and wholesale–retail sales.

A few points in this definition are worth emphasizing. A recession is widespread not only geographically but also across different sectors of the economy. Although a decline in real GDP is the single best indicator of a recession, declines will usually also be observed in income, employment, sales, and other measures of the health of an economy.

How often do recessions occur? Figure 6.4 plots real GDP growth and official U.S. recessions since 1948—this time using quarterly data (expressed as annualized rates) so we can better see the variability over time. There have been 11 recessions since 1948, indicated by the shaded bars. Notice that in addition to recessions, the figure illustrates expansions or booms when real GDP grows at a faster rate than normal. We call the fluctuations of real GDP around its long-term trend, or "normal" growth rate, **business fluctuations** or **business cycles.**

Business fluctuations or **business cycles** are the short-run movements in real GDP around its long-term trend.

Defining when a recession begins and ends is not always obvious, in part because economic data are often revised over time. The estimate of quarterly

FIGURE 6.4

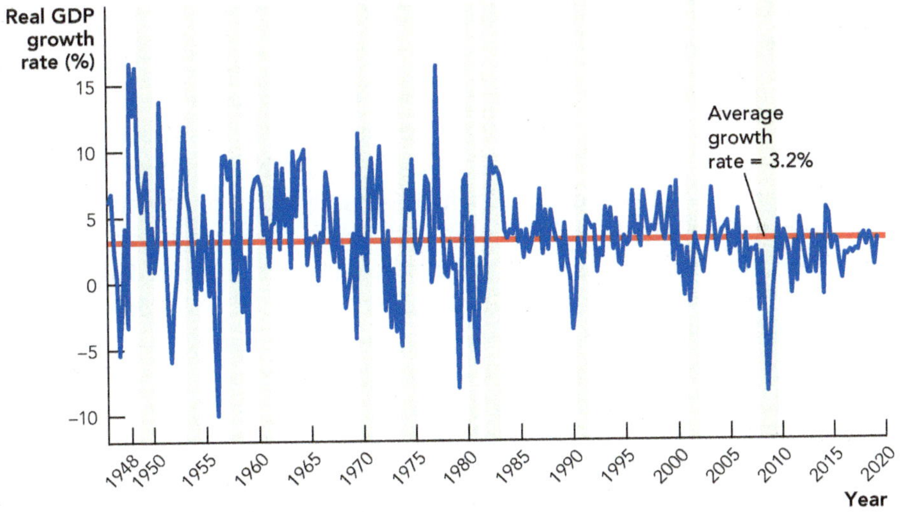

All U.S. Recessions Since 1948, Quarterly Growth Rates Expressed as Annualized Rates

Data from: Bureau of Economic Analysis, https://fred.stlouisfed.org/graph/?g=q6ZE

Economic data take time to collect and evaluate. In April 1991, the NBER announced that a recession had started in July 1990. In 1992, the NBER announced that the recession had ended in March 1991, a few weeks before the recession was first recognized!

CHECK YOURSELF

- What are business fluctuations?
- Why is it sometimes difficult to determine if an economy is in a recession?

GDP, for example, is not ready for release until almost a month after the quarter is over. After that, additional rounds of updated estimates are published in the following two months. The government often makes significant changes in GDP estimates between the original estimate and the final estimate. For example, in 2011 the BEA revised GDP estimates from 2008, and the recession in that year turned out to be even worse than earlier estimates had suggested. The BEA initially estimated that GDP had fallen at an annualized rate of −6.8% in the fourth quarter of 2008. In the revisions, the decline was significantly steeper, −8.9%. Since updates can occur years after the first estimates are released, the usefulness of GDP as a timely indicator is dampened and our understanding of recessions can change over time.

As another example, there is debate about when the 2001 recession started. The official NBER starting date is March 2001, but data revisions have led many people to conclude that the recession actually started in late 2000. Why all the fuss about the timing? If you recall, the presidency changed at the beginning of 2001. Democrats would like to claim that the recession was caused by Republican economic policies, while Republicans want to show that the recession began during President Clinton's final term, before President Bush assumed office.

The Many Ways of Splitting GDP

Another way of understanding GDP is to study its components and how they fit together. Economists split the production of goods and services in many different ways depending on the questions they are asking. We present two common ways of splitting GDP:

1. National spending approach to GDP: $Y = C + I + G + (\text{Exports} - \text{Imports})$
2. Factor income approach to GDP: $Y = \text{Employee Compensation} + \text{Rent} + \text{Interest} + \text{Profit}$

As we will see, both formulas prove useful for understanding business cycles and economic growth.

The National Spending Approach: $Y = C + I + G + (\text{Exports} - \text{Imports})$

Economists have found it useful, especially for the analysis of short-run economic fluctuations, to split GDP into consumption (C), investment (I), government purchases (G) and Exports minus Imports, which is often shortened to Net Exports (NX). To understand why this is equivalent to thinking of GDP as the market value of all finished goods and services produced within a country in a year, note that produced goods can be consumed, invested, or purchased by governments or foreigners. Finally, some consumed, invested, and government-purchased goods are imported. Imported goods are not part of U.S. GDP, so we subtract imports. Thus, GDP can also be written as

$$Y = C + I + G + NX$$

where:

Y = Nominal GDP (the market value all finished goods and services)

C = The market value of consumption goods and services

I = The market value of investment goods, also called capital goods

G = The market value of government purchases

NX = Net exports, defined as the market value of exports minus the market value of imports

We explain each of these factors more in turn.

Consumption is private spending on finished goods and services. Most consumption spending is made by households, such as spending on cars and chickens. Consumption spending, however, also includes spending on health care whether the spending comes from your pocket, an insurance company, or the government (as with Medicaid and Medicare). Note that while economists think of education as an investment in "human capital," the Bureau of Economic Analysis includes education as consumption spending alongside purchases of automobiles, smartphones, and televisions. How would you classify your education spending? Are you here to consume (party!) or invest for the future (study hard!)?

Investment is private spending on tools, plant, and equipment that are used to produce future output. Most investment spending is made by businesses but an important exception is that new home production is counted as investment. It's important to remember that "investment" is spending on tools, plant, and equipment (capital). When a farmer buys a tractor, that is investment. If your university builds new classrooms and labs, that is investment. Buying IBM stock, however, is not investment, as this is a mere change in ownership of some capital goods from one person to another. To make sure that everything adds up, investment also includes changes in inventories.

The third component of GDP is **government purchases,** or spending by all levels of government on finished goods and services. Government purchases include spending on tanks, airplanes, office equipment, and roads, as well as spending on wages for government employees (in this case the government is implicitly thought of as the purchaser of services such as military services). This category includes both government consumption items (like toner cartridges for printers) and government investment items (like roads and levees), and is thus also called government consumption and investment purchases.

A large part of what government does is transfer money from one citizen to another citizen; about 21% of the spending of the federal government, for example, is for Social Security payments. Unemployment and disability insurance, various welfare programs, and Medicare are also large transfer programs. We do not include transfers in government purchases because if we did, we would be double-counting. When the senior citizen buys a television with their Social Security check or consumes health care through Medicare, it is counted in the consumption portion of GDP. Thus, we do not also count the check as part of government purchases. Another way of thinking about this is that we count only government purchases of *finished goods and services.* When the government sends a check to a senior citizen, it is not purchasing a finished good or service—it is transferring wealth.

Net exports is exports minus imports. To understand this term, it's important to remember the *Domestic* in Gross Domestic Product. When we add $C + I + G$ we are adding up all national spending but some of that spending was on imports, goods that were not produced domestically. So we subtract imports from national spending to get national spending on domestically produced goods, $C + I + G - \text{Imports}$. Some of the goods that we *produced* domestically,

Consumption is private spending on finished goods and services.

Investment is private spending on tools, plant, and equipment used to produce future output.

Government purchases are spending by all levels of government on finished goods and services. Transfers are not included in government purchases.

Net exports are the value of exports minus the value of imports.

however, aren't included in *national* spending on domestically produced goods because they weren't bought by nationals but by people in other countries, i.e., some of the goods we produced were exported. Thus, to find domestically produced goods we add exports to national spending on domestically produced goods, to arrive at $C + I + G +$ Exports $-$ Imports or $C + I + G + NX$.

But here is something to avoid. The national spending approach to calculating GDP requires a step in which we subtract imports, but that doesn't mean that imports are bad for GDP! Let's consider a simple economy, one where I, G, and Exports are all zero and $C = \$100$ billion. Our only imports come from a container ship that once a year delivers $10 billion worth of iPhones. Thus when we calculate GDP we add up national spending and subtract $10 billion for the imports: $100 billion − $10 billion = $90 billion. But suppose that this year the container ship sinks before it reaches our port in New York. When we calculate GDP this year, then, there are no imports to subtract. But GDP doesn't change! Why not? Remember that part of the $100 billion of national spending was $10 billion spent on iPhones. So this year when we calculate GDP we will calculate $90 billion − $0 = $90 billion. GDP doesn't change; that shouldn't be surprising since GDP is about domestic production and the sinking of the container ship doesn't change domestic production.

If we want to understand the role of imports (and exports) on GDP and national welfare, we have to go beyond accounting to think about economics. If we permanently stopped all the container ships from delivering iPhones, for example, then domestic producers would start producing more cell phones and that would add to GDP, although producing more cell phones would require producing less of other goods. If we were buying cell phones from abroad because producing them abroad requires fewer resources, then GDP would actually fall when we produced more cell phones at home—this is one of the standard arguments for trade. The standard answer could change, however, if there were lots of unemployed resources in the domestic economy, an issue we will discuss in the chapter on business fluctuations and in later chapters. The point we want to emphasize here is not whether trade is ultimately good or bad, but rather that $Y = C + I + G + NX$ is an accounting identity that can't by itself answer this question.

Figure 6.5 shows the four components of U.S. GDP in 2018. Consumption is by far the largest component, accounting for $13.99 trillion, or 68% of U.S. GDP. Government purchases were $3.59 trillion, or 17.4% of GDP, investment was $3.62 trillion, or 17.6%, and net exports were −$0.63 trillion, or −3.0%. If you look at the "long-term averages" part of Figure 6.5, you'll get an idea of the relative sizes of these numbers in recent times. In later chapters on aggregate demand and business cycles, you will see that changes in these categories represent one way of thinking about the causes or sources of short-run economic downturns and that is one reason why we have covered these particular categories.

FIGURE 6.5

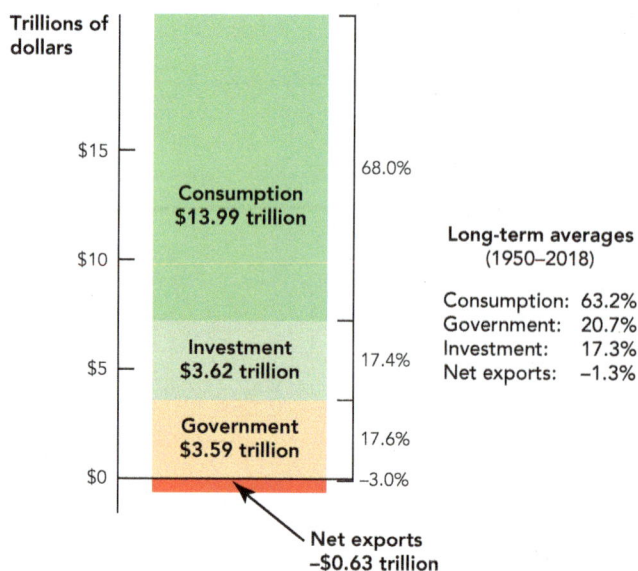

Trillions of dollars

Consumption $13.99 trillion — 68.0%
Investment $3.62 trillion — 17.4%
Government $3.59 trillion — 17.6%
Net exports −$0.63 trillion — −3.0%

Long-term averages (1950–2018)

Consumption: 63.2%
Government: 20.7%
Investment: 17.3%
Net exports: −1.3%

U.S. GDP and Its Components, 2018

Data from: Bureau of Economic Analysis.

The Factor Income Approach: $Y =$ Employee Compensation + Rent + Interest + Profit

When a consumer spends money, the money is received by workers (employee compensation = wages + benefits), landlords (rent), owners of capital (interest), and businesses (profit). Thus, we have yet another way of calculating GDP: We can add up all the spending or we can add up all the receiving. The first method is called the spending approach, while the second is called the factor income approach. Thus, GDP can also be written as

$$Y = \textbf{Employee compensation} + \textbf{Rent} + \textbf{Interest} + \textbf{Profit}$$

As usual, some corrections are necessary to get the accounting right. For example, not every dollar spent on goods and services is a dollar received in income. Sales taxes are one exception with which you can identify. Sales taxes create a difference between what consumers pay and what businesses and workers receive so if we calculate GDP using the income approach, we need to add sales taxes.[*]

For our purposes, the details are less important than the basic idea: Every dollar spent is a dollar of income received so if we are careful in our accounting, we can measure GDP by summing up all the spending on finished goods and services or by summing up everyone's income.

Why Split?

Each of the ways of splitting GDP throws a different light on the economy. Economists who study business fluctuations, for example, are often interested in splitting GDP according to the national spending identity because consumption, investment, government purchases, and net exports behave differently over time. Consumption spending, for example, tends to be much more stable than investment spending. Economists are interested in understanding the causes and consequences of these differences.

The factor income approach is useful if we are thinking about how economic growth is divided between employee compensation, rent, interest, and profits. It turns out, for example, that the largest payment in GDP is to labor. Employee compensation (wages and other benefits) accounts for about 54% of GDP—more than most people expect and much larger than corporate profits, which are around 10% of GDP. The share of GDP going to labor has been quite stable over time, although some evidence suggests that this share has fallen slightly in recent years. Economists are interested in understanding what drives the relative sizes of these shares.

It also helps to have more than one way of counting GDP because different methods are subject to different errors. Calculating GDP in more than one way lets us check our calculations.

No way of splitting GDP is better than another—it all depends on the questions being asked. Many other methods of splitting GDP are also possible and useful. We could look at the market value of food versus all other items, or durable versus nondurable goods, or we could break down GDP into finer

---

[*] We also have to make some corrections for depreciation. Over time machines wear down, factories fall into disrepair, and homes age. Depreciated capital doesn't add to anyone's income but GDP measures production before depreciation, so if we calculate GDP using the income approach, we need to adjust for the depreciation of capital.

geographic areas like regions or states (the latter is called gross state product). In principle, there are millions of ways of building a GDP measure by summing up its smaller parts. Economists continue to refine the idea of GDP, to improve the measurement of GDP, and to develop new ways of splitting GDP.

Problems with GDP as a Measure of Output and Welfare

GDP measures the market value of finished goods and services. *But we do not know the market value of many goods and services.* We don't know the market value, for example, of illegally produced goods and services because neither the buyers nor the sellers are willing to answer questions from government statisticians. An even more serious problem is that we don't know the market value of goods and service that are not bought and sold in markets. We don't know, for example, the market value of clean air because clean air is not bought and sold in a market.

Let's look in more detail at some examples of each of these problems.

GDP Does Not Count the Underground Economy

Illegal or underground-market transactions are omitted from GDP. Sales of crack cocaine, for example, or sales of counterfeit Gucci bags are not reported and so do not show up in government statistics. Legal goods sold "under the table" to avoid taxes also do not show up in GDP.

Nations that have greater levels of corruption and higher tax rates usually have higher levels of underground transactions. In Haiti, the poorest country in the Western Hemisphere, it takes an estimated 203 days of fighting the bureaucracy to start and register a legal business.[4] It is no wonder that so many Haitians keep their commercial activity outside the law. More generally, the size of the informal or "outside the law" sector in Latin America is estimated at 41% of officially measured GDP.[5]

Nations with a great deal of illegal and off-the-books activity are not as poor as they appear in the official GDP statistics. In the United States or Western Europe, the underground economy is likely between 10% and 20% of GDP; that percentage is small relative to the percentage in Haiti or most of Latin America but in absolute terms it is still quite large.

GDP Does Not Count Nonpriced Production

Nonpriced production occurs when valuable goods and services are produced but no explicit monetary payment is made. If a son mows his parent's lawn, the service will not be included in GDP. If a lawn care firm provided the identical work, it would be included in GDP. Yet either way the grass gets cut and economic output increases. Similarly, if you watch videos for free on YouTube, this is not counted in GDP, but if you buy a ticket to the movie theater it is counted in GDP. People search for valuable information on Google, read blogs and newspapers online, and chat with their friends on Facebook but these transactions are not registered in the GDP statistics since they are not priced. Volunteering of all kinds, such as when church workers deliver food to the elderly, people pick up garbage in parks, and book reviewers post reviews on Amazon, is also not counted in GDP. Each of these activities adds to economic output but if the transaction isn't priced, it isn't counted in the GDP statistics.

The omission of nonpriced production introduces two biases into GDP statistics: biases over time and biases across nations.

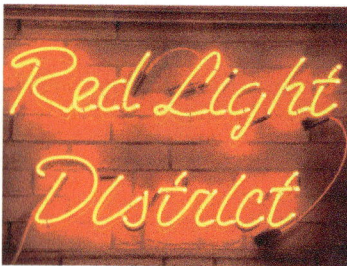

Services are included in GDP Prostitution is legal in the Netherlands and prostitution revenues are included in the Netherlands' GDP.

David Ryznar/Shutterstock

In the United States, the portion of women who are in the official labor force has almost doubled since 1950, rising from 34% to about 60% today. As a result, mothers spend less time working at home than in 1950, but there are more nannies and house cleaners in the economy today. The mothers who worked at home in 1950 were not paid and their valuable services were not counted in GDP. Nannies and house cleaners today are paid and their services are counted in GDP (unless the nanny is hired "under the table" to avoid paying Social Security taxes, of course!). The result is that U.S. GDP in 1950 underestimates a little the real production of goods and services in 1950 relative to that of today.

Nonpriced production also affects GDP comparisons across countries. For example, many cultures discourage women from becoming part of the official workforce. In India, women make up only 28% of the labor force, compared with 46% for the United States.[6] The output of the other 72% of Indian women is not included in Indian GDP, but these women are working. Indian GDP statistics, therefore, underestimate the real production of goods and services in India.

Household production is especially important in poor countries and in rural areas. It is common to read of families, say, in rural Mexico, that earn no more than $1,000 a year. Living off this sum sounds impossible to a contemporary American, but keep in mind that many of these families build their own homes (with help from relatives and friends), grow their own food, and sew their own clothes. Their lives are hard, but much of what they produce is not captured in GDP statistics.

GDP Does Not Count Bads: Environmental Costs

GDP adds up the market value of finished goods and services, but it does not subtract the value of bads. Pollution, for example, is a bad that is produced every year, but this bad is not counted in the GDP statistics. The statistics also do not count the destruction of water aquifers, the accumulation of carbon dioxide in the atmosphere, or the changing supplies of natural resources. Similarly, GDP statistics do not count the loss of animal or plant species as economic costs, unless those animals and plants had a direct commercial role in the economy. Other bads, for example, the bad of crime, are also not counted in GDP statistics. Since more pollution isn't counted as a bad, it's not surprising that less pollution is also not counted as a good. America has cleaner air and cleaner water than it did in 1960, but GDP statistics do not reflect this improvement.

The movement for "green accounting" has tried to reform GDP statistics to cover the environment more explicitly. In 2015, for example, total CO_2 emissions for the United States were 5,270 million tons. The U.S. government estimates that the social cost of CO_2 emissions is $41.20 per ton (using a 3% discount rate and in 2015 dollars), so the total social cost of emissions in that year was $217 billion. Subtracting this bad from the $18,036 billion GDP in 2015 would have given us a slightly smaller estimate of GDP, $17,820 billion. Interestingly, since CO_2 emissions fell over the period 2005 to 2015, such a calculation would also have slightly raised our estimates of growth rates over this period.

Most economists agree with the logic behind green accounting: GDP should measure the market value of all finished goods and services even if those goods and services are not traded in markets. But environmental amenities are often difficult to value. How much, for instance, should be added to GDP because more or fewer polar bears are present in Alaska? How much is a glacier worth? A coral reef? Estimates of the values of these resources may be computed for individual problems, but when it comes to the economy as a whole, the measurement task seems insurmountable. Rather than introduce so much uncertainty into the entire GDP concept, economists usually restrict green accounting (and other GDP modifications) to the analysis of particular problems such as CO_2 emissions.

GDP Does Not Count the Health of Nations

GDP counts the production of goods and services, but the more goods and services we can afford, the more important is another source of wealth, health and longevity. In the seven years between 2007 and 2014, life expectancy increased in the United States by about 1 year. How much was that increase in life expectancy worth? Let's do a back-of-the-envelope calculation to get an idea of the magnitude. By looking at the differences in wages between jobs of different risks (the compensating differential—see your micro text), economists have estimated that people value an additional year of life at about $150,000. Government agencies use numbers like this to value improvements in road safety, reductions in pollution, or new life-saving pharmaceuticals. The U.S. population is about 330 million, but since we are doing a back-of-the-envelope calculation let's simplify it to 300 million. An extra year of life valued at $150,000 for 300 million people is worth a total of $45 trillion!

Our back-of-the-envelope calculation doesn't take into account some important factors. We should be careful about how we compare future and present values (discounting) and we should take into account population growth, but more careful calculations by economists Kevin Murphy and Robert Topel show that we are in the right ballpark—increases in life expectancy are worth tens of trillions of dollars! In fact, Murphy and Topel estimate that the increases in life expectancy between 1970 and 2000 (see Table 6.3) were worth half of all the GDP produced during this period—about $95 trillion dollars.[7]

Numbers like this are important for understanding improvements in welfare over time and also for thinking about how resources should be allocated. Murphy and Topel also calculate, for example, that a 1% reduction in cancer mortality would be worth $500 billion. Or, to put it differently, it would be worth spending $100 billion on a medical "moonshot" program if that program had just a 20% chance of reducing cancer mortality by 1%.

Even though the value of health is not included in GDP, that doesn't mean that society doesn't value health. To understand the trade-offs, however, it is important that we put numbers on the value of health so that we can make appropriate comparisons and make wise choices.

TABLE 6.3 LIFE EXPECTANCY BY AGE GROUP AND YEAR, 1970–2000

	1970	1980	1990	2000	Change in Life Expectancy (1970–2000)
Newborn	70.76	73.88	75.37	76.87	6.11
15 years	57.69	60.19	61.38	62.62	4.93
45 years	30.12	32.27	33.44	34.38	4.26
65 years	15.00	16.51	17.28	17.86	2.86

Data from: Cutler, D. M., Rosen, A. B., and Vijan, S. 2006. The value of medical spending in the United States, 1960–2000. *New England Journal of Medicine*, 355(9): 920–927.

TABLE 6.4 GROWTH IN GDP PER CAPITA CAN BE DISTRIBUTED IN DIFFERENT WAYS

	John	Paul	George	Ringo	GDP	GDP per Capita
Year 1	10	20	30	40	100	25
(a) Year 2	11	22	33	44	110	27.5
(b) Year 2	10	20	30	50	110	27.5
(c) Year 2	20	20	30	40	110	27.5

GDP Does Not Measure the Distribution of Income

GDP per capita is a rough measure of the standard of living in a country. But if GDP per capita grows by 10%, this does not necessarily mean that *everyone's* income grows by 10% or even that the average person's income grows by 10%.

To see why, imagine that we have a country of four people, John, Paul, George, and Ringo, whose factor incomes in year 1 are 10, 20, 30, and 40. Using the factor income approach, we know that GDP is 100 (10 + 20 + 30 + 40) and thus GDP per capita is 25 (100/4). GDP in year 1 and its distribution are shown in the first row of Table 6.4.

Now suppose that in year 2 GDP grows by 10% to 110 and thus GDP per capita grows to 27.5 (110/4). This growth in GDP, however, is consistent with any of the three outcomes shown in rows a, b, and c of Table 6.4. In row a, everyone's income grows by 10%—so John's income grows from 10 to 11, Paul's income grows from 20 to 22, and so forth. In row b, the growth in GDP is concentrated on Ringo, the richest person: His income grows by 25% (from 40 to 50) and everyone else's income stays the same. In row c, the growth in GDP is concentrated on John, the poorest person. His income grows by 100% (from 10 to 20) and everyone else's income stays the same.

GDP and GDP per capita grow by the same amount in each of these cases, but in row a inequality stays the same, in row b inequality increases, and in row c inequality decreases.

In most countries most of the time, growth in GDP per capita is like row *a:* Everyone's income grows by approximately the same amount.[8] Thus, growth in real GDP per capita usually does tell us roughly how the average person's standard of living is changing over time. In examining particular countries and periods, however, we might want to look more carefully at how growth in GDP is distributed. In other words, GDP figures are useful but they will always be imperfect.

Takeaway

The primary topics of macroeconomics are economic growth and business fluctuations. But when we say that "the economy" is growing, what do we mean? And precisely what is fluctuating? If we want to understand growth and fluctuations, we need some concept that defines and measures growth and fluctuations.

The concept of gross domestic product was developed to quantify the ideas of economic growth and fluctuations. GDP, the market value of all finished goods and services produced within a country in a year, is an estimate of the economic output of a nation over a year. When we say that an economy is growing, we mean that GDP, or a closely related concept like GDP per capita, is growing. When we say that an economy is booming or contracting, we mean that growth in real GDP is above or below its long-run trend.

GDP can be measured and summed up in different ways, each of which casts a different light on the economy. The national spending identity, $Y = C + I + G + NX$, splits GDP according to different classes of income spending. The factor income approach, Y = Employee compensation + Interest + Rent + Profit, splits GDP into different classes of income receiving.

GDP per capita is a rough estimate of the standard of living in a nation. Real GDP is GDP per capita corrected for inflation by calculating GDP using the same set of prices in every year. Growth in real GDP per capita tells us roughly how the average person's standard of living is changing over time.

GDP statistics are imperfect. GDP does not include the value of leisure or goods bought and sold in the underground economy, nor does it include the value of goods that are difficult to price, such as the value of having polar bears in Alaska. GDP and GDP per capita also do not tell us anything about how equally GDP is distributed. Economists and statisticians try to refine and improve the measurement of GDP over time. GDP measures are imperfect but they have proven they are useful in estimating the standard of living and the scope of economic activity.

CHAPTER REVIEW

Go online to practice with more examples of these types of problems, including live links to videos, data sources, and feedback.

▶ Problems with this icon relate to optional MRU videos.

KEY CONCEPTS

gross domestic product (GDP), p. 103

GDP per capita, p. 103

gross national product (GNP), p. 105

nominal GDP, p. 106

nominal variables, p. 106

real variables, p. 107

recession, p. 109

business fluctuations (business cycles), p. 109

consumption, p. 111

investment, p. 111

government purchases, p. 111

net exports, p. 111

FACTS AND TOOLS

▶ 1. According to Table 6.1, what country has the highest GDP? What country on the list has the highest GDP per person? What countries on the list have the *second* highest GDP and the *second* highest GDP per person?

▶ 2. What is included in GDP: all goods, all services, or both?

▶ 3. What happened to spending on medical services and recreational activities after 1950?

4. Police officer: "I pulled you over for speeding. You were going 80 miles per hour."

   Driver: "But that's impossible, officer! I've only been driving for 15 minutes!"

   The government reports GDP numbers every quarter. How does this story illustrate the meaning of "GDP per year" when the GDP number is reported every three months?

5. Calculate the annual growth rate of nominal GDP in the following examples:

   Nominal GDP in 1930: $97 billion. Nominal GDP in 1931: $84 billion.

   Nominal GDP in 1931: $84 billion. Nominal GDP in 1932: $68 billion.

   Nominal GDP in 2000: $9,744 billion. Nominal GDP in 2001: $10,151 billion.

   (Data from: Historical Tables, Budget of the United States Government, Congressional Budget Office.)

6. Are the following included in U.S. GDP? Briefly explain why or why not:

   a. Used cars sold at a used car lot/dealership

   b. Your used car you sell to your cousin

   c. Wine made in Napa Valley at a vineyard owned by Australians

   d. Wine made in Australia at a vineyard owned by Americans

   e. The price paid by a French tourist when staying at a San Francisco hotel

   f. The price paid by an American tourist staying at a Paris hotel

   g. A ticket for a Lakers game

7. By definition, is nominal GDP higher than real GDP?

8. In the past 20 years, have recessions been getting more frequent or less frequent than they used to be?

9. According to the National Bureau of Economic Research, which of the following are "normally" part of the definition of a recession?

   A fall in nominal income

   A fall in employment

   A fall in real income

   A fall in the price level

10. Looking back over the past 10,000 years of human history, which is more "normal": for GDP per capita to grow or for GDP per capita to stay about the same?

Discovering DATA

11. Using the Federal Reserve Economic Data (FRED) database (https://fred.stlouisfed.org/), find Real U.S. GDP. Adjust the dates to focus in on the years 2005 to 2016. The recession in 2008–2009 will be highlighted in gray. Look at the quarterly data (click Edit Graph and modify frequency to Quarterly if the data are not already presented quarterly).

   a. What was the highest level of real GDP prior to the recession?

   b. In what year and quarter did U.S. real GDP first exceed its pre-recession level?

Discovering DATA

12. Using the Federal Reserve Economic Data (FRED) database (https://fred.stlouisfed.org/), let's sum up real GDP using its components. Recall that GDP = C + I + G + Net Exports, so start by finding "Real personal consumption expenditures" (C), use the "Billions of Chained 2009 Dollars, Quarterly, Seasonally Adjusted Annual Rate" series. Now click Add Line and find a similar series for real investment (I). Now click Add Line again and look for Real Government Consumption Expenditures and Gross Investment (G), again in billions of dollars. Now click on Add Line one more time and look for real Net Exports (NX) (the last series is only available in this form since 1999).

   a. Graph the result.

   b. In the 2009 recession which series fell by the most?

   c. In the first quarter of 2010 what share of GDP was made up by Consumption? Note that you should *not* have to look up a separate GDP figure to make this calculation.

13. What is the national spending identity? This identity is very important in macroeconomics. It is as important as basic anatomy in medical school: You won't be able to cure anyone until you know what's inside a person.

THINKING AND PROBLEM SOLVING

14. Calculate GDP in this simple economy:

   Consumer purchases: $100 per year

   Investment purchases: $50 per year

   Government purchases: $20 per year

   Total exports: $50 per year

   Total imports: $70 per year

15. Since World War II, who were the only three recession-free U.S. presidents? (We'll revisit the question of how presidents matter for the economy in later chapters.)

16. We noted that "government purchases" don't include all government spending. A big part of what the U.S. government does is transfer

money from one person to another. Social Security (payments to retirees), and Medicare and Medicaid (paying for medical care for the elderly and the poor) make up most of these "government transfers." We'll look into this in more detail in Chapter 17, but right now, let's see how big "government transfers" are and how fast they've grown in the federal government's budget. The figures in this table are all in non-inflation-adjusted dollars. Complete the table.

Year	Total Federal Transfers	Total Federal Spending	Transfers as Percent of Spending
1950	$10.3 billion	$47 billion	_____
2016	$1,961 billion	$4,023 billion	_____
Growth Rate in %	_____	_____	_____

Data from: *Budget of the United States Government: Historical Tables, Fiscal Year 2017.* Washington, DC: U.S. Government Printing Office.

17. Let's figure out GDP for Robinson Crusoe.

a. Initially, he is stuck on an island without the wisdom and local knowledge of Friday. Because Crusoe is a proper Englishman, he wants to keep his accounts. This year, he catches and eats 2,000 fish valued at one British pound (£) each, grows and eats 4,000 coconuts valued at 0.5 British pounds each, and makes two huts (housing) valued at 200 pounds each.

   If government purchases are zero and there is no trade, what is C for Crusoe? What is I? What is Y? (We are going to start using those letters as if they mean something: See question 13 in the previous section.)

b. One year, he learns of a tribe on a nearby island who are willing to trade with him: If he gives fish, they give clams. He produces just as much as before, but he trades 500 of the 2,000 fish and receives 10,000 clams valued at 5 clams per British pound. What is the British pound value of the exported fish? Of the imported clams? What are C, I, and X now? What is GDP now?

c. The following year, Crusoe produces the same as in every other year, but a tribe on the other side of the island steals his two huts

after he makes them, and gives him nothing in return. So he exports, but does not import at all. What are C, I, X, and Y now?

d. In Crusoe's final year on the island, he produces the same as in every other year (he's a reliable worker), but a new shipwreck washes up on his island containing a clock worth £3, a new shirt worth £2, and a copy of Milton's *Paradise Lost* and Shakespeare's complete works, each worth £1. Treat these as imported consumer goods. What is GDP this year? (*Note:* Emphasize the "P" in GDP when considering your answer.) What are C, I, X, and Y this year? (*Note:* One of the four is bigger than usual, one is negative.)

e. Is Crusoe probably happy about what happens in question 17c? Is he probably happy about what happens in question 17d? Keep these answers in mind for when we discuss the economics of trade later on.

18. Let's think about an economically sound way to measure the value of leisure. To keep this simple, we'll just think about the value of leisure to people who *could* work but who decide to stay home. Also, we won't think about how much *actual* workers value their free time, or about how much children and retirees value their time.

In a standard supply and demand labor model, firms "demand" labor, while workers "supply" labor. Let's think about a labor market that is in equilibrium, with a wage of $20 per hour (close to the U.S. average) and with 150 million Americans working out of a total of 225 million working-age Americans.

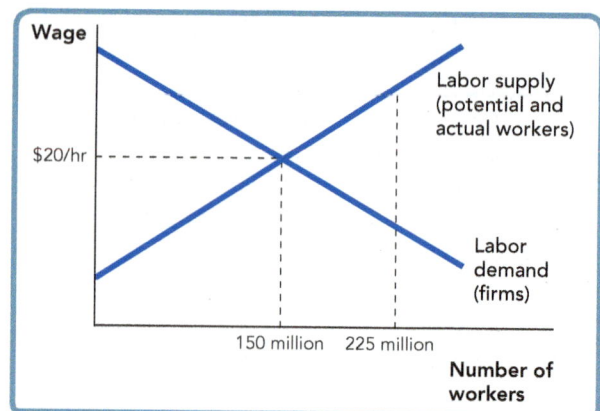

a. According to this simplified model of the U.S. economy, some workers *would* work if the wages were higher, but at the current wage, they'd rather stay home and watch reruns of *Seinfeld* or (don't let this be you!) *Two and a Half Men*. For the workers who are right on the margin between working and not working, what would their wage be if wages rose ever so slightly and they went to work?

b. Let's use this wage as a shorthand for how much nonworkers value their time. After all, the "opportunity cost" of their free time must be at least this high, because otherwise they'd take a job. Now, let's calculate a GDP measure that adds a rough estimate of the value enjoyed by these nonworkers. We'll use the following identity, and we'll round the value of nominal GDP to $14 trillion (close to the actual 2008 level):

Leisure-augmented GDP = Regular GDP + Total monetary value of leisure

If the average working person works 2,000 hours per year (that's a 40-hour week for 50 weeks a year), then what is the leisure-augmented value of U.S. GDP?

19. The underground economy and other nonpriced production make it difficult to accurately measure the precise level of GDP. But GDP could still be very accurate for measuring changes in the economy. If Jerome Powell, the Federal Reserve head, is trying to find out whether the U.S. economy has gone into a recession, are the difficulties of measuring nonpriced production likely to be important problems for his purposes? How is this like always wearing your shoes when you step on the bathroom scale?

20. a. U.S. GDP is approximately $22 trillion and the U.S. population is approximately 330 million. If GDP were divided equally among the U.S. population what would each person get? If you and your nine best friends took almost all U.S. GDP for yourself but gave $3,000 per person to everyone else, how much would you get each year, just for yourself?

b. More seriously, there are currently about 270,000 U.S. taxpayers who earn more than $1.5 million per year. If you could take their money and divide it up equally among the U.S. population of 330 million other Americans, how much money could you give each person? Note that $1.5 million is the cutoff. On average this group earns about $5 million per year so use that number in your calculations.

c. How can large numbers of people get rich? Comment on economic growth versus redistribution.

21. Let's sum up some basic facts of U.S. economic history with numbers:

a. First, let's measure the size of the Great Depression:

Real GDP in 1929 (peak): $323 billion	Real GDP in 1933 (trough): $206 billion
Price level in 1929: 33	Price level in 1933: 24

Calculate the percent change in real GDP and the percent change in the price level from 1929 to 1933. First, calculate the total change, and then divide it by the number of years to get the more typical measure of "percent per year." (*Note:* This is four full years, not three or five.)

b. Second, let's measure how much the economy grew from the lowest depths of the Depression to the peak of World War II's economic boom:

Real GDP in 1933 (trough): $206 billion	Real GDP in 1945: $596 billion
Price level in 1933: 24	Price level in 1945: 38

Again, first calculate the total change, and then divide it by the number of years to get the more typical measure of "percent per year."

c. Finally, let's see if a growing economy must mean growing prices:

Real GDP in 1870: $36 billion	Real GDP in 1900: $124 billion
Price level in 1870: 22	Price level in 1900: 16

Calculate the total and annual growth rates as before. *Note:* The price level fell fairly smoothly across these three decades, a time when the economy grew rapidly and many great American novels were written about life in the growing cities.

(*Data from:* Gordon, Robert J., ed. 1986. *The American Business Cycle: Continuity and Change.* Cambridge, MA: National Bureau of Economic Research.)

22. What is the difference between a nation's *wealth* and its *GDP*? How are the two related?

CHALLENGES

Discovering DATA ∷

23. Consider the following claim:

    Europeans have strong labor unions, so their workers get a bigger share of the pie than U.S. workers.

    Let's use the FRED economic database (https://fred.stlouisfed.org/) to examine this claim. Search for "Share of Labor Compensation in GDP at Current National Prices for United States." Click on the starting date and change it to 1990. (The data for other countries are not always very good before 1990.) Now click Add Line and search for "Share of Labor Compensation Germany." You should find the same series for Germany, click on it and then Add Data Series. Follow the same procedure to add a line for the Share of Labor Compensation in GDP in Italy.

    It is true that Europeans have stronger labor unions than Americans, but is the claim we began with true? What does our analysis of the data tell us about what strong unions and labor regulation can and can't do?

24. During World War II, the government did a good job measuring nominal GDP. But if the price level was calculated incorrectly, we might get a completely wrong idea about what happened with real GDP. During World War II, price ceilings were in place. That means that some things that would've been expensive were instead artificially cheap. Within a few years of the war's end, price controls finally ended, and the price level spiked up about 20%. If the true price level *during the war* was actually 20% higher than reported, would that mean real GDP is higher than the official number in question 21b in the previous section, lower than that number, or is it still the same as that number?

25. If U.S. government statistics counted education spending as part of investment, which of the following would rise, which would fall, and which would remain unchanged? (*Note:* You might use rise, fall, and stay unchanged more than once each or you might not.)

    Consumption

    Investment

    Gross domestic product

26. If U.S. government statistics counted people who are receiving unemployment benefits as people who are "government employees" hired to "search for work," which of the following would rise, which would fall, and which would remain unchanged? (*Note:* You might use rise, fall, and unchanged more than once each or you might not.)

    Consumption

    Government purchases

    Gross domestic product

27. According to legend, some government employees do very little work. If this legend is true enough to be important, then we may be measuring GDP incorrectly. Officially, we say that these are "employed workers," but to a great extent these "employees" are really unemployed in any useful task; they are receiving transfer payments and watching YouTube for 40 hours per week. If, instead, government statistics counted these YouTube-watching government employees as simply retired or unemployed, which of the following would rise, which would fall, and which would remain unchanged? (*Note:* You might use rise, fall, and unchanged more than once each or you might not.)

    Consumption

    Government purchases

    Gross domestic product

WORK IT OUT

For interactive, step-by-step help in solving this problem, go online.

Are the following included in U.S. GDP? Briefly explain why or why not:

a. Used textbooks sold at your college bookstore

b. Used books sold at a garage sale

c. Cars made in the United States at a Toyota factory

d. Cars made in Germany at a General Motors factory

e. The price paid by a German tourist when staying at a New York City hotel

f. The price paid by an American tourist staying at a Berlin hotel

g. A ticket for a Yankees game

▶ MRU VIDEOS

What Is Gross Domestic Product (GDP)?

mru.org/gdp

Problems: **2, 6**

Nominal vs. Real GDP

mru.org/nom-real-gdp

Problems: **7, 20, 21, 24**

Real GDP per Capita and the Standard of Living

mru.org/gdp-per-capita

Problem: **1**

Splitting GDP

mru.org/calc-gdp

Problems: **3, 8, 9, 14–16, 25–27**

7

The Wealth of Nations and Economic Growth

In developed nations, diarrhea is a pain, an annoyance, and, of course, an embarrassment. In much of the developing world, diarrhea is a killer, especially of children. Every year 1.7 million people die from diarrhea, more than from suicide, homicide, war, and terrorism combined. To prevent these deaths, we do not need any scientific breakthroughs, nor do we need new drugs or fancy medical devices. What is needed most is one thing: economic growth.

Economic growth brings piped water and flush toilets, which together cut infant mortality from diarrhea by 70% or more. Malaria, measles, and infections also kill millions of children a year. Again, the lesson is clear: millions of children are dying who would live if there were more economic growth.

Figure 7.1 on the next page illustrates how health and wealth go together. The vertical axis shows GDP per capita and the horizontal axis shows infant survival rates: how many children, out of every 1,000 births, survive to the age of 5. In the United States, one of the world's richest countries, 993 out of every 1,000 children born survive to the age of 5 (i.e., 7 out of every 1,000 die before the age of 5). In Liberia, one of the world's poorest countries, only about 765 children survive to age 5 (i.e., 235 of every 1,000 children die before seeing their fifth birthday). The graph illustrates a strong correlation between a country's GDP per capita and infant survival. The graph doesn't show a perfectly straight line—countries with the same level of income often have different levels of infant mortality, which means that factors other than income, such as government policies, culture, and geography, also matter. However, the correlation between income and infant mortality is quite strong. Notice also that the size of each country's data bubble is proportional to the population of that country; notice that India and China each have populations of more than 1 billion people so economic growth in these countries has the potential to save millions of infants from an early death.

Infant health and wealth tend to move together; indeed, just about *any* standard indicator of societal well-being tends to increase with wealth. Infant survival rates, life expectancy, and nutrition (caloric intake levels), for example, all tend to be higher in wealthier nations. Educational opportunities, leisure, and entertainment also tend to be higher in wealthier nations. Wealthier nations

FIGURE 7.1

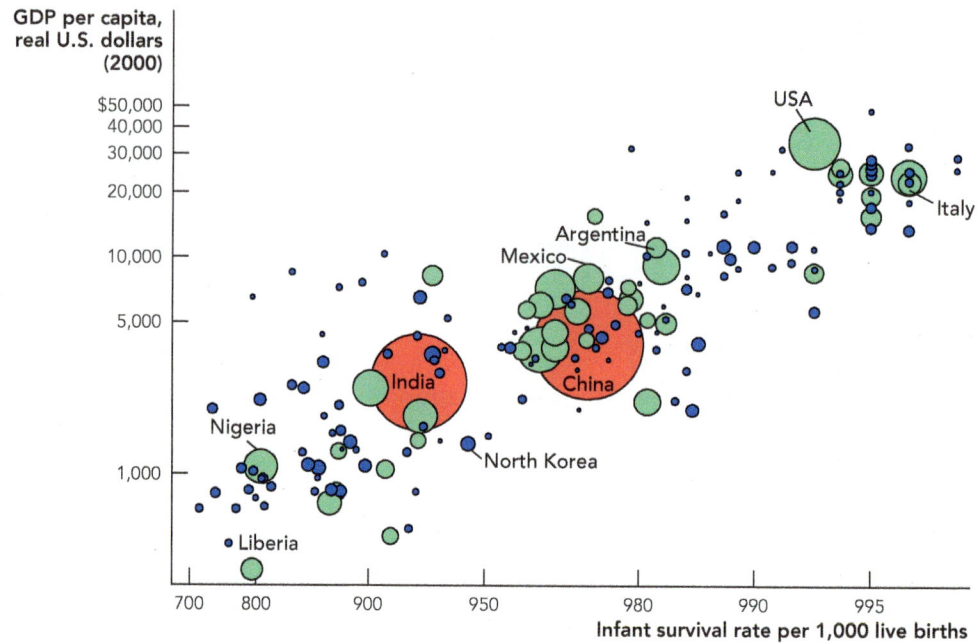

Wealthier Countries Have Higher Infant Survival Rates

Data from: Penn World Tables and World Bank Group, World Development Indicators, 2005.
Note: Not all countries are labeled. GDP on ratio scale. PPP adjusted.

even have fewer conflicts such as civil wars and riots. And, of course, wealthier nations have more material goods such as televisions, iPhones, and swimming pools.

Wealth is clearly important, so we want answers to the following questions. Why are some nations wealthy, while others are poor? Why are some nations getting wealthier faster than others? Can anything be done to help poor nations become wealthy? The answers to these questions are literally a matter of life and death. In this chapter and the next, we will try to answer these questions.

Key Facts About the Wealth of Nations and Economic Growth

Let's begin with some important facts about the wealth of nations and economic growth.

Fact One: GDP per Capita Varies Enormously Among Nations

We already have some understanding of the enormous differences that exist in the wealth of nations and how these differences affect infant mortality and other measures of well-being. Figure 7.2 shows in more detail how GDP per capita differed around the world in recent years. To construct this figure, we start on the left with the world's poorest country, which happens to be the Democratic Republic of the Congo (DRC). The DRC (not labeled) accounts for

MRU

youtube.com/watch?v=JbkSRLYSojo

The Economic History of the World in Less than Five Minutes

FIGURE 7.2

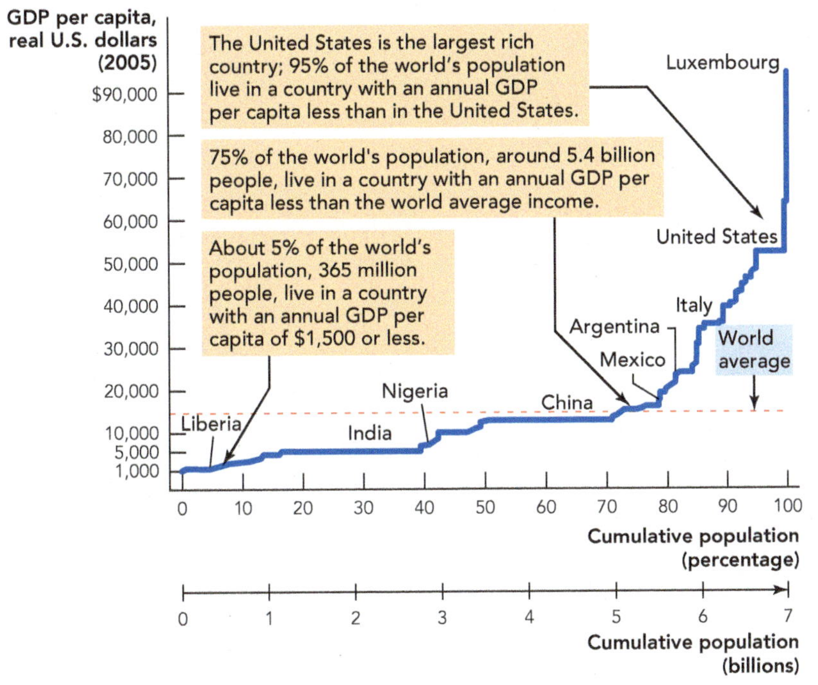

GDP per capita, real U.S. dollars (2005)

The United States is the largest rich country; 95% of the world's population live in a country with an annual GDP per capita less than in the United States.

75% of the world's population, around 5.4 billion people, live in a country with an annual GDP per capita less than the world average income.

About 5% of the world's population, 365 million people, live in a country with an annual GDP per capita of $1,500 or less.

Luxembourg

United States

Italy

Argentina

Mexico

World average

Nigeria

China

Liberia

India

Cumulative population (percentage)

Cumulative population (billions)

The Distribution of World Income (2014)

Data from: Penn World Tables, 8.0. PPP adjusted.

▶▶ **SEARCH ENGINE**

You can find lots of colorful data about the wealth of nations at https://www.gapminder.org/ or https://data.worldbank.org/.

a little more than 1% of the world's population. As we add successively richer countries and their populations, we move further to the right in population and upward in GDP per capita. The graph tells us, for example, that about 10% of the world's population—or 772 million people in 2014—lived in a country with a GDP per capita of less than $2,900—about the level in Bangladesh. Moving farther to the right, we see that about 70% of the world's population lived in a country with a GDP per capita equal to or less than $12,472, about the level in China. The red horizontal dashed line shows the world's average level of GDP per capita in 2014, which is a little less than in Mexico. Fully 73% of the world's population—or 5.2 billion people—lived in a country with a GDP per capita less than average. In other words, most of the world's population is poor relative to the United States.

In thinking about poverty, remember that GDP per capita is simply an average, and there is a distribution of income within each country. In India, GDP per capita was around $5,224, but many Indians have yearly incomes that are less than $5,224 and some have yearly incomes that are higher than the average income in the United States. Around the world, about a billion people have incomes of less than $3 per day.

Fact Two: Everyone Used to Be Poor

The distribution of world income tells us that poverty is normal. It's wealth that is unusual. Poverty is even more normal when we think about human history. What was GDP per capita like in the year 1? No one knows for sure,

FIGURE 7.3

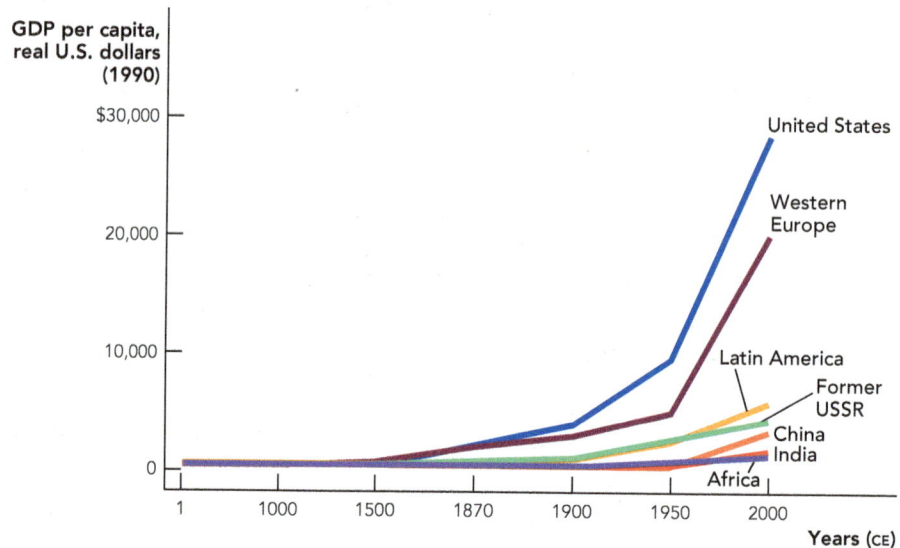

Economic Growth in Major World Regions

Data from: Maddison, Angus. 2007. *Contours of the World Economy: 1–2030 AD.* Oxford: Oxford University Press.
Note: Timeline is not to scale.

MRU

mru.org/hockey-stick

AVERAGE MALE HEIGHT

The Hockey Stick of Human Prosperity

---

but a good guesstimate is around $700–$1,000 per year in 2015 dollars, not much different from the very poorest people living in the world today. What's surprising is not that people in the past were poor, but that *everyone* in the past was poor.

Figure 7.3 shows some estimates of GDP per capita in different regions of the world in different periods from the year 1 to 2000 AD. In the year 1, GDP per capita was about $700–$1,000 and this was approximately the same in all the major regions of the world. Today, GDP per capita is more than 50 times as large in the richest countries as in the poorest countries.

Figure 7.3 illustrates something else of interest: GDP per capita was about the same in year 1 as it would be 1,000 years later and indeed about the same as it had been 1,000 years earlier. For most of recorded human history, there was *no long-run growth in real per capita GDP.* Countries might grow in particular good years, but soon enough a disaster would ensue and the gains would be given back. Only beginning in the nineteenth century does it become clear that some parts of the world began to grow at a rate unprecedented in human history.

Figure 7.3 tells us that economic growth is unusual. But once economic growth begins, it can make some parts of the world rich, while other parts languish at levels of per capita GDP similar to that in the Dark Ages. To see more clearly how small changes in economic growth can have enormous effects on GDP per capita, we pause for a primer on economic growth rates.

A Primer on Growth Rates Recall from the previous chapter on GDP that a growth rate is the percentage change in a variable over a given period such as a year. When we refer to **economic growth,** we mean the growth rate of real per capita GDP.

Economic growth is the growth rate of real GDP per capita:

$$g_t = \frac{Y_t - Y_{t-1}}{Y_{t-1}} \times 100$$

where Y_t is real per capita GDP in period t.

While computing growth rates is simple math, grasping the impact of growth rates on economic progress is critical. Keep in mind that even slow growth, if sustained over many years, produces large differences in real GDP per capita.

To appreciate the power of economic growth, let's consider a few cases. Suppose that the annual growth rate of real GDP per capita is 2%. How long will it take for real per capita GDP to double from $40,000 to $80,000? An average person on the street might answer, "It will take 50 years to double your income at a 2% growth rate." But that is wrong because growth builds on top of growth. This is called "compounding" or "exponential growth."

There is a simple approximation, called the rule of 70, for determining the length of time necessary for a growing variable to double:

> *Rule of 70:* If the annual growth rate of a variable is x %, then the doubling time is $\frac{70}{x}$ years.

At a growth rate of 1%, GDP per capita will double approximately every 70 years (70/1 = 70). If growth increases to 2%, GDP per capita will double every 35 years (70/2 = 35). Consider the impact of a 7% growth rate. If this growth can be sustained, then GDP per capita doubles every 10 years! China has been growing at this rate or a bit higher for several decades, which explains why China has become much richer in the past 30 years. China, however, is still a relatively poor country, so this also tells you how very, very poor they were in the recent past.

The rule of 70 is just a mathematical approximation, but it bears out the key concept that small differences in growth rates have large effects on economic progress. See the appendix to this chapter for a discussion of how you can use Excel to understand the magic of compounding.

Another way of seeing how small changes in the rate of economic growth can lead to big effects is to think about how rich people will be in the future. U.S. per capita GDP is about $50,000 (as of 2014). How many years will it take for real per capita GDP to increase to $1 million? If growth is 2% per year, which would be a little low by U.S. standards, average income will be $1 million per year in just 150 years. If GDP per capita grows at 3% per year, which is a little high by U.S. standards but certainly not impossible, then in just 100 years the average income will be approximately $1 million per year. You and I are unlikely to see this future, but if our grandchildren are lucky, they will see a world in which U.S. GDP per capita is a million dollars, more than 22 times higher than it is today.

MRU

mru.org/rule-of-70

The Rule of 70

MRU

mru.org/growth-rates

Growth Rates Are Crucial

Fact Three: There Are Growth Miracles and Growth Disasters

The United States is one of the wealthiest countries in the world because the United States has grown slowly but relatively consistently for more than 200 years. Can other countries catch up to the United States, and if so, will it take 200 years? Fortunately, other countries can catch up, and amazingly quickly. Figure 7.4 shows two "growth miracles." Following World War II, Japan was one of the poorest countries in the world with a per capita GDP less than that of Mexico. From 1950 to 1970, however, Japan grew at an astonishing rate of 8.5% per year. Remember, at that rate, GDP per capita doubles in approximately 8 years (70/8.5 = 8.2)! Today, Japan is one of the richest countries in the world.

FIGURE 7.4

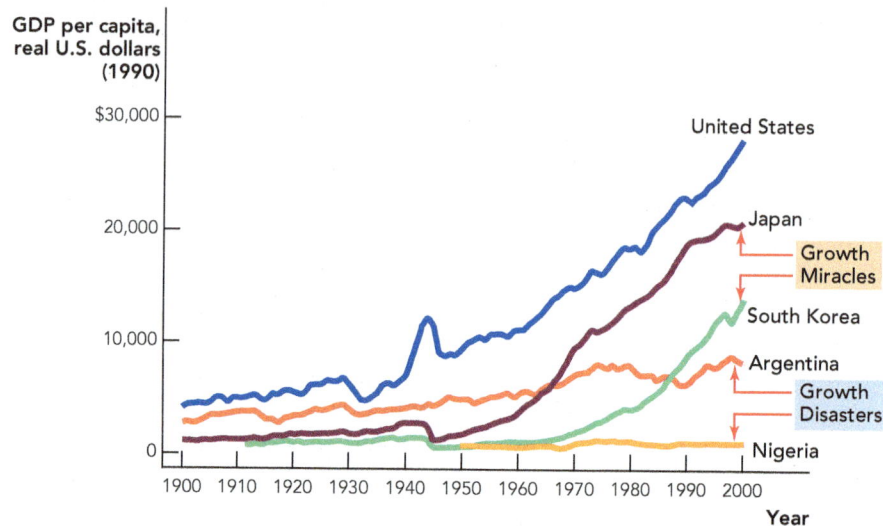

Two Growth Miracles and Two Growth Disasters

Data from: Maddison, Angus. 2007. *Contours of the World Economy: 1–2030 AD.* Oxford: Oxford University Press.

MRU

mru.org/growth-miracle-disaster

ARGENTINA 2015

Growth Miracles and Growth Disasters

In 1950, South Korea was even poorer than Japan with a GDP per capita about the same as that of Nigeria. South Korea's growth miracle began a little later than Japan's, but between 1970 and 1990, South Korea grew at a rate of 7.2% per year. Today, South Korea is a thriving, modern economy on par with many European economies.

Growth miracles are possible but so are growth disasters. Nigeria has barely grown since 1950 and was poorer in 2005 than in 1974 when high oil prices briefly bumped up its per capita GDP. More surprising is the case of Argentina. In 1900, Argentina was one of the richest countries in the world with a per capita GDP almost as large (75%) as that of the United States. By 1950, Argentina's per capita GDP had fallen to half that in the United States. In 1950, however, Argentina was still a relatively wealthy country with a per capita GDP more than twice as high as that of Japan and more than five times as high as that of South Korea. Argentina failed to grow much, however, and by 2000 Argentina's per capita GDP was less than one-third of that of the United States; Japan and South Korea are now much wealthier than Argentina.

The gap between Argentina and many other countries is continuing to grow. China (not pictured) began its own growth miracle in the late 1970s. China is still a very poor nation with a per capita GDP that in 2011 is a little more than half that of Argentina. But China is growing rapidly—remember, if China continues to grow at 7% or 8% per year, it will double its income in about 10 years. Even if Argentina grows modestly, China could pass Argentina in per capita GDP in less than 20 years.

Summarizing the Facts: Good and Bad News

The facts presented above imply both good and bad news. The bad news is that most of the world is poor and more than 1 billion people live on incomes of less than $3 per day. These people have greatly reduced prospects for health, happiness, and peace. The bad news, however, is old news. For most of human history, people were poor and there was no economic growth.

The good news is this: Despite being a relatively recent phenomenon, economic growth has quickly transformed the world. It has raised the standard of living of most people in developed nations many times above the historical norm. Even though economic growth has yet to reach all of the world, there appears to be no reason why, in principle, economic growth cannot occur everywhere. Indeed, growth miracles tell us that it doesn't take 250 years to reach the level of wealth of the United States—South Korea was as poor as Nigeria in 1950, but today has a per capita GDP not far behind Germany or the United Kingdom.

Progress, however, is not guaranteed. The growth disasters tell us that economic growth is not automatic. Some countries such as Nigeria show few signs that they have started along the growth path, while other countries such as Argentina seem to have fallen off the growth path.

Growth miracles and disasters, however, are not purely random events over which people have no control. Inquiring into the nature and causes of the wealth of nations is critical if we are to raise the standard of living and better the human condition.

Understanding the Wealth of Nations

Let's begin with Figure 7.5 on the next page, a guide to the major factors behind the wealth of nations. At the bottom of the figure is what we would like to explain, GDP per capita. As we move up the figure, we see some of the causes of the wealth of nations, beginning with the immediate or most direct causes and moving toward the ultimate or indirect causes.

The Factors of Production

The most immediate cause of the wealth of nations is this: Countries with a high GDP per capita have a lot of physical and human capital per worker and that capital is organized using the best technological knowledge to be highly productive. Physical capital, human capital, and technological knowledge are called factors of production. Let's take a look at each factor of production.

By **physical capital** (or just "capital"), economists mean tools in the broadest sense: pencils, desks, computers, hammers, shovels, tractors, cell phones, factories, roads, and bridges. More and better tools make workers more productive.

Farming is a good illustration of the role of capital. In much of the world, farmers are laborers pure and simple: They dig, seed, cut, and harvest using hard labor and a few simple tools like hoes and plows (often pulled by oxen). In the United States, farmers use a lot more capital—tractors, trucks, combines, and harvesters.

It's not just farmers who use a lot of capital. The typical worker in the United States works with more than $100,000 worth of capital. A typical worker in India works with less than one-tenth as much capital.

It's also not just physical capital that makes U.S. farmers productive. A farmer in the United States riding a tractor uses a GPS receiver to triangulate his exact location using signals from a series of satellites orbiting the earth some 16,500 miles high. The tractor's location is combined with data from other satellites and land-based sensors to precisely adjust the amount of seed, fertilizer, and

Physical capital is the stock of tools including machines, structures, and equipment.

FIGURE 7.5

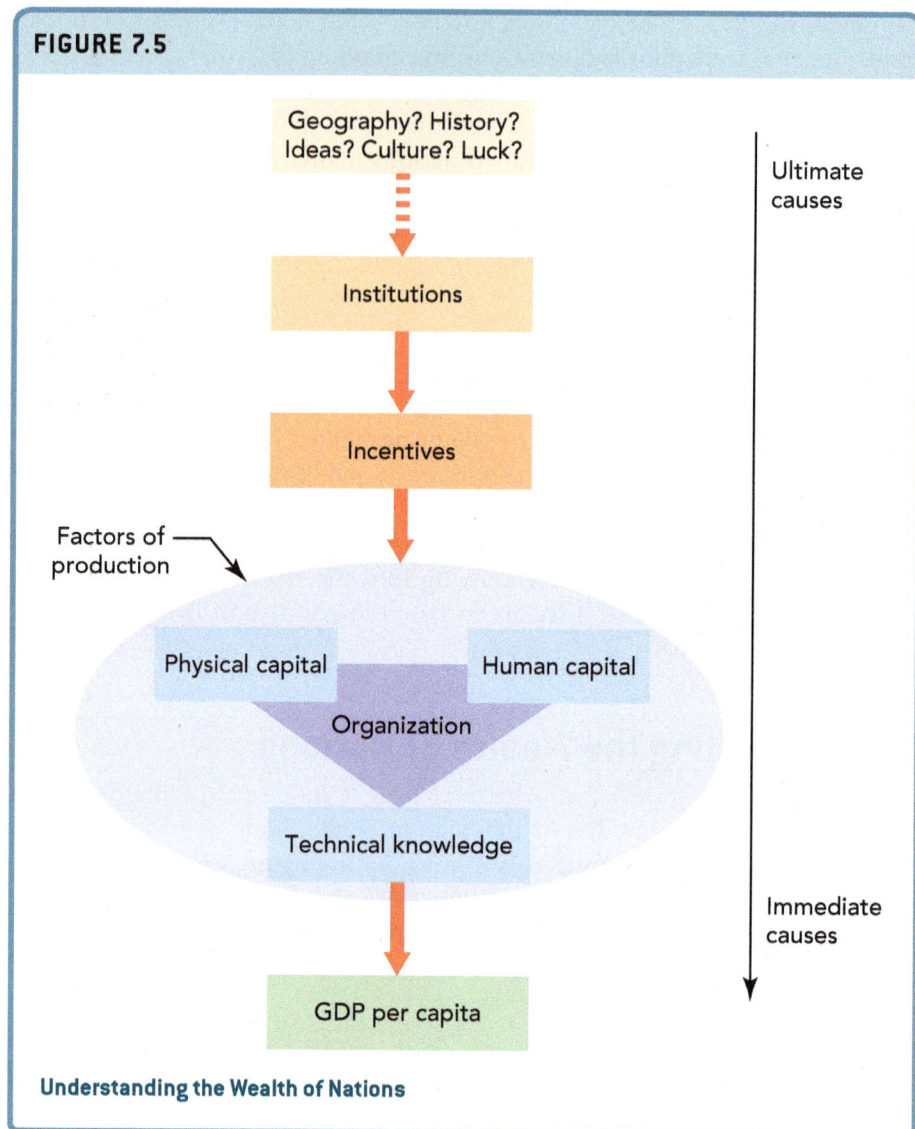

Understanding the Wealth of Nations

water to be applied to the land. The fertilizer has been carefully designed, and the seeds almost certainly have been genetically engineered.

The high-tech nature of farming in the United States draws our attention to the importance of human capital and technological knowledge. **Human capital** is *tools in the mind*, or the stuff in people's heads that makes them productive. Human capital is not something we are born with—it is produced by an investment of time and other resources in education, training, and experience. Farmers in the United States, for example, have more human capital than farmers in most of the world, and it's this human capital that enables them to take advantage of tools like GPS receivers. The same is true in the larger economy—the typical person in the United States, for example, has about 12 years of schooling, while in Pakistan the typical person has less than 5 years of schooling.

The greater quantities of physical and human capital per worker used in U.S. farming make U.S. farmers more productive. U.S. farmers produce more than three times as much corn per acre than do farmers in Pakistan, for example.

Human capital is the productive knowledge and skills that workers acquire through education, training, and experience.

The third factor of production is technological knowledge. This factor includes, for instance, the genetics, chemistry, and physics that form the basis of the techniques used in modern agriculture. (Did you know that the clocks on GPS satellites must be adjusted to account for the effects of Einstein's theory of relativity?)

Technological knowledge and human capital are related but different. Human capital is the knowledge and skills that a farmer needs to understand and to make productive use of technology. **Technological knowledge** is knowledge about how the world works—the kind of knowledge that makes technology possible. We increase human capital with education. We increase technological knowledge with research and development. Technological knowledge is potentially boundless. We can learn more and more about how the world works even if human capital remains relatively constant.

Improved technological knowledge has made U.S. farmers more productive over time. U.S. farms today produce more than two and a half times as much output as they did in 1950 and they do so using *less* land! More physical and human capital has helped to drive this increase in output, but better technological knowledge has been the primary factor.[1]

The final factor, a factor often taken for granted, is organization. Human capital, physical capital, and technological knowledge must be organized to produce valuable goods and services. Who does this organizing and why? To answer this question, we turn to the issue of incentives and institutions.

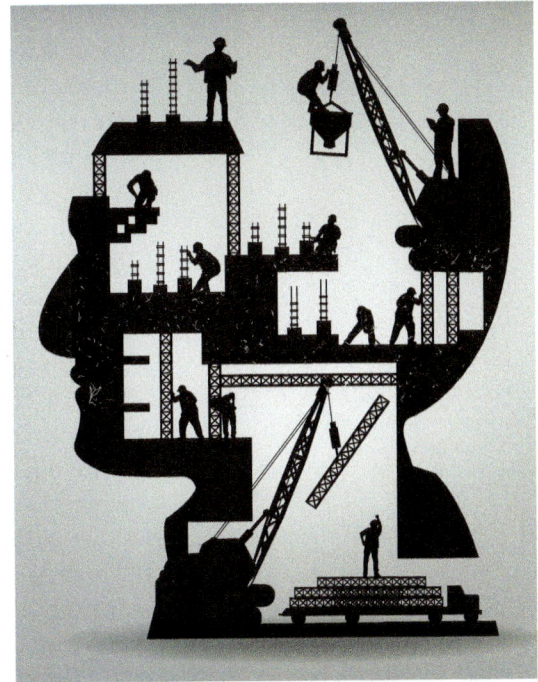

Human capital consists of tools in the mind, the stuff in people's heads that makes them productive.

Technological knowledge is knowledge about how the world works that is used to produce goods and services.

CHECK YOURSELF

- Which country has more physical capital per worker: the United States or China? China or Nigeria?
- What are the three primary factors of production?

Incentives and Institutions

South Korea has a per capita GDP nearly 20 times higher than that of North Korea. Why? In one sense, we have just given an answer: South Korea has more physical and human capital per worker than North Korea.* But this answer is incomplete and partial. The answer is incomplete because we still want to know *why* does South Korea have more physical and human capital than North Korea? The answer is partial because poor countries like North Korea not only have less physical and human capital than rich countries, they also fail to organize the capital that they do have in the most productive ways. To understand the wealth of nations more deeply, we need to take a look at some of the indirect or more ultimate causes.

The example of South and North Korea is useful because we can rule out some explanations for the huge differences in wealth between these two countries. The explanation, for example, cannot be differences in the people, culture, or geography. Before South and North Korea were divided at the end of World War II, they shared the same people and culture—in other words, the same

---

* What about technological knowledge? North Korea has access to most of the world's technological knowledge and is able, for example, to build sophisticated weapons—perhaps even a nuclear bomb; thus differences in technological knowledge explain probably only a small fraction of the differences in the wealth of nations.

Increases in technological knowledge, however, are clearly important for growth at the world level (as opposed to explaining differences in wealth across nations)—as we will discuss at greater length in the next chapter.

human capital. South and North Korea also had similar levels of physical capital—natural resources were about the same in the South as in the North, and if there were any advantages in human-made physical capital, they went to the North, which was at that time more industrialized than the South. When the two regions were split, therefore, South and North Korea were in all important respects the same, almost as if the split was designed as a giant social experiment.

South and North Korea differed in their economic institutions. Broadly speaking, South Korea had capitalism, and North Korea had communism. South Korea was never a pure capitalist economy, of course, but in South Korea the organizers of human capital, physical capital, and technological knowledge are private, profit-seeking firms and entrepreneurs to a much greater extent than in North Korea. In South Korea a worker earns more money if he provides goods and services of value to consumers or if she invents new ideas for more efficient production. Those same incentives do not exist in North Korea, where workers are rewarded for being loyal to the ruling Communist Party. In short, South Korea uses markets to organize its production much more than North Korea and so is able to take advantage of all the efficiency properties of markets discussed in Chapters 3 and 4.

More than fifty years later, the results of the "experiment" splitting North and South Korea are so clear they can be seen from outer space, as seen in Figure 7.6. The differences between these two countries are especially dramatic. But wherever similar experiments have been tried, such as in East and West Germany, or Taiwan and China, the results have been similar.

We said earlier that countries with a high GDP per capita have a lot of physical and human capital that is organized using the best technological knowledge to be highly productive. But factors of production do not fall from the sky like manna from heaven. Factors of production must be produced. Similarly, factors of production do not organize themselves. Physical capital, human capital, and technology must be combined and organized purposively to be productive.

Do you remember Big Idea One and Big Idea Two from the introductory chapter? These ideas were that incentives matter and good institutions align self-interest with the social interest.

Thus, we can now deepen our understanding of the wealth of nations. Countries with a high GDP per capita have institutions that make it in people's self-interest to invest in physical capital, human capital, and technological knowledge and to efficiently organize these resources for production.

In short, the key to producing and organizing the factors of production are *institutions* that create appropriate *incentives*. Let's look at institutions and the incentives that they create in more detail.

FIGURE 7.6

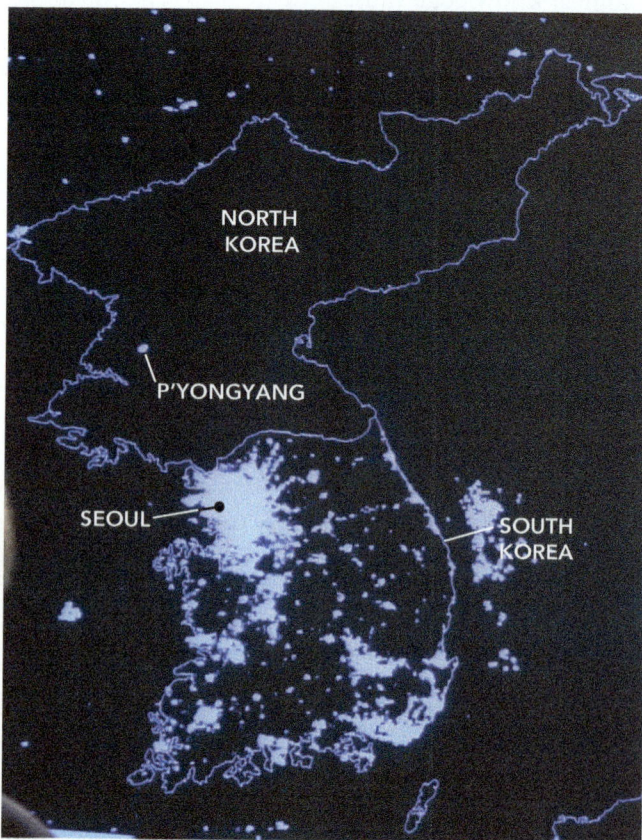

Jason Reed/Reuters/Newscom

Can You Tell Which Country Has Better Institutions? South Korea and North Korea photographed at night from outer space.

Institutions

Institutions include laws and regulations but also customs, practices, organizations, and social mores—institutions are the "rules of the game" that shape human interaction and structure economic incentives within a society.

What kinds of institutions encourage investment and the efficient organization of the factors of production? Understanding institutions is an important area of research in economics, and there is considerable agreement that the key institutions include the following:

- Property rights
- Honest government
- Political stability
- A dependable legal system
- Competitive and open markets

Entire books have been written about each of these institutions and their roles in economic growth. Indeed, much of this book is about property rights and the benefits of open markets and rivalrous economic competition. Thus, we will give only a few examples here of how each of these institutions creates appropriate incentives, incentives that align self-interest with the social interest.

Property Rights When the Communist revolutionaries took control of China, they abolished private property in land. In the "Little Leap Forward," they put farmers to work in collectives of 100–300 families. Communal property meant that the incentives to invest in the land and to work hard were low. Imagine that a day's work can produce an extra bushel of corn. Thus, an extra day's work on a commune with 100 families earned the worker 1/100th of a bushel of corn. Would you work an extra day for a few earfuls of corn? Under communal property, working an extra day doesn't add much to a worker's take-home pay and working a day less doesn't subtract much. Thus, *under communal property, effort is divorced from payment* so there is little incentive to work—in fact, there is an incentive not to work and to **free ride** on the work of others. In the "Great Leap Forward," the incentive to free ride was made even stronger when communes were increased to 5,000 families. But if everyone free rides, the commune will starve. Communal property in agricultural land did not align a farmer's self-interest with the social interest. And, as a result of this and many similar errors on the part of the Chinese leadership, some 20–40 million Chinese farmers and workers starved during this period.

The Great Leap Forward was actually a great leap backward—agricultural land was less productive in 1978 than it had been in 1949 when the Communists took over. In 1978, however, farmers in the village of Xiaogang held a secret meeting. The farmers agreed to divide the communal land and assign it to individuals—each farmer had to produce a quota for the government but anything they produced in excess of the quota that farmer would keep. The agreement violated government policy and, as a result, the farmers also pledged that if any of them was sent to jail, the others would raise their children. The remarkable secret agreement of the Xiaogang farmers is shown at right.

Institutions are the "rules of the game" that structure economic incentives.

mru.org/institutions
The Importance of Institutions

A **free rider** is someone who consumes a resource without working or contributing to the resource's upkeep.

Farmers from 18 households in Xiaogang village signed a secret life-and-death agreement with their thumbprints.

N

The change from collective property rights to something closer to private property rights had an immediate effect: Investment, work effort, and productivity increased. "You can't be lazy when you work for your family and yourself," said one of the farmers.

Word of the secret agreement leaked out and local bureaucrats cut off Xiaogang from fertilizer, seeds, and pesticides. But amazingly, before Xiaogang could be stopped, farmers in other villages also began to abandon collective property. In Beijing, Mao Zedong was dead and a new set of rulers, seeing the productivity improvements, decided to let the experiment proceed.

In the five short years between 1978 and 1983, when China's central government endorsed individual farming, food production increased by nearly 50% and 170 million people were lifted above the World Bank's lowest poverty line. Simply put, the increase in agricultural productivity brought about by the switch to individual farming was the greatest antipoverty program in the history of the world. By 1984, the collective farms were gone and soon after that China's leader Deng Xiaoping announced a new government policy: "It is glorious to be rich."

Property rights in land greatly increased China's agricultural productivity. With fewer workers producing more food, more workers were available to produce other goods. To take advantage of its millions of workers, China opened up to foreign investment, making the label "Made in China" common throughout the world. With their secret pact, the farmers of Xiaogang had begun a second and more successful Chinese revolution.[2]

Property rights are important institutions for encouraging investment in physical and human capital, not just in agriculture but throughout the economy. It can take decades, for example, for an investment in a new apartment building or a factory to pay off. As we will discuss further in Chapter 29, savings are necessary to generate investment and thus growth. But why do people save and invest? Savers won't save and investors won't invest if they don't expect that their property will be secure and they will receive a return for their savings and investment. Property rights are also important for encouraging technological innovation. For instance, investments in new pharmaceuticals take decades to pay off and they are risky—years of research and development sometimes have to be abandoned when the guinea pigs start to die unexpectedly. Just like farmers, investors and workers throughout the economy need to know that they will reap what they sow.

Honest Government China under its former Communist rulers was extreme in abolishing most forms of private property. In many other countries, private property rights exist on paper—but only on paper. In a country like Venezuela, for example, an individual might have a legal right to land or a factory, but everyone knows that the government can take these goods at any moment. Venezuela lacks the rule of law.

More generally, corruption is like a heavy tax that bleeds resources away from productive entrepreneurs. Resources "invested" in bribing politicians and bureaucrats cannot be invested in machinery and equipment, thus reducing productivity. Corrupt government officials will also harass entrepreneurs, creating excessive rules and regulations that force entrepreneurs to pay them to stop making trouble.

Top 10 Least Corrupt Countries	Top Ten Most Corrupt Countries
Denmark	Somalia
New Zealand	South Sudan
Finland	Syria
Singapore	Korea (North)
Sweden	Yemen
Switzerland	Afghanistan
Norway	Equatorial Guinea
Netherlands	Guinea Bissau
Canada	Sudan
Luxembourg	Burundi

Data from: Transparency International, 2016

Data from: Transparency International, 2016

FIGURE 7.7

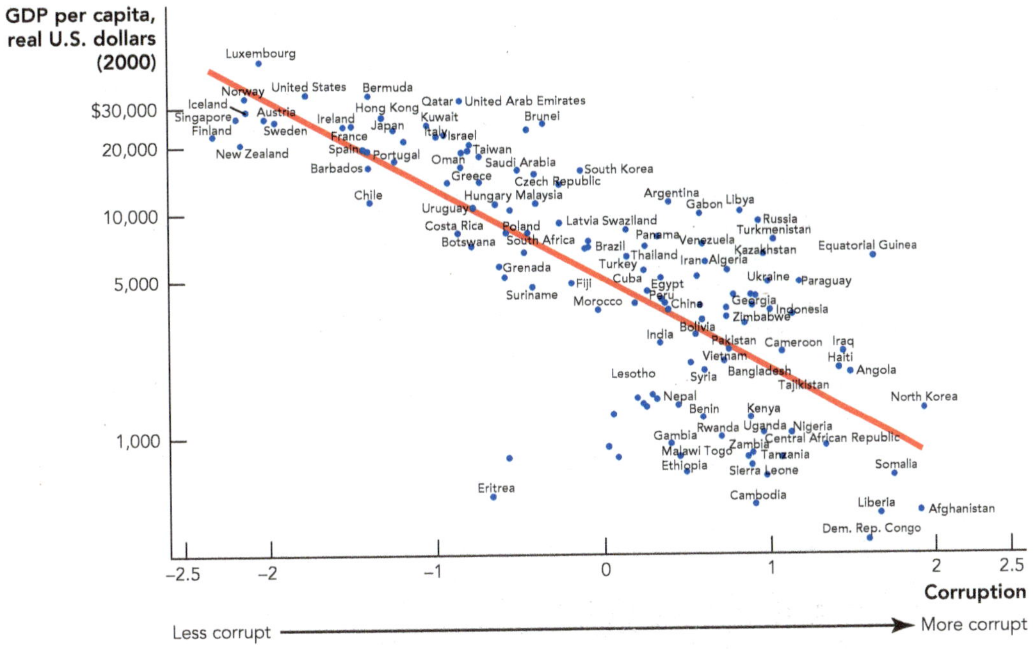

Corrupt Countries Have Lower GDP per Capita

Data from: Penn World Tables and World Bank Group, World Development Indicators, 2005.
Note: Not all countries are labeled. GDP on ratio scale.

Not all taxes are bad, of course. An honest government is one that spends taxpayer funds on public goods like education, infrastructure, and public health. A tax that funds investments in public goods increases the productivity of private investments. Corruption, therefore, is a doubly bad tax because corruption makes it less profitable to be an entrepreneur at the same time as it makes it more profitable to be a corrupt politician or bureaucrat. At some point, corruption can feed on itself, creating a poverty trap: Few people want to be entrepreneurs because they know that their wealth will be stolen and thus there is no wealth to steal.

Figure 7.7 graphs corruption on the horizontal axis. The most corrupt countries like Somalia, Liberia, and North Korea are on the right, scoring about 2 on a 5-point scale running from −2.5 (least corrupt) to 2.5 (most corrupt). The least corrupt countries like Singapore, Iceland, the United States, and Norway are on the left. Real GDP per capita is on the vertical axis. Countries that are more corrupt have much lower per capita GDP.

Political Stability Investors have more to fear than government expropriation—sometimes the threat of anarchy can be even worse. Liberia, for example, has had little but conflict for the past 40 years. Prior to the election in 2006 of President Ellen Johnson-Sirleaf, the first elected female head of state in Africa, it had been 35 years since a Liberian president assumed office by means other than bloodshed. Both the previous two national leaders (Charles Taylor and Samuel Doe) consistently used the force of government to eradicate their opposition. Who wants to invest in the future when civil war threatens to wash away all plans?

AP Photo

A Good Place to Invest? Bullet casings litter a street in the besieged city of Misrata, Libya, Saturday, April 23, 2011.

More generally, in many nations, civil war, military dictatorship, and anarchy have destroyed the institutions necessary for economic growth.

A Dependable Legal System The problem of poorly protected property rights is not always a problem of too much government—sometimes property rights are poorly protected because there is too little government. The legal system in many countries, for example, is of such low quality that no one knows for certain who owns what. In India, residents who purchase land often have to do so two or three times (from different parties), as there exists no reliable record of true ownership. A lawsuit, if you even bother to bring one, can take 20 years or more to resolve. In a major urban area, it's very difficult to build something as simple as a supermarket because developers cannot acquire good title to a modestly sized piece of land. No one wants to build when they cannot protect their investment.

A good legal system facilitates contracts and protects private parties from expropriating one another. Few people think of the U.S. legal system as a paradigm of productivity, but it is compared with the Indian legal system. In the United States, for example, it takes 17 procedures and 300 days to collect on a debt (say, a bounced check). In India, it takes 56 procedures and 1,420 days to do the same thing. That's one reason why it is relatively difficult for people living in India to borrow money in the first place: Lenders know how hard it is to get their money back.

Competitive and Open Markets The factors of production must not only be produced—they must also be organized. Detailed studies from a large number of countries suggest that the failure to organize capital efficiently has a huge effect on the wealth of nations. Poor countries are poor, in other words, not just because they lack capital but also because they use the capital that they do have inefficiently. Overall, about half the differences in per capita income across countries are explained by differences in the amount of physical and human capital (some of those differences in capital spring from deeper differences in institutions) and about half the differences are explained by a failure to use capital efficiently. One study, for example, estimates that if India used its physical and human capital as efficiently as the United States uses its capital, India would be four times richer than it is today.[3]

Why does India use its capital inefficiently? The reasons are numerous, but competitive and open markets are one of the best ways to encourage the efficient organization of resources. India, as well as other poor countries, has many inefficient and unnecessary regulations, which create monopolies or otherwise impede markets.

For instance, Indian shirts are usually made by hand in small shops of three or four tailors who design, measure, sew, and sell, all on the same premises. It sounds elegant but this is not London's Savile Row, where the finest tailors in the world create custom suits for the rich and powerful. India's shirts would be cheaper and of higher quality if they were mass-manufactured in factories—the way shirts for Americans are produced. Why doesn't this happen in India? Shirts in India are produced inefficiently because, until recently, large-scale production was illegal.

In an effort to protect small firms, India prohibited investment in shirt factories from exceeding about $200,000. This restriction meant that Indian shirt manufacturers could not take advantage of **economies of scale**, the decrease in the average cost of production that often occurs as the total quantity of production increases. India has been reforming its economy, which is one reason why economic growth in India has increased in recent years (as we discussed in the previous chapter). India recently lifted the ban on large garment factories, for example, but many, many regulations remain that reduce the productivity of the Indian economy.[4]

Poor countries also suffer from expensive red tape. Economists at the World Bank have estimated the time and cost to do simple tasks such as starting a business or enforcing a contract in a court of law. In the United States, for example, it takes about 4 days to start a business and the total costs of the procedures are minor, about 1% of the average income per capita. In India, starting a business takes 26 days and 13.8% of income per capita. In Haiti, it takes 97 days and 219% of income per capita (data from World Bank, *Doing Business*). Thus, even before a business is begun, an Indian or Haitian entrepreneur must invest extensively in dealing with bureaucracies—that same physical and human capital is not being used to produce goods and services.

Markets can also be made more competitive and open with free trade. Most countries, for example, aren't large enough to support more than a handful of auto manufacturers so free trade is necessary to keep auto manufacturers and other large firms competitive. Perhaps even more importantly, countries that are open to trade are also open to new ideas. Walmart made retailing more efficient in the United States and then it brought these efficiencies to other countries when it expanded internationally. Countries where Walmart was forbidden or discouraged from expanding gained these efficiencies more slowly, if at all. In fact, multinationals like Walmart are the best managed of all firms—they get the most output from the same quantity and quality of inputs—and multinationals are one of the best ways of spreading new and better ideas around the world.[5]

> **Economies of scale** are the advantages of large-scale production that reduce average cost as quantity increases.

The Ultimate Causes of the Wealth of Nations

When China changed its institutions from collective farming to individual farming, agricultural productivity increased dramatically and China began to grow. The example of China is enormously encouraging because it suggests that growth miracles could become common if more countries changed their institutions. But take a look again at Figure 7.5. Institutions have a large effect on increasing and organizing the factors of production, and institutions thus have a large effect on economic growth. But where do institutions come from? Are they products of geography? History? Ideas? Culture? Luck? Try "all of the above" and then some.

Consider geography, which we might also think of as a country's "natural resources." Simple natural resources like oil and diamonds are usually good to have but in rich, developed countries, physical and human capital are typically much more important. But natural resources more broadly conceived—climate, topography, and the prevalence of parasites, to give just a few examples—may help explain why a country is able to accumulate physical and human capital. We said earlier that free trade opens a country up to new ideas and innovation.

FIGURE 7.8

GDP per capita,
1995 (PPP)

Landlocked Nations Have Lower GDP per Capita

Data from: Author calculations based on data from Gallup, Sachs, and Mellinger (1999).

mru.org/geography-growth

Geography and Economic Growth

But free trade is not just a matter of policy or choice—it also depends on natural conditions. It's much cheaper to move goods and people over water than over land, so countries that have easy access to water are naturally more open to trade than countries that are landlocked. In fact, as Figure 7.8 reveals, landlocked countries have lower per capita GDP than countries that have access to a coast. It's not that being landlocked dooms a country to poverty, but countries that are landlocked face the equivalent—from their setting—of permanently high tariff barriers. That can make it more difficult to generate growth, especially in the age before modern communications.

You can also see the importance of history, ideas, geography, and luck in the growth of the United States. The U.S. constitution was written at a time when the ideas of John Locke and Adam Smith were popular and it inherited a tendency toward a market economy and democratic institutions from its colonizer, Great Britain. An open frontier meant cheap land and plenty of freedom to try new ideas and ways of living, perhaps influencing America's entrepreneurial culture even into modern times. And we are very lucky that George Washington had the virtue to stop at two presidential terms, rather than trying to become the next king.

An even more important example of a growth miracle comes from the Industrial Revolution, a period of sustained European technological advances; it is sometimes identified with 1770–1830, but it has deeper roots reaching back to the seventeenth century or earlier. The Industrial Revolution brought us large-scale factories, mass production, the steam engine, the railroad, and the beginnings of a consumer society, among many other benefits. It is the first time that human living standards climbed noticeably above subsistence and stayed there for a long period. We are all still enjoying the benefits of an ongoing industrial revolution in the world's wealthy economies.

The Industrial Revolution, centered in Great Britain, required a combination of multiple distinct advantages. Britain's status as an island and the strong English Navy protected the country against invaders and made property rights more secure. Labor markets had been relatively free for centuries and the ethic of the time encouraged commerce, entrepreneurship, and the accumulation of wealth. The growth of the power of Parliament checked royal tyranny and encouraged economic policies that allowed wealth to spread more widely. Slow increases in agricultural productivity kept living standards above subsistence and enabled the rise of a professional class. Perhaps most important, Britain developed a strong culture of science and engineering and brought the scientific method to bear on economic production, whether it was designing a better spinning jenny or using coal to power a factory more effectively.

From the beginning, positive feedback effects of the Industrial Revolution were strong. More wealth meant more people could devote their lives to science, invention, and turning new ideas into practical commercial developments. That in turn led to new wealth and then again to more applied science. Eventually the Industrial Revolution gave us electricity, the automobile, the flush toilet, and most of the other inventions that define the conveniences of modern life. To sum this all up, the effects of the Industrial Revolution owe much to good institutions for business, science, and governance.

No one understands for certain all the influences that go into creating a nation's institutions, which means that changing institutions isn't easy. When it comes to institutions, we know where we want to go but we don't always know how to get there. Understanding institutions, where they come from, and how they can be changed is thus a key research question in economics.

ted.com/talks/hans_rosling_the_magic_washing_machine

The Magic Washing Machine

Tyler Olson/Shutterstock

Takeaway

It's hard to overstate the importance of economic growth. Once, everyone was poor. Today, GDP per capita is more than 50 times higher in the richest countries than in the poorest. Economic growth has raised billions of people out of near-starvation poverty, but billions more remain in dire poverty with shocking consequences for their quality of life.

Fortunately, poor countries can catch up to rich countries and in a surprisingly short period. Growth "miracles" have brought Japan and South Korea up to European levels of wealth within the lifespan of a single generation. Since the agricultural reforms beginning in 1978, poverty in China has been reduced to an unprecedented degree and China continues to grow rapidly.

What makes a country rich? The most proximate cause is that countries with a high GDP per capita have lots of physical and human capital per worker and that capital is organized using the best technological knowledge to be highly productive.

How do countries get a lot of physical and human capital and how do they organize it using the best technological knowledge? Countries with a high GDP per capita have institutions that encourage investment in physical capital, human capital, technological innovation, and the efficient organization of resources. Among the most powerful institutions for increasing economic growth are property rights, honest government, political stability, a dependable legal system, and competitive and open markets.

CHECK YOURSELF

- List five institutions that promote economic growth.
- When the Pilgrims landed at Plymouth Rock, they established a system of collective farming in which all corn production was shared. Given your understanding of incentives, what do you think happened to the Pilgrims?

CHAPTER REVIEW

Go online to practice with more examples of these types of problems, including live links to videos, data sources, and feedback.

Problems with this icon relate to optional MRU videos.

KEY CONCEPTS

economic growth, p. 128

physical capital, p. 131

human capital, p. 132

technological knowledge, p. 133

institutions, p. 135

free rider, p. 135

economies of scale, p. 139

FACTS AND TOOLS

1. Look at Figure 7.1. About how many babies die before the age of 5 in Nigeria versus Argentina? What is the difference in GDP per person in those two countries?

2. Look at Figure 7.2. About what percentage of the world's population lives in countries richer than Italy? What percentage lives in countries poorer than India?

3. The world's average (mean) GDP per capita is $14,517. There are roughly 7 billion people in the world.

a. What is the world's total GDP?

b. About 20% of the world's population produces 50% of the world's total GDP. (Notice the use of "produces," not "consumes." In popular discussion, you are more likely to hear about the people at the top "consuming" more than their share, not "producing" more than their share. But remember what the last letter of GDP stands for!) How much GDP does the top 20% produce?

c. What is the average GDP per capita of the most productive 20% of the world's population? (*Hint:* 20% of 7 billion people equals how many people?)

4. Now let's look at the productivity of the world's least productive 80%.

a. How much GDP do they produce? (*Hint:* You've already calculated this number in the previous question.)

b. What is the average GDP per capita of the least productive 80% of the world's population?

c. Now, the payoff: How productive is the average person in the top 20% compared with the average person in the bottom 80% of the planet? Answer this by dividing your answer to question 3c by your answer to question 4b. This chapter and the next are devoted to explaining why this ratio is so large.

5. According to Fact Two—Everyone Used to Be Poor—what would your answer to question 4c have been if you calculated it 2,000 years ago?

6. What are the factors of production? Name them and briefly describe them in plain English.

7. Using data from the Penn World Tables, calculate the annual growth rate of real GDP per person for China for the years in the table. The Penn World Tables, available free online, are a reliable source of international economic data, and they are very popular among economists.

Year	Real GDP per Capita (in 1996 U.S. dollars)	Annual Growth Rate
2000	4,001	
2001	4,389	_____
2002	4,847	_____
2003	5,321	_____
2004	5,771	_____

8. Practice with the rule of 70: If you inherit $10,000 this year and you invest your money so that it grows 7% per year, how many years will it take for your investment to be worth $20,000? $40,000? $160,000? (*Note:* Investments in stocks have grown at an average inflation-adjusted rate of 7% per year since the U.S. Civil War. We'll practice this some more in the next chapter.)

Value today: $10,000. Growth rate: 7%

Number of years until money doubles:_____

Number of years until money quadruples:_____

Number of years until your inheritance is 16X larger:_____

9. More practice with the rule of 70: Suppose that, instead, you put your money into a savings account that grows at an inflation-adjusted return of 2% per year. How many years will it take to be worth $20,000? $40,000? $160,000? (*Note:* Bank deposits have grown at roughly this rate over the past 50 years in the United States.)

Value today: $10,000. Growth rate: 2%

Number of years until money doubles:_____

Number of years until money quadruples:_____

Number of years until your inheritance is 16X larger:_____

10. India and China come up a lot in this chapter. You might wonder why so much time is spent talking about just two countries out of more than 180 on the planet. But what fraction of humans live in India and China together?

11. Let's convert Figure 7.5 into words.

Institutions create _____, which in turn affect the amount of _____, _____, and _____ in a country, which, combined with the right kind of _____, generates a level of _____ per person.

12. In the *CIA World Factbook*, GDP per capita in the United States in 2010 was approximately $47,400. The formula for GDP for any given year, y_t, is $y_t = y_0(1 + g_y)^t$, where y_0 is the value of GDP in the beginning year, y_t is the value of GDP for the specific year in question, and t is the number of years after y_0. If y_0 is GDP per capita in 2010 and the economy has continued to grow at approximately 3% as it did in 2010, what will be the value of GDP per capita in 10 years?

Discovering DATA ⠿

13. Using the FRED economic database (https://fred.stlouisfed.org/), let's compare real GDP per capita in Argentina and Korea. First find "Constant GDP per capita for Argentina." Click Edit Graph and then click Add Line and add Constant GDP per capita for the Republic of Korea. Both series should be in U.S. dollars.

   a. What was Argentina's real GDP per capita in 1974? Thirty years later, in 2004?

   b. In what year did South Korea and Argentina have approximately the same real GDP per capita?

   c. What is the ratio of real GDP per capita in South Korea to Argentina today?

14. Using the FRED economic database (https://fred.stlouisfed.org/), let's compare the GDP of the state of California with that of some countries, in this case, France and Canada. Because France's GDP is in euros and Canada's is in Canadian dollars, we will need to convert currencies. In addition, we would like to compare GDP over a similar basket of goods. Comparisons like this are called purchasing power parity (PPP) comparisons. After you have found real GDP for California, click Edit Graph, then click Add Line and find real GDP for France, looking for a series like "Expenditure-side Real GDP at Chained Purchasing Power Parities for France." Now click Add Line again and find a similar series for Canada.

   a. How do California, France, and Canada compare? What does this suggest about the U.S. economy and its role in the world economy?

   b. Using Google, find the population of each of these regions and then do a back-of-the-envelope calculation of real GDP per capita in, say, 2014 in each entity.

THINKING AND PROBLEM SOLVING

15. The average person in Argentina today is about as rich (in inflation-adjusted terms) as their parents. How can this be called a "growth disaster"?

16. Before the rise of affordable automobiles and subways, many people used trolleys—small trains on rails that ran along ordinary streets—to get around in urban areas. On trolleys, there is a literal "free rider problem": Since the trains were right next to sidewalks, and since trolleys were wide open and never had doors, people could hop on and off very easily. How much money will a trolley lose if it is easy to ride for free? If "free riders" are a big problem, what will happen to the supply of trolley rides? What are a few things the trolley industry could do to solve the problem of free riders?

Free riders in Jakarta, Indonesia

17. During the Great Leap Forward, millions of Chinese starved to death because not enough food was produced by farmers. Why didn't farmers grow food? In particular, was it because there wasn't enough human capital or physical capital?

The slogan of the Great Leap Forward was "Long live the People's Commune!" Unfortunately, this patriotic appeal didn't work as well as good economic incentives, and millions lost their lives.
(Information from: Wikipedia, "Great Leap Forward.")

18. Laws that encourage businesses to stay small are often very popular. The laws governing Indian shirt tailors discussed in this chapter are just one example. What are some *noneconomic* (e.g., social,

moral, ethical) reasons why voters might want businesses to stay small? What are some *economic* reasons they might want businesses to grow large?

▶ 19. Economists use the term "human capital" to refer to education and job skills. How is education like a piece of capital?

▶ 20. Many people say that natural resources like oil and minerals are the way to prosperity. Indeed, in an old cartoon by Matt Groening, creator of *The Simpsons*, a professor taught his students, "The nation that controls magnesium controls the universe!" But natural resources have been left out of this chapter completely. Is this a big mistake? (*Information from:* Sala-i-Martin, X., G. Doppelhofer, and R. Miller. 2004. Determinants of long-term economic growth: A Bayesian averaging of classical estimates (BACE). *The American Economic Review* 94(4) (September): 813–835.)

  a. Here are the 10 countries in the world that have the highest amounts of hydrocarbons (oil, natural gas, etc.) per person, in rank order:

     1. Kuwait
     2. United Arab Emirates (UAE)
     3. Saudi Arabia
     4. Iraq
     5. Norway
     6. Venezuela
     7. Oman
     8. Iran
     9. Trinidad and Tobago
     10. Gabon

   Use the *CIA World Factbook*, a convenient online source of information, to see if most of these countries are prosperous. How many of these 10 countries have a GDP per person that is at least half of the U.S. level? How many are less than 10% of the U.S. level? Are any actually higher than the U.S. level?

  b. Now, let's look at the reverse: Let's see if the 10 richest countries in GDP per capita have a lot of hydrocarbon wealth:

     1. Luxembourg
     2. United States
     3. Singapore
     4. Hong Kong
     5. Norway
     6. Australia
     7. Sweden
     8. Canada
     9. Denmark
     10. Japan

   The one country on both lists also makes another list in this chapter. Which one is it?

▶ 21. Economists often refer to the "natural resource curse," by which they mean that large amounts of natural resources tend to create bad politics because as long as the oil keeps flowing or the diamonds remain plentiful, political leaders don't need to care much about what goes on in the rest of the country.

  a. Which one of the three factors of production do you think matters most to a leader of a resource-rich country? Why? (*Note:* Does this help explain what you see happening in many resource-rich countries?)

  b. Which one of the five key institutions do you think matters most to a leader of a resource-rich republic? Why? (*Note:* Does this help explain what you see happening in many resource-rich countries?)

▶ 22. In the Soviet Union, especially in the early decades under Lenin and Stalin, the official doctrine was Communism, and the use of incentives was considered a form of treason. One important exception was the military equipment sector, where bonuses were common for engineers who designed and manufactured jets, nuclear missiles, tanks, and rifles. Why was this an exception?

▶ 23. Free rider problems are everywhere. For example, some restaurants let food servers keep their own tips. Other restaurants require all of the food servers to put their tips into a tip pool, which then gets divided up equally among all of the servers. It's easy to adjust the tip pool so that people who work more hours or serve more tables get their "fair share," so that's not the issue we're concerned about here. Instead, let's think about how the tip pool changes the server's incentive to be nice to the customer.

  a. To keep it simple, let's assume that a server can be "nice" and earn $100 in tips per shift, or be "mean" and earn $40 in tips per shift. If any food servers go from being mean to being nice, how much more will they earn in a non-tip-pooling world? (Yes, this is an easy question.)

b. Now let's look at incentives in a tip pool. If all the servers are mean, how much will the average server earn? If all the servers are nice, how much will the average server earn? What's the change in tips per server if *all* of them switch from being mean to being nice?

c. But in the real world, of course, all food servers makes their own decision to be mean or nice. Suppose that some servers are being nice and others are being mean, and you're trying to decide whether to be nice or mean. What's the payoff *to you* if you switch your behavior? Does your answer depend on how many other servers are being nice?

d. So when are you most likely to be nice: when you're in a tip pool or when you keep your own tips? If the restaurant cares a lot about keeping its customers happy, which policy will it follow?

24. If "everyone used to be poor," then how could some ancient civilizations afford to create massive buildings like the pyramids of Egypt and the Buddhist statues of Afghanistan (sadly, many of the latter were destroyed by the Taliban in the 1990s)?

25. In England during the Wars of the Roses (late 1400s), two parties fought for the crown. Contrast the prospects for economic growth during this period and after this period when Henry VII became the unquestioned head of the country.

CHALLENGES

26. One way to learn about what makes some countries richer is to run statistical tests to see which factors are good at predicting a nation's level of productivity. Sometimes it turns out that a relationship is just a coincidence (like the fact that people in rich countries eat more ice cream), but other statistical tests really can tell you about the ultimate causes of productivity. A statistical test can't tell you everything, but it might help point you in the right direction. In courses on econometrics and statistics, you can learn about how to run sensible tests.

Let's look at one well-known set of tests, to see if what you learned in this chapter matches the statistical evidence. Here are 17 variables that turned out to be very strong predictors of a nation's long-run economic performance in

literally millions of statistical tests (*Information from:* Sala-i-Martin, X., G. Doppelhofer, and R. Miller. 2004. Determinants of long-term economic growth: A Bayesian averaging of classical estimates (BACE). *The American Economic Review,* 94(4) (September): 813–835.) They are in rank order, and a "+" means more of that value was good for long-run productivity:

- Whether a country is in East Asia (+)
- Level of K–6 schooling (+)
- Price of capital goods (−)
- Fraction of land within tropics (−)
- Fraction of population close to the coast (+)
- Malaria prevalence (−)
- Life expectancy (+)
- Fraction of population Confucian (+)
- Whether a country is in Africa (−)
- Whether a country is in Latin America (−)
- Fraction of GDP in mining industries (+)
- Whether a country was a Spanish colony (−)
- Years open to relatively free trade (+)
- Fraction of population Muslim (+)
- Fraction of population Buddhist (+)
- Number of languages widely spoken (−)
- Fraction of GDP spent on government purchases (−)

a. Which of these factors sound like the "three factors of production"? Which ones do they sound like?

b. Which of these factors sound like the "five key institutions"? Which ones do they sound like?

c. Which of these factors sound like geography?

d. The western United States was a Spanish colony until 1849. On average, former Spanish colonies have had poor economic performance. Does the western United States fit that pattern? Why or why not?

27. What do *you* think creates the good institutions that exist in rich countries? Why don't these institutions—property rights, markets, a society where you can usually trust strangers—exist everywhere on the planet?

28. Why do you think expensive red tape is difficult to get rid of in many poor countries? Yes, this is a miniature version of the previous question.

29. Communists believed that their system would be much more efficient than capitalism: They thought that competition between companies was wasteful. Why build three separate headquarters for carmakers (General Motors, Chrysler, and Ford), when you can just build one? Why have three advertising budgets? Why pay for three CEOs? Why not put all the factories together, so that the same engineers can fix problems at all of the plants? Doesn't one large firm maximize economies of scale? These are all good questions. So why do you think Communism turned out to be such an economic disaster, when it sounded like it would be so efficient?

30. The chapter lists five key institutions of economic growth. But isn't there really just one: good government? Support your argument with facts from this chapter.

31. Figure 7.5 and its discussion in the text identify some of the ultimate causes of the Wealth of Nations as *Institutions of Economic Growth*. One of these is honest government. Go to Gapminder at https://www.gapminder.org to explore this relationship. Once there, click on the tab for "Gapminder World" and wait a moment for the first graph to load. Once it has loaded, click on the axes and explore the number of variables available for choosing. For this problem, click on the vertical axis, look under "Society," and choose the "Corruption Perceptions Index (CPI)." You should still have GDP per capita on the horizontal axis.

  a. After noting that higher values in the CPI represent lower levels of corruption, describe what these data are telling you.

  b. Next to the upper-right-hand corner of the diagram is a "Color" box. Click on it and set it to "Geographic regions." Now hover over a color and explore where these regions are in the world. Where are the richest countries? Where are the poorest?

  c. Can you find some very corrupt countries that are also quite rich? Name some of these countries and determine what they have in common.

  d. Does this evidence generally support the claim that an honest government contributes to the wealth of a nation? Why or why not?

32. Figure 7.5 and its discussion in the text identify one of the immediate causes of the wealth of nations as *human capital*. Visit Gapminder World again at Gapminder https://www.gapminder.org and select "Education" and "Literacy Rate, Adult Total" for the vertical axis while leaving GDP per capita on the horizontal axis. (See the previous problem for more detailed instructions.)

  a. What does this display of data convey to you about the value of education?

  b. Now change the vertical axis to the "Mean Number of Years in School" for men older than age 25 and then create a second graph for women older than age 25. How do your conclusions change? Is education still as valuable?

  c. Finally, select eighth-grade math achievement for the vertical axis and determine if this measure of education is also positively associated with GDP per capita.

  d. How do these measures of education work to support or refute the relationship between education levels and GDP per capita?

  e. Now try an additional educational measure using two graphs. Under "Schooling Cost," explore "Expenditures per Student, Primary" and "Expenditures per Student, Secondary." What do you find in these cases and how can you explain these differences?

33. Suppose two countries start with the same real GDP per capita, but country A is growing at 2% per year and Country B is growing at 3% per year. After 140 years, Country B's GDP per capita will be _____ larger than Country A's.

WORK IT OUT

For interactive, step-by-step help in solving this problem, go online.

Let's figure out how long it will take for the average Indian to be as wealthy as the average Western European is today. Note that all numbers are *adjusted for inflation,* so we're measuring output in "piles of stuff," not "piles of money." India's GDP per capita is $5,000, and (somewhat optimistically) let's say that real output per person there grows at 5% per year. Using the rule of 70, how many years will it take for India to reach Italy's current level of GDP per capita, about $36,000 per year?

▶ MRU VIDEOS

Basic Facts of Wealth
mru.org/wealth-nations

Problems: **3, 4**

Growth Rates Are Crucial
mru.org/growth-rates

Problems: **5, 7, 12**

An Orgy of Innovation
mru.org/innovation

Problem: **25**

Growth Miracles and Growth Disasters
mru.org/growth-miracle-disaster

Problem: **15**

The Importance of Institutions
mru.org/institutions

Problems: **11, 16–18, 21, 23, 31–32**

Geography and Economic Growth
mru.org/geography-growth

Problems: **20, 27**

Puzzle of Growth: Rich Countries and Poor Countries
mru.org/puzzle-of-growth

Problems: **6, 11, 17, 19, 24, 28–30**

The Hockey Stick of Human Prosperity
mru.org/hockey-stick

Problem: **5**

The Rule of 70
mru.org/rule-70

Problems: **8, 9**

CHAPTER 7 APPENDIX

The Magic of Compound Growth Using a Spreadsheet

The rule of 70 gives us a quick way to compute doubling times given a growth rate. We can also use a Microsoft Excel spreadsheet to easily answer more difficult questions. We know, for example, that if GDP per capita starts at $40,000 and if the growth rate is 2%, then GDP per capita after 1 year will be $40,800 and after just 35 years it will double to $79,996. We can show this using a simple spreadsheet as in Figure A7.1.

Once we understand the principles, however, we don't need to write each year on a separate line. Instead, we can simplify by using a little bit of mathematical notation.

If our Starting value for GDP per capita is $40,000 and the growth rate is r%, for example, 2%, and we grow for one year, then our Ending value will be $\$40,000 \times (1 + r/100)$. If we grow for two years, our Ending value will be $\$40,000 \times (1 + r/100) \times (1 + r/100)$, which is the same thing as $\$40,000 \times (1 + r/100)^2$. More generally, if the growth rate is r% and we grow for n years, then

$$\text{Ending value} = \text{Starting value} \times \left(1 + \frac{r}{100}\right)^n \quad (A1)$$

We can use this formula to simplify our spreadsheet, as in Figure A7.2.

FIGURE A7.1

C2			f_x =B2*0.02	
	A	B	C	D
	Year	Beginning GDP (per capita)	Increase in GDP	GDP at end of Year
1				
2	1	$40,000	$800	$40,800
3	2	$40,800	$816	$41,616
4	3	$41,616	$832	$42,448
36	35	$78,427	$1,569	$79,996
37				

Compound Growth in a Spreadsheet: The Long Method

FIGURE A7.2

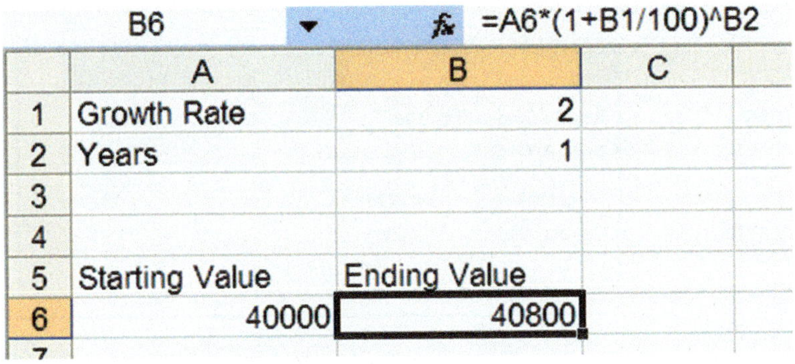

	B6 ▼	f_x =A6*(1+B1/100)^B2	
	A	B	C
1	Growth Rate	2	
2	Years	1	
3			
4			
5	Starting Value	Ending Value	
6	40000	40800	
7			

Compound Growth in a Spreadsheet: The Shortcut

Notice that we put the starting level of GDP per capita, or whatever quantity we are interested in (this could also be the amount of money in a bank account, for example), in cell A6, the growth rate is in cell B1, the number of years we want to grow is in cell B2, and thus the formula in cell B6, "= A6 × (1 + B1/100) ^ B2", is exactly as in equation A1.

By adjusting the Starting value, the Growth rate, and the Number of years, we can find out how much any amount will grow to given any interest rate over any number of years.

We can also use Excel's Goal Seek ability to work backward to find, say, the number of years it will take to reach a certain level of GDP per capita when growth is r% per year. Suppose, for example, that GDP per capita is $46,000 and that growth is 2% per year. How long will it take to reach a GDP per capita of $1,000,000? Here's how you can easily find numbers like this. Go to the Tools menu and click on Goal Seek (in Excel 2007, go to the Data menu and under the submenu What-If Analysis, click on Goal Seek). A box will pop up asking you for three inputs: Set cell _____, To value _____, By changing cell _____. In our case, we want Set cell **B6**, the Ending Value; To value **1,000,000**; By changing cell **B2**; and the number of years. Figure A7.3 shows you what you should see and input. Notice that we also changed the Starting value to $46,000.

FIGURE A7.3

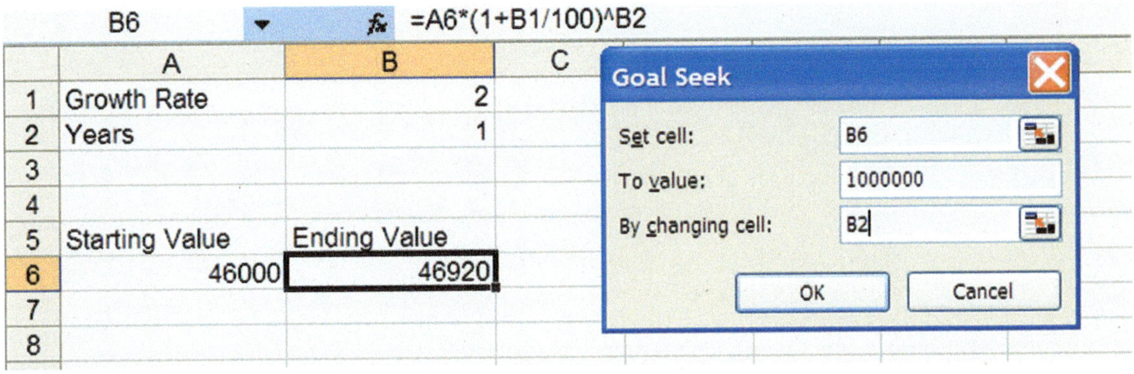

	B6 ▼	f_x =A6*(1+B1/100)^B2		Goal Seek ✕
	A	B	C	
1	Growth Rate	2		Set cell: B6
2	Years	1		To value: 1000000
3				By changing cell: B2
4				
5	Starting Value	Ending Value		OK Cancel
6	46000	46920		
7				
8				

Using Goal Seek

FIGURE A7.4

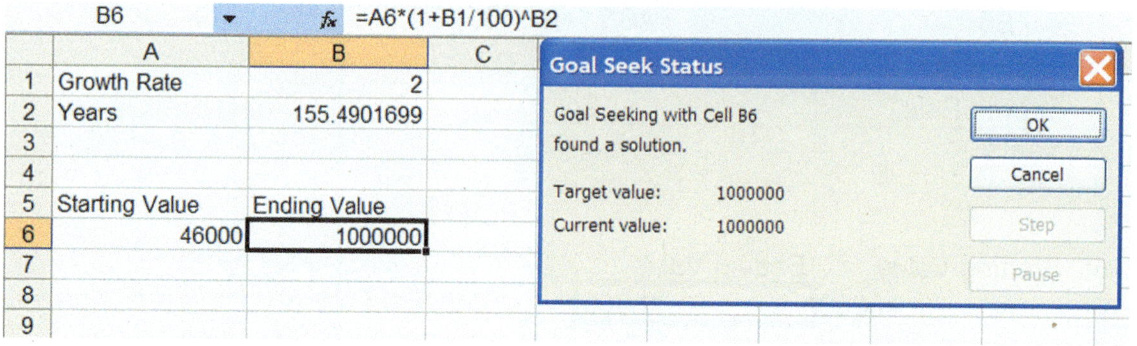

	A	B	C
	B6	▾	f_x =A6*(1+B1/100)^B2
1	Growth Rate	2	
2	Years	155.4901699	
3			
4			
5	Starting Value	Ending Value	
6	46000	1000000	
7			
8			
9			

Goal Seek Status

Goal Seeking with Cell B6
found a solution.

Target value: 1000000
Current value: 1000000

OK

Cancel

Step

Pause

Goal Seek Solves the Problem

Clicking OK produces what you see in Figure A7.4.

Goal Seek has solved the problem! If we start at a value of GDP per capita of $46,000 and we grow at 2% a year, then in 155.49 years we will reach a value of GDP per capita of $1,000,000.

By using Goal Seek and varying the inputs, you can find the answer to all kinds of questions. Can you find, for example, how high the growth rate would have to be to reach a level of GDP per capita of $1,000,000 in, say, 50 years?

Chapter 7 Appendix Questions

■ If a country starts off as rich as the United States, with a GDP per capita of $46,000, and if GDP per capita grows 3% per year, then how many years will it take before GDP per capita is $1,000,000 per year?

■ If a country with a GDP per capita of $4,000 at its start grows at 8% per year, then how many years will it take before GDP per capita is $46,000?

■ If you wanted to double $1,000 in 10 years' time, what average rate of return would you require on your investment?

8

Growth, Capital Accumulation, and the Economics of Ideas: Catching Up vs. the Cutting Edge

In 2010, GDP per capita in China grew by nearly 10%. The same year, GDP per capita in the United States grew by just 2.2%. In its entire history, the U.S. economy has never grown as fast as the Chinese economy grew in 2010. Nor was this an unusual year—the Chinese economy has been growing at extraordinarily high rates for three decades. If these rates continue, China will be richer than the United States in less than 25 years. How can this make sense? Is there something wrong with the U.S. economy? Do the Chinese have a magical potion for economic growth?

Remember, in the last chapter we explained that among the key institutions promoting economic growth were property rights, honest government, political stability, a dependable legal system, and competitive and open markets. But for each and every one of these institutions, the United States ranks higher than China, despite China's having made remarkable improvements in recent decades. So why is China growing so much more rapidly than the United States?

To answer this question, we must distinguish between two types of growth, **catching-up** and **cutting-edge**. Countries that are catching up have some enormous advantages. To become rich, a poor country does not have to invent new ideas, technologies, or methods of management. All it has to do is adopt the ideas already developed in the richer countries. As we will see, catching-up countries like China grow primarily through capital accumulation and the adoption of some simple ideas that massively improve productivity.

The United States is the world's leading economy—it is on the cutting edge. Growth on the cutting edge is primarily about developing new ideas. But developing new ideas is more difficult than adopting ideas already in existence. Calculus isn't easy but it doesn't take a genius to understand calculus; it does

Catching-up growth is growth due to capital accumulation and adopting already existing ideas.

Cutting-edge growth is growth due to new ideas.

take a genius to invent calculus. Countries on the cutting edge grow primarily through idea generation.

In this chapter, we will do two things. First, we will develop a model of economic growth based on capital accumulation. The model will help us understand some puzzles, such as why China is growing so much faster right now than the United States and why the countries that lost World War II, Germany and Japan, grew much faster in the postwar decades than did one of the winners, the United States. We will also discuss how poor and rich countries can converge in income over time.

Our model of economic growth based on capital accumulation does a good job of explaining catching-up growth but it doesn't help much to explain growth on the cutting edge. If we think about growth in the United States, for example, we probably do not think first about more tractors, buildings, and factories—the sorts of things that characterize growth in China. Instead, we think about iPhones, the Internet, and genetic engineering, that is, new products, new processes, and new ideas. Thus, in the second half of the chapter, we turn to cutting-edge growth and the economics of ideas. The economics of ideas explains why growth in the United States is slower than in China, but also why growth in China will slow down. It also suggests, however, that U.S. and worldwide economic growth may become faster in the decades ahead than it has been in the past. To put it bluntly (but regretfully for us), many of you will see more progress in your lifetimes than we will have seen in ours.

The Solow Model and Catching-Up Growth

mru.org/solow-model

Introduction to the Solow Model

Let's begin with a model of the wealth of nations and economic growth called the Solow model (after Nobel Prize–winning economist Robert Solow). The Solow model begins with a production function. A production function expresses a relationship between output and the factors of production, namely the exact way in which more inputs will produce more outputs. For simplicity, we assume that there is only one output Y, which we can think of as GDP, and the three factors of production that we discussed in the last chapter: physical capital, written K; human capital, which we write as eL, and can understand as education, e, times labor, L; and ideas that increase the productivity of capital and labor (technical knowledge), which we write as A. Thus, we can write that output Y is a function F of the inputs A, K, and eL:

$$Y = F(A, K, eL)$$

That equation looks abstract but it represents a simple economic truth. If we look at a typical production process, say, an automobile factory, output depends on capital (the machines K), labor (the workers L adjusted for their level of skill, so eL), and the ideas upon which the whole factory is based (A), namely the invention of the auto and all the machines that help make it.

We also can think of the entire economy as relying on capital, labor, and ideas on a larger scale. We will focus on the Solow production function as a description of an entire economy because we are looking at the causes and consequences of overall economic growth.

For our first look at the Solow model, we will temporarily ignore changes in ideas, education, and labor. If we assume that A, e, and L are constant, then we can simplify our expression for output as $Y = F(K)$. Notice that because

L (the number of workers) is constant, an increase in K (capital) always implies an increase in the amount of capital per worker, K/L, and an increase in Y (output) is also always an increase in output per worker, Y/L.

Capital, Production, and Diminishing Returns

Let's make a quick sketch of what our production function $F(K)$ should look like. More capital, K, should produce more output, Y, but at a diminishing rate. On a farm, for example, the first tractor is very productive. The second tractor is still useful, but not as much as the first tractor. The third tractor is driven only when one of the other tractors breaks down (remember that the amount of labor is constant). What this means is that increases in capital, K, produce less output, Y, the more K you already have—so we should have a production function in which output increases with more K but at a decreasing rate. Following this logic, Figure 8.1 graphs output, Y, on the vertical axis against capital, K, on the horizontal axis, holding L and the other inputs constant.

Notice from Figure 8.1 that the first unit of capital increases output by one unit, but as more and more capital is added, output increases by less and less—this is the "iron logic" of diminishing returns and it plays a key role in the Solow model. Economists call the increase in output when capital increases by one unit the **marginal product of capital.** The graph shows that the marginal product of capital is diminishing.

It can sometimes help to look at a specific production function. In Figure 8.1, we used the production function $Y = F(K) = \sqrt{K}$, which means that output is the square root of the capital input. To see how this works, plug in some numbers. If $K = 4$, then $Y = \sqrt{4} = 2$. If K increases to 16, then $Y = \sqrt{16} = 4$ and so forth.

> The **marginal product of capital** is the increase in output caused by the addition of one more unit of capital. The marginal product of capital diminishes as more and more capital is added.

FIGURE 8.1

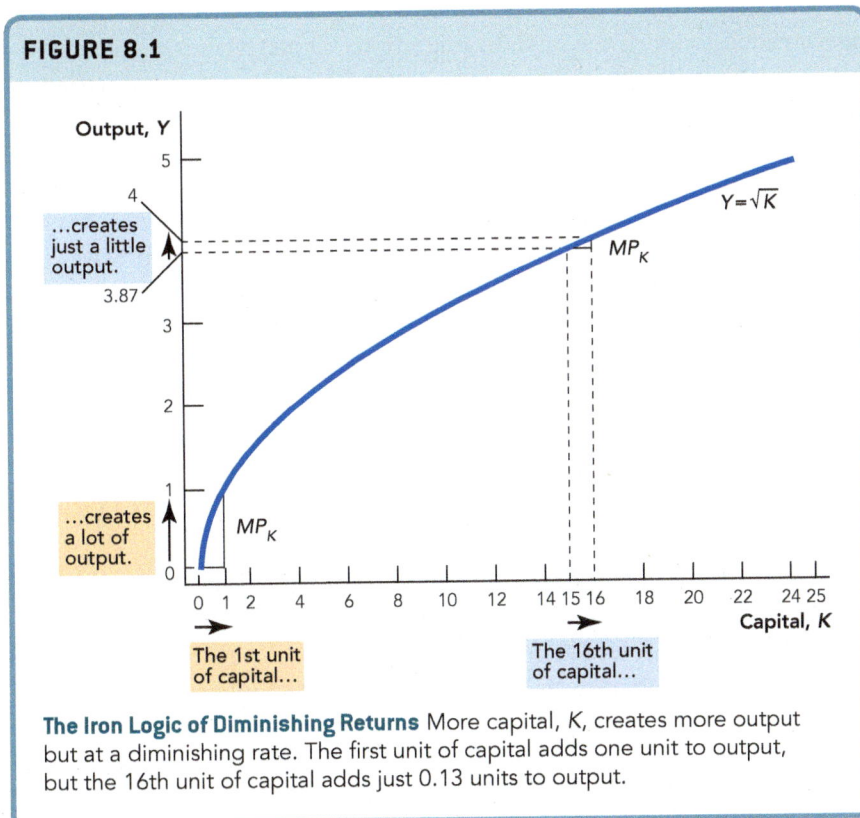

The Iron Logic of Diminishing Returns More capital, K, creates more output but at a diminishing rate. The first unit of capital adds one unit to output, but the 16th unit of capital adds just 0.13 units to output.

As we said, the reason the marginal product of capital diminishes is that the first unit of capital (the first tractor) is applied where it is most productive, the second unit is applied to slightly less productive tasks because the first unit is already performing the most productive tasks, the third unit is applied to even less productive tasks, and so on.

Growth in China and the United States The iron logic of diminishing returns explains quite a bit about why China is now growing so much more rapidly than the United States. Imagine, for example, that a country labors under poor institutions—like a lack of competitive and open markets—so that the incentives to invest in capital are low. Now suppose that new institutions are put into place; perhaps new leaders with better ideas replace the old guard. The new institutions increase the incentives to invest and the capital stock grows. But in a country without a lot of capital but good (or much improved) institutions, the marginal product of capital will be very high. In that case, even small investments pay big rewards and economic growth will be rapid.

This process describes what has happened in China. For most of the twentieth century, China labored under very poor economic institutions. China in the 1950s and 1960s was a growth disaster with mass starvation as a common occurrence. Since the death of Chairman Mao in 1976 and the subsequent move away from Communism and toward markets, China has been growing very rapidly. Chinese growth has been rapid because China began with very little capital, so the marginal product of capital was very high, and with the new reforms the investment rate increased dramatically. In addition, of course, China has benefited by opening up to trade and investment with the developed world.

China also grew rapidly because improved productivity in agriculture—brought about primarily by better institutions, as we discussed in the last chapter—prompted several hundred million Chinese rural peasants, who were no longer needed to work the land, to migrate to Chinese cities. Almost overnight these people went from being subsistence farmers, producing perhaps a few hundred dollars' worth of output a year, to urban workers, producing perhaps a few thousand dollars' worth of output a year in a factory. This is one of the largest economic migrations in human history and for the most part it has been a resounding success.

The iron logic explains why China is catching up to the United States but also why growth in China will slow. China now has its first tractor and indeed its second. As it adds a third and beyond, China's growth rate will fall because the marginal product of capital will fall. Also, China has many problems—from a poor banking system to a lack of experience with the rule of law to a poorly educated population. At the moment, these problems are being swamped by the high productivity of capital. But as capital accumulates and the marginal productivity of capital declines, China's problems will become more of a drag on Chinese growth.

Why Bombing a Country Can Raise Its Growth Rate The iron logic also explains why bombing a country can increase its growth rate. Following World War II, for example, Germany and Japan both grew faster than the United States. It may seem odd that the losers of a war should grow faster than the winners, but the iron logic of diminishing returns predicts exactly this result. During World War II, the capital stock of Germany and Japan—the factories, the roads, and the buildings—was nearly obliterated by Allied bombing. With so little capital remaining, any new capital was highly productive and so Germany and Japan had a strong incentive to invest in new capital. In other words, they grew rapidly as they were rebuilding their economies. It's also the case that Germany and Japan had reasonably good postwar institutions.

But don't make the mistake of envying Germany and Japan their high growth rates. Germany and Japan grew rapidly because they were catching up. Children who have been malnourished often grow rapidly when they are put on a proper diet but it's not good to be malnourished. Similarly, countries whose capital stock has been destroyed will grow rapidly, all else being equal, as they catch up but it is not good to have your capital stock destroyed. Note also that growth in Germany and Japan slowed down as their capital stocks grew and approached U.S. levels; by the 1980s they were growing at close to the U.S. rate. The growth rate in Germany and Japan fell not because they did anything wrong, but, again, because the marginal product of capital declines as a country accumulates more capital.

Figure 8.1 explains that more capital means more output, albeit at a diminishing rate. But where does capital come from and where does it go? Capital is output that is saved and invested, but capital depreciates over time. In the next section, we show how these two aspects of capital—investment and depreciation—fit together. Understanding investment and depreciation will prove important for isolating the ultimate sources of economic growth.

Average Annual Growth Rate of GDP per Capita for Germany, Japan, and the United States		
	1950–1960	1980–1990
Germany	6.6%	1.9%
Japan	6.8%	3.4%
United States	1.2%	2.3%

Capital Growth Equals Investment Minus Depreciation

Capital is output that is saved and invested rather than consumed. Imagine, for example, that 10 units of output are produced. Of the 10 units of output, 7 units might be consumed and 3 units invested in new capital. We write the fraction of output that is invested in new capital as gamma (γ), and in the example just given, $\gamma = \frac{3}{10} = 0.3$.

Figure 8.2 shows how output is divided between consumption and investment when $\gamma = 0.3$. Notice that when $K = 100$, 10 units of output are

FIGURE 8.2

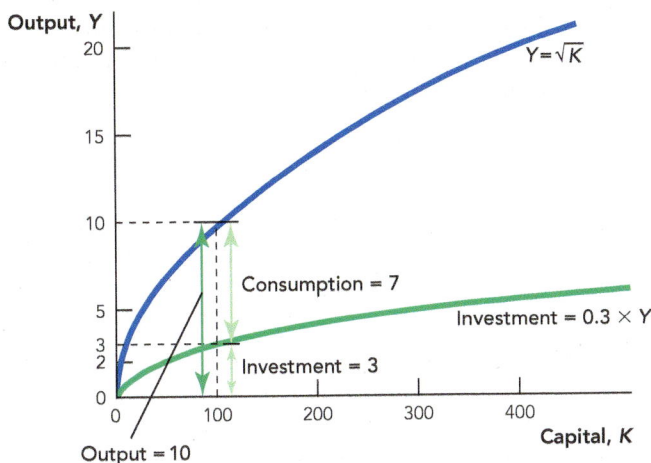

Capital Is Output That Is Invested
The production function $Y = \sqrt{K}$ shows how much output is produced for every level of K, the capital stock. When $K = 100$, 10 units of output are produced. The investment rate is 0.3, so $0.3 \times 10 = 3$ units of output are devoted to investment. The remaining 7 units of output are consumed.

Rome did not replenish its capital stock.

produced and of these 10 units, 7 units are consumed and 3 units are invested in new capital.

Capital also depreciates—roads wear out, harbors become silted, and machines break down. Thus, if there are 100 units of capital in this period, for example, then 2 units might depreciate, leaving just 98 for use in the next period.

We write the fraction of capital that wears out or depreciates as delta (δ); in the example just given, $\delta = \frac{2}{100} = 0.02$. Figure 8.3 shows how much capital depreciates as a function of the capital stock. When the capital stock is 100, for example, then 2 units of capital will depreciate, and when the capital stock is 200, 4 units will depreciate, and so on.

The greater the capital stock, the greater the depreciation, so a country with a lot of roads, harbors, and machines needs to devote a lot of resources to filling potholes, removing silt, and repairing and replacing. In other words, a successful economy must continually replenish its capital stock just to keep going. An economy that does not replenish its capital stock will quickly fall into ruin.

Again, Figure 8.3 shows that capital depreciation increases the greater the capital stock—this will turn out to place another constraint on economic growth.

Why Capital Alone Cannot Be the Key to Economic Growth

We now have everything we need to develop a second important insight from the Solow model. The greater the capital stock, the more capital will depreciate every period (more tractors = more tractor repairs). Thus, at some point, the capital stock will reach a level such that *every* unit of investment is needed just to replace the capital that depreciates in that period. When investment just covers capital depreciation, the capital stock stops growing, and when the capital stock stops growing, output stops growing as well. Thus, the iron logic of diminishing returns tells us that capital alone cannot be the key to economic growth. Let's explore this in more detail.

FIGURE 8.3

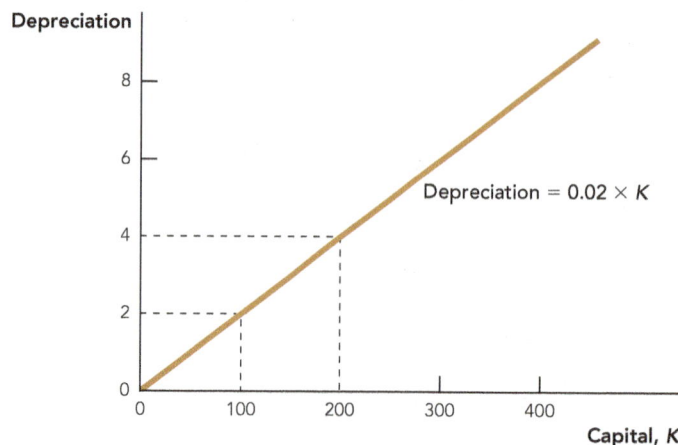

More Capital, More Capital Depreciation Capital depreciates over time, it wears out, it rusts, and it falls apart. If the depreciation rate is 0.02, then $0.02 \times K$ units of capital will depreciate each period (where K is the capital stock). Thus, if $K = 100$, 2 units will depreciate. If $K = 200$, 4 units will depreciate.

Depreciation = 0.02 × K

Figure 8.4 focuses attention on the two key functions, the investment function from Figure 8.2 and the depreciation function from Figure 8.3.

Consider first a case where the capital stock grows larger. For instance, when $K = 100$, 3 units of output are invested in new capital and 2 units of capital depreciate. Investment exceeds depreciation so in the next period, both the capital stock and output will be larger. Thus, when investment is greater than depreciation (*Investment > Depreciation*), we have economic growth.

Investment increases as the capital stock gets larger, but because of the iron logic, investment increases at a diminishing rate. Depreciation, however, increases with the capital stock at a linear (constant) rate. Thus, at some point investment equals depreciation (*Investment = Depreciation*). At this point, every unit of investment is being used to replace depreciated capital, so the amount of net or new investment (investment after depreciation) is zero. We call this the **steady-state** level of capital. At the steady-state level of capital, there is no new (net) investment and economic growth stops.

Finally, suppose that the capital stock is 400. In this case, 8 units of capital would depreciate ($0.02 \times 400 = 8$), but only 6 units of capital would be invested ($0.3 \times \sqrt{400} = 6$) (*Investment < Depreciation*). As a result, when $K = 400$, not all the depreciated capital will be replaced and the capital stock will shrink.

We can summarize as follows:

Investment > Depreciation—The capital stock grows and output next period is bigger.
Investment = Depreciation—The capital stock and output are constant (the steady state).
Investment < Depreciation—The capital stock shrinks and output next period is smaller.

Check the Math

When $K = 100$, $Y = \sqrt{100} = 10$; of these 10 units, $0.3 \times 10 = 3$ units are invested in new capital. Depreciation is $0.02 \times 100 = 2$ units, so *Investment* (3) > *Depreciation* (2), and the capital stock and output grow.

At the **steady state** the capital stock is neither increasing nor decreasing.

Check the Math

As Figure 8.4 is drawn, the steady state occurs when $K = 225$ because
Investment $= 0.30 \times \sqrt{225} = 4.5$
Depreciation $= 0.02 \times 225 = 4.5$
Thus, when $K = 225$,
Investment = Depreciation.

FIGURE 8.4

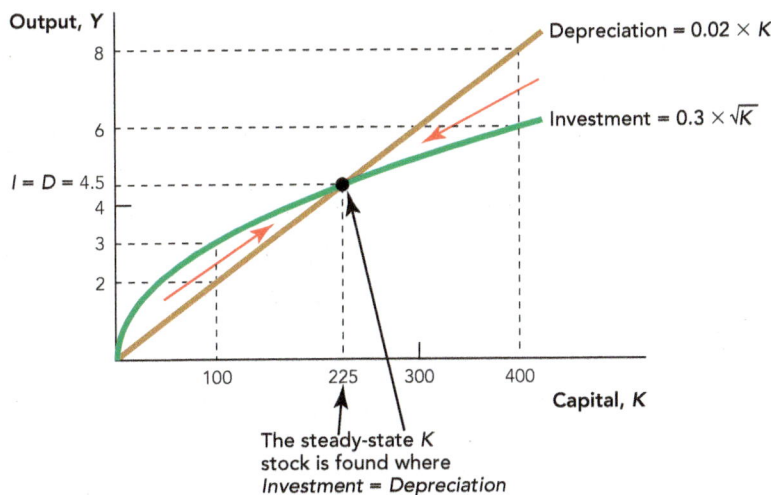

Capital Increases or Decreases Until Investment Equals Depreciation When investment is greater than depreciation, the capital stock grows. When investment is less than depreciation, the capital stock shrinks. When investment equals depreciation, the capital stock stays the same.

▶ MRU

mru.org/solow-steady-state

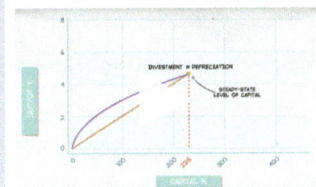

The Solow Model and the Steady State

Human Capital

We learn from our "capital only" model that the economy will move toward a steady state in which there is no capital accumulation. Thus, long-run economic growth cannot be due to capital accumulation. The logic of diminishing returns means that eventually capital and output will cease growing. Economic growth, however, does not seem to be slowing. So what else could drive long-run economic growth? Let's return to the other factors of production discussed in the previous chapter—human capital and technological knowledge.

Can increases in human capital drive long-run economic growth? Human capital is an important contributor to the wealth of nations. Figure 8.5 shows that GDP per capita is higher in countries with more human capital, as measured by average years of schooling.

But human capital is just like physical capital in that it has diminishing returns and it depreciates. In other words, an economic principles class is probably the most important economics class that you will take and all the human capital in the world today will be gone in a hundred years. (Why will all the human capital in the world today be gone in a hundred years? *Hint:* Where will your human capital be in a hundred years?) Thus, within the Solow model, the logic of diminishing returns applies to human capital just as much as to physical capital and neither can drive long-run economic growth.

From Capital Accumulation to Catching-Up Growth

Finally, recall that changes in the capital stock drive output, so when *Investment = Depreciation* and *K* is at its steady-state level, then so is output. We show this in Figure 8.6 simply by adding the output curve back to our diagram. Notice that if *K* is at the steady-state level (*K* = 225, in this case), then *Y*

FIGURE 8.5

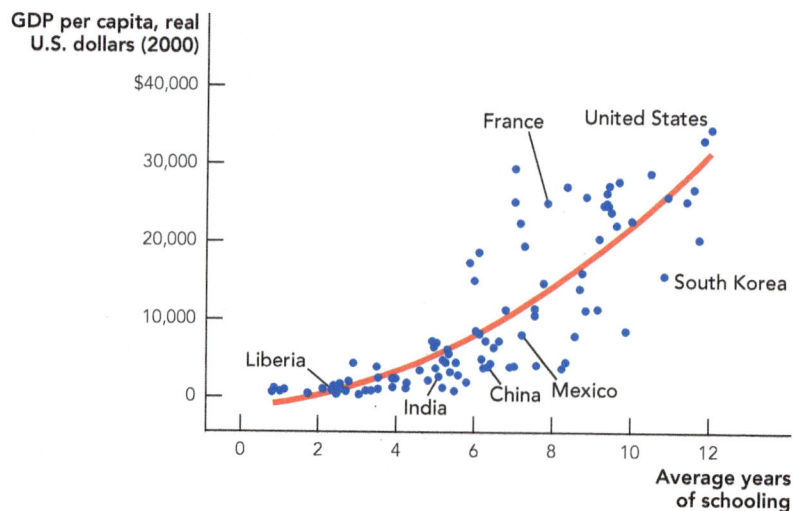

GDP per Capita Is Higher in Countries with More Human Capital (2000)

Data from: Penn World Tables and Barro, Robert J., and Jong-Wha Lee. 2001. International data on educational attainment: Updates and implications. *Oxford Economic Papers,* 53(3): 541–563.

FIGURE 8.6

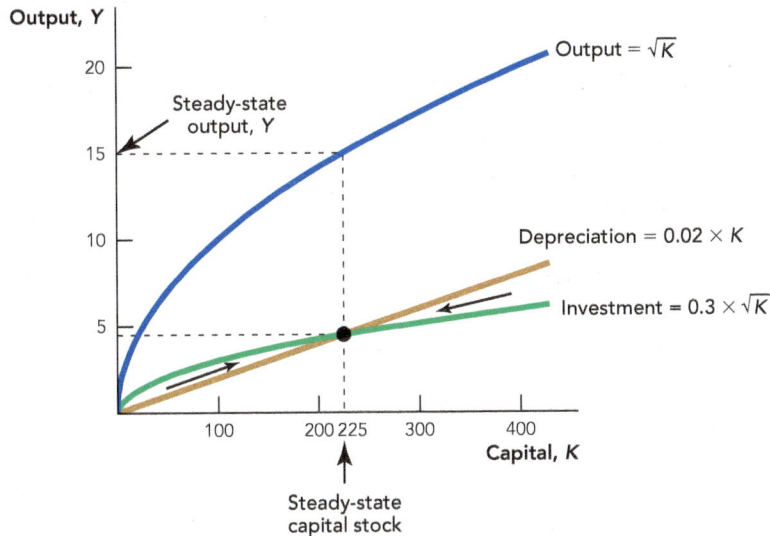

When Capital Is in the Steady State, Output Is in the Steady State The capital stock drives output. At $K = 225$, output is $\sqrt{225} = 15$. At $K = 225$, *Investment = Depreciation*, so the capital stock is neither growing nor shrinking and thus output is neither growing nor shrinking.

will also be at a steady-state level of output, in this case 15. We follow $K = 225$ straight up from the horizontal axis to the point where it meets the $Y = \sqrt{K}$ curve at GDP = 15 on the vertical axis. Similarly, since K drives Y, whenever K is growing, then so is Y. Thus, Figure 8.6 demonstrates in a little more detail than we had before that our theory of capital growth is also a theory of economic growth.

The Investment Rate and Conditional Convergence

Let's stay with the Solow model a little longer and look at investment rates and conditional convergence.

The Solow Model and an Increase in the Investment Rate

What happens in the Solow model if γ, the fraction of output that is saved and invested, increases? It is simple: A greater investment rate means more capital, which means more output. An increase in the investment rate therefore increases a country's steady-state level of GDP. The result just shows that investment increases the number of "tractors" per worker, which raises GDP per worker.

In Figure 8.7 on the next page, we show this intuition in the graph by plotting two investment functions: *Investment* $= 0.3\sqrt{K}$, which means that 3 units of every 10 units of output are saved and invested ($\gamma = 0.3$, as it was in Figure 8.6), and also *Investment* $= 0.4\sqrt{K}$, which means that 4 units of every 10 units of output are saved and invested ($\gamma = 0.4$). Notice that when $\gamma = 0.4$ the new steady-state capital stock increases to $K = 400$ and output increases to 20.

Thus, the Solow model predicts that countries with higher rates of investment will be wealthier. Is this prediction of the Solow model consistent with

CHECK YOURSELF

In Figure 8.6:
- What happens when the capital stock is 400?
- What is investment?
- What is depreciation?
- What happens to output?

FIGURE 8.7

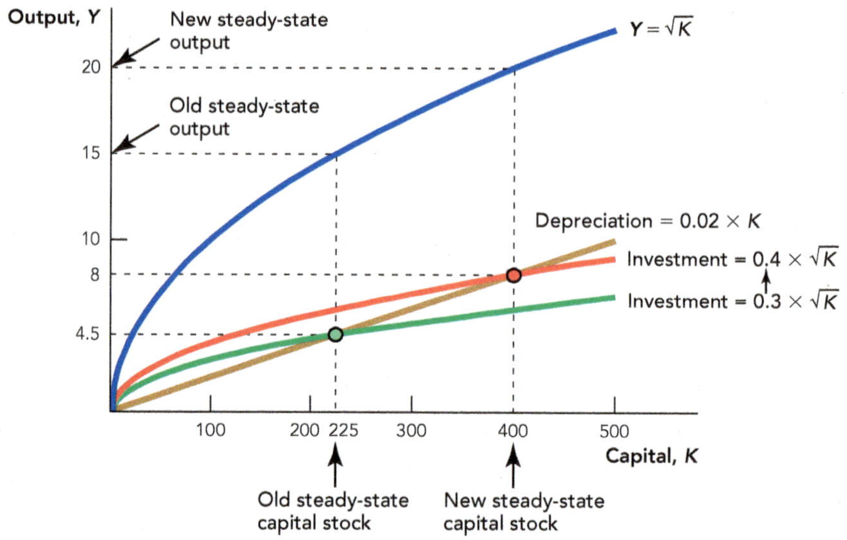

An Increase in the Investment Rate Increases Steady-State Output When the investment rate increases from 0.3 to 0.4, the investment curve shifts up and the steady-state capital stock increases from 225 to 400. Output increases along with the capital stock, rising from 15 to 20.

the evidence? Yes. Figure 8.8 shows that GDP per capita is higher in countries that have higher investment rates.

This makes intuitive sense. More savings mean that more capital goods can be produced and consumers can enjoy a higher standard of living. How wealthy would a country be if it spent all of its resources on partying?

FIGURE 8.8

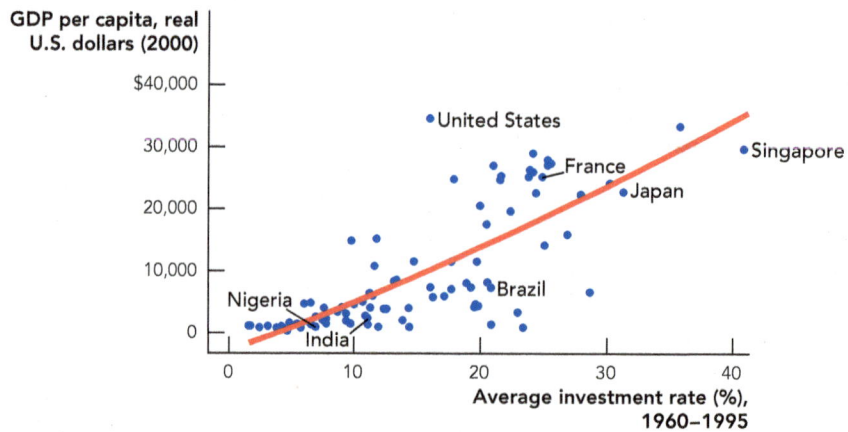

GDP per Capita Is Higher in Countries with Higher Investment Rates

Data from: Penn World Tables and Bernanke, Ben S., and Refet S. Gurkaynak. 2001. Is growth exogenous? Taking Mankiw, Romer and Weil seriously. NBER Working Paper 8365, National Bureau of Economic Research, Inc.

The Solow model says that an increase in the investment rate will increase steady-state output. But in the Solow model, the iron logic of diminishing returns cannot be avoided. When the investment rate increases, we have *Investment > Depreciation* so the capital stock increases and the economy grows. But as more capital accumulates, the iron logic sets in and the economy eventually slows until at the new steady state it stops growing once again. So the level of the capital stock determines the output level but not its growth rate, at least not in the very long run.

For further confirmation of this idea, recall the growth miracle of South Korea from the last chapter. In 1950, South Korea was poorer than Nigeria, while today it is richer than some European nations. The evidence on South Korea's growth is consistent with the Solow model. In the 1950s, the investment rate in South Korea was less than 10% of GDP, but the rate more than doubled in the 1970s and increased to more than 35% by the 1990s. Higher investment rates helped to increase South Korea's GDP, as the country opened many factories and exported cars and electronics to the rest of the world. As South Korea has caught up to Western levels of GDP, however, its growth rate has slowed.

Of course, we should remember that investment rates are themselves caused by other factors such as incentives and institutions. No one wants to invest in an economy, for example, where their investments may be expropriated. One of the reasons the investment rate in South Korea increased is that capitalists believed their investments would be protected.

In this chapter, we have referred to γ as the rate of savings *and* investment, implicitly assuming that savings equals investment. But savings must be efficiently collected and then transformed into investment. The Soviet Union had a high rate of saving but its savings were not invested well, and thus its effective investment rate was very low. In other words, a country that invests its savings poorly is like a country that doesn't invest much at all. A country could also have a low rate of saving but a high rate of investment if it imported savings from other countries. The next chapter will discuss in more detail how financial intermediaries efficiently collect savings, often from around the world, and then transform those savings into productive investments.

The Solow Model and Conditional Convergence

The Solow model also predicts that a country will grow more rapidly the farther its capital stock is below its steady-state value. To understand this result, remember that when the capital stock is below its steady-state value, investment will exceed depreciation. In other words, the capital stock will grow. Now look again at Figure 8.1—when the capital stock is low, it has a very high marginal product. Thus, when a country's capital stock is below its steady-state value, the country will grow rapidly as it invests in capital that has a high marginal product. That's just restating our tractor parable. The tractor is most valuable on the farm that doesn't already have a tractor, as opposed to the farm that is already working with 13 tractors.

We already used this result to explain why China is growing rapidly and why Germany and Japan grew rapidly after World War II. More generally, the Solow model predicts that if two countries have the same steady-state level of output, the country that is poorer today will catch up because it will grow faster. We don't know for certain which countries have the same steady-state

MRU

mru.org/solow-human-capital

Human Capital and Conditional Convergence

FIGURE 8.9

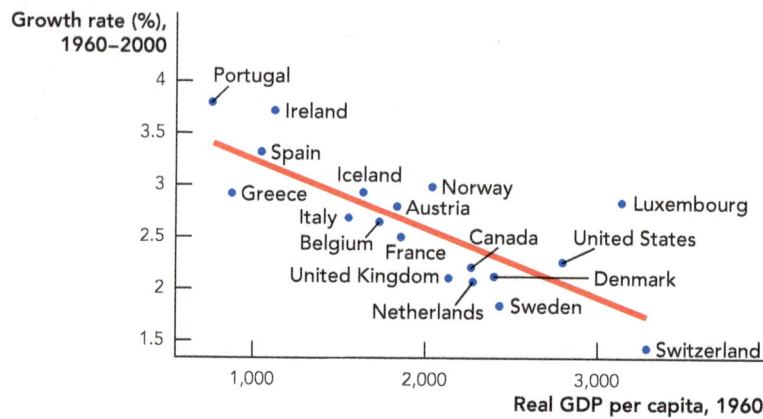

Conditional Convergence The poorer the OECD country in 1960, the faster growth was between 1960 and 2000.

Data from: Penn World Tables.
Note: Data include 18 of the 20 original OECD countries, excluding Germany and Turkey.

level of output, but we might guess, for example, that countries with similar institutions and history have similar steady states. Figure 8.9 tests this prediction using data from 18 of the 20 founding members of the OECD (Organisation for Economic Co-operation and Development).[1] The average annual growth rate between 1960 and 2000 is on the vertical axis, and real per capita GDP in 1960 is on the horizontal axis. The data clearly show that among the OECD countries, the poorer countries grew faster. You can see that lower income in 1960 is associated with higher growth between 1960 and 2000.

Since the poorer countries grow faster, they eventually catch up to the richer countries. Thus, over time the OECD countries have converged to a similar level of GDP per capita. We say that the model and the data exhibit **conditional convergence** because we only see convergence among countries that plausibly have similar steady-state levels of output. As we know from the previous chapter, we do not observe convergence among all countries—the existence of growth disasters such as Nigeria means that some countries are diverging from the rest of the world rather than catching up.

New Ideas and Cutting-Edge Growth

Several predictions of the simple Solow model are consistent with the evidence—countries with higher investment rates have higher GDP per capita, and countries grow faster the farther their capital stock is from its steady-state level. One prediction of the simplest form of the Solow model, however, is inconsistent with the evidence. The simplest form of the Solow model predicts zero economic growth in the long run. Remember, in the long run, the capital stock stops growing because *Investment = Depreciation*, and if the capital stock isn't growing, then neither is output. The United States, however, has been growing for more than 200 years, so we will need to look at a more-developed version of the Solow model. In particular, is there any way to escape the iron logic? Yes, better ideas can keep the economy growing even in the long run.

Conditional convergence is the tendency—among countries with similar steady-state levels of output—for poorer countries to grow faster than richer countries and thus for poor and rich countries to converge in income.

CHECK YOURSELF
- What happens to the marginal product of capital as more capital is added?
- Why does capital depreciate? What happens to the total amount of capital depreciation as the capital stock increases?

Better Ideas Drive Long-Run Economic Growth

Better ideas let us produce more output from the same inputs of physical and human capital. A personal computer today has about the same amount of silicon and labor input as a computer produced 20 years ago, but today's computer is much better—the difference is ideas. Recall our simple production function:

$$Y = \sqrt{K}$$

Remembering that we let A stand for ideas that increase productivity, let's now write our production function as

$$Y = A\sqrt{K}$$

Notice that better ideas or technological knowledge—as represented by increases in A—increase output even while holding K constant, that is, an increase in A represents an increase in productivity. Figure 8.10 graphs two production functions. The first is when $A = 1$, the production function that we have been working with all along. The second is when $A = 2$. Notice that when $K = 16$, output is 4 when $A = 1$, but it's 8 when $A = 2$. Technological knowledge means that we can get more output from the same input.

So long as we develop better ideas that shift the production function upward, economic growth will continue. In a way, it should be obvious that better ideas are the key to long-run economic growth. How much economic growth would there have been without the discovery of electricity or DNA or the development of the internal combustion engine, the computer chip, or the polymerase chain reaction? It's just not enough to throw more effort at a problem; we have to actually know what we are doing and *that* boils down to ideas.

Solow himself tried to estimate how much of U.S. economic prosperity was due to capital and labor, and how much was due to ideas. He came up with the figure that better ideas are responsible for about three-fourths of the U.S. standard of living. Many economists have subsequently debated the exact number, but no one contests the central importance of ideas and technological progress for human well-being.

FIGURE 8.10

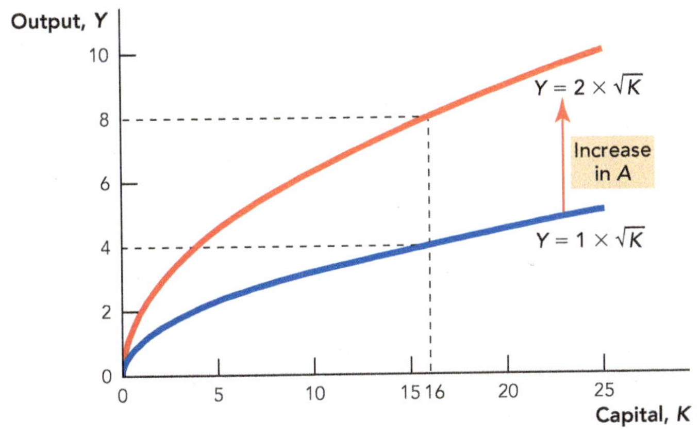

An Increase in *A* Increases Output Holding *K* Constant An increase in *A* represents an increase in productivity. If A = 1, then a capital stock of 16 can produce 4 units of output. If A = 2, then the same capital stock can produce twice as much output.

Solow and the Economics of Ideas in One Diagram

Let's revisit the Solow model one last time and show how better ideas fit within that model. It's simple: Better ideas let us produce more output from the same inputs of capital. But when we produce more output, it makes sense to increase consumption and *investment*. So better ideas also increase capital accumulation.

Figure 8.11 shows the process in a diagram. Okay, the diagram doesn't look simple. Let's take it in steps. Remember that A denotes ideas, and a bigger A means that we are working with better ideas. So imagine that we begin with A = ideas = 1. The economy is in the steady state and output = 15 (at point a'). Now suppose that A increases to $A = 1.5$. Better ideas produce more output from the same capital stock, so output immediately increases from 15 at point a' to 22.5 at point b'. But with greater output, investment also increases, moving from point a to point b. Since investment is now greater than depreciation, capital begins to accumulate. Capital accumulates and the economy grows until investment is once again equal to depreciation at point c, at which point output is now 33.75 (at point c').

Thus, Figure 8.11 shows how the Solow model and the economics of ideas fit together. Better ideas increase output directly and, by so doing, they increase capital accumulation indirectly. Of course, before we ever reach the new level of output, ideas may have gotten even better! And, thus, the process of economic growth is a continuous two-step process of better ideas and more capital accumulation.

FIGURE 8.11

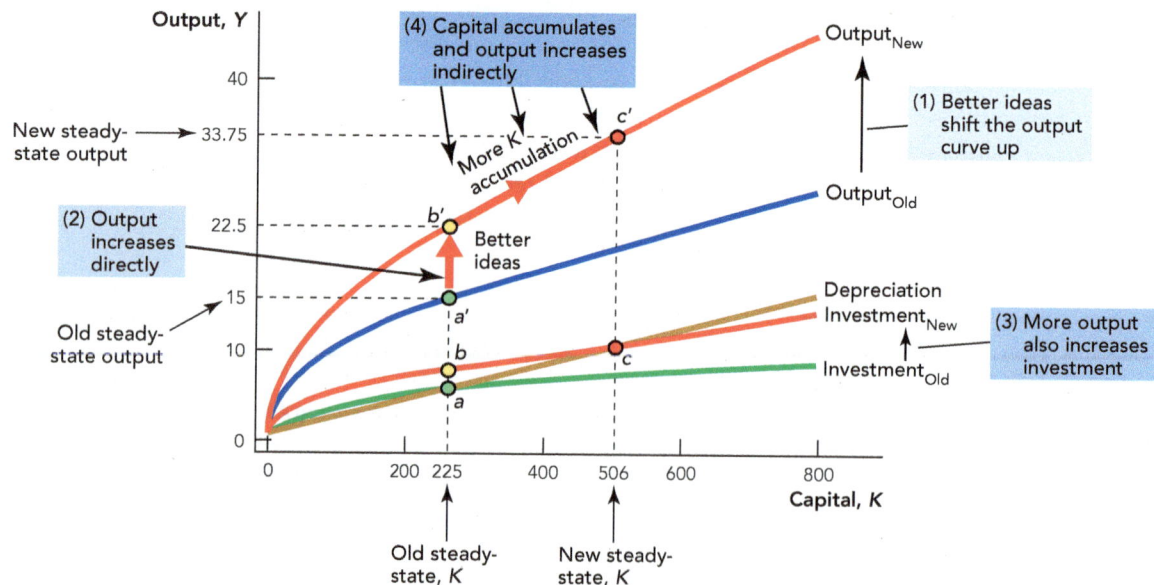

Better Ideas Generate More Output and More Capital Accumulation Better ideas shift the output curve up, which means that (1) more output is produced from the same capital stock so (2) output increases directly from point a' to point b'. More output also means more investment, so the investment curve shifts up (3).

Since investment is now greater than depreciation, the economy begins to accumulate more capital and thus to grow (4). The economy grows until Investment is again equal to Depreciation at point c and output is at point c'. Notice that better ideas increase output directly because of higher productivity and indirectly due to more capital accumulation.

The Economics of Ideas

We have learned from the Solow model that better ideas are the key to economic growth in the long run. Capital accumulation alone will not create much growth in the United States or the other developed economies such as Japan and Western Europe because these economies already have so much capital that investment must be used to replace a lot of depreciated capital every period. Instead, these countries must develop new ideas to increase the productivity of capital and labor.

Ideas have some important and unusual properties: They can be freely shared by an unlimited number of people and they do not depreciate with greater use. As economist Paul Romer emphasizes, ideas often produce more ideas, so growth may be in part self-sustaining. Thus, to better understand economic growth on the cutting edge, we must turn to the economics of ideas.

We will emphasize the following:

1. Ideas for increasing output are primarily researched, developed, and implemented by profit-seeking firms.

2. Ideas can be freely shared, but spillovers mean that ideas are underprovided.

3. Government has a role in improving the production of ideas.

4. The larger the market, the greater the incentive to research and develop new ideas.

Research and Development Is Investment for Profit

In the previous chapter, we emphasized that economic growth was not automatic, and we said that the factors of production do not fall from the sky like manna from heaven. In order to increase output, the factors of production must be produced and organized efficiently. All of this applies to ideas or technological knowledge just as much as to physical and human capital. Once again, incentives are the key. Economic growth requires institutions that encourage investment in physical capital, human capital, and *technological knowledge* (ideas).

In the United States, there are about 1.3 million scientists who research and develop new products, more than in any other country in the world, and most of these scientists and engineers, about 70%, work for private firms. (The ratios are broadly similar in other developed countries.)

Private firms invest in research and development when they expect to profit from their endeavors. Thus, the institutions we discussed in the last chapter—property rights, honest government, political stability, a dependable legal system, and competitive and open markets—also drive the generation of technological knowledge. When it comes to knowledge, other institutions are especially important. These institutions include a commercial setting that helps innovators to connect with capitalists, intellectual property rights such as copyrights and patents, and a high-quality educational system (we will turn to these issues shortly).

It's not just the number of scientists and engineers that matters for economic growth, as many other people come up with new ideas on their jobs, at school, or at home in their garages. Mark Zuckerberg, for example, wrote the software for Facebook as a Harvard student. Just as important, the business culture and institutions of the United States are good at connecting innovators with businesspeople and venture capitalists looking to fund or otherwise take a chance

CHECK YOURSELF

- What happens to investment and depreciation at the steady-state level of capital?
- In Figure 8.7, how much is consumed in the old steady state? How much is consumed in the new steady state?
- Do countries grow faster if they are far below their steady state or if they are close?
- Do countries with higher investment rates have lower or higher GDP per capita?

MRU

mru.org/econ-ideas

The Economics of Ideas

John Kay (1704–1780) invented the "flying shuttle" used in cotton weaving, the single most important invention launching the Industrial Revolution. Kay, however, was not rewarded for his efforts. His house was destroyed by "machine breakers," who were afraid that his invention would put them out of a job. Kay was forced to flee to France, where he died a poor man.

"The patent system . . . added the fuel of interest to the fire of genius." (1859)

Abraham Lincoln (1809–1865). Lincoln is the only U.S. president to have been granted a patent.

on new ideas. Ideas without backers are sterile. In the United States, potential innovators know that if they come up with a good idea, that idea has a good chance of making it to the market. The incentive to discover new ideas is correspondingly strong.

American culture also supports entrepreneurs. People like SpaceX founder Elon Musk, for example, are lauded in the popular media. Historically, however, entrepreneurs were often attacked as job destroyers, as the sidebar on eighteenth-century British entrepreneur John Kay illustrates.

Compared with most other countries, the United States has a very good cultural and commercial infrastructure for supporting new ideas and their conversion into usable commercial products.

Artistic innovation also requires many individuals with a diversity of viewpoints, many sources of support and employment, and businesspeople looking to profit from and support innovations. It's not surprising, therefore, that the United States is also a leader in artistic innovation. American movies, popular music, and dance have spread around the world. But the United States is not just good at popular culture: It is also a leader in abstract art, contemporary classical composition, avant-garde fiction and poetry, and modern dance, to name just a few fields. The lesson is that artistic, economic, and scientific innovations spring from similar sources.

A further significant part of the infrastructure for creativity is property rights. We now turn to one form of intellectual property rights, patents.

Patents Many ideas have peculiar properties that can make it difficult for private firms to recoup their investments in those ideas. In particular, new processes, products, and methods can be copied by competitors. The world's first smartphone was IBM's Simon Personal Communicator introduced in 1992. Ever heard of it? Probably not. Other firms quickly copied the idea and IBM lost out in the race to innovate. Imitators get the benefit of new ideas without having to pay the costs of development. Imitators, therefore, have lower costs so they tend to drive innovators out of the market unless some barrier prevents quick imitation.

Imitation often takes time and this does give innovators a chance to recoup their investments. The Apple iPad design, for example, has been copied by other firms, but until that happened, Apple was able to exploit monopoly power to sell millions of iPads for high profits. That is what makes Apple willing to invest in research and development in the first place and that is why the iPad exists. Firms often compete not by offering the same product at a lower price but by offering substantially new and better products.

Apple also relies on patents to protect its innovations. A patent is a government grant of temporary monopoly rights, typically 20 years from the date of filing. Patents delay imitation, thus allowing innovative firms a greater period of monopoly power. Apple, for example, has patented one of the most distinctive features of the iPad, the multipoint touchscreen. Apple's patent, filed in 2004, gives Apple the right to prevent other firms from copying its technology until 2024. Still, we may well see other similar devices in the near future if Apple licenses its technology to other firms. Furthermore, competitors are finding ways to produce the same effect using different methods—a majority of patented innovations are imitated within five years.

Nevertheless, Apple's patent gives it some monopoly power, and as you know if you studied microeconomics first, firms with monopoly power raise prices above competitive levels. Thus, patents increase the incentive to research and develop new products, but also increase monopoly power once the products are created. Monopoly power not only raises prices, it also means that innovations take longer to spread throughout the economy. The trade-off between creating incentives to research and develop new products while avoiding too much monopoly power is one of the trickiest in economic policy.[2]

Spillovers, and Why There Aren't Enough Good Ideas

Even when a firm has a patent on its technological innovation and other firms cannot imitate in a direct way, ideas tend to spill over and benefit other firms and consumers. A new pharmaceutical will be patented, for example, but the mechanism of action—how the pharmaceutical works—can be examined and broadly copied by other firms to develop their own pharmaceuticals.

Spillovers have good and bad aspects. The good aspect of imitation or spillovers is that ideas are **nonrival**. If you consume an apple, then I cannot consume the same apple. When it comes to eating an apple, it's either you or me—we can't share what we each consume so economists say that apples are rival. But ideas can be freely shared. You can use the Pythagorean theorem and I can use the very same theorem at the very same time. The Pythagorean theorem can be shared by all of humanity, which is why economists say that ideas are nonrival.

Since many ideas can be shared at low cost, they *should* be shared—that's the way to maximize the benefit from an idea. The spillover or diffusion of ideas throughout the world is thus a good thing. For instance, the idea of breeding and growing corn originated in ancient Mexico but now people grow corn all over the world. Spillovers, however, mean that the originator of an idea doesn't get all the benefits. And if the originator doesn't get enough of the benefits, ideas will be underprovided. For this reason, while economists know that idea spillovers are good, they also know that spillovers mean that too few good ideas are produced in the first place.

To understand why spillovers mean that ideas will be underprovided, think about why firms explore for oil. Answer: to make money. So what would happen to the amount of exploration if whenever a firm struck oil, other firms jumped in and drilled wells right next door? Clearly, the incentive to explore would decline if firms didn't have property rights to oil *fields.* Firms explore for ideas just as they explore for oil, and if other firms can set up right next door to exploit the same *field of ideas*, the incentive to explore will decline.

Figure 8.12 illustrates the argument in a diagram. A profit-maximizing firm invests in research and development (R&D) so long as the private marginal benefit is larger than the marginal cost. As a result, private investment occurs until point *a* in Figure 8.12. Spillovers, however, mean that the social benefit of R&D exceeds the private benefit, so that the optimal social investment is found where the marginal social benefit just equals the marginal cost at point *b*. Since the private benefit to R&D is less than the social benefit, private investment in R&D is less than ideal.

Government's Role in the Production of New Ideas

Can anything be done to increase the production of new ideas? We have already mentioned one important government policy that affects the production of new ideas, namely patents. Patents reduce spillovers and thus increase the

FIGURE 8.12

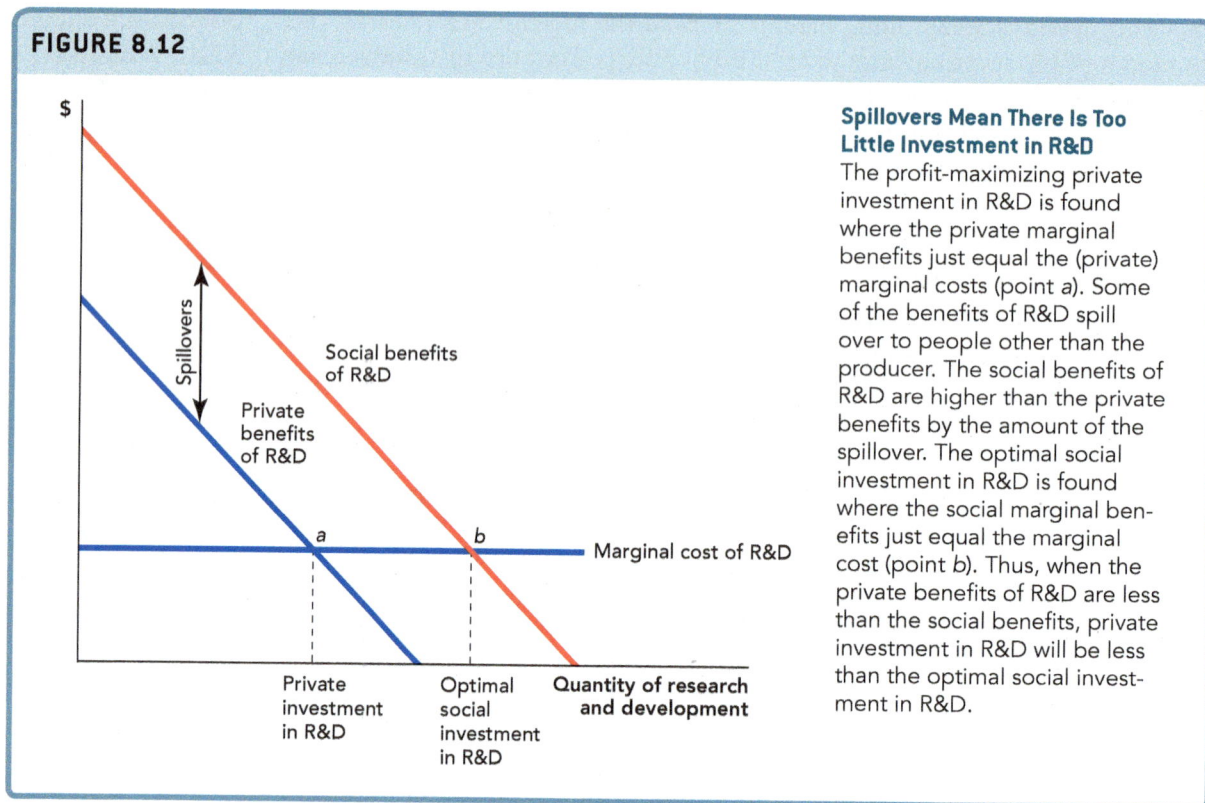

Spillovers Mean There Is Too Little Investment in R&D
The profit-maximizing private investment in R&D is found where the private marginal benefits just equal the (private) marginal costs (point *a*). Some of the benefits of R&D spill over to people other than the producer. The social benefits of R&D are higher than the private benefits by the amount of the spillover. The optimal social investment in R&D is found where the social marginal benefits just equal the marginal cost (point *b*). Thus, when the private benefits of R&D are less than the social benefits, private investment in R&D will be less than the optimal social investment in R&D.

incentive to produce new ideas, but they can also slow down the spread of new ideas. Prizes are another possibility. In 2008, for example, the U.S. Department of Energy offered $10 million to the first inventor to produce a new and more efficient light bulb. In 2011 Phillips claimed the prize with a 10-watt LED bulb that duplicated the light output of a 60-watt incandescent. One advantage of prizes is that the government doesn't have to decide in advance who can best solve a problem. And that's important because new ideas often come from unexpected places. Paying for innovation with a prize, rather than a patent, also means that the idea can spread more rapidly.

The government could also subsidize the production of new ideas. Returning to Figure 8.12, a subsidy or tax break to R&D expenditures, for example, will shift the (private) marginal cost of R&D curve down, thus increasing private investment.

The argument for government subsidies is strongest when the spillovers are largest. The modern world is founded on mathematics, physics, and molecular biology—basic ideas in these fields have many applications so spillovers can be large. But even if the social benefits to basic science are large, the private returns can be small. It's probably easier to make a million dollars producing pizza than it is to make a million dollars producing mathematical theorems. In fact, Thomas S. Monaghan made a billion dollars producing pizza (he's the founder of Domino's), while mathematicians Ron Rivest, Adi Shamir, and Leonard Adleman didn't make nearly so much on their RSA algorithm, even though their algorithm is used to encrypt data sent over the Internet and thus forms the backbone for all Internet commerce.

The large spillovers to basic science suggest a role for government subsidies to universities, especially the parts of universities that produce innovations and the basic science behind innovations. Perhaps most important, universities produce *scientists*. Most of the 1.3 million scientists who research and develop new products in the United States were trained in government-subsidized universities. Thus, subsidies to the hard sciences support the private development of new ideas and those initial subsidies are likely to pay for themselves many times over.

Market Size and Research and Development

Imagine that there are two diseases that if left untreated are equally deadly. One of the diseases is rare, the other one is common. If you had to choose, would you rather be afflicted with the rare disease or the common disease? Take a moment to think about this question because there is a right answer.

If you don't want to die, it's much better to have the common disease. The reason? The costs of developing drugs for rare and common diseases are about the same, but the revenues are greater when the disease is more common. Pharmaceutical companies concentrate on drugs for common diseases because larger markets mean more profits.

As a result, there are more drugs to treat common diseases than to treat rare diseases, and more drugs mean greater life expectancy. Patients diagnosed with rare diseases—those ranked at the bottom quarter in terms of how frequently they are diagnosed—are 45% more likely to die before age 55 than are patients diagnosed with more common diseases.[3]

Larger markets mean increased incentives to invest in research and development, more new drugs, and greater life expectancy. So imagine this: If China and India were as wealthy as the United States, the market for cancer drugs would be eight times larger than it is today.

China and India are not yet wealthy countries but what this thought experiment tells us is that *people in the United States benefit tremendously when other countries grow rich.*

Like pharmaceuticals, new computer chips, software, and chemicals also require large R&D expenditures. As India, China, and other countries, including the United States, become wealthier, companies will increase their worldwide R&D investments.

The Future of Economic Growth

Over the last 10,000 years, growth in per capita world GDP has been increasing. Growth in per capita GDP was approximately zero from the dawn of civilization to about 1500, increased to 0.08% a year between 1500 and 1760, doubled during the next hundred years, and increased even further during the nineteenth and twentieth centuries. Today, worldwide per capita GDP is growing by a little more than 3% per year.

Could economic growth become even faster? Yes. Let's take a look again at our measure of technological progress, A. We can summarize what we have said about the factors causing A to increase in a simple equation:

$$A(\text{ideas}) = \textbf{Population} \times \textbf{Incentives} \times \textbf{Ideas per hour}$$

In words, the number of new ideas is a function of the number of people, the incentives to innovate, and the number of ideas per hour that each person has. Of course, this equation is not meant to be exact—it's just a way of

CHECK YOURSELF

- What would happen to the incentive to produce new ideas if all countries imposed high tax rates on imports?
- What are spillovers and how do they affect the production of ideas?
- Some economists have proposed that the government offer large cash prizes for the discovery of cures for diseases like malaria that affect people in developing countries. What economic reasons might there be to support a prize for malaria research rather than, say, cancer research?

thinking about some of the key factors driving technological growth. So let's go through each of the factors and think about what they imply for the future of economic growth.

The number of people is increasing, which is good for idea generation. More important, the number of people whose job it is to produce new ideas is increasing. In all the world today, there are perhaps 6 million scientists and engineers, of which 1.3 million come from the United States. These 1.3 million represent about one-half of 1% of the U.S. population, a surprisingly small percentage. Yet for the world as a whole, the ratio of scientists and engineers to population is much lower.

Today, because much of the world is poor, thousands of potentially great scientists will spend most of their lives doing backbreaking work on a farm. If the world as a whole were as wealthy as the United States and could devote the same share of population to research and development as does the United States today, there would be more than five times as many scientists and engineers. Thus, as the world gets richer, more people will be producing ideas, and because of spillovers, these ideas will benefit everyone.

The incentives to innovate also appear to be increasing. Consumers are richer and the world is becoming one giant integrated market because of trade; each of these factors boosts the incentives to innovate.

The incentives to innovate also increase when innovators can profit from their investments without fear of expropriation. The worldwide improvement in institutions—that is, the movement toward property rights, honest government, political stability, and a dependable legal system—has been very positive for both innovation and economic growth.

We know the least about the last factor in the equation, the number of ideas per hour or how easy it is to come up with new ideas. In some fields, we are unlikely to ever know much more than we know now. For thousands of years, scientists periodically discovered new human organs, but the last new organ to be found was identified in 1880 (the parathyroid gland). Don't expect more breakthroughs in this field, no matter how hard we look. In some places and times, knowledge grows by leaps and bounds, and in others it stagnates. We don't always know why. In pharmaceuticals and cancer research it seems to take more and more research time to produce the same increase in life expectancy. The power of computers continues to grow but only because we throw more and more researchers at the problem. When the law of diminishing returns is applied to ideas in general as well as to capital, then economic growth will be much slower. There are at least two reasons, however, for thinking that diminishing returns is not the usual state of affairs.

First, many ideas make creating other ideas easier. Sadly, the authors of this book can remember the day when answering even simple questions like who won the 1969 World Series could not be answered without going to a library, consulting a card catalog (don't ask), looking for the appropriate book in the stacks, and then (if the book hadn't been checked out) finding the answer. Today, you can probably find the answer using Google on your cell phone faster than you can read this paragraph. (By the way, it was the New York Mets in one of the greatest upsets in baseball history.) We still have many new ideas, like Google Search and Artificial Intelligence, that are useful for creating even more ideas, so idea production might speed up rather than slow down.

The second reason to think that the number of ideas per hour is not yet strongly diminishing comes from one of the pioneers of the economics of

MRU
mru.org/ted-talk-ideas

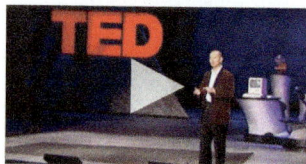

The Future of Economic Growth

ideas, Paul Romer. (Romer is not only a distinguished theorist of ideas, he is a first-class idea entrepreneur; he started Aplia, the online economics test bank and tutorial system that many of you use and that is a good example of an idea that makes learning new ideas easier.) Romer points out that ideas for production are like recipes and the number of potential recipes in the universe is unimaginably vast:

> The periodic table contains about a hundred different types of atoms, which means that the number of combinations made up of four different elements is about $100 \times 99 \times 98 \times 97 = 94,000,000$. A list of numbers like 6, 2, 1, 7 can represent the proportions for using the four elements in a recipe. To keep things simple, assume that the numbers in the list must lie between 1 and 10, that no fractions are allowed, and that the smallest number must always be 1. Then there are about 3,500 different sets of proportions for each choice of four elements, and $3,500 \times 94,000,000$ (or 330 billion) different recipes in total. If laboratories around the world evaluated 1,000 recipes each day, it would take nearly a million years to go through them all.[4]

True, many of the recipes are going to be like chicken liver ice cream (not that good), but the field of ideas that we can explore is so large that diminishing returns may not set in for a very long time.

Putting all this together, economic growth might be even faster in the future than it has been in the past. There are more scientists and engineers in the world today than ever before and their numbers are increasing both in absolute terms and as a percentage of the population. The incentives to invest in R&D are also increasing because of globalization and increased wealth in developing countries such as China and India. Better institutions and more secure property rights are spreading throughout the world.

We have some reasons to be optimistic about the future of economic growth but, of course, nothing is guaranteed. In the twentieth century, two world wars diverted the energy of two generations from production to destruction. When the wars ended, an iron curtain isolated billions of people from the rest of the world, reducing trade in goods and ideas—to everyone's detriment. World poverty meant that the United States and a few other countries shouldered the burden of advancing knowledge nearly alone. We must hope that this does not happen again.

Takeaway

The Solow model is governed by the iron logic of diminishing returns. When the capital stock is low, the marginal product of capital is high and capital accumulates, leading to economic growth. But as capital accumulates, its marginal product declines until per-period investment is just equal to depreciation, and growth stops.

Despite the simplicity of the Solow model, it tells us three important things about economic growth. First, countries that devote a larger share of output to investment will be wealthier. The Solow model doesn't tell us *why* some countries might devote a larger share of output to investment, but we know from the previous chapter that wealthy countries have institutions that promote investment in physical capital, human capital, and technological knowledge. We will also say more about how financial intermediaries channel saving into investment in the next chapter.

Second, growth will be faster the farther away a country's capital stock is from its steady-state value. This explains why the German and Japanese economies were able to catch up to other advanced economies after World War II, why countries that reform their institutions often grow very rapidly (growth miracles), and why poor countries grow faster than rich countries with similar levels of steady-state output.

Third, the Solow model tells us that capital accumulation cannot explain long-run economic growth. Holding other things constant, the marginal product of physical and human capital will eventually diminish, thereby leaving the economy in a zero-growth steady state. If we want to explain long-run economic growth, we must explain why other things are not held constant.

New ideas are the driving force behind long-run economic growth. Ideas, however, aren't like other goods: Ideas can be easily copied and ideas are nonrival. The fact that ideas can be easily copied means that the originator of a new idea won't receive all the benefits of that idea so the incentive to produce ideas will be too low. Governments can play a role in supporting the production of new ideas by protecting intellectual property and subsidizing the production of new ideas when spillovers are most likely to be present.

The non-rivalry of ideas, however, means that once an idea is created, we want it to be shared, which is a nice way of saying copied, as much as possible. There is thus a trade-off between providing appropriate incentives to produce new ideas and providing appropriate incentives to share new ideas.

An important lesson from the economics of ideas is that the larger the market, whether in terms of people or wealth, the greater the incentive to invest in research and development. Similarly, having more people and wealthier countries increases the number of people devoted to the production of new ideas. Thus, the increased wealth of many developing nations, the move to freer trade in global markets, and the spread of better institutions throughout the world are all encouraging for the future of economic growth.

CHAPTER REVIEW

Go online to practice with more examples of these types of problems, including live links to videos, data sources, and feedback.

▶ Problems with this icon relate to optional MRU videos.

KEY CONCEPTS

catching-up growth, p. 151

cutting-edge growth, p. 151

marginal product of capital, p. 153

steady state, p. 157

conditional convergence, p. 162

nonrival, p. 167

FACTS AND TOOLS

▶ 1. Which countries are likely to grow faster: countries doing "cutting-edge" growth or those doing "catching-up" growth?

▶ 2. When will people work harder to invent new ideas: when they can sell them to a market of 10,000 people or when they can sell them to a market of 1 billion? Does your answer tell us anything about whether it's good or bad from the U.S. point of view for China and India to become rich countries?

▶ 3. Many say that if people save too much, the economy will be hurt. They often refer to the fact that consumer spending is two-thirds of GDP to make this point. This is sometimes called the "paradox of thrift."

   a. In the Solow model, is there a paradox of thrift? In other words, is a high savings rate good or bad for a country's long-run economic performance?

b. What about in the real world? According to the data in Figure 8.8, is there a paradox of thrift?

4. Many people say that "the rich grow richer and the poor grow poorer." Is this what Figure 8.9 says about the countries in that graph? Did the rich countries grow more quickly or more slowly than the poor countries?

5. Compared with its fast growth today, is China's economy likely to grow more quickly or more slowly in the future?

6. What is more important for explaining the standard of living in the rich countries: capital or ideas?

7. According to Thomas Jefferson, how are ideas like flames? (Based on Alex Tabarrok's TED talk.)

8. What is a patent?

9. When will people work harder to invent new ideas: when they can patent those ideas for 1 year or when they can patent them for 10 years?

10. Which three countries on the list are good examples of "conditional convergence?"

China

Ireland

Argentina

North Korea

Greece

11. Let's keep track of a nation's capital stock for five years. Mordor starts off with 1,000 machines, and every year, 5% of the machines depreciate or wear out. Fortunately, the people in this land produce 75 machines per year, every year. The key equation for keeping track of capital is quite simple:

Next year's capital = This year's capital + Investment − Depreciation

Fill in the table.

Year	Capital	Depreciation	Investment
1	1,000	0.05 × 1,000	75
2	1,025		75
3			75
4			75
5			75

THINKING AND PROBLEM SOLVING

12. Consider the following three countries that produce GDP this way:

$$Y = 5\sqrt{K}$$

Ilia: $K = 100$ machines

Caplania: $K = 10,000$ machines

Hansonia: $K = 1,000,000$ machines

What will GDP (Y) be in these three countries? Hansonia has 10,000 times more machines than Ilia, so why isn't it 10,000 times more productive?

13. Consider the data in the previous question: If 10% of all machines become worthless every year (they depreciate, in other words), then how many machines will become worthless in these three countries this year? Are there any countries where the amount of depreciation is actually greater than GDP? (This question reminds you that "more machines mean more machines wearing out")

14. Of course, no country makes *only* investment goods like machines, equipment, and computers. They also make consumer goods. Let's consider a case where the countries in question 12 devote 25% of GDP to making investment goods (so γ, gamma, = 0.25). What is the amount of savings in these three countries? In which countries is *Investment < Depreciation*? When is *Investment > Depreciation*?

15. A drug company has $1 billion to spend on research and development. It has to decide on one of two projects:

a. Spend the money on a project to fight a new coronavirus, perhaps called COVID-20.

b. Spend the money on a project to fight a condition of red, itchy skin known as eczema.

The company expects both projects to be equally profitable, all things considered: Yes, project *a* is riskier (since COVID-20 may never cause a pandemic), but if the disease hits, there will be a worldwide market willing to pay a lot of money to cure the disease.

Then one day, before deciding between *a* and *b*, the drug company's CEO reads in the newspaper that the European Union and the United States will not honor patents in the event of a major pandemic. Instead, these governments will "break the patent" and just make the drug available everywhere for $1 per pill. The company will only get $1 per pill instead of the $100 or $200 per pill it had expected.

Given this new information about the possibility that governments will "break the patent," on which project is the company likely to spend its research and development money? (*Note*: In the wake of the deadly anthrax attacks of 2001, the U.S. government threatened to do just this with the patent for Cipro, the one antibiotic proven to cure the symptoms of anthrax infection.)

16. After World War II, a lot of France's capital stock was destroyed, but it had educated workers and a market-oriented economy. Do you think the war's destruction increased or decreased the marginal product of capital?

17. The Solow model isn't only useful for thinking about entire countries: As long as the production function runs into diminishing returns and your total stock of inputs constantly wears out, then the Solow model applies. Consider a professor's knowledge of economics. The more she learns about economics, the more she will forget (depreciation), but the more she knows, the more knowledge she can create (production). So eventually in steady state, she will know only a fixed amount about economics, but what she knows might change over time; some decades she might know a lot about the Federal Reserve, while other decades she might know a lot about the electricity market. In any case, knowledge fades away.

a. Apply the Solow model to a chef's skill at cooking.

b. Apply the Solow model to the size of a navy's fleet of ships.

c. Apply the Solow model to the speed of a cheetah, where the input is calories.

18. Many inventors decide that patents are a bad way to protect their intellectual property. Instead, they keep their ideas a secret. Trade secrets are actually quite common: The formula for Coca-Cola is a trade secret, as is Colonel Sander's secret recipe. What is one major strength of keeping a trade secret rather than applying for a patent? What is a major weakness inherent in going down the trade secret route?

19. Since ideas can sometimes be copied quite easily, many people think that we should put more effort into creating new ideas. Let's see if there are trade-offs to having more people creating new ideas. To keep things simple, let's assume that the growth rate of the economy depends on how many people search for ideas, whether in laboratories, or huddled over laptops in

coffee shops, or while listening to "Stairway to Heaven" at three in the morning. People either produce stuff or produce ideas. Here's how this economy works:

$Y_t = (1 - R) \times A_t L$ (GDP production function)

$A_{t+1} = (1 + R) \times A_t$ (Technology production function)

There are a total of L people in the society, and a fraction $(1 - R)$ of them work in factories and offices making stuff (remember, people working in offices help create output, too!), while the remaining fraction R try to come up with good ideas all day long. To keep the story simple, there are no diminishing returns.

a. What's the trade-off here? If 100% of the people work to make new ideas ($R = 1$), won't that create a prosperous world?

b. In this society, if people are willing to wait a long time for a reward, should they choose a large R or a small R?

c. Plot out GDP in this society for 5 years if A starts off at 100, L starts off at 100, and R is 10%.

Year	A	Y	Y/L
1	100	9,000	90
2	110		
3			
4			
5			

d. Plot out GDP in this society if the society instead chose $R = 20\%$.

20. In Facts and Tools question 2, we saw that big markets create a big *demand* for inventions. This is an example of what Adam Smith meant when he said that "the division of labor is limited by the extent of the market." Now let's look at how big markets impact the *supply* side of inventions. The big idea is quite simple: *More people means more ideas.*

a. In order to create new ideas, you need to have people trying to come up with new ideas. In 1800, there were approximately 300 million humans on the planet—roughly equal to today's U.S. population. If good ideas are "one in a million"—that is, if one person per year out of a million comes up with a world-shaking idea like contact lenses or James Brown's song "The Payback" or the video game Grand Theft Auto—how many great new ideas will occur in the world of 1800? How many will occur in a world of 6 billion people?

b. More realistically, people in the rich countries are most likely to invent earth-shaking ideas and share them with others. There's nothing special about people in rich countries, but they have the education and the laboratories and the Internet connections that will make it practical to invent and spread ideas. If only the top 20% of the earth's population is really in the running to create new ideas, how many new big ideas will come along each year in 1800 and today?

c. If half the population of India and China become rich enough to create new ideas (to simplify, assume populations of 1 billion each), and start coming up with big ideas at the same rate as the top 20%, how many big ideas will India and China alone create for the planet every year?

d. Many people think there are too many people on the planet. (As P. J. O'Rourke once wrote, many people's attitude toward global population is "Just enough of me, way too much of you.") Look at your answer from part b. If the world's population now gets cut in half from the current 6 billion, how many big ideas will come along each year?

21. According to economists Robert Barro and Xavier Sala-i-Martin, convergence isn't just for entire nations: It's also true for states and regions, as well. They looked at state-level GDP per capita in the United States in 1880, and then calculated how fast each state grew over the next 120 years. They found that convergence held almost exactly.

a. With this in mind, draw arrows to connect the GDP per capita data on the left with the long-term growth rates on the right.

GDP per Capita in 1880	Annual Growth Rate, 1880–2000
West: $8,500	1.6%
East: $6,300	1.7%
Midwest: $4,700	2.2%
South: $2,800	1.2%

b. Graph the data from part a in the following figure. Does this look like Figure 8.9's story about the OECD countries, or is it quite different?

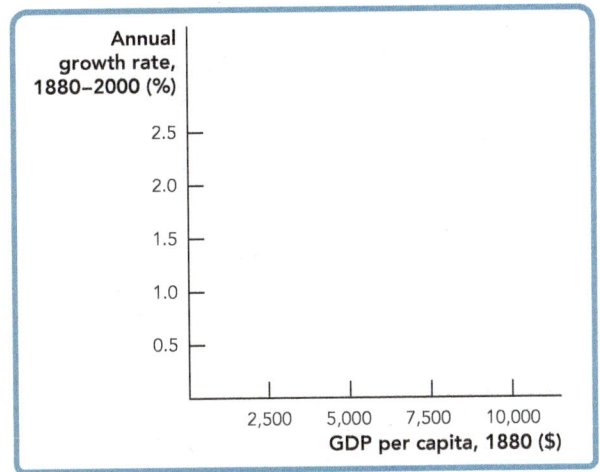

Note: Barro and Sala-i-Martin also found that convergence also held almost exactly for regions of Japan: The areas that were poorest in 1930 grew fastest over the next 70 years. Thus, it is difficult to find major evidence in favor of the commonsense idea that "the poor areas grow poorer."

22. Are we running out of ideas? Economist Paul Romer thinks not. To make things concrete, he notes that if we keep trying out different molecules to search for interesting compounds like new drugs, new plastics, etc., the universe may end from heat death before we finish our search. For example, if we try out 100 different atoms out of the 118 (and increasing!) elements in the Periodic Table, and only look at the 6-atom molecules, this is 100^6 different molecules. And, of course, many common molecules in our bodies consist of hundreds of atoms, so this only scratches the surface of interesting compounds.

a. If it takes a machine 1 minute to test out and fully analyze a new 6-atom molecule, how many years will it take for this one machine to test out all 100^6 molecules? (*Note:* Modern biochemists create computer simulations of molecules to analyze whether potential drugs are likely to work in the molecules that make up the human body, but this is only one narrow form of analysis.)

b. How many machines would it take to test out all of these molecules within 100 years?

c. What about all 10-atom molecules: How many years would it take for one machine to test all of these compounds at one per minute? If your computer can handle it, what about all 100-atom molecules, molecules vastly simpler than many proteins in your body?

CHALLENGES

23. Which country would you expect to have a higher rate of investment: a catching-up country or a cutting-edge country?

24. If the government of a poor catching-up country is trying to decide whether to encourage investment or encourage research and development, which of the two should it favor? (*Note:* In a world of trade-offs, you can't just say, "Both are important!")

25. The Solow model makes it quite easy to figure out how rich a country will be in its steady state. We already know that you're in a steady state when investment equals depreciation. In math, that's

$$\gamma Y = \delta K$$

Since $Y = \sqrt{K}$ in our simplest model, this means that $K = Y^2$:

$$\gamma Y = \delta Y^2$$

There are a lot of ways to solve this for Y—the easiest might just be to divide both sides by Y, and then put everything else on the other side. When you do this, you can learn how steady-state GDP depends on the savings rate and the depreciation rate. Here are a few questions:

a. Many say that if people save more, that's bad for the economy: They say that spending money on consumer goods keeps the money moving through the economy. Does this model say that?

b. Many people say that when machines and equipment get destroyed by bad weather or war, that makes the economy better off by encouraging businesses and families to spend money on new capital goods. Does this model say that?

26. Let's think about two countries, Frugal and Smart. In Frugal, people devote 50% of GDP to making new investment goods, so $\gamma = 0.5$, and their production function is $Y = \sqrt{K}$. In Smart, people devote 25% of GDP to making new investment goods, so $\gamma = 0.25$ and their production function is $Y = 2\sqrt{K}$. Both countries start off with $K = 100$.

a. What is the amount of investment in each country this year?

b. What is the amount of consumption (GDP − Investment, or $Y - I$) in each country this year?

c. Where would you rather be a citizen: Frugal or Smart?

27. Which of the following goods are nonrival?

Sunshine

An apple

A national park

A Mozart symphony

The idea of penicillin

A dose of penicillin

28. According to economist Michael Kremer, as human populations have grown over the last million years, so has the human population growth *rate*. This was true until the 1800s. How does Thinking and Problem Solving question 20 help explain why human populations grew more quickly despite the fact that there were more mouths to feed?

29. Use the Solow diagram to show the impact of a natural disaster that destroys half of a nation's capital stock.

a. Begin with a country in a steady state at $Y^{ss} = \sqrt{K^{ss}}$, and show the short-run effects of the natural disaster destroying half of the steady-state level of capital stock, K^{ss} on the Solow diagram.

b. If $K_1 = \frac{1}{2} K^{ss}$, will output fall by half so that output in period one following the shock is $K_1 = \frac{1}{2} Y^{ss}$? Explain why or why not.

c. What happens in this country in the immediate future and in the long run?

30. A small, less-developed country finds itself the recipient of a large amount of foreign direct investment that adds 50% to its current steady-state level of capital stock. This country seeks your advice about the long-term implications of that kind of help.

a. Assume this country begins in a steady-state condition at $Y^{ss} = \sqrt{K^{ss}}$, and show the short-run effects of a 50% increase in the steady-state level of capital stock such that $K_1 = \frac{3}{2} K^{ss}$ on the Solow diagram.

b. What will the long-term effects of this increase in the capital stock be for this country?

c. What potential problems should this country consider during the adjustment period described in part b?

d. What must this country do in order to gain any permanent long-term benefits from this increase in its capital stock?

e. *Bonus*: Can you think of any examples like these in real life?

31. Change the production function used in the chapter to reflect the contribution of labor in the production process. As with capital, labor also has diminishing returns, so let $Y = \sqrt{KL}$ Now suppose that immigration reform leads to an increase in this country's labor force.

a. Begin with a country in a steady-state condition at $Y^{ss} = \sqrt{K^{ss}L}$, and let K^{ss} equal 400 and $L = 100$. What is the steady-state level of output?

b. Show the short-run effects of a 21% increase in the amount of labor available for use in this country such that $L_1 = 1.21L$ on the Solow diagram.

c. What are the algebraic and numeric outcomes for the short-run level of output, that is, Y^{ss} in terms of K^{ss} and L?

d. Show the new steady-state level of output on the diagram.

e. Demonstrate whether this country will be able to produce 21% more output with a 21% increase in the labor supply. Show this result algebraically. As illustrated in Challenge question 25, you will need to use the steady-state condition $\gamma Y = \delta K$ to show this result.

f. Derive output per worker in the initial steady state (use Y_0^{ss} from part a and divide by the labor force); output per worker in the short run (use Y_1^{ss} from part c and divide by the new labor force); and output per worker in the long run (use Y_1^{ss} from part e and divide by the new labor force).

g. Are the citizens of this country made worse or better off in the long run by a new immigration policy such as this; that is, how does the new long-run level of output per worker compare with the initial level of output per worker?

h. *Bonus:* What is the value for the new steady-state level of capital stock in this country?

WORK IT OUT

For interactive, step-by-step help in solving this problem, go online.

In the Solow model, you've seen that as the total stock of capital equipment gets larger, the number of machines wearing out grows as well. Often, most investment ends up just replacing worn-out machines. This is actually true in the United States and other rich countries. According to the U.S. National Income and Product Accounts (the official U.S. GDP measures), about 12% of total GDP just goes toward replacing worn-out machines and computers and construction equipment.

a. In the Solow model, if the depreciation rate increases, what happens to the steady-state capital level and output level? Answer in words and by using a diagram such as Figure 8.4. (Bonus: If the depreciation rate increases from 0.02 to 0.03, what is the new steady-state level of capital and output?)

b. If the Solow model explains an important part of the real world, should countries hope for high depreciation rates or low depreciation rates? How does this square with the observation that when machines wear out, that "creates jobs" in the manufacturing industries?

▶ **MRU** VIDEOS

Introduction to the Solow Model

mru.org/solow-model

Problems: **1, 23**

Physical Capital and Diminishing Returns

mru.org/solow-physical-capital

Problems: **3, 11–13, 19, 24, 30**

The Solow Model and the Steady State

mru.org/solow-steady-state

Problems: **4, 5, 14, 16, 26, 30, 31**

Human Capital and Conditional Convergence

mru.org/solow-human-capital

Problems: **10, 17, 21, 24, 31**

The Solow Model and Ideas

mru.org/solow-ideas

Problems: **2, 6, 17, 25, 29**

The Economics of Ideas

mru.org/econ-ideas

Problems: **17, 19**

Patents, Prizes, and Subsidies

mru.org/patents

Problems: **8, 9, 15, 18, 27**

The Idea Equation

mru.org/idea-equation

Problems: **20, 22**

The Future of Economic Growth

mru.org/ted-talk-ideas

Problems: **7, 20, 24**

CHAPTER 8 APPENDIX

Excellent Growth

Using a spreadsheet, you can easily explore the Solow model and duplicate all the graphs in this chapter. First, label column A "Capital K" and put a 1 in cell A2. Second, you can create an increasing series by inputting the formula "$= A2 + 1$" in cell A3 and copying and pasting that formula into cells A4 to, say, A500. Your spreadsheet should look like Figure A8.1.

In column B, create a series for Output. Remember that $Y = \sqrt{K}$ so in cell B2, input the formula "$= SQRT(A2)$" and then copy and paste that formula into B3 to B500, as in Figure A8.2.

Now create the headings Investment, Depreciation, Investment Share, and Depreciation Rate in columns C to F, as in Figure A8.3.

In cell E2, put the investment share, 0.3, used in the text, and in cell F2, put the rate of depreciation that we used, 0.02.

In cell C2, which is highlighted, we want to input the formula for investment, which is γY where γ is the investment share. We could input "$= 0.3 \times B2$" into C2 but we would like to be able to easily adjust the investment share and see what happens, so we will input "$= \$E\$2 \times B2$". The $\$E\$2$ says take the investment share from cell E2, and when we copy and paste this formula, it *always* uses cell E2 (not E3, E4, etc.). Copy and paste cell C2 into C3 to C500.

FIGURE A8.1

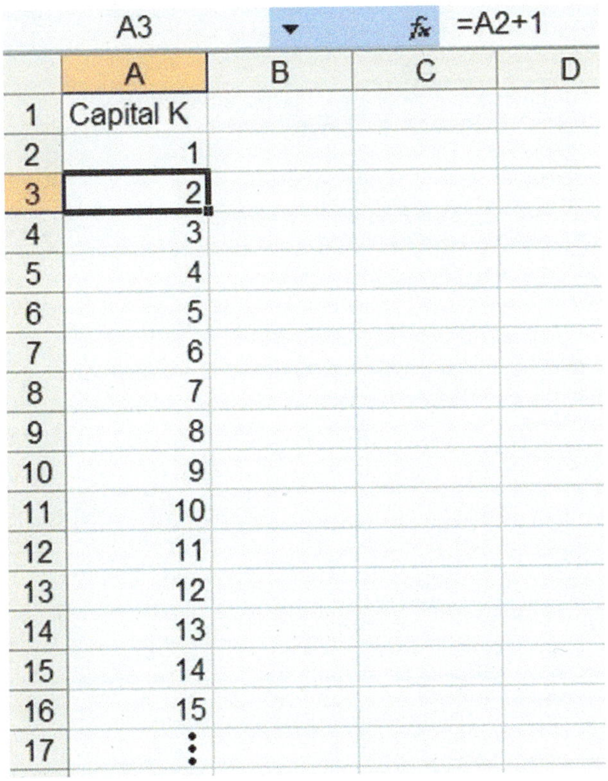

	A3	▼	f_x =A2+1	
	A	B	C	D
1	Capital K			
2	1			
3	2			
4	3			
5	4			
6	5			
7	6			
8	7			
9	8			
10	9			
11	10			
12	11			
13	12			
14	13			
15	14			
16	15			
17	⋮			

FIGURE A8.2

	B2	▼	f_x	=SQRT(A2)	
	A	B	C	D	
1	Capital K	Output			
2	1	1.00			
3	2	1.41			
4	3	1.73			
5	4	2.00			
6	5	2.24			
7	6	2.45			
8	7	2.65			
9	8	2.83			
10	9	3.00			
11	10	3.16			
12	11	3.32			
13	12	3.46			
14	13	3.61			
15	14	3.74			
16	15	3.87			
17	⋮	⋮			

FIGURE A8.3

	C2	▼	f_x	=$E$2*B2		
	A	B	C	D	E	F
1	Capital K	Output	Investment	Depreciation	Investment Share γ	Depreciation Rate δ
2	1	1.00	0.30	0.02	0.3	0.02
3	2	1.41	0.42	0.04		
4	3	1.73	0.52	0.06		
5	4	2.00	0.60	0.08		
6	5	2.24	0.67	0.10		
7	6	2.45	0.73	0.12		
8	7	2.65	0.79	0.14		
9	8	2.83	0.85	0.16		
10	9	3.00	0.90	0.18		
11	10	3.16	0.95	0.20		
12	11	3.32	0.99	0.22		
13	12	3.46	1.04	0.24		
14	13	3.61	1.08	0.26		
15	14	3.74	1.12	0.28		
16	15	3.87	1.16	0.30		
17	⋮	⋮	⋮	⋮		

FIGURE A8.4

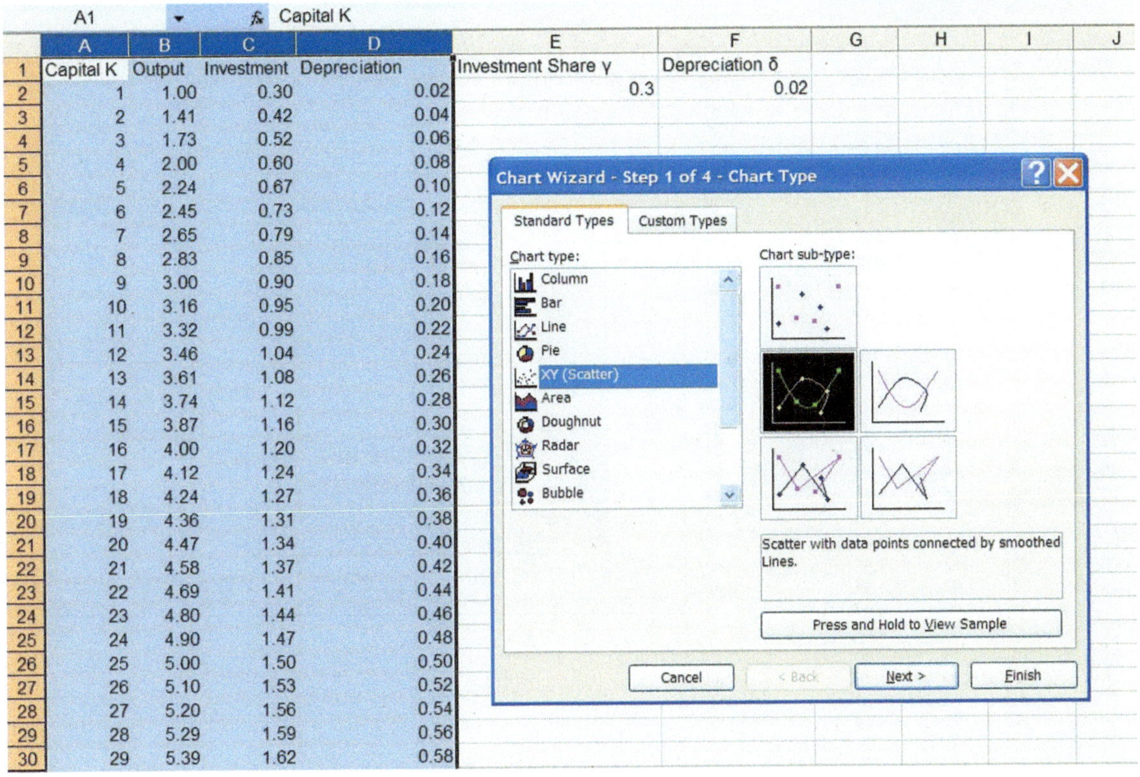

	A	B	C	D	E	F	G	H	I	J
	Capital K	Output	Investment	Depreciation	Investment Share γ	Depreciation δ				
1										
2	1	1.00	0.30	0.02	0.3	0.02				
3	2	1.41	0.42	0.04						
4	3	1.73	0.52	0.06						
5	4	2.00	0.60	0.08						
6	5	2.24	0.67	0.10						
7	6	2.45	0.73	0.12						
8	7	2.65	0.79	0.14						
9	8	2.83	0.85	0.16						
10	9	3.00	0.90	0.18						
11	10	3.16	0.95	0.20						
12	11	3.32	0.99	0.22						
13	12	3.46	1.04	0.24						
14	13	3.61	1.08	0.26						
15	14	3.74	1.12	0.28						
16	15	3.87	1.16	0.30						
17	16	4.00	1.20	0.32						
18	17	4.12	1.24	0.34						
19	18	4.24	1.27	0.36						
20	19	4.36	1.31	0.38						
21	20	4.47	1.34	0.40						
22	21	4.58	1.37	0.42						
23	22	4.69	1.41	0.44						
24	23	4.80	1.44	0.46						
25	24	4.90	1.47	0.48						
26	25	5.00	1.50	0.50						
27	26	5.10	1.53	0.52						
28	27	5.20	1.56	0.54						
29	28	5.29	1.59	0.56						
30	29	5.39	1.62	0.58						

A1   *fx*   Capital K

Chart Wizard - Step 1 of 4 - Chart Type

Standard Types | Custom Types

Chart type:
- Column
- Bar
- Line
- Pie
- XY (Scatter)
- Area
- Doughnut
- Radar
- Surface
- Bubble

Chart sub-type:

Scatter with data points connected by smoothed Lines.

Press and Hold to View Sample

Cancel | < Back | Next > | Finish

Depreciation is just δK where δ is the depreciation rate. As with investment, we might want to alter this parameter, so into cell D2 we will input "= $F$2 × A2".

That's it! To duplicate the graph in Figure 8.4, for example, just highlight columns A, B, C, and D, click the Chart icon (you can also click Chart in the Insert menu), choose XY (Scatter) and the highlighted subtype, and then click on finish. (In Excel 2007 click Insert and then Scatter in the Chart submenu to do the same thing.) See Figure A8.4.

The result is as in Figure A8.5.

If you want to see what happens if the investment share increases to 0.4, as in Figure 8.7 in the chapter, just change cell E2 to 0.4 and the graph will change automatically. You can make other adjustments as well. One thing to watch for is that with parameters too different from the ones we have given, the equilibrium capital stock may be greater than 500. So if you want to see the full picture, you will need to extend the rows even further.

FIGURE A8.5

	A	B	C	D	E	F	G	H	I	J
1	Capital K	Output	Investment	Depreciation	Investment Share γ	Depreciation δ				
2	1	1.00	0.30	0.02	0.3	0.02				
3	2	1.41	0.42	0.04						
4	3	1.73	0.52	0.06						
5	4	2.00	0.60	0.08						
6	5	2.24	0.67	0.10						
7	6	2.45	0.73	0.12						
8	7	2.65	0.79	0.14						
9	8	2.83	0.85	0.16						
10	9	3.00	0.90	0.18						
11	10	3.16	0.95	0.20						
12	11	3.32	0.99	0.22						
13	12	3.46	1.04	0.24						
14	13	3.61	1.08	0.26						
15	14	3.74	1.12	0.28						
16	15	3.87	1.16	0.30						
17	16	4.00	1.20	0.32						
18	17	4.12	1.24	0.34						
19	18	4.24	1.27	0.36						
20	19	4.36	1.31	0.38						
21	20	4.47	1.34	0.40						
22	21	4.58	1.37	0.42						
23	22	4.69	1.41	0.44						
24	23	4.80	1.44	0.46						
25	24	4.90	1.47	0.48						
26	25	5.00	1.50	0.50						
27	26	5.10	1.53	0.52						
28	27	5.20	1.56	0.54						
29	28	5.29	1.59	0.56						
30	29	5.39	1.62	0.58						

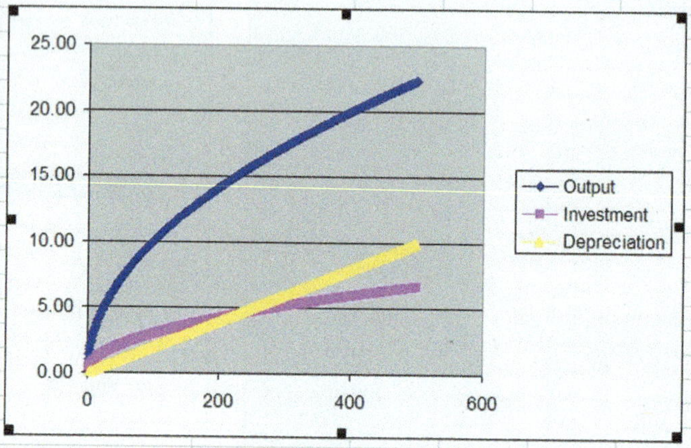

Chapter 8 Appendix Question

1. Use the instructions in the appendix to set up the Solow model in Excel with the Investment Share γ equal to 0.3 and with the Depreciation Rate δ equal to 0.02. Both numbers are just what we used in the chapter. Now increase the Investment Share to 0.36.

   a. What is the new level of steady-state capital? (Remember, the level of steady-state capital is where *Investment = Depreciation*.)

   b. At the new steady level of capital, what is the level of output *Y*?

   Now change the Investment Share back to 0.3 and this time increase the Depreciation Rate to 0.025.

   c. What is the new level of steady-state capital?

   d. At the steady-state level of capital, what is the level of output *Y*?

   e. Fill in the blanks with your conclusions:

   An increase in the investment share _____ the steady-state level of capital and output.

   An increase in the depreciation rate _____ the steady-state level of capital and output.

9

Saving, Investment, and the Financial System

The world's financial system was shaken to its core when on September 15, 2008, the investment bank Lehman Brothers filed for bankruptcy. The Lehman bankruptcy was by far the largest in history. To give you some context, when it went bankrupt Lehman had assets worth $691 billion; when GM went bankrupt several months later it had assets worth just $91 billion. Lehman's bankruptcy triggered stock market crashes around the world. Over the next several weeks the Dow Jones Industrial Average fell by 25%, the British FTSE 100 Index fell by 15%, and the Brazilian BOVESPA fell by 10%, to give just a few examples. The Lehman collapse marked the beginning of the recession of 2008–2009, the most serious recession in the United States since the Great Depression. The Lehman bankruptcy shook the financial world, not simply because it was large but because Lehman Brothers was an important financial intermediary, an institution that works to transform savings into investments.

Lehman Brothers failed because it had lost billions on buying and betting on mortgage securities. So had many other banks and financial institutions. When Lehman failed, many people wondered: Who is next? No one wanted to lend money to a firm that might soon go bankrupt. As a result, credit dried up for firms in many sectors, throwing the American economy and indeed the world economy into what was the scariest moment in many decades. This episode is sometimes called the collapse of the "shadow banking system," a term that we will examine in more detail later in this chapter, but we might also call it the collapse of the financial intermediaries.

This chapter is about savers and borrowers and some of the financial intermediaries—banks, bond markets, and stock exchanges—that bridge the gap between savers and borrowers, as we illustrate in Figure 9.1. We have opened the chapter with a scary story about what can happen when financial intermediaries fail. Fortunately, the collapse of Lehman was an extreme episode and there are plenty of other cases in which intermediation works quite smoothly, to the benefit of all parties involved. Recall from the previous two chapters that savings are necessary for capital accumulation, and the more capital an economy can invest, the greater is GDP per capita. So transforming savings into

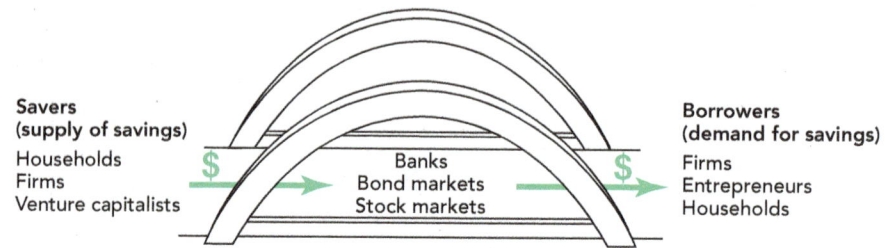

FIGURE 9.1

Savers
(supply of savings)

Households
Firms
Venture capitalists

$

Banks
Bond markets
Stock markets

$

Borrowers
(demand for savings)

Firms
Entrepreneurs
Households

Financial Institutions Bridge the Gap between Savers and Borrowers

The collapse of Lehman Brothers shook the world financial system.

Saving is income that is not spent on consumption goods.

Investment is the purchase of new capital goods.

investment is important. More generally, connecting savers and borrowers increases the gains from trade and smooths the process of economic growth.

Before proceeding, let's make it clear what we mean by the words **saving** and **investment**. Saving is income that is not spent on consumption goods. Investment is the purchase of new capital, things like tools, machinery, and factories. It's important to see that the way economists define investment is not the same as the way a stockbroker defines investment. If Starbucks buys new espresso machines for its stores, that's investment. If John buys stock in Starbucks, that is not investment in the economic sense but merely a transfer of ownership rights of already existing capital (see Chapter 10 for a treatment of how individuals should allocate their funds for their personal "investments"). Most of the trading on stock exchanges is thus not investment in the economic sense because it simply transfers ownership of a stock from one person to another. From an economic point of view, investment requires a purchase of new capital.

Ok, let's see how savings are mobilized and transformed into investment. We will be using the economist's tools in trade—supply and demand—and we'll start with the supply of savings. This is important material in its own right and it also supplies building blocks for understanding banks, bank failures, and what went wrong in the global financial crisis of 2007–2008.

The Supply of Savings

We begin with the left side of Figure 9.1, the supply of savings. Economists have a good but imperfect understanding of what determines the supply of savings. Here are four of the major factors: smoothing consumption, impatience, marketing and psychological factors, and interest rates.

Individuals Want to Smooth Consumption

If you consumed what you earned every year, your consumption over time might look like Path A in Figure 9.2. Along Path A, consumption is equal to income. Consumption is high during your working years, but after retirement consumption drops precipitously—as a result, once you retire and your income falls, you must

FIGURE 9.2

Savings Help to Smooth Consumption If workers spend their entire income every year, their consumption over time will follow Path A. Along Path A, consumption drops tremendously at retirement. By saving during the working years and dissaving during the retirement years, workers can smooth their consumption so that it looks more like Path B.

sell the nice car and give up the fancy lifestyle just to scrape by. Most people would prefer consumption Path B. Along Path B, consumption is less than income during the working years because you save for retirement. But when retirement comes, consumption is greater than income as you spend your savings, or "dissave."

Economists say that Path B is "smoother" than Path A. The desire to smooth consumption over time is a reason to save and, as we will discuss shortly, also a reason to borrow.

The consumption-smoothing theory of saving can tell us something important about AIDS, Africa, and economic growth. Remember from previous chapters that savings are necessary to finance the capital accumulation that generates high standards of living. If there are no savings, investment dries up, economic growth declines, and the standard of living falls.

Now consider that AIDS has dramatically reduced life expectancy in southern Africa. What is your prediction about savings rates? Imagine that you expected to die in a few years—would you save much? Probably not. Similarly, many poorer Africans don't save much because, sadly, they expect to die young.[1] This gives rise to a vicious cycle. The decline in life expectancy caused by AIDS reduces saving rates, which in turn reduces economic growth and the standard of living, and that makes it more difficult to combat diseases like AIDS.

Fluctuations in income are another reason why people save. Some workers, such as salespeople, writers, and home builders, have incomes that fluctuate from year to year. Most workers could have unexpected health problems or they could find themselves unemployed and so they also fear that their income might fluctuate. By saving in the good years, workers can build a cushion of wealth to draw from in the bad years, thereby smoothing their consumption across all years.

Individuals Are Impatient

Another reason why people save, or fail to save, is their level of impatience. Most individuals prefer to consume now rather than later, so saving is not always easy. This is what economists call **time preference**. Time preference

mru.org/save-borrow

Saving and Borrowing

Time preference is the desire to have goods and services sooner rather than later (all else being equal).

reflects the fact that today feels more real than tomorrow. Some people are very impatient; others less so. The more impatient a person, the more likely that person's savings rate will be low.

Impatience is reflected not just in savings but in any economic situation where people must compare costs and benefits over time. The cost of a college degree, for example, comes well before the benefit. To get a college degree, you must pay for tuition and books and, most important, you must give up the income that you could earn from a job, all right now. The benefits of a college degree are large—a typical college graduate will earn nearly twice as much as a typical high school graduate—but the benefits are all in the future. An impatient person will weigh the up-front costs highly and discount the future benefits. Impatient people are unlikely to go to college.

Crime is another economic activity with immediate benefits and future costs so it's not surprising that criminals tend to be impatient people. Similarly, heroin addicts, alcoholics, and smokers all tend to discount the future more heavily than nonaddicts.

Impatience depends, in part, on circumstances and, in part, on the person. In one fascinating study, four-year-old children were offered one marshmallow now or two if they could wait for the tester to return. Many years later, the children were evaluated again—the children who had waited were less impulsive and had higher grades than the children who had not waited.[2]

https://www.ted.com/talks/joachim_de_posada_don_t_eat_the_marshmallow

The Marshmallow Test

Marketing and Psychological Factors

Marketing matters, even for savings. Often individuals save more if saving is presented as the natural or default alternative. In one study, economists studied retirement savings plans. Some employers automatically enrolled all new employees in a retirement savings plan, leaving the employees the choice to opt out, whereas others required employees to request such an account, in effect asking them to opt in. In the businesses that used automatic enrollment, the savings plan participation rate was 25% higher than in the businesses in which employees needed to request a retirement account.

The default also mattered for how much was saved. In one firm, the default savings rate was 3% of salary. More than a quarter of the workers chose that as their savings rate, despite an employer guarantee of a dollar-for-dollar match on contributions of up to 6% of salary. Later, the company switched to a 6% default savings rate; in that setting, hardly any new workers chose the 3% savings contribution rate even though they could have switched with just a phone call.[3]

It's quite surprising how some simple psychological changes, combined with effective marketing and promotion, can change how much people save for their retirement. Behavioral economics, a new and growing field within economics, combines economics, psychology, and neurology to study how people make decisions and how they can be helped to overcome biases in decision making.

The Interest Rate

The quantity of savings also depends on the interest rate, namely how much savers are paid to save. If the interest rate is 5% per year, then $100 saved today returns $105 a year from now. If the interest rate is 10% per year, then $100 saved today returns $110 a year from now. All else being equal, higher interest rates usually call forth more savings.* Figure 9.3 shows the supply curve for savings. The vertical axis of Figure 9.3 measures the interest rate. The horizontal axis measures savings in dollars. In this example, an interest rate of 5% generates total savings of $200 billion and an interest rate of 10% generates total savings of $280 billion.

You might wonder why the supply curve for savings has the interest rate on the vertical axis while other supply curves have had price on the vertical axis. In fact, interest rates are just a convenient way of expressing the price of savings. An interest rate of 5%, for example, means that the saver will be paid $5 (in one year) for every $100 saved. Thus, we could say that when savers are paid a price of $5 per $100 saved, the quantity of savings is $200 billion. It's a bit easier, however, to think in terms of interest rates.

The bottom line is that the interest rate is a market price and it has the same properties of market prices that we discussed in the introductory chapters of this book.

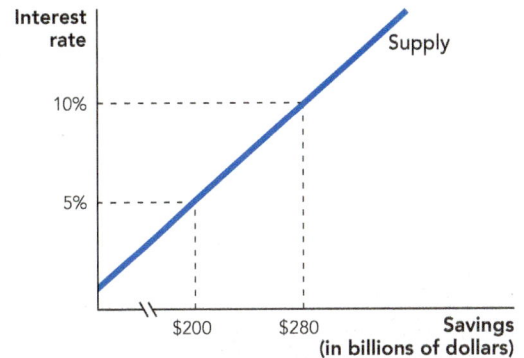

FIGURE 9.3

The Higher the Interest Rate, the Greater the Quantity Saved At an interest rate of 5%, $200 billion is saved. At an interest rate of 10%, $280 billion is saved.

The Demand to Borrow

Why do people borrow? People borrow to smooth their consumption path and especially to finance large investments. Let's look at each of these reasons for borrowing.

Individuals Want to Smooth Consumption

Just as people save in order to smooth consumption, one reason people borrow is to smooth consumption. Many young people, for example, borrow so that they can invest in their education. If they had to pay their tuition expenses all at once, many students would have to sell their car or eat nothing but beans and oatmeal for a year. But if tuition payments can be made over many years, as borrowing makes possible, the sacrifices are spread out and become less painful. A student who can borrow can move some of the sacrifices into future periods when the (now former) student has a job and a regular income. Student borrowing is thus another example of how credit markets let people smooth their consumption over time.

The "lifecycle" theory of savings, pioneered by Nobel Laureate Franco Modigliani, puts the demand to borrow and save together. The lifecycle theory is illustrated in Figure 9.4. Income starts out low during the college years and in the early work years. To finance college and to buy a first home, people borrow so their consumption is higher than their income. As workers enter their prime earning years, they save to pay off their college debt and mortgage

CHECK YOURSELF

- Examining Figure 9.1, what is the crucial function that financial institutions perform?
- Financial advisors have warned that increased life expectancy means that many people have not saved enough for their retirement. If true, what will the consumption path of these people look like as they reach their retirement years? Will this consumption path be smooth?
- Can you think of the other factors that might generate a demand to save? (*Hint:* Apart from retirement, what other factors could cause income to be volatile?)

---

* In principle, it is possible for the supply curve for savings to be negatively sloped. For instance, if an individual wanted exactly $100 in one year's time, then at an interest rate of 10%, they would need to save $90.91, but at an interest rate of 20%, they would need to save only $83.33. Thus, an increase in the interest rate could reduce savings. The evidence, however, indicates that individual savings rates typically respond positively to higher interest rates. In addition, higher U.S. interest rates also encourage lenders in other countries to move some of their savings to U.S. markets. Both forces mean that the supply curve for savings is upwardly sloped in most circumstances.

FIGURE 9.4

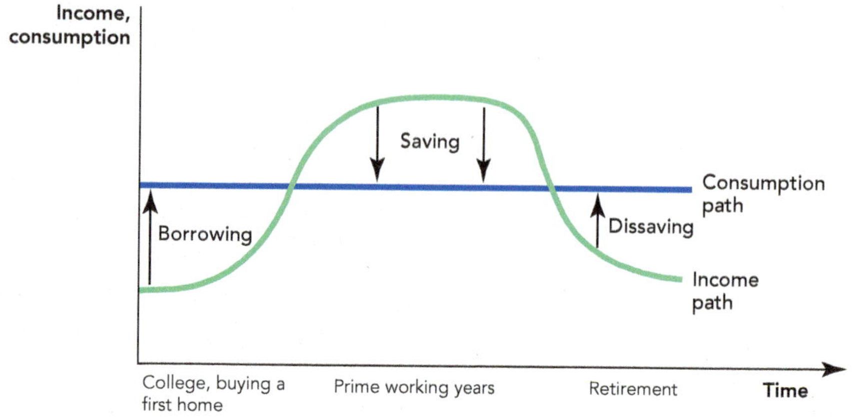

Income, consumption

Saving

Borrowing

Dissaving

Consumption path

Income path

College, buying a first home

Prime working years

Retirement

Time

The Lifecycle Theory of Savings
By borrowing, saving, and dissaving, workers can smooth their consumption path over a lifetime, improving their overall satisfaction. And remember, lifecycle savings isn't just a theory, it's also good advice!

and they prepare for retirement—during this time period consumption is less than income. As people get older and retire, consumption is once again above income as dissaving (i.e., using up savings) occurs. Overall, borrowing, saving, and dissaving help people to smooth out their consumption path over time—although few people would have a consumption path as smooth as the one we have drawn here!

Governments also borrow for reasons much like consumers. Governments may borrow, for example, to finance unusually large expenditures such as those required to pay for a war, or to pay for large investments such as the interstate highway system. We discuss government taxes, spending, and borrowing at greater length in Chapter 17.

Borrowing Is Necessary to Finance Large Investments

Businesses also borrow extensively. Many new businesses can't get under way at all without borrowing. Often the people with the best business ideas are not the people with the most savings, so people with good ideas must borrow funds to start their careers as entrepreneurs.

Fred Smith, the legendary entrepreneur, first laid out the idea for FedEx in an undergraduate paper he had to write for an economics class. Smith's idea, overnight delivery of packages using a hub and spoke system, was great but the problem was that he couldn't start small. To be successful, Smith needed to cover a good part of the country from day 1 and he didn't have enough of his own money to build an entire network. Smith began FedEx with 16 planes covering 25 cities using money he borrowed and also by selling part ownership of FedEx to venture capitalists, investors willing to accept risk in return for a stake in future profits. FedEx, of course, has been a huge success—it changed the way America does business and made Smith a very wealthy man. By the way, Smith's grade on his paper: C!

More generally, businesses borrow to finance large projects. The costs of developing an apartment building are all up front; the revenues don't start flowing until the building is completed and the tenants have moved in. In fact, it may take many years before the revenues fully cover all the up-front costs. If a developer had to wait until he personally had enough funds to pay the up-front costs, he might be able to develop just one or two buildings in his lifetime. By borrowing, developers are able to invest now and develop many more buildings.

The examples of borrowing that we have given share a common theme. A student who can't borrow may not be able to get an education even though the education would be a good investment. A government that can't borrow may not be able to invest in an interstate highway system even though the highway system would pay for itself many times over. A builder who can't borrow may not be able to build an apartment building even though it would be a profitable investment. Thus, borrowing plays an important role in the economy—the ability to borrow greatly increases the ability to invest and, as shown in the previous two chapters, higher investment increases the standard of living and the rate of economic growth.

In Shakespeare's *Hamlet*, Polonius advises, "Neither a borrower nor a lender be." But people forget that Polonius was a fool.

The Interest Rate

Of course, the quantity of funds that people want to borrow also depends on the cost of the loan, or the interest rate. Businesses, for example, borrow when they expect that the return on their investment will be greater than the cost of the loan. Thus, if the interest rate is 10%, businesses will borrow only if they expect that their investment will return *more* than 10%. If the interest rate is 5%, then businesses will only borrow if they expect that their investment will return *more* than 5%. Since a larger number of investments will return *more* than 5% than will return *more* than 10%, the demand to borrow follows the law of demand: The lower the interest rate, the greater the quantity of funds demanded for investment as well as for other purposes.

In Figure 9.5, $190 billion is demanded when the interest rate is 10% and $300 billion is demanded when the interest rate is 5%. But how is the interest rate determined? That is the subject of the next section.

CHECK YOURSELF
- Under the lifecycle theory, when is an individual's savings likely to be at its peak?
- If interest rates fall from 7% to 5% (and all else is the same), what happens to the number of people buying homes? Starting businesses?

FIGURE 9.5

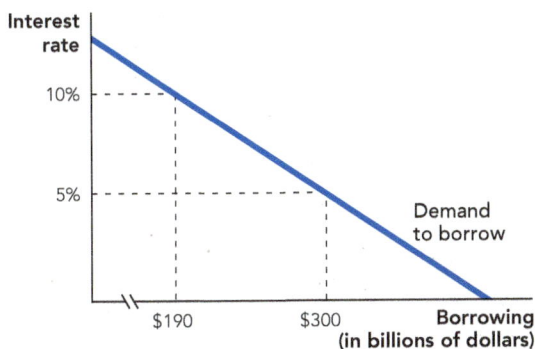

The Lower the Interest Rate, the Greater the Quantity of Funds Demanded At an interest rate of 10%, borrowers would like to borrow $190 billion. At an interest rate of 5%, borrowers would like to borrow more, $300 billion.

Equilibrium in the Market for Loanable Funds

The **market for loanable funds** occurs when suppliers of loanable funds (savers) trade with demanders of loanable funds (borrowers). Trading in the market for loanable funds determines the equilibrium interest rate.

Now that we have covered the supply of savings and the demand to borrow, we can put them together to find an equilibrium in what economists call the **market for loanable funds**. In Figure 9.6, the equilibrium interest rate is 8% and the equilibrium quantity of savings is $250 billion. Notice that in equilibrium, the quantity of funds supplied equals the quantity of funds demanded.

The interest rate adjusts to equalize savings and borrowing in the same way and for the same reasons that the price of oil adjusts to balance the supply and demand for oil. If the interest rate were higher than 8%, the quantity of savings supplied would exceed the quantity of savings demanded, creating a surplus of savings. With a surplus of savings, suppliers will bid the interest rate down as they compete to lend. If the interest rate were lower than 8%, the quantity of savings demanded would exceed the quantity of savings supplied, a shortage. With a shortage of savings, demanders would bid the interest rate up as they competed to borrow. (See Chapter 4 for a review.)

Shifts in Supply and Demand

Changes in economic conditions will shift the supply or demand curve and change the equilibrium interest rate and quantity of savings. Consider an economy in which the citizens become less impatient, and more willing to save for the future. These shifts occurred in South Korea in the 1960s and 1970s, once

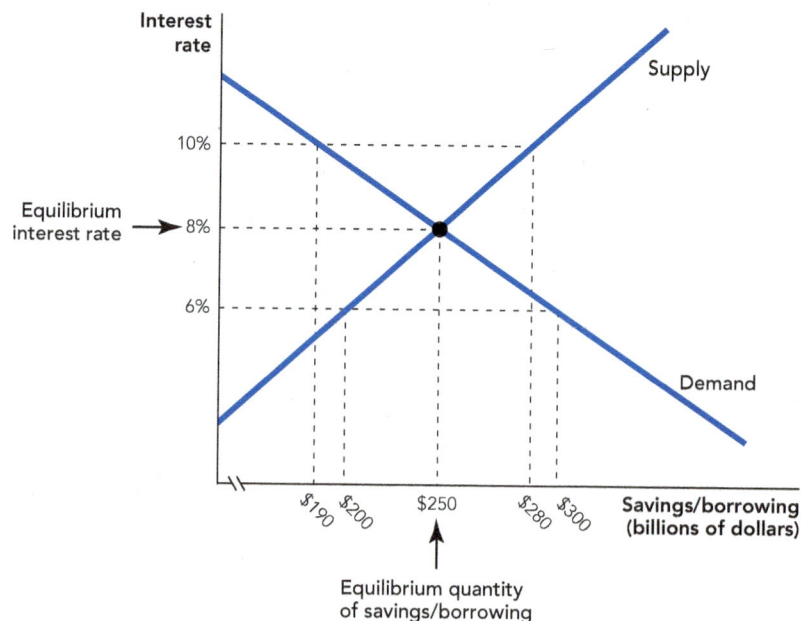

FIGURE 9.6

Equilibrium in the Market for Loanable Funds Determines the Interest Rate and the Quantity of Loanable Funds At an interest rate greater than 8%, there is a surplus of savings and the interest rate is bid down. At an interest rate less than 8%, there is a shortage of savings and the interest rate is bid up. At an interest rate of 8%, the quantity of savings supplied ($250 billion) is exactly equal to the quantity of savings demanded.

many Korean citizens realized they could copy some aspects of the Japanese economic miracle. Across East Asia more generally, growing life spans and fewer children to support (and fewer children to be supported by, in old age) led to a regional savings boom. An increase in the supply of savings is shown by shifting the supply curve to the right and down (indicating more savings at any interest rate or, equivalently, a willingness to save any given amount in return for a lower interest rate).

In Figure 9.7, an increase in the supply of savings causes the equilibrium interest rate to fall from 8% to 6% and the quantity of savings to increase from $250 billion to $300 billion.

What did this shift in savings mean for South Korea? In 1960, Korea was among the poorest countries in the world but today it is a fully developed nation. South Korea's increased savings were plowed into investment and, as we know from our discussion of the Solow model in the previous chapter, one of the key drivers of economic growth is a high rate of investment and capital accumulation.

Of course, a decrease in the supply of savings is shown in the opposite manner, by shifting the supply curve to the left and up.

Sometimes investors become less optimistic, which decreases the demand to invest and borrow. For instance, during a recession many entrepreneurs get scared about the future and they are reluctant to invest. Projects that look good to investors when the economy is booming may look unprofitable when the economy is in the doldrums. The decrease in investment demand can itself help to spread and prolong the recession, as we discuss at greater length in Chapter 14. In Figure 9.8, a decrease in investment demand reduces the interest rate from 8% to 6% and the quantity of savings from $250 billion to $190 billion.

Sometimes, to counteract the decrease in investment demand during a recession, a government offers a temporary investment tax credit. An investment tax credit gives firms that invest in plants and equipment a tax break. The tax credit is usually temporary to encourage firms to invest quickly, when the recession is still in full force. The tax credit means that projects that were unprofitable without the

FIGURE 9.7

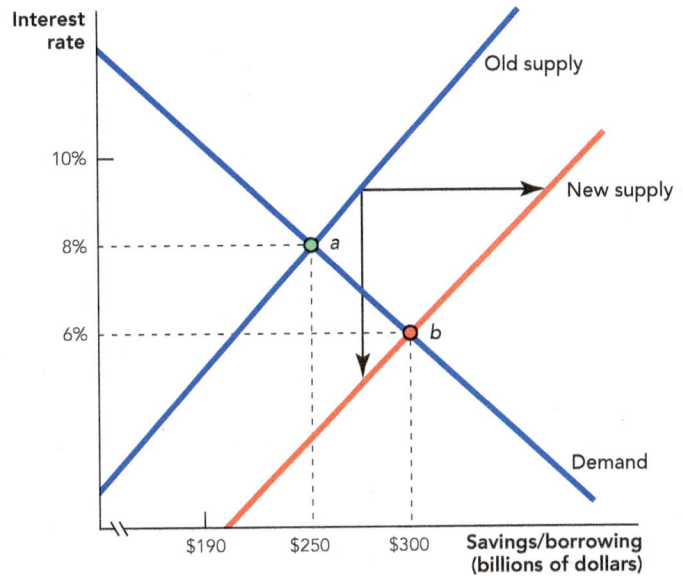

An Increase in the Supply of Savings Increases Savings and Reduces the Interest Rate In the initial equilibrium at point *a*, the interest rate is 8% and the quantity of savings is $250 billion. An increased willingness to save shifts the supply curve to the right and down, shifting the equilibrium to point *b* where the interest rate is 6% and the quantity of savings is $300 billion.

FIGURE 9.8

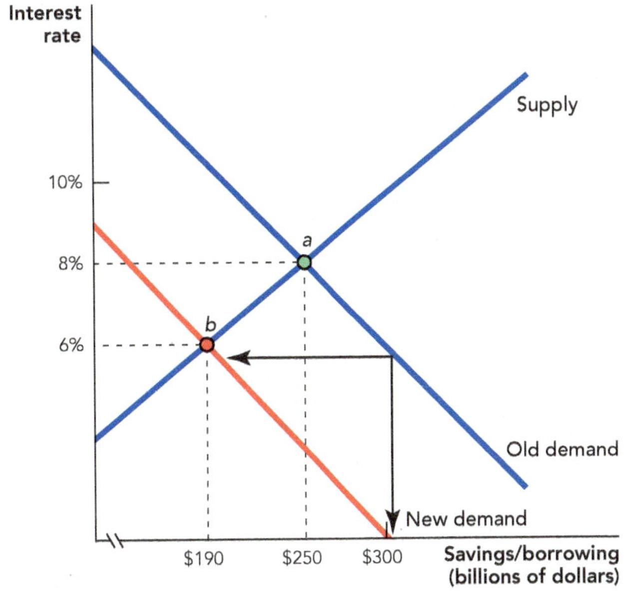

A Decrease in Investment Demand Decreases Savings and the Interest Rate In the initial equilibrium at point *a*, the interest rate is 8% and the quantity of savings is $250 billion. A decreased willingness to invest shifts the demand curve to the left and down, shifting equilibrium to point *b* where the interest rate is 6% and the quantity of savings is $190 billion.

FIGURE 9.9

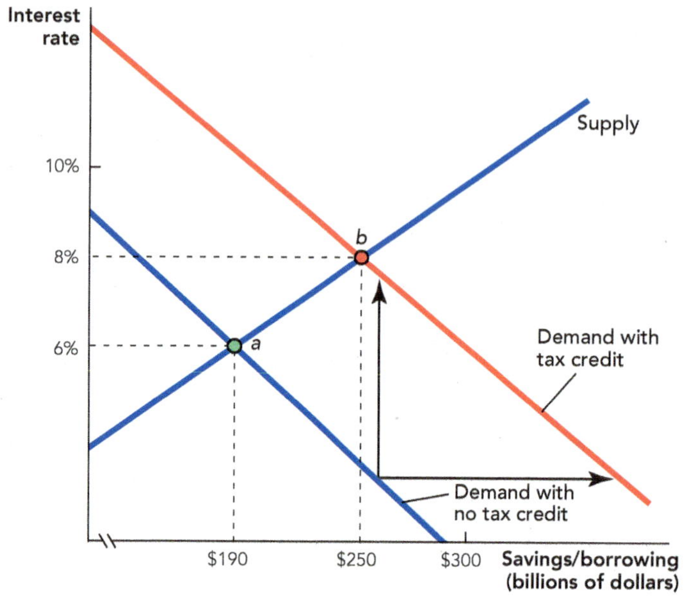

An Investment Tax Credit Increases Investment Demand, Increasing the Quantity of Savings and the Interest Rate In the initial equilibrium at point *a*, the interest rate is 6% and the quantity of savings is $190 billion. An investment tax credit increases the willingness to invest, shifting the demand curve up and to the right, moving the equilibrium to point *b* where the interest rate is 8% and the quantity of savings is $250 billion.

CHECK YOURSELF

- How will greater patience shift the supply of savings and change the interest rate and quantity of savings?
- How will an increase in investment demand change the equilibrium interest rate and quantity of savings?

Financial intermediaries such as banks, bond markets, and stock markets reduce the costs of moving savings from savers to borrowers and investors.

credit are profitable with the credit, so at any given interest rate firms are willing to invest more when a tax credit is available. In other words, the demand to borrow funds shifts to the right (and up), as shown in Figure 9.9.

The Role of Intermediaries: Banks, Bonds, and Stock Markets

Equilibrium in the market for loanable funds does not come about automatically. Savers move their capital, sometimes around the world, to find the highest returns. Entrepreneurs invest time and energy to find the right investments and the right loans. Equilibrium is brought about with the assistance of **financial intermediaries** such as banks, bond markets, and stock markets.

Financial intermediaries reduce the costs of moving savings from savers to borrowers and help mobilize savings toward productive uses. At its core, a financial intermediary is an institution that helps to bring about the equilibrium in Figure 9.6 and to direct resources to more highly valued uses.

Banks

In their role as financial intermediaries, banks receive savings from many individuals, pay them interest, and then loan these funds to borrowers, charging them interest. Banks earn profit by charging more for their loans than they pay for the savings. To earn this money, they must provide useful "middleman" services by evaluating investments and spreading risk.

Imagine that you, as a bank depositor, had to decide which companies were worth lending money to. Is this guy Fred Smith with his FedEx idea a genius or a kook? Banks don't always get it right, but by specializing in loan evaluation, they have a better idea than most of us of which business ideas make sense.

When banks specialize, individual savers don't have to evaluate which factories ought to be built or which businesses deserve to be supported.

Even if individuals could evaluate business ideas, it would be wasteful if every saver spent time evaluating the same business. Imagine that a business needs a million dollar loan. One thousand savers are each willing to lend the business $1,000. If each saver spent a day evaluating the quality of the business, that would be 999 wasted days of effort. It makes more sense for the lenders to appoint a single person to evaluate the business on behalf of all of them. That's exactly what a bank does. Banks coordinate lenders and minimize information costs. Banks are thus an important example of the benefits of specialization and the division of labor.

Banks also spread risk. If Fred Smith, or some other borrower, defaults on his loan, banks spread that loss across the many lenders who deposit money in the bank. This avoids the risk that you have lent Fred Smith $1,000 and suddenly are out the entire sum. It's less risky and no less profitable to lend one thousand firms $1 each than to lend one firm $1,000, so the spreading of risk encourages greater lending and investment.

Banks also play a role in the payments system. Money deposited in a bank can be drawn on with a check or debit card or via the ATM. We discuss banks and the payment system at greater length in our chapter on the Federal Reserve System.

Overall, banks make our lives simpler. We open our accounts, deposit our money, receive our interest payments, and write our checks; at the same time we are participating in the process of economic growth because the bank oversees a process by which our savings are turned into productive investments.

The Bond Market

Instead of borrowing from a bank, well-known corporations can borrow directly from the public. Your local pizza restaurant borrows from a bank, or perhaps even from relatives, because restaurants are a risky business and the finances of that company are difficult for outside investors to evaluate. But when it comes to IBM or Toyota, investors can more easily find information about the firm and so they are willing to bypass the bank as an intermediary and lend to the company directly.

> A **bond** is a sophisticated IOU that documents who owes how much and when payment must be made.

When a member of the public lends money to a corporation, the corporation acknowledges its debt by issuing a **bond**. *A bond is an IOU.* The bond contract lists how much is owed to the bond's owner and when payment must be made. In some cases, all the money is owed on a single day (the day of maturity); in other cases, periodic payments, called coupon payments, must be made in addition to a final payment.

The New York Central and Hudson River Railroad Company borrowed money in 1897 for which they issued bonds, one of which is pictured on the right. The bond is an IOU that promises the Central will pay the owner $1,000 in 1997. In addition, every six months until 1997, the Central promised to pay the owner $17.50. You can see from the picture why the periodic payments are called "coupon payments": The coupons are on the right of the bond and can be clipped and sent to the issuer of the bond to receive payment.

Central's bond illustrates one of the advantages of bond finance—large sums of money can be raised now and invested in long-lived assets such as railroad track. The money can then be paid back over a long period of time, in the case of the Central over a 100-year period.

Alex Tabarrok

A 100-year bond issued by the New York Central and Hudson River Railroad Company in 1897 The bond is an IOU that promised the owner $1,000 in 1997 and $17.50 every six months until that time.

All bonds involve a risk that when the payments come due, the borrower will not be able to pay; this is called "default risk." The Central, for example, eventually defaulted when it went bankrupt, but it did pay its coupons until 1970. Major bond issues are graded by agencies like Moody's and Standard and Poor's. AAA, for example, is the highest grade issued by Standard and Poor's; this grade indicates, according to the rating agencies, that the bond is very likely to be paid. Grades range all the way from AAA to D when a firm is in default. Bonds rated less than BBB- are sometimes called "junk bonds." It's important to remember that risk can never be perfectly quantified and the rating agencies can be wrong—a point we will return to later in this chapter when we discuss the financial crisis of 2007–2008.

If a risky company wishes to borrow money, it has to promise a higher rate of interest because lenders will demand to be compensated for a greater risk of default. Why lend to a risky firm unless you have some prospect of earning higher returns?

Thus, the marketplace grades the risks of major investments and charges interest rates accordingly. In 2016, Berkshire Hathaway, the investment company managed by Warren Buffett, was still a very profitable company. In early 2016, it borrowed $9 billion from the bond market and paid a rate just above that offered to the U.S. government, an extraordinary reflection of its perceived financial soundness. Elsewhere, in the United Kingdom, the soccer team Manchester United was borrowing money at about 9% for a seven-year bond; apparently their players and managers aren't as good!

Can you think of one reason why interest rates on home loans are almost always lower than interest rates on vacation loans? The bank can repossess the house but not the vacation! The house is a form of **collateral**, something of value that by agreement becomes the property of the lender if the borrower defaults on the loan. Thus, the market for loanable funds is really a broad spectrum of markets; the interest rates differ depending on the borrower, repayment time, amount of the loan, type of collateral, and many other features of the loan.

Greater risk can reduce the supply of funds to the market as a whole. If lenders expect a recession, for example, they may become concerned that many firms will go bankrupt and default on their debt. A lender who was willing to lend at 8% when they thought the risk was low will demand a higher return if the lender believes the risk of default has increased significantly.

Governments borrow money as well. As of 2016, the U.S. government owed about $14.4 trillion dollars to private borrowers (individuals, firms, and governments other than the U.S. federal government). When the government borrows a lot of money, private consumption and investment can be **crowded out**. Imagine, for example, that the government borrows $100 billion to cover a budget deficit. In Figure 9.10, the demand curve for loanable funds shifts to the right by $100 billion, increasing the interest rate from 7% to 9%. The higher interest rate has two effects. First, it draws an additional $50 billion of savings into the market so total savings increase from $200 billion to $250 billion. Since greater savings mean less consumption, we can also say that consumption is reduced by $50 billion. Second, the higher interest rate means that some investments and other projects are no longer profitable, so at a higher interest rate, private borrowing falls. In Figure 9.10, we show private borrowing falling by $50 billion. Thus, the $100 billion necessary to cover the government's budget deficit comes from a combination of reduced consumption and reduced private investment and other private borrowing.

Collateral is something of value that by agreement becomes the property of the lender if the borrower defaults.

Crowding out is the decrease in private consumption and investment that occurs when government borrows more.

FIGURE 9.10

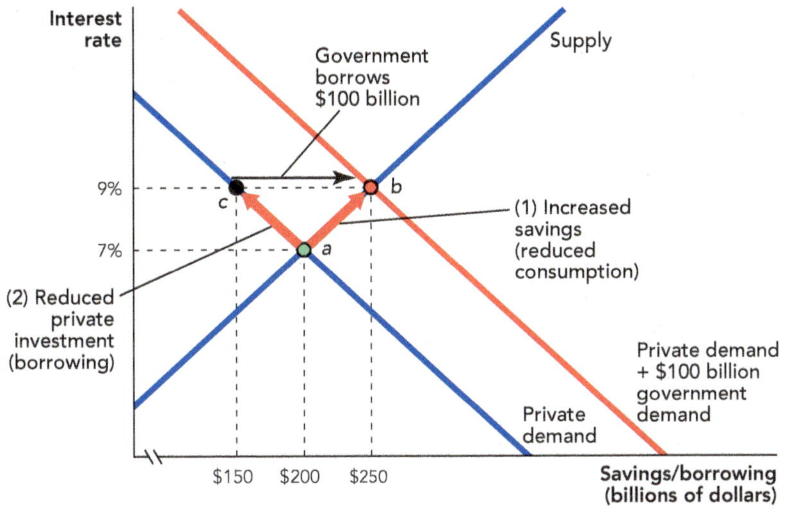

An Increase in Government Borrowing Crowds Out Private Consumption and Investment When the government borrows, it shifts the demand curve to the right, moving the equilibrium from point *a* to point *b*. To reach the new equilibrium at point *b*, two things happen: (1) The higher interest rate draws forth more savings, which means that private consumption falls; and (2) the higher interest rate reduces the demand to borrow and invest. Thus, when the government borrows more, some of the increased borrowing is financed by reduced consumption and some by reduced investment.

We will return to the issues of crowding out, government debt, and deficits in Chapters 17 and 18.

When the U.S. government borrows, it issues a variety of different bonds. U.S. Treasury bonds or T-bonds are 30-year bonds that pay interest every 6 months. T-notes are bonds with maturities ranging from 2 to 10 years that also pay interest every 6 months. T-bills are bonds with maturities of a few days to 26 weeks that pay only at maturity. A bond that pays only at maturity is also called a zero-coupon bond or a discount bond since these bonds sell at a discount to their face value.

Treasury securities are desirable for many investors because they are easy to buy and sell and the U.S. government is unlikely to default on its payments. In general, short-term U.S. government securities tend to be the safest assets, and very short-term bonds, called commercial paper, issued by very large corporations tend to be safe as well. In addition, Treasury securities, especially T-bills, are important in monetary policy; the Federal Reserve buys and sells Treasury securities on a daily basis to influence the money supply (more on this in Chapter 16).

Bond Prices and Interest Rates It's often convenient to express the price of a bond in terms of an interest rate; this is easiest to do with a zero-coupon bond. Suppose, for example, that a bond with very little risk exists that will pay $1,000 in one year's time and that this bond is currently selling for $950. If you were to buy this bond today and hold it until maturity, you would earn $50 ($1,000 − $950), or a rate of return of 5.26% = $\frac{\$1,000 - \$950}{\$950} \times 100$. Thus, every zero-coupon bond has an implied rate of return that can be calculated by subtracting the price from the value at maturity, often called the face value, and then dividing by the price:

$$\text{Rate of return for a zero-coupon bond} = \frac{\text{Face value} - \text{Price}}{\text{Price}} \times 100$$

Sellers of bonds must compete to attract lenders, who compare the implied rate of return on bonds with the rate of return on other assets. Imagine that the interest rate on say a savings account at a bank increases to 10%. Would you buy a bond that pays 5.26%? Would anyone? Of course not. So if the interest rate rises to 10%, what must happen to the price of this bond? The price must fall. In fact, if the interest rate rises to 10%, the price of the bond must fall to $909. Why? Because at a price of $909, the rate of return on the bond is $10\% = \frac{\$1,000-\$909}{\$909} \times 100$. Thus, at a price of $909, sellers of bonds will be able to compete with banks, who are paying 10% on savings accounts. At a higher price they won't find any buyers.

Our simple bond pricing example tells us two important things. First, equally risky assets must have the same rate of return. If they didn't, no one would buy the asset with the lower rate of return and the price of that asset would fall until the rate of return was competitive with other investments. This is called an **arbitrage** principle and we discuss it at greater length in the appendix to this chapter.

The second important lesson is that interest rates and bond prices move in opposite directions. When interest rates go up, bond prices fall. When interest rates go down, bond prices rise. We will be referring to this principle several times throughout the textbook so do study the principle and make a note of it:

■ **Interest rates and bond prices move in opposite directions.**

The inverse relationship between bond prices and interest rates tells us that in addition to default risk, people who buy bonds also face interest rate risk. For instance, perhaps a bond was issued in 2003 at an interest rate of 7%. If interest rates for comparable investments later rise to 9%, having bought a bond yielding 7% was in retrospect a mistake. If, instead, comparable interest rates were to fall to 3%, the bond purchase worked out for the better. The buyer locked in a 7% return when other rates of return were falling to 3%. In other words, bond buyers are making bets that interest rates will fall (bond prices will rise), or at least they are hoping that interest rates will fall. And similarly, bond sellers are betting or hoping that interest rates will rise, which means bond prices will—do you remember?—fall. Again, for more on the relationship between bond prices and interest rates, see the chapter appendix.

The Stock Market

Just as businesses fund their activities by taking out bank loans and selling bonds, they also issue shares of stock. **Stocks** are shares of ownership in a corporation. Owners have a claim to the firm's profits, but remember that profit is revenue minus costs. In other words, profit is what is left over *after* everyone else—creditors, bond holders, suppliers, and employees—have been paid. If profits are high, shareholders benefit. They benefit directly if the firm pays out its profits in dividends or indirectly if the firm reinvests its profits in a way that increases the value of the stock. But if profits are low or negative, shareholders suffer losses.

Stocks are traded on organized markets called stock exchanges. The New York Stock Exchange (NYSE) is the largest in the world. When new stocks are issued, that is called an **initial public offering** or an IPO. An IPO is the first time a stock is sold to the public.

You'll recall from the beginning of this chapter that simply buying and selling existing shares of stock does *not* increase net investment in the economy. But when a firm sells *new* shares to the public, it typically uses the proceeds to fund investment, that is, to buy new capital goods. In addition, the possibility of offering equity or ownership in a firm opens the door to many business

Arbitrage, the buying and selling of equally risky assets, ensures that equally risky assets earn equal returns.

A **stock** or a share is a certificate of ownership in a corporation.

An **initial public offering (IPO)** is the first time a corporation sells stock to the public in order to raise capital.

ventures that might never get off the ground, or might not be able to expand rapidly.

Consider Google. Today Google is a household word, but when the company began in September 1998, it was headquartered in a garage. Yet in August 2004, Google founders Sergei Brin and Larry Page sold $1.67 billion worth of stock in an IPO. The money helped Google to fund new investments and pay for research and development. In addition, Google's IPO turned the founders and the early investors into millionaires and billionaires. This big payoff was a reward for creating the company and making the early and risky investments that were necessary to get Google off the ground. Stock markets help people with great ideas become rich and that encourages innovation. It is no accident that the United States—one of the most innovative countries in the world—also has the best developed stock and capital markets.

Selling part of Google to the public also let the founders diversify. If someday another search service bests Google, Brin and Page will not become paupers. This added safety also encourages innovation. People who come up with new ideas know that their wealth will not be locked into one firm.

See Chapter 10 for more details on stock markets. At this point, the key idea is that stock markets encourage investment and growth.

What Happens When Intermediation Fails?

Economic growth cannot occur without savings and those savings must be processed and intermediated through banks, bond markets, stock markets, and so on. Countries without these institutions have smaller markets for loans, use their savings less effectively, and make fewer good investments.[4] But why do some countries have poorly developed banking and financial systems?

The bridge between savers and borrowers can be broken in many ways, including insecure property rights, inflation and controls on interest rates, politicized lending, and massive bank failures and panics. These problems can break the bridge by (1) reducing the supply of savings, (2) raising the cost of intermediation, and (3) reducing the effectiveness of lending. Figure 9.11 illustrates the main ideas.

CHECK YOURSELF

- What is the primary role of financial intermediaries?
- If your $1,000 corporate bond pays you $60 in interest every year and the interest rate falls to 4%, does the price of the bond rise or fall? What happens if the interest rate rises to 8%?
- Why does an IPO increase net investment in the economy but your purchase of 200 shares of IBM stock does not increase investment?

FIGURE 9.11

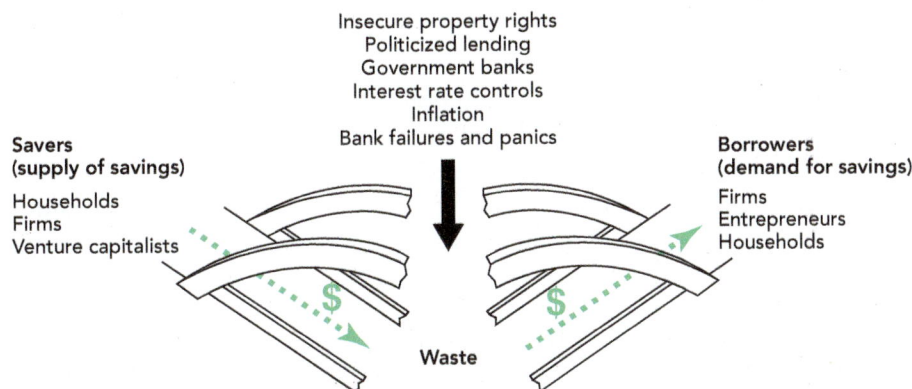

Breaking the Bridge

Insecure Property Rights

Consider, for example, the supply of savings. The expected return on savings depends on more than just the posted rate of interest at the bank. Some governments do not offer secure property rights to savers. That is, saved funds are not immune from later confiscation, freezes, or other restrictions.

During its financial crisis beginning in December 2001, for example, the Argentine government partially froze bank accounts for a year. Many of the banks subsequently went under, which meant that Argentine citizens lost their bank-based savings. This event was not a complete surprise. The Argentine government had a history of freezing bank accounts, such as during 1982 and 1989. Other countries in the region, such as Brazil in 1990, had also frozen bank accounts. Obviously, this repeated pattern means that Argentines and Brazilians save less than they otherwise might wish to. Why save when those funds are simply being put up for grabs? Ana, a 40-year-old teacher from Argentina, kept her savings in dollars in her house and then exchanged them for pesos to pay her bills. She said, "You just can't put your money in banks here."[5] Ana is right, but unlike money in the bank, which can be lent out to fund investment, money under a mattress does not contribute to economic growth.

If individuals expect that contracts will be broken, they will be reluctant to invest in stock markets as well. For instance, the Russian government often does not respect the rights of minority shareholders and at times it has confiscated or restricted the value of their shareholdings. The result is that many foreign investors are unwilling to put money into Russian ventures. They simply do not trust the Russian government, nor do they believe that Russian courts will enforce contracts impartially.

Law is one side of the equation, but custom and informal trust are another. In a healthy economy, shareholders expect that managers are interested in building their long-run reputations, rather than ripping off the company at every possible opportunity. When managers look only to short-run gains, it is hard to run a business enterprise, since investors will not entrust managers with the control of resources. Systems of monitoring and accounting, no matter how well developed, cannot overcome high levels of mistrust. This is a common problem in developing countries around the world but the Enron, WorldCom, and Madoff scandals demonstrate that the United States is also not immune to such problems. Trust is an important asset throughout the world.

Controls on Interest Rates

Price controls on interest rates also cause the loanable funds market to malfunction. Consider a maximum ceiling on the interest rate that can be charged on a loan. Sometimes economists call these ceilings "usury laws"; usury laws date back to medieval times and earlier. Today most American states have usury laws, although often they have loopholes (they don't stop most credit card borrowing, for instance) or they are set at levels too high to influence most loan markets. Nonetheless, a binding and enforceable ceiling on interest rates would look like Figure 9.12.

The equilibrium is just like our analysis of price controls in Chapter 5. At the artificially low price, there is a shortage of credit, and many people who wish to borrow at the controlled interest rate cannot do so. Moreover, the control on interest rates reduces savings. In Figure 9.12, savings fall from $250 billion at the market equilibrium to just $190 billion at the

FIGURE 9.12

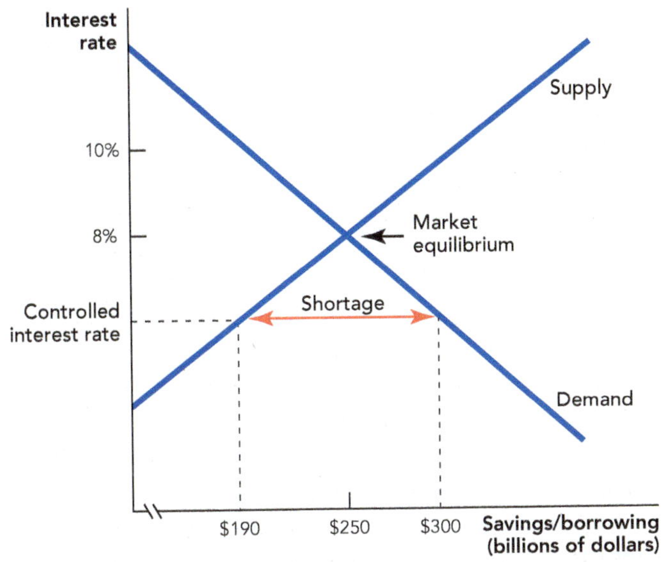

A Ceiling on Interest Rates Creates a Shortage of Savings At the controlled interest rate, the quantity of savings demanded ($300 billion) exceeds the quantity supplied ($190 billion), creating a shortage. At the controlled interest rate, investment is less than at the market equilibrium.

controlled interest rate. Similarly, just as with price controls on oil, an interest rate control will cause a misallocation of savings and a loss of potential gains from exchange. Perhaps most important, investment, which is determined by the supply of savings, will fall below what it would be at the market equilibrium.

Politicized Lending and Government-Owned Banks

Japanese history from about 1990 to 2005 also illustrates the importance of banks in using a nation's savings effectively. During this period, the Japanese continued to save, but Japanese economic growth was zero or negative for most of these years. How can this have been? Many Japanese banks were bankrupt or propped up by the government. They were not allocating funds efficiently. Other banks were pressured to lend money to well-connected political allies, rather than to the most efficient new businesses. During this period, many Japanese banks acted as storehouses for wealth, but they were not effective financial intermediaries. Japanese business innovation, and the Japanese standard of living, suffered accordingly.

In Japan, as in the United States, banks are privately owned, so politicized lending, even when it occurs, is limited. But in many other countries, most large banks are owned by the government. Government-owned banks are useful to authoritarian regimes that use the banks to direct capital to political supporters. While it might be politically wise for the ruler to support his uncle's firm, that uncle is probably not a superior entrepreneur. One important study by economists Rafael La Porta, Florencio Lopez-de-Silanes, and Andrei Shleifer found that the larger the fraction of government-owned banks a country had in 1970, the slower the growth in per capita GDP and productivity over the next several decades.[6]

Bank Failures and Panics

Systematic problems in the banking system usually lead to large-scale economic crises. At the onset of America's Great Depression between 1929 and 1933, 11,000 banks—almost half of all U.S. banks—failed. The ripple effects were grim. Many people lost their life savings; they also had to curtail their spending, which meant that many businesses lost their customers and thus revenue. Many businesses were unable to get loans or daily working capital. Thus, bank failures were followed by a rash of small business failures. It took many years before the American banking system, and the American economy, recovered.

In their seminal work, *A Monetary History of the United States, 1867–1960*, Milton Friedman and Anna Schwartz argued that the Great Depression was brought about, in part, because the Federal Reserve—the U.S. central bank that is charged with overseeing the general health of the banking industry—failed in its job to prevent widespread bank failures.[7] (See Chapter 13 for further discussion of the Great Depression and Chapter 15.) Economist Ben Bernanke later showed that one of the reasons why bank failures were so crucial in the onset of the Great Depression was because banks provide loans to a particular class of borrowers and lenders.[8] According-ing to Bernanke:

> As the real costs of intermediation increased, some borrowers (especially households, farmers, and small firms) found credit to be expensive and difficult to obtain. The effects of this credit squeeze . . . helped convert the severe but not unprecedented downturn of 1929–30 into a protracted depression.

By the way, if you recognize Bernanke's name, it is with good reason: He was chairman of the Federal Reserve between 2006 and 2014 when he had to face the worst intermediation crisis since the Great Depression.

The Financial Crisis of 2007–2008: Leverage, Securitization, and Shadow Banking

Now let's go back to the financial crisis and the collapse of Lehman Brothers, discussed at the beginning of this chapter. To give you an idea of what went on we will need to cover three ideas: leverage, securitization, and the shadow banking system. Let's begin with leverage.

Leverage

As we have seen, consumers, firms, and governments all borrow. Borrowing can be a useful tool but it's also possible to borrow too much. In the years leading up to the financial crisis, Americans borrowed more than ever before, especially in the closely related sectors of home mortgages and banking. It used to be common, for example, for home mortgages to require "20% down," which means that a lender would lend at most 80% of the price of a house. On a $400,000 house, for example, a lender would agree to lend at most $320,000, requiring the buyer to put up at least $80,000 (20% of $400,000) as a down payment.

The difference between the value of a house and the unpaid amount on the mortgage is called the buyer's equity or **owner's equity**. Lenders want buyers to have some home equity because this protects them if the buyer defaults. If a buyer has $80,000 of home equity, for example, then even if the price of the house falls from $400,000 to $350,000 the bank could still recover all of its loan in a foreclosure. The buyer's equity gives the bank a cushion.

In the 1990s and 2000s, however, lenders became convinced that house prices were unlikely to fall and they became willing to lend with much lower down payments, just 5% down or even less. Indeed, at the height of the housing boom in 2006, 17% of mortgages were made with 0% down! Many buyers thought that house prices would continue to rise so buying with zero down was a way to speculate. If house prices rose, they could borrow more or sell at a profit. If house prices fell, they could default and not lose any of their own money. Yet if house prices were to fall and buyers were to begin to default on their loans, the banks no longer would have a cushion.

In finance, the ratio of debt to equity is called the **leverage ratio**. For example, if a buyer of a $400,000 house borrows $320,000 and spends $80,000 of her own savings, then her leverage ratio is $4 = \frac{\$320,000}{\$80,000}$. If the buyer is able to borrow $360,000 to buy a $400,000 house, then the leverage ratio is much greater: $9 = \frac{\$360,000}{\$40,000}$. Put differently, when the leverage ratio is 9, a buyer with $80,000 in cash can borrow $720,000 and buy a house worth $800,000. More leverage means that the same force (your cash) can be used to move (i.e., buy) bigger and bigger assets. As the financial crisis approached, house buyers were using more and more leverage.

Home buyers weren't the only ones leveraging more; so were banks. Lehman Brothers, for example, had assets worth hundreds of billions of dollars but it had borrowed hundreds of billions of dollars to buy those assets. Moreover, just like homeowners, in the 2000s banks had been borrowing more and more with lower and lower "down payments." In 2004, for example, Lehman's leverage ratio was around 20—which meant that for every $105 in assets that the bank owned, it had borrowed $100, leaving it with equity of just $5. A leverage ratio of 20 is already pretty high.

Notice that if the value of Lehman's assets were to fall by just 10%, it would have $94.50 dollars' worth of assets and $100 dollars of debt, which means that a 10% fall in asset prices would make Lehman **insolvent**. An insolvent firm is simply one whose debts or liabilities exceed its assets (liabilities are legal debts plus other amounts owed, e.g., wage payments). Insolvency is usually followed by bankruptcy. Instead of reducing leverage in 2004, however, Lehman increased leverage so that by 2007 Lehman had an astounding leverage ratio of 44![9] At a leverage ratio of 44 even a small decrease in asset prices would bankrupt Lehman and in 2007 housing prices started to fall dramatically.

You might wonder why banks would ever want such a high leverage ratio. As we said, a leverage ratio of 44 means that even a small drop in asset prices would bankrupt Lehman but for exactly the same reasons a small rise in prices meant tremendous profits. When times are good, leverage makes everything better. Moreover, when Lehman did well, Lehman's managers received hundreds of millions, even billions, of dollars in bonuses and stock compensation. But when Lehman went bankrupt did Lehman's managers go bankrupt? No. Most of them lost some money but they still ended up being very rich. Lehman's managers wanted a lot of leverage because when things were going well the

Owner's equity is the value of the asset minus the debt, $E = V - D$.

The **leverage ratio** is the ratio of debt to equity, D/E.

mru.org/great-recession

The Great Recession

An **insolvent** firm has liabilities that exceed its assets.

sky was the limit but when things went poorly most of them had limited downside risk.

Securitization

The second concept we need to understand is securitization. Sometimes mortgage loans are "securitized," or bundled together and sold on the market as financial assets. The seller of a securitized asset gets up-front cash while the buyer gets the right to a stream of future payments. Banks may wish to sell or "securitize" their loans for several reasons. On the positive side, the bank gets more liquid cash and makes its balance sheet safer, and the securitized assets can be held as investments by institutions with a long-term perspective, such as pension funds. It's a way that a lot of institutions can invest indirectly in the American economy. Alternatively, the critics charge that too often banks securitize because they made bad, sloppy, or under-researched loans in the first place and they wish to dump them on unsuspecting suckers somewhere else.

Matt Cardy/Getty Images

Mortgages aren't the only assets that have been securitized Entertainers like David Bowie, Marvin Gaye, and James Brown sold bonds securitized by future royalty payments. Buyers of these bonds are betting that the music of these artists will continue to sell long into the future. The motto of those buying James Brown's bonds? "In the Godfather we Trust."

Once assets are securitized, the revenue streams from them can be sliced and diced and sold in all manner of ways. Mortgage securitization in the 2000s meant that dentists in Germany could easily invest in home mortgages in America. The increased ability to sell mortgages around the world was good for American home buyers because it kept interest rates low and it seemed good for investors who thought they were buying safe and secure assets. What could be safer than American homes? In reality, many of these securitized mortgages turned out to have had much higher risk than had been advertised. In part, some of the securitized bundles were sold on false terms or where the risk was obscured, in part the credit rating agencies performed poorly, and in part people simply estimated risk incorrectly, assuming that house prices would continue rising more or less indefinitely.

When housing prices started to fall dramatically in 2007, many people began to default on their mortgages. Overall delinquency (failure of payment) and foreclosure rates more than doubled. In parts of California, Florida, and Nevada more than 40% of the homes entered foreclosure. Remember that many buyers had only a little equity in their homes so as house prices fell they quickly came to owe more on their mortgage than their house was worth and many chose to default. As a result, the U.S. economy suddenly ended up in a situation in which many banks and other financial intermediaries were holding loans and assets of questionable value. Moreover, since the banks themselves were highly leveraged, when the value of their assets declined, many banks quickly approached insolvency.

The Shadow Banking System

Now let's turn to the last key idea, the "shadow banking system," which has become a common term since the financial crisis. The traditional banking system can be represented by a commercial bank, the bank where you keep your checking account. Commercial banks fund themselves in large part through deposits from people like yourself and from businesses. These deposits are insured by the Federal Deposit Insurance Corporation (FDIC; up to $250,000 and in practice often to an unlimited amount) and so a typical commercial bank always has some source of legally guaranteed funding. Sometimes commercial banks go out of business but because of insurance provided by the FDIC, depositors don't feel that they need to yank out their money at the first sign of trouble.

An investment bank is a bit different from a commercial bank. In a commercial bank the money comes from depositors. In an investment bank, the money comes from investors. Deposits are government guaranteed but investments are not, so investors are much more prone to panic and to withdraw their short-term funding in times of crisis. Investment banks, such as Lehman before its demise, are part of what has been called the shadow banking system. In addition to investment banks, the shadow banking system includes hedge funds, money market funds, and a variety of other complex financial entities. What unites the shadow banking system is that these financial intermediaries act like banks—they typically borrow short term to lend and invest in longer-term and often less liquid assets—but they have traditionally been less heavily regulated and monitored than banks and, unlike deposits, their short-term sources of funds (loans from investors) are not government-guaranteed.

The shadow banking system got its name because it grew up in the shadow of the traditional banking system and for a long time most regulators and policymakers were unaware of its importance. But by the mid-1990s the shadow banking system was lending as much as were traditional banks and at its peak in 2008 the shadow banking system lent $20 trillion, considerably more than did traditional banks.

Stu's Views © Stu All Rights Reserved www.STUS.com

This derivative investment is so complicated that no investor will truly understand it. Thanks!

Fire Sales The financial crisis can be understood as a run on the shadow banking system similar in many respects to bank runs during the Great Depression. Think of an investment bank as being funded by a variety of short-term and long-term loans. The short-term loans disappear most quickly because they are rolled over on a very frequent basis—sometimes nightly. If investors fear that the institution will go bankrupt, each lender will seek to withdraw his money or refuse to renew the loan, as soon as possible, just as depositors rush to withdraw their money from failing banks of the traditional kind. Without the short-term loans, the investment bank no longer has enough operating funds and it is forced to sell off assets quickly in what is often called a "fire sale," shown in Figure 9.13. Furthermore, if enough firms find themselves having to sell assets, fire sales can quickly get out of control. To see how fires sales can become *fire storms*, imagine that there are three financial assets, A, B, and C, and suppose that an external event, such as a fall in housing prices, causes a fall in the price of A. The fall in the price of A worries people who are lending to investment banks or other financial intermediaries who own a lot of A. The worried lenders begin to demand greater collateral on their loans—perhaps some of them even take their funds elsewhere. With less money flowing in, the bank is forced to sell some of its assets. But the bank doesn't just sell asset A, which has already fallen in price, but also some of its holdings of B and C. The natural buyers of these assets are other similar intermediaries, but if they are also under stress they won't want to buy at a normal price. As a result, the prices of

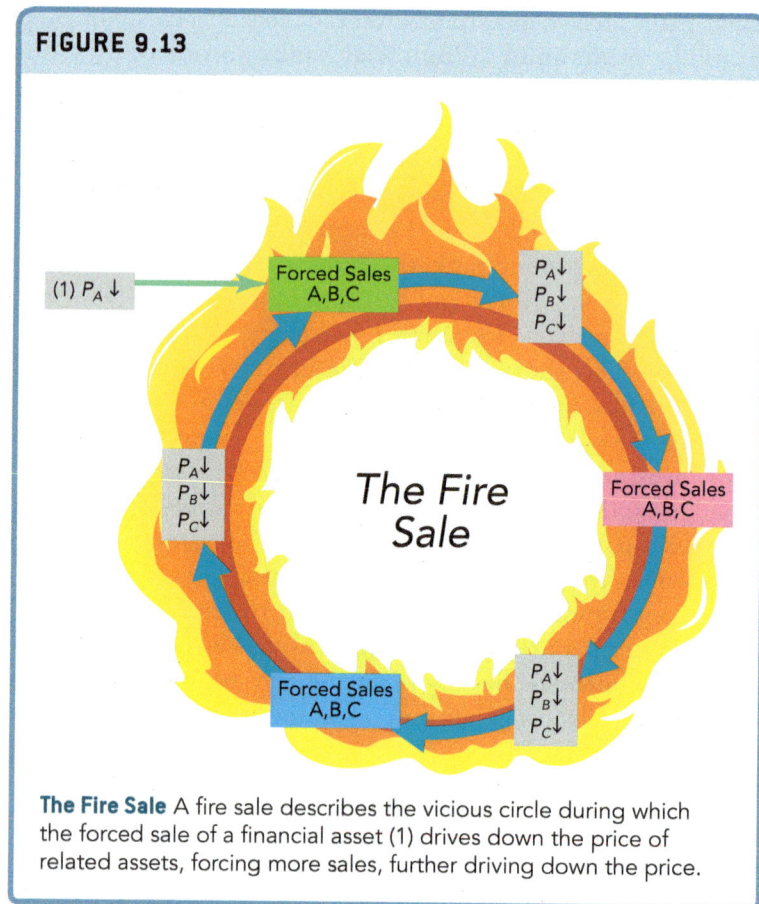

FIGURE 9.13

The Fire Sale

The Fire Sale A fire sale describes the vicious circle during which the forced sale of a financial asset (1) drives down the price of related assets, forcing more sales, further driving down the price.

B and C are also pushed down. As the price of B and C falls, lenders now come to fear that other intermediaries may go bankrupt—even intermediaries who have very little exposure to asset A, which started the problem—and so these lenders start to pull their funds. When these lenders do so, even more intermediaries must sell assets and cut back on lending, and so the problem gets worse.

Thus, in a crisis, the selling of assets by one financial intermediary can set in motion a vicious circle, or cascade, in which other intermediaries are forced to sell, driving asset prices lower, and forcing yet more sales. All of this is very bad for the intermediaries. But remember the intermediaries are bridges that channel funds from savers to borrowers. So when the intermediaries fail, credit dries up and the firms that were relying on that credit also begin to fail, adding yet another vicious cycle to the mix.

The fire sale problem was especially severe in the 2008–2009 recession because many of the participants in the shadow banking system were highly leveraged.

As noted, shortly before its failure, Lehman Brothers had a leverage ratio in the range of 40 and many other major banks were not far behind. As we've already explained, a high leverage ratio puts a bank in a very vulnerable position. When leverage ratios are high, a small decline in asset values can wipe out the equity cushion of the bank and push the bank into insolvency. It was the justified fear of this outcome that caused the short-term lenders to flee from the funding of Lehman, thereby triggering its financial meltdown.

Moreover, because mortgages had been bundled and sold many times over in different combinations, and because many bets had been made on their prices, no one knew exactly which financial institutions faced the biggest losses. As a result, it became increasingly less certain which institutions were profitable and which were in danger of going bankrupt. No one wanted to lend or invest in banks and other intermediaries that might have significant exposure to mortgage-backed assets on their books. Why lend or invest in a bank when the bank might be gone tomorrow? Investors also became wary of any institution that lent money to potentially troubled banks, even if that institution did not itself hold mortgage-backed assets.

The shadow banks in particular relied on short-term funding, which, unlike deposits, was not guaranteed; thus people who lent to shadow banks were anxious to stop lending once they feared a firm might go bankrupt. When lenders withdrew their short-term funding, some shadow banks were forced to sell assets in fire sales, which reduced asset prices and transmitted and amplified insolvency worries to other financial intermediaries. The bundling and division of mortgages and the many side bets made on securitized mortgages were also so complicated that lenders didn't know which intermediaries were safe and which were close to toppling. Just as investors are reluctant to lend to traditional financial intermediaries during these crises, they are reluctant to lend to these shadow banks as well. And as noted earlier, when financial intermediaries can't get new funds, the bridge between savers/lenders and borrowers collapses. Indeed, the reluctance of investors to lend to shadow banks meant that their lending was forced to shrink so that by 2010 shadow banks were lending just $16 trillion—a massive loss of $4 trillion in lending since 2008. It was this credit crunch that threw the entire economy into disarray.

It is now considered a general problem that the short-term loans for the shadow banking system can flee rapidly in times of crisis, causing some financial markets to shut down and credit to freeze up. Some commentators have suggested that the government guarantee loans to the shadow banking system in times of crisis, but that puts a potentially large liability on taxpayers and it is politically unpopular. Nonetheless, the U.S. government already has taken some steps in that direction. After the trauma of the Lehman Brothers failure, the insurance company AIG was on the verge of failure, but this time the Federal Reserve, led by Bernanke, stepped in and took over majority ownership of the company and guaranteed its debts. They didn't want to repeat the credit market freezes that followed the collapse of Lehman. New financial regulations are now bringing the shadow banking system "out of the shadows" and regulating these financial intermediaries in ways similar to traditional banks. A key idea has been to require banks of all kinds to hold more equity, that is, to reduce the amount of their leverage. It remains to be seen how effective and how costly these new regulations will be. Greater government involvement in the allocation of credit also raises the possibility of politicized lending, a problem that, as we discussed earlier, has reduced the efficiency of credit allocation in other countries.

CHECK YOURSELF

- How do usury laws (controls on interest rates) cause savings to decline?
- Besides decreasing the number of banks, how do bank failures hinder financial intermediation?
- How does awarding bank loans by political criteria or by cronyism (to your pals) affect the efficiency of the economy?

Takeaway

Individuals save to prepare for their retirement, to help fund large purchases, and to cushion swings in their income—most generally, savings help individuals, firms, and governments to smooth their consumption over time. Similarly, individuals, firms, and governments borrow to finance large purchases like a home, to invest in new capital, or in the case of governments to finance large expenditures such as those necessary for a war. Once again, borrowing helps agents to smooth their consumption streams. Financial intermediaries bridge the gap between savers and borrowers.

Financial intermediaries also collect savings, evaluate investments, and diversify risk. Banks, bonds, and stock markets help finance new and innovative ideas, such as Google and Federal Express. Financial intermediation is a central part of healthy economic growth.

Without effective financial intermediation, an economy will end up adrift. Insecure property rights, inflation, politicized lending, and bank failures and panics can all contribute to the breakdown of financial intermediation. The 2007–2008 crisis was brought about by high leverage and falling asset prices that created a panic in the shadow banking system that sharply reduced the amount of lending in the economy. The resulting decline in activity demonstrates how important financial intermediaries are to the economy, both when they operate well and when they do not.

CHAPTER REVIEW

Go online to practice with more examples of these types of problems, including live links to videos, data sources, and feedback.

▶ Problems with this icon relate to optional MRU videos.

KEY CONCEPTS

saving, p. 184

investment, p. 184

time preference, p. 185

market for loanable funds, p. 190

financial intermediary, p. 192

bond, p. 193

collateral, p. 194

crowding out, p. 194

arbitrage, p. 196

stock, p. 196

initial public offering (IPO), p. 196

owner's equity, p. 201

leverage ratio, p. 201

insolvency, p. 201

FACTS AND TOOLS

▶ 1. If people want to smooth their consumption over time, what will they tend to do when they win the lottery: spend most of it within a year or save most of it for later?

▶ 2. A large number of economic and psychological studies demonstrate that people who are impatient in one area of their life tend to be impatient in other areas as well. This isn't true in every single case, but of course, that doesn't matter if we're trying to understand the "typical person." Based on your general knowledge and educated guessing:

   a. Who is more likely to smoke: a criminal or a law-abiding citizen?

   b. Who is more likely to shoot heroin: a person who saves 20% of their income or a person who can't ever find a way to save?

   c. Who is more likely to have a lot of credit card debt: a smoker or a nonsmoker?

▶ 3. The typical savings supply curve has a positive slope. If a nation's saving supply curve had a perfectly vertical slope, what would that mean?

   a. People in this country save the same amount no matter what the interest rate is.

   b. People in this country are extremely sensitive to interest rates when deciding how much to save.

▶ 4. Consider three countries: Jovenia (average age: 25), Mittelaltistan (average age: 45), and

Decrepetia (average age: 75). Based on the life-cycle theory, which of these countries will probably have:

a. High savings rates?

b. High rates of borrowing?

c. High rates of dissaving? (That's spending your past savings.)

Note: The way for entire countries to save is to build up the stock of productive capital either at home (through high investment rates) or abroad (by exporting more than importing, i.e., running a trade surplus, and using the proceeds to buy foreign investment goods and assets).

5. Sometimes, in supply and demand models, it is not obvious who "supplies" and who "demands." For instance, in the labor market, individual workers (not firms) supply labor. In the loanable funds market, who is usually the supplier and who is usually the demander? Choose the correct answer.

a. Entrepreneurs supply loanable funds and savers demand loanable funds.

b. Entrepreneurs supply loanable funds and savers also supply loanable funds.

c. Entrepreneurs demand loanable funds and savers demand loanable funds.

d. Entrepreneurs demand loanable funds and savers supply loanable funds.

6. In each of the following, answer either "bank account," "bonds," or "stocks."

a. Which investment is typically the riskiest?

b. Which is a corporate IOU?

c. Which one gives you an ownership "share" in a company?

d. Which one usually lets you "withdraw" part of your investment at any time, for any reason?

e. Which form of investment usually spreads your money over the largest number of investment projects?

f. Which is usually rated by private companies like Moody's or Standard and Poor's?

g. Which one is offered by the U.S. government as well as by private corporations?

7. If savers don't feel safe putting their money in banks or buying bonds, what's the best way to sum up what's happening in the market for loanable funds?

a. Supply of savings falls and the interest rate falls.

b. Supply of savings falls and the interest rate rises.

c. Demand for savings falls and the interest rate falls.

d. Demand for savings falls and the interest rate rises.

8. When governments outlaw high interest rates and the ceiling is binding, what probably happens to the total amount of money borrowed?

a. It rises because borrowers are protected from high interest rates.

b. It falls because savers aren't willing to lend as much money at this low interest rate.

c. Both a and b are usually true.

9. If financial intermediation breaks down, what category of GDP will probably fall the most: consumption, investment, government purchases, or net exports?

10. **a.** In a competitive banking system, what tends to happen to banks that make low-interest rate loans to the banker's friends: Do they tend to be more successful or less successful than other, more ruthless banks?

b. Given your answer to the previous question, how do you suspect that politicized government-owned banks stay in business?

THINKING AND PROBLEM SOLVING

11. Let's work out a simple example in which a person smooths her consumption over time. Gwen is a real estate agent, and she knows that she will have some good years and some bad years. She figures that half the time she'll earn $90,000 per year, and half the time she'll earn $20,000 per year. These numbers are after taxes and after saving for retirement. These numbers are all she has to worry about.

a. If we ignore interest costs just to keep things simple, how much should Gwen consume in the average year?

b. How many dollars will she save during the good years?

c. How many dollars will she borrow during the bad years? (*Note:* "Borrowing," in this context, is basically the same as "pulling money out of savings.")

▶12. Let's think about how the supply of savings might shift in two different cases.

a. Under current U.S. law, businesses are allowed to automatically enroll you in a savings plan that puts 5% of your salary in a retirement fund. Suppose Congress *abolishes* this law: Draw the appropriate shift in the supply curve and label it "a."

b. If Americans all go to see the classic Robin Williams/Ethan Hawke film *Dead Poets Society* and decide to *carpe diem*, or if they read the quotes of a famous Mediterranean preacher who said, "Take therefore no thought for the morrow," or if they watch the appalling 1970s sitcom *One Day at a Time*, what direction is the supply of savings likely to shift? Denote this with a new supply curve labeled "b."

▶13. In this chapter, we focus on three big functions that banks perform:

   i. They evaluate business ideas to see to whom it's worth lending.

   ii. They spread an investment's risk among many different projects.

   iii. They make it easier for people to make payments through checks, ATMs, and wire transfers.

   None of these functions are unique to banks. In the following anecdotes, is the person doing function i, function ii, or function iii?

a. Emmanuel donates a little money to five different charities, in the hopes that at least one of them will do some good in the world.

b. In Lorien's family, she's the one who specializes in deciding which bank everyone else in the family will use.

c. Popeye always has a little cash on hand, so he is always able to lend a little money to Wimpy and Olive Oyl at lunchtime.

d. George spends his time at the Carlyle Group deciding which companies are worth his investment partners' dollars.

e. Scooter wants a good education, so he takes a variety of different classes: some history, some economics, some physics.

f. Frances subscribes to *Consumer Reports* to decide which washing machine to buy.

▶14. In many poor countries, the banking system just isn't advanced enough to lend money for many large investments. Based on this single fact, where would you expect to see more entrepreneurs coming from rich families rather than poor families: in the rich countries or the poor countries? Why?

▶15. The financial analysts at Lexmark have evaluated five major projects. Each project, if it actually goes forward, will be financed by going to a bank to borrow the money. They've calculated a "break-even interest rate": If they can borrow cash to pay for the project at less than that rate, the project will likely be a success; if the rate is higher, then it's not worth it.

	Cost	Break-even Interest Rate
Project A	$100 million	8%
Project B	$50 million	12%
Project C	$200 million	50%
Project D	$25 million	4%
Project E	$150 million	10%

a. If the interest rate is 11%, which projects will Lexmark take on? If the market interest rate is 6%, which projects will it take on?

b. Let's turn this information into a demand curve for loanable funds.

   Organize this data to convert it into Lexmark's "loanable funds demand" curve. *Note:* It will look just like an ordinary demand curve, only with more breaks.

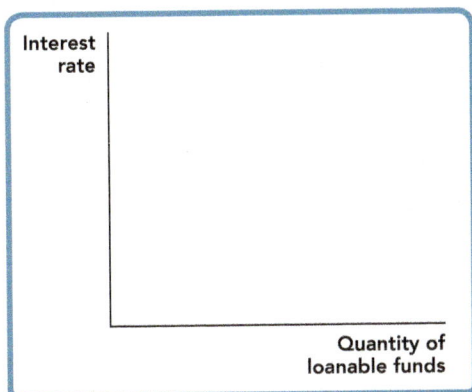

16. In each of the three cases, which bond will usually pay a higher interest rate?

    a. A bond rated AAA, or a bond rated BBB?

    b. A U.S. government bond, or a General Motors bond?

    c. A Citibank bond that gets repaid in 30 years or a Citibank bond that gets repaid in 1 year?

17. Consider your answers to the previous question. When one bond pays a higher interest rate than another bond, is that mostly because savers are less willing to *supply* loanable funds to the higher-rate bond, or because businesses are more interested in *demanding* loanable funds for the higher-rate bond? Why is this so?

18. Consider Figure 9.10. Would a rise in government borrowing make it harder or easier for a new business to sell new stocks in an initial public offering (IPO)? In other words, are government bonds and corporate stocks substitutes for each other or complements to each other?

19. "If the government keeps real interest rates low (either by raising inflation or by decreeing low interest rates), then this encourages extra borrowing by businesses, which leads to more investment purchases, a larger stock of capital equipment, and higher productivity. Therefore, an interest rate ceiling is a good idea." What's wrong with this argument?

20. a. If a zero-coupon bond with a face value of $1,000 payable in 1 year sells for $925, what is the interest rate?

    b. If another bond with the same face value and maturity sells for $900, what is the interest rate on this bond?

    c. Which bond, the one discussed in question a or question b, would you rather invest in? Are you sure? Think again!

Discovering DATA

21. Let's take a look at financial intermediation and the financial crisis and recession of 2007–2009. Using the FRED economic database (https://fred.stlouisfed.org/), search for "all sectors total loans"; you should find a series, All Sectors; Total Loans; Liability. This series is all the lending in the U.S. economy from banks and all other financial intermediaries. When you graph the series you will see that it increases quite smoothly, rising almost without exception every single year from 1945 to 2008. In the third quarter of 2008 the series begins to drop tremendously, and in an unprecedented way—this is the financial crisis.

    a. At the peak, in the third quarter of 2008, how much was being lent in the U.S. economy? (*Hint:* Be careful of the units. The data is given in millions of millions; a million million is a trillion.)

    b. In the third quarter of 2011 how much was being lent in the U.S. economy?

    c. In the space of just three years approximately how much lending disappeared from the U.S. economy?

Discovering DATA

22. One type of debt that you may be familiar with is student loan debt. Using the FRED economic database (https://fred.stlouisfed.org/), search for student loans, then click on "Student Loans Owned and Securitized, Outstanding."

    a. In 2019 approximately how much student debt was owed?

    b. What has happened to the amount of student debt outstanding since 2006?

Discovering DATA ::

23. Using the FRED economic database (https://fred.stlouisfed.org/), find the typical interest rate on a credit card. By searching for "credit card rate," you should find "Commercial Bank Interest Rate on Credit Card Plans, All Accounts."

a. What is the typical interest rate on a credit card in 2019?

b. How does the credit card rate compare to other rates such as mortgage loan rates or government bond rates?

c. Search for "credit card charge off" and you should find a series "Charge-Off Rate on Credit Card Loans, All Commercial Banks." Click Edit Graph and change the frequency to Annual. This series shows the percentage of loans that the banks have to write off as losses. In 2010 what percentage of loans were written off as losses?

d. Why is the credit card rate so much higher than other rates?

CHALLENGES

24. The United States borrows a lot of money from other countries. If you wanted to use the lifecycle theory to explain this, would you say that the United States is acting like a "young" country, an "old" country, or a "middle-aged" country? There's more than one correct way to answer this question.

25. Lenders are more willing to lend if the borrower can put up collateral for the loan. Remember that collateral is something of value that by agreement becomes the property of the lender if the borrower defaults. In the United States, many small business owners borrow money for their business by using their houses or business assets as collateral. But in many developing countries, people don't have secure property rights, or *title*, to the land or house in which they live. In Bangalore, India, for example, it's nearly impossible to say who owns a piece of land and about 85% of the people in that city live on a piece of land for which they have no title. How difficult do you think it would be for a small business person in Bangalore to get a modest-sized loan?

26. Bank savings accounts typically pay an interest rate well below the inflation rate. As of spring 2017, for example, the best interest rates on savings accounts were around 1% per year, while the CPI inflation rate was around 2.5% per year.

What does this mean about the real interest rate on bank savings? Knowing this, why would people still choose to deposit any money in bank savings accounts?

27. How are houses like bonds? With respect only to their home equity (i.e., ignoring all other assets and investments), would home*owners* tend to favor high or low interest rates?

Discovering DATA ::

28. Let's compare 10-year corporate bonds and 10-year government bonds (called Treasuries). Go to the FRED economic database (https://fred.stlouisfed.org/) and search for "10 year corporate bond high quality"; you should find the series "10-Year High Quality Market (HQM) Corporate Bond Par Yield." Click Edit Graph and then Add Line. Now search for "10-Year Treasury" and use the monthly series to match that for the corporate bond.

a. Do 10-year corporate bonds or 10-year Treasuries offer a higher return? Why?

b. Usually the two series move closely together, but graph the two series around the 2008–2009 recession. What happens? Why?

WORK IT OUT

For interactive, step-by-step help in solving this problem, go online.

Predict the effect of each of the following events on the supply of and demand for loanable funds (increase, decrease, or no effect on supply; increase, decrease, or no effect on demand). What would be the likely effect on interest rates?

a. Television newscasters convince most people that the end of the world will occur in 2025.

b. Breakthrough advances in pharmaceuticals increase life expectancy to 100 years.

c. Geologists discover vast new oil deposits under the South Pole. (*Hint:* Drilling in this harsh environment requires extremely large up-front capital expenses.)

d. A business downturn leads to corporate pessimism and increases workers' fears of being laid off (assume workers try to increase their "emergency fund" savings when they're worried about becoming unemployed).

▶ MRU VIDEOS

Saving and Borrowing

mru.org/save-borrow

Problems: **1–5, 11, 12, 24**

What Do Banks Do?

mru.org/banks

Problems: **6, 13, 15**

Intro to Stock Markets

mru.org/stock-market

Problems: **6, 11**

Intro to the Bond Market

mru.org/bonds

Problems: **6, 14, 16–18, 26, 27**

Four Reasons Financial Intermediaries Fail

mru.org/intermediation-failure

Problems: **7–10, 14, 19**

Women in Economics: Anna Schwartz

mru.org/schwartz

The Great Recession

mru.org/great-recession

Problem: **27**

CHAPTER 9 APPENDIX

Bond Pricing and Arbitrage

Bond pricing may seem complicated but it can be understood with a few simple principles. Let's start with something more familiar than bonds. Suppose that you invest $100 in a savings account that pays a 10% rate of interest. How much money will you have in one year? That's easy; every dollar invested at 10% turns into $1.10 in one year so $100 invested at 10% turns into $110, which we can write as $100 × (1.10) = $110.

More generally, let's call the money that you invest the present value (PV), let's call the interest rate r, and let's call the money that you will withdraw from the bank in one year the future value (FV). Then, the relationship between PV, r, and FV is simply

$$PV \times (1 + r) = FV \qquad (1)$$

For example, if you invested $100 in present value at an interest rate of 5%, how much money would you have in a year (FV)? Substituting in equation 1, we have $100 × (1.05) = $105.

Okay, now let's ask a slightly more difficult question. Suppose that the interest rate is 10% and that in one year you would like to have the future value of $100. How much do you need to put in the bank today? In other words, if the interest rate is 10% and you want a future value of $100, what present value do you need to put in the bank? Let's fill in what we know:

$$PV \times (1.10) = \$100$$

To solve for PV, divide both sides by 1.10:

$$PV = \frac{\$100}{1.10} = \$90.91$$

Thus, if the interest rate is 10% and we want $100 in the bank in one year, we need to invest $90.91 today. More generally, we can rewrite equation 1 in any of the following three ways depending on whether we want to solve for FV, PV, or r:

$$PV \times (1 + r) = FV \qquad (1a)$$

$$PV = \frac{FV}{(1 + r)} \qquad (1b)$$

$$(1 + r) = \frac{FV}{PV} \qquad (1c)$$

We now have everything we need to explain bond pricing. Imagine that the interest rate is 10% and suppose that a bond exists that promises to pay $100 in one year's time. Thus, the future value of the bond—conveniently this is also called the face value—is $100, the interest rate r is 10%, and we want to know PV. We can use version 1b of our equation:

$$PV = \frac{\$100}{1.10} = \$90.91$$

In other words, when the interest rate is 10%, a bond promising to pay $100 in one year will sell for $90.91.

Students are often confused by the fact that interest rates and bond prices move in *opposite* directions: That is, when the interest rate rises, bond prices fall, and when the interest rate falls, bond prices rise. But now we can explain this result easily. We know that at an interest rate of 10% a bond that has a future value of $100 will have a price or present value of $90.91. So what happens to the present value of the same bond when the interest rate falls to 5%?

$$PV = \frac{FV}{1 + r}$$

Substituting what we know, we have

$$PV = \frac{\$100}{1.05} = \$95.24$$

Thus, when the interest rate falls from 10% to 5%, the price of the bond rises from $90.91 to $95.23.

We can see from version 1b of our formula that the price of a bond rises when the interest rate falls (and vice versa), but what is the economics behind this result? To understand the economics, we will use version 1c of our equation.

Let's suppose that the interest rate falls from 10% to 5%—in other words, the most that investors can earn on their loanable funds is a 5% rate of return. But imagine that instead of rising to $95.24, the price of a bond paying $100 in one year's time stayed at $90.91. How much could investors earn by investing in this bond? The present value of the bond is $90.91, the future value is $100, so the return *on this bond* is

$$(1 + r) = \frac{FV}{PV} = \frac{\$100}{\$90.91} = 1.10$$

Now what would you do if every other investment in the economy is earning a 5% rate of return, but an equally safe bond exists that earns 10%? Correct, you would buy the bond paying 10%. And what happens when you—and everyone else—start buying this extraordinary bond? Correct, the bond increases in price and, as it increases in price, the return on the bond falls. In fact, the bond will increase in price and its rate of return will fall until it earns a rate of return roughly equal to that on similarly risky investments elsewhere in the economy.

Our last result can be stated more generally: *Buying and selling will equalize the rate of return on equally risky assets.* The buying and selling of equally risky assets is called "arbitrage." Arbitrage is a very important idea with many more implications than we can address here, but if you continue on in economics or finance, you will study arbitrage in more detail.

We have shown how the simplest types of bonds are priced. Many bonds mature in more than one year and many bonds include coupon payments: periodic payments in addition to the final payment at maturity. The formula for determining the present value of a bond that matures in more than one year and that has coupon payments is more complicated than formula 1b, but the ideas are exactly the same. We will give one quick example to illustrate.

Let's begin, once again, with a $100 investment in a savings account that pays a 10% rate of interest. But this time, let's suppose that we invest the money for two years—what is the future value of this investment? We can break our two-year investment into two one-year investments. We first invest $100 at 10%, giving us $110 at the end of the first year. We then invest $110 at 10% for another year, which gives us $121 at the end of two years. In general terms, we can write

$$[PV \times (1 + r_1)] \times (1 + r_2) = FV \qquad \text{(A1)}$$

The term in the square brackets is how much we will have after the first year of investment; we then multiply this amount by $(1 + r_2)$, the rate of interest in year 2, to give us the amount that we will have at the end of two years.

As we did before, we can divide both sides of equation A1 by $(1 + r_1)(1 + r_2)$ in order to rewrite A1 as

$$PV = \frac{FV}{(1 + r_1) \times (1 + r_2)} \qquad \text{(A2)}$$

Let's use formula A2 to figure out the present value or selling price of a bond that pays $100 in two years when the interest rate in year 1 and year 2 is 10%. Substituting what we know, we have

$$PV = \frac{\$100}{(1.10) \times (1.10)} = \$82.64$$

Thus, if the interest rate in year 1 and year 2 is 10%, then a bond that pays $100 two years from now has a present value or selling price of $82.64.

Now here is the big payoff. What is the price of a bond that pays $100 at the end of year 1 and another $100 at the end of year 2? We can easily price this bond because this bond is just a combination of two bonds, one of which pays $100 at the end of year 1 and one of which pays $100 at the end of year 2. But we just calculated the value of these bonds! And, because of arbitrage, the combination bond must sell for the same price as the sum of the two bonds that we calculated earlier, or $173.55 = $90.91 + $82.64.

We can also calculate the value of the combination bond directly. When the interest rate is 10%, the PV of a bond that pays $100 in one year and another $100 in two years is

$$PV = \frac{\$100}{1.10} + \frac{\$100}{(1.10) \times (1.10)} = \$173.55$$

Following through on the same logic, we can now calculate the price of very complicated bonds. The present value of a bond that makes potentially different payments every year for n years is

$$PV = \frac{Payment_1}{(1 + r)} + \frac{Payment_2}{(1 + r)^2} + \frac{Payment_3}{(1 + r)^3} + \ldots \frac{Final\ payment_n}{(1 + r)^n}$$

Bond Pricing with a Spreadsheet

We can calculate the price of bonds like this using a spreadsheet. Figure A9.1 shows a bond that pays $100 in each of the first nine years and then in the 10th year it pays $1,000. The present value of each payment is calculated in Column C. Note that the formula in cell C2, "=B2/(1 + $D$2)^A2", is equivalent to $\frac{Payment_1}{(1+r)}$. Copying this formula for the nine other payments gives us a column

FIGURE A9.1

	C2	▼	f_x =B2/(1+$D$2)^A2	
	A	B	C	D
1	Year	Payment	Present Value	Interest Rate
2	1	$100	$95.24	0.05
3	2	$100	$90.70	
4	3	$100	$86.38	
5	4	$100	$82.27	
6	5	$100	$78.35	
7	6	$100	$74.62	
8	7	$100	$71.07	
9	8	$100	$67.68	
10	9	$100	$64.46	
11	10	$1,000	$613.91	
12				
13		Sum PV		
14		or Price->	$1,324.70	

of present values, which we sum up in cell C14, "=SUM(C2:C11)", to find the price of the bond, $1,324.70.

You can easily vary the interest rate to see what happens to the price of the bond. If the interest rate rises to 10%, for example, we have the result in Figure A9.2.

FIGURE A9.2

	C14	▼	f_x =SUM(C2:C11)	
	A	B	C	D
1	Year	Payment	Present Value	Interest Rate
2	1	$100	$90.91	0.1
3	2	$100	$82.64	
4	3	$100	$75.13	
5	4	$100	$68.30	
6	5	$100	$62.09	
7	6	$100	$56.45	
8	7	$100	$51.32	
9	8	$100	$46.65	
10	9	$100	$42.41	
11	10	$1,000	$385.54	
12				
13		Sum PV		
14		or Price->	$961.45	
15				

And thus, the price of the bond falls to $961.45. Note once again that a higher interest rate means a lower price for the bond. It's also interesting to see that a higher interest rate has a small effect on payments that come soon (compare the PV of the first payment in Figure A9.1 and Figure A9.2), but a very large effect on payments far into the future (compare the PV of the final payment in the two scenarios).

One final point of importance. Bond pricing might seem to be far away from your interests, but the techniques in this appendix can be used to price and understand any kind of asset that has a payment stream over time. A mortgage, for example, is very similar to a bond except instead of receiving bond payments, you will typically be sending mortgage payments. If you want to compare two different mortgages, for example, a 20-year mortgage and a 30-year mortgage where the mortgages have different interest rates, you will want to compute the present value of each mortgage to find the one with the lowest PV. Online mortgage calculators help you to do this. What those calculators do is compute present values using the same types of techniques as found in this appendix.

Chapter 9 Appendix Questions

1. Using a spreadsheet and the material in the appendix, answer the following questions.

   a. Assume the interest rate is 5% (0.05). Calculate the value of a bond that pays $100 at the end of every year for the next 9 years and then at the end of the 10th year pays $1,000.

   b. Calculate the value of this bond if the interest rate is 3%.

2. Answer the following question using a spreadsheet and the material in the appendix.

   You would like to buy a house. Assume that given your income, you can afford to pay $12,000 a year to a lender for the next 30 years. If the interest rate is 7% how much can you borrow today based on your ability to pay? What about if the interest rate is 3%?

10

Stock Markets and Personal Finance

I n 1992, television reporter John Stossel decided to challenge the experts of Wall Street. As a student, Stossel had taken classes from economist Burton Malkiel whose book *A Random Walk Down Wall Street* claimed that the money and fame that went to stock-picking gurus were a sham and a waste. According to Malkiel: "A blindfolded monkey throwing darts at a newspaper's financial pages could select a portfolio that would do just as well as one carefully selected by experts."[1]

Instead of using a monkey, Stossel himself threw darts at a giant wall-sized version of the stock pages of the *Wall Street Journal*. Stossel followed his portfolio for nearly a year and compared the return with the portfolios picked by major Wall Street experts. Stossel's portfolio beat 90% of the experts! Not surprisingly, none of the experts would speak to him on camera about their humiliating loss. The lesson, according to Stossel, is that if you are paying an expert a lot of money to pick your stocks, it is probably you who are the monkey.

In this chapter, we explain why Stossel's amusing experiment is backed up by economic theory and by many careful empirical studies. We will also be giving you some investment advice in this chapter. No, we can't promise you the secret to get rich. Most of the get-rich-quick schemes sold in books, investment seminars, and newsletters are scams. Economics, however, does provide some important lessons for investing wisely. We can't tell you how to get rich quick, but we can perhaps help you to get rich slowly.

Throughout this chapter, we emphasize a core principle of economics: There's no such thing as a free lunch. That's just another way of saying that you shouldn't expect something for nothing, or that trade-offs are everywhere. Let's see how the principle applies to personal finance.

CHAPTER OUTLINE

Passive vs. Active Investing

Why Is It Hard to Beat the Market?

How to Really Pick Stocks, Seriously

Other Benefits and Costs of Stock Markets

Takeaway

▶ MRU Videos

- Should You Listen to the Expert Stock Pickers?
- The Efficient Market Hypothesis
- Diversify, Diversify, Diversify!
- The Rule of 70

Passive vs. Active Investing

Many people invest in the stock market through a mutual fund. A mutual fund pools money from many customers and invests the money in many firms, in return, of course, for a management fee. Some of these mutual funds, called "active funds," are run by managers who try to pick stocks—these mutual funds

FIGURE 10.1

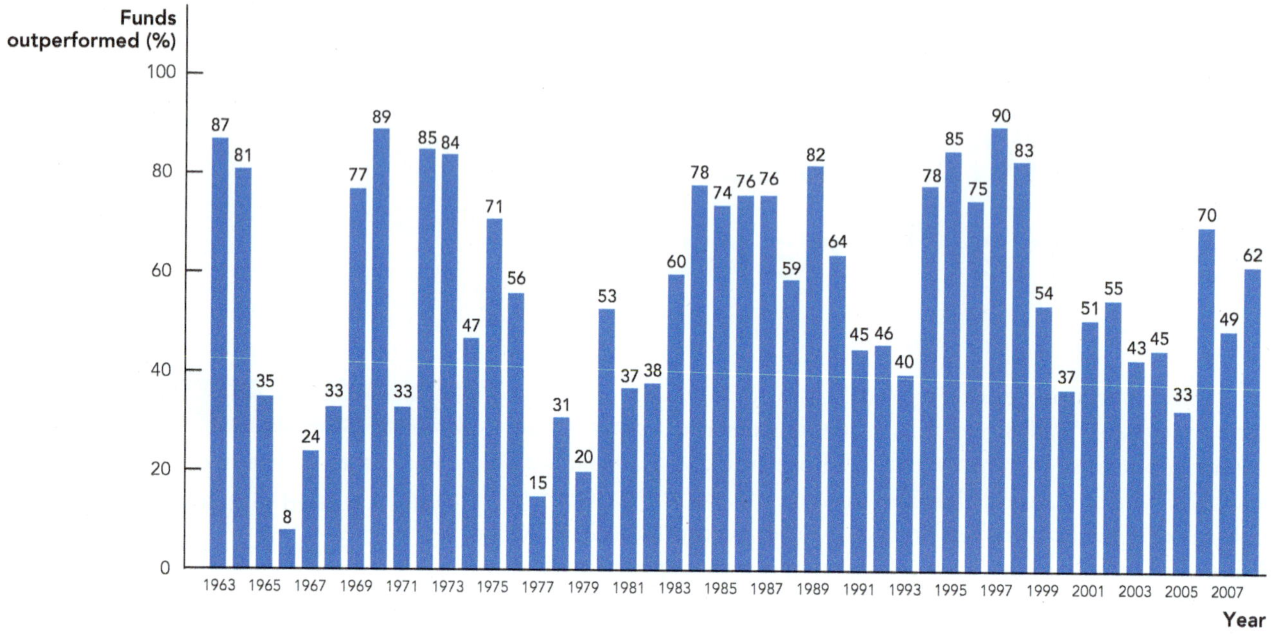

Percent of Mutual Funds Outperformed by the S&P 500

Data from: Bogle, John. 2010. *Common Sense on Mutual Funds.* New York: John Wiley & Sons.

often charge higher than average fees. Other mutual funds are called "passive funds" because they simply attempt to mimic a broad stock market index such as Standard and Poor's 500 (S&P 500), a basket of 500 large firms broadly representative of the U.S. economy.

Figure 10.1 shows that in a typical year passive investing in the S&P 500 Index beats about 60% of all mutual funds. In any given year, some mutual funds beat the index, but what is telling is that the funds that beat the index are different nearly every year! In other words, the funds that beat the index in one year probably just got lucky that year. One study that looked over 10 years found that passive investing beat 97.6% of all mutual funds![2] Overall, it is clear that very few mutual fund managers can consistently beat the market averages.

It is possible that a very small number of experts can systematically beat the stock market. Sometimes Warren Buffett, who promotes long-term investing for value, is cited as an example of a person who sees farther than the rest of the market. He started out as a paperboy and worked his way up to a $52 billion fortune by purchasing undervalued stocks.

Some economists even think that Buffett, and a few others like him, just got lucky. If enough people are out there trying to pick stocks, you're going to have a few who get lucky many times in a row. Take a look at Figure 10.2. At the top of the figure, we start out with 1,000 experts, each of whom flips a coin to predict whether the market will go up or down in the following year. After one year, 500 of the experts will turn out to be right. After two years, 250 experts will have been right two years in a row. At the end of five

FIGURE 10.2

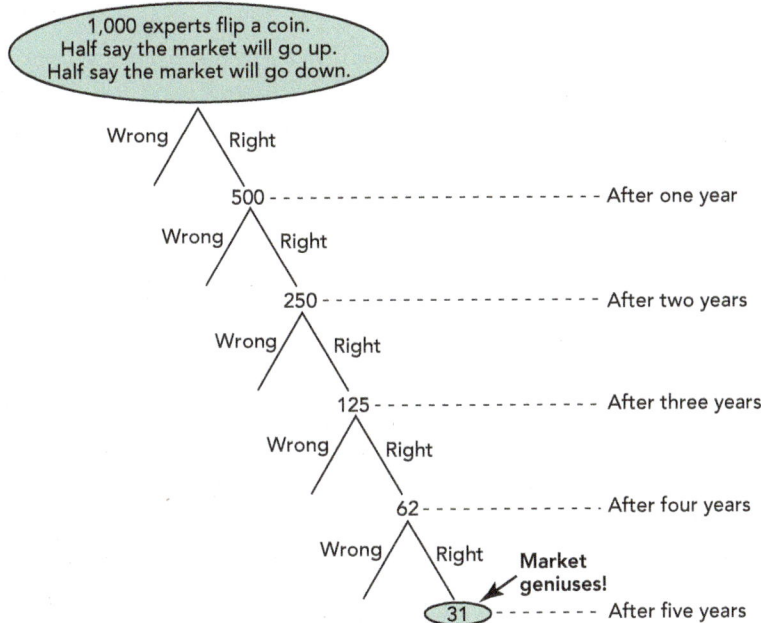

How to Become a Market Genius

years, just 31 out of 1,000 experts will have been right five years in a row. The experts who get it correct every time will be lauded as geniuses on CNBC and their advice will be eagerly sought. But the reality is that they just got lucky.

Is Buffett skilled or lucky? We're not so sure, but we do know this: Right now there is a small industry of people following the moves of Warren Buffett, trying to guess what he will say and do next. It is harder and harder for Buffett to get a big jump on the rest of the stock market. Even if Buffett could beat the market at first, it is not so clear he can beat the market any longer.

Why Is It Hard to Beat the Market?

These results aren't just an accident. Nor is it a statement about the stupidity of mutual fund managers. We know a few of these managers and most of them are pretty smart. Rather, the difficulty of beating the stock market is a tribute to the power of markets and the ability of market prices to reflect information.

Think about it this way: For every buyer of a stock, there is a seller. The buyer thinks the price is going up, the seller thinks the price is going down. There is a disagreement. On average, who do you think is more likely to be correct, the buyer or the seller? Of course, the answer is neither. But if on average buyers and sellers have about the same amount of information, stock picking can't work very well.

Consider the following bit of pseudo investment advice. The number of senior citizens will double by 2050. So the way to make money is to invest in companies that produce goods and services that senior citizens want, things like assisted living facilities, medical care for the elderly, and retirement homes. The baby boom can be a boom for you, If You Invest Now! Sounds plausible, right? So, what's wrong with this argument?

All the premises in the argument are true: The baby boomers are retiring and the demand for goods and services that senior citizens want will increase in the future. But investing in firms that produce goods and services for senior citizens is not a sure road to riches. Why not? If it were, why would anyone sell their stock in these firms? Remember, for every buyer there is a seller. If you think the stock is a good buy, why is the seller selling? It's not a secret that the baby boomers are retiring so the stock price of firms that are likely to do well in the future *already* reflects this information.

Since for every buyer there is a seller, you can't get rich by buying and selling on *public information*. This idea is the foundation of what is called the **efficient markets hypothesis**. The best-known form of this hypothesis states:

The **efficient markets hypothesis** says that the prices of traded assets reflect all publicly available information.

> The prices of traded assets, such as stocks and bonds, reflect all publicly available information. Unless an investor is trading on inside information, they will not systematically outperform the market as a whole over time.

Let's be clear on what this means. It doesn't mean that market prices are always right, that markets are all powerful, or that traders are calm, cool, and rational people. It just means it is difficult for ordinary investors (that probably means you, too!) to systematically outperform the market, again, unless a trader has inside information—information that no one else has. It's restating our point that you might as well throw darts at the stock pages and try to figure out which companies will beat the market. The efficient markets hypothesis is just another way of saying there is no such thing as a free lunch.

So if you do have some information that no one else has, can you make money in the stock market? Yes, but you have to act very quickly. Within *minutes* of the news that the Russian nuclear power plant at Chernobyl had melted down, shares in U.S. nuclear power plant companies tumbled, the price of oil jumped, as did the price of potatoes. Why potatoes? Clever traders on Wall Street figured out that the disaster at Chernobyl meant that the Ukrainian potato crop would be contaminated, so they bought American potato futures to profit from the coming rise in prices. The traders who acted quickly made a lot of money, but as they bought and sold, prices changed and signaled to other people that something was going on. Quite quickly, the inside information became public information and the opportunities for profit evaporated.

The only way you can take advantage of information that other people don't have is to start buying or selling large numbers of shares. But once you start the buying or selling, the rest of the market knows something is up. That is why secrets do not last very long in the stock market and that is another reason why it is so hard to beat the market as a whole.

Some people believe that they have found exceptions to the efficient markets hypothesis. For instance, it is commonly believed that you can make more money by buying stocks when prices are low, or by buying right after prices have fallen. That sounds good, doesn't it? Buying at lower prices. It feels like what you do when you go to Walmart. But buying a stock isn't like buying a lawn chair or a banana. The value of a stock is simply what its price will be in future periods of time. The banana, in contrast, you can simply eat for pleasure, no matter what the future price of bananas. Often lower prices mean that prices are going to stay low or fall even more and that means lower returns on owning stocks. Some studies find that you can do slightly better with your investments by buying right after prices have fallen. But do you know what? If you adjust those higher returns to account for the broker commissions that you have to pay for the extra trading, the higher returns pretty much go away.

A field of study known as "technical analysis" looks for deep patterns in stock and asset prices. Maybe you've heard on the financial news that stocks have "broken through a key support point" or "moved into a new trading range." If you dig deeper, you will find a claim that stock prices exhibit predictable mathematical patterns. For instance, if a stock hovers in the range of $100 a share but does not exceed that level, and one day goes above $100, it might be claimed that the stock is now expected to skyrocket to a much higher level. Hardly. One nice thing about studying the stock market is that there is a lot of very good data. One team of economists studied 7,846 different strategies of technical analysis. Their conclusion was that none of them systematically beat the market over time.[3]

For most investors, the efficient markets hypothesis looks like a pretty good description of reality.

How to Really Pick Stocks, Seriously

Ok, you probably can't beat the market without a lot of luck on your side. But we do still have four pieces of important advice. *Very* important advice. If you apply this advice over the course of your life, you will probably save thousands of dollars, and if you become rich, you may save millions of dollars. (Suddenly, this textbook seems like a real bargain!) No, we don't have a get-rich-quick formula for you, but there are a few simple mistakes you can avoid to your benefit and at no real cost, other than a bit of time and attention. Let's go through each piece of advice in turn.

Diversify

The first secret to picking stocks is to pick lots of them! Since picking stocks doesn't work well, the "secret" to wise investing is to invest in a large basket of stocks—to diversify. Diversification lowers the risk of your portfolio, how much your portfolio fluctuates in value over time.

By picking a lot of stocks, you limit your overall exposure to things going wrong in any particular company. When the energy company Enron went bankrupt in 2001, many Enron employees had put most of their life's wealth in . . . can you guess? . . . Enron stock. That's a huge mistake, whether you work at the company or not. If you put all your eggs in one basket, it is a disaster if the handle on that basket breaks. Instead, you should buy many different stocks, in many different sectors of the economy, and, yes, in many countries, too. You'll end up with some Enrons, but you'll also have some big winners, such as Google and Apple. And if Google and Apple have become Enrons and gone under

CHECK YOURSELF

- Is it better to invest in a mutual fund that has performed well for five years in a row or one that has performed poorly for five years in a row? Use the efficient markets hypothesis to justify your answer.

since this book was published, well, that is just further reason why you should diversify!

Modern financial markets have made diversification easy. Mutual funds let you invest in hundreds of stocks with just one purchase. And since stock picking doesn't work well, diversification has no downside—it reduces risk without reducing your expected return.

We are focusing on diversification across stocks but there are all kinds of risks in the world and you should diversify across as many of those risks as possible. U.S. stocks, for example, tend to fluctuate in value along with the growth rate of the U.S. economy. You can reduce this source of risk by including a large number of international firms in your portfolio. Bonds, art, housing, and human capital (your knowledge and skills) all have associated returns and risks, and for a given amount of return, you minimize your risk by diversifying across many assets.

If you accept the efficient markets hypothesis, and you accept the value of diversification, your best trading strategy can be summed up very simply. It is called **buy and hold**. That's right, buy a large bundle of stocks and just hold them. You don't have to do anything more. You will be diversified, you will not be trying to beat the market, and you can live a peaceful, quiet life.

Some of the simplest ways to buy and hold mean that you replicate the well-known stock indexes. Just for your knowledge, here are a few of those indexes:

The *Dow Jones Industrial Average* (or the Dow for short) is the most famous stock price index. The Dow is composed of 30 leading American stocks, each of these counted equally, whether the company is large or small. The Dow is not a very diversified index.

The *Standard and Poor's 500* (S&P 500) is a much broader index of stocks than the Dow; as the name indicates, it consists of the prices of 500 different stocks. Unlike in the Dow, the larger companies receive greater weight in the index than the smaller companies. The S&P 500 is a better indicator of the market as a whole than the Dow.

The *NASDAQ Composite Index* averages the prices of all the companies traded on NASDAQ, or National Association of Securities Dealers Automated Quotations, more than 3,000 securities. The NASDAQ index contains more small stocks and high-tech stocks relative to the Dow or the S&P 500.

Notice that diversification changes our understanding of what makes a stock risky, or not risky. You might at first think that a risky stock is one whose price moves up and down a lot. Not exactly. If investors are diversified, and indeed most of them are, their risk depends on how much their portfolio moves up and down, not on how much a single stock moves up and down. A single stock might move up and down all the time but still an overall diversified portfolio won't change in value much if some of your stocks are moving up while others are moving down.

According to finance economists, the riskiest stocks are those that move up and down in harmony with the market. For instance, many real estate stocks are risky because they are highly cyclical. They move up a lot when times are good (and the rest of the market is high) and they move down a lot when times are bad. When a recession comes, a lot of people just can't afford to buy

---

To **buy and hold** is to buy stocks and then hold them for the long run, regardless of what prices do in the short run.

> MRU
>
> mru.org/stock-diversify
>
> Diversify, Diversify, Diversify!

a new house. In contrast, for an example of a relatively safe stock, consider the discount outlet Walmart. When bad times come, yes, Walmart loses some business. But Walmart also gains some business because people who used to shop at Nordstrom now have less money and some of them will now shop at Walmart. In this regard, Walmart is partly protected from business downturns.[4] Many health-care stocks are safe in a similar way. Even if times are bad, you're probably not going to postpone that triple bypass operation; if you do, you won't be around to see when times are good again. In other words, if you care about the risk of a stock, don't just look at how the price of that stock moves. Look at how the price varies with the rest of the market. In the language of finance economists or statisticians, the riskiest stocks are those with the highest *covariance* with the market as a whole.

The lesson here is that if you are worried about risk, think about your portfolio as a whole, rather than obsessing over any single stock. Or let's be more specific: If you are going to become an aerospace engineer, don't buy a lot of stock in aerospace companies. The value of your human capital—which is worth a lot—is already tied up in that industry. Don't make your overall portfolio riskier by putting more eggs in that basket. If anything, buy stocks that do well when aerospace does poorly. More generally, finance theorists say that the least risky assets *for you* are assets that are *negatively correlated* with *your portfolio*. What this means is that you should try to buy assets that rise in value when the rest of your portfolio is falling in value. Are you afraid that high energy prices will cripple the prospects for your career? Buy stock in a company that builds roads in Saudi Arabia. If oil prices stay high, the gains of that road-building company will partially offset your other losses. The lesson applies to more than stocks. If you become a dentist, you run the risk that a new technology will eliminate cavities. So try to limit your risk by diversifying your portfolio: Marry an optician or an engineer, not another dentist!

Avoid High Fees

We have some other advice for picking stocks. Avoid investments and mutual funds that have high fees or "loads," as they are sometimes called. It simply isn't worth it.

Let's say for instance that you wish to invest in the S&P 500. Some funds charge management and administrative fees of 0.05% of your investment, but other funds can charge up to ten or twenty times as much for investing in exactly the same basket of stocks.

The funds with the higher fees don't give you much of value in return. The lesson is simple: Don't pay the higher fees!

Even small fees can add up to large differences in returns over time. Let's say you are investing $10,000 over 30 years. If you invest with a firm that charges 0.10% a year in fees and the stock market gives a real return of 7% a year, then in 30 years you will have earned $74,016. If you invest in a firm that charges 1% a year, then in 30 years you will have about $57,434. The higher fees cost you $16,582 and, as we have shown, you probably got nothing for your extra fees. Small differences in growth or loss rates, when compounded over time, make for a big difference. The same is true for your portfolio.

That brings us to a corollary principle, to which we now turn.

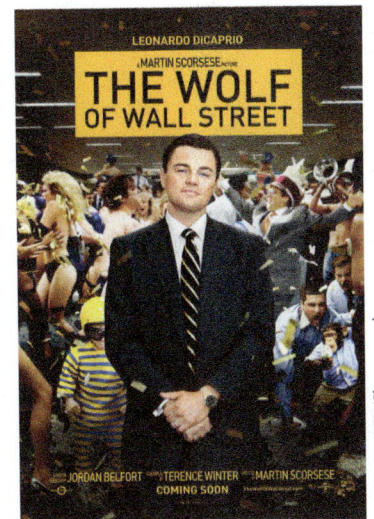

What are the Wolf's incentives? Jordan Belfort, the New York stockbroker whose life was chronicled in Martin Scorsese's movie *The Wolf of Wall Street,* made millions by charging small investors high fees to buy dubious investments.

Moviestore/REX/Shutterstock

Compound Returns Build Wealth

If one investment earns a higher rate of return each year than another investment, in the long run that makes a big difference. Imagine you buy a well-diversified portfolio of stocks and every year you reinvest all of your dividends. A simple approximation, called the rule of 70, explains how long it will take for your investment to double in value given a specified rate of return.

Rule of 70: If the rate of return (annual percent increase in value including dividends) of an investment is x%, then the doubling time is $70/x$ years.

Table 10.1 illustrates the rule of 70 by showing how long it takes for an investment to double in value given different returns. With a return of 1%, an investment will double approximately every 70 years (70/1 = 70). If returns increase to 2%, the value of your investment will double every 35 years (70/2 = 35). Consider the impact of a 4% return. If this rate of return is sustained, then the value of an investment doubles every 17.5 years (70/4 = 17.5). In 70 years, the value doubles 4 times, reaching a level 16 times its starting value!

The rule of 70 is just a mathematical approximation but it bears out the key concept that when compounded, small differences in investment returns can have a large effect. To make this more concrete, if you have a long time horizon, you probably should invest in (diversified) stocks rather than bonds.

TABLE 10.1 YEARS TO DOUBLE USING THE RULE OF 70

Annual Return (%)	Years to Double
0	Never
1	70
2	35
3	23.3
4	17.5

In the long run, stocks offer higher returns than bonds. Since 1802, for example, stocks have had an average real rate of return of about 7% per year, while bonds have paid closer to 2% per year.[5] Using our now familiar rule of 70, we know that money that grows at 7% a year will double in 10 years, but money that grows at 2% a year won't double for 35 years. Alternatively, growing at 7% a year, $10,000 will return $76,122 in 30 years, but if that investment grows at 2% a year, the return over that same period of time will be only $18,113.

Stocks, however, have the potential for greater losses than do bonds because bond holders and other creditors are always paid before shareholders. You are unlikely to lose much money if you buy high-grade corporate or government bonds, but the stock market is highly volatile and it does periodically crash. Nonetheless, in American history, stocks almost always outperform bonds over any 20-year time period you care to examine, including the period of the Great Depression and World War II. Stocks are usually the better long-term investment.

Of course, that doesn't mean that everyone should invest so heavily in stocks. In any particular year, or even over the course of a month, week, or day, stocks can go down in value quite a bit. If you are 80 years old and managing your retirement income, you probably shouldn't invest much in stocks. If you have to send your twins to college in two years' time, you might want some safer investments, as well. Nor does the past necessarily predict the future—just because stocks outperformed bonds in the past doesn't mean that will continue to happen. Remember to diversify!

MRU

mru.org/rule-70

The Rule of 70

The No-Free-Lunch Principle, or No Return Without Risk

The differences between stocks and bonds, as investment vehicles, reflect a more general principle. There is a systematic **trade-off between return and risk**. Figure 10.3, for example, shows the trade-off between return and risk on four asset classes. U.S. T-bills are safe but have low returns. You can get a higher return by buying stock in a group of large firms such as in the S&P 500, but the value of those firms fluctuates a lot more than the value of T-bills, so to get the higher return, you need to bear higher risk.[*]

If you want even more risk than an investment in the stock market, numerous schemes give you a chance of making a killing. The simplest of such strategies is to take all your money, fly to Las Vegas, and bet on "black" for a spin of the roulette wheel. Yes, there is a 47.37% chance that you double your wealth. That's a high return, sort of. Sadly, there is also a 52.63% chance that you will lose everything you have, including your credit rating and the trust of your spouse and children. That's what we call high risk.

Remember this story when you hear about a high-flying "hedge fund" or other fancy investment device. It's easy to generate high returns for a few years by getting lucky and doubling down (betting all your winnings again). Take a look again at Figure 10.3. Higher returns come at the expense of higher risk.

This no-free-lunch principle can help you evaluate some other investments, as well. Let's say you come into a tidy sum of money and you start wondering

The **risk–return trade-off** means higher returns come at the price of higher risk.

FIGURE 10.3

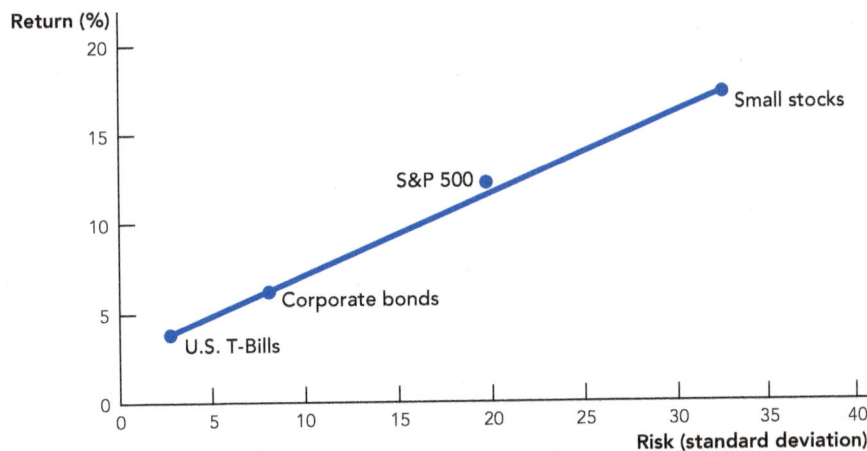

The No-Free-Lunch Principle: Higher Returns Come at the Price of Higher Risk

Note: Ibbotson Associates. 2007. *Returns and Standard Deviations on the Arithmetic Averages of Nominal Returns, 1926–2006. Classic Yearbook.*

[*] We measure risk using the standard deviation of the portfolio return. The standard deviation is a measure of how much the return tends to fluctuate from its average level: thus, the larger the standard deviation, the greater the risk. A rule of thumb is that there is a 68% probability of being within ±1 standard deviation of the mean return. For the S&P 500, for example, the mean return is about 12% and the standard deviation is about 20% so in any given year, there is a 68% probability that the return will be between −8% and 32%. Of course, there is a 32% probability that something else could happen! But beware! The rule of thumb is only an approximation. Risk in the real world can rarely be modeled with perfect mathematical accuracy.

whether you should invest in art. Overall, should you expect art to be a better or inferior financial investment, compared with the market as a whole?

A lot of people—probably most people—buy art because they want to look at it. They enjoy hanging it on their walls. In the language of economics, art yields "a nonmonetary return," which is just our way of saying it is fun to look at. Now suppose that investments in art earned just as high a return as investments in stocks. In that case, art would be fun to have on the wall *and* would be an excellent investment. But wait, that sounds like a free lunch doesn't it? So what does the no-free-lunch principle predict?

We know that the expected returns on different assets, adjusted for risk, should be equal. So if some asset yields a higher "fun" return, those assets should, on average, yield a lower financial return. And that is exactly what we find with art. On average, art underperforms the stock market by a few percentage points a year. You can think of the lower returns as the price of having some beautiful art on your wall. Again, it's the no-free-lunch principle in action.

This kind of analysis applies not just to art but also to real estate. Let's say you want to buy a home. Can you expect superior or inferior financial returns over time? This question is a little trickier than the art question because two different and opposing forces operate. Let's look at each in turn.

First, a home tends to be a risky asset for most purchasers. Let's say you buy a $300,000 home by putting down $200,000 and borrowing the remainder. That home is probably a fairly big chunk of your overall wealth and it puts you in a relatively nondiversified position. That's risk, people don't usually like risk, and as we saw above, riskier assets earn, all other things equal, higher expected returns (the risk-return trade-off).

Second, and probably more important, if you buy a house, you get to live in it. The house, like the painting, provides you with personal services and in this case those services are valuable. Many people enjoy their backyard and the feeling of owning a home and being able to paint the walls any color they want. These nonmonetary returns mean that houses can be expected to pay a relatively low financial return.

Indeed, if we look at the financial returns on real estate over a long time horizon, it turns out they are fairly low. In fact, for long periods of time, the average financial rate of return on real estate is not much different from zero. One lesson is that houses must be lots of fun!

If you want to see that the downside of real estate investments is not just a recent phenomenon, take a look at Figure 10.4.

In the 50 years from 1947 to 1997, real housing prices hardly changed at all, although with some blips upward in the late 1970s and late 1980s. Beginning in 1997, a housing boom pushed prices well above any before seen in U.S. history. As you probably know, prices tumbled dramatically starting in 2006, but since 2011 they have risen and are now once again higher than at any time in the twentieth century.

The lesson is that most of the time a house is a good place to live but not a good place to invest. When prices started to rise in 1997 and kept rising year after year, many people thought that real estate was the investment of the century—"they ain't making any more," people said. But the no-free-lunch principle tells us that precisely because houses are a good place to live, we should not also expect them to be a good investment. All other things equal, fun activities yield lower financial returns than nonfun activities.

When prices rose, some people got lucky and made a killing, but other people tried to do the same and ended up bankrupt. So don't expect to make a

FIGURE 10.4

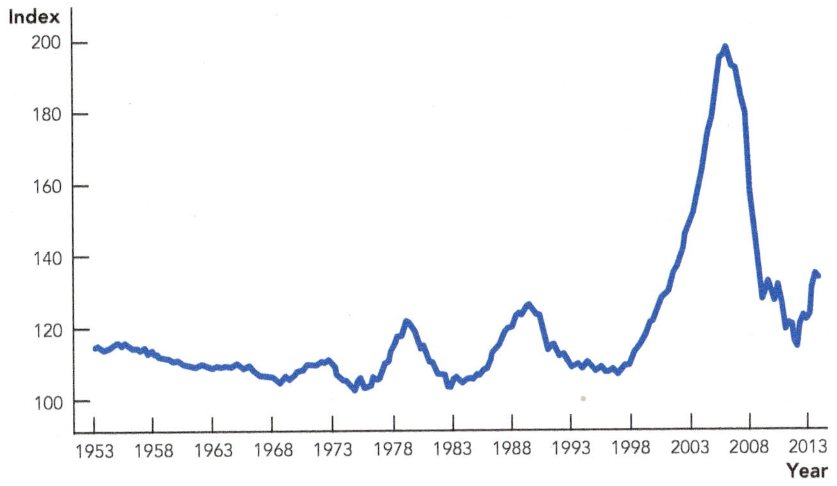

Index of Real U.S. Housing Prices, 1953–2013

Data from: Robert Shiller's *Irrational Exuberance*, www.irrationalexuberance.com.

killing in the real estate market, and remember to diversify! One more point. Are you one of those people who doesn't like to mow the lawn? Do you dread the notion of choosing homeowner's insurance or worrying about when your roof will fall in? The lesson is simple: Don't buy a house, you won't have fun, and the financial returns won't make it worth your while.

Other Benefits and Costs of Stock Markets

Throughout this chapter, we've recommended against gambling with all or most of your money. We've recommended buy and hold, based on a diversified portfolio. But hey, maybe some of you are into gambling. You know what? If you want to take risk for the sake of risk alone, the U.S. stock market offers the best odds in the world, better than Las Vegas and better than your local bookie. People on average make money in the U.S. stock market and that is because the productive capacity of the U.S. economy is expanding through economic growth. There is more profit to go around and that means you have a good chance of making some really lucrative investments.

Stock markets have uses beyond investment. First, new stock and bond issues are important to a company as a means of raising capital for new investment (investment now in the economic sense of increasing the capital stock). Stock markets also reward successful entrepreneurs and thus encourage people to start companies and look around for new ideas. The founders of Google are now very rich and selling company shares to the stock market helped make them so. A well-functioning stock market helps companies such as Google get going or expand.

Second, the stock market gives us a better idea of how well firms are run. The stock price is a signal about the value of the firm. When the stock price is increasing, especially when it is increasing relative to other stocks, this is a signal that the firm is making the right investments for future profits. When the stock is declining, especially when it is declining relative to other stocks, this is

CHECK YOURSELF

- How does investing in stocks of other countries help to diversify your investments?
- Many people dream of owning a football or baseball team. Would you expect the return on these assets to be relatively high or low?

a signal that something has gone wrong and perhaps management needs to be replaced. Some critics allege that Google has dominated Web search but failed with its maps, blog search services, and email accounts. It is not necessarily clear whether these endeavors are making money for the company. Will Google make YouTube into a profitable venture? Are the charges true that "Google has lost it"? It's hard to say in the abstract. But we can look at Google's share price and see if it is going up or down. Market prices give the public a daily report on whether the managers of a company are succeeding or failing.

Third, stock markets are a way of transferring company control from less competent people to more competent people. If a group of people think they know the right way to run a company, they can buy it and put their money where their mouth is, so to speak. Maybe a company should be merged, broken up, or simply taken in a new direction. The stock market is the ultimate venue where people bid for the right to make these decisions.

Bubble, Bubble, Toil, and Trouble

It's worth pointing out that stock markets (and other asset markets) have a downside, namely that they can encourage speculative bubbles. A speculative bubble arises when stock prices rise far higher, and more rapidly, than can be accounted for by the fundamental prospects of the companies at hand. Bubbles are based in human psychology and often they are hard to understand. Nobel Prize–winning economist Vernon Smith, whom you met in Chapter 4, has found that speculative bubbles and crashes occur in experimental markets, even when traders are given enough information to easily calculate an asset's true value.[6] Inexperienced traders are more prone to bubbles, but even experienced traders can fall for bubbles when the trading environment changes. Speculative bubbles and crashes have significant costs, as we will discuss, so economists are trying to better understand bubbles and how market institutions can be designed to help avoid them.

During the dot.com era, circa 2000, many Internet or dot.com stocks had very high prices even though many of these companies had never earned a dime of profit or for that matter any revenue. Many of the tech stocks were listed on the NASDAQ stock exchange. As you can see in Figure 10.5, in the space of five years the NASDAQ Composite Index more than tripled from a monthly average of about 1,200 to more than 4,000 before falling back down again. Many people made a lot of money on the ride up and many people— maybe the same people, maybe others—lost a lot of money on the ride down.

If you can spot speculative bubbles on a consistent basis, yes, you can become very wealthy. But, of course, a speculative bubble is usually easier to detect with hindsight than at the time. Apple and Google might have looked like speculative bubbles, too; the only problem is that they never burst. Betting too soon that high prices will end is also one way to go bankrupt.

Speculative bubbles, and their bursting, can hurt an economy. During the rise of the bubble, capital is invested in areas where it is not actually very valuable. A second wave of problems comes when the bubble crashes. Lower stock prices (or lower home prices) mean that people feel poorer and so they will spend less. The collapse of the bubble also means that workers must move from one sector to another, such as from high tech to retailing, or from real estate to export industries. Shifting labor from one sector of an economy to another creates labor adjustment costs.

We saw both of these problems with the dot.com bubble and the real estate bubble leading up to the crash of housing prices in 2007–2008. During the dot.com

FIGURE 10.5

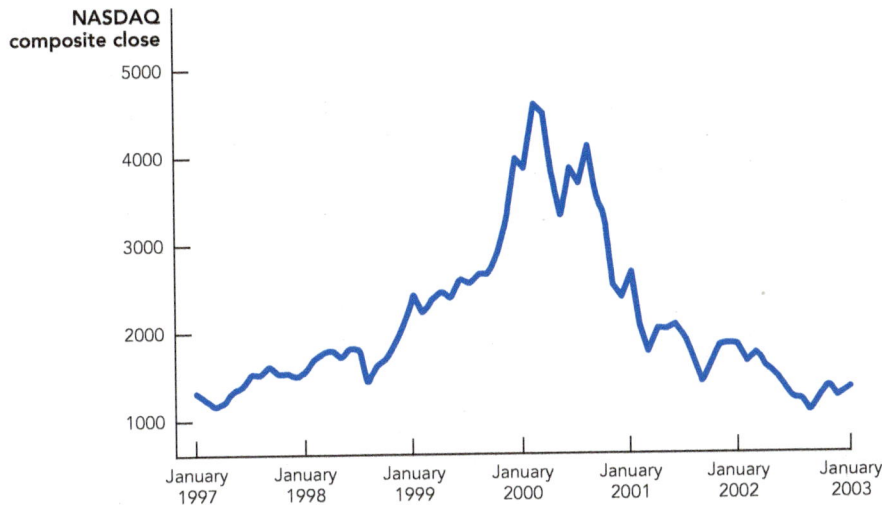

The Boom and Bust in Tech Stocks: Monthly Close on NASDAQ Composite Index, 1997–2002

Data from: NASDAQ.

boom years, for example, we invested too much in stringing fiber-optic cable across the world's oceans—cable that later proved to be unprofitable. Similarly, during the housing boom we invested too much in houses that later were abandoned. In addition, the boom in housing prices led banks to be much too lax about the value of financial assets backed by portfolios of mortgages. When housing prices started to fall and people began to default on their mortgages, the value of these asset-backed securities plummeted and banks found themselves nearing bankruptcy. To stave off bankruptcy, these banks cut back on lending, transmitting problems in the housing markets to the wider economy and helping to generate the lengthy recession beginning in late 2007.

Yes, bubbles can be a problem, but few people doubt that we are better off with active trading in stock and asset markets. One partial solution is to have greater transparency in assessing the value of companies and assets. Economists continue to research asset markets and the possibility of limiting bubbles and subsequent crashes. But, for now, there is no surefire solution for getting rid of asset bubbles.

Takeaway

We have stressed some simple and practical points. It is difficult for an investor to consistently beat the market over long periods. You are well-advised to diversify your investments. Avoid fees and try to generate a high compound return over time. Understand that the promise of higher returns is often accompanied by higher risk.

Viewed as a whole, stock markets and other trading markets give investors a chance to earn money, diversify their holdings, express opinions on the course of the market, and hedge risks. Stock markets also play a role in financing innovative new firms. Stock markets appear to be subject to speculative bubbles, but active stock markets are an important part of a healthy growing economy.

CHECK YOURSELF

- The Federal Reserve was criticized for not stepping in and bursting the housing bubble, which would have prevented the housing collapse. Do you think this criticism is valid, based on what you read in this section?

CHAPTER REVIEW

Go online to practice with more examples of these types of problems, including live links to videos, data sources, and feedback.

▶ Problems with this icon relate to optional MRU videos.

KEY CONCEPTS

efficient markets hypothesis, p. 220

buy and hold, p. 222

risk-return trade-off, p. 225

FACTS AND TOOLS

1. Before we plunge into the world of finance, let's review the rule of 70. Suppose your rich aunt hands you a $3,000 check at the end of the school year. She tells you it's for your education. But what should you *really* do with that extra money? Let's see how much it would be worth if you saved it for a while.

   a. If you put it in a bank account earning 2% real annual return on average, how many years would it take before it was worth $6,000? Until it was worth $12,000?

   b. If you put it in a Standard and Poor's 500 (S&P 500) mutual fund earning an average 7% real return every year, how many years would it take before it was worth $6,000? Until it was worth $12,000?

   c. Suppose you invest a little less than half your money in the bank and a little more than half in a mutual fund, just to play it somewhat safe, so that you can expect a 5% real return on average. How many years now until you reach $6,000 and $12,000?

2. Let's do something boring just to drive home a point: Count up the number of years in Figure 10.1 in which more than half of the mutual funds managed to beat the S&P 500 index. (Recall that the Standard and Poor's 500 is just a list of 500 large U.S. corporations—it's a list that overlaps a lot with the Fortune 500.) What percentage of the time did the experts actually beat the S&P 500?

3. Consider the supply and demand for oranges. Orange crops can be destroyed by below-freezing temperatures.

   a. If a weather report states that oranges are likely to freeze in a storm later this week, what probably happens to the demand for oranges *today*, before the storm comes?

   b. According to a simple supply and demand model, what happens to the price of oranges today given your answer to part a.

   c. How does this illustrate the idea that stock prices *today* "bake in" information about *future* events? In other words, how is a share of Microsoft like an orange? (*Note:* Wall Street people often use the expression, "That news is already baked into the price," when they talk about the efficient markets hypothesis.)

4. In the United States, high-level corporate officials have to publicly state when they buy or sell a large number of shares in their own company. They have to make these statements a few days after their purchase or sale. What do you think probably happens (choose a, b, c, or d) when newspapers report these true "insider trades"? (*Note:* The right answer according to theory is actually true in practice.)

   a. When insiders sell, prices rise, since investors increase their demand for the company's shares.

   b. When insiders sell, prices fall, since investors increase their demand for the company's shares.

   c. When insiders sell, prices fall, since investors decrease their demand for the company's shares.

   d. When insiders sell, prices rise, since investors decrease their demand for the company's shares.

5. Let's see how fees can hurt your investment strategy. Let's assume that your mutual fund grows at an average rate of 7% per year—before subtracting the fees. Using the rule of 70:

   a. How many years will it take for your money to double if fees are 0.5% per year?

   b. How many years will it take for your money to double if fees are 1.5% per year (not uncommon in the mutual fund industry)?

   c. How many years to double if fees are 2.5% per year?

6. **a.** If you talk to a broker selling the high-fee mutual fund, what will they probably tell you when you ask them, "Am I getting my money's worth when I pay your high fees?"

   b. According to Figure 10.1, is your broker's answer likely to be right most of the time?

THINKING AND PROBLEM SOLVING

7. Your brother calls you on the phone telling you that Google's share price has fallen by about 25% over the past few days. Now you can own one small slice of Google for only $540 a share (the price on the day this question was written). Your brother says he is pretty sure the stock is going to head back up to $700 very soon and you should buy.

   Should you believe your brother? (*Hint:* Remember someone is selling shares whenever someone else is buying.)

8. In most of your financial decisions early in life, you'll be a buyer, but let's think about the incentives of people who sell stocks, bonds, bank accounts, and other financial products.

   a. Walking in the shopping mall one day, you see a new store: the Dollar Store. Of course, you've seen plenty of dollar stores before, but none like this one: The sign in the window says, "Dollars for sale: Fifty cents each." Why will this store be out of business soon?

   b. If business owners are self-interested and fairly rational people, will they ever open up this dollar store in the first place? Why or why not?

   c. This dollar store is similar to stories people tell about "cheap stocks" that you might hear of on the news. Fill in the blank with any prices that make sense: "If the shares of this company were really worth _____, no one would really sell it for _____."

9. How is "stock market diversification" like putting money in a bank account?

10. Warren Buffett often says that he doesn't want a lot of diversification in his portfolio. He says that diversification means buying stocks that go up along with stocks that go down; but he only wants to buy the stocks that go up! From the point of view of the typical investor, what is wrong with this reasoning?

11. There are three stocks available: a solar energy firm, an oil firm, and an airline. You can invest in two. Which two?

Discovering DATA ⠿

12. How easy is it to spot a bubble? Go to the FRED economic database (https://fred.stlouisfed.org/) and search for NASDAQ. You should find the NASDAQ Composite Index. Graph it and click Max to show all the data available.

    a. What happened to the index between November of 1998 and February of 2000? Then what happened?

    b. What happened to the index between October of 2009 and October of 2014? Then what happened?

    c. Are you willing to make a bet about the future direction of the NASDAQ?

CHALLENGES

13. What is so bad about bubbles? If the price of Internet stocks or housing rises and then falls, is that such a big problem? After all, some people say, most of the gains going up are "paper gains" and most of the losses going down are "paper losses." Comment on this view.

14. Mr. Wolf calls you with what he says is a tremendous opportunity in the stock market. He has inside knowledge about a pharmaceutical company and he says that the price will go up tomorrow. Of course, you are skeptical and decline his offer. The next day the price does go up. Mr. Wolf calls again and says not to worry, tomorrow the price will go down and that will be a good time to buy. Again, you decline. The next day the price does go down. Mr. Wolf calls you over the next several weeks and every time he calls his predictions about the stock price prove to be amazingly accurate. Finally, he calls to tell you that tomorrow is the big one, the day the price will skyrocket. Mr. Wolf has been accurate many times in a row so you empty your bank account to buy as much stock as possible. The next day the price of the stock goes nowhere. What happened?

WORK IT OUT

For interactive, step-by-step help in solving this problem, go online.

Let's see how fees can hurt your investment strategy. Let's assume that your mutual fund grows at an average rate of 5% per year—before subtracting the fees. Using the rule of 70:

a. How many years will it take for your money to double if fees are 0.5% per year?

b. How many years will it take for your money to double if fees are 1.5% per year (not uncommon in the mutual fund industry)?

c. How many years to double if fees are 2.5% per year?

MRU VIDEOS

Should You Listen to the Expert Stock Pickers?

mru.org/pick-stocks

Problem: **6**

The Efficient Market Hypothesis

mru.org/beat-market

Problems: **7, 8, 10, 14**

Diversify, Diversify, Diversify!

mru.org/stock-diversify

Problem: **5**

The Rule of 70

mru.org/rule-70

Problems: **1, 5**

11

Unemployment and Labor Force Participation

Thirty-six thousand travel agents lost their jobs on November 10, 1999. Actually, it didn't happen quite that fast, but when Expedia.com went public, there were 124,000 travel agents in the United States and by 2006 there were fewer than 88,000. Travel agents became less common as more people booked their own travel online.

The disappearance of the travel agent represents a recurring story in American history. Many jobs have disappeared—blacksmiths, chimney sweeps, and darkroom technicians, for example, are no longer in demand. Employment in other fields has greatly declined. For example, in 1910 there were 11.5 million farm workers in the United States; today there are less than one million. New jobs, however, have replaced old jobs. There are now more than 1.6 million jobs in the "App economy," jobs related to writing apps for mobile phones and devices. Before the introduction of the iPhone in 2007, there were zero jobs in this industry. Jobs are growing rapidly in high-tech areas like software engineering and the biosciences, but a wealthier society also means more and better paying jobs in professions that have been around for a long time. Today, for example, there are more than 200,000 professional athletes, coaches, umpires, and related workers in the United States—more than any other time in history.

A growing economy is a changing economy and *some* unemployment is a necessary consequence of economic growth. The unemployment rate in France, however, has hovered around 10% for several decades. High and long-lasting unemployment is unlikely to be caused by economic growth. During a recession, unemployment increases quickly and in many different industries at once and that too is unlikely to be caused by economic growth. Thus, there are different types of unemployment with different causes.

Figure 11.1 on the next page illustrates the organization of this chapter. We are going to start at the top with the issue that is most prominent in the economics and business news, namely unemployment. We explain how unemployment is defined and then the different types of unemployment and their causes.

233

FIGURE 11.1

Employed

Unemployed

Adults not in labor force
(e.g., students, homemakers,
retirees, others)

Employed + Unemployed = Labor force

Unemployment rate
= Unemployed/Labor force

Adults not in labor force + Labor force
= Adult noninstitutionalized civilians

Labor force participation rate
= Labor force/(Adult noninstitutionalized civilians)

Plus children, military personnel,
and institutionalized civilians

U.S. population

Employment, Unemployment, and Labor Force Participation in the U.S. Population

Data from: Bureau of Labor Statistics.

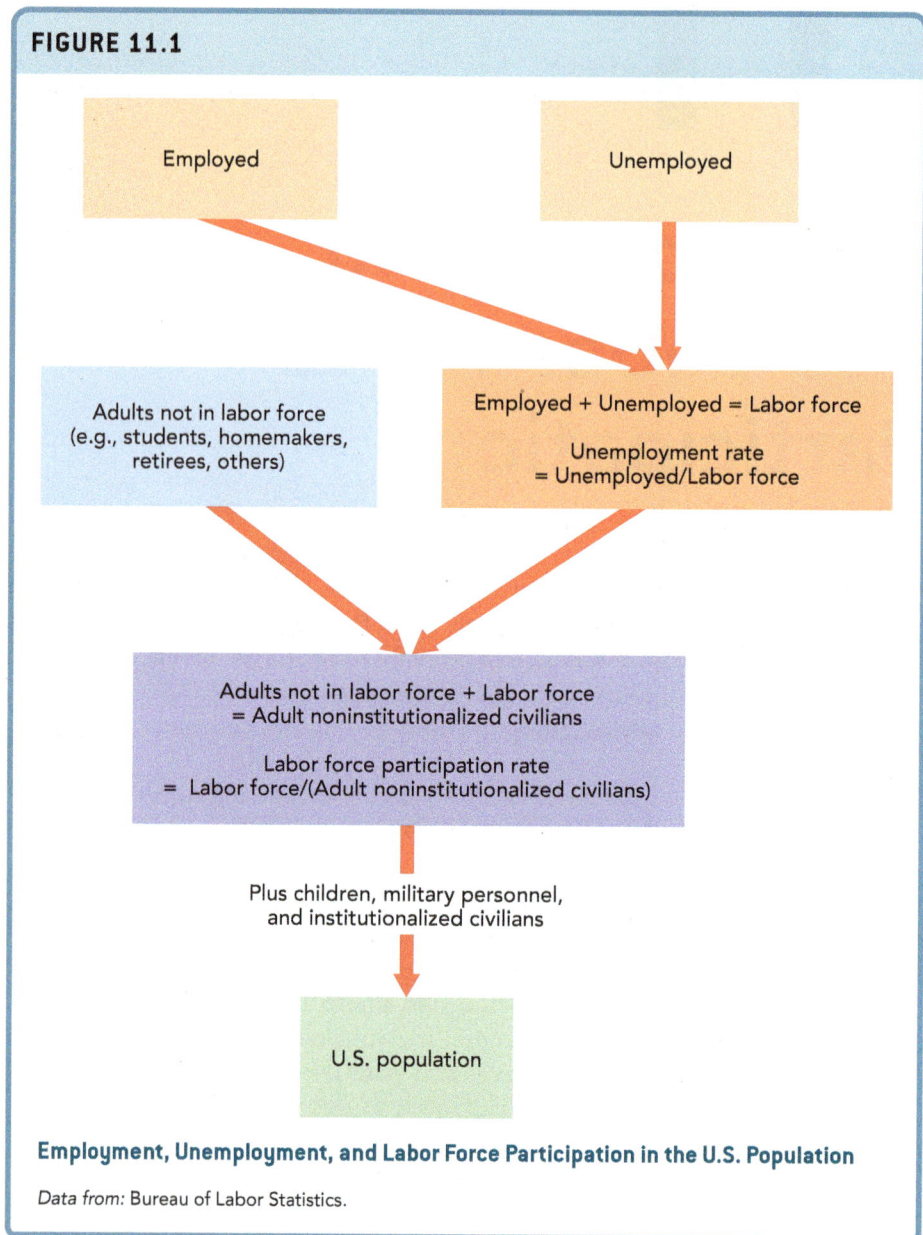

Don't forget, however, that many individuals neither have a job nor are looking for work—these individuals are not part of the labor force. As we move down the tree, we will ask: Why do some people choose to be in the labor force while others do not? Why is it, for example, that most women are in the (paid) labor force today even though this was uncommon in the 1950s? And why is labor force participation for some workers much higher in some countries than in others? The topic of labor force participation makes up the second half of the chapter. And what about total population, at the very bottom of this structure? For that you must take a demography course, but you'll find a brief discussion of birth control at the close of the chapter.

Defining Unemployment

Unemployed workers are adults who do not have a job but who are looking for work.

Is a 6-year-old without a job unemployed? Is someone in prison unemployed? What about a retired 60-year-old? In all cases the answer is no. We count someone as **unemployed** only if they are *willing and able to work but cannot find a job.*

In practice, this means that to be counted as unemployed, a person must be an adult (16 years or older), not institutionalized (e.g., not in prison), a civilian, and, most important, that person must be *looking for work*. Similarly, to be counted as employed, a person must be an adult, noninstitutionalized civilian with a job.

In June 2017, there were 7.0 million unemployed persons in the United States and 153.2 million employed persons. Together, the employed and the unemployed make up the labor force of 160.2 million (7.0 + 153.2).

The **unemployment rate** is the percentage of the labor force without a job:

The **unemployment rate** is the percentage of the labor force without a job.

$$\text{Unemployment rate} = \frac{\text{Unemployed}}{\text{Unemployed} + \text{Employed}} \times 100$$

$$= \frac{\text{Unemployed}}{\text{Labor force}} \times 100$$

Thus, in June 2017, the unemployment rate was 4.4%:

$$= \frac{7.0 \text{ million}}{7.0 \text{ million} + 153.2 \text{ million}} \times 100 = \frac{7.0}{160.2} \times 100 = 4.4\%$$

mru.org/unemployment

How Is the Unemployment Rate Defined?

Once we have examined the issue of unemployment, we will investigate some of the determinants of the **labor force participation rate,** the percentage of the adult, civilian, noninstitutionalized population (adults for short) in the labor force.

The **labor force participation rate** is the percentage of adults in the labor force.

How Good an Indicator Is the Unemployment Rate?

We are interested in the unemployment rate because unemployment, especially long-term unemployment, can be financially and psychologically devastating. Unemployment also means that the economy is underperforming—labor that could be used to produce valuable goods and services is being wasted. The unemployment rate is the single best indicator of how well the labor market is working in both of these senses, but it is an incomplete indicator.

Individuals without a job are not counted as unemployed if they are not actively looking for work. But some people who are unemployed for a long period of time may get discouraged and stop looking for work even though they want a job. It's difficult to know exactly how many **discouraged workers** there are because the concept is not well-defined. Many people who are happily retired would take a job if the wage were high enough, but should every retired person count as a discouraged worker? The Bureau of Labor Statistics (BLS) keeps statistics on one definition of discouraged workers, which it defines as workers who want and are available for work, and who have looked for a job sometime in the last year but not in the last month because they believe that no jobs were available for them.

Discouraged workers are workers who have given up looking for work but who would still like a job.

Using this definition, the number of discouraged workers in the United States is small relative to the number of unemployed workers, so counting discouraged workers as unemployed increases the unemployment rate only modestly. The number of discouraged workers has increased since the recession in 2009, but as Figure 11.2 illustrates, the unemployment rate with and without discouraged workers is similar and the two rates track each other closely.

FIGURE 11.2

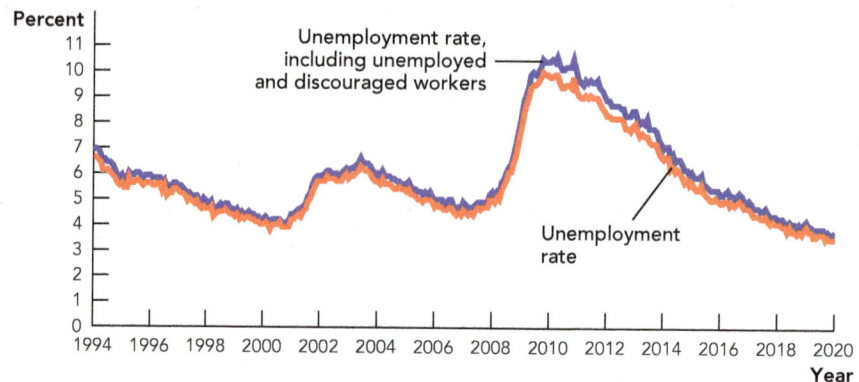

The Unemployment Rate With and Without Discouraged Workers

Data from: Bureau of Labor Statistics, https://fred.stlouisfed.org/graph/?g=oYtZ.

The unemployment rate also doesn't measure the quality of the jobs people take or how well workers are matched to their jobs. A taxi driver with a PhD in chemistry, for example, is counted as fully employed by the BLS. Similarly, a worker who has a part-time job but who wants a full-time job is counted as fully employed. If we counted these workers as partially unemployed, the unemployment rate would be higher, but defining and measuring partial employment isn't easy. If a taxi driver has a BA in English, should that be counted as almost fully employed? Nearly everyone wants a better job in some dimension (more hours, fewer hours, closer to home, higher wages, better benefits, etc.) so is everyone less than fully employed?

Underemployment rate is a Bureau of Labor Statistics measure that includes part-time workers who would rather have a full-time position and people who would like to work but have given up looking for a job.

Even though any definition is imperfect, the BLS also looks at one measure of the **underemployment rate**. This includes part-time workers who would rather have a full-time position and also people who would like to work but have given up looking for a job. As of February 2017, this rate was 9.5 in the American economy.

Given these imperfections in the official unemployment rate, economists also look at other measures of labor underutilization and indicators of how well the labor market is performing, such as the labor force participation rate, the number of full-time jobs, and average wages. Fortunately, most of these other indicators (and probably many other job characteristics that are more difficult to measure) correlate well with the unemployment rate, so the unemployment rate is a good summary indicator of the state of the labor market. (See Thinking and Problem Solving question 22 for more on this.)

Economists distinguish three types of unemployment: frictional, structural, and cyclical. We start with frictional.

Frictional Unemployment

What is the fastest way to sell a house? Lower the price! At a low enough price, any house will sell quickly. So selling houses is easy: It's finding a price that the seller is willing to accept and the buyer is willing to pay that is difficult. In the same way, it's always easy to find a job if you are willing to work for peanuts. Finding a job that you want at a wage that you will accept and the employer will pay, however, takes time and effort. The difficulty of matching employees to employers creates friction in the labor market, and the resulting temporary unemployment is called frictional unemployment. Thus, **frictional unemployment** is short-term unemployment caused by the ordinary difficulties of matching employee to employer.

Scarcity of information is one of the causes of frictional unemployment. Workers do not know all the job opportunities available to them, and employers do not know all the available candidates and their respective qualifications. The Internet has probably lowered the underlying rate of frictional unemployment by making it easier for workers to search for jobs and for firms to search for workers.

Frictional unemployment usually doesn't last very long. If the economy is not in a recession, it might take a few weeks to find a new job, or for specialized workers perhaps a few months but not much longer. Figure 11.3 shows the typical duration of unemployment in 2018, a nonrecession year, and also in 2010 as the economy slowly exited the 2007–2009 recession. In 2018, most unemployment was of fairly short duration: 34.3% of the unemployed were jobless for less than five weeks and 29.8% were jobless for only 5 to 14 weeks. The remaining 36% were jobless for more than 14 weeks, with 21.4% jobless for more than half a year. In the United States in a nonrecession year, a significant fraction of unemployment is frictional.

The situation was very different in 2010 when a majority of the unemployed had been unemployed for more than 14 weeks. Indeed, in mid-2010, 43.3% of the unemployed had been unemployed for more than 6 months. Not since the

> **Frictional unemployment** is short-term unemployment caused by the ordinary difficulties of matching employee to employer.

FIGURE 11.3

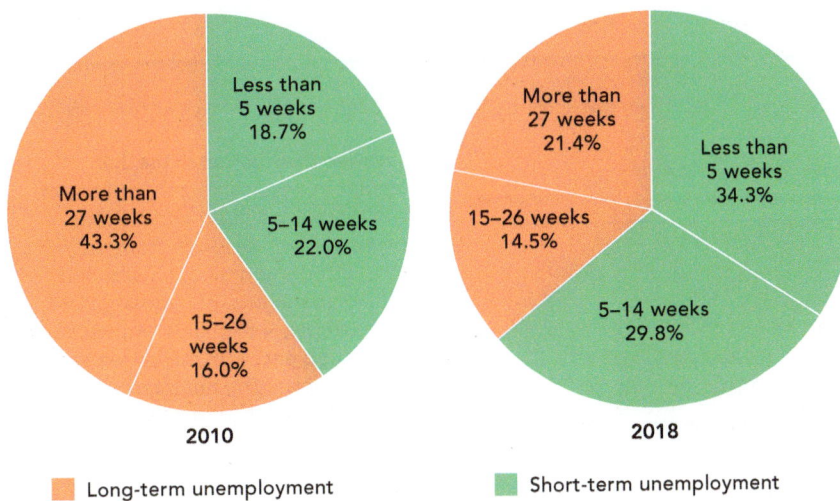

2010

Less than 5 weeks 18.7%

5–14 weeks 22.0%

15–26 weeks 16.0%

More than 27 weeks 43.3%

2018

More than 27 weeks 21.4%

Less than 5 weeks 34.3%

5–14 weeks 29.8%

15–26 weeks 14.5%

■ Long-term unemployment   ■ Short-term unemployment

U.S. Unemployment Duration in 2010 and 2018 In 2010, when the economy was recovering from the big 2008–2009 recession, a large fraction of unemployment was long term. In 2018, a more normal year, a majority of unemployment was short term.

Data from: https://fred.stlouisfed.org/graph/?g=p4UF.

Great Depression had so many unemployed workers been unemployed for such an extended period of time.

Frictional unemployment is typically a large share of total unemployment because the U.S. economy is dynamic. Innovation and the relentless pressure of competition drive progress. Progress, however, is not simply creating new jobs and adding them to the old. Rather it's about creating new jobs and destroying old jobs. Webmasters are in; travel agents are out. We can see this process in more detail by looking at statistics on job creation and destruction.

As shown in Figure 11.4, the U.S. economy had around 210,000 more jobs at the end of February of 2014 than it had at the beginning. This number, however, hides an underlying reality of much greater change. In that same month, 4.59 *million* new jobs were created but during the same month there were also 4.38 million job separations (quits, layoffs, and other separations). The net figure, the one often reported in the news, is the difference between hires and separations (4.59 − 4.38 = 0.21 million, or 210,000 new jobs). These figures are typical. In any given month, millions of jobs are created and millions of jobs are destroyed. "Creative destruction," a term coined by economist Joseph Schumpeter, describes this process well.

Structural Unemployment

Structural unemployment is persistent, long-term unemployment. Isn't it redundant to say that unemployment is persistent *and* long-term? Not quite. In France, Germany, Italy, and Spain, for example, approximately 40% to 50% of the unemployed have been unemployed for more than one year and this has been true for about 25 years.[1] In 2010 in the United States, 29% of the unemployed had been unemployed for more than a year, but this had been true for only about one year. The phrase "persistent, long-term unemployment" means that a substantial fraction of the unemployed have been unemployed for more than one year and that this problem has lasted for a long time. Persistent

CHECK YOURSELF
- What is a key cause of frictional unemployment?
- To minimize frictional unemployment, unemployed workers would have to accept the first job they were offered no matter what the wage. Is frictional unemployment always a bad thing?

Structural unemployment is persistent, long-term unemployment caused by long-lasting shocks or permanent features of an economy that make it more difficult for some workers to find jobs.

FIGURE 11.4

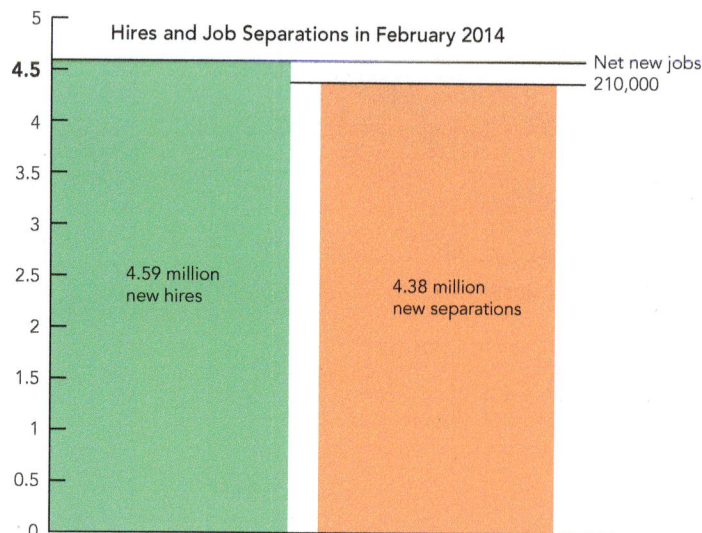

Hires and Job Separations in February 2014

4.59 million new hires

4.38 million new separations

Net new jobs 210,000

Creative Destruction in the Job Market In a typical month, millions of workers will be hired and millions of workers will separate from their jobs, through quitting, layoffs, and other separations. In February 2014, for example, 4.59 million workers were hired and 4.38 million workers left their jobs. The net increase of 210,000 new jobs hid an underlying job market that is extraordinarily dynamic.

long-term unemployment has traditionally been much less of a problem in the United States than in Europe. Long-term unemployment following the 2008–2009 recession, however, has been more persistent than in the past. By 2015, 18.7% of the unemployed had been unemployed for more than one year—a high rate for the United States but less than half the rate of the European Union average.

What causes structural unemployment? One cause is large, economy-wide shocks that occur relatively quickly. Adjusting to these shocks can create long-lasting unemployment as the economy takes time to restructure. In addition to the oil shocks, the U.S. economy has had to restructure in recent decades because of the shift from a manufacturing to a service economy, because of globalization and because of new information technologies such as the computer and the Internet.

Labor Regulations and Structural Unemployment

The late 1970s oil shock (as well as the other shocks previously mentioned) hit the United States as hard as it did Europe, but in the United States unemployment tends to increase with a shock and then decrease, while in Europe (especially in the big four continental economies—France, Germany, Italy, and Spain), unemployment has increased with shocks and then remained at high levels. Table 11.1 shows that unemployment in the big four European countries hovered around 10% or higher for 20 years and a large fraction of this unemployment has been long term. Why did unemployment rates in the United States and Europe behave so differently?

Structural unemployment has been a more serious problem in Europe than in the United States because of labor regulations. More specifically, unemployment benefits, minimum wages, unions, and employment protection laws benefit some workers, but these regulations can also increase unemployment rates. All of these regulations are more generous and wide-ranging in Europe than in the United States, and that helps explain why structural unemployment is a more serious problem in Europe than in the United States. Let's go through each labor market intervention in turn.

TABLE 11.1 UNEMPLOYMENT RATES IN EUROPE VS. THE UNITED STATES, 1980–2004

Country	1980–1984	1985–1989	1990–1994	1995–1999	2000–2004	Fraction Unemployed for More Than One Year (2004)
France	7.3%	9.3%	9.6%	10.8%	8.4%	41.6%
Germany	5.9%	6.4%	6.7%	9.8%	8.8%	51.8%
Italy	8.8%	11.6%	10.9%	11.8%	9.3%	49.7%
Spain	15.9%	19.9%	19.6%	20.0%	11.7%	37.7%
United States	8.3%	6.2%	6.6%	4.9%	5.2%	12.7%

Data from: OECD Statistics and OECD Employment Outlook, 2005.

TABLE 11.2 UNEMPLOYMENT BENEFIT REPLACEMENT RATES IN EUROPE VS. THE UNITED STATES, 1994

	First Year	Second and Third Year	Fourth and Fifth Year
France	80%	62%	60%
Germany	74%	72%	72%
Spain	70%	55%	39%
United States	38%	14%	14%

Note: The data cover a worker with a dependent spouse and are net rates after taking into account taxes and other benefits.
Data from: Ljungqvist L. and T. Sargent. 1998. The European unemployment dilemma. *Journal of Political Economy* 106(3): 514–550.
Martin, John P. 1996. Measures of replacement rates for the purpose of international comparisons: A note. *OECD Economic Studies* 26(1): 99–115.

Unemployment Benefits Unemployment benefits are the most obvious labor regulation that can increase unemployment rates. Unemployment benefits include unemployment insurance, but also other benefits such as housing assistance that may be available in some countries. Table 11.2 shows how much of a worker's take-home pay was replaced by unemployment benefits in France, Germany, Spain, and the United States in 1994.[2] (We focus on 1994 because this is about midway through Europe's long spell of unemployment.)

In the first year of unemployment in France, the unemployment benefit system replaced 80% of a worker's income. A worker who lost their job in France, in other words, faced only a 20% cut in pay. In fact, if we look only at income, and not at the satisfaction that comes from having a job, a French worker who lost their job was probably better off—after all, an unemployed worker had 80% of the income of an employed worker and much more leisure time ("unemployed workers" may also work for pay in the black market). In comparison, the unemployment benefit system in the United States replaced only 38% of a worker's pay so a worker who lost their job faced a 62% cut in pay.

Unemployment benefits also last much longer in Europe than in the United States. In the United States, for example, unemployment benefits typically fall by more than half after just one year (although unemployment benefits are often extended in the United States when the unemployment rate is especially high). But in France, Germany, and Spain, unemployment benefits never decrease by so wide a margin.

Given these figures, it shouldn't be surprising that long-term unemployment is much more common in Europe than in the United States (see the last column in Table 11.1). In Europe, the price of unemployment is low, so more unemployment (leisure) is demanded. Or, if you like, workers in Europe can afford to remain unemployed for longer periods than workers in the United States.

In summary, unemployment benefits reduce the incentive for workers to search for and take new jobs. Now switching to look at the demand side of the labor market, minimum wage, unions, and employment protection laws reduce the incentive of firms to create and offer new jobs.

FIGURE 11.5

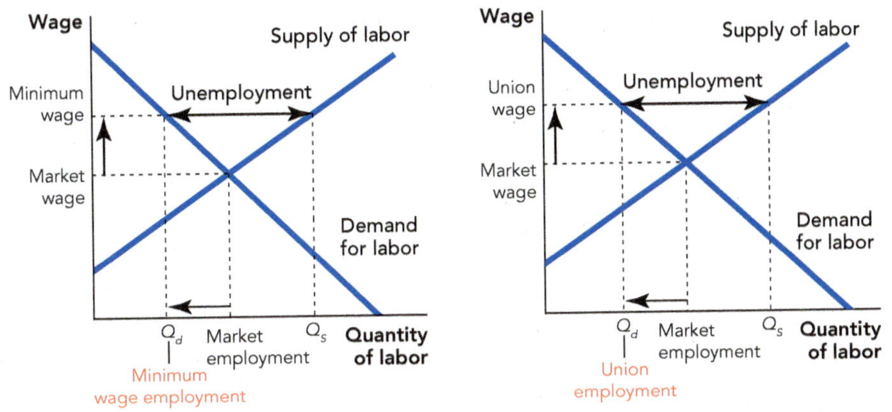

The Minimum Wage and Unions Increase Unemployment In the left panel, the minimum wage raises the wage, thus decreasing the quantity of labor demanded. In the right panel, the union threatens to strike unless the firm pays the union wage. The increase in the wage decreases the quantity of labor demanded.

Minimum Wages and Unions In the left panel of Figure 11.5, we analyze the minimum wage (see Chapter 5 for a more extensive discussion). The minimum wage raises the price of labor from the market wage to the minimum wage, and as labor becomes more expensive, firms reduce employment from market employment to minimum wage employment Q_d. At the minimum wage, the number of workers looking for work Q_s exceeds the number of jobs Q_d—thus, the minimum wage creates unemployment in the amount $Q_s - Q_d$.

In Western Europe, minimum wages have been higher than in the United States. In recent years, for example, the minimum wage in France was about 32% higher than in the United States. Minimum wages in Western Europe have also been higher relative to the **median wage** than in the United States. (The median wage is defined so that half of all workers earn less than the median and half more.) In France, the minimum wage has been about 62% as large as the median wage. In the United States, the minimum wage has only been about 32% as large as the median wage.[3] What this means is that the minimum wage will affect more workers and create more unemployment in France than in the United States. As discussed in Chapter 5, the minimum wage is more likely to create unemployment among young workers, who tend to be less productive, than among older workers. Thus, in both France and the United States, unemployment rates are higher among the young than the old, but in France in 2014, 23% of workers under the age of 25 were unemployed, while in the United States 13% of these workers were unemployed.

Unions are also more powerful in Europe than in the United States. A union is an association of workers that bargains collectively with employers over wages, benefits, and working conditions. In the United States, most (87%) workers are not governed by a union contract; instead, they have an individual contract (written or unwritten) with employers. In many European countries, however, 80% or more of workers are governed by a union contract.

Unions can provide value for workers and employers alike, but excessively strong unions have a very similar effect as minimum wages. Unions demand higher wages by using their power to strike and to prevent the firm from hiring substitute labor. In the right panel of Figure 11.5, the union raises the price of labor from the market

The **median wage** is the wage such that one-half of all workers earn wages below the median and one-half of all workers earn wages above the median.

A **union** is an association of workers that bargains collectively with employers over wages, benefits, and working conditions.

wage to the union wage. As labor becomes more expensive, firms reduce employment from market employment to union employment Q_d. At the union wage, the number of workers looking for work Q_s exceeds the number of jobs Q_d—thus, unions increase unemployment by the amount $Q_s - Q_d$.

Employment Protection Laws

In the United States, an employee may quit and an employer may fire at any time and for any reason. This is called the **employment at-will doctrine**. There are many exceptions to the at-will doctrine, the most important being that the doctrine can be changed by contract. Many workers, for example, have contractually guaranteed severance packages and tenured university professors cannot be fired at will. Employees can also be restricted by contract. Employees in some industries with a lot of trade secrets are often asked to sign a noncompete agreement when they are hired. If an employee who signs a noncompete agreement quits, they may be forbidden, for example, from working for a competitor for a set period. Public law also imposes certain restrictions; employers, for example, are forbidden from hiring or firing on the basis of race, religion, sex, sexual orientation, national origin, age, or handicap status. Despite many exceptions, the at-will doctrine can be thought of as the most basic U.S. labor law.

In most of Europe, labor law is quite different. Portugal's constitution, for example, forbids at-will employment and requires employers to notify the government whenever a worker is dismissed. Moreover, if a Portuguese firm needs to lay off a group of workers, it must get the government's permission. Nor can the firm choose which workers to lay off; instead, it must follow strict guidelines determining which workers will be laid off first (generally, the most junior workers are fired first). In addition, laid-off workers must be given 60 days' notice, severance pay, and other benefits. Throughout Western Europe, public law and collective bargaining—not contracts—govern things like the length of the workweek, overtime pay, paid leave, temporary employment, notice periods, severance pay, and more.

Hiring and firing costs make labor markets less flexible and dynamic. A European firm with an unexpected increase in orders, for example, will not simply hire more workers. If the firm hires more workers and orders then decline, it would be stuck with workers it could not lay off without incurring great expense. Thus, hiring and firing costs make firms more cautious and slower to act.

Greater job security is valuable to workers with full-time jobs, but the more expensive it is to hire and fire workers, the more difficult it will be for new workers and unemployed workers to find jobs. Imagine, for example, how difficult it would be to get a date if every date required marriage! In the same way, it's more difficult to find a job when every job requires a long-term commitment from the employer.

The World Bank calculates a "rigidity of employment index," which summarizes hiring and firing costs, as well as how easy it is for firms to adjust hours of work (e.g., whether there are restrictions on night or weekend hours). A higher index number means that it is more expensive to hire and fire workers and more difficult to adjust hours. Figure 11.6 plots the rigidity index against the percentage of unemployment that is long term (lasting more than one year). The red line shows the trend in the data; greater rigidity in labor markets is clearly associated with greater long-term unemployment. Notice especially that France, Germany, Italy, and Spain all have high rigidity and high

---

The **employment at-will doctrine** says an employee may quit and an employer may fire an employee at any time and for any reason. There are many exceptions to the at-will doctrine, but it is the most basic U.S. employment law.

FIGURE 11.6

Hiring and Firing Costs Increase Long-Term Unemployment

Data from: World Bank and OECD Statistics, 2003 data.

---

long-term unemployment, while the United States has the least rigid labor markets and one of the lowest rates of long-term unemployment.

A Tale of Two Riots The tale of two riots illustrates another effect of employment protection laws. Paris, the city of lights, was lit up by hundreds of burning vehicles in November 2005 as angry, predominantly immigrant youth rioted in the streets. The riots were triggered by accusations of police brutality, but poverty and unemployment were the larger underlying frustrations. Unemployment rates among the rioting youth were above 30%.[4]

French firms were reluctant to hire young, minority workers—perhaps, in some instances, because of discrimination, but also because the more expensive it is to hire and fire, the more reluctant firms will be to hire workers without experience and workers for which there is any perceived uncertainty about quality. Once again, if every date required marriage, would you go on a blind date? A blind date might be worth some risk if you can dump a loser, but who will go on a blind date if a date means forever? So with regard to firms, young workers are riskier than older workers. Workers without a job are riskier than workers with a job (recall our discussion of the unemployment trap). And minority workers or workers who in some way differ from the "norm" may be regarded as more risky than typical workers by some employers.

Outsider riot Paris suburbs, 2005

Insider riot Central Paris, 2006

Thus, employment protection laws tend to have the most negative effects for young, already unemployed, and minority workers.

The French government was aware of these problems and in response to the riots it proposed to change labor law so that for workers under the age of 26, employment would be at-will for the first two years. The idea was to reassure firms that hiring a young, immigrant worker could be more like a blind date and less like marriage. Of course, this at-will employment is the norm in the United States. For elite French youth, however, the idea that they could be fired at will was upsetting and an infringement of what they considered to be their rights. Several hundred students barricaded themselves in the Sorbonne, the famous Paris university, and called on students everywhere to protest.

Now it was time for the insiders, the young elite, to riot and they proved every bit as adept at burning cars as had the impoverished youth of the year before. Not surprisingly, the elite riots were effective—the French government quickly backed down from the at-will employment doctrine. Unemployment in France, especially among young, immigrant workers remains high.

Summarizing, employment protection laws have the following effects. They:

■ Create valuable insurance for workers with full-time jobs.

■ Make labor markets less flexible and dynamic.

■ Increase the duration of unemployment.

■ Increase unemployment rates among young, minority, or otherwise "riskier" workers.

Labor Regulations to Reduce Structural Unemployment

In recent years, Europe has begun to change some of its labor regulations to try to reduce long-term unemployment. In Denmark, for example, unemployment benefits were limited to four years, and after one year workers who wish to continue receiving benefits must either enroll in job search or job training programs or take public employment. Denmark also subsidizes employers who are willing to train unemployed workers. Denmark and other countries now also have work tests—requirements that unemployed workers who want benefits must prove that they are actively seeking work.[5] These types of laws are called **active labor market policies**.

The United States has been a leader in testing active labor market programs. One of the most successful programs is the simplest—pay workers to get a job! In several large-scale experiments, randomly chosen unemployed workers were told that they would be paid a bonus if they found work early. The workers who were told about the bonus got jobs significantly sooner than those not promised bonuses.

Europe has also been slowly moving toward more flexible labor markets by allowing some exceptions to collective bargaining agreements for certain categories of workers, such as young workers, temporary workers, and part-time workers. Remember, however, the tale of the two riots. "Insiders" have been very reluctant to give up their benefits for the sake of the unemployed "outsiders."

Factors That Affect Structural Unemployment

Let's summarize the factors that can increase structural unemployment:

With **active labor market policies**, like work tests, job search assistance, and job retraining programs, the focus is on getting unemployed workers back to work.

Riots and Structural Unemployment

mru.org/structural

- Large, long-lasting shocks that require the economy to restructure:
  - Oil shocks
  - Shift from manufacturing to services
  - Globalization and global competition
  - Fundamental technology shocks (computers, the Internet, and—maybe—artificial intelligence)
- Labor regulations:
  - Unemployment benefits
  - Minimum wages
  - Powerful unions
  - Employment protection laws

We also discussed some active labor market policies that can reduce structural unemployment:

- Job retraining
- Job-search assistance
- Work tests
- Early employment bonuses

Cyclical Unemployment

The final category of unemployment is **cyclical unemployment**, or unemployment correlated with the ups and downs of the business cycle. Figure 11.7 graphs the U.S. unemployment rate since 1948. The shaded areas are recessions. Notice that during every recession, unemployment increases dramatically.

CHECK YOURSELF
- Define structural unemployment.
- Why does the term "employment at-will" accurately describe the United States but not Western European countries?

Cyclical unemployment is unemployment correlated with the business cycle.

FIGURE 11.7

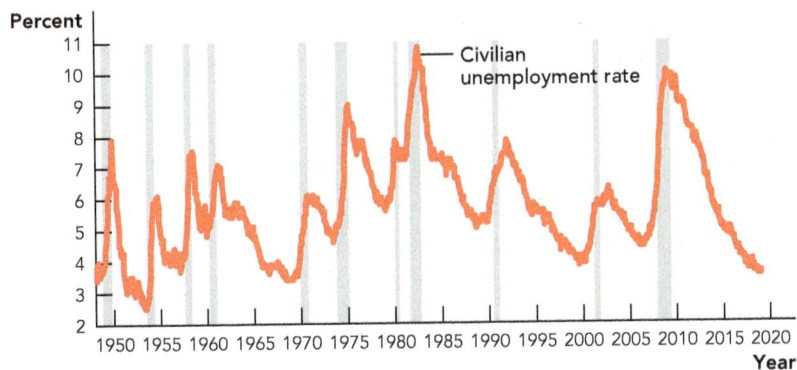

The Unemployment Rate Increases During a Recession: U.S. Civilian Unemployment Rate, 1948–2016

Note: Recessions are shaded.
Data from: Bureau of Labor Statistics; National Bureau of Economic Research, https://fred.stlouisfed.org/graph/?g=IFU9.

Lower growth is usually accompanied with higher unemployment for two reasons. First and most obviously, when GDP is falling, firms often lay off workers, which increases unemployment. The second reason is more subtle. Higher unemployment means that fewer workers are producing goods and services. When workers are sitting idle, it's likely that related capital is also sitting idle (e.g., factories are boarded up). An economy with idle labor and idle capital cannot be maximizing growth, and that will hurt the ability of that economy to create more jobs.

Figure 11.8 emphasizes the flip side of the idea that lower growth is correlated with increases in unemployment—faster growth is correlated with decreases in unemployment. Figure 11.8 plots changes in the U.S. unemployment rate on the vertical axis against growth on the horizontal axis. As you can see, faster growth in real GDP decreases unemployment. In fact, unemployment tends to fall when growth is above average and it tends to rise when growth is below average. Consider 1982 when the economy was in a deep recession and the unemployment rate increased by 2.1%. On the other hand, just two years later in 1984, real GDP was growing rapidly, at 7.2% a year, unemployment was falling, and, partly as a consequence, President Ronald Reagan was reelected in a landslide.

Although we define cyclical unemployment as unemployment correlated with the business cycle, the cause of cyclical unemployment is a subject of debate among economists, largely because the cause of business cycles is a subject of debate. Some economists think that business cycles are mostly a response to real shocks that require a reallocation of labor across industries. For these economists, a business cycle is nothing more than the economic growth

FIGURE 11.8

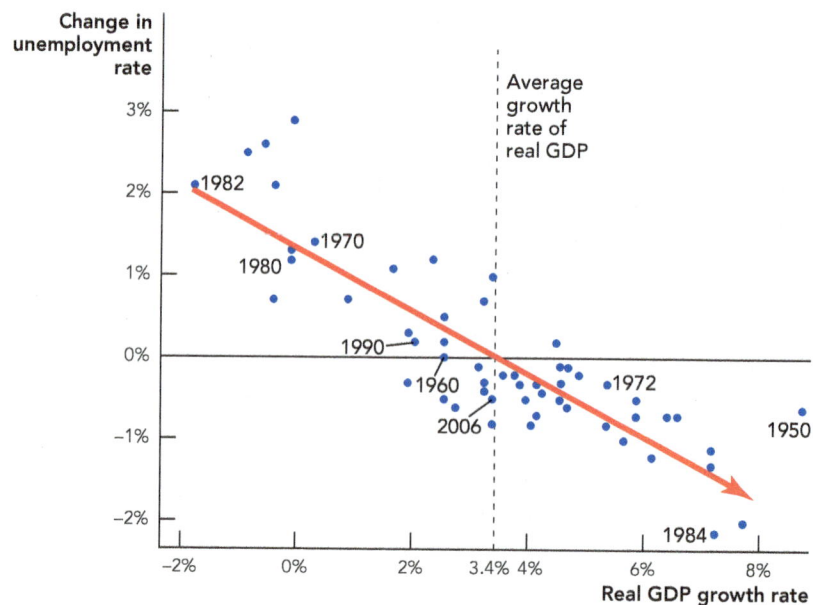

Faster Growth in Real GDP Decreases Unemployment

Data from: Bureau of Labor Statistics and Bureau of Economic Analysis.

process in action—growth is volatile, not smooth. Thus, for these economists, cyclical unemployment is just another example of frictional and structural unemployment.

Other economists, typically of the "Keynesian" persuasion, think that cyclical unemployment is caused by deficiencies in aggregate demand. This concept will be explained in later chapters, but for the time being, we can think of this notion of cyclical unemployment as caused by a mismatch between the aggregate level of wages in an economy and the level of prices. The wages demanded by workers are out of synch with the level of prices, so workers are too expensive to hire from the point of view of firms.

We will return to the concepts of real shocks, mismatches between aggregate wages and prices, business uncertainty, and potential government policy to reduce cyclical unemployment in greater detail in upcoming chapters.

The Natural Unemployment Rate

The **natural unemployment rate** is defined as the rate of structural plus frictional unemployment. Economists typically think of the underlying rates of frictional and structural unemployment as changing only slowly through time as major, long-lasting features of the economy change. Cyclical employment, however, can increase or decrease dramatically over a matter of months. Figure 11.9 plots one estimate of the natural rate against the actual unemployment rate. The natural rate changes only slowly through time and the actual rate of unemployment varies around the natural rate.

The concepts of cyclical, structural, and frictional unemployment are not always clear and distinct. If times are good, an employer will place more ads and search harder for workers. We might say that the frictional rate of unemployment has fallen, but we also might say that the cyclical rate of unemployment has fallen. Both descriptions of the improvement are true. Similarly, how well an economy absorbs, say, displaced auto workers (structural unemployment) will depend on the overall strength of economic conditions. One type of unemployment can even turn into another. Cyclical unemployment, for example,

> The **natural unemployment rate** is the rate of structural plus frictional unemployment.

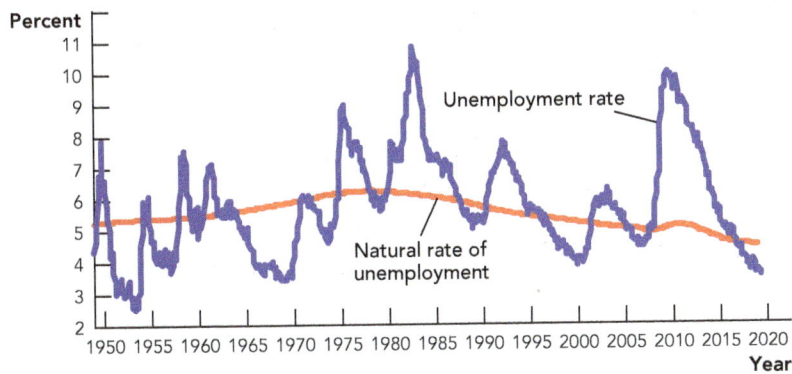

FIGURE 11.9

The Natural Unemployment Rate: United States, 1948–2016

Data from: Bureau of Labor Statistics and author calculations, https://fred.stlouisfed.org /graph/?g=oYu9.

can turn into structural unemployment if workers remain unemployed for too long, thereby leading to a decline in skills and employment prospects. As we showed earlier, the increase in unemployment that began with the 2007–2009 recession is taking a very long time to decline, leading to worries that unemployment that perhaps started out as cyclical may become structural.

Most economists view observed unemployment as a mix of structural, frictional, and cyclical characteristics. The three categories nonetheless give us some useful ideas for organizing the sources of unemployment.

CHECK YOURSELF

- What happens to cyclical unemployment during the business cycle?
- How are economic growth and unemployment related?

Labor Force Participation

So far we've focused on whether people can get a job if they want one, but it is also important to ask whether people *want* a job. We therefore turn from the unemployment rate to the labor force participation rate. Recall that the labor force participation rate is the percentage of the adult, noninstitutionalized, civilian population (adults for short) who are working or actively looking for work. In other words, the labor force participation rate is the percentage of adults who are in the labor force:

$$\text{Labor force participation rate} = \frac{\text{Unemployed + Employed}}{\text{Adult population}} \times 100$$

$$= \frac{\text{Labor force}}{\text{Adult population}} \times 100$$

In the United States (circa 2017), there were 160.1 million members of the labor force and 255.0 million adult, noninstitutionalized civilians, so the labor force participation rate was

$$\frac{160.1 \text{ million}}{255.0 \text{ million}} \times 100 = 62.8\%$$

What determines the labor force participation rate? We will discuss two factors.

1. Lifecycle effects and demographics
2. Incentives

Lifecycle Effects and Demographics

Baby boomers are the people born during the high birthrate years, 1946–1964.

Table 11.3 shows how labor force participation rates vary with age. Not surprisingly, most young adults are full-time students not workers. Labor force participation peaks in the prime working years, ages 25–54, when most adults are in the labor force. After age 65, most people retire and only a small minority remain in the labor force.

Lifecycle effects can interact with demographics to change national labor force participation rates. For example, as more **baby boomers** reach retirement age, the labor force participation rate will decline. In 2000, 12.4% of the population was 65 years or older, but by 2030 nearly 20% of the population will be 65 years or older. In fact, by 2030 it's estimated that 18.2 million people in the United States will be

TABLE 11.3 THE LABOR FORCE PARTICIPATION RATE AT DIFFERENT AGES

Age Range (years)	Labor Force Participation Rate
16–19	34%
25–54	80.9%
65+	18.6%

Data from: Bureau of Labor Statistics, 2014.

85 years or older.[6] Since older people are less likely to participate in the labor force, the aging of the U.S. population will lower the labor force participation rate.

Many economists are concerned because falling labor force participation means lower tax receipts. Of greater concern, tax receipts will be falling just as the demands on Social Security and Medicare rise. The head of the U.S. Government Accountability Office, whose job it is to analyze the long-term financial health of the U.S. government, has said in this regard, "When those boomers start retiring en masse, then that will be a tsunami of spending that could swamp our ship of state if we don't get serious."[7] We take up these important issues at greater length in Chapter 17.

A natural response to rising life expectancies and better health at older ages is later retirement. The "normal" retirement age is partly a matter of culture and convention but it is also partly determined by economic incentives, especially taxes—a subject to which we now turn.

Incentives

Why do people join the labor force? A few artists (and some professors!) love to work, but most people work because work pays more than leisure. More specifically, the choice to work depends on the difference between what work pays and what leisure pays. The choice to work, therefore, can be influenced by taxes on workers and benefits paid to nonworkers. Taxes discourage work and benefits encourage nonwork. We can see both of these effects in action by looking at how retirement systems in different countries change the incentives that older people have to work.

Taxes and Benefits Figure 11.10 shows labor participation rates for men ages 55–64 in different countries in 1998. In Belgium, only one-third of men

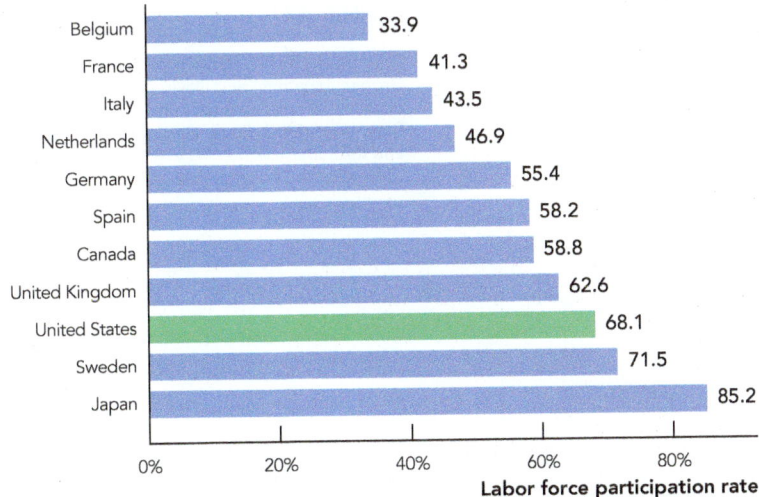

FIGURE 11.10

Country	Labor force participation rate
Belgium	33.9
France	41.3
Italy	43.5
Netherlands	46.9
Germany	55.4
Spain	58.2
Canada	58.8
United Kingdom	62.6
United States	68.1
Sweden	71.5
Japan	85.2

Labor Force Participation Rates of Older Workers Differ Significantly Across Countries (Males Aged 55–64, 1998)

Data from: OECD Labor Force Statistics.

in this age range were working, while in the United States only one-third of men of this age range were retired! Why are there such large differences in labor force participation rates? It's not just cultural differences concerning the right age for retirement.

In the United States, a worker of retirement age who continues working is not penalized.* But many countries penalize workers who work past the normal or early retirement age because many countries do not allow a worker to work *and* receive the same government pension. For example, in the Netherlands in the 1990s, a worker who worked past the age of 60 lost one year of benefits. The lost benefits can be thought of as a tax on working. Workers who kept working also had to pay payroll taxes on their wages. The net result was that a worker who worked past the age of 60 in the Netherlands earned less money than a worker who retired! In other words, a worker who did not retire at age 60 had to pay to work. If you had to pay to work, how much work would you do?

Figure 11.11 graphs the labor force participation rate in the 1990s of older men against a measure of the penalty, the implicit tax on working. Countries with a high implicit tax have a low labor force participation rate.

Early retirement is beneficial for workers if they want to retire early, but taxing older workers at significantly higher rates than younger workers (sometimes at rates above 100%!) does not benefit the older workers. Pushing older workers into retirement also imposes significant costs on younger workers who must pay higher taxes because older workers are not contributing to GDP.

In the 1990s, as the costs of their retirement systems rose, many European governments began to make benefits less generous and also to reduce the implicit tax on working. As the penalty on working fell, the labor force

FIGURE 11.11

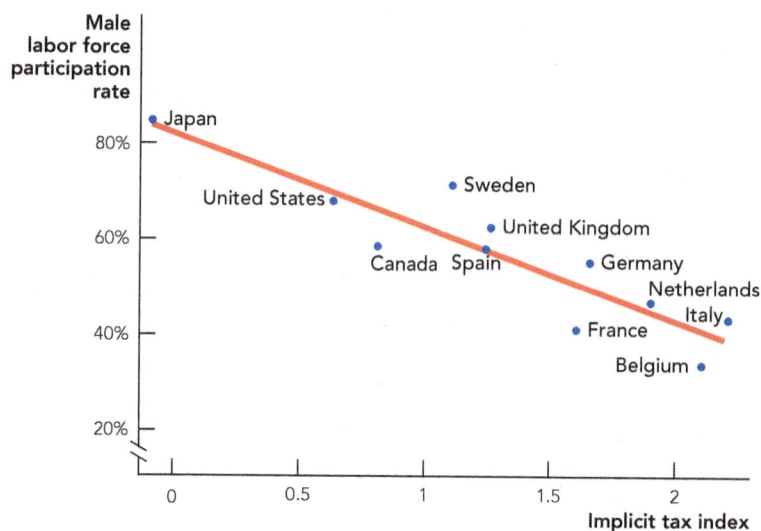

Male Labor Force Participation Declines the Higher Are Implicit Taxes (Males Aged 55–64)

Data from: OECD Labor Force Statistics, 2005. Gruber, Jonathan, and David A. Wise. 1999. Introduction and summary. In J. Gruber and D. A. Wise (Eds.), *Social Security Programs and Retirement Around the World*. Chicago: University of Chicago Press.

* After age 65, Social Security payments are not reduced at all by earnings. Between the ages of 62 and 65, a worker's Social Security payment is reduced when the worker continues to work but payments beginning at age 65 are increased in rough proportion—thus, there is very little penalty to continuing work even at age 62. See Gruber, J., and P. Orszag. 2003. Does the Social Security earnings test affect labor supply and benefits receipt? *National Tax Journal* 56(4): 755–773.

participation rates of older workers increased. In 1998, only 33.9% of older male workers in Belgium worked, but by 2015 this had increased to 52.2%. The Netherlands also reduced the tax on working and the labor force participation rates of older workers increased from 46.4% to 77.6%. These changes illustrate how incentives powerfully influence the choice to work.

Incentives and the Increase in Female Labor Force Participation

Incentives have also played a role in the dramatic increase in the U.S. labor force participation rates of women. In 1948, only 35% of women aged 25–54 were in the (paid) labor force. By the mid-1990s, 75% of these women were in the labor force. Figure 11.12 plots U.S. labor force participation rates for women since 1948. Notice that the 1970s brought especially large increases in labor force participation rates.

Cultural factors such as the rise of feminism and the growing acceptance of equality for women certainly played a role in rising female labor force participation. But cultural changes do not happen in a vacuum. Changes in the economy such as the move from a manufacturing to a service economy also brought more women to work. Even today, for example, there are almost three times as many male semiskilled factory and machine operators as female operators, but there are more female professionals (lawyers, professors, accountants, etc.) than there are male professionals.[8] As the manufacturing sector declined and the service sector rose, there was less demand for machine operators and more demand for professionals. This raised wages in sectors where females had a comparative advantage, thereby drawing more females into the labor force. In turn, the phenomenon of women in the workplace fueled the rise of feminism.

The growth in women working was especially dramatic in the professions. Figure 11.13 shows the percentage of the first-year students who were female in medical school, dentistry, law, and business programs from 1955 to 2005. From 1955 to about 1970, fewer than 10% of first-year students in the professions were females. Beginning around 1970, however, female participation shot up—more than doubling in all professions in just 10 years and continuing to increase until between 40% to 50% of all students in professional programs are female.

FIGURE 11.12

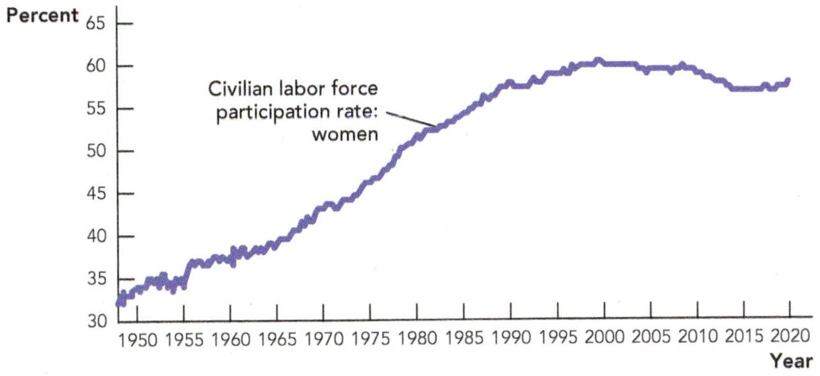

Female Labor Force Participation Increased Rapidly from 1955 to 2019

Data from: Bureau of Labor Statistics, https://fred.stlouisfed.org/graph/?g=mQyk.

FIGURE 11.13

Females Entered Professional Degree Programs in Large Numbers Beginning in the 1970s

Data from: Goldin, Claudia. 2006. The quiet revolution that transformed women's employment, education, and family. *American Economic Review* 96(2): 1–21.

Why did females start entering professional schools in increasing numbers beginning around 1970? Economists Claudia Goldin and Lawrence Katz have an intriguing and controversial answer—the contraceptive pill, known simply as the pill.[9]

How the Pill Increased Female Labor Force Participation

The pill has been called the greatest technological advance of the twentieth century. For the first time in history, women were given a low-cost, reliable, and convenient method of controlling fertility, the pill. Condoms can also prevent unwanted pregnancy, but the pill is easier to use, less prone to error, and more reliable. Among typical users, the pill is seven times more reliable than condoms, and among those who always use the pill according to directions, it is 60 times more reliable.

Economists Goldin and Katz argue that the pill lowered the costs of earning a professional degree by giving women greater certainty about the consequences of sex. It takes years of effort to earn a professional degree, and earning a degree while bearing or taking care of a baby is very difficult. Thus, women who wanted a professional degree before the advent of the pill had either to bear the costs of abstinence or risk pregnancy. The pill lowered these costs and increased the incentive of women to invest in a long-term education.

The availability of the pill and the increase in women entering college and professional degree programs do coincide. Although the pill was first sold for contraceptive use in 1960, at that time 30 states banned advertisements for birth control devices and some even banned the sale of contraceptives. It wasn't until 1965 in the landmark case *Griswold v. Connecticut* that the U.S. Supreme Court said states could not ban the sale of contraceptives to *married couples*. Single women could still be prohibited from buying contraceptives until 1972. As laws banning the sale of contraceptives fell, more women bought contraceptives and according to Goldin and Katz, more women began to plan for long-term careers.

▶ **MRU**

mru.org/employ-women

Women Working: What's the Pill Got to Do with It?

Goldin and Katz make a plausible argument for their hypothesis (and they provide more evidence than we discuss here); nevertheless, it would be interesting to know if similar effects happened in other countries as the pill became available. In much of the world today, women have fewer opportunities to be educated and to fully participate in the paid workforce than men—this failure to fully utilize the talents of women is an enormous loss to these women and to the economy. Questions like these are on the cutting edge of economics—perhaps some of you will help to answer them.

The Decline in Male Labor Force Participation

Over the past half century as shown in Figure 11.14, male labor force participation rates in the United States have been declining, slowly but steadily. In 1965, nearly 97% of all males in their prime working years (ages 25–54) were in the labor force but only 88% of such men were working or looking for work in recent years. In other words, in recent years about 12% of the male prime-aged population haven't been participating in the labor force—that's about 7.5 million potential workers who aren't working or looking for work. Trying to understand the causes and consequence of this decline is an active area of research.

We can usefully organize our thinking around the supply and demand for labor. In the supply and demand model, two forces can explain a decline in the labor force participation rate, a decrease in the demand for labor or a decrease in the supply of labor, as shown in Figure 11.15.

Let's begin with a decrease in the supply of labor as shown in the right panel of Figure 11.15. Suppose that the alternatives to working—engaging in leisure, home production, or working outside the formal labor market—become more attractive. In this case, the labor-supply curve will shift upward and to the left, which means that men require a higher wage to enter the workforce or equivalently fewer men are willing to work at a given wage. The equilibrium moves from point a to point b and employment declines from Q_1 to Q_2.

CHECK YOURSELF

- The marginal tax rate (the tax on additional income) for married couples was reduced significantly during the 1980s. How would this affect the female labor force participation rate?
- Some politicians want to raise the age at which people can collect Social Security benefits, likely postponing retirement for many. How will this change affect the labor force participation rate?

FIGURE 11.14

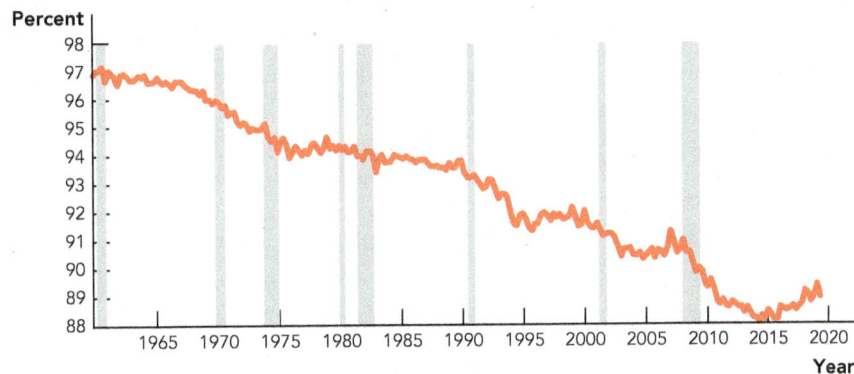

Percent

The Slowly but Steadily Declining Male Labor Force Rate

Data from: OECD, Main Economic Indicators—complete database, Main Economic Indicators (database), https://dx.doi.org/10.1787/data-00052-en; https://fred.stlouisfed.org/graph/?g=p5vm.

FIGURE 11.15

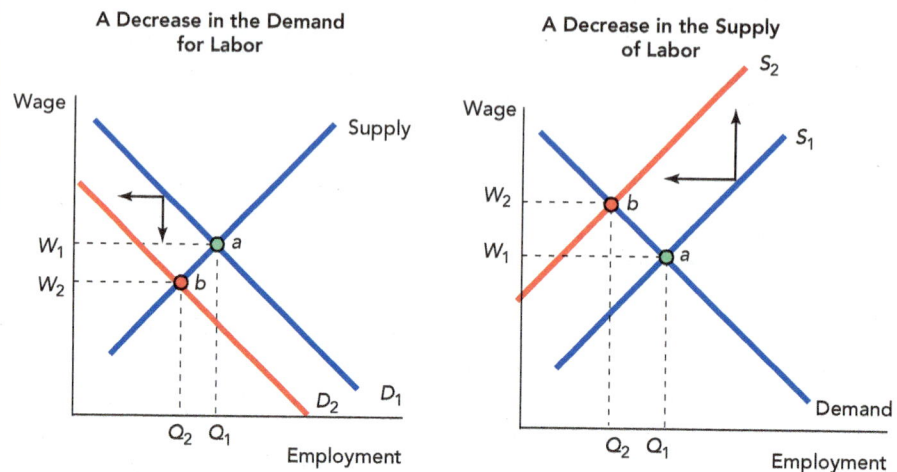

Two Explanations for Falling Labor Force Participation

A Decrease in the Demand for Labor

A Decrease in the Supply of Labor

Two Explanations for Falling Labor Force Participation A decrease in the demand for labor and a decrease in the supply of labor will both reduce the quantity of labor supplied from Q_1 to Q_2 but a decrease in the demand for labor reduces wages while a decrease in the supply of labor increases wages.

One simple theory for why men might be reducing their supply of labor is that married men might be staying at home more often while their spouses work. In other words, with more women working and earning higher incomes, some families might choose to switch "traditional" roles with the men staying at home and engaging in greater child care and home production and their partners working. From this perspective, the decline in male labor force participation would not be concerning. The data, however, do not support this explanation.

If changing gender roles were responsible for declining male labor force participation, we would expect that married men would be the ones reducing their supply of labor but it's unmarried men who are working less. Indeed, men who are out of the labor force are less likely to be married than in the past.[10]

In addition, the American Time Use Survey collects data on how Americans spend their time on a minute-by-minute basis and prime-aged males out of the labor force are not spending large amounts of time in child care or household production. Table 11.4 shows that prime-aged males who were in the labor force spent an average of 29 minutes per day caring for household members. In contrast, prime-aged males out of the labor force spent one minute *less* caring for household members. (By the way, if you are wondering, females spend about 42 minutes a day caring for household members. If that seems low, keep in mind that this is an average for all women, even those without any household members who need caring for.) The major difference between males in and out of

TABLE 11.4 MINUTES PER DAY SPENT ON VARIOUS ACTIVITIES BY PRIME-AGED MALES

	In the Labor Force	Out of the Labor Force
Caring for Household Members	29	28
Household Activities and Services	84	111
Socializing, Relaxing, Leisure	251	472
Watching Television	154	335

Data from: Council of Economic Advisers, 2016.

the labor force is leisure. Prime-aged males out of the labor force spent nearly 8 hours a day (472 minutes) on socializing, relaxing, and leisure compared with a little more than 4 hours (251 minutes) per day for those in the labor force.

Prime-aged males out of the labor force do have a lot of leisure time. Older men watch television. Younger men play video games. Indeed, one hypothesis is that video games have gotten so cheap and are so much fun to play that they are pulling young men out of the labor force.[11] One difficulty with the video game hypothesis is that video games do not seem to have reduced labor force participation in other countries. Also, prime-aged males out of the labor force report being less happy and more stressed than those in the labor force which is not consistent with men being pulled out of the labor force by better games. It seems more plausible that playing video games is an effect of not working rather than a cause of not working.

A common belief is that people are being pulled out of work by an increasingly generous welfare state. Not surprisingly, prime-aged males out of the labor force do rely on government more than their working counterparts. But government support of prime-aged men is not extravagant, a little under $7,000 per year on average (2014). Rather than relying on government, most prime-aged males out of the labor force rely on family. The average white male aged 25–34 who is out of the labor force receives approximately $3,300 in disability insurance benefits and $1,000 in food stamp assistance annually but $21,800 from other household members. About one-quarter of these men live at home with a parent.[12] (The numbers for blacks of the same age are $2,400 from disability benefits, $1,200 from food stamps, and $18,600 from other family members and more than 40% of these men live at home with a parent.)[13]

Government support is not extravagant nor, for the most part, has it increased over time. One exception is that there has been a large increase in persons receiving Social Security Disability Insurance (SSDI). In 1970, 1.5 million potential workers were receiving disability benefits but by 2019 the number of beneficiaries had increased to more than 8.4 million potential workers. This is a large increase, especially given that the health of the U.S. population has improved since 1970 and the number of workplace injuries has fallen in half.

Workers who are accepted to the SSDI program decrease their labor force participation rates significantly compared with similar workers who are denied benefits.[14] SSDI, however, appears to explain only a part of the declining rate of *prime-aged male* labor force participation. The reason is that half of SSDI recipients are women and many of the male beneficiaries are above prime age. Disability insurance is part of the reason why some older males have dropped out of the labor force, but overall economists think that disability insurance is not the major reason for declining male labor force participation.

Finally, let's return to the right panel of Figure 11.15 and note a key implication of the model. If declining labor force participation is caused by a decrease in labor supply then we should see rising wages for the workers who remain in the labor force (note in the right panel of Figure 11.15 that the wage increases from W_1 to W_2). The idea is simple: If leisure or home production is becoming more valuable, then to get workers to stay in the labor force employers must pay them higher wages. But the type of workers who are most in danger of leaving the workforce—most notably less educated workers—are precisely the workers who have seen their wages *fall* in recent decades. A fall in wages combined with a decrease in participation is more consistent with the story told in the left panel of Figure 11.15, a decrease in the demand for (some types) of labor. Let's examine this hypothesis in more detail.

FIGURE 11.16

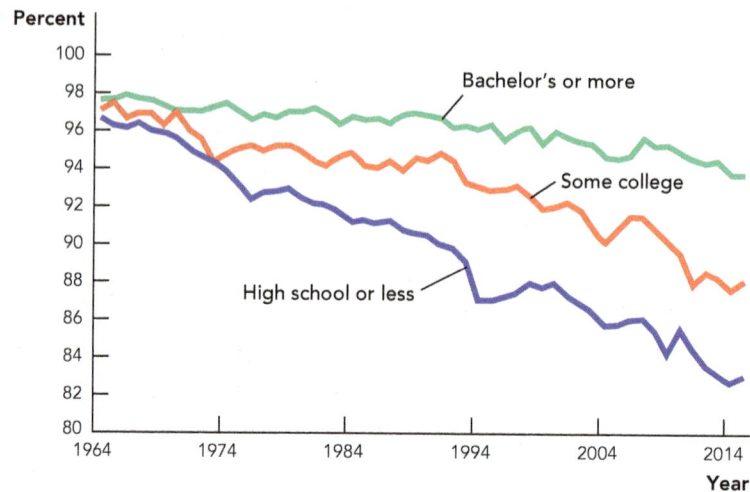

Prime-Aged Male Labor Force Participation by Educational Attainment

Data from: Bureau of Labor Statistics, *Current Population Survey* (Annual Social and Economic Supplement), CEA calculations.

The workers who are leaving the labor force are less educated than the average worker. In 1965, almost all prime-aged men were in the labor force, regardless of education level. Since that time, male labor force participation has declined especially strongly for men with less education. As a result, males with a bachelor's degree or higher are significantly more likely to be in the labor force today than workers with a high school degree or less, as illustrated in Figure 11.16.

The relative wages of less-educated men have been falling at the same time as their labor force participation rates have fallen, as shown in Figure 11.17.

Wages for less educated workers have declined relative to more educated workers because of changes in technology working through the demand for labor. Manufacturing jobs that could be done with workers with a high school education, for example, have declined in number because of trade and especially because of technology and automation. At the same time, high-paying jobs have been created in service industries but these typically require more education and the ability to work with computers or other advanced technologies.

By the way, you might wonder if the increasing participation of women in the labor market could explain the declining participation of men? It's a logical hypothesis, but the women entering the workforce have tended to be more educated while the men exiting the labor force have tended to be less educated. As a result, the types of jobs that the women have competed for have tended be in higher-skill service-sector industries while the decline of jobs has been in lower-skill manufacturing industries. In other words and to simplify, low-skill men are leaving the labor force because jobs such as those in coal mining are disappearing not because women are competing for those jobs and driving down wages.

Thus, as the simple supply and demand model suggests, the workers with declining wages have also seen declining labor force participation. But there are puzzles. The supply and demand model is about the absolute level of wages but although the wages of less-educated men have declined substantially relative to more educated men, that's mostly because the wages of more educated workers

▶ MRU

mru.org/econ-career-choice

MORE POWERFUL

The Economics of Choosing the Right Career

FIGURE 11.17

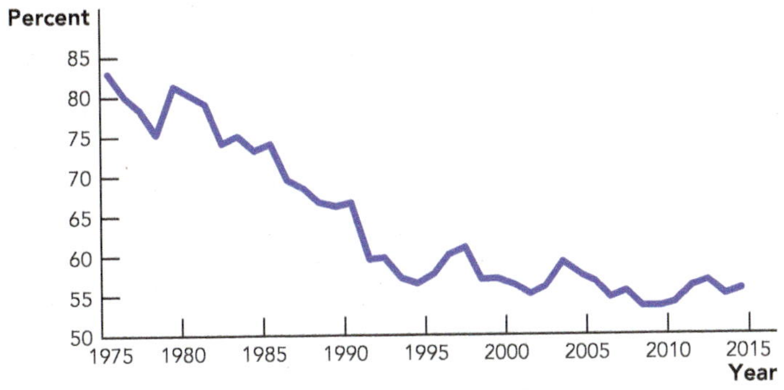

Ratio of High School Graduates' Wages to College Graduates' Wages

Note: The earnings ratio compares the median full-time, full-year worker over age 25 with just a high school degree to the same type of worker with at least a bachelor's degree. Prior to 1992, bachelor's degree is defined as four years of college.
Data from: Bureau of Labor Statistics, *Current Population Survey* (Annual Social and Economic Supplement), CEA calculations.

FIGURE 11.18

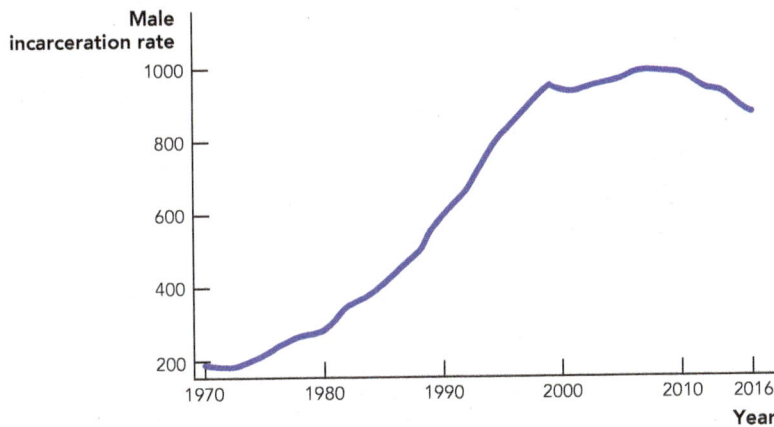

The Male Incarceration Rate The male incarceration rate increased by a factor of five from 1970 to its peak in 2007.

Data from: Bureau of Justice Statistics, Corrections Statistical Analysis Tool (CSAT) and *BJS Bulletin: Prisoners 1925–1981.*

have been rising. In absolute terms, the wages of less educated men have been flat or declined only slightly and not enough in absolute terms to explain the decline in labor force participation. Thus, the simple supply and demand model is useful for organizing our thoughts but is probably not enough to explain all of the data.

Another factor that may be important in explaining the decline in the labor force participation of less-skilled men is the rise in mass incarceration. The male incarceration rate in the United States increased from 200 per 100,000 in 1970 to nearly 1,000 per 100,000 at its peak in 2007, as shown in Figure 11.18.

Incarceration doesn't reduce the labor force participation rate directly because the rate is measured as the ratio of the labor force to the adult *noninstitutionalized* population (see Figure 11.1). But what happens to prisoners when they are released? It's difficult to get a job with an arrest record let alone a prison record, In fact, due to occupational licensing, it's illegal for ex-felons to work in many industries. Approximately 7% of prime-aged men have been incarcerated.[15] Thus, the rising incarceration rates of the past could be causing some of today's low labor force participation rates.

Overall, the decline in male labor force participation is a puzzling and worrying phenomenon with many causes and consequences that economists and others are investigating. Finally, we have focused on declining male labor force participation because the big story about female labor force participation over the past 50 years has been increasing rates, as we discussed in the previous section. But take another look at Figure 11.12. Female labor force participation peaked in 2000 at approximately 60% and since then participation has declined slightly. Thus, the forces that have reduced male labor force participation may now have started to reduce female labor force participation.

Takeaway

Perhaps the most important lesson of this chapter is that even in the best of times, unemployment will exist and fluctuate. The economy is always changing and only through change is there growth. It is important to help workers who are buffeted by change, but there is a difference between helping workers to adjust and trying to prevent adjustment—ultimately, we can do the former but not the latter. As we discussed in this chapter, some labor market policies intended to protect workers have increased structural unemployment in Western Europe compared with the United States. Labor market policies that make it easier for workers to retrain and move to employment have had greater success in keeping long-term unemployment low.

After reading this chapter, you should know how unemployment, the unemployment rate, and the labor force participation rate are defined. You should also be able to apply these definitions to data. For example, there are 10 people; 6 have jobs, 1 is looking for work, 1 is a child, 1 is in prison, and the last is retired. What is the labor force? What is the unemployment rate? What is the labor force participation rate?[16] You should also know something about frictional, structural, and cyclical unemployment, which includes defining each and giving examples of their causes.

Finally, it's important to know something about the factors that increase or decrease the labor force participation rate. Changing demographics such as aging baby boomers, technology like the pill, cultural attitudes toward women and work, and government policy such as taxes and pension benefits can all change the labor force participation rate. At the most basic and important level, the labor force participation rate responds to the incentive to work.

Changes in the labor force participation rate can have a large impact on an economy. The declining labor force participation rate of prime-aged males is a worrying trend that economists do not fully understand.

CHAPTER REVIEW

Go online to practice with more examples of these types of problems, including live links to videos, data sources, and feedback.

▶ Problems with this icon relate to optional MRU videos.

KEY CONCEPTS

unemployed, p. 234

unemployment rate, p. 235

labor force participation rate, p. 235

discouraged workers, p. 235

underemployment rate, p. 236

frictional unemployment, p. 237

structural unemployment, p. 238

median wage, p. 241

union, p. 241

employment at-will doctrine, p. 242

active labor market policies, p. 244

cyclical unemployment, p. 245

natural unemployment rate, p. 247

baby boomers, p. 248

FACTS AND TOOLS

1. Which of the following people are counted as unemployed?

   A person out of work and actively searching for work

   A person in prison

   A person who wants to work but stopped searching six months ago

   A person who works part-time but who wants full-time work

2. According to Figure 11.1, what adults are considered not to be in the labor force?

3. If we count "discouraged workers" as unemployed when calculating the unemployment rate, does the rate more than double, less than double, or remain unchanged?

4. Decide whether each of the following are frictional, structural, or cyclical unemployment:

   a. The economy gets worse, so General Motors shuts down a factory for four months, laying off workers.

   b. General Motors lays off 5,000 workers and replaces them with robots. The workers start looking for jobs outside the auto industry.

   c. About 10 workers per month at a General Motors plant quit their jobs because they want to live in another town. They start searching for work in the new town.

5. Let's connect the minimum wage model back to the supply and demand model of the chapter on Price Ceilings and Price Floors. Is a minimum wage a price ceiling or a price floor? Does it create a surplus or a shortage in the labor market?

6. In France, why do employment protection laws tend to have negative effects on the young, already unemployed, and minority workers?

7. Let's look at how the unemployment rate changes during and after a typical recession. In Figure 11.7, does the unemployment rate tend to reach its peak *during* the recession, or does it usually reach its peak *after* the recession?

8. According to Figure 11.10, during which decade was the natural unemployment rate the highest?

9. Take a look at Figure 11.12. About how big is the difference in labor force participation rates between countries with the highest implicit tax rate on older men compared with countries with the lowest implicit tax rate? Round to the nearest 10%.

10. Based on the ideas in this chapter, name three labor market policy changes that would be likely to decrease the rate of structural unemployment. There are many more than three possible answers.

THINKING AND PROBLEM SOLVING

11. When the following events happen, does the unemployment rate rise, fall, or stay the same?

    a. Workers are laid off and start looking for work.

b. People without jobs who are looking for work find work.

c. People without jobs who are looking for work give up and stop looking.

d. People without jobs who are not looking for work become encouraged and decide to start looking for work.

e. People without jobs who are not looking for work take a job immediately.

12. Let's see how many jobs have to be destroyed for one *net* job to be created. As noted in the text, millions of jobs are created and destroyed every month. Suppose that 5 million jobs are destroyed every month and about 5.25 million jobs are created. What is net job creation? What is total job destruction divided by net job creation? So how many total jobs are destroyed for every net job created?

13. Take a look at Table 11.2. If you have to pick a country to lose your job in, and you know you're going to be out of work for one year, which country offers the highest one-year average replacement rate? Which offers the highest two-year average replacement rate? If you're going to be out of work for three years, which country offers the highest average rate of wage replacement?

14. When a government raises the minimum wage by $2.00 per hour, where would we expect more jobs to be lost: in the fast-food industry or in city government? Why?

15. Let's see how GDP per person can be affected by changes in the fraction of citizens who work. This fraction is better known as the employment–population ratio. To keep things simple, let's assume that every employed worker produces $50,000 worth of output. If the employment–population ratio is 50%, what is GDP per *person*? If the employment–population ratio rises to 55%, what is GDP per *person*?

16. Calculate the unemployment rate and the labor force participation rate in the following cases:

a. Employed: 100 million. Population: 200 million. In labor force: 110 million.

b. Unemployed: 10 million. Population: 200 million. Employed: 90 million.

c. In labor force: 30 million. Population: 80 million. Unemployed: 3 million.

17. Goldin and Katz looked for the link between birth control and women's labor force participation by examining the difference between states that acted early to make birth control legal and states that waited until later. Which states do you think had the biggest jump in women joining the labor force: states that legalized birth control earlier or those that legalized it later? (*Note:* Goldin and Katz provide evidence for the correct answer in their paper.)

18. Here's a story economists tell one another: A Nobel Prize–winning economist flew to New York City for a conference. He got into a cab, and started talking with the cab driver. The cab driver said, "Oh, you're an economist? Let me tell you, this economy is terrible. I'm an unemployed architect." The economist immediately replied, "No you're not, you're an employed cab driver." According to the way the U.S. government measures unemployment, who is right?

19. Between 1984 and 2001, the U.S. government made it much easier to get payment for disability and the number of disabled people more than doubled from 3.8 million to 7.7 million. Most of the people who try to qualify for disability payments have a tough time finding jobs, and spend a lot of time "out of work and actively searching for work." Once people start receiving disability payments, however, they rarely work again and continue to get the disability payments for decades: These citizens then count as "out of the labor force." What effect did reducing the requirements to get disability payments have on the unemployment rate?

Discovering DATA ••

20. Let's examine the labor force participation rates of teenagers. Using the FRED economic database (https://fred.stlouisfed.org/), search for "Labor force participation rate 16 to 19 years." Graph the rate that is Not Seasonally Adjusted and click on 5Y to get the rate for the last 5 years.

a. Why is the rate so choppy?

b. In the peak month, approximately what percentage of teenagers are in the labor force? What about in trough months? Over the year, therefore, by approximately how much does the labor force participation rate of teenagers change?

21. It's been said that "once you reach the top of the ladder of opportunity, the first thing to do is pull up the ladder behind you." Let's consider the implications of this adage for labor market outcomes.

a. When doctors, schoolteachers, and beauticians encourage the government to make it more difficult for people to enter their industries, does this tend to lower or raise the supply of these professionals?

b. If government requires higher educational and training standards for doctors, schoolteachers, and beauticians, does this tend to raise or lower the demand for the services of these professionals?

c. In equilibrium, taking into account your answers to parts a and b, what is the total effect of this lobbying on the wages of these professionals: Do wages rise, fall, or is the total effect ambiguous? Does the total number of people employed in these professions rise, fall, or is the total effect ambiguous?

Discovering DATA

22. It is sometimes said that the official unemployment statistic undercounts unemployment rates because it doesn't count discouraged workers, defined as workers who have given up looking for work but who would take a job if one were offered to them. As we noted in the text, in addition to the official unemployment rate the Bureau of Labor Statistics (BLS) also tracks a rate that does include discouraged workers, defined as people who say they want a job and who have looked for a job in the last year but not in the last month. In fact, the BLS defines six different measures of unemployment called U1 through U6. The official unemployment rate is the U3 Rate. U1 and U2 are more strict definitions of unemployment. With the U1 rate a person has to be without a job for 15 weeks or more before they count as unemployed. U4, U5, and U6 are less strict definitions. For example, U4 is the rate that includes discouraged workers.

Using the FRED economic database (https://fred.stlouisfed.org/), let's graph all six rates. Start with the civilian unemployment rate—also known as the U3 Rate. Then click Edit Graph followed by Add Line. Search for the U1Rate (all one word) then follow the same procedure to add the U2Rate, U4Rate, U5Rate, and U6Rate.

a. In 2010 what was the highest unemployment rate by any of the BLS's definitions? At this same time what was the lowest unemployment rate by any of the BLS's definitions? Were any of the BLS's definitions wrong?

b. What can you say about how the rates move together? Does it matter much which rate of unemployment you use to describe the labor market?

Discovering DATA

23. Using the FRED economic database (https://fred.stlouisfed.org/), find the "Youth Unemployment Rate in the United States" then click Edit Graph and Add Line and find the "Youth Unemployment Rate for France."

a. In 2006 what was the youth unemployment rate in the United States and what was the rate in France?

b. As discussed in the text, give two possible reasons why the youth unemployment rate in France is higher than the youth unemployment rate in the United States.

CHALLENGES

24. Long-term, structural unemployment is higher in Europe than in the United States, but some European countries have it worse than others. Take a look at Table 11.1. Spain has a lower fraction of long-term unemployment than the other European countries, but a higher rate of unemployment than the other European countries in that table. What can we conclude about the kind of unemployment taking place in Spain?

25. a. If European governments set rules for marriage the same way they set rules for employment—with tough, preset rules that make it hard to end the relationship—would you expect rates of divorce to rise, fall, or can't you tell with the information given?

b. Would the length of marriages rise, fall, or can't you tell with the information given?

c. Would married couples probably be happier (more productive) or less happy (less productive) than under more flexible marriage rules? The last of these three questions might have more than one correct answer.

26. When are workers more likely to get a job: six weeks before their unemployment benefits run out, or a week before their unemployment benefits run out? (*Note:* The correct answer to this question is solidly backed up by U.S. job data.)

27. Take a look at Figure 11.5. In that figure, we're holding "job quality" or "working conditions" constant, and looking at how changes in wages impact the quantity of labor supplied and demanded. In many union negotiations, the union and its workers don't push for higher wages. Instead, they push for better working conditions: safer machines, better insurance coverage, or cleaner restrooms.

So now let's model this: Let's hold *wages* constant, and look at how changes in *working conditions* impact the quantity supplied and quantity demanded of labor. Thus, set it up just like a real-life labor negotiation. Draw a conventional supply and demand chart, but on the vertical axis, just put "job quality—high or low" instead of "wage." Then, show what happens to the amount of unemployment created when a union successfully negotiates a higher-than-equilibrium job quality.

28. Even though most Americans who become unemployed are only unemployed for a short period of time, when you look at who is unemployed *at a given moment in time*, you'll find that most of the unemployed have been without a job for quite a while. Let's imagine a simple economy to see how to resolve this paradox. In this economy, there are two types of workers: Type A workers take one month to find a new job and Type B workers take 10 months to find a new job.

Each month, let's assume that *one* Type A and *one* Type B worker lose their jobs. Notice that *we're assuming that half of all people who lose their jobs today will find new jobs in a month.* But, as we shall see, this implies that most of the unemployed will have been unemployed for a long period.

a. In the long run (or "steady state"), there will be 11 workers out of work in this simple society at any given point in time. Show that this is true by keeping track of the "pool" of unemployed workers in this society for two years. You can start off assuming that the pool is empty at time zero—that no one is unemployed—but you'd get the same steady-state answer regardless of your starting point. You can prove that 11 will be out of work just with pencil and paper or much more quickly with Excel. To help you out, here's an example of what the pool of unemployed will look like in month 7. Keep going with this calculation until you see that the number of workers in the pool no longer changes month to month—this is called the "steady state."

The Unemployment Pool: Month 7	
Shallow End (Type As)	Deep End (Type Bs)
1 Type A worker enters pool (loses job).	1 Type B worker enters pool.
1 Type A worker exits pool (finds work).	6 Type B workers are already in the pool.
	0 Type B workers exit the pool.
Total: 1 Type A worker is in the pool (unemployed).	Total: 7 Type B workers are in the pool (unemployed).

b. In the steady state—that is, when your pool starts having the same numbers every month—how many of the 11 workers in the unemployment pool have been unemployed for "one month"? How many of the 11 workers in the unemployment pool have been unemployed for more than one month?

c. If you see an economy where most *currently* unemployed workers have been out of work for a long time, does this mean that most people who have been unemployed in the last few years were unemployed for a long time? How does this example illustrate your answer?

Discovering DATA ⠸

29. Overall, labor force participation rates have been declining in the U.S. economy but not for every demographic. Let's examine the labor force participation rates of teenagers and older people. Using the FRED economic database (https://fred.stlouisfed.org/), search for "Labor force participation rate 16 to 19 years." Graph the seasonally adjusted rate since we are interested in long-term trends. Then click Edit Graph and Add Line and then search for and add "Labor Force Participation Rate: 55 years and over."

   a. Since the 1990s whose labor force participation rate has increased and whose has decreased?

   b. For the group whose labor force participation rate has increased, make two hypotheses or stories about why the trend is up. Try to make one hypothesis a good or positive story and one a bad or negative story. Do the same for the group whose labor force participation rate has declined.

Discovering DATA ⠸

30. Using the FRED economic database (https://fred.stlouisfed.org/), let's compare employment in manufacturing and construction. First, find manufacturing employment and then click Edit Graph and Add Line to add in construction employment. Graph the data from 1990 to the present.

   a. What is the long-term trend in manufacturing employment? What would you guess are the reasons for the trend?

   b. What is the long-term trend in construction employment?

   c. Both employment series fell during the 2008–2009 recession. For which series would you expect employment to recover?

WORK IT OUT

For interactive, step-by-step help in solving this problem, go online.

Who is more likely to ask politicians for stronger labor unions and laws, making it harder to fire workers: insiders who have jobs or outsiders who don't have jobs?

▶ MRU VIDEOS

The Economics of Choosing the Right Career

mru.org/econ-career-choice

Problem: **21**

How Is the Unemployment Rate Defined?

mru.org/unemployment

Problems: **1–3, 8**

Is Unemployment Undercounted?

mru.org/unemploy-measure

Problems: **18, 22**

Frictional Unemployment

mru.org/frictional

Problems: **4, 12**

Riots and Structural Unemployment

mru.org/structural

Problems: **4, 6, 10, 13, 15, 19, 24, 27**

Cyclical Unemployment

mru.org/cyclical

Problems: **4, 7, 11, 14**

Labor Force Participation

mru.org/lfpr

Problems: **16, 28**

Taxing Work

mru.org/taxing-work

Problems: **9, 19, 25, 26**

Women Working: What's the Pill Got to Do with It?

mru.org/employ-women

Problem: **17**

12

Inflation and the Quantity Theory of Money

R obert Mugabe had a problem. The dictatorial president of Zimbabwe needed money. Unfortunately, Mugabe's policy of seizing commercial farms had driven productive farmers and entrepreneurs out of the country, frightened off foreign investors, and pushed Zimbabwe, once called the breadbasket of Africa, to the verge of mass starvation. Zimbabwe had almost nothing left to tax, but Mugabe still needed money to bribe his enemies and reward his supporters, especially the still loyal Zimbabwean army. Mugabe thus turned to the last refuge of needy governments, the printing press.

Governments and counterfeiters alone can pay their bills by printing money. Beginning in 2001, when inflation was already running at 50% per year, Mugabe pushed the printing presses to breakneck speed. Whenever a bill came due or soldiers needed paying, it was no problem—just print more money. In May 2006, for example, the government announced plans to print 60 *trillion* Zimbabwean dollars to finance a 300% increase in pay for soldiers. Ironically, the payment was delayed because Zimbabwe didn't have enough U.S. dollars to buy ink and paper.[1]

When the ink and paper arrived, the government flooded the economy with more money. The economy, however, could not produce more goods. When more money chases the same goods, the consequences are easy to see: inflation. In Zimbabwe, the inflation rate quickly increased from 50% a year to 50% a month to more than 50% a day! By the end of 2008, prices in Zimbabwe were doubling overnight and the monthly inflation rate hit 79,600,000,000% per month. Finally, in 2009, the government legalized transactions in foreign currencies and the Zimbabwe dollar effectively ceased to exist.

In this chapter, we explain how inflation is defined and measured, the causes of inflation, the costs and benefits of inflation, and why governments sometimes resort to inflation.

Defining and Measuring Inflation

Inflation is an increase in the average level of prices. We measure the average level of prices with an index, the average price from a large and representative basket of goods and services. Thus, inflation is measured by changes in a price

▶ **MRU**

mru.org/hyperinflation

Who Wants to Be a Trillionaire?

Inflation is an increase in the average level of prices.

265

FIGURE 12.1

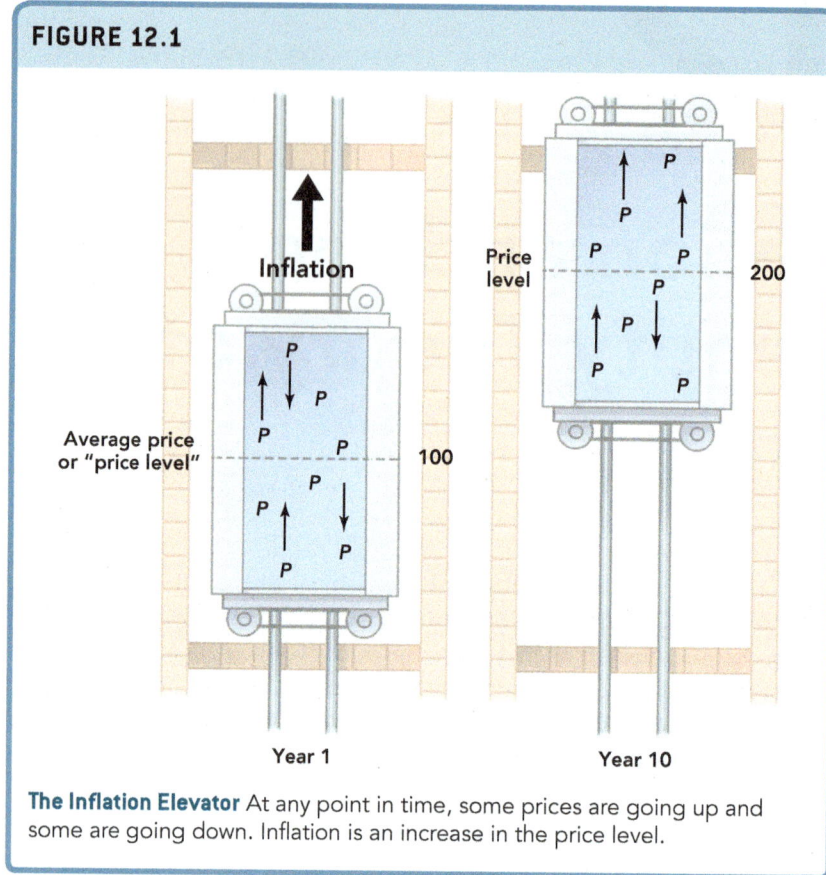

The Inflation Elevator At any point in time, some prices are going up and some are going down. Inflation is an increase in the price level.

The **inflation rate** is the percentage change in the average level of prices (as measured by a price index) over a period of time.

$$\text{Inflation rate} = \frac{P_2 - P_1}{P_1} \times 100$$

index and the **inflation rate** is the percentage change in a price index from one year to the next:

$$\textbf{Inflation rate} = \frac{P_2 - P_1}{P_1} \times 100$$

where P_2 is the index value in year 2 and P_1 is the index value in year 1. A 10% inflation rate means, quite simply, that goods and services are priced (on average) 10% higher than they were a year ago.

Shifts in supply and demand push prices up and down all the time, but inflation is an increase in the average level of prices. We can think of inflation as an elevator lifting all prices over time. In Figure 12.1, some prices in year 1 are going up and some are going down, but overall the average level of prices is 100. Inflation tends to lift all prices, so by year 10 the average level of prices is 200.

Price Indexes

Economists measure inflation using several different price indexes that are based on different bundles of goods:

1. *Consumer price index (CPI):* Measures the average price for a basket of goods and services bought by a typical American consumer. The index covers some 80,000 goods and services and is weighted so that an increase in the price of a major item such as housing counts for more than an increase in the price of a minor item like kitty litter.

2. *GDP deflator:* The ratio of nominal to real GDP multiplied by 100 (discussed in Chapter 6). The GDP deflator covers all finished goods and services.

3. *Producer price indexes (PPI):* Measure the average price received by producers. Unlike the CPI and GDP deflator, producer price indexes measure prices of intermediate as well as finished goods and services. PPI exist for different industries and are often used to calculate changes in the cost of inputs.

For most Americans, the CPI is the measure of inflation that corresponds most directly to their daily economic activity; for businesses and governments, the other indexes take on greater relevance. We focus on the CPI unless otherwise indicated.

One point to remember about the CPI is that the basket of goods and services bought by the average consumer is changing all the time. The CPI, for example, contains a category for audio media like music. In 1975 music typically came on a vinyl record, but if the Bureau of Labor Statistics (BLS) measured the price of music by the price of vinyl records today, it would report that there has been a tremendous increase in the price because vinyl records are now expensive collector's items. To avoid this problem, the BLS periodically updates the basket to reflect the introduction of new goods. Changes in quality present a similar challenge. In 2007, when it was introduced, an iPhone cost $499, which is slightly less expensive than today, but the first iPhone had a 320-by-480-pixel resolution screen, a 2-megapixel camera, and 4 gigabytes of storage. At the time of publication, the latest iPhone has a 1792-by-828-pixel resolution screen, two 12-megapixel cameras that also take HD movies, and up to 256 gigabytes of storage, among many other improvements. Thus, the true price of an iPhone—the price accounting for quality—is much lower today than in 2007. The BLS, which computes the CPI, tries to take both of these factors—new goods and better-quality goods—into account when computing the CPI, but it's challenging. As a result of these challenges, some economists suggest that the CPI may actually overstate inflation by a little bit every year (0.9% is one estimate). That may not seem like much, but it can matter when making comparisons over several decades or more.

Inflation in the United States and Around the World

Figure 12.2 shows the annual inflation rate in the United States since 1950. The average inflation rate over this period was 3.6%, but in many periods, especially in the 1970s, inflation was significantly higher. Over the past 10 years (2010–2020), inflation in the United States has averaged about 1.8%.

Figure 12.3 illustrates the cumulative effect of inflation on a large basket of goods. A basket that cost about $10 in 1913 would have cost $36.70 in 1969, $100 in 1982, $207 in 2007, and $256 in 2019. The height of the line represents the level of the CPI during each year.

The CPI is often used to calculate "real prices." A **real price** is a price that has been corrected for inflation. Real prices are used to compare the prices of goods over time. Suppose, for example, that you are told that the average price of a gallon of gasoline was $1.25 in 1982 but double that, $2.50, in 2006. These prices are correct, but should we conclude that gasoline was twice as expensive in 2006 than in 1982? No. The CPI was 100 in 1982 and 202 in 2006 so the price of most products doubled during this time period; wages rose, as well. Thus, the price of gasoline did not increase over this time period relative to other goods, so the real price of gasoline was about the same in 1982 as 2006. Challenge Problem 22 at the end of this chapter shows how you can easily convert nominal to real prices using the FRED online economic database.

A **real price** is a price that has been corrected for inflation. Real prices are used to compare the prices of goods over time.

FIGURE 12.2

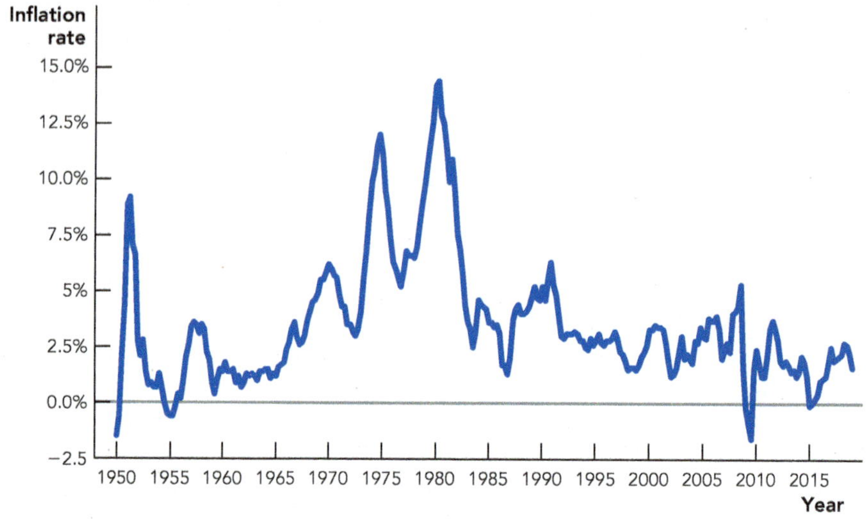

The Inflation Rate in the United States, 1950–2019

Data from: https://fred.stlouisfed.org/graph/?g=qAKP

Most prices go up over time, but there are exceptions. Pocket calculators now cost a few dollars; in 1972, they cost $395. In 1927, two-way radio phone service, America to London, cost $75 for five minutes. Today, a five-minute phone call to England costs mere pennies with Skype. In some cases, technological progress is so rapid that for particular goods and services, it overcomes the general tendency of prices to rise.

FIGURE 12.3

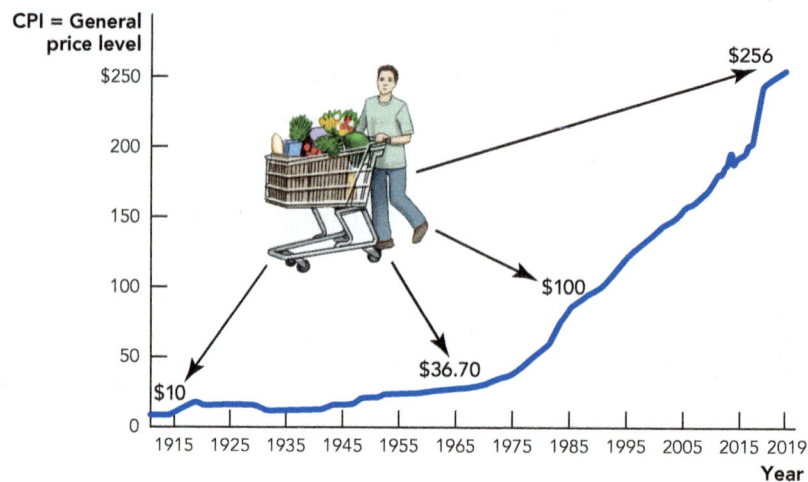

The Effect of Inflation on the Price of a Basket of Goods

Data from: U.S. Bureau of Labor Statistics.

Recent U.S. inflation experience is moderate compared with international inflation rates and the historical record. Table 12.1 displays selected international inflation rates in 2016. South Sudan and Venezuela had the highest inflation rates in the world—each approached 500% that year. Inflation in the United States was just over 1% per year and some countries such as Italy, Greece, and Japan had slight deflations.

Table 12.2 presents some figures for major "hyperinflations." The numbers in Table 12.2 are so high, they are hard to believe, but they are true. In Germany, for example, what cost 1 Reichsmark in 1919 cost half a trillion Reichsmarks in 1923.

Hungary's postwar hyperinflation is the largest on record. The numbers are so high, they are difficult to describe. What cost 1 Hungarian pengo in 1945 cost 1.3 septillion pengos at the end of 1946. Seeing numbers like this, the physicist Richard Feynman said that really big numbers should not be called "astronomical" but "economical."

The Quantity Theory of Money

We already have a good idea about the causes of inflation from the opening discussion of Zimbabwe. We can now examine the inflationary mechanism in more detail by explaining the quantity theory of money. The quantity theory of money does two things: First, it sets out the general relationship between money, velocity (to be defined soon), real output, and prices; second, it helps to explain the critical role of the money supply in determining the inflation rate.

Imagine that every month you are paid $4,000 and you spend $4,000. In a year, you spend $4,000 12 times, so your total yearly spending is $4,000 \times 12 = $48,000$. Another way of figuring out your total yearly spending is to add up all the goods that you buy and multiply by their prices. We can write this identity (an equation that must hold true by definition) as

$$M \times v = P \times Y_R$$

where M is the money you are paid, v is the number of times in a year that you spend M (we call v the "**velocity of money**," hence the v), P is prices, and Y_R is a measure of the real goods and services that you buy. A similar identity holds for the nation as a whole, where we interpret M as the supply of money, v as the average number of times in a year that a dollar is spent on finished goods and services, P as the price level, and Y_R as real GDP.

Thus, for the nation as a whole, we can write

$$Mv = PY_R$$

M = Money supply P = Price level
v = Velocity of money Y_R = Real GDP

TABLE 12.1   INFLATION RATE IN SELECTED COUNTRIES, 2016

Country	Inflation Rate (%)
South Sudan	476.02
Venezuela	475.806
Suriname	67.109
Angola	33.683
Malawi	19.782
Brazil	9.019
Mexico	2.824
China	2.075
United States	1.188
United Kingdom	0.743
Germany	0.399
France	0.346
Netherlands	0.103
Italy	−0.05
Greece	−0.1
Japan	−0.162

Data from: International Monetary Fund, World Economic Outlook Database, October 2016.

CHECK YOURSELF

- If the CPI was 120 this time last year and is 125 right now, what is the inflation rate?
- If the inflation rate goes from 1% to 4% to 7% over two years, what will happen to the prices of the great majority of goods: Will they go up, stay the same, or go down, or do you not have enough information to say?
- Why do we use real prices to compare the price of goods across time?

v, **velocity of money**, is the average number of times a dollar is spent on finished goods and services in a year.

TABLE 12.2 SELECTED EPISODES OF HYPERINFLATION

Nation	Period	Cumulative Inflation Rate (%)	Maximum Inflation Rate on a Monthly Basis (%)
America	1777–1780	2,702	1,342
Bolivia	1984–1985	97,282	196
Peru	1987–1992	17,991,287	1,031
Yugoslavia	1993–1994	1.6×10^9	5×10^{15}
Nicaragua	1986–1991	1.2×10^{10}	261
Greece	1941–1944	1.60×10^{11}	8.5×10^9
Germany	1919–1923	0.5×10^{12}	3,250,000
Zimbabwe	2001–2008	8.53×10^{23}	7.96×10^{10}
Hungary	1945–1946	1.3×10^{24}	4.19×10^{16}

Data from: Fisher, Stanley, Ratna Sahay, and Carlos A. Vegh. 2002. Modern hyper- and high inflations. *Journal of Economic Literature, American Economic Association* 40(3): 837–880.
Anderson, Robert B., William A. Bomberger, and Gail E. Makinen. 1988. The demand for money, the "reform effect," and the money supply process in hyperinflation: The evidence from Greece and Hungary reexamined." *Journal of Money, Credit and Banking* 20: 653–672, https://en.wikipedia.org/wiki/Hyperinflation, https://www.sjsu.edu/faculty/watkins/hyper.htm, and https://www.cato.org/zimbabwe.

Since Mv is the total amount spent on finished goods and services and PY_R is the price level times real GDP, both sides of this equation are also equal to nominal GDP.

With some additional assumptions, the simple identity, $Mv = PY_R$, helps us think through how money affects output and prices. We proceed with two further assumptions, namely that both real GDP (Y_R) and velocity (v) are stable compared with the money supply (M).

Let's discuss why these assumptions are usually reasonable. Over the period we are interested in, real GDP is fixed by the real factors of production—capital, labor, and technology—exactly as discussed in Chapters 7 and 8. We know that inflation can be 10%, 500%, 5,000% a year, or much higher. Real GDP, in contrast, rarely changes by more than, say, 10% a year, so changes in real GDP don't seem like a plausible candidate for explaining large changes in prices.

Let's also assume that v, the velocity of money, is stable. The velocity of money is the average number of times a dollar is used to purchase finished goods and services within a year. In the preceding example, v was 12 because you were paid monthly and you spent your entire monthly income of $4,000 12 times in a year. In the U.S. economy today, v is about 7 and it is determined by the same kind of factors that might determine your personal v, factors such as whether workers are paid monthly or biweekly, how long it takes to clear a check, and how easy it is to find

A 500,000,000,000 dinar bank note from a world hyperinflation leader, Yugoslavia c. 1993. At the time, 500 billion dinars could buy about $5 worth of goods.

and use an ATM. These factors change over time but only slowly. Other factors that we will discuss at greater length in the chapters on business fluctuations can change v more quickly, but not by enough to account for large and sustained increases in prices. For these reasons, changes in v also do not seem like a plausible candidate for explaining large and sustained increases in prices.

The Cause of Inflation

If Y_R is fixed by the real factors of production and v is stable, then it follows immediately that the only thing that can cause increases in P are increases in M, the supply of money. In other words, inflation is caused by an increase in the supply of money.

How well does this theory hold up? The left panel of Figure 12.4 plots the price level (P) and the supply of money (M) in Peru during its hyperinflation. A product with a price of 1 Peruvian intis in 1980 would have cost more than *10 million* intis by 1995. (To reduce the number of zeroes, the Peruvian government changed the name of the currency twice during this period, first from intis to soles de oro and then to the nuevo sol.) As you can see, the supply of money also increased about 10 million times in lockstep with the increase in prices.

The quantity theory of money can also be written in terms of growth rates. We denote the growth rate of any variable with a little arrow over the variable, so $\overrightarrow{M}$ is the growth rate of the money supply, $\overrightarrow{P}$ is the growth rate of prices, and so forth. If $Mv = PY_R$, then it is also true that:[*]

$$\overrightarrow{M} + \overrightarrow{v} = \overrightarrow{P} + \overrightarrow{Y}_R$$

We have a special word for the growth rate of prices $\overrightarrow{P}$: inflation! (Inflation is also often written with a special symbol, π.) If we assume that velocity isn't

$$M\bar{v} = P\bar{Y}_R$$

The Quantity Theory of Money in a Nutshell When v and Y are fixed (indicated by a top bar), increases in M must cause increases in P.

FIGURE 12.4

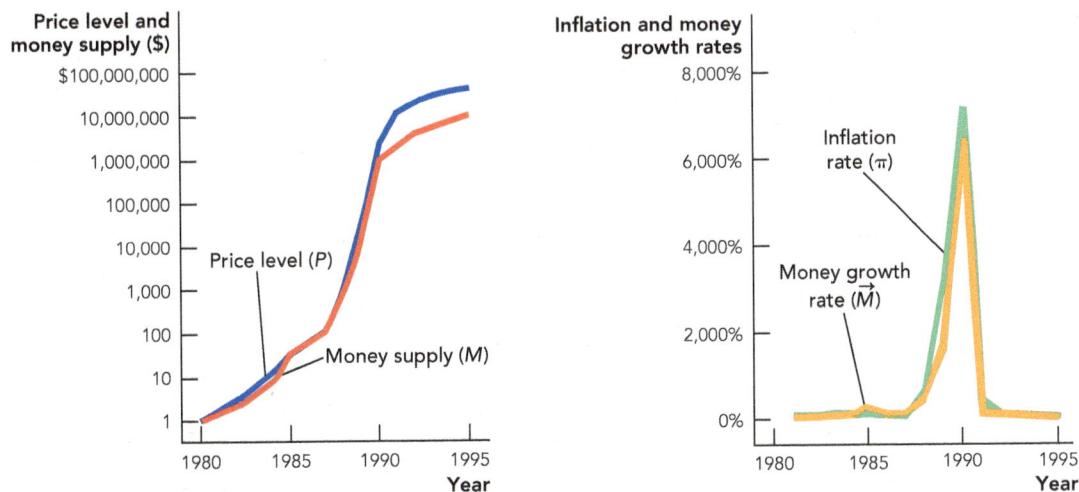

Inflation Is a Monetary Phenomenon in Peru

Data from: International Monetary Fund, International Financial Statistics.

---

[*] To derive this equation, we have used a convenient mathematical fact that if $Y = A \times B$, then the growth rate of Y is approximately equal to the growth rate of A plus the growth rate of B.

changing much, as we just did, then the growth rate of velocity $\vec{v}$ will be zero or very low. We also know that $\vec{Y}_R$, the growth rate of real GDP, is relatively low, say, between 2% and at most 10%. Thus, if we ignore these two factors, we see immediately that $\vec{M} \approx$ *Inflation Rate* (π), where $\approx$ means approximately equal. In other words, the quantity theory of money says that the growth rate of the money supply will be approximately equal to the inflation rate.

The right panel of Figure 12.4 shows that during Peru's hyperinflation, this was true: As the supply of money grew faster, so did the inflation rate, peaking in 1990 at a rate of 7,500% per year.

What about other times and places? Figure 12.5 plots inflation rates on the vertical axis versus money growth rates on the horizontal axis for 110 nations between 1960 and 1990. Nations with rapidly growing money supplies had high inflation rates. Nations with slowly growing money supplies had low inflation rates. In fact, as the red line indicates, on average, the relationship is almost perfectly linear, with a 10 percentage point increase in the money growth rate leading to a 10 percentage point increase in the inflation rate.

If we are thinking about sustained inflation, a significant and continuing increase in the price level, then Nobel Prize–winner Milton Friedman has it exactly right: "Inflation is always and everywhere a monetary phenomenon." This is one of the most important truths of macroeconomics.

Even though large and sustained increases in prices stem from increases in the money supply, changes in v and Y_R can have modest influences on inflation rates. Suppose, for example, that M and v are fixed; then increases in Y_R (real GDP) must lower prices. In the past, many countries used a commodity such as gold or silver as money. The dollar, for example, was defined as 1/20th of an ounce of gold between 1834 and 1933. Since the supply of gold or silver

FIGURE 12.5

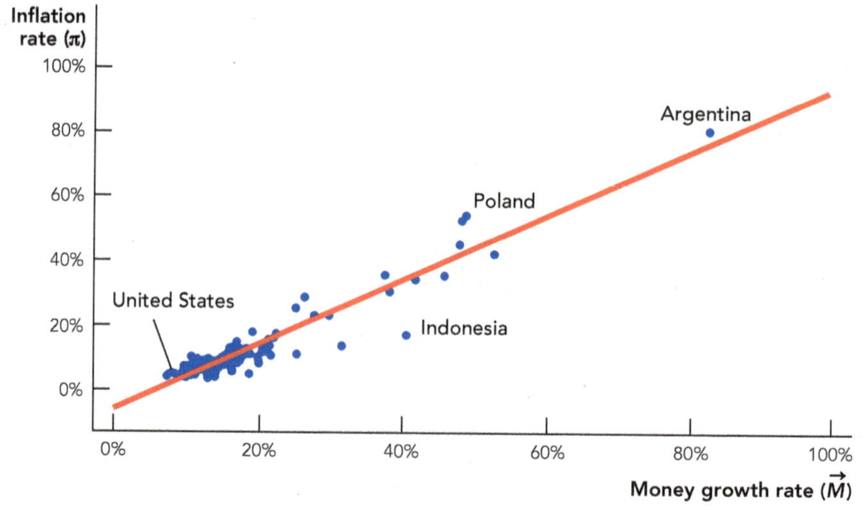

Inflation Is Always and Everywhere a Monetary Phenomenon

Note: Inflation rates and money growth rates over 1960–1990.
Data from: McCandless, G., and W. Weber. 1995. Some monetary facts. *Federal Reserve Bank of Minneapolis Quarterly Review* 19(3):2–11.

usually increases slowly under commodity-money standards, prices typically decrease a bit every year as Y_R increases faster than M.

Finally, even taking the influence of M into account, changes in the velocity of money will affect prices. For instance, increases in the velocity of money can accelerate an already existing inflation. At the height of the German hyper-inflation in 1923, prices were increasing by the minute. Velocity increased in response to this extreme condition. Instead of being paid weekly, for example, workers would be paid as often as three times a day and they would hand off their earnings to their wives, who would rush to the stores to buy food, soap, clothes, *anything* before prices rose even further. Inflation itself caused an increase in velocity, which further fueled inflation.

The velocity of money can also decrease. In an economic panic, individuals may simply hold their money and be afraid to spend it. People might believe that keeping money under the mattress could be less risky than putting money in a bank. During the Great Depression, many people in the United States behaved in precisely this way and the decrease in monetary velocity helped to fuel a **deflation**, a decrease in prices, that worsened the depression. More moderate decreases in velocity or in the growth rate of the money supply would reduce the inflation rate, a **disinflation** rather than a deflation. (We discuss deflation and the Great Depression at greater length in Chapters 13 and 16.)

Deflation is a decrease in the average level of prices (a negative inflation rate).

A **disinflation** is a reduction in the inflation rate.

The quantity theory also assumes that changes in M cannot change Y_R. In the long run, this makes sense because we know that real GDP is determined by capital, labor, and technology and changes in M won't change any of these factors. Thus, in the long run money is neutral. Imagine, for example, that we doubled the money supply. In the long run, the quantity theory says that prices will double and nothing else will change. We will return to the long-run neutrality of money again and again so let's make a special note of this principle:

In the long run, money is neutral.

Although money is neutral in the long run, it's possible that changes in M can change Y_R in the short run. In particular, under some circumstances increases in M can *temporarily increase* real GDP and decreases in M can *temporarily decrease* real GDP. To see how changes in M could cause changes in real GDP in the short run, let's look at an inflation parable that illustrates how new money works its way through an economy.

An Inflation Parable

Consider a mini economy consisting of a baker, tailor, and carpenter who buy and sell products among themselves. Now consider what happens when a government like that in Zimbabwe starts paying its soldiers with newly printed money. At first, the baker is delighted when soldiers walk through his door with cash for bread. To satisfy his new customers, the baker works extra hours, bakes more bread, and is able to raise prices. "How wonderful," he thinks, "with the increase in the demand for bread, I will be able to buy more clothes and cabinets." Meanwhile, the tailor and carpenter are thinking much the same thing as soldiers are also buying goods from them.

When the baker arrives at the tailor to buy shirts, however, he finds that he has been fooled. The soldiers have bought shirts for themselves and the price of shirts has now gone up. Similarly, the tailor and carpenter discover that the prices of the goods that they want to buy have also increased. Although they earned more dollars, their real wages—the amount of goods that the baker, tailor, and carpenter can buy with their dollars—have decreased.

When the government next wants to buy goods, it faces higher prices and must print even more money to buy just as many goods as before. Moreover, as the new money enters the economy, the baker, for example, will now *race* to the tailor and carpenter to try to spend the money before prices rise. Unfortunately, the tailor and carpenter are likely to have had the same idea and the result is that prices increase even more quickly than the time before.

Eventually, as the government continues to print money and buy goods, the baker, tailor, and carpenter will come to expect and prepare for inflation. Instead of working extra hours, the baker, tailor, and carpenter will realize that by the time they get to spend their new money, the prices of the goods that they want to buy will have risen in price. Knowing this, the baker, tailor, and carpenter will no longer be so happy to see the soldiers enter their shop waving fistfuls of dollars and they will no longer work extra hours baking more bread, sewing more clothes, or building more cabinets.

The inflation parable tells us that an unexpected increase in the money supply can boost the economy in the short run, but as firms and workers come to expect and adjust to the new influx of money, output will not grow any faster than normal. The inflation parable serves us well for now, but the short-run relationship between unexpected inflation and output is a key idea in economics and one we will return to in much greater detail in the next chapter.

CHECK YOURSELF

- In the long run, what causes inflation?
- What is the equation that represents the quantity theory of money?

The Costs of Inflation

To the person in the street, the costs of inflation are obvious—prices are going up; what could be worse? But most people rarely consider that inflation also raises their wages. (No doubt, we all have a tendency to think that bad events, like price increases, are the fault of others but good events, like higher wages, are due to our own virtues.) If all prices, including wages, are going up, then what is the problem with inflation?

If everyone knew whether the rate of inflation was 2% or 8%, then everyone could prepare and the exact inflation rate would not matter very much. But instead of everyone knowing the rate, it's more often the case that no one knows the rate of inflation! In the United States, inflation was 1.3% in 1964; the rate more than quadrupled to 5.7% in 1970 and increased to 11% per year by 1974. Inflation caught most people by surprise. And when inflation decreased from 13% in 1980 to 3% in 1983, most people were surprised again. Inflation also tends to be more variable and thus more difficult to predict when the inflation rate is high. Take a look again at the right panel of Figure 12.4. Inflation in Peru went from 77% in 1986 to 7,500% in 1990 and then back down to 73% in 1992. Who can predict such changes?

High rates of inflation do create some problems, as we will explain, but volatile or uncertain inflation is even more costly. We now cover some specific problems or costs introduced by high and volatile inflation. Keep in mind the picture of inflation as a kind of insidious, slow-moving cancer. Inflation destroys the ability of market prices to send signals about the value of resources and opportunities.

Price Confusion and Money Illusion

Prices are signals and inflation makes price signals more difficult to interpret. In our inflation parable, for example, the baker initially thought that the increase in the demand for bread signaled that the real demand for bread had increased. In fact, since all prices were rising, the real demand for bread had not increased. Confusing a nominal signal with a real signal has real consequences. The baker thought that prices were telling him to work harder and produce more bread. When he later discovered that all prices had risen, he knew that he had made a costly mistake.

Now imagine that one day the *real demand* for bread does increase, only now the baker is so used to inflation, he ignores the signal. Instead of working harder, the baker continues to bake the same number of loaves of bread as before. Opportunities are missed because signals have become obscured.

In a modern economy, it might seem easy enough to figure out whether an increase in demand for bread reflects a real increase in demand or just an increase in the money supply. Just pick up the *Wall Street Journal* and read the articles about monetary policy. But it's not actually so easy. Sometimes the money supply is increasing and the real demand for bread is going up, both at the same time. It is difficult to sort out the relative strength of both influences. Or perhaps the baker never understood the principles of economics, or, unlike you (!), never read a really good economics textbook.

Human beings are not always perfectly rational, which makes reading signals even more difficult. Even when we should know better, we sometimes treat the higher wages and prices that result from inflation as higher wages and prices in real terms. If the price of a movie goes up 10% and other prices including wages go up by about the same amount, we ought to conclude that the real price of a movie has stayed more or less the same. But many people conclude, mistakenly, that movies have become "more expensive." They treat this as a change in relative price: They may see fewer movies or make other decisions based on this new price. Economists call this the "money illusion." **Money illusion** is when people mistake changes in nominal prices for changes in real prices.

In short, inflation usually confuses consumers, workers, firms, and entrepreneurs. When price signals are difficult to interpret, the market economy doesn't work as well—resources are wasted in activities that appear profitable but in fact are not, entrepreneurs are less quick to respond to real opportunities, and resources flow more slowly to profitable uses.

mru.org/inflation-cost1

Price Confusion and Money Illusion

Money illusion is when people mistake changes in nominal prices for changes in real prices.

Inflation Redistributes Wealth

In our inflation parable, the government bought bread, shirts, and woodwork simply by printing paper. Where did these real goods come from? They came from the baker, tailor, and carpenter. Inflation transfers real resources from citizens to the government. Thus, *inflation is a type of tax*.

The inflation tax does not require tax collectors, a tax bureaucracy, or extensive record keeping. You can hide from most taxes by keeping your transactions secret and saving your money under the bed. But you can't hide from the inflation tax! Money under the bed is precisely what inflation does tax because as prices rise, the value of the dollars under the bed falls. It's not surprising, therefore, that money-strapped governments in danger of collapsing typically use massive inflation. Almost all the hyperinflations in Table 12.2 involved governments with massive debts or spending that could not be paid for with regular taxes.

Inflation does more than transfer wealth to the government—it also redistributes wealth among the public, especially between lenders and borrowers. To see why, suppose that a lender lends money at an interest rate of 10% but that over the course of the year the inflation rate is also 10%. On paper, the lender has earned a return of 10%—we call this the "nominal return." But what is the lender's real rate of return? The lender is paid 10% interest, but she is paid in dollars that have become 10% less valuable. Thus, the lender's real rate of return is 0%.

Thus, inflation can reduce the real return that lenders receive on their loans, in effect transferring wealth from lenders to borrowers. In the 1970s, for example, high inflation rates meant the real value of 30-year fixed-rate mortgages that were taken out in the 1960s declined tremendously, redistributing billions of dollars from lenders to borrowers. Borrowers benefited but many lenders went bankrupt.

In the late 1970s, however, many people began to expect that 10% inflation was here to stay, so home buyers were willing to take out long-term mortgages with interest rates of 15% or higher. When inflation fell unexpectedly in the early 1980s, these borrowers found that their real payments were much higher than they had anticipated. Wealth was redistributed from borrowers to lenders.

We can explain the relationship between inflation and wealth redistribution more precisely by writing the relationship between the lender's real rate of return, the nominal rate of return, and the inflation rate as follows:

$$\textbf{Real interest rate = Nominal rate} - \textbf{Inflation rate} \qquad (1)$$

or, in symbols,

$$r_{\textbf{Real}} = i - \pi$$

Real rate of return is the nominal rate of return minus the inflation rate.

Nominal rate of return is the rate of return that does not account for inflation.

In words, the **real rate of return** is equal to the **nominal rate of return** minus the inflation rate.

Lenders, of course, will not lend money at a loss. Thus, when lenders expect inflation to increase, they will demand a higher nominal interest rate. For example, if lenders expect that the inflation rate will be 7% and the equilibrium real rate (determined in the market for loanable funds—see Chapter 9) is 5%, then lenders will ask for a nominal interest rate of approximately 12% (7% to break even given the expected rate of inflation plus the 5% equilibrium rate). If lenders expect that the inflation rate will be 10%, lenders will demand a nominal interest rate of approximately 15% (10% to break even given the expected rate of inflation plus the 5% equilibrium rate).

The **Fisher effect** is the tendency of nominal interest rates to rise with expected inflation rates.

The tendency of nominal interest rates to increase with expected inflation rates is called the **Fisher effect** (after economist Irving Fisher, 1867–1947). As an approximation,[*] we can write the Fisher effect as

$$i = \textbf{E}\pi + r_{\textbf{Equilibrium}} \qquad (2)$$

i = Nominal interest rate, $\text{E}\pi$ = Expected inflation rate
$r_{\text{Equilibrium}}$ = Equilibrium real rate of return

---

[*] The Fisher effect equation in the text is only approximate. The exact Fisher effect equation is $(1 + i) = (1 + r)(1 + \pi)$. If a lender wants a real rate of return of 5% ($r = 0.05$) and the inflation rate is 10% ($\pi = 0.1$), then the lender must charge a nominal rate of 1.155 (1.10×1.05), or 15.5%. When inflation rates are low, the approximation works well, but it does not during hyperinflations.

FIGURE 12.6

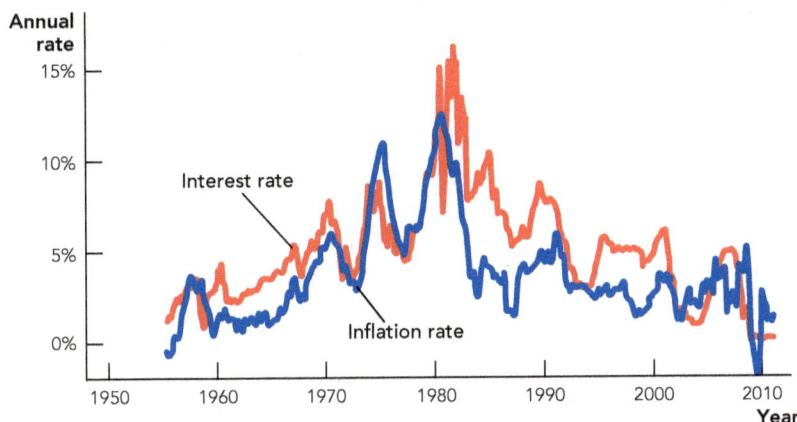

Nominal Interest Rates Tend to Increase with Inflation Rates

Data from: U.S. Bureau of Labor Statistics and Board of Governors of the Federal Reserve System.

The Fisher effect says that the nominal interest rate is equal to the expected inflation rate plus the equilibrium real interest rate. Most important, the Fisher effect says that the nominal rate will rise with expected inflation. We can see the Fisher effect in Figure 12.6, which graphs the inflation rate and short-term nominal interest rate in the United States from 1955 to 2010.

Thus, repeating equations 1 and 2, we have

$$r_{Real} = i - \pi \tag{1}$$

and

$$i = E\pi + r_{Equilibrium} \tag{2}$$

If we substitute *i* from equation 2 into equation 1, we see that the real rate of return will be determined in large part by the difference between expected inflation and actual inflation:

$$r_{Real} = (E\pi - \pi) + r_{Equilibrium}$$

If $(E\pi < \pi)$, that is, if expected inflation is less than actual inflation, then the real rate of return will be less than the equilibrium rate and will quite possibly be negative. Wealth will be redistributed from lenders to borrowers.

If $(E\pi > \pi)$, that is, if expected inflation is greater than actual inflation or equivalently if there is an unexpected "disinflation," then the real rate of return will be higher than the equilibrium rate. Wealth will be redistributed from borrowers to lenders.

Only when $E\pi = \pi$, that is, when expected inflation is equal to actual inflation, will the real return be equal to the equilibrium return. In this case, there will be no unexpected redistribution of wealth between borrowers and lenders. We summarize the effects of inflation on the redistribution of wealth in Table 12.3.

Governments are often borrowers so governments benefit from unexpected inflation. Thus, a government with massive debts has a special incentive to increase the money supply—called **monetizing the debt**. Why doesn't the

Monetizing the debt is when the government pays off its debts by printing money.

TABLE 12.3 THE REDISTRIBUTION OF WEALTH CAUSED BY INFLATION

Unexpected inflation ($E\pi < \pi$)	Unexpected disinflation ($E\pi > \pi$)	Expected inflation = Actual inflation ($E\pi = \pi$)
Real rate less than equilibrium rate	Real rate greater than equilibrium rate	Real rate equal to equilibrium rate
Harms lenders Benefits borrowers	Benefits lenders Harms borrowers	No redistribution of wealth

government always inflate its debt away? One reason is the Fisher effect. If lenders expect that the government will inflate its debt away, they will only lend at high nominal rates of interest. To avoid this outcome, the government may try to make a credible promise to keep the inflation rate low.

Another reason the government doesn't always inflate its debt away is that people who buy government bonds are typically voters who would be upset if their real returns were shrunk to zero or less. But what do you think would happen to inflation rates if a nation's debt was owed to foreigners? A government would probably have a stronger incentive to inflate away debt owed to foreigners than debt owed to voters. The U.S. debt is increasingly owed to foreigners, which makes some economists predict a return of inflation in the United States, especially if a future U.S. government finds it difficult to cover its debt with other taxes (see Chapter 17).

Inflation and the Breakdown of Financial Intermediation

Sometimes a government will combine inflation with controls on interest rates, making it illegal to raise the nominal rate of interest and preventing the Fisher effect from operating. When nominal interest rates are not allowed to rise and the inflation rate is high, the real rate of return will be negative. In this way, bank savings accounts are turned into wasting accounts.

When real interest rates turn negative, people take their money out of the banking system, using the cash to invest abroad (if they can), or to buy a real asset like land that is appreciating in value alongside inflation, or to simply consume more. In any of these cases, when many people pull their money out of the banking system, the supply of savings declines and financial intermediation becomes less efficient. Table 12.4 shows a number of examples of severely negative real interest rates. In every case, economic growth was also negative. Countries with negative real interest rates usually have many problems so we can't blame all of the poor economic growth on inefficient financial intermediation. Nonetheless, studies show that even after controlling for other factors, negative real interest rates reduce financial intermediation and economic growth.

Hyperinflation and the Breakdown of Financial Intermediation

If inflation is moderate and stable, lenders and borrowers can probably forecast reasonably well and loans can be signed with rough certainty regarding the real value of the future payments. But when inflation is volatile and unpredictable, long-term loans become riskier and they may not be signed at all. Thus, the real problem of unexpected inflation is not simply that it redistributes wealth, but—even worse—that few long-term contracts will be signed when borrowers and

MRU
mru.org/inflation-cost2

Financial Intermediation Failure

TABLE 12.4 NEGATIVE INTEREST RATES AND ECONOMIC GROWTH

Country	Years	Real Interest Rate (%)	Per Capita Growth (%)
Argentina	1975–1976	−69	−2.2
Bolivia	1982–1984	−75	−5.2
Chile	1972–1974	−61	−3.6
Ghana	1976–1983	−35	−2.9
Peru	1976–1984	−19	−1.4
Poland	1981–1982	−33	−8.6
Sierra Leone	1984–1987	−44	−1.9
Turkey	1979–1980	−35	−3.1
Venezuela	1987–1989	−24	−2.7
Zaire	1976–1979	−34	−6.0
Zambia	1985–1988	−24	−1.9

Data from: Easterly, W. 2002. *The Elusive Quest for Growth. Economists' Adventures and Misadventures in the Tropics.* Cambridge, MA: MIT Press.

lenders both fear that unexpected inflation or deflation *could* redistribute their wealth.

High and volatile inflation rates have decimated many developing nations. When Peru experienced hyperinflation between 1987 and 1992, private loans virtually disappeared. When firms cannot get loans, they cannot build for future expansion and growth. The price level in Peru is approximately 10 million times higher today than it was in 1997. Who could have predicted these rates of increase or built them into a contract?

The virtual elimination of inflation in Mexico shows how much capital markets can flourish in a stable environment. In the 1980s, the rate of Mexican inflation at times exceeded 100%. Long-term loans were very hard to come by. In the United States, it's relatively easy to borrow money for 10, 20, or 30 years or even longer. But as recently as the early 2000s, 90% of the local currency debt in Mexico matured within one year.

In the 1990s, the inflation rate in Mexico came down to about 10% and more recently it has been close to 3%, not that far from the rate in the United States. Mexican capital markets have grown rapidly as inflation has been stabilized. In 2006, the Mexican government was able to introduce a 30-year bond, denominated in Mexican pesos; this would have been unheard of as recently as the mid-1990s.

The greater ease and predictability of long-term borrowing also has caused the Mexican mortgage market to take off. It is now relatively easy to obtain a long-term mortgage in Mexico—due largely to lower and less volatile inflation—and many more middle-class Mexicans have been able to afford homes.

It's not only lenders and borrowers that need to forecast future inflation rates. Any contract involving future payments will be affected by inflation. Workers and firms, for example, often make wage agreements several years in advance, especially when unions or other forms of collective bargaining are in place. If the rate of inflation is high and volatile, they are more likely to set wages at the wrong level. Either wages will be too high, and the firm will be reluctant to use more overtime or hire more workers, or wages will be too low, in which case workers are underpaid, they will slack off, and some will quit their jobs altogether.

Unexpected inflation redistributes wealth throughout society in arbitrary ways. When the inflation rate is high and volatile, unexpected inflation is difficult to avoid and society suffers as long-term contracting grinds to a halt.

Inflation Interacts with Other Taxes

Most tax systems define incomes, profits, and capital gains in nominal terms. In these systems, inflation, even expected inflation, will produce some tax burdens and tax liabilities that do not make economic sense.

To make this concrete, let's say you bought a share of stock for $100, and over several years inflation alone pushed its price to $150. The U.S. tax system requires that you pay profits on the $50 gain even though the gain is illusory. Yes, you have more money in nominal terms, but that money is worth less in terms of its ability to purchase real goods and services. In real terms, the stock hasn't increased in price at all yet you must still pay tax on the phantom gain.

In this case, inflation leads to people paying capital gain taxes when they should not. The overall tax burden rises. The long-run effect is to discourage investment in the first place.

Depending on the details of particular tax systems, inflation can also push people into higher tax brackets or make corporations pay taxes on phantom business profits. In short, inflation increases the costs associated with tax systems.

Inflation Is Painful to Stop

Once inflation starts, it's painful to stop—this is one of the biggest costs of inflation. Imagine that the inflation rate has been 10% in an economy for some time so that loans, wage agreements, and all kinds of business contracts are based on the expectation that inflation will continue at 10%. The government can reduce inflation by reducing the growth in the money supply, but what will happen to the economy? When workers, firms, and consumers expect 10% inflation, a lower rate is a shock. At first, firms may interpret the lower rate as a reduction in real demand and thus they may reduce output and employment. Furthermore, contracts signed on the expectation of 10% inflation are now out of whack with actual inflation. Wage bargains that promised raises of 12% per year were modest when inflation was 10%, but are huge increases in real wages when the inflation rate is 3%. Workers may be thrown out of work as the unexpected increase in their real wage makes them unaffordable. Only in the long run, as expectations adjust, does the economy move to a point where both inflation and unemployment are low.

In the United States, for example, Ronald Reagan was elected to the presidency in 1980 after inflation in the United States hit 13.5% a year. By 1983, tough monetary policy had reduced the inflation rate to 3%, but the consequence was a severe recession and an unemployment rate of a little more than 10%. Only in 1988 did unemployment return to near 5.5%.

Takeaway

Inflation is an increase in the average level of prices as measured by a price index such as the consumer price index (CPI). A price index can be used to convert a nominal price into a real price, a price corrected for inflation.

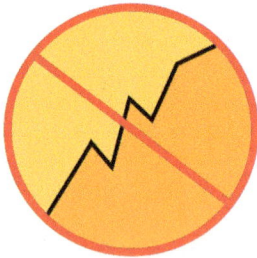

Just Say No Inflation has been likened to a drug addiction. At first the highs (a booming economy) are good. But soon bigger and bigger doses are needed to generate the same high as before (unexpected inflation becomes expected inflation). Eventually, all that is left is the fear of withdrawal (disinflation).

CHECK YOURSELF

- Consider unexpected inflation and unexpected disinflation. How is wealth redistributed between borrowers and lenders under each case?
- What happens to nominal interest rates when expected inflation increases? What do we call this effect?
- What does unexpected inflation do to price signals?

Sustained inflation is always and everywhere a monetary phenomenon. In the long run, real GDP is determined by the real factors of production—capital, labor, and technology—so changes in the money supply cannot permanently increase real GDP. Thus, the quantity theory of money is a good guide to how prices respond to changes in the money supply in the long run. Although money is neutral in the long run, changes in the money supply can influence real GDP in the short run for a variety of reasons.

Inflation makes price signals more difficult to interpret, especially when people may suffer from money illusion. Inflation is a type of tax. Governments with few other sources of tax revenue often turn to inflation because the inflation tax is difficult to avoid.

Workers and firms will adjust to a predictable inflation by incorporating inflation rates into wage contracts and loan agreements. The tendency of the nominal interest rate to increase with expected inflation is called the Fisher effect. But inflation is often difficult to predict. When inflation is greater than expected, wealth is redistributed from lenders to borrowers. When inflation is less than expected, wealth is redistributed from borrowers to lenders. The possibility of arbitrary redistributions of wealth in either direction makes lending and borrowing more risky and thus breaks down financial intermediation.

Anything above a mild sustained rate of inflation is generally bad for an economy. Economists disagree, however, as to whether and how much small amounts of well-timed inflation can benefit an economy. In the next chapter and Chapter 16, we discuss at greater length how policymakers might use the short-run trade-off between inflation and output to smooth recessions and booms. This remains one of the most important and controversial "fault lines" in modern macroeconomics.

CHAPTER REVIEW

Go online to practice with more examples of these types of problems, including live links to videos, data sources, and feedback.

▶ Problems with this icon relate to optional MRU videos.

KEY CONCEPTS

inflation, p. 265

inflation rate, p. 266

real price, p. 267

v, velocity of money, p. 269

deflation, p. 273

disinflation, p. 273

money illusion, p. 275

real rate of return, p. 276

nominal rate of return, p. 676

Fisher effect, p. 276

monetizing the debt, p. 277

FACTS AND TOOLS

▶ 1. What is a "price level"? If the "price level" is higher in one country than another, what does that tell us, if anything, about the standard of living in that country?

▶ 2. What are some forces that could cause shocks to v, the velocity of money?

▶ 3. What is probably a bigger problem: a steady rate of inflation of, say, 15% or a rate of inflation that varies unexpectedly year to year from 0% to 15%, so that, on average the rate is well below 15%? Why?

▶ 4. Who gets helped by a surprise inflation: people who owe money or people who lend money?

5. Who is more likely to lobby the government for fast money growth: people who have mortgages or people who own banks that lent money for those mortgages?

6. Consider the interaction between inflation and the tax system (assume the inflation is expected). Does high inflation encourage people to save more or discourage saving? If a government wants to raise more tax revenue in the short run, should it push for higher or lower inflation?

7. Which tells me more about how many more goods and services I can buy next year if I save my money today: the nominal interest rate or the real interest rate? Which interest rate gets talked about more in the media?

8. If everyone expects inflation to rise by 10% over the next few years, where, according to the Fisher effect, will the biggest effect be: on nominal or real interest rates?

THINKING AND PROBLEM SOLVING

9. Calculate inflation in the following cases:

Price Level Last Year ($)	Price Level This Year ($)	Inflation Rate
100	110	
250	300	
4,000	4,000	

10. What does the quantity theory of money predict will happen *in the long run*? According to the quantity theory, a rise in the money supply can't change v or Y in the long run, so it must affect P. Let's use that fact to see how changes in the money supply affect the price level. Fill in the following table:

M	v	P	Y
150	5		50
200	5		50
100	5		50

11. In the long run, according to the quantity theory of money, if the money supply doubles, what happens to the price level? What happens to real GDP? In both cases, state the percentage change in either the price level or real GDP.

12. Much of the economic news we read about can be reinterpreted into our "$Mv = PY$" framework. Turn each of the following news headlines into a precise statement about M, v, P, or Y:

a. "Deposits in U.S. banks fell in 2015."

b. "American businesses are spending faster than ever."

c. "Prices of most consumer goods rose 12% last year."

d. "Workers produced 4% more output per hour last year."

e. "Real GDP increased 32% in the last decade."

f. "Interest rates fall: Consumers hold more cash."

13. It's time to take control of the Federal Reserve (which controls the U.S. money supply). In this chapter, we're thinking only about the "long run," so Y (real GDP) is out of the Fed's control, as is v. The Fed's only goal is to make sure that the price level is equal to 100 each and every year—that's just known as "price stability," one of the main goals of most governments.

In question 10, you acted like an economic *forecaster:* You knew the values of M, v, and Y and had to guess what the long-run price level would be. In this question, you will act like an economic *policymaker:* You know the values of v and Y, and you know your goal for P. Your job is to set the level of M so that you meet your price-level target.

In some years, there will be long-lasting shocks to v and Y, so your job as a policymaker is to offset those shocks by changing the supply of money in the economy. Some of these changes might not make you popular with the citizens, but they are part of keeping P equal to the price-level target. Fill in the following table:

Year	M	v	=	P	Y
1	25,000	2		100	500
2		4		100	500
3		4		100	400
4		4		100	200
5		2		100	400
6		1		100	600

14. Nobel laureate Milton Friedman often said that "inflation is the cruelest tax." Who is it a tax on? More than one answer may be correct:

a. People who hold currency and coins in their wallet, purse, or at home

b. Businesses that hold currency and coins in their cash registers

c. People or businesses who keep deposits in a checking account that pays zero interest

d. People or businesses who keep deposits in a savings account that pays an interest rate higher than the rate of inflation

e. People or businesses who invest in gold, silver, platinum, or other metals

▶ 15. In countries with hyperinflation, the government prints money and uses it to pay government workers. How is this similar to counterfeiting? How is it different?

▶ 16. The Fisher effect says that nominal interest rates will equal expected inflation plus the real equilibrium rate of return:

$$i = E\pi + r_{\text{Equilibrium}}$$

i = Nominal interest rate

$E\pi$ = Expected inflation rate

$r_{\text{Equilibrium}}$ = Equilibrium real rate of return

Economists and Wall Street experts often use the Fisher effect to learn about economic variables that are hard to measure because when the Fisher effect holds, if we know any two of the three items in the equation, we can calculate the third. Sometimes, for example, economists are trying to estimate what investors *expect* inflation is going to be over the next few years, but they have good estimates only of nominal interest rates and the equilibrium real rate. Other times, they have good estimates of expected inflation and today's nominal interest rates, and want to learn about the equilibrium real rate. Let's use the Fisher effect just as the experts do: Use two *known* values to learn about the *unknown* third one.

i	$E\pi$	$r_{\text{Equilibrium}}$
5%	2%	3%
5%	1%	
5%		8%
	10%	2%
6%		2%
0%	−2%	

Note: The last entry is an example of the "Friedman rule," something that we'll come back to in a later chapter.

Discovering DATA ⠿

17. How much did a typical basket of goods increase in price between 1990 and 2010? Let's use the FRED economic database (https://fred.stlouisfed.org/) to answer this question. Search for the CPI (the consumer price index). Click Edit Graph and change the frequency to Annual.

a. What was the CPI in 1990? What was the CPI in 2010?

b. What was the total inflation rate over this 20-year period?

CHALLENGES

18. If I get more money, does that typically make me richer? If society gets more money, does it make society richer? What's the contradiction?

19. Why is it so painful to get rid of inflation? Why can't the government just stop printing so much money?

▶ 20. Who gets hurt most in the following cases: banks, mortgage holders (i.e., homeowners), or neither?

$E\pi$	π	Who gets hurt?
4%	10%	
10%	4%	
−3%	0%	
3%	6%	
10%	10%	

▶ 21. Let's see just how much high expected inflation can hurt incentives to save for the long run. Let's assume the government takes about one-third of every extra dollar of nominal interest you earn (a reasonable approximation for recent college graduates in the United States). You must pay taxes on nominal interest—just like under current U.S. law—but if you're rational, you'll care mostly about your real, after-tax interest rate when deciding how much to save.

To make the economic lesson clear, note that in every case, the real rate (before taxes) is an identical 3%. In each case, calculate the nominal after-tax rate of return and the real after-tax rate of return. Notice that as inflation rises, your after-tax rate of return plummets.

i	$E\pi = \pi$	$\frac{2}{3} \times i$	$\left(\frac{2}{3} \times i\right) - \pi$
Nominal Interest Rate	Inflation (no surprises)	Nominal After-tax Return	Real After-tax Return
15%	12%	10%	–2%
6%	3%		
12%	9%		
90%	87%		
900%	897%		

Discovering DATA ⠒

22. Let's get some practice with converting nominal to real series using the FRED economic database at https://fred.stlouisfed.org/. Go to FRED and find the series, "Median Sales Price for New Houses Sold in the United States." Click on Edit Data and modify Frequency to Annual.

a. What was the median price of a new house in 1980 and in 2019?

b. What was the percentage increase in the price of a median new house between 1980 and 2019? Is this a real price increase or a nominal price increase?

To find the real price increase, click Edit Graph, then under "Customize data" search for the CPI (the consumer price index). Click Add. Notice that the median house price data is series (a) and the CPI is series (b). Under Formula we can create a new formula for the real median price of new houses. Enter "a/b★100". Click Apply.

c. Using the real price series, what was the median price of a new house in 1980 and in 2019? What was the percentage increase in the real price of a median house between 1980 and 2019?

d. Can you think of any other reasons why the median price of a new house might have increased between 1980 and 2019?

Discovering DATA ⠒

23. Let's look at the inflation rate and the interest rate on 30-year mortgages in the United States. We will use the FRED economic database (https://fred.stlouisfed.org/). First search for the CPI, and then click Edit Graph and change Units to Percent Change from Year Ago and the Frequency to Annual, for the annual inflation rate. Now click Add Line and search for Mortgage. You should find a 30-year mortgage rate for the United States. Add that Data Series and then change the Units to Percent (not Percent Change from Year Ago) and change frequency to Annual.

a. As inflation rose in the 1970s and fell in the 1980s and 1990s, what happened to mortgage interest rates? What do we call this effect?

b. In 1981, what was the average interest rate on a 30-year mortgage? What was the inflation rate in 1981? Over the next 30 years, what very approximately was the inflation rate?

c. Did home buyers who took out 30-year mortgages in 1981 get a good deal or bad deal? Why?

d. In 1981, do you think banks and homebuyers predicted what would happen to the inflation rate over the next 30 years? Discuss some problems with high and volatile inflation.

WORK IT OUT

For interactive, step-by-step help in solving this problem, go online.

What does the quantity theory of money predict will happen *in the long run* in these cases? According to the quantity theory, a rise in the money supply can't change v or Y in the long run, so it must affect P. Let's use that fact to see how changes in the money supply affect the price level. Fill in the following table:

M	v	P	Y
100	5		50
150	5		50
50	5		50

▶ MRU VIDEOS

Who Wants to Be a Trillionaire?
mru.org/hyperinflation

Problem: **15**

Measuring Inflation
mru.org/inflation-def

Problems: **1, 9**

Quantity Theory of Money
mru.org/quant-theory-money

Problems: **10–12**

Causes of Inflation
mru.org/inflation-cause

Problems: **2, 10–12**

Price Confusion and Money Illusion
mru.org/inflation-cost1

Problem: **3**

Financial Intermediation Failure
mru.org/inflation-cost2

Problems: **3–5, 16, 20**

Why Governments Create Inflation
mru.org/govt-inflation

Problem: **15**

Office Hours: Costs of Inflation
mru.org/inflation-cost3

Problem: **21**

13

Business Fluctuations: Aggregate Demand and Supply

Economic growth is not a smooth process. Real GDP in the United States has grown at an average rate of 3.2% per year over the past 65 years. But the economy didn't grow at this rate every day or every month or even every year. The economy advances and recedes, it rises and falls, it booms and busts.

In Chapters 7 and 8, we looked at why some countries are rich and others are poor. In answering that question, we could safely ignore booms and recessions and focus on average rates of growth over periods of many years. We now turn from average growth rates to focus on the deviations from average, namely the booms and the recessions.

Figure 13.1 on the next page illustrates the booms and recessions of the U.S. economy by quarter since 1948. The average rate of growth of real GDP is 3.2% per quarter (on an annual basis), as marked by the red line, but the economy rarely grew at an average rate. In a typical recession, the growth rate might drop to −5% in some quarters, and in a boom, the economy can grow at a rate of 7 to 8% or higher. We call the fluctuations of real GDP around its long-term trend or "normal" growth rate **business fluctuations** or business cycles. **Recessions**, which we defined in Chapter 6 as significant, widespread declines in real income and employment, are shaded.

Recessions are of special concern to policymakers and the public because unemployment increases during a recession. Notice in Figure 13.2, for example, how unemployment increases dramatically within each of the shaded regions that are the periods of U.S. recessions.

More generally, a recession is a time when all kinds of resources, not just labor but also capital and land, are not fully employed. During a recession, factories close, stores are boarded up, and farmland is left fallow. We know that some unemployment is a natural or normal consequence of economic growth—in the previous chapter, we called this level of unemployment the

Business fluctuations are fluctuations in the growth rate of real GDP around its long-term trend growth rate.

A **recession** is a significant, widespread decline in real income and employment.

287

FIGURE 13.1

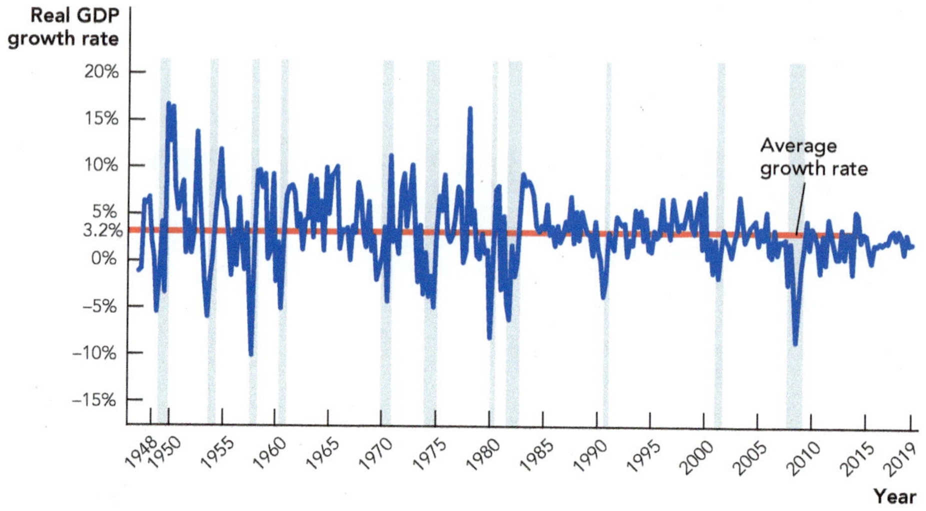

Economic Growth Is Not Smooth: Quarterly Growth Rate in Real GDP, 1948–2019

Data from: U.S. Bureau of Economic Analysis.
Note: Quarterly growth rates calculated on an annual basis. Recessions are shaded.

FIGURE 13.2

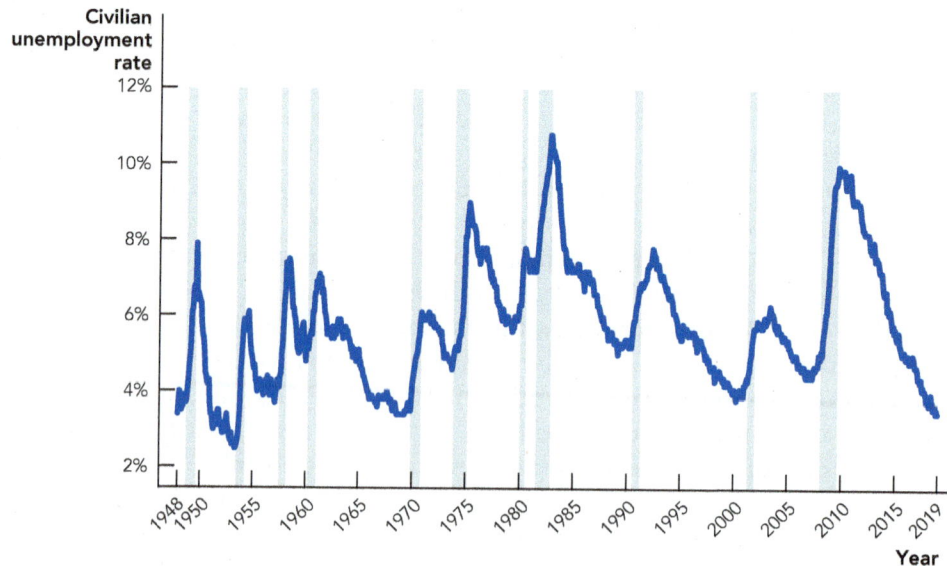

The Unemployment Rate Increases During a Recession: U.S. Civilian Unemployment Rate, 1948–2019

Data from: U.S. Bureau of Labor Statistics; National Bureau of Economic Research.
Note: Recessions are shaded.

natural unemployment rate—but often unemployment exceeds the natural rate. More generally, when there are a lot of unemployed resources, it suggests that resources are being wasted and the economy is operating below its potential. One of the goals of economic thinking is to better understand the causes of booms and recessions, and perhaps learn how policy might help to smooth out these fluctuations. Recessions are the exception rather than the norm, but still we would all be richer and more secure if we could limit the frequency and severity of recessions.

To understand booms and recessions, we are going to develop a model of aggregate demand and aggregate supply (AD–AS). Our model will show how unexpected economic disturbances or "shocks" can temporarily increase or decrease the economy's rate of growth. We will focus on how an economy responds to two types of shocks, real shocks (also called aggregate supply shocks) and aggregate demand shocks.

Ultimately, our AD–AS model will have three curves: the aggregate demand curve, the long-run aggregate supply curve, and the short-run aggregate supply curve. Let's begin with the aggregate demand curve.

The Aggregate Demand Curve

The **aggregate demand curve** tells us all the combinations of inflation and real growth that are consistent with a *specified* rate of spending growth. The easiest way to explain an AD curve is to derive it using the quantity theory of money from the previous chapter. Recall that we can write the quantity theory in dynamic form as

$$\overrightarrow{M} + \vec{v} = \overrightarrow{P} + \overrightarrow{Y}_R \qquad (1)$$

where $\overrightarrow{M}$ is the growth rate of the money supply; $\vec{v}$ is growth in velocity (how quickly money is turning over); $\overrightarrow{P}$ is the growth rate of prices, that is, the inflation rate, which we also write as $\boldsymbol{\pi}$; and $\overrightarrow{Y}_R$ is the growth rate of real GDP, which we simplify and call real growth. Thus, we can also write equation 1 as

$$\overrightarrow{M} + \vec{v} = \textbf{Inflation} + \textbf{Real growth} \qquad (2)$$

Now imagine that $\overrightarrow{M} = 5\%$, $\vec{v} = 0\%$, and real growth is 0%. What is the inflation rate? To answer that question, we substitute what we know into equation 2. Thus, 5% + 0% = Inflation + 0%, so Inflation = 5%. Intuitively, if the money supply is growing by 5% a year ($\overrightarrow{M} = 5\%$) and velocity is stable ($\vec{v} = 0\%$), then spending is growing by 5% a year. But if there are no additional goods to spend the money on, that is, if real growth is 0%, then prices must rise by 5%. In short, more spending plus the same goods equals higher prices.

An AD curve tells us *all* the combinations of inflation and real growth that are consistent with a specified rate of spending growth ($\overrightarrow{M} + \vec{v}$). We have just discovered *one* such combination; an inflation rate of 5% and a real growth rate of 0% are consistent with a spending growth rate of 5%. But what other combinations of inflation and real growth are consistent with a spending growth rate of 5%?

What would the inflation rate be if, just as before, $\overrightarrow{M} = 5\%$ and $\vec{v} = 0\%$, but now real growth = 3%? Once again, we substitute what we know into equation 2. Thus, we have 5% + 0% = Inflation + 3%, so Inflation = 2%. The intuition is quite simple. Inflation is caused when more money chases the same goods. So, if more money is chasing an increased quantity of goods, then, all else being equal, the inflation rate will be less than the increase in money growth.

Thus, we now have *two* combinations of inflation and real growth that are consistent with a spending growth rate of 5%. In Figure 13.3, point *a* shows an

The **aggregate demand curve** shows all the combinations of inflation and real growth that are consistent with a specified rate of spending growth ($\overrightarrow{M} + \vec{v}$).

Key Equation

$\overrightarrow{M} + \vec{v} = $ Inflation + Real growth

MRU

mru.org/AD-curve

$\overrightarrow{M} + \overrightarrow{V} = $ INFLATION + REAL GROWTH

The Aggregate Demand Curve

Check the Math

If the money supply is growing at 5% per year ($\overrightarrow{M} = 5\%$) and velocity is stable ($\vec{v} = 0\%$), then Inflation + Real growth must equal 5%. If Real growth is 3%, then Inflation must be 2%.

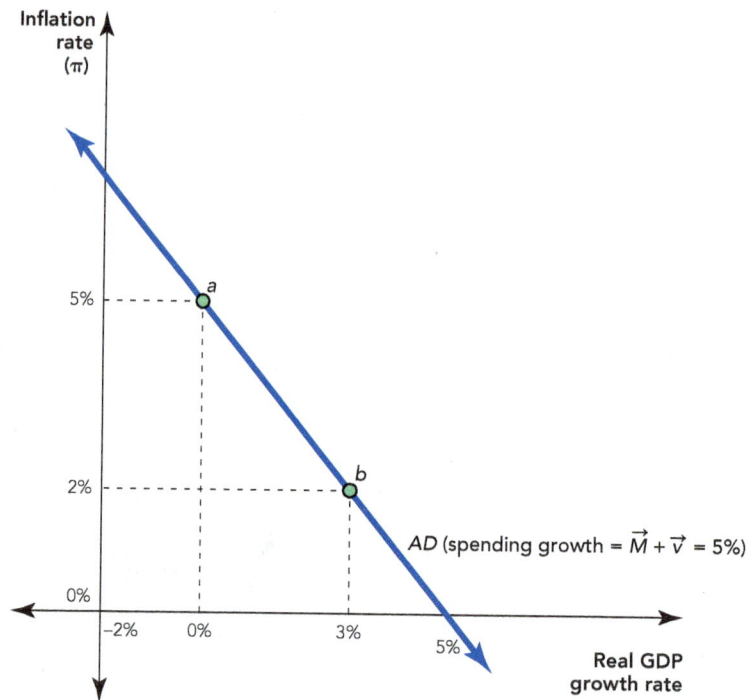

FIGURE 13.3

The Aggregate Demand Curve If spending is growing by 5% per year but real growth is 0%, then prices must be rising by 5%—that is, the inflation rate must be 5% (point *a*). If spending is growing by 5% and real growth is 3%, then inflation must be 2% (point *b*). If spending is growing by 5% and real growth is 5%, then what is the inflation rate?

inflation rate of 5% and a real growth rate of 0%, and point *b* shows an inflation rate of 2% and a real growth rate of 3%. Both of these combinations are consistent with a spending growth rate of 5%, *so they belong on the same AD curve.* In fact, from equation 2 we know that all the combinations of inflation and real growth that are consistent with a spending growth rate of 5% must satisfy the equation 5% = Inflation − Real growth. In other words, any combination of inflation and real growth that adds up to 5% is on the same AD curve. Figure 13.3 shows the AD curve for a spending growth rate of 5%. Thus, all the points on this line add up to 5%.

Notice also that the AD curve is a straight line with a slope of −1.[*] This means that, given the rate of spending growth, a 1 percentage point increase in real growth reduces inflation by 1 percentage point.

Shifts in the Aggregate Demand Curve

The AD curve for a spending growth rate of 5% is all the combinations of inflation and real growth that add up to 5%. So, what is the AD curve for a spending growth rate of 7%? Right, all the combinations of inflation and real growth that add up to 7%. Now that we know what an AD curve is, we also know how the

---

[*] We can easily show this by rewriting equation 2 in the familiar $Y = b + mX$ format, Inflation = $(\vec{M} + \vec{v}) - 1 \times$ Real growth. Notice that m, the slope of the curve, is −1.

FIGURE 13.4

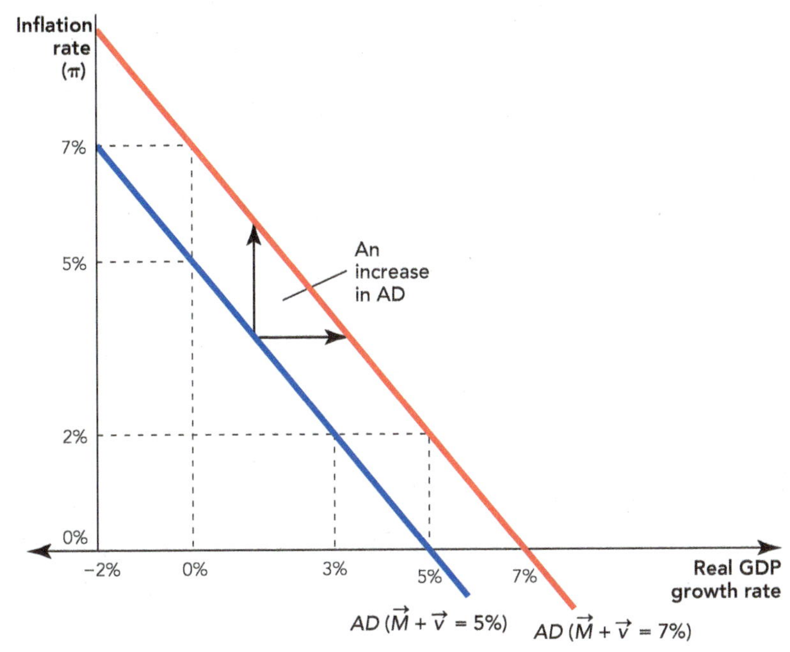

An Increase in Spending Growth Shifts the AD Curve Up and to the Right (Outward) An increase in spending growth, $\vec{M} + \vec{v}$, increases AD, shifting the curve up and to the right (outward). Note that each curve is defined by a specified level of spending growth. For example, along the curve $AD\ (\vec{M} + \vec{v} = 5\%)$, each combination of inflation and real growth must add to 5%. Along the curve $AD\ (\vec{M} + \vec{v} = 7\%)$, each combination of inflation and real growth must add to 7%.

AD curve shifts. In Figure 13.4, for example, notice that all the combinations of inflation and real growth along the AD curve denoted $AD\ (\vec{M} + \vec{v} = 5\%)$ add up to 5% and all the combinations of inflation and real growth along the AD curve denoted $AD\ (\vec{M} + \vec{v} = 7\%)$ add up to 7%. Thus, if spending growth increases to 7%, either because of an increase in $\vec{M}$ or because of an increase in $\vec{v}$, then the AD curve shifts up and to the right (outward). The intuition is that increased spending must flow into either a higher inflation rate or a higher growth rate. Thus, an increase in spending growth shifts the AD curve outward, up and to the right, and, of course, a decrease in spending growth shifts the AD curve inward.

As we have said, an increase in spending growth can be caused by either an increase in $\vec{M}$ or $\vec{v}$. Later on in this chapter and in Chapters 16 and 18, we explain exactly what this means in practice. For now, we just need to remember that increased spending growth shifts the AD curve outward and decreased spending growth shifts the AD curve inward.

The Long-Run Aggregate Supply Curve

We learned earlier in Chapters 7 and 8 that economic growth depends on increases in the stocks of labor and capital and on increases in productivity (driven by new and better ideas and better institutions). Thus, every economy

CHECK YOURSELF

- If we have an aggregate demand curve with $\vec{M}$ = 7% and $\vec{v}$ = 0%, what will inflation plus real growth equal? If we find out that real growth is 0%, what is inflation?

- Increased spending growth shifts the aggregate demandcurve which way: inward or outward?

FIGURE 13.5

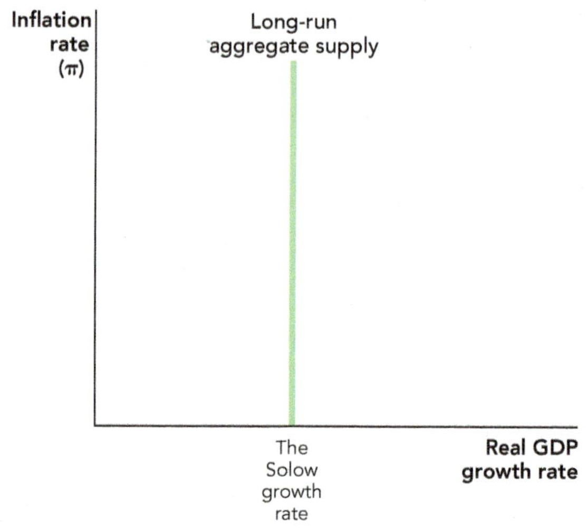

The Long-Run Aggregate Supply Curve The long-run aggregate supply curve is vertical at the economy's potential growth rate, which we also call the Solow growth rate.

has a potential growth rate given by these fundamental, or real, factors of production. We call the rate of growth, as given by the real factors of production, the "Solow" growth rate. We call it that because Robert Solow, one of the giants of economics, created an important model of an economy's fundamental growth rate. In Chapter 8, we described Solow's model in more detail, but if you skipped that section don't worry: Just think of the **Solow growth rate** as the rate of economic growth given flexible prices and the existing real factors of capital, labor, and ideas.

In the long run money is neutral, as we emphasized in the previous chapter. Thus, when we put the inflation rate on the vertical axis of a graph and real growth (the growth rate of real GDP) on the horizontal axis, the **long-run aggregate supply curve** is very simple—it's a vertical line at the Solow growth rate. Figure 13.5 illustrates the long-run aggregate supply curve.* Once again, the fundamental growth rate of the economy depends on factors such as the amount and quality of labor and capital, not on the rate of inflation.

The **Solow growth rate** is an economy's potential growth rate, the rate of economic growth that would occur given flexible prices and the existing real factors of production.

The **long-run aggregate supply curve** is vertical at the Solow growth rate.

A **real shock**, also called a productivity shock, is any shock that increases or decreases the potential growth rate.

Shifts in the Long-Run Aggregate Supply Curve

Let's put the AD and long-run aggregate supply curve together. This will let us explain how business fluctuations can be caused by real shocks, a way of thinking about business fluctuations often called the "real business cycle" (RBC) model. Figure 13.6 shows an AD curve in which the growth rate of spending is 10% a year and a long-run aggregate supply (LRAS) curve that has a growth rate of 3%. Since $\overline{M} + \vec{v} = $ Inflation + Real growth, and $\overline{M} + \vec{v} = 10\%$, and Real growth = 3%, we know that inflation is 7% a year. Thus, in this model, the equilibrium inflation rate and growth rate are determined by the intersection of the AD and LRAS curves.

Take a look again at Figure 13.1, which shows the growth rate of U.S. GDP over time. Although the growth rate has averaged about 3% (at an annual rate) per quarter for many years, it has fluctuated around this average. Why?

One reason that the growth rate fluctuates is that economies are continually being hit by shocks, which shift the Solow growth rate. As an example, consider an agricultural economy: Good weather can increase crop production—driving the growth rate up—while bad weather can decrease production, thereby driving down the growth rate.

We call these shocks **real shocks** or productivity shocks because they increase or decrease an economy's fundamental ability to produce goods and services and, thus, they increase or decrease the Solow growth rate.

---

* Saying that potential growth does not depend on the rate of inflation is a strong form of the money neutrality result that we discussed in the previous chapter. Unexpected and variable inflation can reduce a country's potential growth rate, and there are a variety of reasons why even an expected inflation rate might have a small influence on potential growth. Dealing with these issues, however, would complicate our model without leading to a better understanding of our current topic, business fluctuations.

FIGURE 13.6

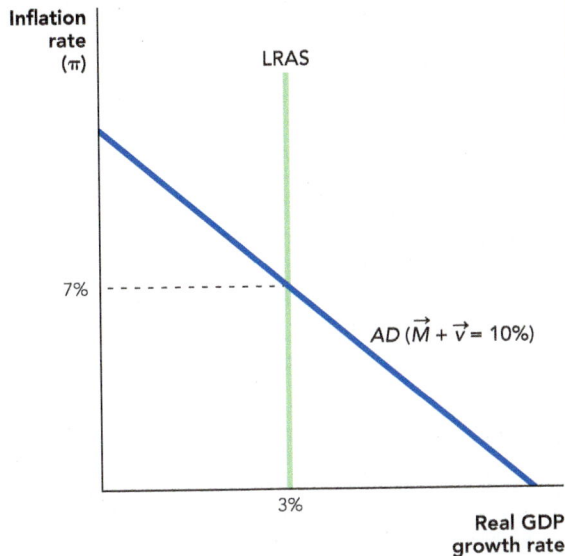

The AD and Long Run Aggregate Supply (LRAS) Curves
If $\overline{M} + \overline{v}$ is 10% and real growth is given by the Solow growth rate at 3%, then the inflation rate will be 7%.

FIGURE 13.7

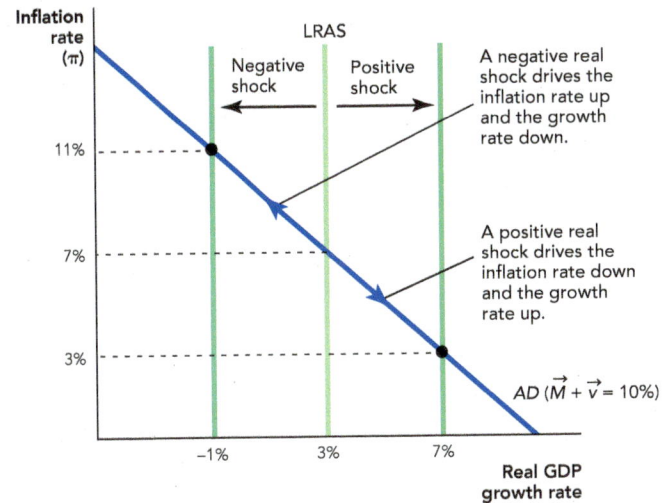

Real Shocks Can Shift the LRAS Curve to the Right and to the Left A positive real shock shifts the LRAS curve to the right, increasing real growth and reducing inflation. A negative real shock shifts the LRAS curve to the left, decreasing real growth and increasing inflation. Negative and positive real shocks are hitting the economy at all times.

A positive real shock shown in Figure 13.7 shifts the LRAS curve to the right, increasing real growth. The increase in the supply of goods brought about by a higher real growth rate reduces the inflation rate. During the late 1990s, for example, the Internet revolution, a positive real shock, increased the growth rate of the economy. Faster, more powerful computers at lower prices helped to keep inflation low.

A negative real shock shifts the LRAS curve to the left, decreasing real growth. The slower growth rate means fewer new goods to spend money on so the inflation rate increases. In the 1970s, for example, a negative real shock—a sudden, sharp decrease in the relative supply of oil that led to several big jumps in the price of oil—reduced the growth rate and increased inflation.

Shocks to the LRAS curve will change the growth rate and the inflation rate temporarily because the LRAS curve is always shifting back and forth as new shocks hit the economy. Remember from Figure 13.1 that growth is not smooth. Thus, growth rates fluctuate from quarter to quarter, as positive shocks increase growth temporarily and negative shocks reduce growth temporarily. In the United States, growth has fluctuated around approximately 3% for about a century. In different times and places, the average Solow growth rate could be higher or lower depending on growth in the fundamentals—capital, labor, ideas, and institutions—but every economy will always be subject to real shocks so growth will always fluctuate.

This way of looking at booms and recessions—the real business cycle (RBC) model or perspective—is a natural extension of the Solow growth model. In the RBC framework, business fluctuations are simply changes in economic growth in the short run driven by real shocks.

Real Shocks

Let's take a closer look at real shocks. Real shocks are rapid changes in economic conditions that increase or diminish the level or productivity of capital and labor, which in turn influences GDP and employment. To understand shocks and to see why they matter, we start with poorer economies, where shocks are easier to see and understand. Later in the chapter, we move to how shocks can create problems for the United States and other developed economies.

There are several billion farmers in the world and for many countries agriculture remains the single largest contributor to GDP. How much a farm produces depends on the quantity and quality of the inputs of capital and labor, but agricultural output also depends on the weather. When the weather fluctuates, so does output and therefore so does GDP, especially in agricultural economies.

Figure 13.8 shows how shocks to the weather influence India's agricultural output and GDP. The blue line is the percentage deviation in India's yearly rainfall from the average (from 1970 to 1990). Above-average rainfall is good for the crops so in 1975, for example, rainfall was 10.8% above average, and in the left-hand panel, we see that agricultural output (the green line) in that year grew by a bountiful 12.8%. In 1979, however, much of India had a drought. Rainfall was 11% below average and agricultural output fell by nearly 13%, compared with the year before.

Agriculture has been the largest contributor to India's GDP, so the shocks to agricultural output caused by the weather have had a big impact on GDP growth. It is not just that agriculture contributes to GDP directly but, if farmers struggle, many other sectors of the Indian economy suffer as well. For instance,

FIGURE 13.8

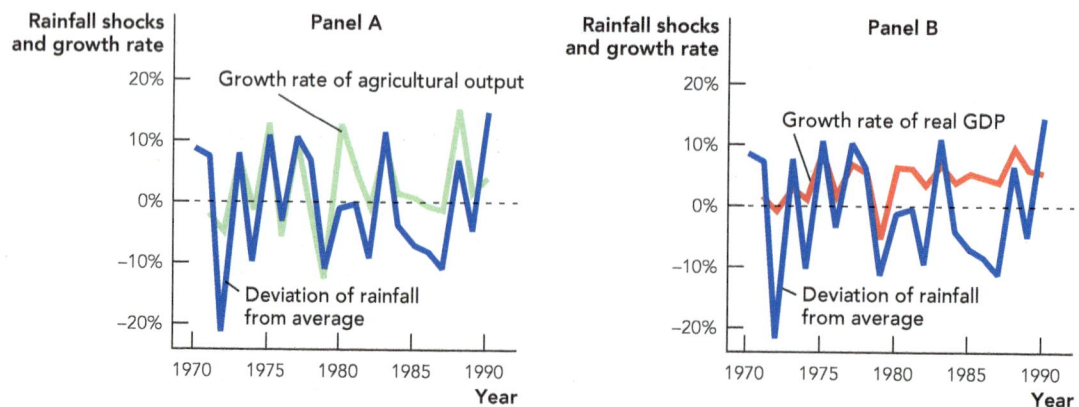

Rainfall Shocks in India Correlate Well with Agricultural Output and GDP Panel A: Rainfall shocks and the growth rate of India's agricultural output. **Panel B:** Rainfall shocks and the growth rate of India's GDP.

Data from: Reserve Bank of India and Indian Institute of Tropical Meteorology.

the demand for tractors will go down and farmers will buy fewer items for their own consumption. Thus, the shock spreads to other sectors of the economy. In Panel B of Figure 13.8, the red line shows the growth rate of India's GDP. As expected, GDP boomed in 1975, growing by nearly 10%, and busted in 1979 with a decline of 5.2%. Note that the booms and busts in GDP are not as strong as the booms and busts in agricultural output because other sectors, less influenced by the weather, also contribute to GDP.

By the way, take a close look at Panel B of Figure 13.8. Does it seem to you that shocks to rainfall have become less important to India's GDP since 1980? If so, you are probably correct. Agriculture contributed 40% of India's GDP in 1970, but because the Indian economy has grown and diversified, it contributed only 20% of India's GDP in 1990. Therefore, shocks to the weather are becoming less economically important in India over time. In the United States, agriculture contributes less than 1% to GDP, so yearly variations in the weather don't have much of an effect on GDP. Other shocks, however, can rock the U.S. economy.

Oil Shocks

In an economy with a large manufacturing sector, a reduction in the oil supply is like a reduction in rainfall in an agricultural economy. Oil and machines are complementary, which means they work together, along with labor, to produce output. Thus, when the oil supply is reduced, capital and labor become less productive. Oil greases the wheels of industry, sometimes literally, and with less oil the wheels do not turn as well.

The first oil shock came in late 1973, when many of the oil-producing nations under the guise of OPEC (Organization of the Petroleum Exporting Countries) reduced the global oil supply to protest America's support of Israel in the Middle East. The result was that the price of oil more than tripled in just two years. This became a significant problem for the American economy.

The higher price of oil, for instance, also meant a much higher price for gasoline (oil is one input into gasoline). Higher gas prices reduced the demand for larger cars and increased the demand for smaller cars. The U.S. auto industry was specialized in the production of larger cars and had a difficult time adjusting. Factories cannot simply be switched from the production of one type of car to another—much of the physical capital in an auto factory is specialized. A machine that is used to bend steel is no longer useful when production switches to lightweight, fuel-saving plastic composites. Workers are specialized, too, in both knowledge and location. Thus, the oil shock meant that many auto plants producing larger cars shut down or were used at less than full capacity. Similarly, autoworkers became unemployed and many had to learn new skills, and often they had to move to new jobs.

Not every part of the American economy was harmed. The demand for smaller cars increased, for example, but the U.S. auto industry could not immediately meet that demand. It can take a decade to design and build a new car, so it took considerable time for capital and labor to reallocate to the production of smaller American cars. In the meantime, output and employment in the auto industry fell. Similarly, over time, the city of Houston (which services much of the American oil industry) became populated with many former residents of Detroit (which made large American cars), but the transition was costly and disruptive.

Since oil is an important input in many sectors of the economy, high oil prices—or oil shocks—hurt many American industries. Thus, sharp increases

FIGURE 13.9

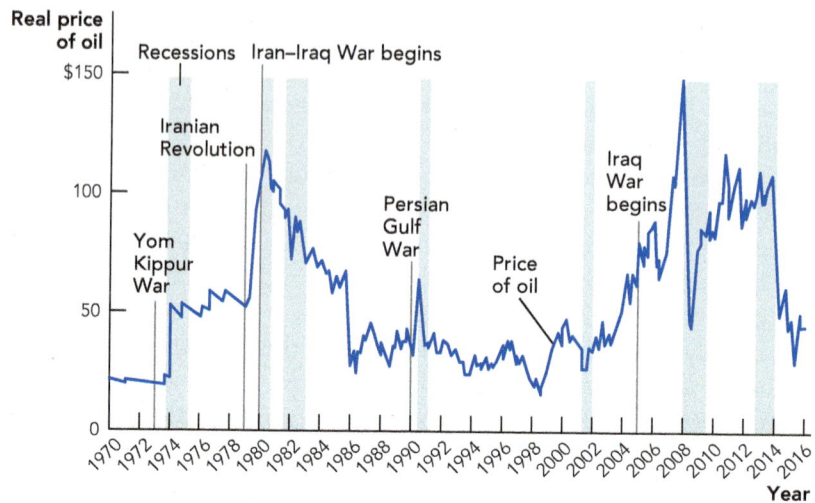

The Price of Oil and U.S. Recessions

Data from: St. Louis Federal Reserve Economic Database. Corrected for inflation using CPI. Real price in 2016 dollars.

in the price of oil can disrupt the economy as a whole. Figure 13.9 shows the price of oil and the last six U.S. recessions. In each case, there was a large increase in the price of oil just prior to or coincident with the onset of recession (oil prices were still very high during the 1981–1982 recession, which was almost a continuation of the 1980 recession). The pattern is especially clear with the 1974, 1980, and 1991 recessions in the graph. In these cases, the onset of a war reduced the supply of oil, driving up the price unexpectedly. Unexpected shocks are the most costly to deal with.

It's fairly easy to see the impact on the economy of a large increase in the price of oil but it's harder to eyeball the effect of smaller shocks. Careful statistical analysis, however, can disentangle the effect of oil shocks from the many other shocks that keep on hitting the economy. In Figure 13.10, we show how the economy responds to an unexpected and permanent increase in the price of oil of 10%.

Starting from the normal or trend rate of growth (which is fixed at the zero point on the vertical axis of the graph), Figure 13.10 shows that a 10% increase in the price of oil slows the economy down gradually, with the biggest slowdown occurring about 5 quarters (a little more than a year) after the onset of the increase in price. After 5 quarters, the growth rate begins to pick up again quite quickly, and after 10 quarters (two and a half years), the economy has adjusted to the higher price and the growth rate returns to normal.

Thus, a 10% increase in the price of oil lowers the GDP growth rate, from what it would have been without the price increase, for a little more than two years. The total effect on GDP is a decrease of about 1.4%. In other words, if the price of oil had not increased, real GDP would have been about 1.4% higher.

FIGURE 13.10

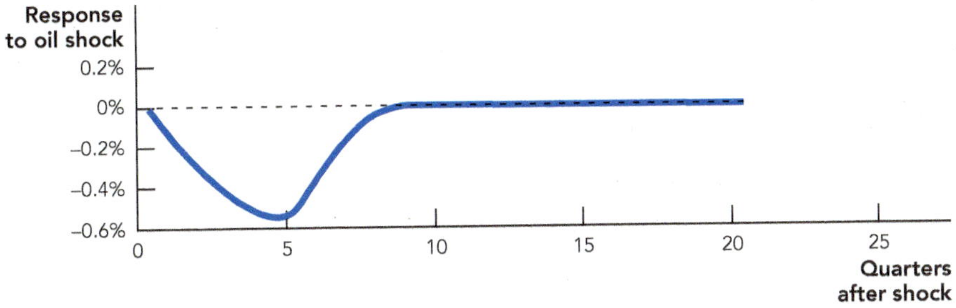

Response to oil shock

Real Output Growth Response to a 10% Increase in Oil Price

Note: Stylized graph of response of real GDP to a 10% increase in oil prices based on dynamics estimated over the 1984–2005 period.
Data from: Sill, Keith. 2007. "The Macroeconomics of Oil Shocks." Federal Reserve Bank of Philadelphia, *Business Review* Q1: 21–31.

More Shocks

Oil and rainfall shocks are only two among many shocks that might hit an economy. In 2020, the world was hit with a major negative supply shock due to the COVID-19 virus. To reduce contagion, many countries quarantined entire cities and required millions of people to stay home. That meant a big decline in *L*, labor, and a big decline in productivity as workers could no longer work together. In addition, workers are integrated into supply chains, so when some workers aren't producing goods and services, the productivity of workers throughout the world is reduced. If the tire factory shuts down, so does the automobile factory, even if the automobile factory is fully staffed. Thus, the negative supply shock reduced GDP throughout the world—even in places less directly hit by the virus. Other possible shocks are wars, terrorist attacks, major new regulations, tax rate changes, mass strikes, and new technologies such as the Internet. Most generally, economies are continually hit by many small shocks. Some of the shocks are good, like a productive new technology, and some are bad, like a drought. In a typical year, the good shocks outweigh the bad and the economy grows. People build on previous knowledge and most of the time they are able to do better and produce a bit more than in previous years. In a bad year, however, an economy may be hit with a big shock, like an oil shock, or by several small negative shocks that outweigh the positive ones. In either case, a recession may result. It is a bit like playing poker. Every now and then you get a hand of cards that simply cannot be played well, no matter what you do. Table 13.1 lists some major factors that shift the LRAS curve left (negative shock) or right (positive shock).

In addition to shocks, there are also forces that amplify and transmit shocks across sectors of the economy and through time. In the next chapter, we will take a closer look at amplification and transmission mechanisms and show how a shock to, for example, the agricultural sector can be amplified and transmitted to many other sectors of the economy in a way that can make the shock have bigger effects and last longer than might be expected from the size of the shock alone.

MRU

mru.org/LRAS

The Long-Run Aggregate Supply Curve

CHECK YOURSELF

- Consider the ubiquity of cell phones throughout the world. How can this ubiquity be considered a positive shock? (*Hint:* Compare with 10 years ago.)

- How would a large and sudden increase in taxes—for example, a tax on energy—shift the long-run aggregate supply curve?

TABLE 13.1 SOME FACTORS THAT SHIFT THE LONG-RUN AGGREGATE SUPPLY CURVE

Negative Shocks (LRAS Curve Moves Left)	Positive Shocks (LRAS Curve Moves Right)
Bad weather (important in agricultural economy)	Good weather (important in agricultural economy)
Higher price of oil or other important input	Lower price of oil or other important input
Productivity slump/technology slump	Productivity boom/technology boom
Higher taxes or regulation	Lower taxes or regulation
Disruption of production by war, earthquake, pandemic	Smooth production without disruption

Aggregate Demand Shocks and the Short-Run Aggregate Supply Curve

An **aggregate demand shock** is a rapid and unexpected shift in the AD curve (spending).

Aggregate demand shocks are another type of shock that can hit the economy. An **aggregate demand shock** is a rapid and unexpected shift in the aggregate demand curve. Since the AD curve is all about spending, we can also say that an aggregate demand shock is a rapid and unexpected shift in spending. To explain why AD shocks matter, we need to introduce the short-run aggregate supply (SRAS) curve and explain the importance of "sticky" (not perfectly flexible) wages and prices.

Before we introduce the SRAS curve, however, let's give some intuition about where we are going. It takes time for an aggregate demand shock to work its way through the economy. Recall the inflation parable from the previous chapter. In that parable, the government of Zimbabwe prints more money to pay its soldiers. The soldiers use the new money to buy more goods such as bread—that's an increase in spending, a positive shock to aggregate demand. At first, the baker is delighted when soldiers walk through her door with cash for bread. To satisfy her new customers, the baker works extra hours and bakes more bread. "How wonderful," she thinks, "with the increase in the demand for bread I will be able to buy more clothes and cabinets." The baker is *expecting* to buy clothes and cabinets at the same prices as she paid before the soldiers started to buy more bread. Only later does the baker realize that the soldiers have been buying more of everything, pushing up prices throughout the economy so that her money buys her less than it did before. Once the baker comes to expect rising prices throughout the economy, she raises the price of bread and goes back to producing at the old output level.

In 1936, John Maynard Keynes published a revolutionary book, *The General Theory of Employment, Interest and Money. The General Theory* explained that when prices were not perfectly flexible, deficiencies in aggregate demand could generate recessions.

The parable tells us that a positive shock to spending increases output at first, but in the long run only increases prices. We know from our basic equation $\vec{M} + \vec{v} = \text{Inflation} + \text{Real growth}$ that an increase in spending $\vec{M} + \vec{v}$ must either increase the inflation rate π or the real growth rate. But we also know that in the long run, the real growth rate will be equal to the Solow rate, which is not influenced by the inflation rate, so in the long run an increase in spending will increase the inflation rate alone. The parable, however, tells us that the inflation rate does not necessarily increase immediately in direct proportion to

FIGURE 13.11

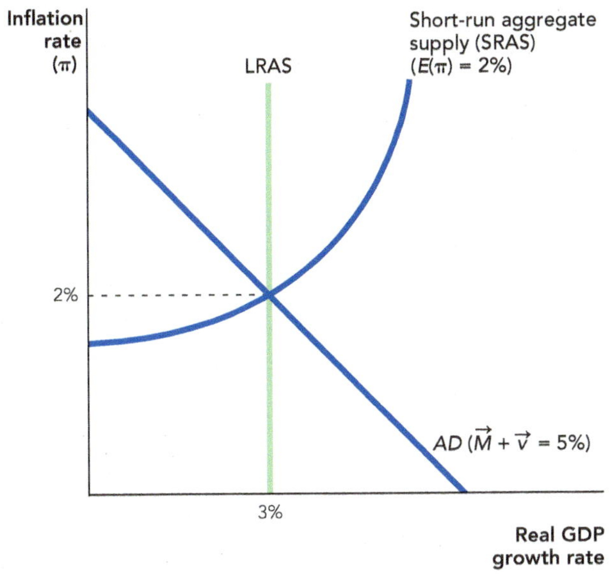

The Short-Run Aggregate Supply Curve Inflation and real growth are positively related in the short run when prices are sticky. We illustrate this relationship with an upward-sloped, short-run aggregate supply curve.

an increase in spending. In the short run, an increase in spending will be split between increases in inflation and increases in real growth—that is, the essence of the short-run aggregate supply curve to which we now turn.

Short-Run Aggregate Supply Curve

The **short-run aggregate supply (SRAS) curve** is upward-sloping, like that shown in Figure 13.11, An upward-sloping SRAS means that in the short run an increase in aggregate demand will increase both the inflation rate and the growth rate, and a decrease in demand will decrease both the inflation rate and the growth rate.

Figure 13.12 illustrates the same ideas from the parable but now using the AD, SRAS, and LRAS curves. We start from a position of long-run equilibrium, which means that the inflation rate consumers and firms are expecting must be equal to the actual inflation rate and that the real growth rate must be at the Solow level. Thus, in Figure 13.12, the initial equilibrium is at point *a* where the real growth rate is at the Solow rate (3%), the inflation rate is 2%, and the expected inflation rate is 2%. Economists often use the symbol π for inflation and $E(\pi)$ for the *expected* inflation rate. As we will show shortly, each SRAS curve is associated with a particular rate of expected inflation, so the initial SRAS curve is labeled with $E(\pi) = 2\%$.

Now suppose that the growth rate of the money supply increases unexpectedly from 5% to 10%. The injection of more money into the economy increases AD, which, in turn, creates a temporary boom at point *b*. At *b* the economy is growing at a 6% rate of real growth with inflation of 4%. Notice that $\overrightarrow{M}$ has increased by 5 percentage points. Some of that increase in spending is reflected in the inflation rate, which increases by 2 percentage points, but some of the increase in spending is reflected in real growth, which increases by 3 percentage points. In the short run, an increase in spending growth is split between increases in inflation and increases in real growth.

The **short-run aggregate supply curve (SRAS)** shows the positive relationship between the inflation rate and real growth during the period when prices and wages are sticky.

The rate of inflation that workers and producers expect is written $E(\pi)$.

FIGURE 13.12

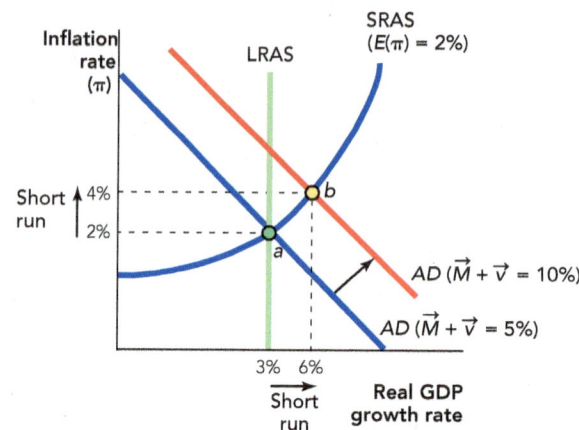

An Increase in $\vec{M}$ Shifts the AD Curve Out An increase in AD increases real growth in the short run. The equilibrium moves from point *a* to the short-run equilibrium at point *b*.

To further explain how a spending increase can create a temporary increase in growth, let's return to our baker but now imagine that she owns a large bakery. An increase in spending encourages the baker to expand, so she offers her workers more overtime opportunities at a higher wage. At first the workers are pleased since they see that their nominal wage—the number on their paychecks—has increased. But as the workers spend their money, they discover that prices elsewhere in the economy are rising so much that even with the overtime, their wages are buying fewer goods and services than before—more work for less real pay! Although the workers' nominal wages have increased, their real wages—namely the amount of goods and services they can buy with that wage—have decreased. The workers' eagerness to work harder is what economists call a **nominal wage confusion**. Eventually, the workers will come to expect the higher inflation rate and they will demand even higher wages to catch up to the higher inflation rate, but in the short run an increase in spending can cause an increase in output.

Prices also don't move instantly to their new long-run equilibrium because it is costly to change prices. Economists call the costs of changing prices **menu costs** because an obvious example is the costs of printing new menus when a restaurant changes its prices. Menu costs also include the costs of upsetting customers with frequent price changes. Menu costs mean that businesses don't like to change prices every day or even every quarter, so price changes take time.

Firms may also not be sure whether a change in market conditions is temporary or permanent. If firms are unsure, they will hold off on changing prices, at least for a while. Imagine that the price of eggs increases. Does the restaurant change the price of an omelette? If the restaurant knew the price change was permanent, then it probably would. But maybe the price of eggs will decrease tomorrow. If the change in the price of eggs is temporary and the firm prints new menus today, it might also have to print new menus again tomorrow, or perhaps incur the risk that consumers search around for a cheaper breakfast. Better to wait and see before changing the prices and printing the new menus.

Over time, however, firms will begin to realize that the price of eggs isn't coming back down—the increase in price really was permanent and so firms will adjust their menus. Similarly, as prices rise and workers begin to realize that

Nominal wage confusion occurs when workers respond to their nominal wage instead of to their real wage, that is, when workers respond to the wage number on their paychecks rather than to what their wage can buy in goods and services (the wage after correcting for inflation).

Menu costs are the costs of changing prices.

their real wage hasn't risen, they will demand higher wages. Since wages are a cost to firms, higher wages will in turn lead to higher prices. Wages and prices will continue to increase until the new long-run equilibrium is achieved.

The Long Run

In Figure 13.13, we show what happens in the long run. In the long run, *unexpected inflation always turns into expected inflation* and the SRAS curve shifts up and to the left; from Old SRAS ($E[\pi]$ = 2%) to New SRAS ($E[\pi]$ = 7%). As expectations and prices adjust, more and more of the increase in $\overrightarrow{M}$ is reflected in the inflation rate and less is reflected in the real growth rate. In the long run, after all transitions are complete, all of the increase in $\overrightarrow{M}$ is reflected in the inflation rate—$\overrightarrow{M}$ increases by 5 percentage points, the inflation rate increases by 5 percentage points, the growth rate returns to the Solow level, and the actual inflation rate comes to equal the expected inflation rate (7%). Thus, an increase in $\overrightarrow{M}$ increases real growth in the short run—during the period in which prices and wages are sticky.[*]

Here is a hint about shifting the SRAS curve. In the long run, people will always come to expect the actual inflation rate (you can't fool people forever), and in the long run, the inflation rate is found where the LRAS curve intersects the AD curve. In the long run, the economy must be on the LRAS curve, thus the SRAS curve is always moving toward the point where the LRAS curve intersects the new AD curve (point *c* in Figure 13.13). Notice that in the new long-run equilibrium, the inflation rate is 7% and the expected inflation rate is 7%. Also, in the long-run equilibrium at point *c*, growth is equal to the Solow rate—this reflects our intuition that in the long run, money doesn't influence real growth (money is neutral) but does influence the inflation rate (inflation is a monetary phenomenon).

We also see here a preview of several profound dilemmas in macroeconomic policy. Once we are at the new equilibrium at point *c*, consumers and

mru.org/SRAS

The Short-Run Aggregate Supply Curve

FIGURE 13.13

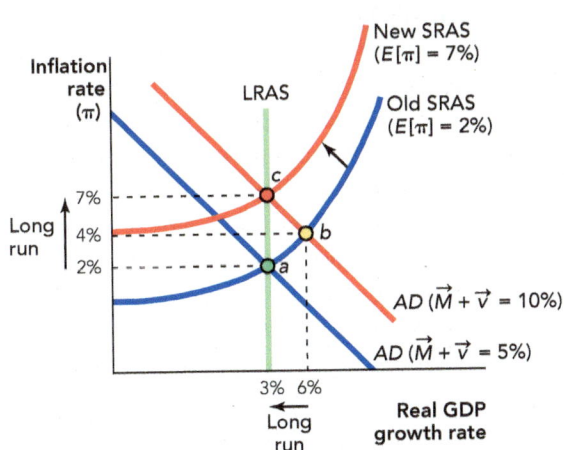

In the Long Run, Real Growth Eventually Returns to the Solow Rate In the long run the SRAS curve shifts upward as inflation expectations adjust and wages become unstuck. As a result, real growth will eventually return to the Solow rate as given by the LRAS curve and inflation will increase. In the long run, after all transitions are complete, the economy will end up at point *c*. In the long run, unexpected inflation always becomes expected inflation.

[*] For the purpose of making the models simple, we've focused on showing the initial short-run change and then the long-run results, after all the necessary transitions and adjustments have worked their way through the system.

FIGURE 13.14

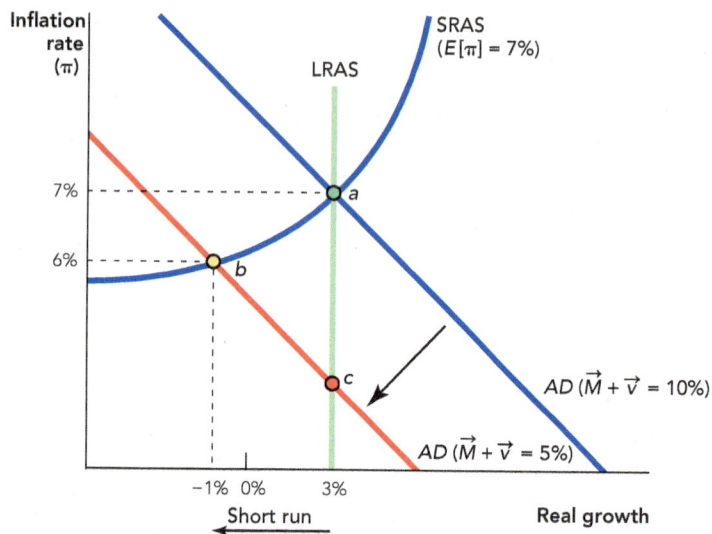

A Fall in Aggregate Demand Could Induce a Lengthy Recession At point *a*, spending is growing at a rate of 10% and real growth is 3%, so inflation is 7%. Suppose spending growth decreases to 5%. In the short run, wages are sticky, so although spending growth declines, wage growth does not. As a result, real growth falls to –1% and the inflation rate falls to 6% at point *b*. In the long run, as wages become unstuck, the economy will move to a new long-run equilibrium at *c*, but getting to point *c* could take a lengthy recession.

producers are expecting an inflation rate of 7%, so to increase the real growth rate above the Solow rate once again, policymakers would have to increase the actual rate of inflation above 7%. Can you see how a policymaker might become trapped in a spiral of ever-increasing inflation rates? We will return to this issue in Chapter 16. Of course, you might ask why not just reduce aggregate demand and return to a lower inflation rate? Unfortunately, prices and wages adjust even more slowly to a fall in AD than to an increase in AD, so a fall in AD can create a severe recession.

Figure 13.14 shows what happens when AD falls due to a fall in $\overrightarrow{M}$. From an initial equilibrium at point *a*, the fall in AD shifts the economy to a new short-run equilibrium at point *b*, creating a small reduction in the inflation rate and a large reduction in real growth. Eventually, the economy will adjust to the fall in $\overrightarrow{M}$ and it will return to a long-run equilibrium at point *c*. We don't show this in detail in Figure 13.14, however, because we want to focus on the recession and why an economy can take a long time to adjust to a decrease in aggregate demand.

It takes time for a decrease in spending to make its way through the economy for all the reasons that we have already discussed in the case of an increase in spending: namely wages are sticky, menu costs and uncertainty make businesses reluctant to change prices immediately, and expectations take time to adjust. As a result, in the short run, a fall in spending growth is split between a fall in inflation rates and a fall in growth. Most economists, however, believe that prices and wages are especially sticky in the downward direction. Here is one phrase to keep in mind: Prices rise like rockets and fall like feathers.

No one likes to have their wages cut or even wage growth reduced, which is one reason that wages are especially sticky in the downward direction. In addition, large union contracts often fix wage growth for several years in advance. So imagine that prices have been going up by 5% and wages by 7% every year for a number of years. Contracts may even have been written guaranteeing wage growth of 7%. Now, however, the inflation rate falls to 2% a year. Workers are expecting wage increases of 7%, but if firms paid that amount, they would be unprofitable. Firms could cut wage growth to 4%, which would give workers the same increase in real wages of 2% that they had before, but how will workers feel when their salary increase is much less than expected? What will happen to morale and motivation? How will a union feel when the company tries to renegotiate its contract? Very often, morale goes down and the union threatens a strike. As a result, firms may find it easier to fire workers or reduce hours than to lower wages. In other words, a fall in aggregate spending will reduce the growth rate.

MRU

mru.org/sticky-wages

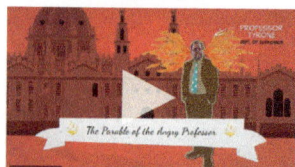

Sticky Wages and the Parable of the Angry Professor

The economist Truman Bewley interviewed employers and labor leaders, asking them why wages don't fall during a recession. He concluded that the main reason employers don't like to cut wages is that if workers see smaller numbers on their paycheck, their morale declines and they often take their anger out on their employers. In contrast, layoffs get the misery out the door. As a result, a fall in aggregate demand can be very dangerous because wages can take a long time to fall, and during that time output declines can be especially large. This is one reason why we have drawn the SRAS curve so it is flatter to the left of the LRAS curve. A decrease in spending that requires expected wage growth to decrease will tend to create a large decrease in the growth rate.

Shocks to the Components of Aggregate Demand

We have already looked at how changes in $\overline{M}$ can create AD shocks. Now we consider the other term in our equation: $\vec{v}$. We can think of changes in $\vec{v}$ as increasing or decreasing the spending rate, holding the money supply constant. To understand why the spending rate might change, it's useful to recall the national spending identity, $Y = C + I + G + NX$. The national spending identity reminds us that spending is spending on something. For example, if $\vec{v}$ increases, that means the growth rate of C, I, G, or NX must increase—that is, an increase in $\vec{v}$ must be apportioned among an increase in $\vec{C}$, $\vec{I}$, $\vec{G}$, or $\overline{NX}$.

It's often easier to think about changes in $\vec{v}$ working through changes in $\vec{C}$, $\vec{I}$, $\vec{G}$, or $\overline{NX}$ because each of these factors has somewhat different causes and consequences. Let's look at a change in $\vec{C}$.

Changes in $\vec{v}$ can be broken down into changes in $\vec{C}$, $\vec{I}$, $\vec{G}$, or $\overline{NX}$.

A Shock to $\vec{C}$

Why might $\vec{C}$ decrease? Fear could be one reason. Imagine that consumers suddenly become more pessimistic and fearful about the economy, as they did in 2008 when the banking system was in danger of collapse. The "animal spirits," to use the famous phrase of John Maynard Keynes, turn negative. Workers, for example, might be worried about becoming unemployed, so they decide to postpone buying a new car or remodeling their kitchen. The decrease in consumption purchases will temporarily reduce spending growth, $\vec{C}$. Let's look at Figure 13.15. We begin at point *a* with an inflation rate of 7%, an expected inflation rate of 7%, and a real growth rate of 3%. A decrease in spending growth, a negative AD shock, shifts the AD curve inward and to the left, reducing the real growth rate in the short run. With lower spending growth, wage growth should fall to match the reduction in price growth, but because wages are sticky, especially in the downward direction, wage growth remains high so firms are unprofitable, employment falls, and the economy slows.

Thus, in the short run, the economy moves from point *a* to point *b*, where the inflation rate is lower and the real growth rate is also lower—in this example at point *b*, growth is negative and the economy is in a recession.

In the long run, fear recedes, wages adjust, and the spending growth rate returns to normal so the economy returns to long-run equilibrium at point *a*. Let's explain the shift back of the AD curve in the long run in greater detail.

Why Changes in $\vec{v}$ Tend to Be Temporary

Changes in $\vec{v}$ (i.e., changes in the *growth rate* of C, I, G, or NX) differ from changes in $\overline{M}$ in one respect. $\overline{M}$ can be permanently set at any rate—5%,

FIGURE 13.15

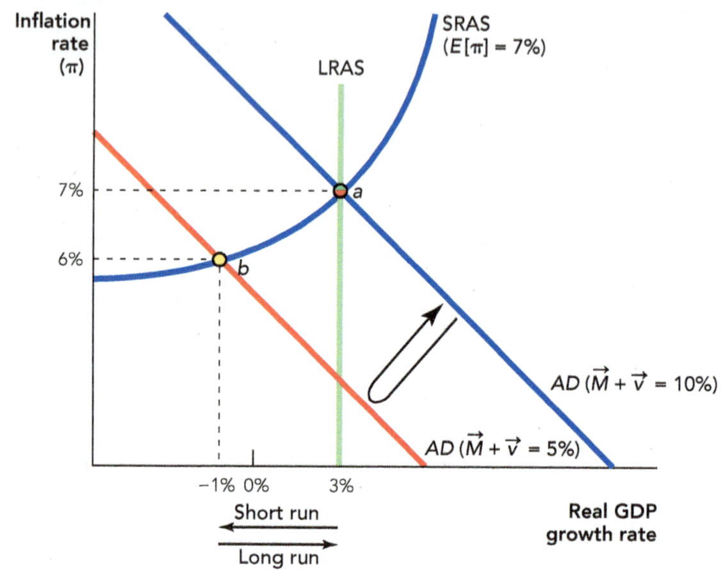

A Temporary Decrease in AD Reduces the Inflation Rate and the Growth Rate in the Short Run At point *a*, spending is growing at a rate of 10% and real growth is 3%, so inflation is 7%. If consumers become fearful and reduce their spending, $\vec{v}$ declines, so the AD curve shifts inward. In the short run, wages are sticky, so although spending growth declines, wage growth does not. As a result, real growth falls to −1% and the inflation rate falls to 6% at point *b*. In the long run, as fear recedes and wages become unstuck, $\vec{v}$ returns to its normal rate, as does real growth.

mru.org/AD-AS

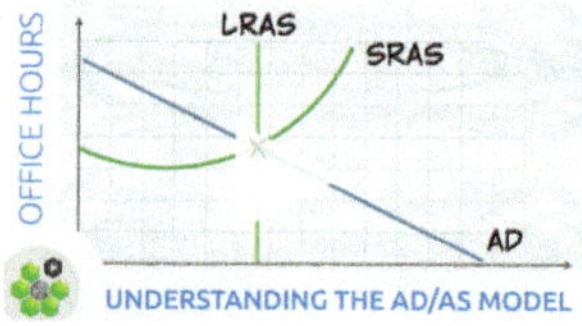

Office Hours: Using the AD–AS Model

17%, 103%—but changes in $\vec{v}$ tend to be temporary. How do we know this? Recall that in our example, consumers were worried about becoming unemployed, so they cut back on purchases like buying a new automobile, that is, a decrease in $\overline{C}$ in this period. In the next period, consumers might cut back on some other purchase, but as they cut back, the consumption that remains (like groceries and rent) becomes even more important and consumers stop cutting back. Also, as consumers cut back on consumption, their savings increase and they become more reassured about spending. Thus, if nothing else changes, consumption will return to its normal growth rate.

As another example, consider an increase in government spending to stimulate the economy (a strategy that will be discussed in Chapter 18). An increase in spending will temporarily increase $\overline{G}$, shifting the AD curve out. The government can do this in the short run, but if $\overline{G}$ were to grow at an unusually high rate year after year, government purchases would soon dominate the economy. In fact, even if voters did not object, eventually $\overline{G}$ would have to fall because in the long run, government spending cannot grow faster than the rate of economic growth (otherwise, government spending on real output would eventually be more than GDP, and that is not possible). The analysis is similar for the other components of Y because as we know from Chapter 6 the shares of GDP devoted to *C*, *I*, *G*, and *NX* have been quite stable over time, so changes in $\overline{C}$, $\overline{I}$, $\overline{G}$, or $\overline{NX}$ tend to be temporary.

Thus, returning to Figure 13.15, we show that a decrease in $\overline{C}$ reduces AD and the rate of inflation in this period. In future periods, however, $\overline{C}$ will return to its normal rate and, as it does, AD and inflation will return to their previous rates. Notice that because the AD curve shifts back in the long run, *changes in* $\overline{C}$, $\overline{I}$, $\overline{G}$, *or* $\overline{NX}$ *do not change the rate of inflation in the long run.* In other words, long-run or sustained inflation requires ongoing increases in the money supply, a truth we've already outlined in the previous chapter.

Other AD Shocks

We have already said that fear could decrease consumption spending (and, thus, confidence could increase consumption spending). What other factors could change $\overline{C}$, $\overline{I}$, $\overline{G}$, or $\overline{NX}$?

Fear and confidence play a similar role in investment spending as in consumption spending. If businesspeople fear that the economy is entering a recession, they may want to wait to make large investments in a new plant and equipment. Similarly, confidence about the future will encourage businesspeople to make significant investments.

Wealth shocks can also increase or decrease AD. Imagine, for example, that the stock market or the housing market tumbles. Before the fall in prices, consumers might have spent freely, expecting that in their retirement years or in an emergency they could sell their stocks or their homes and live on the proceeds. When prices fall, consumers suddenly realize that their wealth has fallen so that they now need to save more; thus, they cut back on their spending. In 2008, for example, a simultaneous fall in stock and housing prices caused a very large decrease in consumption spending. (A positive wealth shock works the opposite way. As the stock market rises, for example, consumers spend more today as their increasing wealth gives them confidence that they will have plenty in the future.)

Taxes are another important shifter of $\vec{C}$ and $\vec{I}$. An increase in taxes can reduce consumption growth and a decrease in taxes can increase consumption growth. Taxes targeted at investment spending—such as an investment tax credit—can have a similar effect on investment growth. Changes in taxes are also a part of fiscal policy to be studied in Chapter 18.

Big increases in the growth rate of government spending will increase AD, and decreases in the growth rate of government spending will reduce AD. During a war, for example, government spending usually increases at a high rate, thereby shifting the AD curve outward. Government spending can also be timed to try to offset the business cycle. (Again, see Chapter 18).

The category called net exports consists of exports minus imports. We look at exports and imports more closely in Chapters 19 and 20, but for now the basic idea is simple. If other countries increase their spending on our goods (exports), that increases our AD. If we shift our spending away from domestic goods to foreign goods (imports), that reduces our AD.

Table 13.2 summarizes some of the factors that can shift the AD curve. Let's now apply the insights from the AD–AS model to understanding the so-called Great Depression, a watershed event in U.S. history.

CHECK YOURSELF

- What always happens to unexpected inflation in the long run?
- What happens to the aggregate demand curve if consumers fear a recession is coming and cut back on their expenditures?

TABLE 13.2 SOME FACTORS THAT SHIFT THE AGGREGATE DEMAND CURVE

Positive Shocks (Increase AD) (= Higher Growth Rate of Spending)	Negative Shocks (Decrease AD) (= Lower Growth Rate of Spending)
A faster money growth rate	A slower money growth rate
Confidence	Fear
Increased wealth	Reduced wealth
Lower taxes	Higher taxes
Greater growth of government spending	Lower growth of government spending
Increased export growth	Decreased export growth
Decreased import growth	Increased import growth

Understanding the Great Depression: Aggregate Demand Shocks and Real Shocks

The Great Depression (1929–1940) was the most catastrophic economic event in the history of the United States. GDP plummeted by 30%, unemployment rates exceeded 20%, and the stock market fell to less than a third of its original value. America went from confidence to desperation. In fact, the Great Depression was a worldwide event, plaguing almost all the developed nations. In some cases, such as Germany, the economic downturn led to totalitarian regimes followed by war. The 1930s and 1940s were terrible years for the world and bad economic policy was partly at fault.

Aggregate Demand Shocks and the Great Depression

The Great Depression occurred in the United States as follows. In 1929, the stock market crashed, creating a mood of pessimism among the American public. In part, this stock market crash had been brought on by a tight monetary policy, aimed at limiting a stock market bubble. The fall in stock prices was a wealth shock that made many people feel poorer and so they limited their spending, causing $\overline{C}$ to fall. This, combined with the initial monetary contraction, that is, a reduction in $\overline{M}$, reduced aggregate demand, shifting the AD curve inward to the left.

But that is only the beginning of the story. In 1930, depositors lost confidence in their banks and, as they withdrew their money, they created a wave of bank failures. These bank failures meant that people lost their money, again diminishing aggregate demand. Moreover, at the time there was no government deposit insurance so when the first banks failed, people became suspicious of other banks and rushed to withdraw their money even from banks that were otherwise sound. From 1930 to 1932, there were four waves of banking panics; by 1933, more than 40% of all American banks had failed.

The fear and uncertainty created by bank failures, rising unemployment rates, falling consumer confidence, and inconsistent policymaking in Washington also reduced investment spending. Between 1929 and 1933, for example, investment spending fell by nearly 75%. In many years, spending on new investment was not enough to replace the tools, machines, and buildings that had depreciated due to natural wear and tear. Astoundingly, the U.S. capital stock was lower in 1940 than it had been in 1930.[1]

Furthermore, in 1931, instead of increasing $\overline{M}$, the Federal Reserve allowed the money supply to contract even further. In the early 1930s, the U.S. money supply fell by about a third, *the largest negative shock to aggregate demand in American history*. At that time, the Fed should have been expanding the money supply to drive up output in an emergency situation and also to boost the reserves of failing banks (we analyze monetary policy further in Chapter 16). Instead, the Fed allowed the money supply to contract and a disaster ensued. Bad decision making caused an additional monetary contraction during 1937–1938, which led to yet another wave of economic distress. It made the Great Depression much longer than it needed to be.

Figure 13.16 shows the story in a diagram. In the late 1920s, the economy was growing at a rate of about 4% per year with no inflation. Starting in 1929, a series of brutal shocks to aggregate demand reduced $\overline{C}$, $\overline{I}$, and $\overline{M}$ and by 1932 pushed real growth to a rate of −13% and inflation to −10% per year. Note that although drawn separately, all these shocks were interconnected, as previously discussed.

FIGURE 13.16

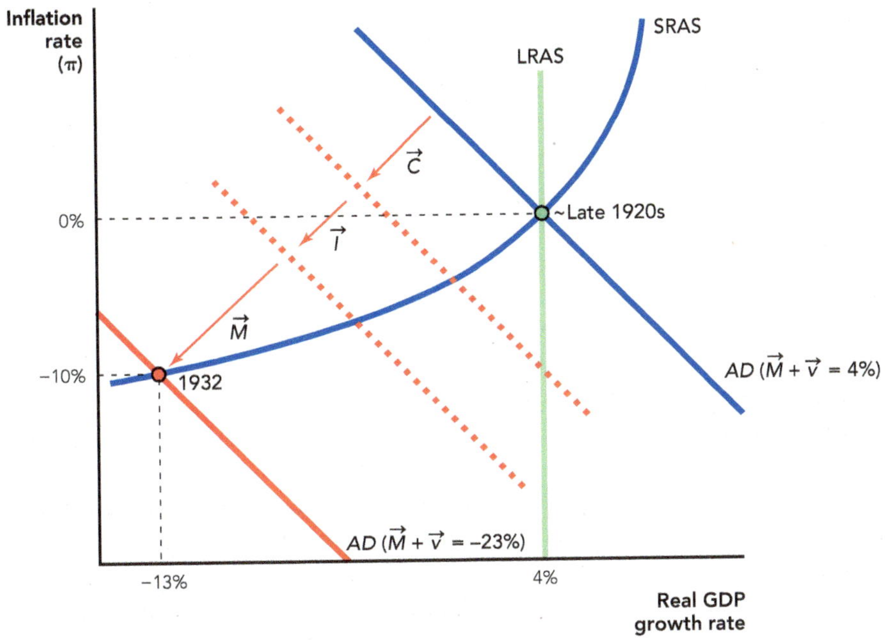

The Great Depression and the Great Fall in Aggregate Demand During the Great Depression, the growth rate of consumption, investment, and the money supply declined dramatically, creating deflation and an unprecedented decline in real growth.

To make all these problems worse, the decrease in aggregate demand caused prices to fall (as shown in the figure) and that, in turn, raised the real value of debts. One feature of virtually all loans is that they are denominated in terms of dollars, and the debt is not adjusted for inflation or deflation. So if a person or company has borrowed $10,000 and the price level falls by 10% (as it did in some of the Depression's worst years), the real, inflation-adjusted value of that debt burden is now 10% higher than before. That makes life more difficult for debtors, and many of them will not be able to meet their obligations and perhaps they will go bankrupt, disrupting the economy further. Furthermore, many debtors will spend less money, thereby decreasing aggregate demand even more than from the initial shocks. While the real income of creditor banks goes up for the same reason that the real value of the debt goes up, these banks don't have such a high propensity to spend or invest as do the desperate debtors, and so, the transfer of wealth from debtors to creditors still means that aggregate demand goes down.

Thus, the Great Depression was due primarily to the *great fall in aggregate demand*. Real shocks, however, also played a role in the Great Depression and in the failure of the economy to recover more quickly from the great fall. Let's take a look at how real factors contributed to the Great Depression.

Real Shocks and the Great Depression

We have already mentioned one real shock—the bank failures—and you can see why bank failures are a real shock by thinking back to Chapter 9.

Bank failures reduced the money supply and spending (an aggregate demand shock), but they also reduced the efficiency of financial intermediation. As we discussed in that earlier chapter, banks play a key role in bridging the gap between savers and investors, and as banks failed, this bridge collapsed. Some firms could rely on internally generated funds for investment, and large firms could turn to the stock and bond markets for new funds. But many small businesses relied on loans from local banks that understood these businesses, and thus many small firms were especially harmed by bank failures.

To sum up the causal chain of events: A fall in $\overline{M}$ reduced aggregate demand, which led to bank failures, which led to a reduction in the productivity of financial intermediation, a real shock. As you would by now expect, the real shock reduced growth even further. One of the broader lessons of this episode—which is true more generally—is that shocks to AD and shocks to the LRAS curve are linked in most recessions. In some cases, the shock to AD creates a real shock, and in other cases, a real shock creates a shock to AD; for instance, the fear and uncertainty created by a real shock can reduce AD by inducing people to cut back on spending and investment.

Some economic policy mistakes during the Great Depression also impeded recovery. As we have already mentioned, the Federal Reserve failed to use its power over the money supply to increase aggregate demand. In addition, there were other policy failures. For example, the National Industrial Recovery Act (NIRA) and the Agricultural Adjustment Act (AAA), both of 1933, tried to combat falling prices not by increasing aggregate demand but by reducing supply. Under NIRA, businesses were encouraged not to invest in machinery (in order to keep labor demand high), and they were encouraged to raise prices by creating cartels. Under the AAA, the government paid farmers to kill millions of pigs and plow under cotton fields in order to increase prices. Neither of these policies is likely to have increased economic growth. The Supreme Court ruled in 1935 and 1936, respectively, that both laws were unconstitutional.

Most famously (but perhaps not most importantly) the Smoot–Hawley Tariff of 1930 raised tariffs (taxes) on tens of thousands of imported goods.[2] In principle, a tariff, by taxing foreign goods, can boost demand for domestic goods, thereby increasing AD. (Notice from our list of factors that can shift AD in Table 13.2, that a decrease in imports can increase AD.) In reality, retaliations against the Smoot–Hawley Tariff by other countries created a spiraling decline in world trade. When other countries raised their tariffs, U.S. exports fell. Remember that a reduction in exports reduces aggregate demand. Unfortunately, the large decline in world trade meant that the net effect of the tariff was to reduce aggregate demand.

In addition to being a shock to AD, a second negative effect of the tariff occurred because *a tariff is also a negative productivity shock*. We get the most output from our capital and labor when we specialize in fields in which we have a comparative advantage and then trade for the goods that we produce at a comparative disadvantage (see Chapter 2 for more on comparative advantage). A tariff pushes capital and labor into lower productivity sectors, thereby reducing total output. Another way of seeing this point is to recognize that a tariff has exactly the same effects as an increase in transportation costs. Therefore, a tariff is like a negative productivity shock to the shipping industry, which ripples out to all the other industries dependent on shipping.

As if these shocks were not enough, the United States was beset during the early years of the Great Depression by a natural shock, namely the onset of the so-called Dust Bowl. A severe drought and decades of ecologically unsustainable

MRU

mru.org/AD-AS-depression

Understanding the Great Depression

farming practices turned millions of acres of farmland in Texas, Oklahoma, New Mexico, Colorado, and Kansas to dust. Dust storms blackened the sky, reducing visibility to a matter of feet. Hundreds of thousands of people were forced to leave their homes and millions of acres of farmland became useless.

In a good year, the real shocks of the Great Depression could have been absorbed without major difficulty, but in a bad year, the shocks compounded one another and made a desperate situation even worse.

Takeaway

We've covered a lot in this chapter, but the basic point is that the model of aggregate demand and supply can be used to analyze business fluctuations, fluctuations in the growth rate of real GDP.

Using our model, we laid out how to analyze two types of shocks, real shocks and aggregate demand shocks. Real shocks are analyzed through shifts in the LRAS curve. Aggregate demand shocks are analyzed using shifts in the AD curve.

When you combine the aggregate demand curve, long-run aggregate supply curve, and short-run aggregate supply curve into a single diagram, you can analyze a wide variety of economic scenarios and how they affect the growth rate of the economy. As you will see in future chapters, our model will also help us to explain when government policy can and cannot be used to successfully smooth business fluctuations.

The aggregate demand curve can be broken down into changes in $\overline{M}$ and $\vec{v}$, and slopes downward. In addition changes in $\vec{v}$ can be broken down into changes in $\vec{C}$, $\vec{I}$, $\vec{G}$, or $\overrightarrow{NX}$. Factors including nominal wage and price confusion, sticky wages, sticky prices, menu costs, and uncertainty create an upward-sloped short-run aggregate supply curve.

We outlined the history of America's Great Depression from the 1930s using our model. The Great Depression resulted from an unfortunate, concentrated, and interrelated series of aggregate demand and real shocks.

The material in this chapter is central to macroeconomics. If you understand where these curves come from and how to shift them, you will have a basic toolbox for many macroeconomic questions. You are now ready to tackle many of the core topics of macroeconomics and business cycles.

CHECK YOURSELF

- What happened to the U.S. money supply in the early 1930s? Did this initially affect aggregate demand or the long-run aggregate supply curve, and in which direction?
- If, as was said earlier in this chapter, real shocks hit the economy all the time, should we ignore them in explaining the Great Depression?

CHAPTER REVIEW

Go online to practice with more examples of these types of problems, including live links to videos, data sources, and feedback.

▶ Problems with this icon relate to optional MRU videos.

KEY CONCEPTS

business fluctuations, p. 287

recession, p. 287

aggregate demand curve, p. 289

Solow growth rate, p. 292

long-run aggregate supply curve, p. 292

real shock, p. 292

aggregate demand shock, p. 298

short-run aggregate supply curve, p. 299

nominal wage confusion, p. 300

menu costs, p. 300

FACTS AND TOOLS

1. Sort the following shocks into real shocks or aggregate demand shocks. Remember that "shocks" include both good and bad events.

   A fall in the price of oil

   A rise in consumer optimism

   A hurricane that destroys factories in Florida

   Good weather that creates a bumper crop of California oranges

   A rise in sales taxes

   Foreigners watch fewer U.S.-made movies

   Fear

   New inventions occur at a faster pace

   A faster money growth rate

2. Look at Figure 13.2. Let's sum up some basic facts about the link between unemployment rates and recessions. Notice that the shaded bars indicate periods of recession, and wider bars mean longer recessions.

   a. How many recessions have there been since World War II?

   b. Since World War II, how many recessions had unemployment rates greater than 10%?

   c. Often, the unemployment rate seems to peak after the recession ends: The economy goes back to growing, while the unemployment rate rises for a while. As the figure shows, the recessions of 1990 and 2001 have been clear examples of such "jobless recoveries." Approximately how many times did the unemployment rate peak after the recession ended?

3. Look at Figure 13.5. When inflation rises, does the Solow growth rate rise, fall, or remain unchanged?

4. Are "real shocks" negative shocks, by definition?

5. When negative real shocks hit, what typically happens to the long-run aggregate supply curve: Does it shift left, shift right, or stay in the same place?

6. When negative real shocks hit, what typically happens to the aggregate demand curve? Does it shift left, shift right, or stay in the same place?

7. As Figure 13.1 implies, for the United States, the long-run aggregate supply curve has, on average, been approximately 3% real growth per year. If a negative real shock hits, shifting it by 2 percentage points, what will happen to real growth: Will

it be positive or negative? Would you call the resulting economic conditions a recession?

8. a. What does a negative real shock do to inflation: Does it rise, fall, or remain unchanged?

   b. What does a negative real shock do to spending growth: Does it rise, fall, or remain unchanged?

   c. What does a fall in spending growth—that is, a shift inward of the AD curve—do to real growth: Does it rise, fall, or remain unchanged?

9. In the following cases, will real growth rise, fall, or remain unchanged?

   a. Expected inflation = 5%
      Actual inflation = 7%

   b. Expected inflation = 3%
      Actual inflation = 1%

   c. Expected inflation = 6%
      Actual inflation = 6%

   d. Expected inflation = 7%
      Actual inflation = −10%

   e. Expected inflation = −1%
      Actual inflation = 0%

10. Consider the following figure. In this relatively unsuccessful economy, the Solow growth rate is 1% per year:

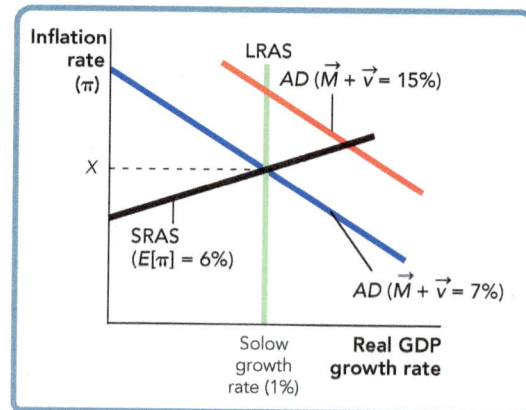

   a. Calculate the inflation rate at X in this economy. (*Hint:* Use the quantity theory.)

   b. If spending growth were 15% in this economy, what would the inflation rate be in the long run, assuming the Solow growth rate stays fixed?

11. a. The short-run aggregate supply (SRAS) curve is very predictable. When inflation is

greater than people expect, SRAS eventually shifts (*choose one:* up, down) over the next year or so, and when inflation is less than people expect, SRAS eventually shifts (*choose one:* up, down) over the next year or so.

b. Here's another, equally valid way to look at the SRAS curve: When real GDP growth is above the Solow growth rate, SRAS eventually shifts (*choose one:* right, left) over the next year or so, and when real GDP growth is below the Solow growth rate, SRAS eventually shifts (*choose one:* right, left) over the next year or so.

c. Explain why the two ways of looking at the SRAS curve are equivalent.

THINKING AND PROBLEM SOLVING

12. Complete the following sentences:

With a real shock, when real growth is worse than usual, inflation is _____ than usual.

With an aggregate demand shock, when real growth is worse than usual, inflation is _____ than usual.

13. a. In the 1970s, the United States had slow growth and high inflation. Which kind of shock best fits these facts?

Negative real shock

Positive real shock

Negative aggregate demand shock

Positive aggregate demand shock

b. Using the same categories, explain the late 1990s, when the United States experienced fast growth and falling inflation.

c. Again using the same four categories, explain the early 2000s, when the United States experienced slow growth and falling inflation.

d. Which shock best explains the 1981–1982 recession, when inflation fell quickly and unemployment rose quickly?

e. Which shock best explains the Great Recession of 2007–2008?

▶ **14.** To keep things simple, let's put this into a familiar supply and demand story and assume that in the long run, workers offer a fixed supply of labor: In other words, while they may be picky about jobs in the short run, in the long run they'll work regardless of the going wage.

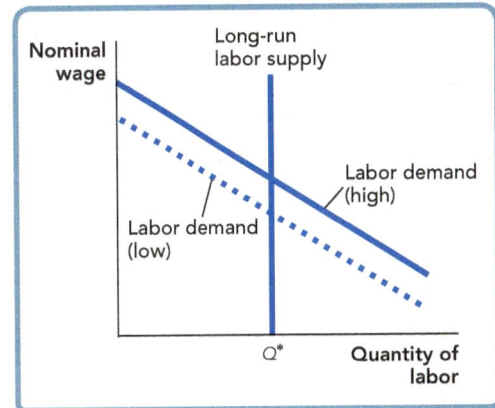

It's the businesses who *demand* labor and workers who *supply* labor. Currently, let's assume the economy starts off at long-run equilibrium, so that the normal number of workers, Q★, are working.

a. Suppose labor demand falls, shifting to the left, as in the figure. What does the short-run supply curve for labor look like if workers refuse to take pay cuts even if it means losing their jobs (we can call this the "take this job and shove it" strategy after a famous country and western song). Indicate your answer by drawing a new line on the figure, labeling it "Short-run labor supply." You only need to focus on the area to the left of Q★.

b. Recalling your basic supply and demand model, does this fall in labor demand then create a "surplus" of workers or a "shortage" of workers?

c. According to the basic supply and demand model, what will happen to the price of labor over time as a result of this fall in labor demand?

15. a. If the media report a lot of good news about the economy, what is likely to happen to velocity?

b. If the Federal Reserve wants to keep aggregate demand (i.e., spending growth) stable, what will it do to the growth rate of the money supply when a lot of good news comes out about the economy: increase it, decrease it, or leave it unchanged? (*Hint:* In practice, central bankers often call this "leaning against the wind.")

▶ **16.** After a monetary shock hits aggregate demand, which curve will shift to bring output growth back to the Solow growth rate: the short-run aggregate supply curve or the aggregate demand curve? (*Hint:* Which curve is more like a microeconomic story about prices adjusting in order to bring supply and demand into balance?)

17. What happens when bad aggregate demand shocks hit the economy? Consider the following graph.

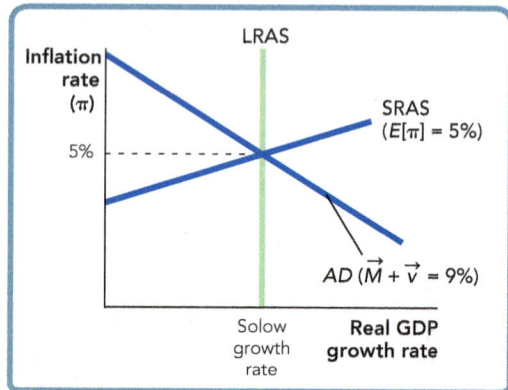

a. Before we get to the bad aggregate demand shock, let's find out what the potential growth rate is in this economy. Use the quantity theory to find your answer.

b. Because of a fall in the growth of the money supply, spending growth falls to 4% per year. Draw the immediate result on aggregate demand in the graph.

c. This fall in money growth lasts for many years. Eventually, in the long run, workers, business owners, and consumers all adjust their inflation expectations enough so that the economy returns to the potential growth rate. Draw this new SRAS curve in the figure.

d. In the long run, after spending growth falls to 4% per year, what will the potential growth rate be? What will inflation be?

18. Real-world economies get hit with lots of shocks to aggregate demand and real shocks. Some shocks clearly fit into the first category, some into the second, and some include a generous mix of both. Let's categorize the following shocks. Only one is a clear case of "both."

Steelworkers go on strike, so less steel is produced.

Businesses read about the glories of mobile commerce, so demand for high-tech investment purchases increases.

U.S. senators read about the glories of the Internet, so demand for high-tech government purchases increases.

A series of investment banks like Lehman Brothers and Bear Stearns go bankrupt.

Around 2000, the glories of the Internet fade a bit so innovations increase at a somewhat slower rate for a few years.

The U.S. government launches two costly wars almost simultaneously, so government purchases increase dramatically (referring to World War II, of course).

The U.S. government launches two costly wars almost simultaneously, using the draft to force many men to work much longer hours and supply more labor than they would otherwise.

19. Let's have some practice with the aggregate demand curve. If you want to draw it in your familiar $y = b + mx$ format, you can think of it this way:

Inflation = (Growth in money + Growth in velocity) − Real growth

a. When you look at a fixed aggregate demand curve, like the one in Figure 13.3, what is being held constant? (*choose one*):

Spending growth (growth in M + growth in v)

Real GDP growth (growth in Y)

Inflation (growth in P)

b. When you look at a shifting aggregate demand curve, like the one in Figure 13.4, what *had* to change to make the curve shift? (*choose one*):

Spending growth (growth in M + growth in v)

Real GDP growth (growth in Y)

Inflation (growth in P)

c. According to the quantity theory, which of the following statements *must be* false, and why? More than one may be false.

"Last year, spending grew at 10%, real growth was 4%, and inflation was 6%."

"Last year, spending grew at 4%, real growth was −2%, and inflation was 6%."

"Last year, spending grew at 100%, real growth was 0%, and inflation was 20%."

"Last year, spending grew at 5%, real growth was 5%, and inflation was 2%."

"Last year, spending grew at 10%, real growth was 5%, and inflation was −5%."

20. In the aggregate demand and supply model, what is "sticky"? More than one may be true: wages, real growth, prices, velocity, money growth, unemployment.

21. During the Great Depression, which of the following were mostly aggregate demand shocks and which were mostly negative real shocks?

The fall in the growth rate of money

The fall in farm productivity

The Smoot–Hawley Tariff Act

22. Recall that $Y = C + I + G + NX$.

a. If government spending increases, then we model that as an increase in:

   i. v.

   ii. M.

   iii. Q.

   iv. T.

b. An increase in G:

   i. shifts the AD curve inward.

   ii. shifts the AD curve outward.

   iii. doesn't move the AD curve.

   iv. shifts the LRAS curve.

c. A shift outward in the AD curve will tend to:

   i. increase inflation and reduce growth.

   ii. decrease inflation and increase growth.

   iii. decrease inflation and decrease growth.

   iv. increase inflation and increase growth.

CHALLENGES

23. Here is a puzzle. A country with a relatively small positive aggregate demand shock (a shift outward in the AD curve) may have a substantial economic boom, but sometimes countries that have massive increases in the AD curve (hyperinflation countries like Germany before World War II, e.g.) don't seem to have massive economic booms. Why does a small AD increase sometimes raise GDP much more than a giant AD increase?

24. Some companies raise their workers' pay by giving raises, but others prefer to give one-time bonuses instead. Think about two steel mills facing a big two-year drop in steel demand: In one steel mill, workers have received pay raises every year for five years. In the second mill, most of the pay increases have occurred through big bonuses at the end of each year. Which steel mill will probably keep more jobs during the two-year downturn? Why? Would you draw a perfectly vertical curve, a curve with a positive slope, or a curve with a negative slope?

25. Reconsider your answer to Facts and Tools question 3. If you wanted to draw the long-run aggregate supply curve accurately, taking into account the idea that very high rates of inflation are likely to reduce real growth, how would you draw the long-run aggregate supply curve?

26. a. If aggregate demand shocks are the most important drivers of business fluctuations, then should we expect real wages to be procyclical (rising when GDP growth is high) or countercyclical (rising when GDP growth is low)?

b. If real shocks are the most important drivers of business fluctuations, then should we expect real wages to be procyclical or countercyclical?

c. Macroeconomists find mixed evidence on the link between business fluctuations and inflation. But there's more agreement on the link between business fluctuations and real wages: The real wage is procyclical, growing quickly during good times and growing slowly or falling during bad times. Which of the two shocks (real or aggregate demand) is this most consistent with? (We'll revisit this question in the next chapter.)

27. Often, more than one kind of shock hits the economy at once. When this happens, the different shocks *could* push inflation (or real growth) in different directions in the short run, leaving the final short-run result ambiguous. What is most likely to happen to inflation and real output growth in the following cases: Will they rise or fall, or can't you tell with the information given? Note that you will often (maybe always) be able to definitely know the answer for one but not the other.

a. A nation's scientists invent many new Internet search tools, raising current productivity and making investors optimistic about future inventions as well.

b. A government raises taxes and its economy experiences a year of excellent weather for growing crops.

c. Oil prices skyrocket and the central bank slows the rate of money growth.

28. Use Figure 13.11 as a starting point for this problem and consider the initial impact of the following circumstances on the aggregate demand, long-run aggregate supply, and short-run aggregate supply curves.

a. A war in the Middle East rapidly increases the price of oil.

b. More and more consumers develop a fear that they are in danger of losing their jobs and businesses fear that they are in danger of losing their customers.

c. Add to this set of problems the uncertainty that a new administration introduces by pushing through significant social reform expected to increase business costs and reduce consumers' discretionary income.

29. Continuing from your short-run results in the previous problem, what do you believe will happen in the long run as these adjustments work their way through the economy?

30. A significant productivity slowdown occurred during the 1970s and 1980s. A large part of it occurred in industries closely related to the energy crises of the 1970s. (Besides the "Oil Shocks" section in this chapter, you can read a brief summary about these developments in the *NBER Digest*, http://nber.org/digest/jun05/w10950.html.)

    a. Use the aggregate demand and supply model to show the effects of the energy crises and productivity slowdown on the economy if spending growth remains unchanged.

    b. Suppose that unaware of the productivity slowdown at the time, monetary authorities increased the growth rate of money in order to stimulate spending growth, or AD, and boost employment. What impact would this have on the economy?

    c. Review Figures 13.1, 13.2, and Figure 12.2 from the previous chapter and determine if it seems like the scenario described in this problem might have been possible. Why?

31. Following the productivity slowdown discussed in question 30, the U.S. economy experienced a relatively quick transition to the electronic age of computers and the Internet, and many of the outward effects of the 1970s energy crises faded as a result.

    a. Use the aggregate demand and supply model to show the effects of widespread computer and Internet usage on the economy if spending growth remains unchanged.

    b. Suppose that velocity increases due to greater consumer confidence because of your findings in part a. First, does greater consumer confidence make sense? Why?

    c. Second, how will this affect inflation and GDP growth in the long run?

WORK IT OUT

For interactive, step-by-step help in solving this problem, go online.

From the equation of exchange, $MV = PY$ we know that spending growth ($\vec{M} + \vec{v}$) equals inflation (π) + Real growth. Recall from the chapter that in the long run (1) the inflation rate is found where the AD curve intersects the LRAS curve (reading off the vertical axis) and (2) the expected inflation rate is found where the short-run aggregate supply curve intersects the LRAS curve. With these things in mind, assume that the Solow growth rate is 3% and answer parts a through d.

a. If spending growth equals 10%, what will π equal in the long run? What will $E\pi$ equal?

b. If spending growth equals 6%, what will π equal in the long run? What will $E\pi$ equal?

c. If spending growth equals 4%, what will π equal in the long run? What will $E\pi$ equal?

d. What can we say about inflation π and expected inflation $E\pi$ in the long run?

▶ MRU VIDEOS

The Aggregate Demand Curve

mru.org/AD-curve

Problems: **1, 19**

The Long-Run Aggregate Supply Curve

mru.org/LRAS

Problems: **1, 5, 7, 8**

The Short-Run Aggregate Supply Curve

mru.org/SRAS

Problems: **11, 16**

Sticky Wages and the Parable of the Angry Professor

mru.org/sticky-wages

Problem: **14**

Changes in Velocity (and Shifts in the AD Curve)

mru.org/AD-AS-velocity

Problem: **22**

Understanding the Great Depression

mru.org/AD-AS-depression

Problem: **21**

Office Hours: Using the AD–AS Model

mru.org/AD-AS

Problem: **27**

14

Transmission and Amplification Mechanisms

In the previous chapter, we explained the basics of the aggregate demand–aggregate supply model. The driving forces in that model were real shocks (shifts in the long-run aggregate supply curve) and aggregate demand shocks (shifts in the AD curve). In this chapter, we explain in greater detail how economic forces can amplify shocks and transmit them across sectors of the economy and through time. When a shock is amplified, a mild negative shock can be transformed into a more serious reduction in output and a positive shock can be transformed into a boom. In addition, we will show in this chapter how real shocks and aggregate demand shocks can interact—one type of shock can lead to the other, for example.

We focus on five transmission mechanisms: intertemporal substitution, uncertainty and irreversible investments, labor adjustment costs, time bunching, and shocks to collateral and net worth, which we call collateral damage.

Intertemporal Substitution

Let's go back to our farm example from the previous chapter. We showed that when the weather fluctuates, so does output and therefore so does GDP, especially in agricultural economies such as India. Once again, Figure 14.1, on the next page, shows how rainfall shocks are correlated with the growth rate of agricultural output (Panel A) and GDP (Panel B) in India.

When rainfall is below average, the same capital and labor inputs produce less agricultural output—that is the direct effect of the negative rainfall shock. But the shock to GDP is caused not simply by less rainfall but also by how people respond to less rainfall. If rainfall is below average, for example, farmers may work less hard and devote less capital to their fields.

Why would farmers choose to use less labor and capital in response to a negative shock? Think about it this way: When the crops are bountiful, it makes sense to work from dawn till dusk because each hour of additional work pays a lot—remember the old saying, make hay when the sun shines? But when the crops are poor, the returns to an additional hour of work are low and so

FIGURE 14.1

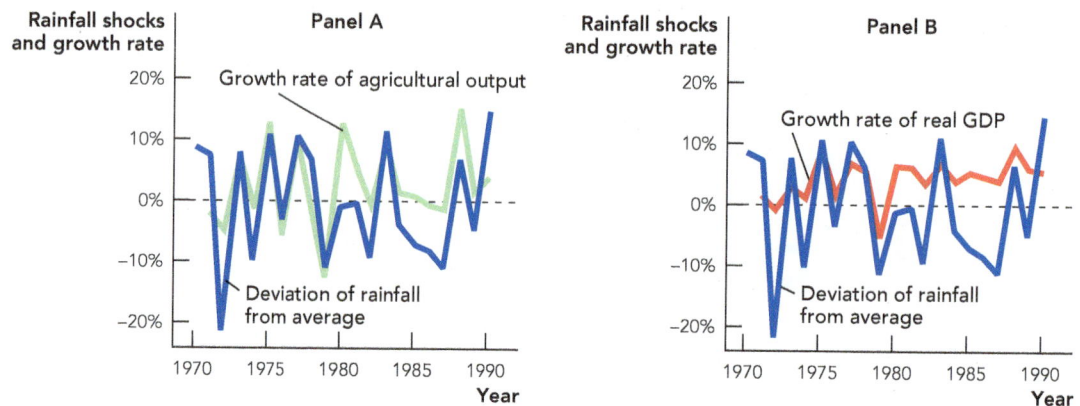

Rainfall Shocks in India Correlate Well with Agricultural Output and GDP Panel A: Rainfall shocks and the growth rate of India's agricultural output. **Panel B:** Rainfall shocks and the growth rate of India's GDP.

Data from: Reserve Bank of India and Indian Institute of Tropical Meteorology.

farmers may rationally decide to work less. The same is true for applications of capital. When planted crops will blossom, it may be worth paying the fuel costs to run the tractor an extra hour. When planted crops will in any case wither, why bother spending the money on fuel? Just leave the tractor in the shed.

Economists call this effect **intertemporal substitution**. The term means that a person or a business is most likely to work hard when working hard brings the greatest return. We work hard in some times and rest in others, and of course we pick and choose the spots when we try hardest. We are substituting effort across time and thus the expression *intertemporal substitution*.

When you study for a test, do you practice intertemporal substitution or do you study an equal amount every day? As a test approaches, you probably study harder, turning down some opportunities for fun. Once the test is over, you study less and have more fun. Intertemporal substitution means that when you study, you study a lot, and when you party, well, you know.

Intertemporal substitution, however, is not just about substituting between work and leisure. We pointed out in Chapter 1, for example, that when jobs are plentiful and wages are increasing, there is a tendency for fewer people to enter college, but when jobs are scarce and wages are stagnant, more people decide to invest in an education. Students understand that the opportunity cost of getting an education falls when jobs are scarce.

During a boom, people are less likely to retire or take early retirement—why not stay another year or two and bank the high wages? Similarly, homemakers and other people who might otherwise not work will choose to enter the workforce during boom periods. During recessions, people are more likely to take early retirement or focus on homemaking. Figure 14.2 shows that when GDP is growing faster than trend, the employment to population ratio also tends to grow faster than trend. The implication is that the supply of labor increases in a boom and falls during a recession.

Intertemporal substitution is the allocation of consumption, work, and leisure across time to maximize well-being.

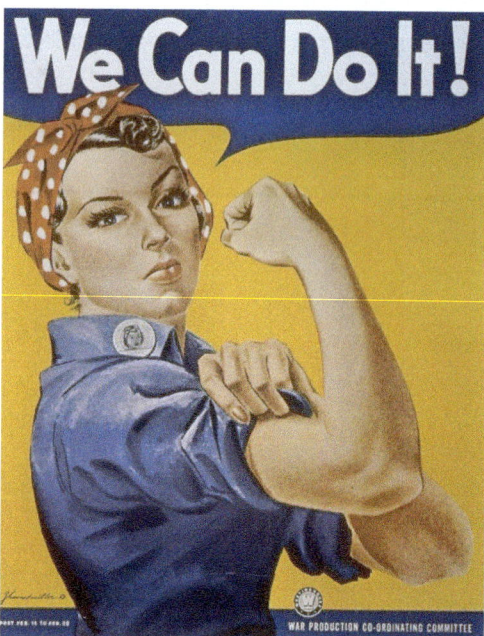

Intertemporal substitution at work during World War II.

FIGURE 14.2

Intertemporal Substitution: Percentage Deviation from Trend in GDP and the Employment–Population Ratio, 1950–2010 When growth rates increase above trend, a greater fraction of the population enters into the workforce, suggesting intertemporal substitution at work.

Data from: U.S. Bureau of Labor Statistics and Bureau of Economic Analysis.

Notice that intertemporal substitution magnifies negative economic shocks. When things go a bit bad, the return to work and investing fall, and often people work less and invest less, which makes things go just a little worse. The ripple effects of this process help turn an initial shock into a broader recession. Of course, on the upside, intertemporal substitution can feed an economic boom and make it more intense. If things are going well, many people will be inclined to work harder, which will in turn increase output and make things go even better. Figure 14.3 shows how intertemporal substitution amplifies shocks to the long-run aggregate supply (LRAS) curve. Intertemporal substitution is hardly the only force behind employment decisions (see Chapter 11) but it does play a role in magnifying shocks, both on the upside and the downside.

Let's turn to another transmission mechanism, uncertainty and irreversible investments.

Uncertainty and Irreversible Investments

Negative shocks also increase uncertainty, which is bad for business investment. Bad news usually also means uncertain news, since the arrival of the bad news causes

FIGURE 14.3

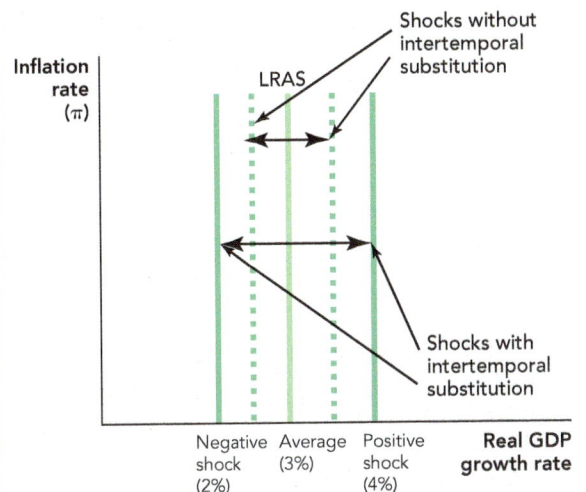

Intertemporal Substitution Amplifies Shocks

people to rethink how the world works. For instance, when the 9/11 attacks hit the United States, uncertainty about the future increased. All of a sudden many people started worrying—rightly or wrongly—that subsequent terrorist attacks would be a big problem. The initial response was to hold off on business investment. Until it became clear that such attacks would not become regular occurrences, for instance, many investors were reluctant to fund new construction in New York City. When investors are uncertain, often they prefer to wait and sample more information before committing themselves.

The key idea here is that many investments involve sunk costs, that is, they are **irreversible investments**, or very costly to reverse. Once a new office building has been constructed on Wall Street, for example, it is difficult to tear down that building and redeploy the steel and glass to other economic uses. So, before investors build a new skyscraper, they will try to make sure that there will be a demand for the offices. Of course, investors sometimes get this wrong, just as commercial real estate overexpanded in the mid- to late 1980s, or too many homes were built in the years preceding the real estate crash of 2007. But prior to expansion, investors want to see many strong signals that market conditions will validate their plans.

The more uncertain the world appears, the harder it is for investors to receive definite signals about where to invest their resources. Investors may see that the demand to watch television programs is shrinking, as it has been for years, but investors do not know which new sectors will be expanding. Will all those extra TV-watching hours be replaced by time spent on Facebook or Netflix, or by time spent outdoors? When investors wait to see what happens, that means resources are sitting idle rather than being productive. That means lower GDP and it contributes to the economic slowdown.

To see the logic of irreversible investment, consider the decision to marry. Marriage is a kind of investment and not just in the financial sense. It is a commitment to the future and it is often for a very long period. Given the seriousness of this commitment, you ought to make (relatively) sure that your marriage is a good idea. If you receive some information causing you to doubt your potential partner (did someone hint they have a gambling problem?), maybe you should wait a while and discover the truth before proceeding. Of course, if you wait to decide on marriage, you may also wait to buy a house together, even if buying a house is a good idea. That's just common sense. The point is that the same logic applies to economic investments. Uncertainty usually slows investment and keeps resources in less-productive uses.

Irreversible investments have high value only under specific conditions—they cannot be easily moved, adjusted, or reversed if conditions change.

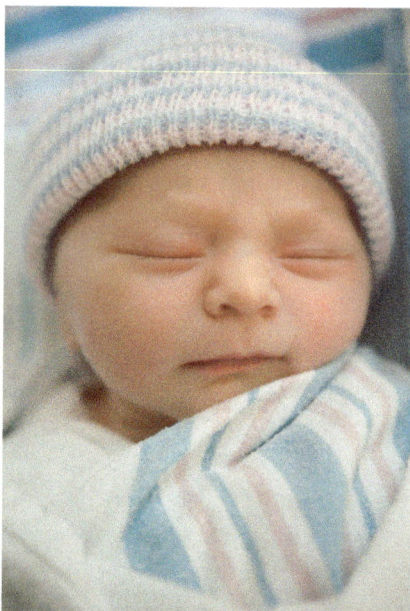

Tim Tadder/Getty Images

One of the most irreversible investments of them all

Labor Adjustment Costs

Once a negative shock hits the economy, labor must adjust. Workers must look for new jobs, move to new areas, and sometimes change their wage expectations. Recall from Chapter 11 how search—looking for a new job—is one reason for unemployment. A negative shock to the economy, by remixing opportunities, induces more search and thus causes more search-related unemployment. **Labor adjustment costs** are the costs of shifting workers from declining sectors of the economy to growing sectors.

Labor adjustments to shocks are not always rational in the narrowly economic sense of that term. If an automobile worker is laid off from the General Motors assembly line and loses their formerly unionized job, they may not be able to find the same wage elsewhere. Currently, the less-unionized automakers in the United States pay a lower hourly wage than the more-unionized GM. Some automobile workers without a high school degree may make up to $100,000 per year. It may

Labor adjustment costs are the costs of shifting workers from declining sectors of the economy to the growing sectors.

take a while for that person, if thrown out of work, to admit that they must settle for a lower wage. In the meantime, they are looking for a job and perhaps even rejecting offers that are as good as they will ever find.

The high cost of reversing job decisions can lead to unemployment, just as the costs of reversing investment can cause investors to wait. Again, consider the closure of a Detroit automobile plant and the fate of the former workers. These workers face at least three options: They can wait for the plant to reopen, they can seek another job in Detroit, or they can move to a more prosperous part of the country. Which course of action is best?

It's not always easy to say which choice is best, yet the choice involves a costly-to-reverse decision. Once the house is sold and the belongings are packed and moved to Houston, it is costly to go back to Detroit. The unemployed autoworker, rather than moving to Houston, might wait for a while to see what happens, even if he knows the probability of finding a job in Houston is higher than in Detroit. Or if that person opens up a pet shop, it will be difficult to shift back into automobile manufacturing. So, when faced with these uncertainties, many workers simply bide their time until the future is clearer. Maybe they'll do some part-time or casual work (or maybe they'll put a new deck on the house), but they probably won't be employed at full productivity. The result is ongoing unemployment, or at least underemployment, and again the initial negative real shock is magnified.

In sum, changes to the world require people to adjust their jobs and their careers. People can't always make those adjustments right away, and in the meantime output and employment will be lower than normal.

Time Bunching and Network Effects

People often bunch their activities at common points in time. Most people work from 9 AM to 5 PM rather than from 10 PM to 6 AM. One reason is that these are daylight hours, but another reason is because everyone else is working during this time. If you and your coworker are in the office at the same time, it is easier to collaborate. Furthermore, working is more fun when you do it with other people.

We also like to party at the same time and to see movies and concerts with other people. It's not just a question of fun—it is also economics. If you want to cook an elaborate meal, order some fancy bottles of wine, or clean up the house for a party, you want to make sure that enough people attend for those efforts to be worthwhile.

Most generally, many economic activities **bunch** or **cluster in time** because it pays to coordinate your economic actions with those of others. That just means that we want to be investing, producing, and selling at the same time that others are investing, producing, or selling. In short, economic activity tends to cluster together in time just as it clusters together in space. (What do we call a cluster of economic activity in space? A city.)

Time bunching is the tendency for economic activities to be coordinated at common points in time.

Bunching occurs across different time frames. There is bunching across the course of a single day; GDP grows more during the 9-to-5 hours than late at night, for example. But there is also bunching across weeks, months, and quarters. The "seasonal business cycle" is one form of economic clustering in time. The fourth quarter of the year—October through December—brings more economic activity than any other time. Production is higher, sales are higher, and GDP grows faster, relative to the other parts of the year. After Christmas is over, however, the party ends and GDP in the next period is typically lower. GDP also tends to grow slowly during the summer months. The point is not that we should abolish Christmas or summer vacation, but rather that seasonal cycles help us understand some features of regular business cycles.

Once some economic activity is moving in the upward or downward direction, other parts of economic activity tend to follow that momentum in order to gain the advantages of time bunching. The clustering of economic activity in time makes buying and selling more efficient, but it also causes shocks to spread through the economy and to spread through time. Let's say that a negative economic shock arrives and the economy slows down in the current period. Many people are less keen to work, and they will save up their working for some point in the future (intertemporal substitution, as discussed earlier). This effect will induce others to cut back on their work as well. If the Indian farmers work less when the weather is bad, then tractor salespeople will probably work less as well. Similarly, if fewer people are showing up at the office, you might be less productive as well. You'll be more likely to stay home and more likely to make your big work effort during some other period, perhaps when you expect the office to be up and running at full speed. So if some people retreat from full-speed work, these decisions spill over onto others and cause them to cut back their effort as well. The time bunching effect is magnified when production is organized in networks or supply chains. We gave an example in the last chapter. When the tire factory in China shuts down due to a strike or a natural disaster like the COVID-19 pandemic, then so does the U.S. automobile factory even if the automobile factory has no problems of its own. The tire factory also stops buying rubber, so shocks propagate upwards to suppliers and downwards to customers. Overall, the lesson is that fluctuations in key industries can ripple or cascade throughout an economy.

Supply chains and network effects become especially important when there are large shocks to supply or demand because a single failure along the supply chain can disrupt entire industries. When the demand for hand sanitizer skyrocketed with the COVID-19 pandemic, for example, one problem with producing more sanitizer was simply getting enough plastic bottles. Similarly, when we needed to run millions of tests for the virus, one bottleneck was finding enough cotton nose swabs.

Collateral Damage

"For whoever has, to him shall be given; and whoever has not, from him shall be taken even that which he seems to have" (Luke 8:18). In the parable of the lamp, Jesus was talking about knowledge but the message also applies to banking. Banks like to lend to people who already have lots of money. When banks lend to firms, they typically will insist that the firm have some cash on hand, strong assets, and positive net worth (assets > debts). As a rule, banks are more concerned about downside risk than upside gain because if the firm does poorly, the bank could lose the entire value of its loan, but if the firm does incredibly well (like Google), the bank simply gets its loan back plus interest. Banks, therefore, don't make a lot of investments in startups or firms with debts that exceed assets.

The bank's incentives make sense for the bank, but for the economy as a whole this type of behavior amplifies booms and busts. Consider a firm that makes televisions and that wants to expand into manufacturing computer monitors. The market for monitors is growing, the firm has expertise in electronics, and it has good contacts with retailers. The firm writes a business plan and applies to a bank for a loan. The firm is making lots of profits in its television division and, as a result, it has high net worth. The firm's net worth acts like a kind of **collateral** for the bank—a cushion or guarantee that even if the

Collateral is a valuable asset that helps to secure a loan. If the borrower defaults, ownership of the collateral transfers to the lender.

monitor division fails, the firm will still have cash to pay back the loan. Satisfied that the loan is safe, the bank makes the loan.

Now consider the same scenario during a recession. As before, we will assume that the market for computer monitors is growing and the firm, of course, still has the same expertise in electronics and contacts with retailers. What differs now is not the potential profitability of the monitor division. But the firm's television business is not going so well and, as a result, the firm has lower net worth and the bank has lost its safety cushion, a **collateral shock**. The bank now evaluates the loan as risky and says no. Now that the firm cannot expand into monitors, a growing field, it is left with a dying television division and it ends up going bankrupt and firing its workers. For whoever has, to him shall be given; and whoever has not, from him shall be taken.

More generally, during a boom, asset prices are increasing and firms have cash flow. As a result, banks are willing to approve more loans, which makes the boom even bigger. But as an economy enters the downward phase of business cycles, asset prices fall, cash flow is reduced, and firms have lower net worth. Lenders see loans as being riskier and they cut off or restrict credit. This process drives more firms under, increasing joblessness and making the bust worse.[1]

This scenario is a good example of how real shocks and aggregate demand shocks can reinforce and amplify one another. In general, the real shock mechanisms in this chapter involve lower wealth, greater risk, and greater difficulties of adjustment, in various combinations. Those same economic problems will mean lower consumer spending, less business investment, and also less borrowing and lending, all factors that will feed into lower aggregate demand.

Collateral shocks also affect consumers. Say John bought a house near Orlando, Florida, one center of the 2000–2006 real estate bubble, for $200,000. As was common practice at the time, suppose that John paid no money down, so he borrowed the entire purchase price, $200,000, from a bank. Once the real estate bubble burst and home prices fell, that same house suddenly was worth $120,000. Because the value of John's house is now less than what he owes on it, John is said to be "underwater," or John has negative equity in the house. It's difficult to get an exact estimate, but around the year 2010, nearly 20% of all American homes were underwater to some degree.

Now imagine that John receives a job offer in Houston, Texas, where the economy isn't as depressed as in Orlando. It's hard to rent out the Orlando house but it's also hard to sell it. If John sells the house, he has to pay roughly $200,000 back to the bank (the exact sum depends on how long ago the loan was taken out and how many payments the buyer has made in the interim). Yet the sale yields only $120,000, or less if you take brokerage commissions into account. In other words, John has to come up with $80,000 or more in cold hard cash. For a lot of people, that's extremely difficult to do, especially during a recession. The end result is that the move to Houston does not happen and John does not take the better job. "Underwater" positions make moving more difficult and the adjustment of the economy to business cycles is therefore slower.

An alternative scenario is that John takes the job in Houston and "mails in the keys." In other words, John defaults on his mortgage. The home, as a financial asset, has a value of negative $80,000 to John so walking away makes financial sense. John is better off but the bank is worse off. That is a transfer of wealth, but the problem is worse than this.

A **collateral shock** is a reduction in the value of collateral. Collateral shocks make borrowing and lending more difficult.

When many homeowners have no positive equity in their homes, and thus are "underwater," their incentive to maintain the value of those homes declines as the time of default approaches. They do less maintenance or may even abuse the property. If John is thinking that he might default in the near future, does he take tender, loving care of the flowers and garden? Does he check carefully for cracks in the walls and ceilings and have them repaired promptly? It is common that when banks have to foreclose, the bank loses 25% or even more of the value of that home.[2] It's also true that the value of other homes in the neighborhood declines when there are a lot of foreclosures nearby. In 2010 in the wake of the recession, about 1 in 12 houses with mortgages below $1 million were in foreclosure, so that is a lot of wealth being dissipated.

When the nominal owner of a property doesn't have much **equity** in the property, very often they don't do a good job taking care of the property. The lesson applies to more than just homes. We've talked about how the bank loses on these deals, so what happens if a bank made too many bad loans to too many insolvent homeowners? Well, then it's not just the home with low capital value—the bank itself has low capital value or sometimes it is said that the bank is thinly capitalized. And what do we know about individuals or organizations with low capital value? Return to the sentence earlier in this paragraph: "When the nominal owner of a property doesn't have much equity in the property, very often they don't do such a good job taking care of the property."

In other words, when the bank itself is "underwater" or nearly so, the bank managers don't do a very good job of taking care of the bank. No, they don't usually take out a sledgehammer, but there are other ways of eroding the capital value of a bank. Bank employees won't see the bank as a place for a career if it is tottering and, as a result, they won't invest in their relationship with the bank or its customers. The managers will fail to build up new business opportunities and they will take dubious risks, all in the knowledge that since the bank is already on the verge of destruction, they don't have to worry about the downside so much. Bank employees take the same "nothing left to lose" attitude as our defaulting homeowner. The banks with low capital values will not be run very well because there is little value to protect and the chance of "foreclosure" on the bank—in this case, called bankruptcy—is fairly high. Banks in this situation are commonly referred to as "zombie banks," and, indeed, during 2009–2010 the number of bank failures reached an all-time high.

The net result is this: When asset prices fall, there is a lot of collateral damage.

Takeaway

In sum, at least five factors amplify economic shocks and help bring about business downturns. Those factors are labor supply and intertemporal substitution, uncertainty and irreversible investment, labor adjustment costs, the desire to bunch or cluster economic activity together in time, and collateral shocks. The core lesson is this: A medium-sized negative economic shock is capable of causing a disproportionately large downturn in economic production and employment.

An owner's **equity** is the value of the asset minus the debt, $E = V - D$.

▶ **MRU**

mru.org/great-recession

The Great Recession

CHECK YOURSELF

- Immediately after 9/11, most U.S. companies eliminated business travel temporarily. After a few weeks, business travel started to pick up again. Which transmission mechanism came into play? Go through as many aspects of business travel as you can think of: air travel, transportation to and from airports, hotel stays, meals out, contact with people remaining back in the office. Explain how the unexpected near-cessation in business travel amplified the original shock.

CHAPTER REVIEW

Go online to practice with more examples of these types of problems, including live links to videos, data sources, and feedback.

▶ Problems with this icon relate to optional MRU videos.

KEY CONCEPTS

intertemporal substitution, p. 318

irreversible investments, p. 320

labor adjustment costs, p. 320

time bunching, p. 321

collateral, p. 322

collateral shock, p. 323

equity, p. 324

FACTS AND TOOLS

1. Take a look at Figure 9 in the previous chapter. In the past few decades, what has usually happened to the price of oil just before or during a recession?

2. When oil price shocks force people to switch jobs, how much GDP are they producing when they are out of work?

Discovering DATA ✦✦

3. Banks require a valuable asset, or collateral, to be pledged to secure a loan. Using the FRED economic database (https://fred.stlouisfed.org/), find the chart for the Percent of Value of Loans Secured by Collateral for Commercial Banks.

a. In the years prior to 2014, what was the (approximate) average percent of loan value secured by collateral?

b. In 2019, what was the average percent of loan value secured by collateral?

c. What does this change indicate about how willing commercial banks were to lend in 2019 compared with earlier years?

4. When an investment is irreversible, are you likely to a decision about it in a hurry or wait until more information comes in?

5. When do you want to study for a test: when your friends are studying for the same test or when they are not? How can this help explain seasonal business fluctuations?

▶ 6. If the long-run aggregate supply curve increased because of a sudden fall in the price of oil, what would happen to inflation? Assume that spending growth (aggregate demand) does not change—only the LRAS curve shifts. Draw the shift in the following figure. (*Note*: In the real world, this happens fairly often. Big declines in the price of oil happened in 1986 and again in 1998, and the price of oil fell by 50% in late 2008.)

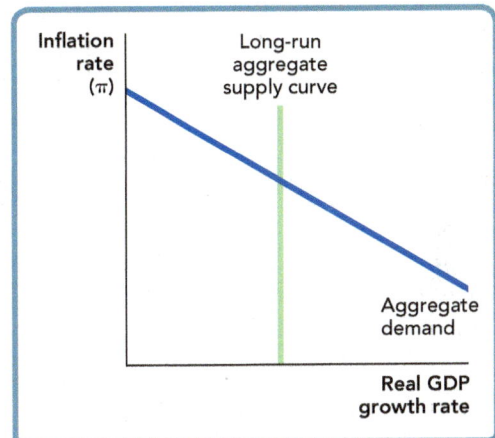

7. Office buildings have a boom-bust cycle every day. At what hours of the weekday do grocery stores have an economic boom? What days of the week do shopping malls have an economic boom?

THINKING AND PROBLEM SOLVING

8. In India, the economy grows faster when there's a lot of rain and grows more slowly when there is a drought. This creates big fluctuations in the economy. If the government wrote laws to smooth out these fluctuations by paying people to work more in the dry years and by taxing people so that they would work less in the heavy-rain years, would that make the average Indian better off? Why or why not? (Keep your

answer in mind during the next recession, when pundits and politicians recommend tax breaks to encourage more hiring.)

9. **a.** According to Figure 10 in the previous chapter, about how long does it take for an oil price shock to have its biggest impact on the economy? How long does it take before the oil shock's effects completely go away?

   b. What might be happening in the labor market that might explain why it takes so long for an oil shock to do its worst?

   (Glance through the transmission mechanisms listed in the chapter for some ideas.)

10. When would a restaurant owner prefer to open a new restaurant: one year after an oil shock hits or two years after the oil shock hits?

11. How is marriage like a decision to build a new factory? Which decision is easier to reverse?

12. **a.** Who would you be more likely to hire at your company: someone who has stayed in the same career for years, or someone who tries an entirely new career every time they become unhappy with their job?

    b. How does this help explain why workers are reluctant to quickly move on to a new career when they get laid off?

13. People sometimes use the expression, "Kicking the can down the road." It refers to putting a big decision off until later—it's almost (but not quite!) a synonym for procrastinating, and it's usually used in a negative sense. "Fred graduated and decided to spend a year waiting tables in New York. Grad school? He's kicking the can down the road on that one." What economic idea is equivalent to "kicking the can down the road," and how can it be a good thing?

14. As we note in the chapter, an oil price shock will probably increase the size of an oil-centered city like Houston, Texas. During the time that people are moving to Houston, looking for jobs, and switching jobs to find the best job possible, do you think GDP will be lower than usual or higher than usual? (Try focusing on the *production* part of GDP in answering this question.)

15. Can you think of some reasons why the following examples of time bunching and intertemporal substitution might be true? (Yes, you'll notice that there's a blurry line between the two.)

    a. People who work outside work more when the weather is good.

    b. People work when others are also working.

    c. Even nonreligious people who don't give gifts shop more as Christmas time approaches.

    d. Food servers at a restaurant prefer to work the dinner shift.

    What do all of these examples have to do with the business cycle?

16. Consider the following economic events. Which of them will have the effect of amplifying a negative real shock and which are intended to offset a shock?

    a. Several large financial institutions become insolvent as a housing bubble bursts and subprime mortgages begin to default in large numbers.

    b. Many financial institutions begin issuing fewer loans and increasing their excess reserve holdings in anticipation of higher default rates on existing loans.

    c. The Federal Reserve expands the money supply and lowers interest rates.

    d. Instead of building for future demand, home builders delay their usual building so they can wait and see whether demand increases.

    e. As unemployment rises, consumers begin cutting back on their expenditures and paying down personal debt.

    f. The government passes a stimulus package increasing spending on roads and other infrastructure.

    g. Firms accumulate cash reserves and delay expansion projects pending the outcome of potential government actions influencing business conditions.

    h. Students decide to stay in college for longer periods of time due to the poor job market, and older workers retire early.

Discovering DATA ::

17. When a borrower fails to make a scheduled payment on a mortgage, the mortgage is called delinquent. Delinquency is the first step toward foreclosure. Using the FRED economic database (https://fred.stlouisfed.org/), find the chart for the Delinquency Rate on Single-Family Residential Mortgages in the United States.

    a. What was the approximate delinquency rate in a typical year prior to the 2008–2009 recession?

    b. What was the peak delinquency rate and when?

    c. What was the delinquency rate in 2019? Compare this rate with prerecession levels.

CHALLENGES

18. In 1971, Intel invented the first computer micro-processor. In early 1993, the National Center for Supercomputing Applications released the first Web browser, Mosaic (which later became Netscape). Both inventions seem like good news, and both inventions created great uncertainty about which business models would succeed in the future: They were game changers. Would these uncertainty-creating inventions encourage businesses to make massive investments quickly, or would they encourage businesses to wait a few years to see how it all pans out?

Boyan Jovanovic and his coauthors discuss this topic in several papers. For an introduction, see Bart Hobijn and Boyan Jovanovic, 2001. The information-technology revolution and the stock market: Evidence. *American Economic Review* 91(5): 1203–1220.

19. For the sake of the economy, should the government ban Christmas and instead encourage people to give gifts throughout the year? Why or why not?

20. How is the previous question similar to this question: Should the government encourage people to move from the East and West coasts to the Midwest and Rocky Mountain states, where the population is less dense?

21. Do workers *choose* to work more *because* wages are temporarily high and do workers *choose* to work less *because* wages are temporarily low? This is key to the "intertemporal substitution" story of this chapter. The following chart shows how much wages change in the short run: Except in the 1970s, the moves are almost always in a 2% range, running from 1% higher than average to 1% lower than average.

So, when wages move up or down for a year or two, does the number of Americans working move in the same direction at the same time? Let's see. The following economic simulation is based on actual U.S. data and shows how a 1% rise in wages usually impacts the number of Americans employed. Sometimes the effect is bigger than this, and sometimes smaller, but this is the average.

In practice, a 1% rise in wages apparently causes a 0.2% rise in the number of Americans with jobs. It takes nine months for this to happen.

How much would wages have to rise to raise employment by 1% or 2%, according to these estimates? (*Note:* This is roughly how much employment rises during a boom.) Is this "wage-channel" effect large enough to explain most of the job fluctuations we see during real-world business cycles?

22. a. If long-run aggregate supply shocks do largely explain business fluctuation, while the aggregate demand curve mostly stays fixed, then should prices be higher than usual or lower than usual during a recession?

b. The following chart portrays historical U.S. data on the relationship between the price level and real GDP. If you take a look at the big swings in the 1970s and early 1980s, especially during recessions, do the data roughly suggest that long-run aggregate supply curve shocks or aggregate demand shocks were the primary disturbance?

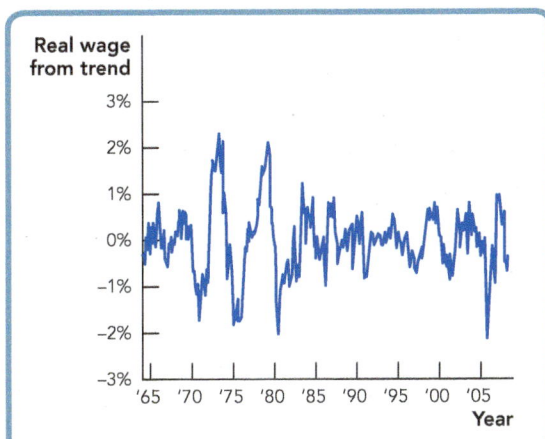

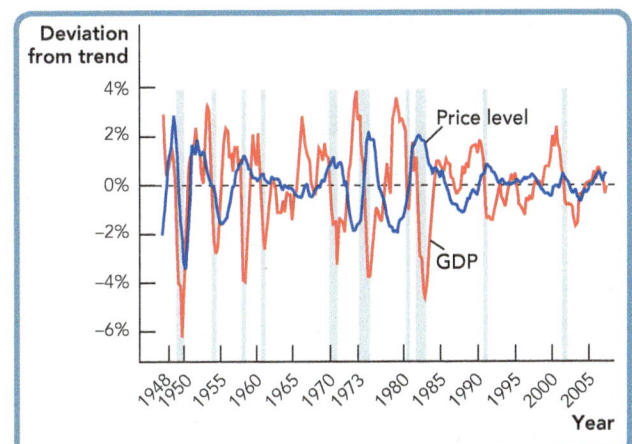

(Data from: U.S. Bureau of Economic Analysis and author calculations.)

23. In the context of this chapter, identify what each of the following scenarios has in common and explain how they will affect an economy suffering from a recession.

   a. Joe and Julie married, saved, and bought a modest home several years ago when housing prices were rising. They love their home and its location, are now expecting their second child, and need more space. Financially, they can afford a larger house payment, or a second mortgage, but their bank has informed them that despite their significant down payment, they are ineligible for a home equity loan because the current value of their home has declined to below the balance on their mortgage.

   b. A bank has many potential borrowers with good prospects but due to problems with previous real estate loans, it has begun to build up its excess reserves in order to strengthen its balance sheets in the event of defaults on those assets.

   c. A car dealership finds itself in the path of a tornado that destroys all of its stock of both used and new cars. Sales have been good because the recession has mostly spared this region of the country, but the dealership's insurance does not cover weather-related events and the dealer now has no assets and a negative net worth.

Discovering DATA ⁘

24. Capacity utilization is an estimate of how close an economy is to its maximum output, defined as the highest level of output sustainable given its resources. Using the FRED economic database (https://fred.stlouisfed.org/), search for a series on capacity utilization and graph it.

   a. Capacity utilization has never been measured at 100%. Why might an economy be at less than 100% capacity utilization even in good times?

   b. What was the capacity utilization level in January of 2008 and what about in June of 2009?

   c. What was happening to unemployment between January of 2008 and 2009?

   d. Suppose that wages are sticky but that other prices are flexible. Comment on how sticky wages may contribute to reduced capacity utilization.

WORK IT OUT

For interactive, step-by-step help in solving this problem, go online.

In the chapter, we discussed how intertemporal substitution can amplify a boom by causing people to work more and by causing more people to work (while the reverse is true in a recession). Capital is also subject to intertemporal substitution. For example, it's possible to run a factory at close to capacity in one period, while putting off maintenance to a later period. How do you think capacity utilization varies across the business cycle? Is capacity utilization procyclical (varies positively with GDP) or countercyclical (varies negatively with GDP)?

▶ MRU VIDEOS

Five Minutes on Real Business Cycle Theory

mru.org/rbc

Problem: **6**

The Great Recession

mru.org/great-recession

Problem: **16**

CHAPTER 14 APPENDIX

Business Fluctuations and the Solow Model

A way of summarizing some of the lessons of this chapter is that at least some business fluctuations are just economic growth in the short run. Economic growth happens in fits and starts rather than smoothly. The economists Finn Kydland and Edward Prescott developed key aspects of the real business cycle (RBC) model in the 1980s and were awarded the Nobel Prize in 2004 for their work. One advantage of thinking about business fluctuations in this way is that they can then be analyzed using a version of the Solow growth model called the real business cycle (RBC) model. A complete understanding of the real business cycle model requires quite a bit of advanced mathematics, but we can briefly describe the main ideas. Consider the following production function, which is just like that used in Chapter 8 but with the addition of labor as well as capital:

$$Y = A_t \times F(K, L)$$

To recap, output Y is a function of the inputs of capital K and labor L. In the earlier chapter, we talked about the A factor as an index of ideas. Better ideas mean a larger A, which means that more output can be produced from the same inputs of capital and labor. That is a good interpretation of A in the long run, but we can also think about A as representing *any* factor that influences the productivity of K and L. Thus, if Y is the output of corn, then A could be deviations of rainfall from the average. Above-average rainfall, say, $A = 2$, means that the inputs of K and L produce a lot of corn. Below-average rainfall, say, $A = \frac{1}{2}$, means that the same inputs of K and L produce less corn.

When we are thinking about long-run economic growth, it doesn't hurt to simplify and think about A as increasing smoothly through time. To analyze business fluctuations, however, we need to recognize that A jumps around. Thus, in the business fluctuation, or RBC, model, A is a productivity shock variable.

The second complication we need to add to the Solow growth model to analyze business fluctuations is to give a more sophisticated account of investment and labor supply. In the Solow growth model, investment is a simple function of output, Investment $= \gamma Y$, where the investment rate γ is a constant proportion like 0.3. That's not a very realistic assumption. Will savers and investors want to invest the same proportion of output during a recession as during a boom? Probably not, for the reasons we discussed in the chapter (uncertainty, for example). How do savers and investors decide how much and when to invest? This is a complicated decision that requires savers and investors to forecast future events. Solving this problem is difficult, which is where the complicated mathematics come in, but we know that γ will vary over time.

Similarly, in the growth version of the Solow model, we assumed that L was population and that L was fixed. (It's also easy to think about L as increasing slowly and steadily.) But in the short run, we need to recognize that workers may choose to enter or exit the workforce and choose to take jobs or search for work—intertemporal substitution. As a result, L becomes the labor force and L can change due to changes in the participation rate and the unemployment rate. How do workers decide how much and when to work? Again, this is a complicated decision that requires workers to forecast the future and carefully optimize.

Adding shocks to the Solow model and giving a more sophisticated account of how savers, investors, and workers make decisions create what is known as the real business cycle model or the standard "neoclassical" model of business cycles. The intuitive account of business fluctuations that we have given in this chapter is based on this model.[*]

Explaining a full RBC model is too advanced for this appendix, but we recall that we showed how to simulate the Solow model using Excel in the appendix to Chapter 8. We can easily modify that model to include productivity shocks. Figure A14.1 shows our Excel model with a new column (column B) labeled A. Excel's RAND( ) formula creates a random number between 0 and 1. If we want a number between X and Y, we can write $= \text{RAND}( )*(Y - X) + X$. We will use our random number as a productivity shock A_t, so we want a number that can be a little bigger than 1 or a little smaller than 1. Thus, when we get a random number that is greater than 1, that is a positive productivity shock (output increases), and when we get a random number that is less than 1, that is a negative productivity shock (output decreases). Thus, we input into cell $B2 = \text{RAND}( )*(1/0.95 - 0.95) + 0.95$, which creates a random number between $1/0.95$ and 0.95; over many draws this random number is designed so that it will average out to approximately 1. We now modify our output formula in D2 so it reads $= B2*C2\wedge(1/2)$; in other words, we multiply the contribution of capital $(C2\wedge 1/2)$ by the productivity shock A_t, which we generated in column B.

FIGURE A14.1

		B2	▼	f_x =RAND()*(1/0.95-0.95)+0.95							
	A	B	C	D	E	F	G	H	I	J
1	Time	A	Capital K	Output	Investment	Depreciation	Capital Growth	Y Growth	Investment Share γ	Depreciation δ
2	1	0.956905382	200	13.53	4.06	4.00	0.06		0.3	0.02
3	2	0.967909022	200.06	13.69	4.11	4.00	0.11	1.17		
4	3	0.983678593	200.17	13.92	4.18	4.00	0.17	1.66		
5	4	0.952410981	200.34	13.48	4.04	4.01	0.04	-3.14		
6	5	1.018061434	200.37	14.41	4.32	4.01	0.32	6.90		
7	6	1.036326744	200.69	14.68	4.40	4.01	0.39	1.87		
8	7	0.976878889	201.08	13.85	4.16	4.02	0.13	-5.64		
9	8	0.990237834	201.22	14.05	4.21	4.02	0.19	1.40		
10	9	0.963290803	201.41	13.67	4.10	4.03	0.07	-2.68		
11	10	0.994149412	201.48	14.11	4.23	4.03	0.20	3.22		
12	11	1.041301257	201.68	14.79	4.44	4.03	0.40	4.80		
13	12	1.028858954	202.08	14.63	4.39	4.04	0.35	-1.10		
14	13	0.995156067	202.43	14.16	4.25	4.05	0.20	-3.19		
15	14	0.953711687	202.63	13.58	4.07	4.05	0.02	-4.12		
16	15	0.984056799	202.65	14.01	4.20	4.05	0.15	3.19		
		⋮								
377	376	0.997989023	225.44	14.98	4.50	4.51	-0.01	3.46		
378	377	0.973955736	225.42	14.62	4.39	4.51	-0.12	-2.41		
379	378	1.032046001	225.30	15.49	4.65	4.51	0.14	5.94		
380	379	0.961868177	225.44	14.44	4.33	4.51	-0.18	-6.77		
381	380	0.982599886	225.27	14.75	4.42	4.51	-0.08	2.12		

[*] For a more complete but still accessible explanation of this model, see Plosser, Charles I. Summer 1989. Understanding real business cycles. *Journal of Economic Perspectives* 3(3): 51–77.

This model works very much like the Solow model in Chapter 8, but now the random shocks increase or decrease growth around the average Solow growth rate. Figure A14.2, for example, simulates 100 periods of the Solow model around the equilibrium output of 15. Notice how shocks can generate business fluctuations.

FIGURE A14.2

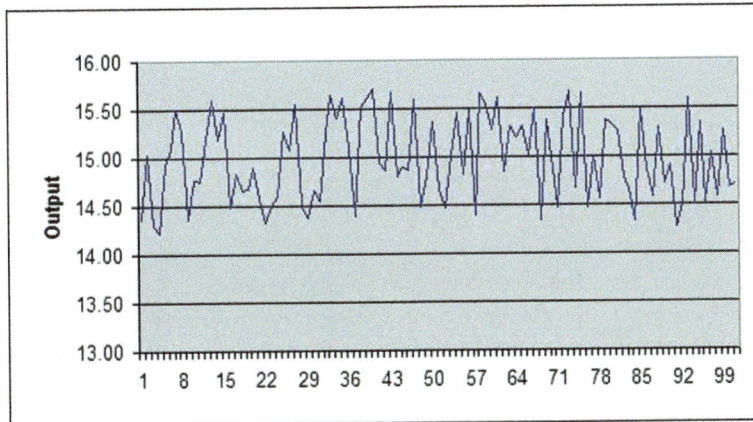

The Solow Model with Shocks

15

The Federal Reserve System and Open Market Operations

Imagine that you wanted to borrow $2 *trillion*. Whom would you ask? In 2008, the worldwide financial system was in a crisis and banks and other financial institutions wanted to borrow more than $2 trillion—they turned to the only person in the world capable of lending that kind of money, a mild-mannered, former professor of economics named Ben Bernanke. As chairman of the Federal Reserve System (the Fed), Bernanke was sometimes said to be the second most powerful person in the world, after the president of the United States. Bernanke was able to make the loans because he could draw on the awesome power of the Federal Reserve Bank to create money.

What is the Federal Reserve? How does it create money? What does it use its power for?

If you read this chapter, you'll come away with an understanding of the Federal Reserve and its powers. The quick and dirty answer is that through its influence over the money supply, the Federal Reserve usually has more influence over aggregate demand than any other institution and shifts in aggregate demand can greatly influence the economy in the short run (as we first showed in Chapter 13). So, let's take a look at the Federal Reserve System first, then examine what is meant by the money supply, and finally focus on the tools that the Fed uses to influence the money supply, aggregate demand, and the economy.

CHAPTER OUTLINE

What Is the Federal Reserve System?

The U.S. Money Supplies

Fractional Reserve Banking, the Reserve Ratio, and the Money Multiplier

How the Fed Controls the Money Supply

The Federal Reserve Is the Lender of Last Resort

Revisiting Aggregate Demand and Monetary Policy

Who Controls the Fed?

Takeaway

Appendix: The Money Multiplier Process in Detail

▶ **MRU** Videos

- The U.S. Money Supplies
- How the Fed Works: Before the Great Recession
- How the Fed Works: After the Great Recession
- The Federal Reserve as Lender of Last Resort

What Is the Federal Reserve System?

The Federal Reserve acquires its unique powers through its ability to issue money. Open your wallet or your purse and take a look at some bills. At the top, you will see the words "Federal Reserve Note." In the past, many banks issued their own bank notes, which were used as money. But today the money we use in the United States is provided by just one bank, the Federal Reserve. Thus, the Federal Reserve has the power to create money—an awesome power that forms the centerpiece of this chapter. The Fed doesn't have to literally print money. It can, as we shall see, also create money "by computer" by adding reserves to bank accounts held at the Fed. This new money can then be lent out in a way that increases aggregate demand.

If the Federal Reserve is a bank, who are its customers? The Fed is both the government's bank and the banker's bank. As the government's bank, the Fed maintains the bank account of the U.S. Treasury. When you write a check to the IRS to pay your taxes, the money ends up in the Treasury's account at the Fed. In addition to receiving money, the U.S. Treasury also borrows a lot of money and the Fed manages this borrowing—that is, the Fed manages the issuing, transferring, and redeeming of U.S. Treasury bonds, bills, and notes. Since the U.S. Treasury is by far the world's largest bank customer—it has more income and it also borrows more than any other bank customer—the Federal Reserve is a large and powerful bank.

In addition, the Fed is also the bankers' bank. Large private banks keep their own accounts at the Fed—in part, because some banks are required to hold accounts with the Federal Reserve and in part because other banks and financial institutions want a safe and convenient place to hold their money. The Fed also regulates other banks and it lends money to other banks. Finally, the Fed manages the nation's payment system—the system of accounts that makes it possible to write checks from one bank to another—and it protects financial consumers with disclosure regulations. Many of these and other duties are shared with other state and federal agencies.

Now that we know what the Fed is, let's turn to its most important function: regulating the U.S. money supply. But first we have to understand what the money supply is.

The U.S. Money Supplies

Just about everyone expects to be paid in money. If you show up with money—at least in its appropriate form—hardly anyone will turn you away. In other words, **money** is a widely accepted means of payment.

Money is a widely accepted means of payment.

But money is more than cash. Cash, or currency, is paper bills and coins, which serve as a quick and efficient way of making small transactions. But currency is not so useful for larger transactions, especially between businesses. Often it is easier to pay by check or debit card (which can be thought of as an electronic check) or by credit card (and then pay your bill later by check). For larger purchases, you might transfer money from a savings account to a checking account and then pay by check or debit. All these means of payment are money but they are not currency.

The most important assets that serve as means of payment in the United States today are:

1. Currency—paper bills and coins.
2. Total reserves held by banks at the Fed.
3. Checkable deposits—your checking or debit account.
4. Savings deposits, money market mutual funds, and small-time deposits.

Figure 15.1 shows the magnitude and proportions of the major means of payment in the United States (there are also some smaller items, such as traveler's checks, that we have omitted).

Let's say a few words about each of these means of payment. Currency is coins and paper bills (Federal Reserve Notes) held by people and nonbank firms. If you look at the total for currency (almost $1.7 trillion) and divide it

FIGURE 15.1

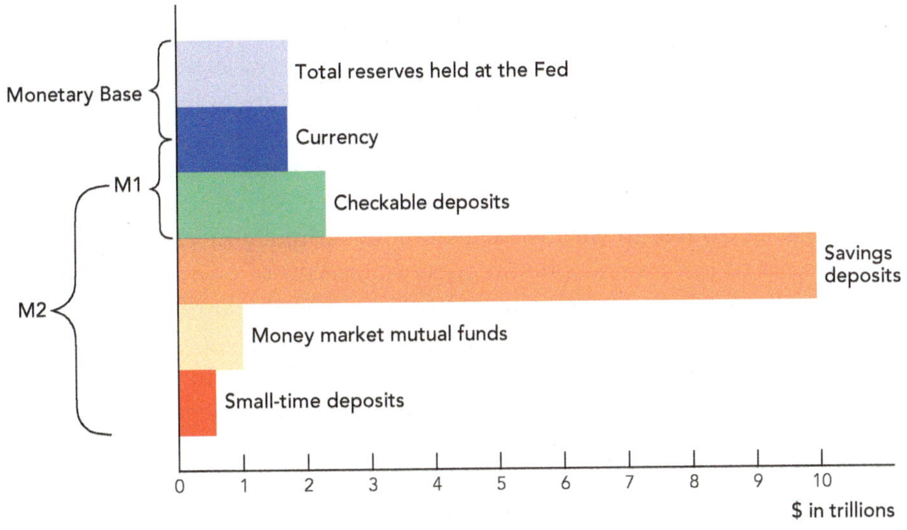

The U.S. Money Supplies

Data from: Board of Governors of the Federal Reserve System, February 2020.

by the American population (about 329 million), that amounts to about $5,200 per person (and even more per adult). Who has this much cash on hand? Of course, some of the money is in cash registers and some drug dealers do hold a lot of cash, but the real explanation for why so much U.S. cash exists is that quite a bit is used in other countries. Panama, Ecuador, and El Salvador all use the U.S. dollar as their official currency, as do some other small nations like the Republic of Palau. Dollars are also used unofficially in many other unstable countries as a means of preserving and protecting wealth. When Iraqi dictator Saddam Hussein was captured, he had $750,000 in U.S. hundred dollar bills in his hideaway.

"Total reserves" held by banks at the Fed is the means of payment you probably don't have personal experience with, but total reserves play a very important role in the financial system. All major banks have accounts at the Federal Reserve System—accounts that they use for trading with other major banks and for dealings with the Fed itself. It's not currency in these accounts but electronic claims that can be converted into currency if the bank wishes.

Checkable deposits are just like they sound, namely deposits that you can write checks on or can access with a debit card. These are the sorts of deposits we use most often in making daily transactions. Often these are also called demand deposits because you can access this money "on demand."

The largest means of payment are savings accounts, money market mutual funds, and small time deposits (also called certificates of deposit or CDs). Each of these components can be used to pay for goods and services, but typically with a little bit of extra work or trouble. Payments from a savings account can be made, for example, by first transferring the money to a checkable account. A money market mutual fund is a mutual fund invested in relatively safe short-term debt and government securities. Money market mutual funds typically allow you to write some number of checks per year or you can always sell part of your fund and transfer the money to a checkable account. Small time deposits cannot be withdrawn without penalty before a certain time period has elapsed, usually six months or a year.

A **liquid asset** is an asset that can be used for payments or, quickly and without loss of value, be converted into an asset that can be used for payments. The more liquid the asset, the more easily it can serve as money. Currency is usually the most liquid asset since currency can be spent almost everywhere. Checkable deposits and reserves are also very liquid, since they can also be spent easily and they can be turned into currency without loss. Money market mutual funds and time deposits are less liquid since sometimes it takes time and a little bit of trouble to turn these assets into currency or checkable deposits. It's possible to use even less liquid assets as a means of payment (we will take your house in return for, say, a copy of this textbook), but it is inconvenient. Economists therefore have found that these components are the most useful for analyzing the effect of "money" on the economy. It should be clear, however, that the money supply can be defined in different ways depending on exactly which kinds of liquid assets are included in the definition.

Economists have created many definitions of the money supply. The three most important, as shown in Figure 15.1, are:

- The monetary base (MB): Currency and total reserves held at the Fed
- M1: Currency plus checkable deposits
- M2: M1 plus savings deposits, money market mutual funds, and small time deposits

The Fed has direct control only over the monetary base. But it's the other components of the money supply—M1 and M2—that have the most significant effects on aggregate demand. As we will discuss later in the chapter, the Fed can increase bank reserves, but if the banks aren't lending, the increase in reserves won't do much to increase aggregate demand.

More generally, the central bank tries to use its control over MB to influence M1 and M2, but there are many other influences on M1 and M2 so each monetary aggregate can shrink or grow independently of the others. The Fed ultimately wants to steer aggregate demand, but once again its steering is sometimes wobbly because, although M1 and M2 influence aggregate demand, there are also other influences.

To understand how the Fed influences M1 and M2 but also why its influence is sometimes tenuous, we must introduce the concepts of fractional reserve banking, the reserve ratio, and the money multiplier.

Fractional Reserve Banking, the Reserve Ratio, and the Money Multiplier

When you open a bank account, the teller doesn't take your money and put it into a box labeled with your name. Instead, the bank holds a *fraction* of your account balance in reserve—hence the term **fractional reserve banking**— and it uses the rest of your money to make loans.

Banks earn profit on these loans. So do you. Competition among banks to attract your funds means that if the bank lends out your money and charges 5% interest, the bank must share some of that return with you. The bank will pay you, say, 2% for providing the money that they lend. The bank doesn't just pay you interest, it also gives you useful services like check writing and check clearing, which are in part funded from bank

---

A **liquid asset** is an asset that can be used for payments or, quickly and without loss of value, be converted into an asset that can be used for payments.

CHECK YOURSELF

- Define the monetary base.
- What is the amount of currency in circulation compared to the amount of checkable deposits?

Under **fractional reserve banking**, banks hold only a fraction of deposits in reserve, lending the rest.

profits on loans. Of course, you don't get the full 5% return because the bank is bearing the risk on the loans, plus paying the costs of making the loans and monitoring the loan borrowers.

How much does the bank keep in reserve and how much does it lend? Banks need reserves to meet ordinary depositor demands for currency and payment services. Who would patronize a bank where the ATM was always empty? A variety of regulations (Basel III and Dodd–Frank, if you must know) also encourage banks to hold low-risk, high-quality assets such as reserves. On the other hand, banks don't want to hold too many reserves because money held in reserve isn't being lent and lending is how banks earn most of their profits. Thus, there are opportunity costs to holding onto reserves. Banks balance these benefits and costs and thus they decide on the ratio between reserves and deposits. We define the **reserve ratio, RR**, as the ratio of reserves to deposits. If $1 in cash is held in reserve for every $10 of deposits, the reserve ratio is 1/10.

The reserve ratio is determined primarily by how liquid banks wish to be, with some constraints imposed by regulation. When banks are worried that depositors might want to withdraw their cash or when loans don't seem so profitable anyway, they want a reserve ratio that is relatively high; when banks aren't worried about depositors demanding cash and when loans are profitable, they want to have a relatively low reserve ratio.

It's also useful to work with the inverse of the reserve ratio, called the **money multiplier, MM**. The money multiplier is the ratio of deposits to reserves, or in this case 10. Why is it called the money multiplier? Imagine that the Federal Reserve creates $1,000 of new money by crediting your bank account with an additional $1,000. Does that sound incredible? In fact, the Fed can create new money at will either by printing it or—the more modern method— by adding numbers to bank accounts held at the Fed. As we shall see, the Federal Reserve creates billions of dollars in just this way on a regular basis. So let's imagine that your bank account has been credited with an additional $1,000. Your bank now has $1,000 in extra reserves, but remember that banks don't want to keep all of their depositors' money in reserve. Banks make a profit by lending so now that your bank has extra reserves, it will also feel comfortable making more loans. To restore its reserve ratio to 1/10, your bank will want to keep $100 in reserve and make additional loans of $900. So let's say it lends $900 to Sam.

Now here's where it gets tricky. You have an extra $1,000 in your account but in addition Sam now has an extra $900 in his bank account, which we will assume is held at another bank. Now Sam's bank has an extra $900, but it too doesn't want to hold all of its new money in reserves so it will keep $90 in reserve and make $810 in new loans—thus, the bank's reserve ratio stays at 1/10. The process does not stop there as Sam's bank now lends money to Tom and Tom's bank lends money to Dick and . . . well you get the idea. This process keeps going through a ripple effect as one bank increases its loans, leading to an increase in deposits in another bank, which in turn increases its loans, which leads to an increase in deposits in another bank, which increases its loans . . . and so forth.

What is the end result of the ripple process? There are two ways to see the end result, the long way and the shortcut. We are going to save the long way for the appendix. Here's the shortcut. If banks want a reserve ratio of 1/10, then when the Federal Reserve increases reserves by $1,000, deposits must ultimately increase by $10,000. Now remember that the money multiplier is the inverse of the reserve ratio, or 10. Did you notice that deposits eventually

The **reserve ratio, RR,** is the ratio of reserves to deposits.

The **money multiplier, MM,** is the amount the money supply expands with each dollar increase in reserves. MM = 1/RR.

mru.org/money-supply

The U.S. Money Supplies

increase by the increase in reserves *multiplied* by the money multiplier? That's why it's called the money multiplier.

Let's summarize: The money multiplier tells us how much deposits expand with each dollar increase in reserves. If the money multiplier is 10, for example, then an increase in reserves of $1,000 will lead to an increase in deposits of $10,000. Since checkable deposits are part of the money supply (M1 and M2), we can also say that an increase in reserves of $1,000 increases the money supply by $10,000. Thus, we have

Change in money supply = Change in reserves × Money multiplier

or

$$\Delta MS = \Delta \text{Reserves} \times \text{MM}$$

CHECK YOURSELF

- If the reserve ratio is 1/20, what percent of deposits is kept as reserves?
- If the reserve ratio is 1/20, what is the money multiplier?
- If the Fed increases bank reserves by $10,000 and the banking system has a reserve ratio of 1/20, what is the change in the money supply?

How the Fed Controls the Money Supply

Now that we have seen what the money supply is and why the money multiplier multiplies a change in reserves, let's look at the two major tools the Fed uses to control the money supply. These are:

1. Open market operations—the buying and selling of (usually) short-term U.S. government bonds on the open market
2. Paying interest on reserves held by banks at the Fed

Open Market Operations

Suppose that the Federal Reserve wants to increase the money supply. How does it do it? As explained earlier, if the Fed wants to create money, it can simply print money or add numbers to bank accounts. But how does the new money find its way into the economy? Imagine, for example, that the Fed added money to its own bank account and bought apples with the new money. At first, the money would flow to apple farmers and then the apple farmers would buy more tractors and television sets and vacations, and the money would flow out to other people who themselves would buy more goods. In this way, the Fed's increase in the money supply would spread throughout the economy. And if the Fed wanted to reduce the money supply, it could sell some of the apples that it had bought earlier.

The Fed, however, doesn't want to buy and sell apples. Apples are difficult to store, expensive to ship, and available in very large quantities during only part of the year. So instead of apples, the Fed buys and sells government bonds, usually short-term bonds called Treasury bills or T-bills (these are also often called Treasury securities or "Treasuries"). Government bonds can be stored and shipped electronically and the market for government bonds is liquid and deep, which means that the Fed can easily buy and sell billions of dollars' worth of government bonds in a matter of minutes.

Open market operations occur when the Fed buys or sells government bonds.

So, if the Fed wants to change the money supply, it usually does so by buying or selling government bonds. This is called an **open market operation**. To pay for the T-bills, the Fed electronically increases the reserves of the seller, usually a bank or a large dealer in Treasury securities. With more reserves on hand, that bank will respond by increasing its loans beginning the ripple process just described. That is, banks will make additional loans, the loans will in turn be used to buy goods and pay wages, and people will deposit some of these payments into other banks. The new deposits will increase the reserves of these other banks, which will now also be able to make more loans. Thus, the purchase of bonds by the Federal Reserve leads to a ripple process of increasing deposits, loans, deposits, loans, deposits, more loans, and so forth.

We noted earlier that the change in the money supply is equal to the change in reserves multiplied by the money multiplier, $\Delta MS = \Delta \text{Reserves} \times \text{MM}$. It's important to remember, however, that the size of the money multiplier is not fixed. The multiplier is the inverse of the reserve ratio and the reserve ratio is determined by banks. When banks are confident and eager to lend, they will want to keep their reserves relatively low so the money multiplier will be large ($\text{MM} = 1/\text{RR}$). In this case, small changes in reserves will have a relatively large effect on the money supply.

But when banks are fearful and reluctant to lend—that is, they wish to hold a high level of reserves—the money multiplier will be low and a change in the monetary base need not change the broader monetary aggregates much at all.

Thus, even though the Fed controls the monetary base, the Fed may not know how much or how quickly changes in the base will change loans and the broader measures of the money supply.

Summarizing, (1) the Federal Reserve can increase or decrease reserves at banks by buying or selling government bonds, (2) the increase in reserves boosts the money supply through a multiplier process, and (3) the size of the multiplier is not fixed but depends on how much of their assets the banks want to hold as reserves.

Open Market Operations and Interest Rates

Conducting monetary policy by buying and selling government bonds rather than, say, apples has another advantage. You may recall from Chapter 9 that bond prices and interest rates are inversely related: When bond prices go up, that is another way of saying interest rates go down, and when bond prices go down, that means interest rates go up. Thus, when the Fed buys or sells bonds, it changes the monetary base and influences interest rates at the same time. Let's go through this in more detail.

When the Fed buys bonds, it increases the demand for bonds, which pushes up the price of bonds, thus lowering the interest rate. So, buying bonds stimulates the economy through two distinct mechanisms, namely higher money supplies and lower interest rates. In a sense, the increase in the money supply increases the supply of loans and the lower interest rates increase the quantity of loans demanded.

When the Fed sells bonds, the process works in reverse. Selling bonds reduces the money supply as people give up their reserves to buy the bonds. Selling bonds also lowers the price of bonds, which means that interest rates increase. Instead of stimulating the economy, an open-market sale of bonds will slow the economy.

When you hear that "the Fed has lowered (or raised) interest rates," do not be confused. The Fed does not "set" interest rates in the same way that the owner of a New York bodega "sets" the price of milk in the store. Instead, interest rates are determined in a broad market through the supply and demand for loans as outlined in Chapter 9. The Fed works through supply and demand, and if the Fed wants short-term interest rates to fall, it has to buy more bonds, thereby influencing market prices.

MRU

mru.org/fed-pre-2008

How the Fed Works: Before the Great Recession

The Fed Controls a Real Rate Only in the Short Run Lending and borrowing decisions depend on the real interest rate, the interest rate after inflation has been taken into account (see Chapter 12). It's important to understand, therefore, that the Fed has influence on real interest rates only in the short run. Remember that money is neutral in the long run—that neutrality includes real interest rates. Similarly, remember from Chapter 13 that an increase in aggregate demand (AD) increases the real growth rate only in the short run. Thus, the long-run neutrality of money, the long-run neutrality of aggregate demand, and the long-run neutrality of Federal Reserve influence over real rates are all different sides of the same "coin."

The Fed has the most influence over a short-term interest rate called the Federal Funds rate. The **Federal Funds rate** is simply the *overnight* rate (that's really short term!) for a loan from one major bank to another. Banks lend not only to entrepreneurs, consumers, and home buyers but also to other banks and financial institutions.

> The **Federal Funds rate** is the overnight lending rate from one major bank to another.

Jekyll Island Club—Creation of the Fed The Federal Reserve has been a controversial institution in American politics ever since the secret 1910 meeting on Jekyll Island, where plans were drafted for the central bank.

Since the Federal Reserve can easily change the reserves of major banks through open market operations, it can exercise especially tight control over the Federal Funds rate. In fact, monetary policy is usually conducted in terms of the Federal Funds rate. For example, instead of deciding to increase the money supply by $50 billion, the Fed might decide to reduce the Federal Funds rate by a quarter of a percentage point—the Fed will then buy bonds until the Federal Funds rate drops by a quarter of a point. Similarly, if the Fed wants to increase the Federal Funds rate, it will sell bonds until the Federal Funds rate increases by the desired amount.

Quantitative Easing The Fed usually focuses on the Federal Funds rate because it is a convenient signal of monetary policy, it responds very quickly to actions by the Fed, and it can be monitored on a day-to-day basis. During the recession of 2008–2009, however, the Fed dramatically increased the supply of reserves—so much so that it pushed the Federal Funds rate very close to zero. In fact, between January 2009 and December 2016 the Federal Funds rate was kept below 0.5%. When the Federal Funds rate is close to zero, it is said to be at or near the **zero lower bound**.

> When the Federal Funds rate is close to zero, it is said to be near the **zero lower bound**.

In 2009, the Fed pushed the Federal Funds rate to near the zero lower bound, and still the economy wasn't booming. So, in order to push longer-term interest rates down, the Fed moved from primarily buying and selling the short-term debt of the federal government to also buying and selling longer-term government bonds in the 10- to 30-year range. During the financial crisis the Fed even bought more than a trillion dollars' worth of mortgage-backed securities to help sustain liquidity in that market. This kind of policy is called **quantitative easing** and it is used when the federal funds rate is near the zero lower bound.

> **Quantitative easing** is when the Fed buys longer-term government bonds or other securities.

Payment of Interest on Reserves

In the midst of the financial crisis, the Federal Reserve began to use a new method to control the money supply: payment of interest on reserves. Most other central banks continue to focus on open market operations and the Fed may someday go back to these older methods, but for the time being it is necessary to learn both sets of operating procedures.

So what exactly changed and how does it matter?

Prior to October 2008, the supply of reserves and the Federal Funds rate were tied closely together. As we discussed earlier, when the Fed increased the supply of reserves the Federal Funds rate would be pushed down, and when the Fed decreased the supply of reserves the Federal Funds rate would be pushed up. During the crisis, however, the Fed wanted to separate these two aspects of monetary policy. To avoid any hint of a bank run, for example, the Fed might want banks to have lots of reserves. Yet, the Fed might also want to keep interest rates close to a certain level. Paying interest on reserves allowed the Fed to separate the two channels of monetary policy. The Fed could now choose to supply the banking system with whatever level of reserves it thought best and, by setting the interest rate the Fed paid on those reserves, it could influence other interest rates in the economy. Notice, for example, that when the Fed pays interests on reserves, it puts a floor on the Federal Funds rate because no bank would want to lend to another bank at a rate that was less than what they could get just by holding onto their reserves.

As we said, during the financial crisis the Fed wanted to put a lot of reserves into the system. How much? Prior to 2008, bank reserves in excess of required reserves were about 2 billion dollars. But starting in 2008, excess reserves increased from 2 billion to 2.8 trillion! (See Figure 15.2.) Even though the Fed pays only a very low interest rate on reserves, banks are willing to hold lots of

MRU
mru.org/fed-post-2008

FED AFTER GREAT RECESSION

How the Fed Works: After the Great Recession

FIGURE 15.2

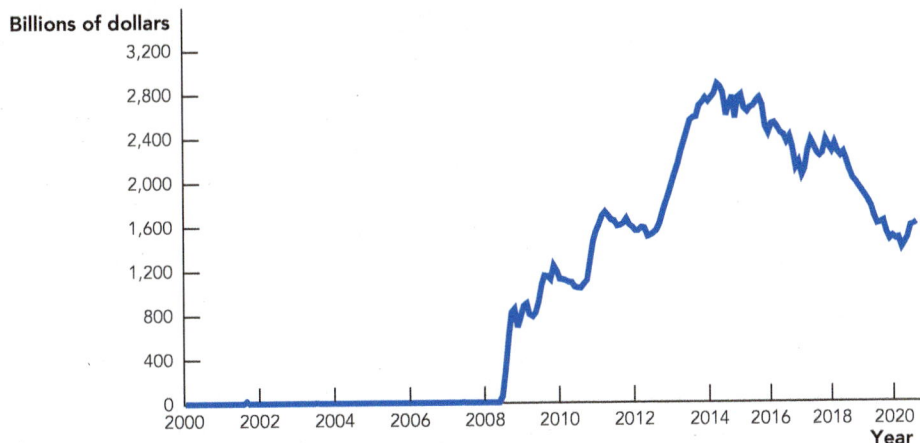

Excess Reserves of Financial Institutions, 2000–2020

Data from: https://fred.stlouisfed.org/graph/?g=pmwA

reserves because interest rates in the wider economy are also close to zero, at least for low-risk investments. Even a low interest rate on reserves encourages banks to hold a lot of reserves when it's hard to find superior returns at a comparable level of risk elsewhere.

So how does the Federal Reserve conduct monetary policy now that reserves are so large? On its own, changing the supply of reserves is no longer very effective in boosting loans because banks have more than enough reserves for all their requirements. Since banks already hold trillions of dollars in reserve, just adding more reserves won't translate into more lending; lending is no longer constrained by reserves.

What the Fed can do, however, is change the demand for reserves. Suppose, for example, that the Fed wants to pursue a relatively *contractionary monetary policy*, as was the case in late 2015. First, the Fed raises the rate of interest that it pays on reserves. That increases the demand for reserves and also places upward pressure on other short-term interest rates. Since banks can now earn a higher interest rate on reserves, they are less willing to lend those reserves, which pushes up market interest rates. Higher market interest rates and a higher demand to hold reserves mean that borrowing declines and broader measures of the money supply grow less quickly than otherwise would have been the case.

Now let's say the Fed wants to pursue an *expansionary monetary policy*. To do so, the Fed would lower the rate of interest paid on reserves. As a result, banks would be less inclined to simply sit on their reserves. Instead, they would want to lend more and that in turn would lower market rates of interest and increase the flow of money through the economy.

At least that is the way it is supposed to work in theory and the way the Fed hopes it will work. There is considerable uncertainty as to how much these actions can influence real economic activity, however. Interest rates are already very low, so even if the Fed were to drop the interest rate paid on reserves to zero, how much is that really going to affect bank decisions? Maybe not very much. As we said above, bank lending is no longer constrained by reserves and when interest rates are very low it may not be constrained very much by interest rates either. When interest rates are so low that lowering them even further is not possible or is not effective at increasing aggregate demand, the economy is sometimes said to be in a **liquidity trap**.

The Federal Reserve Is the Lender of Last Resort

During a panic, when depositors are running to their banks to withdraw their money, lenders are refusing to lend, fire sales are lowering asset prices, and no one knows where to turn, everyone turns to the Fed—the lender of last resort.

Panics can be especially dangerous because under the right circumstances they can be set in motion by the tiniest of tremors, and yet they can quickly grow and spread so that they become self-fulfilling. A panic, for example, might start with a simple rumor that a financial institution, like a bank, is insolvent. An **insolvent institution** is one with more liabilities than assets. If depositors and lenders fear that a bank is insolvent, they will rush to withdraw their money, knowing that the last people attempting to withdraw will be the ones holding the bag.

The rumor could even be false. Perhaps the bank has plenty of assets but its assets are illiquid. An **illiquid asset** is an asset that cannot be quickly converted into cash without a large loss in value; perhaps because the asset is difficult to

The economy is said to be in a **liquidity trap** when interest rates are close to the zero lower bound, so pushing them lower is not possible or not effective at increasing aggregate demand.

CHECK YOURSELF
- Underline the correct answers. The Fed wants to lower interest rates: It does so by (buying/selling) bonds in an open market operation. By doing this, the Fed (adds/subtracts) reserves and through the multiplier process (increases/decreases) the money supply.
- If the Fed increases the amount that it pays on reserves, will that tend to increase/decrease aggregate demand?

An **insolvent institution** has liabilities that are greater than its assets.

An **illiquid asset** is an asset that cannot be quickly converted into cash without a large loss in value. A bank may be illiquid but not insolvent.

value and it takes time to find the right buyer. The main assets that banks hold are loans that are difficult to value and that won't pay off until some point in the future, so banks hold lots of illiquid assets. If the bank is forced to liquidate early to pay its depositors or lenders, there could be a lot of waste.

Banks establish long-term relationships with their customers. Consider, for example, a software project. The team behind the project works closely with a bank to get a loan. The team finishes half of the code and needs another loan. It makes sense to go back to the same bank—no one else will understand the project as well. If that bank can't fund the project, the whole project will probably die, wasting the work that has already gone into it. Not only will it be hard to explain the project to other investors, but those investors may fear an adverse selection problem—why isn't the bank that best knows the project making the loan? A bank run can break the continuity necessary to fund long-term projects.

The depositors, however, can't tell whether the bank is really insolvent or just illiquid and any hint that the bank isn't ready to pay everyone on demand could make the panic spread.

That's where deposit insurance and the Federal Reserve come in. Deposit insurance tells depositors: don't worry, even if the bank is insolvent you will still be paid. And because of that guarantee, there is no run and the bank isn't forced to stop funding the software project before it is finished.

When deposit insurance isn't enough or when the financial institution isn't covered by deposit insurance, then the Fed can step in as the lender of last resort. The Fed provides the bank with enough cash to pay off any depositor who wants to be paid off; again, without requiring the bank to liquidate its assets too early.

Traditionally, the Fed lent to solvent but illiquid banks to get them through a temporary squeeze and it wound down insolvent banks. But during a panic the Fed may also lend to insolvent banks—to bail them out.

The problem during a panic is the problem of **systemic risk**—if one financial institution goes down it's likely to take others with it, like dominos. Thus, because the bankruptcy of one insolvent financial intermediary could take illiquid but solvent institutions down with it, the Fed sometimes has to bail out some insolvent banks in order to protect the entire system.

At the height of the 2008–2009 financial crisis, for example, the Federal Reserve, the Federal Deposit Insurance Corporation (FDIC), and the U.S. Treasury stepped in to support the financial system on an unprecedented scale. In addition to buying trillions of dollars' worth of longer-term government bonds and mortgage-backed securities, the Federal Reserve also lent banks hundreds of billions of dollars. The Fed also extended its lending beyond banks to become the lender of last resort to other financial intermediaries in the commercial paper and asset-backed securities markets. All told, the Fed lent financial intermediaries more than a trillion dollars, as shown in Figure 15.3.

The Fed also went from lender of last resort to owner of last resort (!) when it assumed a majority ownership stake in the insurance company AIG. Even though AIG wasn't a bank, the Fed worried that if it went bankrupt it would threaten many other financial intermediaries. The Fed wanted to create a line break and stop the dominoes from toppling over.

The Fed was joined in these actions by the FDIC. Deposit insurance, which traditionally had been limited to $100,000 for each bank account, was in effect

mru.org/lender-last-resort

The Federal Reserve as Lender of Last Resort

Systemic risk is the risk that the failure of one financial institution can bring down other institutions.

FIGURE 15.3

Total Fed Lending, January 2007–January 2013

Data from: Federal Reserve H.4.1 Statistical Release, Table 1. Factors Affecting Reserve Balances of Depository Institutions and Condition Statement of Federal Reserve Banks.

Moral hazard occurs when banks and other financial institutions take on too much risk, hoping that the Fed and regulators will later bail them out.

The Fed steps in as a lender of last resort to stop the spread of a financial panic.

extended to all accounts, increasing the amount insured by some 8 trillion dollars. In addition, the U.S. Treasury guaranteed trillions of dollars in money market funds. Finally, the U.S. government stepped in as a lender of last resort and partial owner of General Motors when GM couldn't get funding from banks.

But here's the problem. What would you do if you were told that you could invest in anything and the government would step in and bail you out if you failed? It's obvious. You would take more risk since you would get the benefit of the upside and wouldn't have to deal with the downside! When individuals or institutions are insured, they tend to take on too much risk. This is the problem of **moral hazard**. Big financial institutions that are "too big to fail" have too little incentive to make responsible financial investments.

This is in part why the Fed also has the role of regulating banks: to minimize reckless bank behavior, the Fed imposes conditions on what assets the bank can and must hold. Regulations like this, however, have costs of their own, including a more bureaucratic and less flexible banking system.

Limiting systemic risk while checking moral hazard is the fundamental problem the Fed faces as a bank regulator. In addition, the financial system has become more complex and intertwined as financial assets are packaged, subdivided, bought, and sold more than ever before. The shadow banking system has become as important as traditional banks in the financial system, but it is less well understood. As a

FIGURE 15.4

Open market operations—the buying and selling of short-term U.S. government bonds. The Fed buys bonds to lower interest rates and expand the money supply, and sells bonds to raise interest rates and contract the money supply.

Raising or lowering the interest rate paid on reserves. The Fed lowers the rate paid on reserves to decrease reserve demand and expand bank lending, and raises the rate to increase reserve demand and reduce bank lending.

Quantitative easing—the buying and selling of longer-term U.S. government bonds or other securities. Used to influence longer-term rates directly or to support borrowing and lending in especially distressed markets in a crisis.

Lender of last resort—lending to banks and other financial intermediaries in a crisis to maintain borrowing and lending.

Four Tools Used by the Federal Reserve

result, the Fed's lender of last resort and regulatory functions have become much more important and more complex.

The Fed is trying to steer a course between two problems. If a panic occurs, it may be best to bail out some firms, even bad actors, to protect the system, and yet the promise to bail out firms in a future panic encourages risk taking and increases the probability that a panic will happen in the first place. It is not obvious that the Fed has the tools to steer clear of both problems. This is the great dilemma of modern banking regulation.

Figure 15.4 summarizes four of the most important Fed tools.

Revisiting Aggregate Demand and Monetary Policy

Now that we have covered the major tools of the Federal Reserve, let's remember that what the Fed ultimately wants to do is to use its tools to influence aggregate demand (AD). Let's imagine, for example, that the Fed wants to increase aggregate demand and it chooses to do so by buying bonds in an open market operation. The bond purchase increases the monetary base and decreases short-term interest rates. The increase in the base increases deposits and loans through the multiplier process, and the decrease in interest rates stimulates investment (and consumption) borrowing. As a result—if all goes well—AD increases. The increase in AD then influences the economy as discussed in Chapter 13 and is shown in Figure 15.5. Beginning at point a, an increase in $\overline{M}$ shifts the aggregate demand curve outward, moving the economy to point b, where inflation and the real growth rate are higher. In the long run, after transition the economy will move to point c with a higher inflation rate (money neutrality again) but a growth rate given by the fundamentals at the long-run potential level.

We now know that the process is not quite so simple. The Fed can buy bonds and increase the monetary base, but these actions do not increase aggregate demand by any guaranteed amount, since we don't know exactly how

FIGURE 15.5

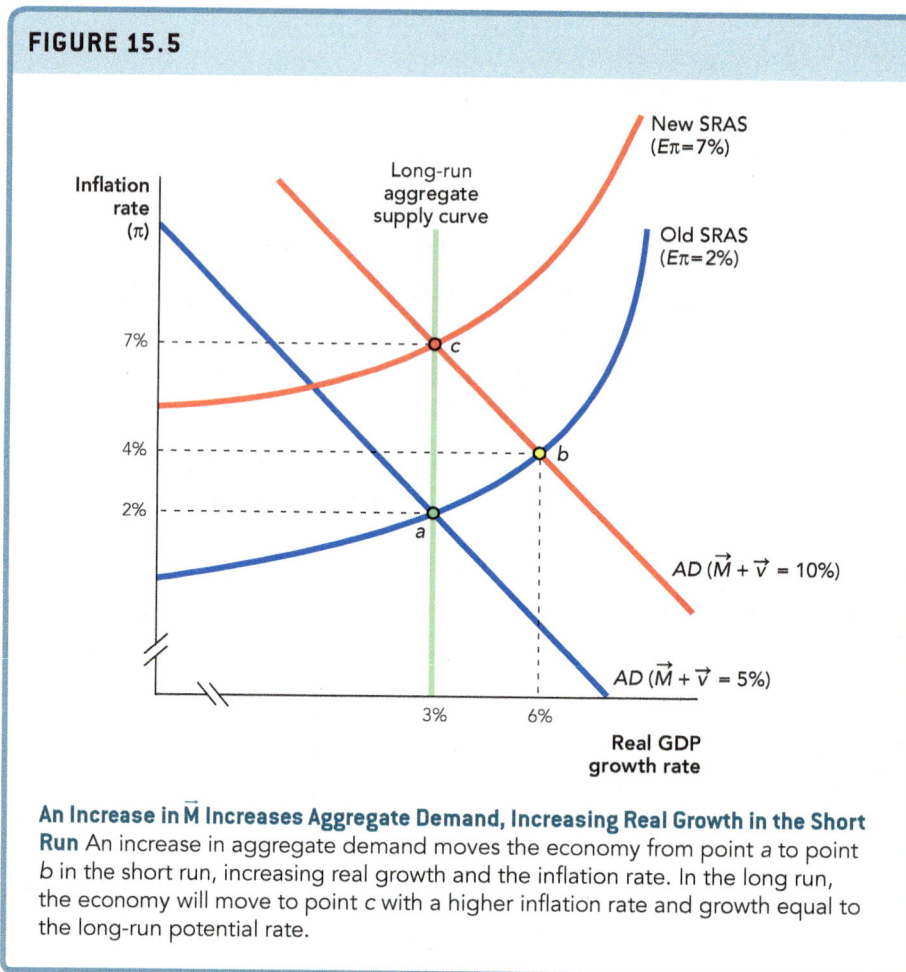

An Increase in $\vec{M}$ Increases Aggregate Demand, Increasing Real Growth in the Short Run An increase in aggregate demand moves the economy from point *a* to point *b* in the short run, increasing real growth and the inflation rate. In the long run, the economy will move to point *c* with a higher inflation rate and growth equal to the long-run potential rate.

much M1 and M2 will go up in response to the higher monetary base. Nor do we know exactly how much the lower interest rates will stimulate investment spending, especially since the Fed has the most influence over *short-term* rates, while most investment spending will depend on longer-term rates. In addition, all of these processes take time and the lags from action to response are not fixed but may vary. If the Fed acts to reduce interest rates today, for example, it may take 6 to 18 months before aggregate demand and economic growth begin to respond significantly. In the meantime, economic conditions may change.

Thus, to estimate the effect of its actions on aggregate demand, the Fed must try to predict and monitor many variables determining the size and timing of the response to its actions. Some of the things the Fed must try to predict and monitor are:

■ Will banks lend out all the new reserves or will they lend out only a portion, holding the rest as excess reserves?

■ How quickly will increases in the monetary base translate into new bank loans and thus larger increases in M1 and M2?

■ Do businesses want to borrow? How low do short-term interest rates have to go to stimulate more investment borrowing?

■ If businesses do borrow, will they promptly hire labor and capital, or will they just hold the money as a precaution against bad times?

The Federal Reserve's power should not be underestimated but increasing or decreasing aggregate demand is not like turning a tap on and off. The Fed has a limited set of tools and it must constantly adapt those tools to new circumstances and conditions. We will be taking up the difficulties and dilemmas of monetary policy in the real world at greater length in the next chapter.

Who Controls the Fed?

The power to create money out of thin air and to lend trillions of dollars is an awesome power. How is this power controlled?

The Fed has a seven-member Board of Governors, who are appointed by the president and confirmed by the Senate. Governors are appointed for 14-year terms and cannot be reappointed—this means a single president will rarely appoint a majority of the board. Once appointed, members of the Board of Governors cannot be easily fired. The chairperson of the Fed is appointed by the president from among the members of the Board of Governors and confirmed by the Senate for a term of four years. In addition, the Fed has to periodically report to overseers in both houses of Congress.

Although we say "the Fed," the Fed is not just one bank but 12 Federal Reserve Banks, each headquartered in a different region of the country.* The regional structure of the Fed explains another peculiarity: The Fed is a quasi-private, quasi-public institution. Each regional bank is a nonprofit bank with nine directors: Six of these directors are elected by commercial banks from the region and three are elected by the Board of Governors. Six of the directors must be nonbankers and these are drawn from business, labor, academia, and other fields. In 2017, for example, the vice president of Costco was a director at the San Francisco Fed, the president of George Mason University was a director at the Richmond Fed, and the president of the Chicago Federation of Labor was a director at the Chicago Fed. The directors of the regional banks appoint a regional bank president. Finally, the seven members of the Board of Governors, along with five rotating presidents of the regional Fed banks, make up the Federal Open Market Committee. The Federal Open Market Committee determines the stance of monetary policy by controlling open market policy. It is therefore the most important and influential part of the Fed system.

Confused? Yes, it is confusing and we have spared you many of the details! Perhaps it will help to know that the confusing structure of the Federal Reserve system has a purpose. The Federal Reserve is powerful, so in keeping with the U.S. system of checks and balances, the power of the Fed is dispersed—no single president appoints all the governors of the Fed, the governors do not have complete control over Fed policy, the regional bank presidents come from all over the United States, and they are appointed by directors who are drawn not just from banking but from a wide variety of fields.

The bottom line is that the Federal Reserve is usually one of the most independent agencies in the U.S. government. It is relatively insulated from politics, party, and elections—perhaps only the Supreme Court is more independent.

CHECK YOURSELF

- If money is neutral in the long run, why would the Fed want to increase the money supply in the short run?
- How will fear about the economy entering a recession affect the disposition of banks to lend? How will this affect the Fed's ability to shift aggregate demand in a recession?

Dr. Mary Daly, the President of the San Francisco Federal Reserve, dropped out of high school and drove a doughnut truck for her first job. Her expertise in labor markets helps her to debate and determine interest rate policy as a member of the Federal Open Market Committee.

Bloomberg/Getty Images

---

* The headquarters of the 12 regional banks are located in Boston, New York, Philadelphia, Cleveland, Richmond, Atlanta, Chicago, St. Louis, Minneapolis, Kansas City, Dallas, and San Francisco.

That said, in the financial crisis of 2008, the Fed had to work closely with the Treasury Department (for one thing, Treasury resources were required to recapitalize banks) and in that sense it was much less independent than usual. In general, the independence of the Federal Reserve worries some people who would prefer that the Fed be more directly accountable to democratically elected politicians. Other people are concerned that if the Federal Reserve could be controlled directly by, say, the president, this would give the president the power to order the Federal Reserve to expand the money supply and boost the economy just before an election.

Political pressures have been put on the Federal Reserve and some chairpersons have been less independent than others. In 1972, President Nixon asked Arthur Burns, the chair of the Fed, to stimulate the economy before the election. Burns did stimulate the economy and Nixon won in a landslide, but the economic gains were temporary. Not surprisingly, inflation was too high for the rest of the 1970s. This was not a proud moment in the history of the Federal Reserve or the presidency.

Overall, an independent Federal Reserve is defended by most economists as part of the U.S. system of checks and balances.

Takeaway

To return to the opening of this chapter, we now have a sense why the Fed chairperson is (possibly) the second most powerful person in the world. The Federal Reserve is the government's bank and the bankers' bank, and it has the power to create money. The ability to create money, regulate the money supply, and potentially lend trillions of dollars means that the Fed has significant powers to influence aggregate demand in the world's largest economy.

The concept of "the money supply" can refer to several different measures. It is important to know the major definitions of the money supply (MB, M1, and M2) and how they differ. The Fed controls the money supply by buying and selling government bonds in what are called open market operations.

By buying and selling bonds, the Fed changes bank reserves. A change in reserves changes the money supply through a multiplier process of rippling loans and deposits. The final result is that $\Delta MS = \Delta \text{Reserves} \times \text{MM}$. The money multiplier, however, changes over time, so the Fed's influence over aggregate demand is subject to uncertainty in both impact and timing.

When the government buys securities, the interest rate decreases and that stimulates consumption and investment borrowing. When the government sells securities, the interest rate increases, thereby reducing borrowing for either consumption or investment. The Fed can also influence interest rates by raising or lowering the interest rate the Fed pays on bank reserves. For day-to-day operations, in normal times, the Fed focuses its attention on the Federal Funds rate, the interest rate on overnight loans between major banks. The Fed has the most influence over real rates of interest in the short run. The Fed has little influence over long-run real rates of interest.

In emergency situations, the Fed serves as a "lender of last resort" for banks and for major financial institutions that find themselves in trouble. Preventing "systemic risk"—or the spread of financial problems from one institution to another—while also minimizing the moral hazard that comes when banks assume too much risk, assuming that they will be bailed out in the future, are two of the Fed's most important jobs.

CHAPTER REVIEW

Go online to practice with more examples of these types of problems, including live links to videos, data sources, and feedback.

▶ **Problems with this icon relate to optional MRU videos.**

KEY CONCEPTS

money, p. 334

liquid asset, p. 336

fractional reserve banking, p. 336

reserve ratio (RR), p. 337

money multiplier (MM), p. 337

open market operations, p. 338

Federal Funds rate, p. 340

zero lower bound, p. 340

quantitative easing, p. 340

liquidity trap, p. 342

insolvent institution, p. 342

illiquid asset, p. 342

systemic risk, p. 343

moral hazard, p. 344

FACTS AND TOOLS

▶ 1. Let's find out what counts as money. In this chapter, we used a typical definition of money: "a widely accepted means of payment." Under this definition, are people using "money" in the following transactions? If not, why not?

   a. Lucy sells her Saab to Maya for $1,000 in cash.

   b. Lucy sells her Saab to Maya for $1,000 worth of old Bob Dylan records.

   c. Lucy sells her Saab to Maya for $1,000 in checking account balances (transferred by writing a check).

   d. Lucy sells her Saab to Maya by Maya promising $1,000 worth of auto detailing services over the next year.

   e. Lucy sells her Saab to Maya for $1,000 worth of Revolutionary War–era continental dollars.

▶ 2. Define the following:

   a. The monetary base, MB

   b. M1

   c. M2

▶ 3. **a.** Suppose that banks have decided they need to keep a reserve ratio of 10%—this guarantees that they'll have enough cash in ATMs to keep depositors happy, and enough electronic deposits at the Federal Reserve so that they can redeem checks presented by other banks. What is the money multiplier in this case?

   b. If depositors start visiting the ATM a lot more often, will banks want to have a higher reserve ratio or a lower reserve ratio? Will this increase the money multiplier or lower it?

4. If the Federal Reserve wants to lower interest rates via open market operations, should it buy bonds or should it sell bonds?

▶ 5. Practice with money multipliers. Think of the "money supply" (MS) as equal to either M1 or M2.

   a. RR = 5%, Changes in reserves = $10 billion, MM = ?, Change in MS = ?

   b. RR = ?, Change in reserves = $1,000, MM = 5, Change in MS = ?

   c. RR = 100%, Change in reserves = $10 billion, MM = ?, Change in MS = ?

▶ 6. In the previous question, one example assumed that banks kept a 100% reserve ratio. Some economists have recommended that *all* banks be required by law to keep 100% of their deposits in the bank vault, at the Federal Reserve, or invested in ultrasafe investments such as short-term U.S. Treasury bills.

   a. If this happened, what would the money multiplier be equal to?

   b. If this happened, would the interest rate on bank deposits probably go up or down?

   c. If this happened, would people be more likely or less likely to invest their savings in bank alternatives, such as bonds, mutual funds, or their cousin's lawn mowing business?

7. The main interest rate that the Federal Reserve tries to control is the Federal Funds rate, the interest rate that banks charge on short-term (usually overnight) loans to other banks. Let's see how much interest a bank can earn if it lends money at the Federal Funds rate.

Virginia Community Bank has $2,000,000 of extra cash sitting in its account at the Federal Reserve Bank of Richmond. It gets a call from Bank of America asking to borrow the whole $2,000,000 for 24 hours. (This is typical: It's usually the smaller banks lending money overnight to the bigger banks.)

a. If the *annual* interest rate on federal funds is 4%, what (approximately) is the *one-day* interest rate on federal funds? (Note that interest rates, like GDP growth rates, are usually reported as "per year," just as speeds are reported as miles "per hour.")

b. How many dollars of interest will Virginia Community Bank earn for lending this money for one day?

c. If Virginia Community Bank lent this amount every day at the same rate for an entire year, how much interest would it earn?

8. Let's use the model of the supply and demand for bank reserves to explain how the Federal Reserve can change aggregate demand in the short run. Remember that the Federal Reserve controls the *supply* of bank reserves, but private banks create *demand* for bank reserves.

a. After a meeting, the Federal Reserve's Open Market Committee votes to cut interest rates from 2% to 1.5%. How will they make this happen: Will they increase the supply of reserves or decrease the supply?

b. As a result of your answer to part a, will banks usually lend more money in response, or will they lend less money? Will this tend to increase the nation's money supply, lower it, or will it have no net effect on the money supply?

c. Will this typically increase aggregate demand or lower it?

Discovering DATA ::

9. Using the FRED economic database (https://fred.stlouisfed.org/), graph the effective Federal Funds rate from 2007 to the present.

a. Approximately what was the Federal Funds rate in 2007?

b. What was the Federal Funds rate around the first week of January 2009?

THINKING AND PROBLEM SOLVING

10. Whether an asset is "liquid" often depends on what situation you are in. For each of the following pairs of assets, which is more liquid in the particular setting?

You want to buy a sofa:

A savings account or currency

You want to trade for a bologna sandwich in elementary school:

A peanut butter and jelly sandwich or sushi

You want to buy a house:

Currency or a checking account

You live in a postapocalyptic wasteland:

Rice or currency

You are traveling across Europe during the Middle Ages:

Gold coins or works of art

You are an investment banker buying a corporation:

U.S. Treasury bonds or currency

11. a. Who is more likely to take bigger risks: a trapeze artist with a safety net underneath or a trapeze artist without a safety net?

b. Who is more likely to take bigger risks with his deposits: a bank CEO in a country where there is a lender of last resort or a bank CEO in a country where there is no lender of last resort?

c. Who is more likely to spend more time searching for a well run, safe bank: a depositor living in a country with government-run deposit insurance or a depositor living in a country without government-run deposit insurance?

d. Do government-run central banks and deposit insurance both increase moral hazard problems, both decrease moral hazard problems, or do they push in different directions when it comes to moral hazard?

12. a. In the short run, if the Fed wants to cut short-term, nominal interest rates, what does it do: Does it increase the growth rate of money or decrease the growth rate of money? Why? Will this tend to lower the real rate or will it tend to lower inflation?

b. In the long run, if the Fed wants to cut short-term, nominal interest rates, what does it do: Does it increase the growth rate of money or decrease the growth rate of money? Why? Will this tend to lower the real rate or will it tend to lower inflation?

13. Let's watch a bank create money. Last Wednesday, the Bank of Numenor opened for business. The first customer, Edith, walked in the door with 100 silver coins called Thalers to deposit in a new checking account. The second customer, Max, walks in the door a few minutes later, asking to borrow 50 Thalers for a week. The bank lends Max the Thalers. Just to keep things simple, assume these are the *only* financial transactions in Numenor. And just to be clear: Thalers are either "currency" or "reserves": Silver in Max or Edith's hands is "currency," while Thalers in the bank is "reserves."

   a. How much "money" is there in the Numenor economy before Edith walks into the bank?

   Monetary base:

   M1:

   b. How much "money" is there in the Numenor economy after Edith makes her deposit, but before Max walks in for his loan?

   Monetary base:

   M1:

   c. How much "money" is there in the Numenor economy after the Bank makes Max the loan?

   Monetary base:

   M1:

   d. Which action created money: Edith's deposit or Max's loan?

14. You are a bank regulator working for the Federal Reserve. It is your job to see whether banks are solvent or insolvent, liquid or illiquid. Fit each of the following banks into one of the following four categories:

   1. *Liquid and solvent (best)*

   2. *Illiquid but solvent (probably needs short-term loans from other banks or from the Fed)*

   3. *Liquid but insolvent (should be shut down immediately: could fool people for a while if not for your good efforts)*

   4. *Illiquid and insolvent (should be shut down immediately)*

   a. Bank of DelMarVa

Short-term assets	*Short-term liabilities*
$10 million	$6 million
Total assets	*Total liabilities*
$40 million	$50 million

   b. Bank of Escondido

Short-term assets	*Short-term liabilities*
$6 million	$10 million
Total assets	*Total liabilities*
$50 million	$40 million

   c. Bank of Previa

Short-term assets	*Short-term liabilities*
$12 million	$10 million
Total assets	*Total liabilities*
$50 million	$40 million

   d. Bank of Cambia

Short-term assets	*Short-term liabilities*
$8 million	$10 million
Total assets	*Total liabilities*
$30 million	$40 million

   e. Bank of Marshall

Short-term assets	*Short-term liabilities*
$120 million	$100 million
Total assets	*Total liabilities*
$500 million	$400 million

15. Does the House of Representatives get to vote on who becomes the chairperson of the Federal Reserve Board? If not, who *does* get to vote?

CHALLENGES

16. We mentioned how difficult it can be for the Federal Reserve to actually control aggregate demand: Its control over the broader money supply (M1 and M2) is weak and indirect, plus it can't control velocity very much at all. Let's translate the following bullet points from the chapter into an expanded aggregate demand equation. You know that increasing AD means increasing spending growth, $\vec{M} + \vec{v}$, but now you know that $\vec{M}$ (growth in M1 or M2, money measures that include checking accounts) depends on growth in the monetary base (MB) and on the money multiplier (MM). That means an increase in AD requires an increase in $\overrightarrow{MB} + \overrightarrow{MM} + \vec{v}$.

Let's apply this fact to the following cases mentioned in the chapter. In all cases, the Federal Reserve is trying to boost AD by raising $\overrightarrow{MB}$ But if there's a fall in $\overrightarrow{MM}$ or a fall in $\vec{v}$ at the same time, the Fed's actions might do nothing to AD. In each case below, what are we concerned about: a fall in $\overrightarrow{MM}$ or a fall in $\vec{v}$?

a. Will banks lend out all the new reserves or will they lend out only a portion, holding the rest as excess reserves?

b. Will increases in the monetary base translate into new bank loans?

c. If businesses do borrow, will they promptly hire labor and capital, or will they just hold the money as a precaution against bad times?

17. In the past, the Federal Reserve didn't pay interest on reserves kept in Federal Reserve banks: For an ordinary U.S. bank, money kept at the Fed earned zero interest, just like money stored in a vault or in an ATM. In 2008, the Fed started paying interest on deposits kept at the Fed.

a. Once the Fed started paying interest, what would you predict would happen to demand for reserves by banks: Would they demand more reserves or fewer reserves from the Fed?

b. If a central bank starts paying interest on reserves, will private banks tend to make more loans or fewer loans, holding all else equal? (*Hint:* Does the opportunity cost of making a car loan rise or fall when the central bank starts paying interest on reserves?)

c. Let's put parts a and b together, keeping in mind the fact that bank loans create money. That means your answer to part b also tells you about the money supply, not just about the loan supply. If a central bank starts paying interest on reserves, will the reserve ratio chosen by banks tend to rise or fall? And will the money multiplier tend to rise or fall?

d. Your answer to part c tells us that when the central bank starts paying interest on reserves, there's going to be a shift in M1 and M2, the broad forms of money supply that include money created through loans. But there are a lot of ways to affect the money supply, so if one force is pushing the money supply in one direction, we can find another tool to push the money supply in the opposite direction. Therefore, if a central bank chooses to start paying interest on reserves,

but it wants M2 to remain unchanged, what should the bank do to the supply of reserves: Should it increase the supply of reserves or decrease the supply of reserves?

18. Economist Bennett McCallum says that in order to push interest rates down in the long run, the central bank needs to raise interest rates in the short run. How can this be true?

Discovering DATA ⠞

19. Using the FRED economic database (https://fred.stlouisfed.org/), find and graph the amount of mortgage-backed securities held by the Federal Reserve since 2007.

a. What quantity of mortgage-backed securities did the Fed hold prior to 2009?

b. Approximately what quantity of mortgage-backed securities did the Fed hold in 2016?

c. Why did the Federal Reserve purchase these securities?

d. What problems may this cause moving forward?

Discovering DATA ⠞

20. Using the FRED economic database (https://fred.stlouisfed.org/), graph the Effective Federal Funds rate from 2007 to the present. Now click Edit Graph and then Add Line. Add the Unemployment rate. Click Format and change the y-axis position of line 2 (unemployment) to the right—this will give you one axis for the Federal Funds rate on the left and one axis for the Unemployment rate on the right.

a. How did the Fed respond to increasing unemployment?

b. Did monetary policy work to lower unemployment? Can you tell from this graph?

c. What happens if unemployment spikes back up? Can the Fed lower the Federal Funds rate much more? Could the Fed push the Federal Funds rate below zero?

WORK IT OUT

For interactive, step-by-step help in solving this problem, go online.

We mentioned that the central bank can influence a short-run real interest rate—this is because in the short run the inflation rate is relatively constant but the central bank can adjust the nominal rate on short-term loans. Recall that after investing in a T-bill, the real rate that investors receive is

$$\text{Real interest rate} = \text{Nominal interest rate} - \text{Inflation}$$

a. If inflation is 3% and the Fed wants the real rate on short-term loans to be 2%, what should it set the nominal Fed Funds rate equal to?

b. If inflation is 3%, and the Fed wants to encourage borrowing by cutting the real rate on short-term loans to −1%, what should it set the nominal Fed Funds rate equal to?

c. If inflation is 6%, and the Fed wants to discourage borrowing by raising the real rate on short-term loans to 4%, what should it set the nominal Fed Funds rate equal to?

MRU VIDEOS

The U.S. Money Supplies

mru.org/money-supply

Problems: **1, 2**

The Money Multiplier

mru.org/money-multiplier

Problems: **3, 5, 6**

The Federal Reserve as Lender of Last Resort

mru.org/lender-last-resort

Problem: **11**

CHAPTER 15 APPENDIX

The Money Multiplier Process in Detail

Just to recap from the chapter, when the Federal Reserve conducts an open market operation, we said that the money supply changes by the change in reserves times the money multiplier, $\Delta MS = \Delta \text{Reserves} \times \text{MM}$. If the Fed buys government bonds, for example, this increases bank reserves, which increases the money supply by the increase in reserves times the money multiplier.

We've already mentioned the idea of a ripple effect: As one bank increases its loans, this leads to an increase in deposits in another bank, which in turn increases its loans, which leads to an increase in deposits in another bank, which increases its loans . . . and so forth. Now it is time to look at this multiplier process in more detail.

It's helpful to examine a simple form of accounting statement called a T-account. On the left side of a T-account, we list the bank's assets, and on the right side, we list the bank's liabilities. An asset is simply something that represents wealth or value to the bank. In our simple T-accounts, the only assets a bank can have are its reserves and its portfolio of loans. A liability refers to a debt or something owed to someone else. In our simple T-accounts, the only liabilities a bank can have will be deposits (the bank owes depositors the money in their accounts).

Now suppose that the Fed buys a government bond for $1,000 from a dealer in Treasury securities. The dealer has an account at the First National Bank and thus the Federal Reserve adds $1,000 to the dealer's account. As a result, the First National Bank's liabilities (its deposits) increase by $1,000, but the bank now also has an extra $1,000 in reserves. The First National Bank's T-account looks like this:

First National Bank	
Assets	**Liabilities**
Reserves: +$1,000	Deposits: +$1,000
Loans:	

But what will the First National Bank do with its reserves? The bank wants to make a profit so it will take a portion of its reserves and lend them out. Suppose that the bank keeps $100 in reserves and lends out $900. The bank's T-account now looks like this:

First National Bank	
Assets	**Liabilities**
Reserves: $100	Deposits: $1,000
Loans: +$900	

Notice that the ratio of the bank's reserves to deposits is $100/$1,000 or 0.1; thus, the reserve ratio = 0.1. Now the firm or person that borrowed the $900 did so to purchase goods and services. Let's suppose that the borrower wrote a check for a cruise to Luxury Vacations Inc., which has an account at the Second National Bank. Luxury Vacations Inc. deposits the check into its account at the Second National Bank so the T-account of the Second National Bank now looks like this:

Second National Bank	
Assets	Liabilities
Reserves: +$900	Deposits: +$900
Loans:	

Notice that the Second National Bank's reserves have increased by $900. What does the bank want to do with these reserves? Lend them! Suppose that the Second National Bank also wants a reserve ratio of 0.1 so the Second National Bank keeps $90 in reserves and lends out $810. Its T-account now looks like this:

Second National Bank	
Assets	Liabilities
Reserves: $90	Deposits: $900
Loans: +$810	

Are you beginning to see the multiplier in action? Let's do one more. Suppose that the person or firm who borrowed money from the Second National Bank wanted the money to buy a computer. The borrower writes a check to Apple, which deposits the money in its account at the Third National Bank. The T-account of the Third National Bank now looks like this:

Third National Bank	
Assets	Liabilities
Reserves: +$810	Deposits: +$810
Loans:	

The Third National Bank also wants to make a profit, so it lends out a portion of its reserves, leading to a T-account like this:

Third National Bank	
Assets	Liabilities
Reserves: $81	Deposits: $810
Loans: +$729	

So let's summarize what we have so far:

The Banking System			
	Assets		Liabilities
	Reserves	Loans	Deposits
First National Bank	+$100	+$900	+$1,000
Second National Bank	+$90	+$810	+$900
Third National Bank	+$81	+$729	+$810
. . .	. . .	. . .	. . .

Notice that the process doesn't stop with the Third National Bank but continues onward. What is the final result of this process of expansion? Let's focus on what is happening to deposits and see if we can get to the answer a little more quickly by figuring out the pattern.

At the First National Bank deposits increase by $1,000, at the Second Bank deposits increase by $900, or $0.9 \times \$1,000$, at the Third Bank deposits increase by $810 or $0.9^2 \times \$1,000$. If you guessed that at the Fourth Bank deposits would increase by $729 or $0.9^3 \times \$1,000$, you are correct so the total process looks like this:

$$\$1,000 \times (1 + 0.9 + 0.9^2 + 0.9^3 + \cdots 0.9^n)$$

This is an example of an infinite geometric series and mathematics can show that $(1 + 0.9 + 0.9^2 + 0.9^3 + \cdots 0.9^n)$ converges to $\dfrac{1}{1-0.9}$ so deposits will increase by

$$\$1,000 \times \frac{1}{1-0.9} = \$1,000 \times \frac{1}{0.1} = \$1,000 \times 10$$

The last expression should look familiar. Remember that we assumed in our derivations that each bank wanted a reserve ratio of 0.1 so the money multiplier $MM = 1/RR = 10$. Thus, the last statement says that deposits increase by the increase in reserves ($1,000) times the money multiplier, 10. The increase in the money supply can be measured by the increase in deposits. Thus, we have $\Delta MS = \Delta \text{Reserves} \times MM$, exactly as we said in the chapter. Aren't you glad we saved the details for the appendix!

We can summarize by looking at how the initial increase in reserves created by the Fed open market purchase of bonds affects the entire banking system. A multiplier similar to that for deposits applies to reserves and loans so the final result looks like this:

The Banking System			
	Assets		Liabilities
	Reserves	Loans	Deposits
First National Bank	+$100	+$900	+$1,000
Second National Bank	+$90	+$810	+$900
Third National Bank	+$81	+$729	+$810
. . .	. . .	. . .	. . .
Total	$1,000	$9,000	$10,000

Note that we can measure the increase in the money supply by either the increase in the banking system's assets, Reserves + Loans, or by the increase in the banking system's liabilities, namely deposits. Thus, either way the money supply increases by the $10,000, or more generally $\Delta MS = \Delta \text{Reserves} \times MM$ as we have said before.

Let's make one qualification. In the multiplier process we went through, we assumed that every borrower wrote a check for every dollar of its loan and kept none of the money in cash. Thus, if a loan was made for $900, then somewhere in the banking system deposits increased by $900. If any of the borrowers keep some of their loan in cash, however, then the multiplier process does not operate on the cash component. For example, if a borrower receives a loan for $900 and writes a check for $800, keeping $100 in cash, then the multiplier process works only on the $800. Thus, the public's demand for cash also influences the multiplier process and complicates the Fed's job because the demand for cash can change over time.

16

Monetary Policy

The Nobel Prize–winning economist Milton Friedman once likened monetary policy to throwing money from a helicopter. Thus, when *Businessweek* asked in 2008, "Will 'Helicopter Ben' Ride to the Rescue?" they were asking whether Ben Bernanke, then the chairman of the Federal Reserve, would be able to use monetary policy to jolt the economy out of a looming recession.

In reality, the Federal Reserve rarely uses helicopters in its rescue operations. As discussed in the previous chapter, the Fed uses three primary tools to influence aggregate demand (AD): (1) open market operations in which the Fed buys bonds, which increases the money supply and reduces interest rates, or the Fed sells bonds, which decreases the money supply and increases interest rates; (2) lending to banks and other financial institutions; and (3) changes in the interest rate paid on reserves. These are the essential methods through which the Fed affects the real economy.

In this chapter, we take for granted *how* the Fed influences AD and turn more directly to three key practical questions: When *should* the Fed try to influence AD, when *will* the Fed be able to influence AD, and when will the influence on AD *result* in higher GDP growth rates?

We start with the best case for monetary policy: where it is clear what the Fed should do in general terms, such as responding to negative monetary shocks, and when the Fed has a good chance of being successful. We then consider some reasons why even in the best case the Fed doesn't always know which detailed course of action is best. We next consider why some of the other cases—such as negative real shocks—are much harder for the Fed to respond to effectively. Finally, we learn that there are some times when the Fed itself can contribute to a boom and subsequent bust. We end with a look at the financial crisis that started in 2007.

Monetary Policy: The Best Case

Let's start with the most straightforward case, namely a negative shock to aggregate demand driven by what John Maynard Keynes called "animal spirits," emotions and instincts, confidence and fear. Suppose, for example, that the economy has been growing at 3% and the inflation rate is 7%. Now imagine that consumers become more pessimistic and they borrow and spend less, banks lend less, entrepreneurs cut back on expansions and invest less—all of this causes a negative AD shock. The AD curve shifts left, moving the economy from point *a* to point *b* as shown in Figure 16.1.

▶ **MRU**

mru.org/intro-fed

Monetary Policy and the Fed

FIGURE 16.1

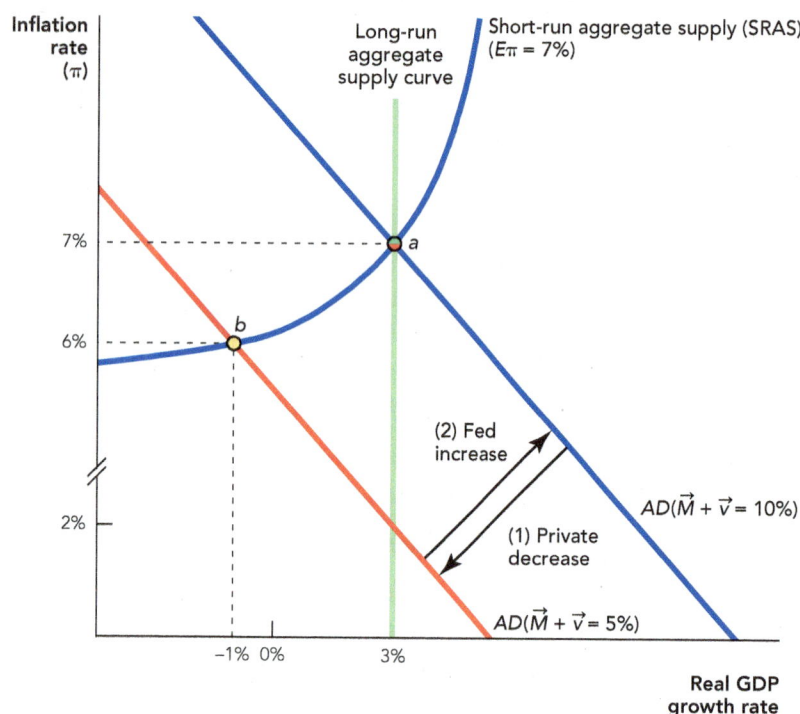

In the Best-Case Scenario, the Federal Reserve Can Offset a Negative Shock to AD with an Increase in $\vec{M}$ A decrease in AD (step 1) shifts the AD curve inward, shifting the equilibrium from point *a* to point *b*. If the Federal Reserve acts quickly, an increase in $\overline{M}$ (step 2) will move the economy back to point *a* without a prolonged recession.

As you can see, the negative shock (if not counteracted by the Fed) means that the growth rate of output will decline. If the contraction is severe enough, the rate of output growth can even turn negative, bringing the economy into a recession, just as we have discussed in Chapters 13 and 15. Eventually, the economy will recover from the negative AD shock. As fear recedes we'll return to our steady state growth level but not without some sluggish growth and increased unemployment, or even a recession in the meantime.

Could the Fed combat this sluggish growth with monetary policy? Yes! If the Fed can increase the rate of growth of the money supply, reducing interest rates and encouraging more bank lending and investor borrowing, then the AD curve shifts back up and to the right.

Using the policy tools described in the previous chapter, the Federal Reserve is able to push the AD curve back to its original position so the economy will transition from point *b* to *a*, thereby reducing the severity and length of the recession. In essence, instead of allowing the economy to adjust to a decrease in AD, which may require lower growth and higher unemployment, the Federal Reserve quickly restores AD to its previous level.

But Figure 16.1 makes monetary policy look too easy—what could be easier than shifting a curve? Two difficulties make it hard for the Fed to get this right all the time:

1. **The Federal Reserve must operate in real time when much of the data about the state of the economy is unknown.** More specifically, it takes time for data to be gathered. Data are often released on a monthly or quarterly basis. Sometimes data are amended, after the fact. Then, it takes time for data to be interpreted and for problems to be recognized.

Was the dip in employment last month a precursor of a recession or was it an exception? If the price of oil went up last month, does that indicate a longer-term trend or was it the result of some temporary shock? Is a decline in the stock market predicting a future recession or not? In the recent financial crisis, the first major signs of trouble in the subprime market came in August 2007, but most investors—and also the Fed—had no idea that so many banks and financial firms would fail, or be on the brink of failing, over the next year. In fact as late as the spring of 2008, GDP growth figures were still strongly positive and not everyone thought the United States was headed for a recession.

2. **The Federal Reserve's control of the money supply is incomplete and subject to uncertain lags.** Recall from the previous chapter that an increase in the money supply typically affects the economy with a lag that can vary in time from 6 to 18 months. And remember, in atypical situations, if banks aren't willing to lend, then although the Fed may increase the monetary base, the larger monetary aggregates and thus aggregate demand won't increase very much in response. Thus, if banks are slow to lend, then the Fed can easily undershoot, generating a smaller shift in AD and a smaller increase in the rate of economic growth than is desirable. But a larger stimulus is not necessarily better because if the economy recovers before the money supply works its magic, the Fed can easily end up overshooting its goal—producing a higher rate of inflation than is desirable.

Figure 16.2 on the next page portrays the more realistic case for monetary policy in which too little stimulation pushes the economy only to point c where growth is still sluggish. But "too much" monetary stimulation pushes the economy to point d with a higher than desirable inflation rate at 9% (and a growth rate that is high but unsustainable in the long run). Only with the "just right" or Goldilocks amount of stimulation does the economy quickly return to its long-run balanced growth path at point a. We would like it if the Fed hit the Goldilocks amount of stimulation every time, but don't forget: Goldilocks is a fairy tale.

Reversing Course and Engineering a Decrease in AD

Suppose that the Federal Reserve does overstimulate, pushing the aggregate demand curve to "Too much" in Figure 16.2. What then? Remember from our discussion in Chapter 12 that inflation makes price signals more difficult to interpret, creates arbitrary redistributions of wealth, and makes long-term planning and contracting more difficult, among other problems. Thus, we don't want inflation to be too high. But, we also know from Chapters 12 and 13 that bringing down the rate of inflation is costly because prices and wages are not fully flexible in the downward direction. That means economies sometimes get stuck between a rock and a hard place—between continuing a costly rate of inflation or reducing it at the risk of a recession.

Many economists think that the Federal Reserve did overstimulate the economy in the 1970s; and, as a result, by 1980, the inflation rate hit 13.5% a year. Ronald Reagan was elected to the presidency in part to change economic policies. By 1983, tough monetary policy under Reagan and cigar-chomping Federal Reserve Chairman Paul Volcker had reduced the inflation rate to 3%, but the consequence was a very severe recession with an unemployment rate of just over 10%.

mru.org/monetary-best
Monetary Policy: The Best Case Scenario

FIGURE 16.2

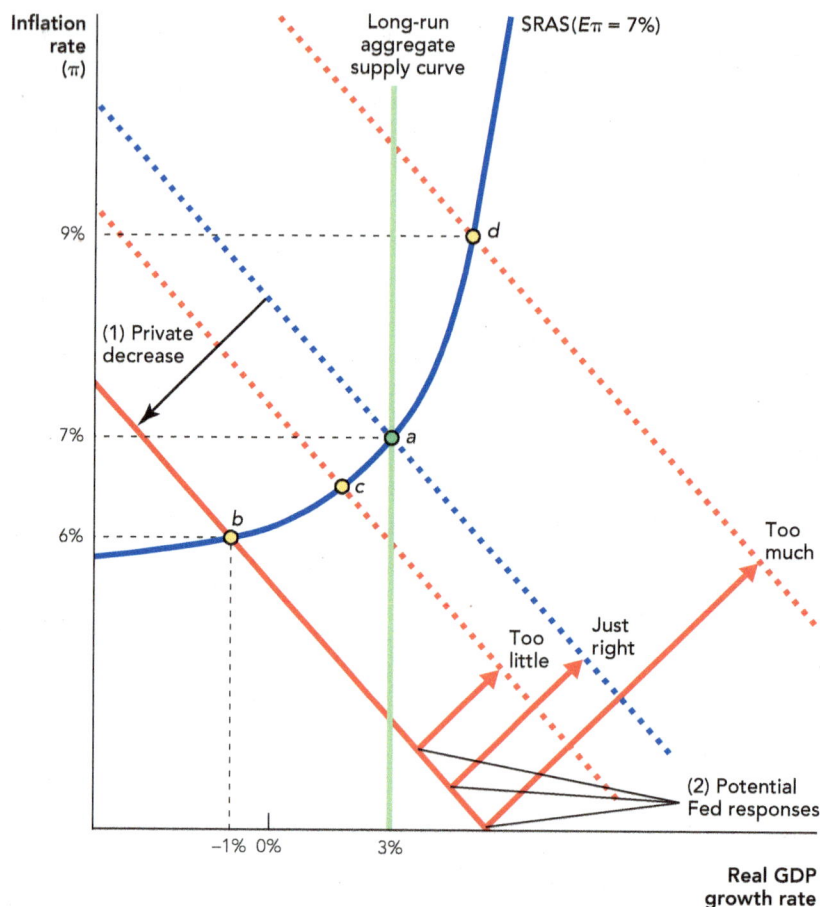

Getting Monetary Policy "Just Right" Is Not Easy The Federal Reserve operates in real time when much of the data about the economy is unknown. In addition, the Fed's control of aggregate demand is of uncertain magnitude and timing. As a result, the Fed may respond to a fall in AD (step 1) with too little, too much, or just the right amount of stimulus (step 2).

A **disinflation** is a significant reduction in the rate of inflation.

A **deflation** is a decrease in prices, that is, a negative inflation rate.

The **disinflation** experiment was costly, but unlike the **deflation** of the Great Depression, when prices fell, it was a policy chosen on purpose. The 1980s disinflation broke the back of inflation and provided the foundation for the 25 or so years of successful economic growth—and mostly low unemployment—that the American economy enjoyed until the recession of 2008–2009.

Since World War II there have been six episodes when the Fed deliberately put the brakes on money growth, most prominently the shift beginning with the 1980 presidential election just mentioned. In every case, the tighter monetary policies were followed by declines in output. On average, industrial production 33 months later was 12% lower than otherwise would have been expected. But again, these contractions aren't always bad. Sometimes a contraction is necessary to bring down the rate of inflation. Of course, economists debate which of these contractions were needed and which were not.

A monetary policy is **credible** when it is expected that a central bank will stick with its policy.

Whether or not a particular contraction is a good idea, economists do agree on one point: A monetary contraction goes best when it is **credible,** namely when market participants expect the central bank to carry through its tough stance. This makes sense if you think through exactly why a disinflation is difficult for an economy. A sufficiently radical disinflation leads to unemployment because wages and prices are sticky, especially in the downward direction (as explained in Chapter 12). If nominal wage growth is too high, some workers will end up being very expensive and employers will choose to lay them off. So, the key to a less painful disinflation is to increase nominal wage flexibility. Now imagine that a central bank has announced a disinflation but no one really believes it, or people believe it only halfheartedly. Nominal wages probably aren't going to grow more slowly, and when the disinflation comes, if indeed it does come, the unemployment cost will be high. Alternatively, if the coming disinflation is widely expected, then workers will be prepared for slower wage growth and will quickly adjust to what they know is inevitable. Thus, a credible disinflation reduces the unemployment effects of disinflation. So, the lesson is this: If a central bank wishes to undertake a disinflation, it has to be ready to stay the course and it should announce and explain its policy very publicly. This is called making monetary policy credible.

The Fed as Manager of Market Confidence

Fear and confidence are some of the most important shifters of aggregate demand. And one of the Federal Reserve's most powerful tools is not its influence over the money supply but its influence over expectations, namely its ability to boost **market confidence**. Recall from Chapter 14 that when investors are uncertain, they often prefer to wait, to delay, and to try to gather more information, before they commit themselves. In addition, remember that one reason we see a lot of time bunching or clustering of investments is that it pays to coordinate your economic actions with those of others—that is, you want to be investing, producing, and selling at the same time that others are investing, producing, or selling. Uncertainty, therefore, can create what economists call a *bandwagon effect* on investment—I am uncertain and so delay my investments, you follow suit not because of uncertainty alone but because your investment is less likely to work well if it doesn't happen at the same time as my investment (time bunching or coordination of investment). Moreover, the fact that you cut back investment verifies that my decision to cut back was a good idea so no one can be accused of behaving irrationally.

> **Market confidence:** One of the Federal Reserve's most powerful tools is its influence over expectations, not its influence over the money supply.

Uncertainty drives people away from investment spending and toward assets like cash. Holding cash isn't very productive but cash and other similar assets are what you want when you are in "wait and see" mode. In terms of our model of aggregate demand, an increase in the demand for cash is indicated by a decrease in $\vec{v}$. At the same time, increased uncertainty will lead to a fall in $\overline{M}$, as both borrowers and lenders will cut back, and M1 and M2 will grow at slower rates. Changes in both the $\vec{v}$ and the $\overline{M}$ work together to shift the aggregate demand curve inward or to the left, as you can see in Figure 16.1 near the beginning of this chapter.

To cite an example, uncertainty increased after the terrorist attacks of September 11, 2001. Although the devastation in Manhattan was extreme, the economic cost of the attack was small relative to the size of the U.S. economy. Nevertheless, if enough people had taken the attack as a signal to reduce investment, the bandwagon effect could have created a severe recession. The Federal Reserve stepped in to try to prevent this from happening by lending billions of dollars to banks. In the week before September 11, for example, the Federal Reserve lent about $34 million to banks, a trivial amount. On September 12, the Federal Reserve lent $45.5 *billion* to banks.

The mere fact that the Federal Reserve sent a countersignal—we are going to massively maintain or increase AD if necessary—helped stabilize expectations, reduce fear, and raise confidence. In addressing the COVID-19 pandemic, for example, the Federal Reserve announced early on a slew of emergency actions, including buying hundreds of billions of dollars' worth of government bonds and private securities, lending to banks and major corporations, and helping the Small Business Administration lend to small businesses. In a very unusual live interview, Chairman Jerome Powell said, "When it comes to lending, we are not going to run out of ammunition. That just doesn't happen." The Fed's actions have direct effects on the economy but are also about raising confidence to prevent $\vec{v}$ from falling. The Federal Reserve can't always prevent an increase in uncertainty from reducing $\vec{v}$ and $\overline{M}$; sometimes uncertainty really does increase, such as when a war is imminent, and waiting is the appropriate response. But the Fed often can reduce the bandwagon effect and stabilize expectations toward a more positive outcome.

Monetary policy is often about changing expectations and perceptions, rather than just manipulating numbers and equations. That's one reason why central banking can be so difficult and why it is an art as well as a science.

CHECK YOURSELF

• How do problems with data affect the Fed's ability to set monetary policy that is "just right"?

The Negative Real Shock Dilemma

A very difficult case for monetary policy is when the economy is hit by a negative real shock such as a rapid oil price increase. As we saw in Chapters 13 and 14, a negative real shock shifts the long-run aggregate supply (LRAS) curve to the left, moving the equilibrium from point *a* to point *b*, as shown in Figure 16.3. That means a higher rate of price inflation and a lower growth rate for GDP, again as previously covered. How should monetary policy respond?

FIGURE 16.3

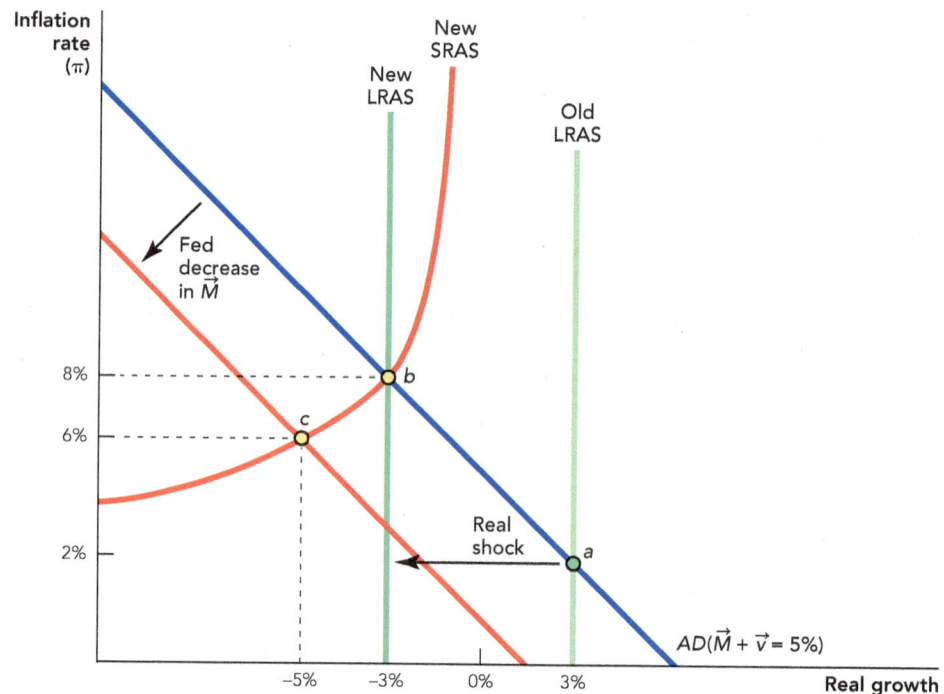

The Federal Reserve's Dilemma When Responding to a Real Shock (1) A real shock shifts the long-run aggregate supply (LRAS) curve to the left, moving the economy from point *a* to a recession at point *b*. If the Federal Reserve concentrates on the higher inflation rate, it may decide to reduce AD, with a cut in $\overline{M}$, moving the economy to point *c* with a lower inflation rate but an even lower growth rate. Note that for clarity we have suppressed the old SRAS curve running through point *a*.

One approach is to focus on the inflation rate, which has jumped from 2% to 8%. What is the recipe for reducing inflation? Correct—a *decrease* in $\vec{M}$. In the 1970s, for example, the Federal Reserve often responded to supply shocks, such as an oil shock, by decreasing $\vec{M}$ and *reducing* aggregate demand. That means taking the AD curve and shifting it farther back to the left through the use of monetary policy. In Figure 16.3, we show the new equilibrium at point *c*. The reduction in $\vec{M}$ reduces the inflation rate from 8% to 6%, but also reduces economic growth and by more than the supply shock alone would have done.

Some economists have argued that the Federal Reserve's actions in trying to stem inflation were even worse for the economy than the oil shocks. Interestingly, the most prominent critic of the Federal Reserve's actions in the 1970s was Ben Bernanke. Consistent with his criticism, when he was Fed chairman and faced with rising oil prices in 2007–2008, he did not contract the rate of growth of the money supply.[1]

Today, central bankers are more likely to believe that a central bank should respond to a negative real shock by increasing aggregate demand but that, too, has its problems.

The Federal Reserve can increase aggregate demand by increasing the money growth rate, but, when the economy is facing a negative real shock, it is less productive than at other times, due to the real shock. As a result, an increase in $\vec{M}$ will not move the economy back to point *a*. Instead, most of the increase in $\vec{M}$ will show up in inflation rather than in real growth so the economy will shift from point *b* to point *c*, as shown in Figure 16.4 with a much higher inflation rate and a slightly higher growth rate.

MRU

mru.org/monetary-neg-shock

The Negative Real Shock Dilemma

FIGURE 16.4

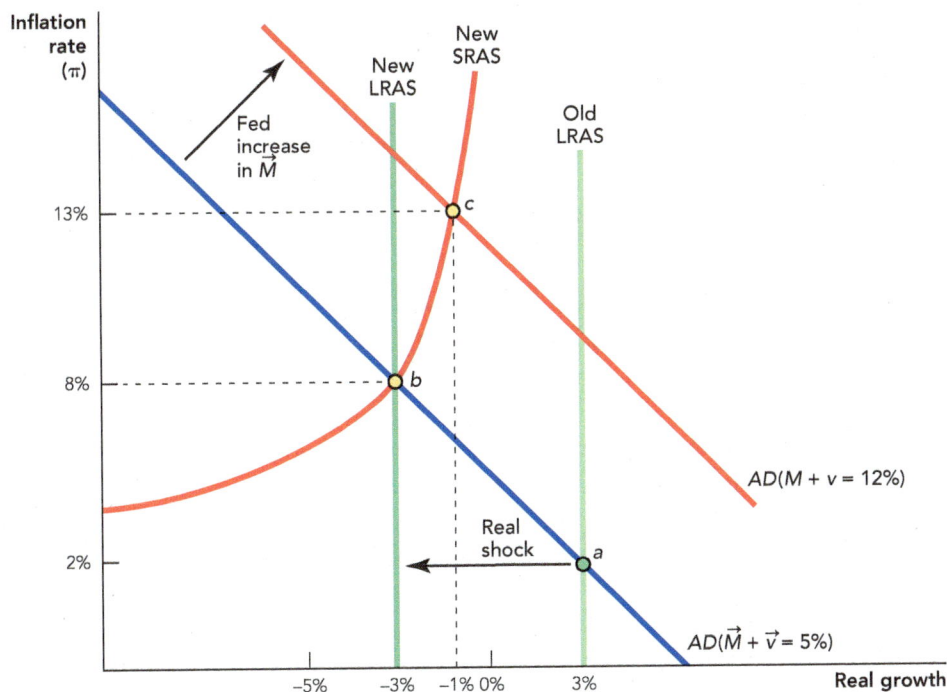

The Federal Reserve's Dilemma When Responding to a Real Shock (2) A real shock shifts the LRAS curve to the left, moving the economy from point *a* to a recession at point *b*. If the Federal Reserve concentrates on the lower growth rate, it may decide to increase AD, with an increase in $\vec{M}$ moving the economy to point *c* with a little bit higher growth rate but a much higher inflation rate. Note that for clarity we have suppressed the old SRAS curve running through point *a*.

Is it worthwhile responding to a real shock with an increase in AD? Maybe not. Although an increase in $\overline{M}$ may increase the growth rate a little, the inflation rate increases by a lot and, as we just saw in our discussion of the Volcker disinflation, higher inflation now can cause serious problems later. In particular, if the inflation rate gets too high, the Fed has to reduce inflation, thereby creating a lot of unemployment. Perhaps you wondered in the previous section on engineering a disinflation, why the rate of inflation might have ended up too high in the first place. Now you know at least one way inflation can end up too high and that also helps us understand why the dilemmas of monetary policy arise so frequently.

Moreover, recall from Chapters 13 and 14 that real shocks are often accompanied by aggregate demand shocks, so the figures are considerably simplified. Consider, for example, the coronavirus shock of 2020. Social distancing and the lockdown orders created a recession—this was a real shock that monetary policy could not fix. Indeed, since the idea was to keep people at home, an economic "stimulus" wasn't desirable. At the same time, however, the shock reduced aggregate demand as consumers could no longer buy many goods, such as restaurant meals and concert tickets, nor did they need new cars or fancy clothes. Fear and uncertainty caused people to spend less and, for those that could, save more. The Fed, therefore, did have a role to play in keeping interest rates low, as well as in lending to banks and other businesses to help tide them over during the crisis. Confused? Don't worry; that is exactly how the economists at the Federal Reserve felt. We are quite serious when we say that a combination of shocks can confuse economists at the Federal Reserve. Don't forget that in addition to the problems you face as students, the Federal Reserve is looking at real-time data, which as we have noted are often uncertain and subject to revision.

The bottom line is that with a real shock, the central bank faces a dilemma: It must choose between too low a rate of growth (with a high rate of unemployment) and too high a rate of inflation. The central bank, in fact, stands a good chance of getting a mix of both problems. The lesson is this: If you are a central banker, hope that you don't face too many negative real shocks in your term.

When the Fed Does Too Much

The Fed has considerable power to influence aggregate demand but, as we argued earlier, that power is constrained by uncertainty and by an inability for anyone to fully understand the complexity of the economy. As a result, it's possible for the Federal Reserve to make booms and recessions worse rather than better. For example, a number of economists have argued that Federal Reserve policy in 2001–2004 contributed to the housing boom and eventual bust that led to the financial crisis in 2007–2008. Of course, many factors contributed to the financial crisis, including too much leverage and irrational exuberance, as discussed in Chapters 9 and 10. The financial crisis and the Fed's role in it are highly debated topics among economists and a consensus has not yet been reached. Nevertheless, to see how the Fed might have contributed to the financial crisis, let's go back to the late 1990s and the recession of 2001.

In the late 1990s, the American economy was the envy of the world. Economic growth was strong and the unemployment rate was low, even

CHECK YOURSELF

- If the Fed wanted to restore some growth in the economy to deal with high unemployment, what would it do? What would be the problem with acting in this way?
- Suppose that the Fed reacts to a series of negative real shocks by increasing AD every time. What will happen to the inflation rate?

MRU

mru.org/fed-limits

When the Fed Does Too Much

FIGURE 16.5

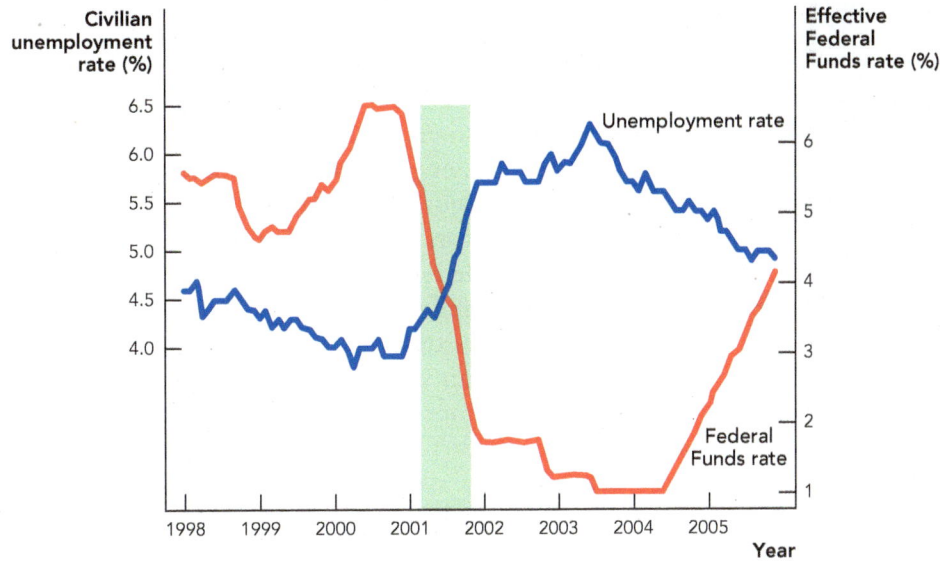

Unemployment and the Federal Funds Rate, 1998–2005

Data from: St. Louis Federal Reserve.

dipping below 4% in 2000. The recession that began in early 2001 didn't last long but there were troubling signs that not all was well. In particular, notice from Figure 16.5 that the unemployment rate continued to increase *even after the recession had officially ended.*★ From a rate of 4% in 2000, unemployment increased during the recession to 5.5% and then kept increasing until it peaked at 6.3% (almost a 50% increase) in June 2003. In fact, even three years after the recession ended, the unemployment rate remained near its recession high.

The Federal Reserve was very concerned about the unemployment rate and it also worried about the psychological blow to consumer confidence after the terrorist attacks on 9/11. To combat the high unemployment rate, the Fed tried to increase aggregate demand through expansionary monetary policy. Figure 16.5 shows one measure of the Fed's efforts, the Federal Funds rate. As described in the previous chapter, the Federal Funds rate is a short-term interest rate that is largely under the control of the Federal Reserve. During the recession, the Fed pushed down the Federal Funds rate from about 6.5% in 2000 to 2% at the end of 2001 when the recession ended. But even after the recession ended, the Fed pushed the Federal Funds rate even lower to below 2%. Indeed, from mid-2003 to mid-2004, the Fed held the Federal Funds rate at 1%, an extraordinarily low rate.

★ Recall from Chapter 6 that the exact dates of a recession are a judgment call made by the National Bureau of Economic Research. The unemployment rate is one piece of information that goes into defining when a recession begins and ends but it is quite possible for economic activity as measured by other factors such as GDP, sales, and income to be increasing even when the unemployment rate is not declining.

Subsidized bananas sometimes do encourage crashes.

The low Federal Funds rate helped to make credit cheap throughout the economy. This meant it was relatively easy to borrow money and it encouraged people to take out more mortgages, bidding up the price of homes. Unfortunately, easy credit can start or intensify a bubble.

The concept of a speculative bubble was introduced in Chapter 9, but to restate the fundamental idea here, a bubble arises when asset prices rise far higher, and more rapidly, than can be accounted for by the fundamental prospects of the asset. Investors get carried away by the prospect for gain and they underestimate the prospect of loss. Prices are instead driven by shifts in market psychology and successive waves of irrational exuberance.

Now imagine an investor who is thinking of buying a bunch of homes, not to live in them, but rather to resell them quickly for a profit (known as "flipping"). Cheap, easy credit makes it easier for investors of this kind to operate and thus it can intensify bubbles. The low interest rates are, in essence, signaling to market participants that credit is easy and it is a good idea to borrow money. In the words of the Austrian economists Ludwig von Mises and Friedrich A. Hayek, these are *distorted price signals*. A distorted price signal arises when government policy, or in this particular case the Fed's monetary policy, moves a price in a manner that encourages investors to take risks. Of course, the investors didn't have to take foolish risks. If you stockpile bananas on your roof and the roof caves in, it's your mistake even if the government subsidized the purchase of bananas. Nevertheless, cheap bananas and cheap credit probably make these mistakes more likely. The mistakes here were not exclusive to the Fed: The government-sponsored mortgage agencies, called Fannie Mae and Freddie Mac, guaranteed and subsidized a lot of low-quality mortgages, as did the private insurance firm AIG, and that also made the housing bubble worse.

The Fed began to raise interest rates in mid-2004 but rates remained very low until at least mid-2005. In 2006 housing prices peaked, and by 2007 were in free fall. Figure 16.6 illustrates what happened.

The problem for the economy, of course, came when the price of real estate started to fall in 2006. New home construction dropped very quickly. Homeowners felt poorer and started to spend less, reducing aggregate demand. In addition, the real estate crash contributed to a freezing up of financial intermediation as banks and other intermediaries took huge losses on poor investments in mortgage securities (as discussed in Chapter 9). Since bank lending is a main generator of M1 and M2, this means lower rates of growth for the money supply. As a result, economic growth rates started to decline. By the fall of 2008, the growth rate was negative, meaning that the American economy was shrinking.

Dealing with Asset Price Bubbles

The Fed probably made a mistake holding the Federal Funds so low for so long. But more generally, how should the Fed respond to asset price increases? It's easy to say in retrospect that the Fed should have raised rates sooner or should have raised rates more quickly in response to the housing bubble, but there are several problems with this line of thinking. First, few people expected

---

FIGURE 16.6

The Housing Boom and Bust: Index of Real House Prices, 1990–2010

Data from: Robert Shiller's Irrational Exuberance, http://www.irrationalexuberance.com/

---

that a fall in housing prices would wreak as much havoc as it did on financial intermediaries and the general economy. The economy, for example, had quickly recovered from the much larger drop in stock prices during the tech bubble that ended with the recession of 2001. The Fed may have believed that trying to reduce unemployment was worth the risk of generating a bubble in asset prices.

Second, it's not always easy to identify when a bubble is present. If everyone knew it was an unsustainable bubble, then all should have invested accordingly and bet against the bubble, thereby enriching themselves and also stopping the bubble in the first place. Of course, that isn't what happened and the bursting of the bubble was in large part a surprise to many people, including the Fed. Also, don't make the mistake of thinking that if prices rise a lot and then fall, that must mean a bubble was present. Prices can rise and fall for reasons closely related to fundamentals and still cause macroeconomic problems.

Third, monetary policy is a crude means of "popping" a bubble. Monetary policy can influence *aggregate* demand, or target credit markets at the aggregate level, but monetary policy can't push the demand for housing down and keep the demand for everything else up. Thus, popping a bubble means reducing the growth rate of GDP for the broader economy as a whole. Is it worth the price, especially when we do not always know when we have an unsustainable bubble on our hands?

Note, however, that in addition to monetary policy, the Fed does have the power to regulate banks and it probably could have restrained some of the "subprime," no-questions-asked mortgages that were sold during the boom and later went into

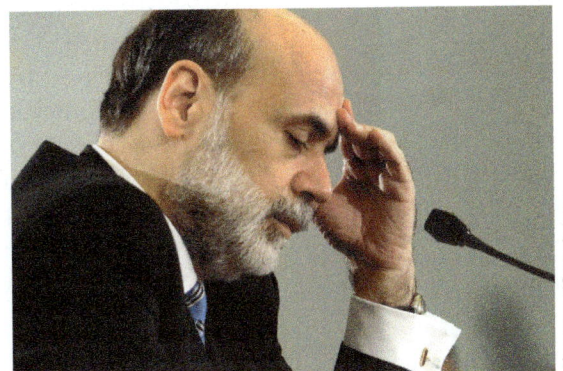

Former Federal Reserve Chairman Ben Bernanke
It seemed so much easier in the textbook.

CHECK YOURSELF

- How can the Fed tell when increases in asset prices reach the bubble stage?
- If the Fed thinks there is a bubble in housing prices and contracts the growth in the money supply to pop it, what collateral damage can it cause?

default. That would have been the best way of limiting the bubble without taking down the broader economy.

Economists have not settled on what to do when asset prices like housing prices or stock prices boom. The bottom line is this: Monetary policy is difficult in the worst of times and it's not easy in the best of times.

Rules vs. Discretion

The possibility of the "Too little" and "Too much" responses, or in other words the imperfections of monetary policy, has led to a debate over rules versus discretion when it comes to monetary policy. Ideally, monetary policy tries to adjust for shocks to aggregate demand, but it is often debated whether these adjustments are effective in reducing the volatility of output. If the Fed responds too often in the wrong direction or with the wrong strength, GDP volatility will increase rather than decrease.

Economists who think that the Fed is likely to make a lot of mistakes believe that apart from extreme cases, the Fed is best advised to follow a consistent policy and not try to adjust to every aggregate demand shock. A typical monetary rule would set target ranges for the monetary aggregates like M1 or M2 or for the rate of inflation. Nobel Prize winner Milton Friedman, for example, advocated a strict rule in which the money supply would grow by 3% a year every year, since the U.S. economy has a long-run growth rate near 3%.

A monetary rule, however, works best only when v, monetary velocity, doesn't change rapidly. To see one problem with a monetary rule, let's return to the quantity theory of money and the relationship

$$Mv = PY_R$$

where M is the money supply, v is velocity, P is the price index, and Y_R is real GDP.

A monetary rule says keep M constant (or growing at a constant rate) but that means that the Fed must ignore changes in v. In times of crisis such as the Great Depression or the Great Recession, we have seen that v can fall rapidly as consumers and businesses cut back on their spending and banks reduce lending. If M is constant and v falls, then either P must fall or Y_R must fall. Since prices are sticky, the usual outcome is that both P and Y_R fall, and a fall in Y_R means a recession.

To avoid some of the defects of a monetary rule but still constrain the Federal Reserve from too much discretion, other economists have suggested a nominal GDP rule. The nominal GDP rule is simple: it says keep Mv constant (or growing at a constant rate). If Mv doesn't change or grows smoothly, then so does PY_R, and that would be ideal.

Figure 16.7 shows nominal GDP from 2003 to 2013. Before the recession, which began in December of 2007, nominal GDP had been increasing at a little over 5% a year. As the recession began, however, nominal GDP began to increase more slowly, and then in the third quarter of 2008 it started to plunge.

A nominal GDP rule would have required the Federal Reserve to increase M by as much as it takes to keep nominal GDP growing at around 5% a year (along the path given by the dotted red line). As you can see, the Fed did not follow a nominal GDP rule.

If the Fed had followed a nominal GDP rule, the recession of 2008 would have been much milder. But it's not clear that the Fed *could* have followed a nominal GDP rule. To be fair, the Fed was not asleep at the wheel in 2008 and

FIGURE 16.7

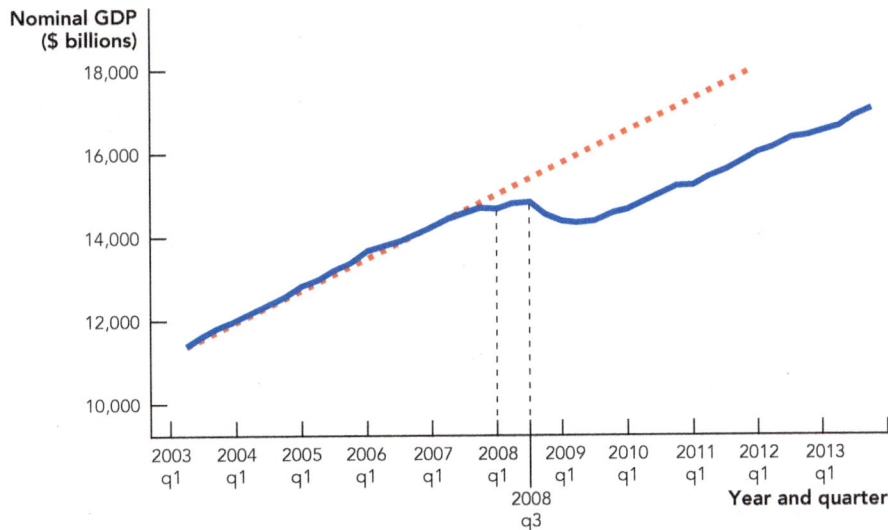

Would a Rule Have Been Better? Nominal GDP fell significantly beginning in the 3rd quarter of 2008. The Fed did not increase *M* enough to make up for a fall in *v*. Whether the Fed should have or could have kept nominal GDP on track is debated.

they did respond to the fall in nominal GDP by increasing the monetary base. Indeed, between August of 2008 and December of 2008, the monetary base doubled! That is by far the largest increase in the monetary base in the Fed's entire history. Proponents of a nominal GDP rule say the Fed did too little, too late. In this view, if the Fed had acted sooner and given the markets clearer guidance, then *v* would have stayed higher and the Fed could have more easily returned nominal GDP to its trend.

As emphasized earlier, much of what the Fed does is to try to manage market confidence and expectations. A rule such as a nominal GDP rule might help to stabilize expectations, especially in normal times. But if a rule suggests that the Fed must do things it has never done before, market participants may wonder whether the Fed will really follow the rule or even if it *can* follow the rule. It may be hard for the Fed to maintain a growth path for *Mv* when credit is collapsing, for instance. Moreover, if a rule suggests that the Fed should do something it has never done before, should and will the Fed follow the rule? It's difficult to know the results of a rule when it requires the Fed to take actions that are outside historical experience.

Takeaway

The Fed has some influence over the growth rate of GDP through its influence over the money supply and thus AD. An increase in $\overline{M}$ increases AD and a decrease in $\overline{M}$ decreases AD.

When faced with a negative shock to AD, the central bank can restore aggregate demand through an expansionary monetary policy. Monetary policy, however, is subject to uncertainties in impact and timing and getting it "Just right" is not guaranteed. Poor monetary policy can decrease the stability of GDP.

CHECK YOURSELF
- Why did Milton Friedman argue for a set rule of 3% money growth per year? Why not 2% or 0%?

MRU

mru.org/yellen

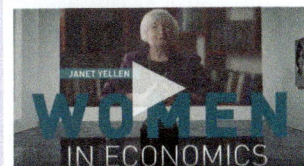

Women in Economics: Janet Yellen

If in responding to a series of recessions, the Fed increases $\overline{M}$ too much, it may find that it later has to contract $\overline{M}$ when inflation becomes too high. Usually, this process—called a disinflation—is painful and it results in a recession. A disinflation goes best when the central bank has some degree of credibility in its attempt to set things right.

A central bank would like low unemployment and low inflation, but it is not always possible to achieve both goals. When a negative real shock comes, the Fed must choose between allowing low rates of growth, excessively high rates of inflation, or some combination of both. There is no easy way out of this dilemma.

Monetary policy is difficult in the worst of times and it's not easy in the best of times. The Federal Reserve has significant power but that power is not always easy to wield. Sometimes the central bank itself contributes to booms that eventually lead to painful busts. How to recognize and respond to asset price booms is not obvious and the economics of asset price booms is unsettled.

Real shocks and aggregate demand shocks are always mixed and not easy to disentangle. The data on which central bankers operate are often slow to arrive and subject to revision. As a result, central banking is as much art as science.

CHAPTER REVIEW

Go online to practice with more examples of these types of problems, including live links to videos, data sources, and feedback.

▶ Problems with this icon relate to optional MRU videos.

KEY CONCEPTS

disinflation, p. 360

deflation, p. 360

credible, p. 360

market confidence, p. 361

FACTS AND TOOLS

1. This chapter is concerned mostly with how monetary policy might be able to return an economy *quickly* to the potential growth rate after a shock. But as we saw in the discussion of the quantity theory of money in Chapter 12, a market economy has a correction mechanism to return itself *slowly* to the potential growth rate after a shock: flexible prices. Let's review the quantity theory, and remember that in the quantity theory, inflation does all of the adjusting.

Recall that: $\overline{M} + \vec{v} =$ Inflation + Real growth

a. Consider the nation of Kydland. Before the shock to Kydland's economy, $\overline{M} = 10\%$, $\vec{v} = 3\%$, real growth = 4%. What is inflation?

b. In Kydland, $\vec{v}$ falls to 0%, but $\overline{M}$ stays the same. In the long run, what will inflation equal? What will real growth equal?

c. Consider the nation of Prescottia. Before the shock to Prescottia's economy, $\overline{M} = 2\%$, $\vec{v} = 4\%$, real growth = 2%. What is inflation?

d. In Prescottia, $\vec{v}$ rises to 8%. In the long run, what will inflation equal? What will real growth equal?

e. Consider the nation of Friedmania. Before the shock to Friedmania's economy, $\overline{M} = 3\%$, $\vec{v} = 0\%$, real growth = 3%. What is inflation?

f. In Friedmania, $\overline{M}$ falls to 1%. In the long run, what will inflation equal? What will real growth equal?

2. We've just reviewed the quantity theory of money, which is a theory that shows how the economy fixes itself in the long run. But as economist John Maynard Keynes famously said, "In the long run we are all dead." Let's bring SRAS back into the model, and play the role of a central banker reacting to a rise in velocity growth.

a. The following diagram shows the economy growing at the potential growth rate with 10% inflation. Illustrate what happens if consumers and investors become more optimistic. Clearly label the new growth rate on the x-axis with the words "High-AD real growth," and label the new inflation rate on the y-axis with the words "High-AD inflation."

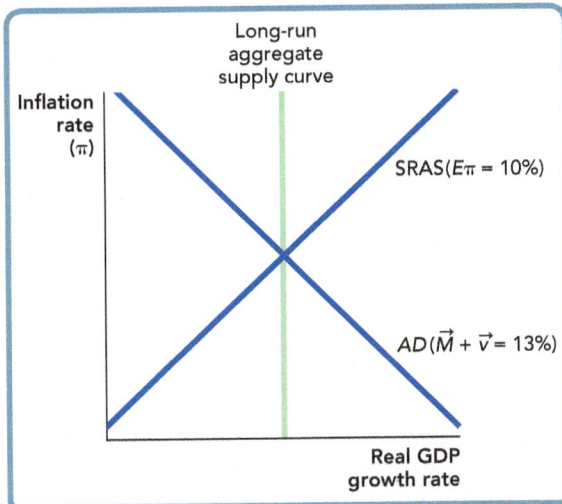

b. Once the central banker sees this rise in AD, she decides to fully reverse it with monetary policy. In the graph, illustrate what happens if she does her job "Just right."

c. If she does her job "Just right," what will the inflation rate be? Provide an exact number.

3. Let's look at the Federal Reserve's dilemma when there's a positive shock to the long-run aggregate supply curve. We'll consider the reverse of Figures 16.3 and 16.4.

a. In the following figure, illustrate the effect of this positive potential growth shock, ignoring the possible effect of sticky wages and prices.

b. If the central bank kept AD fixed, would inflation be higher or lower after this positive

real shock? Would real growth be higher or lower after this positive real shock?

c. If the central bank wants to return inflation to its old level, should it raise money growth or lower it?

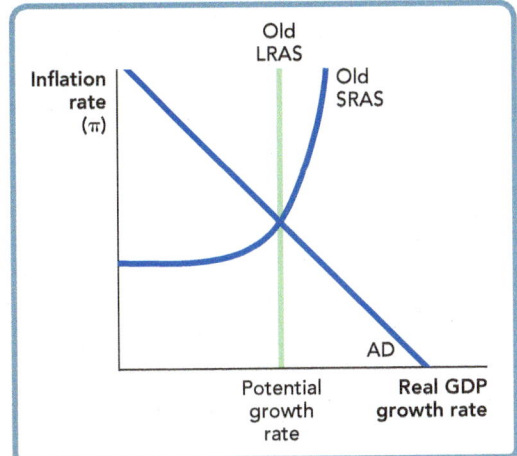

d. If the central bank wants to return real growth to its old level, should it raise money growth or lower it?

e. Economists say that central bankers face a "cruel trade-off" between inflation and real growth when a potential growth shock hits. Do your answers to parts c and d fit in with this theory?

4. All of the following are called "rules." Which of the following so-called rules are actually like "rules" and which are more like "discretion"? How can you tell the difference?

a. Congress passes a law providing automatic cost-of-living increases to Social Security every year. (*Note:* This is current U.S. law.)

b. Congress follows a rule to vote every few years on how much to increase Social Security payments—votes that usually occur just before an election. (This was the law before 1972.)

c. The Federal Reserve follows the famous "Taylor rule" for setting the Federal Funds rate:

Nominal rate = 2% + Inflation +
0.5 × (Real growth rate
− Potential growth rate)

d. The Federal Reserve follows a rule of "doing whatever seems right at the time."

e. The police follow a rule of questioning anyone loitering outside of a bank who looks suspicious.

f. The police follow a rule of questioning anyone loitering outside of a bank who is dressed in bulky clothing that could conceal a weapon.

5. Let's consider a case that has some similarities to Figure 16.2. We mentioned that it's difficult for the Fed to know what's really happening to the economy in real time. This is similar to the well-known "fog of war," where wartime news accounts often turn out to be exaggerations of the real story. In this question, the Federal Reserve thinks that consumer pessimism has pushed AD down by 10%, but in reality, the pessimism has pushed AD down by only 5%.

a. In the following figure, illustrate two AD curves: "AD with false shock" (AD-F to save room) and "AD with true shock" (AD-T).

b. If the central bank wants to use monetary policy to reverse a 10% shock to AD, it will have to raise money growth by 10%. Now draw two more AD curves on the figure: "Fed reacts to false shock" (FR-F to keep it short) and "Fed reacts to true shock" (FR-T).

c. After the central bank overreacts to the exaggerated news reports of economic calamity, what is the final result: Will real growth be higher or lower than before the shock hits? Will inflation be higher or lower than before the shock hits?

6. Which of the following would be methods that the Fed could use to "maintain market confidence" when a negative AD shock hits?

a. Slow the growth rate of the monetary base.

b. Raise the interest rate on "discount window" loans.

c. Promise to increase the growth rate of money if the economy worsens further.

d. Sell Treasury bills and buy bank reserves through open market operations.

e. Pay a higher interest rate on reserves.

7. When talking about the economy, people often make a distinction between policies that work "only in theory" compared to those that work "in practice." In theory, a fall in money growth slows down the economy in the short run. In the six episodes since World War II when, as discussed, the Fed deliberately put the brakes on money growth, did this theory work "in practice" every single time, most of the time but not all of the time, or did this theory fail most of the time?

8. A monetary policy is said to be *credible* if the central bank will have an incentive to do tomorrow what it says today that it will do tomorrow. Other policies may be credible or noncredible. Which of the following policies are credible?

a. A student promises to study for the final after going to the frat party.

b. A long established store offers "Guaranteed satisfaction or your money back."

c. A government promises never to bail out banks that take on too much risk and go bankrupt.

9. **a.** When a financial bubble collapses, is that more like a fall in aggregate demand or a fall in the potential growth rate?

b. When a financial bubble collapses, what is more likely to happen as a result: a fall in inflation or a rise in inflation?

10. Central banks and voters alike usually want higher real growth and lower inflation. What kind of shock makes that happen? (*Note:* This is similar to the type of shock that causes higher quantity and lower price in a simple supply and demand model.)

11. An economy has been growing for many years at just 1% per year, which most people consider slow. An adviser to the government suggests that faster growth in the money supply could increase the growth rate. How would you respond?

THINKING AND PROBLEM SOLVING

12. Let's reenact a simplified version of the 1981–1982 Volcker disinflation. Expected inflation and actual inflation are both 10%, real growth is 3%, and to keep it simple, velocity growth is zero. (*Historical note:* In fact, velocity growth shifted quite a lot during this period, which made

Volcker's job harder than in this problem. Otherwise, the numbers are close to the historical facts.) Thus, we have

AD: Money growth = Inflation + Real growth

Let's define a simple SRAS curve:

SRAS: Inflation = Expected inflation + 1 × (Real growth rate − Potential growth rate)

Notice that this equation gives a positive relationship between inflation and real growth for a fixed potential growth rate and expected inflation rate.

a. First, let's calculate how fast the money supply grew back when inflation was 10% in 1980 and real growth was at the rate of 3%. How fast did the money supply grow at this point, before Volcker started fighting inflation? (*Hint:* Use the AD equation.)

b. Now, let's calculate how fast Volcker will let the money supply grow in the long run, after he pulls inflation down to 4% per year. Remember, he'll assume that in the long run, the economy will just grow at the potential growth rate. (*Hint:* Use AD again.)

c. In the short run, when Volcker cuts money growth to the rate you calculated in part b, the economy won't grow at the potential growth rate. Instead, real output will grow at whatever rate the SRAS dictates. In terms of algebra, this means you have to combine SRAS and AD; it's a system of two equations and two unknowns: inflation and real growth. You know the values of money growth, expected inflation, and the potential growth rate already. In the short run, what will real growth and inflation be?

13. Now, let's reenact the Volcker disinflation in an alternate universe where wages are more flexible and workers are much more willing to accept slower growing wages when the inflation rate falls. This will make the SRAS steeper, as we saw in our original discussion of short-run aggregate supply.

Our model economy is thus as follows:

SRAS: Inflation = Expected inflation + 2 × (Real growth rate − Potential growth rate)
AD: Money growth = Inflation + Real growth

a. Answer part *c* of the previous question again, now in this world with a steeper SRAS.

b. Let's see how far this can go: What if workers pay constant attention to the Fed's every move and will slow their wage demands the moment they see Volcker tightening the money supply? Answer the previous question with "100" in the place of "2" in the SRAS equation. Feel free to round your answers to the nearest percent.

c. If you were a central banker trying to cut inflation, and you want to keep real growth as close as possible to the potential growth rate, what would you prefer: a steep SRAS (i.e., workers with flexible wages), or a flatter SRAS (i.e., workers with sticky wages)?

14. The Fed plays an important role in maintaining market confidence. As former Chairman Alan Greenspan put it in a 1997 address: "In [financial crises] the Federal Reserve *stands ready* to provide liquidity, if necessary. . . . The objectives of the central bank in crisis management are to . . . prevent a contagious loss of confidence." [emphasis added]

Just by *standing ready* to provide loans to banks in an emergency, the Fed can often prevent emergencies from happening in the first place. In each of the following examples, how does the fact that someone or something stands ready to cure the bad outcome help prevent the bad outcome from ever happening in the first place?

a. A security guard stands inside a bank.

b. Federal agents guard Fort Knox, where about one-half of the U.S. government's gold is stored.

c. The Federal Reserve promises to insure almost 100% of bank deposits.

d. Police, worried about possible riots during spring break in Palm Springs, California, bring in police from other cities.

15. We discussed how hard it is to keep AD stable or put it back "where it belongs" after a shock. Alan Blinder, a former vice chairman of the Federal Reserve, noticed that this was a major problem. In his book *Central Banking in Theory and Practice*, he argued that this was a good reason for the Fed to take baby steps whenever it needed to make big shifts in AD. Sometimes you're better off taking two years to slowly and carefully undo an AD shock rather than shift it back quickly and inaccurately in one year.

To illustrate, let's see how things turn out if you, the central banker, take two years rather than one year to react to a negative velocity shock. You have better control over AD if you make small moves than if you make big moves, but big moves can get you back to the potential growth rate more quickly: As so often in economics, you face a trade-off.

In this question, your ultimate goal is to get AD back to 5% per year, the potential growth rate is 3%, and expected inflation is always 2% per year.

Starting point (substitute what you know into these equations and solve):

AD: 1% = Inflation + Real growth rate

SRAS: Inflation = Expected inflation + (Real growth rate − Potential growth rate)

a. Slow approach: Add 2% per year to AD for two years (through some mix of money growth and higher confidence). What will real growth equal each year?

	Start	End of Year 1	End of Year 2
Real Growth			

b. Fast approach: Assume that you tried to add 4% to AD in Year 1, but you mistakenly add 7% instead (through some mix of excess bank lending and irrational exuberance). In the second year, you tried to correct by cutting back by 3%, but you mistakenly cut back by 4% (through some mix of slower bank lending and investors' loss of confidence). What will real growth equal each year?

	Start	End of Year 1	End of Year 2
Real Growth			

c. You can see how the "best approach" is a matter of taste, but which method would you expect a central banker to prefer if Congress has to decide whether to reappoint the central banker to a new four-year term in a few months?

16. Milton Friedman and Anna Schwartz argued in the last chapter of their *Monetary History of the United States* that a shift in money growth will usually cause velocity to shift in the same direction: So higher money growth causes optimism, and slower growth causes pessimism. They believed that velocity had its own shocks, as well.

a. Let's run through some examples of how this might work, in a setting where the Fed wants to keep AD growth stable at 10%. To keep things simple, we'll just assume that the Fed can control money growth perfectly, and we'll assume that a 1% change in money growth causes a 0.5% shock to velocity growth in the same direction. Fill in the table.

In each case, AD = Initial velocity shock + Money growth + Velocity shock caused by money growth.

Year	Initial Velocity Shock	Money Growth	Velocity Shock Caused by Money Growth
1	4%	4%	4% × 0.5 = 2%
2	3%		
3	16%		
4	8%		
5	4%		
6	0%		

b. If velocity does tend to move in the direction of money growth, how does this change the Fed's response to economic shocks? Should it take bigger moves or smaller moves in money growth when a shock comes along?

17. We saw that real shocks and AD shocks often occur simultaneously. When this happens, unless we know the exact size of each shock, we can't be sure of the effect on both inflation *and* real growth: We'll know only one or the other for sure.

In each of the following cases, we can be *sure* that *one* of the four events will happen:

A fall in inflation

A rise in inflation

A fall in real growth

A rise in real growth

In the following cases, which changes can we confidently predict? (*Hint:* Draw an AD/LRAS curve graph. Try several different combinations of the indicated shifts and see which outcomes are possible on the graph.)

a. The banking system becomes less efficient at building bridges between savers and borrowers, and investor confidence declines: A negative real shock and a negative velocity shock occur simultaneously.

b. The banking system becomes less efficient at building bridges between savers and borrowers, and the Federal Reserve increases money growth: A negative real shock and a positive money shock occur simultaneously.

c. Biologists learn how to use computer simulations to rapidly search for molecules that would make promising medicines, and investors become optimistic about future profit opportunities: A positive real shock and a positive velocity shock occur simultaneously.

18. One argument for giving discretion to central bankers is that sometimes emergencies come along that a simple rule can't solve. Suppose there's a massive, permanent negative shock to velocity. Naturally, if the central bank has discretion, it will immediately respond by boosting money growth. But let's look at the alternative:

a. Suppose that the central bank follows a fixed 3% annual monetary growth rule, as Milton Friedman sometimes recommended. In the short run, what will the velocity shock do to real growth and to inflation?

b. In the long run, what will this velocity shock do to real growth and to inflation?

c. If voters are concerned only about real growth in the long run, will they favor rules, will they favor discretion, or will they be indifferent between the two?

d. If voters are impatient, and concerned only about real growth in the short run, will they favor rules, will they favor discretion, or will they be indifferent between the two?

e. Which kind of voters favor discretion: those with a long-run horizon or those with a short-run horizon?

Discovering DATA ⁚⁚

19. Using the FRED economic database (https://fred.stlouisfed.org/), find the velocity of M2 from 2005 to 2019. Click Edit Graph and change the units to Percent Change. What happened to the growth rate of velocity in the 4th quarter of 2008? What kind of shock is this?

This chapter has more Challenge questions than usual. Take this as a sign of how difficult monetary policy really is!

20. Practice with the best case: You are the central banker, and you have to decide how fast the money supply should grow. Your economy gets hit by the following AD shocks and your job is simply to neutralize them: Just push money growth in the opposite direction of the shock.

In all of the following cases, assume that there's no change whatsoever to the potential growth rate, and assume that before the shock, you're at your optimal inflation rate and optimal real growth rate. (Yes, this really is the best case!) These are all shocks, so think of each case study as preceded by the word, "Suddenly. . . ." Given the shocks to $\vec{v}$, velocity, should the central bank react by raising money growth or by cutting money growth?

a. Investors become pessimistic about future profit opportunities.

b. State governments increase spending on schools, prisons, and health care.

c. The federal government passes a national sales tax.

d. The federal government increases military spending.

e. Foreigners buy fewer American-made airplanes and movies.

f. American consumers start buying fewer domestically made Hondas and more imported Hondas.

g. Domestically made computers, cars, and furniture all become much more durable and longer-lasting.

21. Milton Friedman famously said that changes in money growth affect the economy with "long and variable lags." That means that if the government increases growth in the monetary base this month, the money multiplier takes a few months to turn this into growth in checking and savings deposits, and it takes a few months more before businesses and consumers actually spend this money to purchase goods and services. Let's see how this changes our views of the previous question.

In each case from Problem 20, the Fed predicts how long the velocity shock itself will last: We call this "shock duration" in the next table. After that time, velocity growth will go back to its old level. Additionally, in each case, the Fed's staff of PhD economists estimates how many months it will take for a change in money supply to actually push AD in the desired direction: This is the "monetary lag."

The question is quite simple: If monetary lags are shorter than the shock duration—if the Fed has "fair warning"—then a shift in AD will be stabilizing. If not, then a shift in AD will be like mailing a birthday card to your mother the day before her birthday: possibly destabilizing. So, in which of these cases should the Federal Reserve change money growth?

Case	Monetary Lag (months)	Shock Duration (months)	Shift in Money Growth: Stabilizing or Destabilizing?
a.	14	8	
b.	18	12	
c.	20	Permanent	
d.	12	24	
e.	16	9	
f.	10	Permanent	
g.	18	Permanent	

22. One of the reasons it's difficult to be a monetary policymaker is because it's so hard to tell what's actually going on in the economy. It's a lot like being a doctor in a world before X-rays, MRIs, and inexpensive blood tests: When the patient complains about a stomachache, you don't know if it's caused by food poisoning or by a tumor the size of a grapefruit.

In each of the cases from Problem 20, consider the fact that your data are often quite unreliable. (Fed Chair Alan Greenspan was famous for holding meetings with 100 staff economists, peppering them with questions about the quality of their data on the economy, and often knowing more than his own staff economists about the strengths and weaknesses of various surveys of the U.S. economy.) To make matters more difficult, the Federal Reserve has to forecast the behavior of Congress, which is at least as difficult as predicting the behavior of businesses: Politicians often claim they are going to raise or cut spending or taxes, but then fail to do so.

If in cases a, b, and d from Problem 20, the Fed chairman decides that the forecasted shocks really

aren't very likely to happen, then taking into account your answers to questions 20 and 21, in which cases should the Fed actually do nothing whatsoever in response to news about the economy?

23. We explained how a central bank has an important role in maintaining confidence: "High confidence" keeps velocity growth and the money multiplier from falling. But as we've seen, sometimes one has to be cruel to be kind.

President Franklin Roosevelt followed this "tough love" approach during the Great Depression. Soon after taking office, he closed all banks for a four-day "bank holiday." During this holiday, he gave his first Fireside Chat, a radio address where he explained his policies to the American people in plain language. After the four-day holiday, he still kept one-third of all U.S. banks closed (mostly small farmer banks with one or two branches). Over the next few years, only half of this one-third eventually reopened.

Thus, FDR's bank holiday pushed the broad U.S. money supply (M1 or M2) down. Nevertheless, the economy grew quickly during FDR's first year, 1933. Why? Because FDR promised that the banks that reopened were the safest banks, and he promised that the federal government would keep these safer banks open through generous discount window lending. This boosted confidence and encouraged people to borrow from and lend to the remaining banks.

As Milton Friedman and Anna Schwartz put it in their classic book *A Monetary History of the United States*, "The emergency revival of the banking system contributed to recovery by restoring confidence in the monetary and economic system and thereby inducing the public . . . to raise velocity . . . rather than by producing a growth in the stock of money" (p. 433).

Let's see how an emotional concept like "confidence" shows up mathematically. To keep things simple, we'll look at AD in terms of growth in nominal GDP (growth in dollar sales) rather than growth in real GDP (growth in actual output). We'll compare the "before" and "after," so we'll skip over 1933, the year of the biggest banking crisis and of FDR's solution to the crisis:

Year	M2	v
1932	$35.3 billion	2.16
1934	$33.1 billion	2.36

a. What was the level of nominal GDP in 1932 and 1934?

b. What was the growth of M2 between these two years?

c. What was the growth of velocity between these two years?

d. What was the growth of nominal GDP between these two years?

e. If velocity growth had been zero during this period (perhaps due to low confidence), but money growth stayed the same, what would have happened to nominal GDP growth?

24. Central bankers often believe that their hands are tied by the public. Arthur Burns, the Fed chairman under President Nixon, reportedly said in the November 1970 Federal Reserve board meeting that "he did not believe the country was willing to accept for any long period an unemployment rate in the area of 6 percent." In other words, if AD shocks or potential growth shocks came along that pushed the unemployment rate up, Burns believed he had to boost AD to help the economy: The voters wouldn't tolerate anything else.

a. In the early 1970s, the economy was hit with some negative potential growth shocks, the most famous of which were the massive oil price increases caused by the OPEC oil embargo. Inflation started off at 4%, and Burns actually behaved according to his stated philosophy. What did Burns do to AD in the 1970s: Did he raise it or lower it?

b. If Burns had kept AD fixed instead of shifting it as he did, would inflation have been lower or higher than it actually turned out to be?

c. According to our model, did Burns' actions raise, lower, or have no impact on the long-run aggregate supply curve?

d. If in the 1970s the United States had been hit by negative AD shocks instead of negative potential growth shocks, and Burns had followed his same philosophy, would inflation have been higher or lower than it actually turned out to be?

25. Central bankers are reluctant to try to pop alleged bubbles. Which topics covered in this chapter might explain why they are reluctant to do so?

26. We mentioned Milton Friedman's advice that central bankers should follow a "fixed money growth rule," where the broad money supply (M1 or M2) grows at the same rate every year. Other economists have instead recommended that central bankers follow "nominal GDP targeting," which is similar to a fixed AD curve. Assume that the central bank really can control money growth and velocity growth within a reasonable period of time if it tries to do so.

a. What is the difference between a fixed money growth rule and nominal GDP targeting from the point of view of the AD equation?

b. If velocity shocks never occur, what's the best policy for keeping AD as stable as possible: fixed money growth, nominal GDP targeting? Or are both equivalent?

c. If velocity shocks are common, what's the best policy for keeping AD as stable as possible: fixed money growth, nominal GDP targeting? Or are both equivalent?

27. The previous question assumed that the central bank can really control money growth and velocity growth within a reasonable period of time. Instead, let's work with the more realistic assumption that it takes about a year for a change in monetary policy to actually influence money growth: Even though the central bank can increase bank reserves literally within minutes through open market operations or the term auction facility, it takes months for banks to determine whom they should lend to. And as you know, most money is created through bank loans.

In this question, the central bank tries to follow nominal GDP targeting so that AD grows at 7% per year. In other words, the central banks tries to set the money growth rate so that velocity growth plus money growth equals 7%. Each year, it responds to that year's velocity growth, but the response won't actually kick in until next year. (Think of this as driving a car with loose steering: You steer to the right, but the car only starts moving to the right about 2 seconds later.)

a. Fill in the following table. Notice that in each year, Actual AD = Velocity growth + Money growth. In the first year, the central bank observes velocity growth of 3% and thus targets money growth of 4%. The next year money grows at 4% as targeted, but velocity growth in that year is 1% so actual AD grows at 5%. In Year 2, the central bank observes velocity growth of 1% and thus targets money growth of 6%. Keep going.

Year	Velocity Growth	Target Money Growth	Money Growth	Actual AD
1	3%	4%	n/a	n/a
2	1%	6%	4%	5%
3	9%	–2%	6%	15%
4	6%			
5	2%			
6	5%			
7	0%			
8	4%			
9	6%			
10	5%			

b. Every year, the central bank tries to keep AD = 7%, yet it never accomplishes its goal. How do "long lags" explain this failure?

c. How would this table look if you had followed Friedman's 3% money growth rule instead? Don't calculate any numbers, just answer verbally: Would the swings tend to be bigger than in the table or smaller?

28. a. Central bankers must manage expectations. Suppose that inflation is running at 10% and the central banker would like to lower inflation to 2% without reducing real growth. What should the central banker tell the public? And at what level should the central banker set money growth? Assume that velocity shocks are zero and that the potential growth rate is 3%.

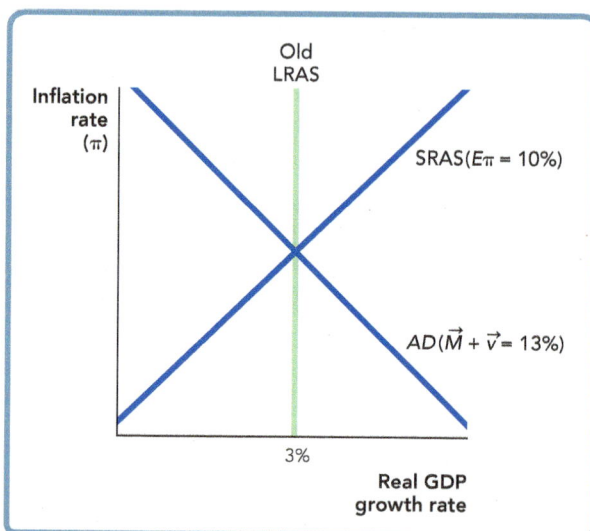

b. Suppose that the public does believe the central banker. What temptation might the central banker face? (*Hint:* Imagine that it is an election year and the central banker would like to see the current administration reelected.)

c. If the central banker is not believed, what will happen? Use your answers to parts a and b to discuss the importance of independent central banks.

29. In response to the housing bust and its fallout discussed at the end of this chapter, the U.S. economy entered into recession in December 2007. That recession officially ended in June 2009, but more than two years later at the end of 2011, many people still felt that the "recession" was not really over. As evidence, they cited high unemployment rates and the failure of some areas of the economy such as the housing market and lending to fully recover. Observers cited lack of confidence and elevated levels of uncertainty for reasons both economic and political. The Federal Reserve implemented several policies to lower both short- and long-term interest rates and increase confidence, but the private sector of the economy did not respond as it had following earlier recessions.

a. Use the AD–AS model to describe how the bursting of the housing bubble affected the economy, how the Fed responded, and the impact it had. In your discussion, be sure to point out which parts of this chapter apply to which behaviors in the economy and which parts apply to the role of the Fed in these events.

b. Critics of the Fed's response in lowering and keeping interest rates so low for so long argued that the Fed was risking increased inflation. Use the AD–AS model again to explore the validity of these claims.

WORK IT OUT

For interactive, step-by-step help in solving this problem, go online.

In the United States, the government's data on real growth improve over time. For instance, we now know that in the early 1970s, the economy was actually growing 4% faster than people believed. At the time, the Fed thought the economy was in a deep recession, so it mistakenly boosted money growth. The Fed's overreaction caused inflation. Real-time surveys in the early 1970s depicted an awful economy, but as economic historians have gone back to the data, they have discovered that the economy wasn't as awful as they thought: Someone just put the thermometer in the fridge.

Economists at the Philadelphia Federal Reserve have collected data on how our view of the economy has changed over time. These "real-time data" are summarized by Croushore and Stark in a review article entitled "A Funny Thing Happened on the Way to the Data Bank: A Real-Time Data Set for Macroeconomists" (Federal Reserve Bank of Philadelphia, *Business Review*, September/October 2000, 15–27). Let's use their summary of the data and a six-sided die to see just how inaccurate our real-time views of the economy actually are.

a. We're going to reenact the 1970s, and we'll start figuring out how error-filled the government's growth estimates will be. Croushore and Stark report that, on average:

   i. One-sixth of the time, measured growth is 2% better than actual growth.

   ii. One-third of the time, measured growth is 1% better than actual growth.

   iii. One-third of the time, measured growth is 1.5% worse than actual growth.

   iv. One-sixth of the time, measured growth is 3% worse than actual growth.

Find a six-sided die (or use Excel to simulate rolling the die) and record your rolls in the following table. If you've rolled a 1, count that in category i; if you roll a 2 or 3, place that in category ii; a 4 or 5 goes in category iii; and if you roll a 6, place that in category iv. Then write down how much measurement error you'll have for that year.

Example: If your first roll was a 4, that places you in category iii, so write down "−1.5" as the amount of measurement error for 1971.

(Note: Psychologists and behavioral economists have found that people are fairly bad at generating truly random numbers on their own, so it's best just to roll the die.)

Year	Roll (value)	Category	Measurement Error (%)
1971			
1972			
1973			
1974			
1975			
1976			
1977			
1978			
1979			
1980			

b. Let's see what values we get when we add together the true real growth rate (which economists will only know years later) with the measurement error in the previous table. For "true real growth," we use the most recent data in the following table—but of course even these estimates could change in the future. The sum is the actual government data that will wind up in the Federal Reserve chair's hands.

Example: If your first roll was a 4, that placed you in category iii, so subtract 1.5% from the true 1971 growth rate to yield a real-time government report of 1.9% annual growth.

Year	True Real Growth	Government Data (%)
1971	3.4%	
1972	5.3%	
1973	5.8%	
1974	−0.5%	
1975	−0.2%	
1976	5.3%	
1977	4.6%	
1978	5.6%	
1979	3.2%	
1980	−0.2%	

c. In your simulation, how many times was the government data off by 2% or more?

d. If the potential growth rate in the 1970s was actually 3.6% (the average growth rate in the 1970s), then in how many years did your government data give values *below* 3.6% when true real growth was *above* 3.6%? How often did the reverse occur, with your government data *above* the potential rate while true real growth was *below*?

e. Add together your two values from part d. This is the number of times that even a *very good* central banker would have wanted to push AD in the wrong direction: it's the number of times this weather vane was pointing in entirely the wrong direction.

(*Note:* You might be wondering whether the U.S. government tends to exaggerate extra good economic news just before an election. As far as economists can tell, the answer is no, at least when it comes to the official GDP number. U.S. GDP estimates contain mistakes before an election just as often as usual, but those mistakes don't tend to favor the political party in power. In Japan, though, GDP reports do tend to be extra optimistic just before an election. For more, see Faust, Rogers, and Wright, "News and Noise in G-7 GDP Announcements," online at the Federal Reserve Board's Web site.)

▶ MRU VIDEOS

Monetary Policy and the Fed

mru.org/intro-fed

Problem: **11**

Monetary Policy: The Best Case Scenario

mru.org/monetary-best

Problems: **2, 12, 20**

Women in Economics: Janet Yellen

mru.org/yellen

The Negative Real Shock Dilemma

mru.org/monetary-neg-shock

Problem: **17**

When the Fed Does Too Much

mru.org/fed-limits

Problems: **4, 27, 29**

17

The Federal Budget: Taxes and Spending

Some people do better from the federal government than others. Take Ida May Fuller. In 1940, Ida May received Social Security check #00-000-001, the very first in the program's history. Ida May's working career had almost ended by the time Social Security began, so she had paid just $24.75 in Social Security taxes and she got almost all of that back with her first check, which was for $22.54. Ida May lived to be 100, so by the time she died in 1975, she had received a total of $22,888.92 in benefits.

You can see why Ida May is smiling. But will you be smiling from federal taxes and spending? After all, you will pay Social Security taxes throughout your working life, and what about the benefits? You can be fairly sure that unlike Ida May, you won't receive almost a thousand times more than what you put in.

More generally, since about the mid-1950s, the federal government has spent about 20% of GDP and raised about 18% of GDP. That's a lot of money, almost $5 trillion in spending in 2020. Where does all that money come from? Where does it all go? And for how long can the U.S. government keep spending more than it raises in taxes?

Tax Revenues

The federal government takes in about $3.6 trillion, or approximately $11,000 for every man, woman, and child in the United States. The federal government takes in money in many ways, but three sources—the individual income tax, the Social Security and Medicare taxes, and the corporate income tax—account for more than 90% of the revenue. Figure 17.1 shows the major sources of revenue for the U.S. government.

The individual income tax is the single largest source of revenue for the federal government. The second category, Social Security and Medicare taxes (a few other smaller taxes are also included in this category), includes the "FICA tax" you have seen on your paycheck—these taxes are so named because unlike the income tax, the revenue from these taxes is tied to specific programs. Corporate income taxes are a distant third. The other sources are much smaller and they include excise taxes such as taxes on gasoline and alcohol, user fees,

Ida May Fuller received the very first Social Security check.

FIGURE 17.1

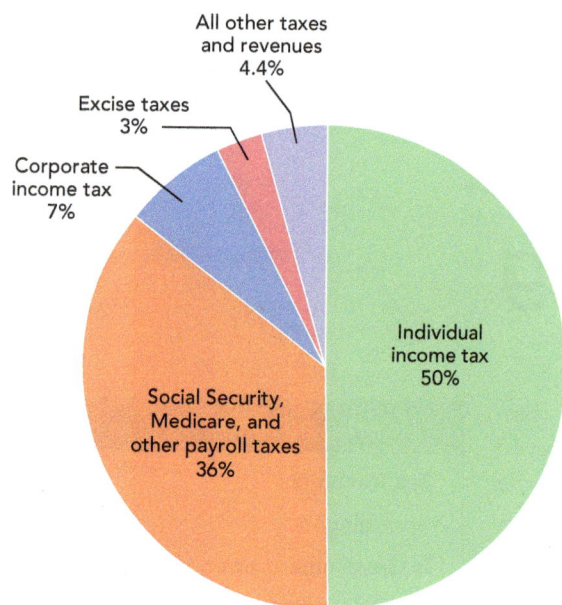

U.S. Federal Tax Receipts (2020)

Tax	Amount ($b)	Percentage
Individual income tax	$1,824	50%
Social Security, Medicare, and other payroll taxes	$1,295	36%
Corporate income tax	$255	7%
Excise taxes	$109	3%
All other taxes and revenues	$161	4.4%
Total federal taxes	$3,644	100.0%

Data from: Budget of the United States Government, fiscal year 2020.
Note: Percentages are subject to rounding error.

estate and gift taxes, and custom duties or tariffs. Let's take a closer look at the three largest sources of revenue.

The Individual Income Tax

Most Americans are required to file an income tax return with the federal government. On this form a person reports their income and the tax code determines how much money is due. The 2020 schedule of marginal tax rates for someone who is married and filing jointly with a spouse is shown in Figure 17.2.

The **marginal tax rate** is the tax rate that you must pay on an additional dollar of income. Figure 17.2 tells us that if you earn less than $19,750, then the marginal tax rate, the rate on an additional dollar of income, is 10% (some deductions are allowed). If you earn between $19,750 and $80,250, the rate of tax on an additional dollar of income is 12%. If you earn between $80,250 and $171,050, you must pay 22% of any additional income to the federal government. Marginal tax rates increase in uneven steps until the top marginal tax rate of 37% is reached on any income earned greater than $622,050.

We care about the marginal tax rate because, as usual in economics, it's the *marginal* rate that matters for determining things like the incentive to work additional hours. If you are considering doing an extra carpentry job for spare cash, you don't care what tax you are paying on the money you've already earned. You care about how much additional tax you will be paying on the extra money that you might earn if you choose to take the job.

The **marginal tax rate** is the tax rate paid on an additional dollar of income.

FIGURE 17.2

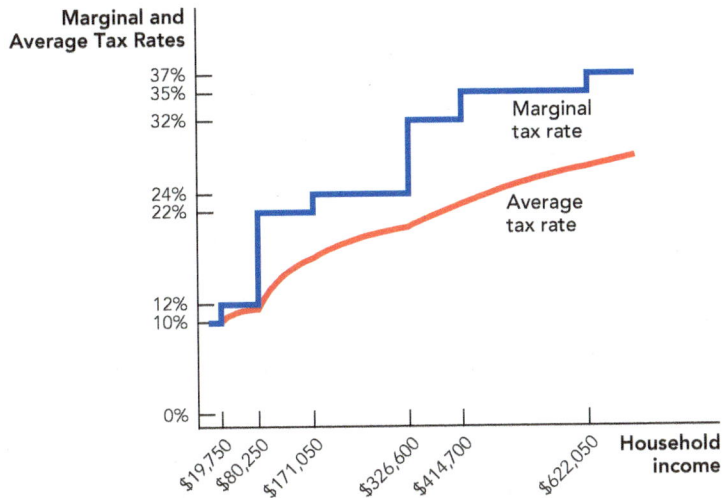

U.S. Marginal and Average Tax Rates (Married, Filing Jointly, 2020)

Data from: U.S. Internal Revenue Service.

Marginal tax rates today are lower and flatter than they have been in the past. In 1960, for example, the lowest marginal tax rate was 20% and the highest rate was 91%! Of course in the further past, rates were much lower than today. In 1913, when the income tax began, the top marginal rate was just 7% and that rate didn't take effect until annual income was over $10 million (in today's dollars).

Your **average tax rate** is simply your total tax payment divided by your total income. If your income is $50,000, for example, then your total income tax under the current system can be calculated as follows. You pay 10% on the first $19,750, or $1,975, then you pay 12% on the next $30,250, or $3,630, for a total tax of $5,605. Your average tax rate is then

$$\frac{\$5,605}{\$50,000} \times 100 = 11.2\%$$

The **average tax rate** is the total tax payment divided by total income.

However, the tax system is not quite as simple as we have presented so far because you are also allowed to deduct some income from your total taxable income. The standard deduction for a married couple in 2020 is $24,800, which means that someone with an income of $100,000 is taxed as if they had an income of $75,200 and a person with an income of $24,800 is considered to have zero taxable income. Most people take the standard deduction, but there are also deductions for certain types of "special" spending such as mortgage interest, state and local taxes, and charity, and if these items add up to more than your standard deduction you can take the itemized deductions instead.

Taxes on Capital Gains and Interest and Dividends
The income tax is a tax on your labor income and also on any income you receive from your investments, namely your interest income, your dividends, and your capital gains. You may receive interest income, for instance, on your savings accounts, and this income usually is taxed as if it were labor income.

The taxation of capital gains is more complicated. You receive a capital gain, for instance, if you buy stock at $110 a share and later resell it at $210 a share. Your capital gain is the extra $100 you made from the rise in the value of the stock. You pay a tax on those profits and currently the standard capital gains tax rises from 0% for those with low incomes to 15% for most taxpayers to 20% for those whose income puts them in the highest income tax bracket. Capital gains taxes are paid only when the assets are actually sold and not while the assets are simply being held.

As is often the case in our tax system, the real rates people pay are not the same as the rates written into the tax code. For instance, capital gains allow for "loss offsets." If you gain $100 selling one stock and lose $100 selling another, usually the two sums cancel each other out in the calculation of your tax liability. If you know how to group your winners and losers together at the right time, the true rate of capital gains taxation you face may be much lower than the published rate of 15%.

The Alternative Minimum Tax (AMT) There is yet another complication to the American tax system, and that is the **alternative minimum tax**, or AMT. The AMT was started in 1969 after a televised congressional hearing revealed that 155 households with income over $200,000 (about $1.2 million in today's dollars) had paid no income tax. These families had done nothing illegal, but they had managed to take advantage of tax laws to avoid income taxes. Thus, the original goal of the AMT was to make sure that it would not be possible for anyone to avoid all income tax.

The AMT requires taxpayers to make two computations. First, they must compute what they owe under the standard tax code; then, they must compute what they owe under the AMT, which is typically based on a flat rate of either 26% or 28%, with no deductions allowed. The taxpayer must then pay whichever number is higher.

The marginal note reads:

> **Alternative minimum tax (AMT)** is a separate income tax code that began in 1969 to prevent the rich from not paying income taxes. It was not indexed to inflation and is now an extra tax burden on many upper middle class families.

Social Security and Medicare Taxes

Almost all workers in the United States pay the Federal Insurance Contributions Act tax, better known as the FICA tax, the acronym that you will see on your payroll check. The FICA tax is 6.2% of your wages on the first $137,500 of income. In addition, your employer also pays a 6.2% tax on the same earnings so the total FICA tax is 12.4%. The FICA taxes fund Social Security payments.

Many Americans believe, "I pay half of this tax, my employer pays the other half," but this isn't quite right. As you probably recall from microeconomics, the person who appears to pay a tax isn't always the person who actually pays. In reality, economic research shows that the employer's payment is mostly taken out of the worker's prospective wage; in other words, if your employer didn't have to pay the FICA tax, your wages would be higher.[*] Much of the burden of the FICA tax falls on workers, not on employers.

---

[*] In fact, exactly this situation occurred in Chile when it privatized its social security program in 1981. Beginning in 1981, employers no longer had to pay social security taxes for their employees. The fall in employer taxes, however, did not result in extra profits. Instead, wages rose as the payroll tax fell—exactly as predicted by tax incidence theory. Other studies in the United States show that when the government mandates that firms provide benefits to their employees such as health benefits, wages fall. Thus, employees rather than employers pay for mandated benefits. On Chile and for references to other studies, see Gruber, J, 1997. The incidence of payroll taxation: Evidence from Chile, *Journal of Labor Economics* 15(3), S:72–S101.

Medicare is partly financed out of general revenues and partly financed out of special payroll taxes. For most workers, 1.45% is withheld from their paychecks in the form of a Medicare premium and the employer pays another 1.45%. Again, workers pay much of the employer's premium in the form of lower wages. Self-employed individuals pay the full 2.9% themselves.

The Corporate Income Tax

In 2017, after a contentious debate, the corporate tax rate in the United States was reduced from 35% to 21%. Those rates are applied to the (accounting) profits of the corporation, rather than to sales or gross income and so, at least in theory, corporations that are more profitable pay more.

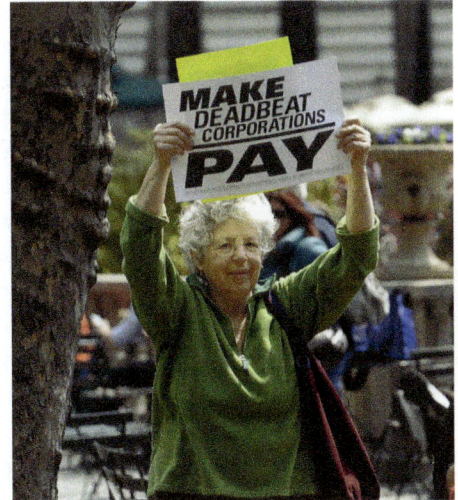

Who pays the corporate tax isn't as simple as a slogan.

Who gets the benefits of a corporate tax cut? The answer might seem obvious. Corporations! But a corporation is just a legal structure for organizing people. Every penny of corporate tax revenue must come from consumers who pay higher prices, workers who receive lower wages, or capitalists who receive lower profits. The answer might still seem obvious. As a matter of accounting, the corporate tax means that there are fewer profits to pay to capitalists so perhaps capitalists (investors) pay the corporate tax and, as a result, also get the benefits of a tax cut? Capitalists benefit first from a cut in the corporate tax but the first round impact is not the whole story. We need to delve deeper into the *incidence* of the corporate tax.

A cut in the corporate tax rate increases the incentive to invest in the corporate sector. As more capital enters the corporate sector, the return to capital and to the capitalists in that sector falls. Thus, some of the gains from a corporate tax must flow elsewhere. Where? Some of the increased capital in the corporate sector will come from the noncorporate sector (sole proprietorships, partnerships, S-corps). As capital moves from the noncorporate sector to the corporate sector, the return in the corporate sector falls and the return in the noncorporate sector increases until we reach equality. Thus, one lesson is that all capitalists will benefit from a cut in the corporate tax rate, not just capitalist investors in the corporate sector.

A cut in the corporate tax rate, therefore, will increase the return to capital overall but that too is not the end of the story. A higher return to capital overall will increase the incentive to invest overall. As investment increases, the return to capital in all sectors will decline. Thus, some of the gains from a corporate tax must flow elsewhere. Where? In order to be productive, capital needs workers. Thus, increased investment increases the demand for workers, which increases wages. Greater production also means lower prices. It may seem surprising that some of the gains from a corporate tax cut will flow to workers and consumers but that's just another way of saying that capitalists will pass on some of the costs of a tax *increase* to workers and consumers!

A useful rule to remember is that *elasticity = escape*. The more elastic factors can escape a tax, which will thus be borne by the less elastic factors. Capital tends to be highly elastic—it moves between sectors and countries with relative ease. Thus, capital can often escape some of a tax increase but remember that's just another way of saying that capital will also pass on some of the gains of a tax cut. Elasticity cuts both ways.

So who pays the corporate tax? Each of the relevant elasticities is difficult to measure so the answer is uncertain but two recent estimates find that a majority of the corporate tax is borne by capital but a substantial 30% to 50% of the corporate tax is born by workers and consumers.[1]

Even if workers and consumers bear a significant portion of the corporate income tax, that doesn't mean raising (or lowering) the corporate tax is a bad idea. We have to raise revenue somehow and comparing corporate taxes with other taxes such as income taxes and sales taxes is complicated. The important lesson, however, is that slogans like "make corporations pay their fair share!" don't make sense. We can call it a "corporate tax" but that doesn't mean that corporations or even capitalists end up paying the final bill. Understanding tax incidence isn't easy but neither can it be wisely ignored.

The Bottom Line on the Distribution of Federal Taxes

Once we add in deductions, exemptions, corporate taxes, payroll taxes, excise taxes, the AMT, and assumptions about tax incidence (who pays the tax), what is the final result? It's not an easy calculation, but the best estimate of the distribution of federal taxes by income is shown in Figure 17.3.

The left panel of Figure 17.3 shows that if we divide households into categories according to how much they earn, then households with incomes in the bottom 20% pay very little in federal tax, less than 5% of their total income. As income increases so does the average rate, so those with incomes in the top 20% pay an average tax rate of just over 25%. The average tax rate continues to rise if we look at those in the top 1% who pay more than 30% of their income to the federal government.

It is sometimes said that the rich do not pay taxes in the United States. That is false. Whether they pay *enough* taxes depends on your point of view, but despite all the deductions, exemptions, loopholes, and so forth, the U.S. tax system is **progressive**—people with higher income pay a higher percentage of their income in tax to the federal government than people with lower income.

A **progressive tax** has higher tax rates on people with higher incomes.

FIGURE 17.3

Average Tax Rate by Income Category

Share of Federal Taxes Paid by Income Category

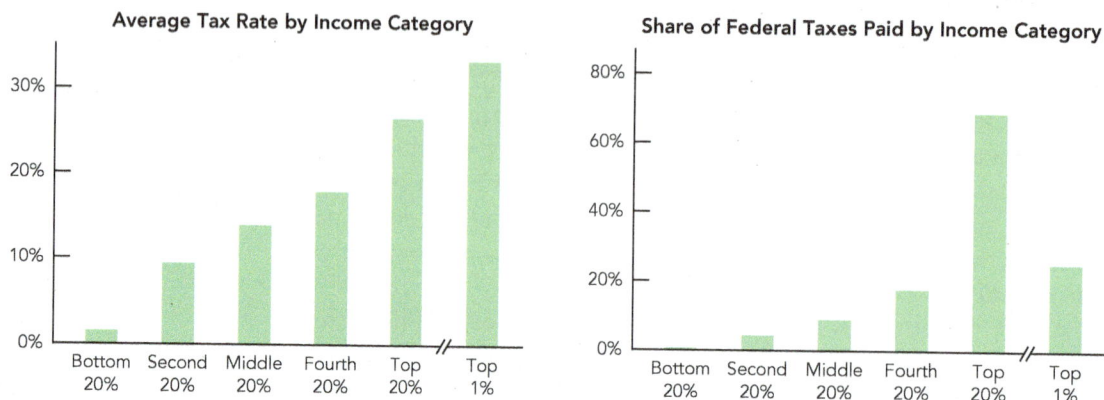

Who Pays Federal Taxes?

Data from: Congressional Budget Office, 2019 based on 2016 data.
Note: Income includes market income and government transfers.

In contrast to a progressive tax is a **flat tax**, which has a constant tax rate applied to income at all levels of earning. If the tax code were radically simplified to eliminate almost all deductions, including the deductions for mortgage interest and charitable giving, then by some calculations a flat rate of around 19% would raise approximately the same revenue as today.[2] A flat tax has a number of desirable properties. Simplification of the tax code would be appreciated by many taxpayers and elimination of deductions and loopholes would encourage people to make investment, consumption, and work decisions for good economic reasons rather than merely to reduce tax payments.

A **flat tax** has a constant tax rate.

The disadvantage of a flat tax is that moving to a flat tax would require lowering rates on the rich and raising rates on the middle class and poor. If you compare the average tax rate paid by different income classes under the current tax code—shown in the left panel of Figure 17.3—with a flat rate of 19%, you can see that tax rates for the rich and poor could change quite dramatically under a flat tax.

Even if a flat tax were significantly more efficient than our current tax code, it's hard to see how the United States could ever move to such a system because too many interest groups would oppose major changes. Other countries, however, including Russia, the Czech Republic, and Estonia, have flat taxes and some states, such as Colorado, Utah, and Illinois, also have flat taxes on income.

Returning to the current federal U.S. tax code, the average tax rate is higher on the rich and the rich have more money—put these two things together and we can calculate who pays for the federal government. The right panel in Figure 17.3 shows the share of federal tax revenues that is paid for by each income category. The finding is that the rich, and especially the very rich, bear by far the largest share of the federal tax liability. Almost 70% of federal taxes are paid by people in the top 20% of income earners. The top 1% alone pay about one-quarter of all federal taxes.

State and Local Taxes

In addition to federal taxes, most people pay state and local taxes, so the federal tax burden is not the end of the story. Overall, state and local taxes are about half the level of federal taxes, just under 9% of GDP. Compared with the federal government, states raise more of their revenues, about 20% on average, from sales taxes. Since sales tax rates are the same for everyone, regardless of income, state and local taxation as a whole is less progressive than income taxation. Thus, state and local taxes probably make the overall tax system a little bit less progressive than the federal tax system, but it does depend on the state.

CHECK YOURSELF

- Individual income taxes plus Social Security and Medicare taxes represent what percent of federal revenues? (Review Figure 17.1 if necessary.)

Spending

Almost two-thirds of the U.S. federal budget is spent on just four programs in a typical year: Social Security, defense, Medicare, and Medicaid, as seen in Figure 17.4. Interest on the national debt and various unemployment insurance programs and welfare programs are also large. Everything else—spending on roads, education, police, prisons, science and technology, agriculture, the environment, and the various stimulus programs intended to boost the economy— account for the remainder of the budget. Let's take a closer look at the big items to see just where our tax money goes.

FIGURE 17.4

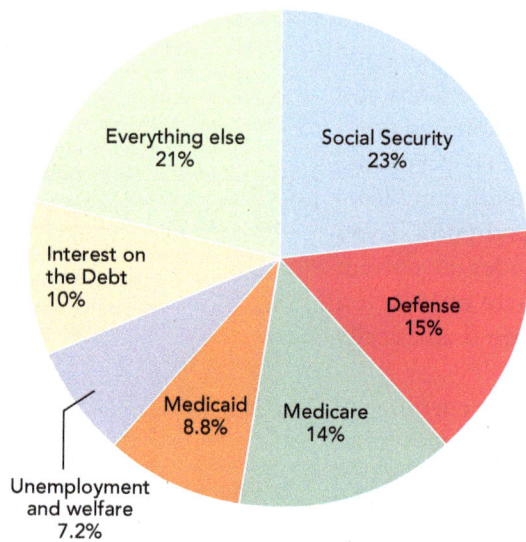

Program	Spending ($b)	Percentage
Social Security	$1,102	23%
Defense	$726	15%
Medicare	$679	14%
Medicaid	$418	8.8%
Unemployment and welfare	$340	7.2%
Interest on the Debt	$479	10%
Everything else	$1,002	21%
Total federal spending	$4,746	100.0%

U.S. Federal Spending: Major Programs (2020)

Data from: U.S. Government Printing Office: Budget of the United States Government.
Note: Percentages are subject to rounding error.

Social Security

If measured in terms of dollars paid out, Social Security is the single largest government program in the world. The Social Security programs pay more than 1 trillion dollars in benefits annually to more than 62 million beneficiaries.

We've already seen how the Social Security tax works. If you are wondering where that money goes, Social Security is run on a pay-as-you-go basis. That means that when the government takes in your dollars, the money does not go into an account or trust with your name on it. The money is shipped out right away to the current elderly, who of course are receiving benefits. When you become old, you'll get your benefits from taxes on the young at that later point in time.

Every year the federal government sends Americans letters telling us how much money is in "our" personal social security accounts. Don't be misled. There is no money in "your account"; there isn't a "your account" at all. Those letters are just the government's prediction of how much you'll get back some day. Of course, since you are in the meantime a voter, don't be surprised if those predictions turn out to be a little bit optimistic.

Social Security benefits are defined by a complex formula depending on how many years a worker worked, what their average earnings were over their working life, whether or not they are married, what year they retire, and at what age. In recent years, the average retiree and spouse have been paid $1,440 a month so one immediate lesson is that you shouldn't count on Social Security alone to support you in your old age.

The complexity of the formula means that Social Security is not equivalent to a simple forced savings program under which the government requires everyone to save 12.4% of their income. Rather, the Social Security system redistributes wealth in complex ways, some intended and some probably not intended. One intended benefit, for example, is that Social Security is more generous the lower a worker's lifetime earnings. In other words, workers with low lifetime incomes tend to get more out of the system than if they had saved their tax payments, while workers with high lifetime incomes tend to get less out of the system than if they had saved the same amount as they paid in Social Security taxes.

Social Security is also much more generous to married people than to singles. Consider two retirees, one married, one not, who paid exactly the same amount in lifetime Social Security taxes. The retirees receive the same retirement benefit for themselves but the spouse is also eligible for a spousal benefit, even if the spouse never worked. When it was common for one spouse to work and the other not to work, married couples got much more out of Social Security for every dollar they put in than did singles. Now that it's more common for both spouses to work, the spousal benefit isn't as large as it once was because workers whose own benefits exceed the spousal benefit don't get the spousal benefit. By the way, the spousal benefit can also be paid to a divorced spouse, so with multiple marriages and divorces you can imagine how complicated the system can get.

President Franklin D. Roosevelt signing the Social Security bill.

The age at which workers can claim their full retirement benefits was 65 for many years but, because the Social Security program was getting very expensive, in 1983, the full retirement age was made to slowly increase depending on when the worker was born. You—assuming you were born after 1960—must wait until age 67 to claim your full retirement benefits. Some people advocate increasing the full retirement age again, so you may want to keep an eye on the age at which you will be able to claim full benefits. A worker can start claiming some benefits as early as age 62, but people who opt for early retirement get a lower monthly payment. Benefits are indexed to the level of wages in the United States, so over time benefits rise automatically with general increases in prosperity.

Do you recall Ida May Fuller from the introduction? She paid $24.75 in Social Security taxes and received $22,888.92 in payments. Ida May's example is extreme but the basic idea is quite general. Workers who retired in the early years of Social Security received full benefits even though they paid Social Security taxes for only a portion of their working life. In addition, the Social Security tax rate increased over time, rising from 2% in 1940 to today's rate of 12.4%. The higher tax rate on today's workers funds larger benefits for *yesterday's* workers—even though yesterday's workers paid a lower tax rate on their earnings.

Social Security has become less generous over time for another reason—the labor force has been growing more slowly in recent decades because fewer people are working and because the growth rate in the population has declined. It's harder to fund benefits to yesterday's workers when there are fewer workers to tax today.

Increased life expectancy makes the Social Security system more generous over time. If life expectancy continues to increase, then future Social Security benefits will be *very* generous. But don't count your chickens before they hatch. Social Security spending currently exceeds Social Security taxes—the difference is made up by interest on past excess contributions. The Congressional Budget Office projects, however, that interest payments will cover the Social Security deficit only until 2029.[3] In 2029, the difference between benefits spending and Social Security taxes will have to be made up by revenues from taxes other than the Social Security tax, increases in Social Security taxes, or decreases in benefits, such as increases in the retirement age. No one is quite sure what will happen so there is a lot of uncertainty about future benefits.

Defense

The official budget for the Department of Defense is about $726 billion. Even this figure, however, doesn't include spending on veterans' benefits, homeland security, nuclear weapons research, or costs of military-style operations that run through the CIA or other non-Defense Department agencies. A broader definition for defense would increase defense spending by at least another $100 billion or more depending on what is included.

The United States spends much more on its military than does any other country in the world. Table 17.1 presents some data on the top 10 countries by military expenditure in 2018. Do we get value for our money? Unfortunately, assessing how much we should spend on the military goes well beyond standard economics and into issues of foreign policy. That is an important question but it isn't a topic for this book.

Medicare and Medicaid

Medicare reimburses the elderly for much of their medical care spending, covering hospital stays, doctor bills, and prescription drugs. To be eligible for Medicare, an individual should be 65 or older and have worked for at least 10 years in a job paying Medicare premiums. Many of the disabled are covered as well, even if they have not held such jobs.

In fiscal year 2020, Medicare spending amounted to $679 billion. Social Security and Medicare, taken together, are by far the largest undertakings of the U.S. government, and both are programs that transfer wealth to the elderly.

Medicare does not pay all medical bills outright. Instead, beneficiaries are required to pay some percent of the charges, known as a "copayment." A beneficiary also has to pay for relatively small charges, which is known as a "deductible." Many of the elderly buy private insurance to pay for the gaps in their Medicare coverage.

In addition to Medicare, you may have heard of Medicaid. Whereas Medicare covers the elderly, Medicaid covers the poor and the disabled. Of course, some of the elderly are poor as well and these people are eligible for both programs. The federal government and state governments pay for Medicaid jointly, but the program itself is run through state governments. As of fiscal year 2020, Medicaid expenditures were around $418 billion. Spending on Medicaid has been increasing in recent years as more people are covered under Medicaid due to the Affordable Care Act.

TABLE 17.1 TOP TEN COUNTRIES BY MILITARY EXPENDITURE (BILLIONS OF U.S. DOLLARS)

	Country	Military Expenditure (billions)
1	United States	$648.0
2	China	250.0
3	Saudi Arabia	67.6
4	India	66.5
5	France	63.8
6	Russia	61.4
7	United Kingdom	50.0
8	Germany	49.5
9	Japan	46.6
10	South Korea	43.1

Note: 2018 data.
Data from: SIPRI Military Expenditure Database, https://www.sipri.org/

Unemployment Insurance and Welfare Spending

It is a common myth that most of the money spent by our federal government goes to welfare programs. In reality, federal welfare payments (not including Medicaid or unemployment insurance) amount to $200–$400 billion a year (depending on exactly what one counts and whether the economy is in a recession). These are substantial figures, but other programs are much larger.

Remember, other than defense, the largest spending programs are Social Security and Medicare, and these programs primarily transfer wealth to the elderly, not to the poor. Since we will all be elderly sooner or later (at least if we are lucky), these transfers eventually go to virtually all Americans.

Most welfare payments fall into a few common categories. First, personal welfare payments are made to poor households with children. The largest of these is called Temporary Assistance for Needy Families (TANF). Since 1996, an individual cannot receive these benefits for more than five years in a lifetime. Housing vouchers under the Section 8 program give poor households a voucher that subsidizes a portion of their rent.

Especially important is the Earned Income Tax Credit (EITC), which is now the main form that antipoverty policy takes at the federal level. The EITC, quite simply, pays poor people cash through the tax system depending on how much they earn. So, for instance, if you are married, have a child, and earn $20,000 a year, you are below the poverty line and the EITC will supplement your income, giving you over $3,000 for the year. With more than one child, the credit goes up to almost $4,000. In recent years, about $65 billion was spent on the EITC and these federal programs are supplemented by a wide variety of state and local welfare programs for the poor.

Unemployment insurance (UI) makes payments to people who are out of work and is not restricted to the poor. UI is a large program that can expand rapidly during recessions. In 2007, for example, just $35 billion was spent on UI, but with the recession and emergency benefits, that number increased to $160 billion in 2010 before falling back to $35 billion in 2016. Extraordinarily large unemployment insurance payments were made in 2020 to deal with the economic shutdown due to the COVID-19 pandemic.

Everything Else

Before discussing paying interest on the national debt, let's look at everything else. Everything else accounts for all the other spending programs of the federal government, which include:

- Farm subsidies
- Spending on roads, bridges, and infrastructure
- The Disaster Relief Fund
- The Small Business Administration
- The Food and Drug Administration
- All federal courts
- Federal prisons
- The FBI
- Foreign aid
- Border security
- NASA

- The National Institutes of Health
- The National Science Foundation
- Financial assistance to students
- The wages of all federal employees

All of these programs add up to a large amount of money, but none of these programs is large compared with Social Security, defense, or Medicare.

A common misconception about the budget involves foreign aid. When polled, 41% of Americans said that foreign aid is one of the two largest sources of federal expenditure. In reality, foreign aid is about 1% of the overall federal budget; the exact number depends on how that term is defined since sometimes "foreign aid" and "military assistance" are difficult to distinguish.

Is Government Spending Wasted?

You have probably also heard a lot about government waste. In fact, there are good reasons for thinking that governments might not spend money as carefully as you or I, namely weak incentives and lack of information on how to spend the money effectively. Suppose you get an A on your economics midterm and decide to spend $100 on a treat for yourself. What's the best possible use of that $100? A new pair of jeans? A dinner date? Part of a ski trip? Whatever the answer, you have good information about your wants and needs and you have good incentives to shop carefully—researching quality, comparing prices, and searching for high value—after all, *your* enjoyment and *your* money are at stake!

Now suppose that you must spend $100 on a gift for someone else. (Perhaps you are obligated to exchange Christmas gifts with your coworkers.) You still want to get value for your money but your information about what the recipient wants or needs is much less and your incentive to investigate and research quality are diminished compared with when you were spending the money on yourself. Economist Joel Waldfogel, estimated that billions of dollars are wasted every Christmas because most gifts cost the giver more than they are valued by the recipient.[4] To avoid this waste, we give the administrative assistants in our department cash. But Christmas might not be as fun if every present under the tree was money.

Now suppose that you must spend someone else's money on a gift for someone else. (Perhaps your boss gives you some money to buy a Christmas gift for one of her other employees.) You probably don't want to waste the money entirely (perhaps your boss will notice if you pocketed the cash) but you don't have good information about what the recipient wants or needs and now you are spending someone else's money so your incentives to shop carefully are very much diminished. A lot of government spending falls into this category—some people spending other people's money on yet other people. As a result, we should not be surprised when a lot of government spending results in some waste and inefficiency.

In Afghanistan and Iraq, for example, the United States spent more than a hundred billion dollars on reconstruction efforts, but audits revealed many billions of dollars in waste, fraud, and abuse. Projects were started and never completed. Hospitals were built but never provided with equipment to operate. Fraud was rampant. On one project the auditor questioned 40% of the costs it reviewed, including $900 for a control switch valued at $7.05. Perhaps most infamously, $10 billion(!) in shrink-wrapped packages of $100 bills was flown from New York to Iraq, but then simply disappeared.[5]

MRU

mru.org/econ-xmas

An Economist's Christmas

Spending in Iraq and Afghanistan was probably especially likely to be wasted because the U.S. government lacked information about local wants and needs, which were very different from those of people in the United States, and because the ultimate boss—the American taxpayer—was far away and could not easily monitor how the money was being spent. Problems of information and incentives, however, plague all kinds of government spending, both at home and abroad.

Government spending can be wasteful, but if a politician claims that they will pay for new spending programs or tax cuts by cutting "waste"—beware! First, the problem of government waste is not due to a few bad apples but rather due to deeper problems of information and incentives that are difficult to solve. Second, our trip through the federal budget shows that cutting waste may sound good, but the reality is that most of the money is being spent on the big programs. Consider Social Security, the largest government spending program. Social Security transfers cash—it's like the perfect Christmas gift recommended by economists—and because the program is well-known, it's well monitored. As a result, despite some fraud, the overhead costs of the Social Security program are low.

Overall, it's difficult to cut spending on big programs without cutting benefits. If we want more spending on those programs, ultimately taxes must rise or we must cut spending somewhere else. If we want lower taxes, spending and benefits must fall. There is no such thing as a free lunch.

The National Debt, Interest on the National Debt, and Deficits

The final category of spending we will discuss is interest on the national debt. If you Google the "U.S. national debt," you will probably find a number around $25 trillion, but quite a bit of this debt is held by other branches of the federal government. The Social Security Trust Fund, for example, holds billions of dollars in Treasury bonds, which simply represent an IOU on future Social Security payments.

A better measure of our current debt is the **national debt held by the public,** which is all federal debt held by individuals, corporations, state or local governments, foreign governments, and other entities other than the federal government itself. The national debt held by the public as of 2020 is just over $18 trillion. From now on when we talk about the national debt, the federal debt, or just the debt, we mean the national debt held by the public.

The **national debt held by the public** is all federal debt held by individuals, corporations, and governments other than the U.S. federal government.

Eighteen trillion dollars is a very big number, but it has to be compared with another very big number, GDP, which is about $22 trillion. Thus, the United States has a debt-to-GDP ratio of over 80%. Is this a big number? Figure 17.5 shows the debt-to-GDP ratio since 1939. Today's debt-to-GDP ratio is high by past standards, especially outside of a world war. More worrying is that in 2007 the debt to GDP ratio was only 35% so the national debt is rising very quickly.

The highest debt-to-GDP ratio in U.S. history occurred in 1946 at 108%. As we discussed in Chapter 9, it makes sense for you to borrow to pay for large expenses, thereby smoothing your consumption, and the same thing is true for the U.S. government. The government borrowed heavily to finance emergency expenditures for World War II, but following the war the debt-to-GDP ratio slowly declined until the 1980s. In the 1980s, a combination of tax cuts and increases in defense spending increased the debt-to-GDP ratio. The ratio then fell as the economy expanded and the federal government briefly

FIGURE 17.5

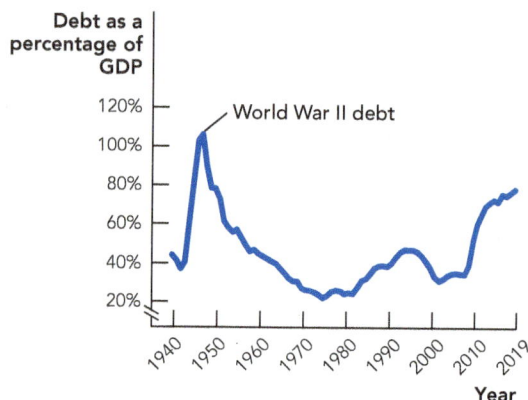

Debt as a percentage of GDP

World War II debt

The Debt-to-GDP Ratio, 1939–2019

Data from: https://fred.stlouisfed.org/graph/?g=mXsy.
Note: Gross federal debt held by the public as percent of gross domestic product.

The **deficit** is the annual difference between federal spending and revenues.

CHECK YOURSELF

- When you retire, you will receive Social Security benefits and most Americans will also receive Medicare benefits. Right now, what percentage of federal spending is represented by Social Security plus Medicare payments?

- Why is it important to consider the debt-to-GDP ratio rather than just the absolute amount of the national debt? What does this ratio tell us?

ran a series of budget surpluses under President Bill Clinton in the 1990s. More recently, the debt-to-GDP ratio increased slightly due to further tax cuts and defense spending under former President George W. Bush. The debt-to-GDP ratio increased sharply due to the recession that began in late 2007, which lowered GDP (hence raising the debt-to-GDP ratio), and led to increased government spending designed to stimulate the economy under President Barack Obama. The debt-to-GDP ratio will rise tremendously due to falling GDP and much higher spending associated with the COVID-19 pandemic and shutdown. It might have been better had we saved some more in the past.

Every year, the government must pay interest to the people who lent it money, namely the bondholders. If your debt is $100 and the interest rate is 5%, then you owe the lender $5 a year in interest payments. It works the same way with the national debt. The U.S. debt in 2020 was about $25 trillion and the average interest rate on the debt was a little more than 2%, so the federal government paid approximately $500 billion in interest payments to bondholders. Interest payments of $500 billion sound like a lot, but the Federal government collects $3.6 trillion in taxes, so as a share of revenues, interest payments are only 13%. An interest rate on the debt of 2%, however, is low. In 2007, for example, the interest rate on the debt was 5%. The low rate appears to be due to a large amount of world savings, sometimes called the savings glut, and a big demand for the relatively safe assets of the U.S. government. If interest rates were to increase significantly, interest on the debt would also increase significantly, putting big pressure on other items inthe U.S. budget.

Sometimes commentators suggest it makes a big difference if the debt of the U.S. government is held by foreigners or Americans. From a purely economic point of view, however, this distinction isn't very important. What is important is how wisely the federal government spends the borrowed money. If, years later, interest payments go to foreigners, that is because the foreigners offered to lend us money at the best rates. You can make a moral or ethical judgment that Americans ought to be spending less and saving more (which would mean less borrowing from foreigners), but low savings would be an even greater problem without foreign lenders.

We now need to make a distinction between the national debt and the deficit. The debt is the total amount of money owed by the federal government at a point in time. It is a cumulative total of previous obligations. The **deficit** is the difference—in any given year—between what the government is spending and what the government is collecting in revenues. You can think of the deficit as the annual change in the national debt.

The top half of Figure 17.6 shows federal government spending (green) and revenues (blue) as a percentage of GDP from 1960 to 2019. When spending is greater than revenues, the government must borrow to make up the difference—the difference is the deficit, shown in the bottom half of Figure 17.6 (red) also as a percentage of GDP (and as a negative value). In 1990, for example, the federal government spent almost 22% of GDP, but it collected only 18% of GDP in tax revenues. Since government spending was greater than revenues, the government had to borrow the difference, so in 1990 the deficit was about 4% of GDP (22% − 18%). Since 1960 the government has a run a deficit in almost every year.

FIGURE 17.6

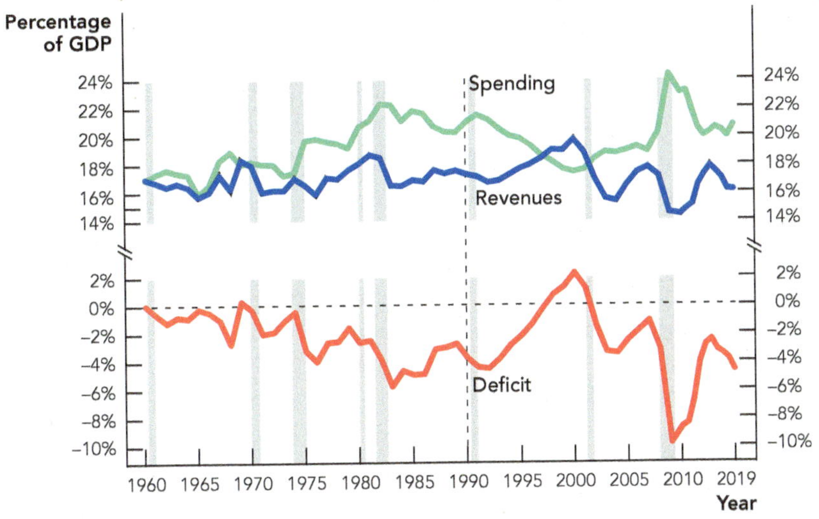

Spending, Revenues, and Deficits of the U.S. Government as a Percentage of GDP, 1960–2019

Data from: Federal Reserve Bank of St. Louis, U.S. Office of Management and Budget. https://fred.stlouisfed.org/graph/?g=pyN2.

Should We Have a Balanced Budget Amendment?

The Nobel Prize–winning economist James Buchanan argued that deficits are a natural consequence of political incentives because future taxpayers don't have a current vote.[6] Spending today without taxing today imposes an externality on future generations. Buchanan argued for a balanced budget amendment that would require today's spending to match today's taxation and thus would internalize the fiscal externality.

The main argument against a balanced budget amendment is that it would make it more difficult to aggressively respond to a recession with greater spending. To overcome this objection, most balanced budgets make exceptions for war, national emergency, or recession. The United States has not passed a balanced budget amendment at the federal level (most states, however, have balanced budget rules), but other countries have adopted versions of a balanced budget law. The Polish constitution, for example, prohibits debt greater than 60% of GDP and Germany passed a constitutional "debt brake" in 2009 that prohibits the federal government from having a structural deficit greater than 0.35% of GDP.

Sweden has one of the most interesting fiscal rules. Since 2000, Sweden's central government has been required to budget for a 1% surplus over the business cycle. In other words, rather than prohibiting deficits, Sweden's rule says that the government must plan on average to have budget surpluses. The Swedish government is thus free to spend during a recession so long as they save during a boom. In a similar way, Joseph in the Bible didn't advise the Pharaoh to balance the budget. Instead, Joseph warned the Pharaoh to save during the seven fat years so the country was prepared for the seven lean ones. Joseph may have been on to something.

Will the U.S. Government Go Bankrupt?

We said earlier that the current debt-to-GDP ratio of 80% is large but not unprecedented. Nevertheless, many economists are worried about the future debt-to-GDP ratio.

The COVID-19 pandemic is pushing the debt-to-GDP ratio much higher and faster than was predicted, but like a war, we hope the COVID-19 disaster is temporary. The main forces driving these worries are not disasters or recessions but demographics and increasing health-care costs. The U.S. population is getting older. At the turn of the twenty-first century, 12.4% of the U.S. population was aged 65 years and older, but by 2030 more than 20% of the population will be elderly. The increase in the number of elderly people means higher Social Security and Medicare payments. As a fraction of GDP, for example, Social Security payments will have to increase by about 41% if benefits are to be maintained at promised levels. More elderly people also means we will see increases in Medicare payments, although in this case an even bigger problem than demographics is rising health-care costs per person.

Because of Medicare, Medicaid, and health insurance subsidies, health-care costs will consume a larger and larger share of the federal budget. As health-care costs increase, pressure will be put on everything else and some combination of increased taxes, reduced spending on other items, or higher debt must come to pass.

In recent decades, health-care costs per person have been rising more than twice as fast as GDP per capita. If health-care costs continue rising at their current rate, those costs will account for a larger and larger part of the economy.

The Future Is Hard to Predict

So what will happen? Will spending decrease or will taxes increase? No one knows. The American public has yet to decide which way it will vote. On the one hand, the United States does have a history of relatively low taxes. Americans fought the Revolutionary War, in part, as a protest against British taxes even though British Americans had one of the smallest tax burdens in the world! The modern income tax didn't begin until 1913 and that required a separate amendment to the Constitution. Prior to the income tax, about a third of the federal government was financed by taxes on alcohol, which is one reason why prohibitionists lobbied for the income tax! Even as late as 1916, the federal government accounted for less than 5% of GDP.

Taxes and federal spending increased dramatically during 1916–1919 and 1942–1945, corresponding to World War I and World War II, respectively. But since that time federal taxes and spending have been fairly stable—as we noted, around 18% of GDP. When taxes have increased, there have often been backlashes with Americans electing politicians who promise to cut taxes. So, will Americans accept much higher tax rates in the future than they ever have in the past? Will you?

If taxes and spending in the United States do increase, this would make the United States more like other developed countries. Figure 17.7 shows total government spending by country, including spending by federal, state, and local governments. Today, the U.S. federal government spends a smaller fraction of GDP than do the governments of most other developed countries. As a result, spending could increase substantially in the United States over the next several decades and the United States would still be spending at levels comparable to Germany, Italy, and the Netherlands today.

The federal government has not planned for future expenses. Have you?

Stockbyte/Getty Images

FIGURE 17.7

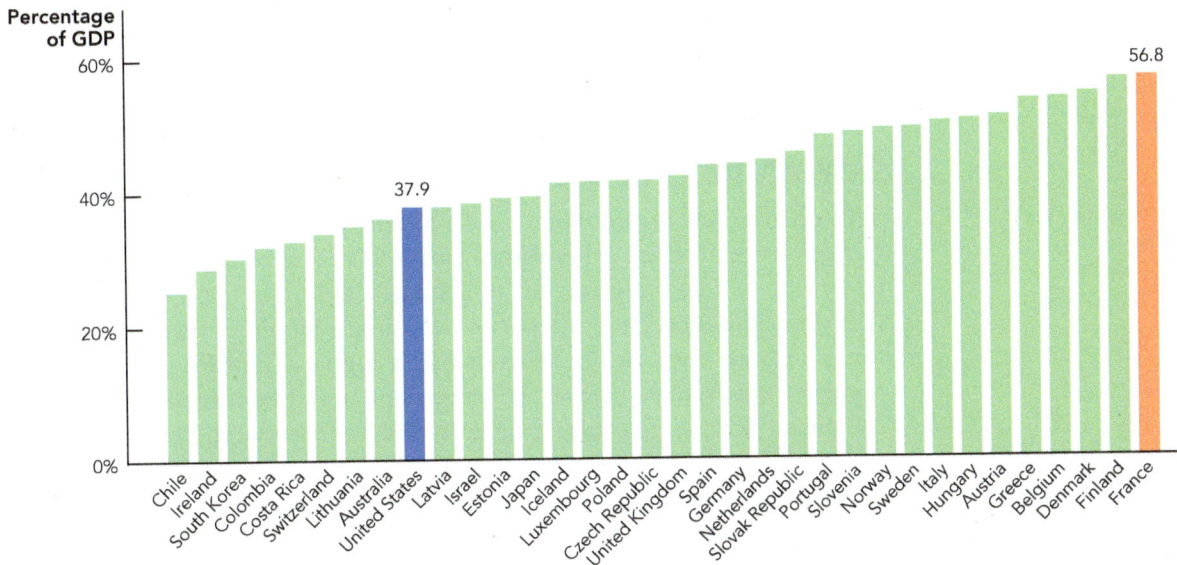

Government Spending in the United States Today Is Lower Than in Most Other Developed Countries

General government spending includes spending by federal, state, and local governments.
Data from: OECD (2019), General government spending (indicator). doi: 10.1787/a31cbf4d-en

Could spending be cut? We have already cut some projected Social Security spending by increasing the age of retirement. Perhaps we can cut spending even more—but don't expect the elderly to take this sitting down! And remember a large part of the growth in spending is due to rising health-care costs. Many people talk about slowing the growth of health-care costs but it isn't so easy. There is a lot of waste in health-care markets, but also there are many wonderful innovations. Drugs known as statins lower our cholesterol and new surgical procedures save many lives; a triple bypass operation is now more or less standard procedure. It's not so easy to sort out the good medical procedures from the bad ones, and so by most accounts health-care costs will continue to rise. Other countries do spend a significantly smaller fraction of their GDP on health-care costs, but the *growth* in health-care costs is fairly similar throughout the developed world.

Don't forget that whatever happens, the news is actually quite good for the most part. Americans are living longer than ever before and many medical advances are paying off. Let's say you thought you would live to be 80 but then you learn you will live to be 100 instead. You might worry about how to finance your now-longer retirement and perhaps you might even despair that it seems impossible. But this is the kind of problem that we can live with!

Another scenario is that GDP will grow faster in the future than it has in the past. We outlined one case for optimism in Chapter 8. Nevertheless, although we hope for the best, it's probably wise to plan, if not for the worst, then at least for the most likely outcome, and that will require some painful tax increases or spending cuts.

One general lesson is that we cannot judge the fiscal health of the federal government simply by looking at today's budget or today's deficit. New

CHECK YOURSELF

- Projecting forward for the next 40 years, what categories of spending are likely to increase or decrease? What does this mean for overall government spending? Will it grow, fall, or stay the same?
- If the pace of idea generation quickens, as was discussed in Chapter 8, the long-run aggregate supply growth curve might shift permanently. If this happens, how would it affect the debt-to-GDP ratio? Explain what this means for our nation's ability to pay for increased benefits for retirees.

government programs often grow over time and we ought to think about implicit future spending commitments when evaluating these new programs. Politicians in the past made many promises to spend in the future and today we are dealing with the legacy of these promises.

Revenues and Spending Undercount the Role of Government in the Economy

This chapter has mostly been about federal revenues and expenditures. But our government does many things and imposes many costs that do not show up on any formal budgetary accounts. The Environmental Protection Agency (EPA), for instance, has a budget of only about $9 billion yet its real reach, in terms of both costs and benefits, is much higher. The EPA has the power to regulate how business affects the environment and its mandates involve many billions of dollars of costs and benefits. Government spending is one measure of how government affects the economy, but it is not a complete or fully accurate measure.

Governments take many other actions that commandeer resources from the private sector but do not show up as full budgetary expenditures. For instance, until 1973 the United States ran a military draft. Drafted soldiers, of course, are relatively cheap if you just look at their paychecks, but the draft involves a very significant opportunity cost. Many people who were ill suited to be soldiers were removed from their jobs or their studies. The real cost of the draft—the opportunity cost—was pointed out by Milton Friedman, who advocated a move to a volunteer army. The United States had to pay soldiers more, so military costs appeared to go up. In reality, the volunteer army reduced the total cost to society of providing national defense by freeing up more productive labor, even if that efficiency was not reflected in the government's budget statements.

Takeaway

An examination of the current federal budget reveals some key points. First and foremost is the simple point that the federal government takes in and spends a great deal of money. It is hard to imagine revenues and spending of over $3.5 *trillion*.

Next, it is useful to recognize where this money comes from. Contrary to what some people might think, the huge majority of tax revenues comes from individuals in the form of individual income taxes and tax on wages linked to Social Security and Medicare.

For many people, it is surprising to learn what the federal government spends its money on. The obvious category of defense spending represents around 15% of spending. About one-third of the federal budget goes for Social Security and Medicare payments. Comprehensive general transfers to the elderly represent far more money than do welfare expenditures per se.

What about the future? The U.S. tax system is very complicated and not always transparent in its effects. Nevertheless, we can estimate future expenditures and revenues as a way of understanding the fiscal strength or weakness of a nation. It is very likely that federal expenditures will rise in the future, most of all because of rising health-care expenditures. One question is whether and how federal revenues will rise to keep the budget sufficiently close to balancing.

CHAPTER REVIEW

Go online to practice with more examples of these types of problems, including live links to videos, data sources, and feedback.

▶ Problems with this icon relate to optional MRU videos.

KEY CONCEPTS

marginal tax rate, p. 382

average tax rate, p. 383

alternative minimum tax (AMT), p. 384

progressive tax, p. 386

flat tax, p. 387

national debt held by the public, p. 393

deficit, p. 394

FACTS AND TOOLS

1. a. Consider Figure 17.3. We can use these data to find out what percentage of federal taxes is paid from the "top down" by the top 40%, top 60%, or top 80% of income earners. Likewise, we can count from the "bottom up" by the bottom 40%, 60%, or 80% of income earners. Fill in the table.

Share of Total Federal Tax Revenue		Share of Total Federal Tax Revenue	
Everyone	100%	Everyone	100%
Bottom 20%	0.8%	Top 80%	
Bottom 40%	4.9%	Top 60%	
Bottom 60%		Top 40%	85.6%
Bottom 80%		Top 20%	68.7%

b. Given these data, which of the following are true?

   i. The bottom 60% of taxpayers pay less than 25% of federal taxes.

   ii. The top 80% of taxpayers pay over 98% of federal taxes.

   iii. The top 40% of taxpayers pay less than 60% of federal taxes.

2. In 2017, corporate income taxes were about 9.9% of total federal revenue. Use Figure 17.6 to help estimate what fraction of GDP represents corporate income taxes.

3. a. Let's explore the difference between the average income tax rate and the marginal income tax rate. In the simple land of Rabushka, there is only one tax rate, 20%, but workers don't have to pay tax on the first $10,000 of their income. For every dollar they earn above $10,000, they pay 20 cents on the dollar to the Lord High Mayor of Rabushka.

The easy way to calculate the tax bill is the same way that America's IRS does: Subtract $10,000 from each person's income and call the remainder "taxable income." Multiply taxable income by 0.20, and the result is "tax due." Fill in the table.

Income	Taxable Income	Tax Due	Marginal Tax Rate	Average Income Tax Rate
$5,000	$0	0	0%	0%
$10,000	$0	0	0%	0%
$15,000	$5,000	$1,000	20%	6.7%
$20,000				
$50,000				
$100,000				
$1,000,000				

b. Is the marginal tax rate ever lower than the average tax rate?

c. As a worker's income rises and rises past $1,000,000, will the average tax rate ever be greater than 20%?

d. Just to make sure you know what these terms mean in plain English: For an accountant making $50,000 per year, what percentage of her income goes to the Lord High Mayor?

Note: This simple tax system is quite similar to the plan that economist Robert Hall and political scientist Alvin Rabushka spell out in their book, *The Flat Tax*, widely available for free online. Hall and Rabushka estimate that a system like this one would raise roughly the same amount of revenue as the current federal income tax.

4. **a.** Do most federal government transfers of cash go to the elderly or to the poor?

   b. Do most federal government purchases of health care go to the elderly or to the poor?

5. Based on the information in this chapter, let's see who gets a better deal, a greater net benefit, from Social Security. In each pairing, choose one, or write "unclear."

   Women or men?

   Married couples or singles?

   People born in 1910 or people born in 1965?

   High-income earners or low-income earners?

6. There are a lot of ways to slice up the U.S. budget. With this in mind, which of the following statements are true, according to Figure 17.4?

   i. Most of the federal budget is spent on welfare and foreign aid.

   ii. About half of the federal budget goes toward Medicare, Medicaid, and Social Security combined.

   iii. More than half of the federal budget goes toward Medicare, Medicaid, Social Security, and interest on the debt combined.

   iv. The federal government spends about $2,200 on the military per person in the United States.

7. Pundits and commentators often state (correctly) that entitlement spending (spending on Medicare, Medicaid, and Social Security) is going to explode in the future. But by lumping all three together, we obscure the source of the explosion.

   a. Which of the three really won't be "exploding" all that much compared with the other two?

   b. Which category of federal spending is projected to actually decline in future decades?

THINKING AND PROBLEM SOLVING

8. By U.S. law, your employer pays half of the payroll tax and you, the worker, pay the other half. We mentioned that according to the basics of supply and demand, the part of the tax paid

by the employer is likely to cut the worker's take-home pay. Let's see why. We'll start off in a land without any payroll taxes and then see how adding payroll taxes (like FICA and Medicare) affects the worker's take-home pay.

   a. Who is it that "supplies labor"? Is it workers or firms? And who demands labor? Workers or firms?

   b. The following chart illustrates the pretax equilibrium. Mark the equilibrium wage and quantity of labor in this market. In part c, remember that this "wage" is the amount paid directly to workers.

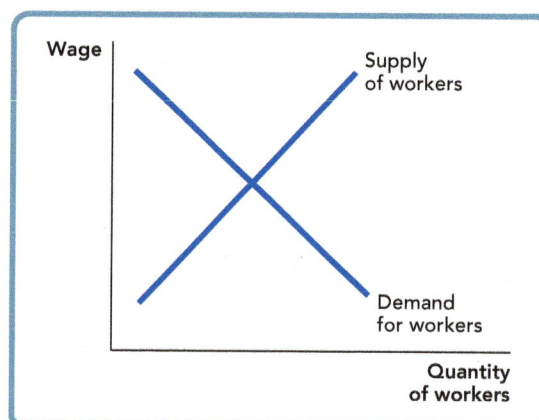

   c. Suppose the government enacts a new payroll tax of 10% of worker wages, "paid" fully by employers. What will happen to the typical firm's demand for labor? In other words, when firms learn that every time they hire a worker, they have to pay not only that worker's wage but also 10% of that worker's wage to the government, will that increase or decrease their willingness to hire workers? After you answer in words, also illustrate the shift in the graph.

   d. So, in the equilibrium with a new fully-employer-paid payroll tax, will worker's take-home wages be higher or lower than beforehand?

   e. Imagine that most workers want full-time jobs to support their families whether the wage is high or low. What does this imply about the shape of the supply curve? Redo the analysis with the new supply curve and discuss the exact effect on wages of the payroll tax.

9. It's easy to confuse the "federal deficit" with the "federal debt." We'll work out an example

to make the differences clear. To keep the math simple, we'll falsely assume that in this land of Barrovia, the government can borrow from the public at an interest rate of 0%—so there is no interest on the debt. We will also assume that the government is unwilling to print money to finance its budget, so the only way to finance a deficit is by borrowing. The debt inherited from 2017 is 4,000 credits (C4,000, in the local notation). Fill in the accompanying table.

Note: The relationship between deficits and debts is similar to the relationship between investment and the capital stock, which we investigated back in Chapters 7 and 8: The first is a "flow," while the second is a "stock"; the first is like a river, while the second is like a lake.

Year	Revenue	Spending	Deficit	Debt
2018	C100	C120	C20	C4,020
2019	C80	C130	C50	
2020	C110	C140		
2021	C120	C150		
2022	C120	C160		

10. Social Security is primarily a pay-as-you-go program, which means that the government pays retirees their promised benefits by taxing today's workers. Imagine that Social Security moved to a fully funded program in which today's workers (or the government on their behalf) invested in assets, such as stocks and bonds, to pay for their own retirement.

a. Discuss some of the costs and benefits of a fully funded program.

b. Discuss some of the difficulties of transitioning to the new system. (*Hint:* Think about today's retirees.)

11. Calculating taxes on capital gains takes a little work, but if you buy and sell stocks, bonds, works of art, or homes, you'll probably have to do this at some point. Let's practice. In a few of the following cases, the price will fall—just record that as a negative rise (a "capital loss," in tax jargon). (In some cases, you can use these to offset taxes on capital gain but we won't get into that detail here.)

a. Fill in the table.

Item	Purchase Price 2015	Sale Price 2020	Capital Gain	Tax Due at 15% Rate
10 Shares of Microsoft stock	$1,200	$1,250	$50	$7.50
1 Share of Berkshire Hathaway stock	$8,000	$11,000		
100 Shares of GM stock	$1,000	$500		
1 Picasso napkin sketch	$15,000	$14,000		
1 Mexican Amate folk painting	$2,000	$3,500		

b. One nice thing about the capital gains tax is that you can choose what year to pay it by choosing what year to sell your investment. If you wanted to sell your single share of Berkshire stock and your Picasso in the same year, how much tax would you pay?

12. A handful of states allow tax exemptions for dependents, which basically means you can subtract a given amount (which differs by state) from your taxable income. States also have their own income tax rates. How big is the tax break for having a dependent child in each of the following states?

a. Michigan, where the dependent exemption is $4,750 and the state marginal income tax rate is 4.25%.

b. Alabama, where the dependent exemption is $500 and the highest state marginal income tax rate is 5%.

c. Ohio, where the dependent exemption is $2,350 and the state marginal income tax rate is 4.797%.

d. Rhode Island, where the dependent exemption is $4,100 and the highest state marginal income tax rate is 5.99%.

13. a. If 1% of federal spending goes toward foreign aid, then what percent of U.S. GDP goes toward foreign aid? Figures 17.4 and 17.6 will help.

b. If 20% of federal spending goes toward defense spending, then what percent of U.S. GDP goes toward defense spending?

c. If $30 billion of federal spending goes toward earmarked appropriations, what percent of federal spending goes toward earmarks?

14. Some people argue that a large national debt will make future generations poorer. One way to test this is to see what happened after the last time the United States had a large national debt: after World War II. As Figure 17.5 shows, the debt-to-GDP ratio was over 100%, a bit higher than even today's ratio. Let's compare this to Figure 6.3 in Chapter 6 and Figure 11.6 in Chapter 11, which show the growth rate of GDP and the unemployment rate, respectively.

a. During the 1950s, was the growth rate lower than average? How about during the 1960s?

b. During the 1950s, was the unemployment rate higher than average? How about during the 1960s?

c. Overall, is it fair to say that the two decades after the massive World War II debt were worse than average?

Note that this single case doesn't count as conclusive proof: Perhaps the United States just got lucky, or the federal government did an unusually good job spending its World War II expenditures to build up its capital stock (a point emphasized in the excellent Francis Ford Coppola film *Tucker: The Man and His Dream*), or perhaps a massive short-term debt doesn't cause much economic trouble. You can learn more about these possible explanations in other economics courses.

15. Which of the following actual government programs show up as costs in the federal budget?

The Department of Labor mandates the minimum wage for workers.

The Environmental Protection Agency mandates that cars have equipment to keep pollution levels low.

The National Oceanic and Atmospheric Administration forecasts the weather.

The Coast Guard rescues sailors from a sinking yacht off the coast of Cape Cod.

The Border Patrol requires that all vehicles driving on highways out of San Diego be stopped to inspect for the presence of undocumented immigrants.

Discovering DATA ⦂⦂

16. Using the Fred economic database (https://fred.stlouisfed.org/), create a series showing federal expenditures as a share of GDP. First find Federal Government current expenditures. Then Edit Graph and, under Customize Data, add Gross Domestic Product (since expenditures are in billions, look for GDP in billions, not real GDP). After adding GDP, go down to the Formula field and use a/b*100.

a. Approximately how much of GDP was spent by the federal government in 2019?

b. In the 2008−2009 recession, what happened to federal spending as a share of GDP? Give two reasons why.

Discovering DATA ⦂⦂

17. Let's take a look at one aspect of the U.S. tax system over the past 100 years. Using the Fred economic database (https://fred.stlouisfed.org/), look for "U.S. Individual Income Tax: Tax Rates for Regular Tax: Highest Bracket."

a. When the income tax was first introduced, what was the rate on the highest bracket?

b. The rate on the highest tax bracket shot up shortly after the income tax was introduced; it then fell in the 1920s before shooting up again. Suggest a theory for why this happened.

CHALLENGES

18. In 1989, Senator Bob Packwood asked Congress's Joint Committee on Taxation how much extra revenue the government would raise if it just started taxing 100% of all income over $200,000 per year. The Joint Committee crunched some numbers and reported an answer: $204 billion per year.

a. What is wrong with this answer?

b. Under Packwood's proposal, what would the marginal tax rate be at $250,000 per year? At $500,000 per year?

Note: Packwood asked the Joint Committee this question not because he wanted to raise taxes that high, but to make a point. The tale of his efforts—and the efforts of Ronald Reagan, Dan Rostenkowski, Bill Bradley, and many others—to improve the U.S. tax code in the 1980s is compellingly told in Birnbaum and Murray's book *Showdown at Gucci Gulch: Lawmakers, Lobbyists, and the Unlikely Triumph of Tax Reform.*

19. Today, many government transfer programs are run through the tax code. The Earned Income Tax Credit (EITC), which we discussed in this chapter, is one important example. The federal government also has a variety of other "refundable tax credits," that is, spending programs run through the tax code. These blur the line between "tax breaks" and "government spending." This may explain their popularity: Voters and politicians who like tax breaks can claim that these programs are tax breaks, while voters and politicians who like higher government spending can claim that these programs are government spending.

a. Your income is $20,000 per year. You pay your initial tax bill of $5,000 but the government sends you a $1,000 tax refund because you have a young child. What is your after-tax income, including the value of the government check?

b. Your income is $20,000 per year. You pay your initial tax bill of $5,000 and the government sends you a $1,000 check because you have a young child. What is your after-tax income, including the value of the government check?

c. Your income is $20,000 per year. You pay your initial tax bill of $500 but the government sends you a $1,000 tax refund because you have a young child. What is your after-tax income, including the value of the government check?

d. Your income is $20,000 per year. You pay your tax bill of $500 and the government sends you a $1,000 check because you have a young child. What is your after-tax income, including the value of the government check?

e. In which of these cases does the government check seem like "government spending" to you, and why? You may find more than one case applicable—this question borders on the philosophical.

20. a. If the debt-to-GDP ratio rose to 100% and the interest rate on the debt were 5% per year, what fraction of GDP would go toward paying interest on the debt?

b. If this happened, would interest on the debt be a bigger share of GDP than Social Security is today?

c. In your opinion, do you think that Americans would tolerate spending this much of the national income on interest payments for past spending? More important, do you think Americans would want their politicians to stop making the interest payments and just default on some or all of the federal debt? Why or why not?

21. In the past, the U.S. government offered "food stamps" to poor Americans. These "stamps" were pieces of paper that looked like Monopoly money and could be spent just like money at many grocery stores. The government has a complex formula that determines how much each poor person gets each month which is now given in the form of government-provided debit cards.

Let's suppose that instead, the government decides to pay 95% of every poor person's food bill, as long as it is purchased at a typical grocery store: The poor person would make a "copayment" of 5% of the total bill, and the federal government would reimburse the grocery store for the remaining 95%. Just to keep things simple, let's assume that the government has a good way to make sure that poor people can't resell this food to others.

a. Which method would probably lead to more spending on food: the current method or the 5% copayment method? Why?

b. If food companies like Kellogg's and Quaker Oats start inventing new, more delicious dishes at a rapid rate, under which method will the federal government's food spending grow fastest: the current method or the 5% copayment method?

c. Which method is more like how most people pay for health care, including the elderly and the poor under the federal government's Medicare and Medicaid programs: the current method or the 5% copayment method?

d. Recall that health care is a field of rapid innovation. How can your answer to parts b and c explain the rapid growth of medical spending?

22. When discussing the statements sent to you by the federal government that predict your future Social Security payments, we said, "Don't be surprised if those predictions turn out to be a little bit optimistic." Consider why this might be *wrong*: Why might these predictions be too *pessimistic*, precisely because Social Security recipients are also voters? (*Hint:* Senior citizens are more likely to vote than younger citizens.)

23. There are many ways to help poor people in foreign countries. You can find charities, for example, that will buy a cow or shoes for people in poverty or help to dig a well in a low-income village. Which of these programs do you think is the best way to help the poor? What are the pros and cons of simply giving cash?

MRU VIDEO

An Economist's Christmas

mru.org/econ-xmas

Problem: **23**

WORK IT OUT

For interactive, step-by-step help in solving this problem, go online.

Under current law, homeowners can get a big tax break: The details of the tax break really don't matter as much as the mere fact that if you make mortgage payments on a home that you live in, your taxes might be lower than otherwise.

a. Suppose that Congress eliminated the tax break for homeowners. What will this law do to the demand for homes: raise, lower, or have no impact?

b. What will be the net effect of eliminating the break on the price of houses?

c. Given your answers to parts a and b, comment on who gets the benefits of the tax break. Is it people who buy homes? Sellers? (Be careful, sellers were buyers once!) Why could eliminating the tax break prove difficult?

18

Fiscal Policy

The U.S. economy was falling into a severe recession. The S&P 500 stock index was plummeting. And in the third quarter of 2008, consumer spending dropped by 3.7%, the largest drop in 28 years. Consumer spending is a large fraction of GDP (as you will recall from Chapter 6), so the sudden drop in spending pushed down the growth rate of GDP. To encourage more spending, President George W. Bush authorized the Treasury to send checks to some 130 million taxpayers, paying up to $600 to individual taxpayers and up to $1,200 for married couples. Could the new money jump-start the economy? Not this time. Consumer confidence was ebbing. Even with a few extra bucks in their pocket, consumers weren't ready to spend. The economy continued to worsen and in 2009 President Barack Obama tried a different approach: hundreds of billions of dollars in new government spending on roads, bridges, education, and other infrastructure, combined with additional tax cuts and also aid for state governments. If the American consumer wouldn't spend, then the American government would.

Fighting a recession with tax cuts and increased government spending are two forms of fiscal policy. **Fiscal policy** is federal government policy on taxes, spending, and borrowing that is designed to influence business fluctuations.

In this chapter, we use the aggregate demand and aggregate supply curves, familiar to you from Chapter 13, to understand fiscal policy. We begin by asking why fiscal policy works and we then go into more detail on when it works best.

Fiscal policy is federal government policy on taxes, spending, and borrowing that is designed to influence business fluctuations.

Why Should Fiscal Policy Work?

Let's begin by answering a basic question. Why should fiscal policy work at all? In other words, why should spending more increase the real production of goods and services? We said earlier that the real production of goods and services is determined by fundamental factors like the amount and quality of human capital, physical capital, and technology. Spending more does not increase any of these factors in any obvious way, so why should spending more increase output? That's a good question, and in ordinary times when the economy is at full employment, spending more won't appreciably increase output.

Let's imagine, for example, that the government wants to build a dam. Building the dam requires the production of lots of new goods and services, like water turbines and financial accounting, but will that production increase GDP? No. If the economy is operating at full employment, then the goods and services used to build the dam would have been used to build other goods and services, such as office buildings. In other words, at full employment the goods and services used to build the dam have a high opportunity cost. Once the dam begins to operate, it will increase the production of electricity and that will increase GDP, but if the economy is at full employment the construction of the dam will pull resources from other sectors of the economy. Thus the net effect on GDP will be approximately zero. We also say that at full employment the increase in government spending will mostly **crowd out** production by the private sector, so, again, the net effect on GDP is approximately zero.

Crowding out is the decrease in private spending that occurs when government spending increases.

But now consider a situation in which many workers and resources are unemployed. In this case, building the dam doesn't necessarily reduce the production of goods and services elsewhere in the economy. In fact, if all the workers and resources used to build the dam would have been unemployed without the dam, then every dollar spent on the dam will add one dollar to GDP. In some situations, spending a dollar could even increase GDP by more than a dollar. Suppose that the government hires some unemployed construction workers and suppose that the construction workers use some of their new income to buy meals at restaurants. Increased spending by construction workers encourages restaurants to hire more waiters and cooks, some of whom were themselves unemployed. Because every dollar spent on construction workers is thus multiplied by the spending of the newly hired construction workers, every dollar spent on the dam could generate, say, $1.45 of new goods and services. The **multiplier effect** is the additional increase in spending caused by an increase in government spending.

The multiplier effect is the additional increase in spending caused by the initial increase in government spending.

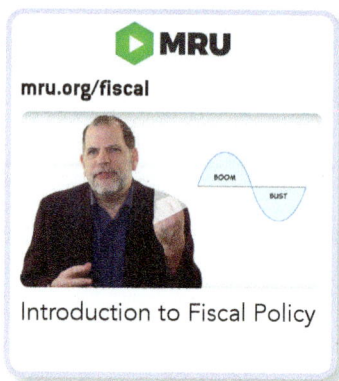

The fundamental reason that fiscal policy can work is that when resources are unemployed, the economy is operating inefficiently. If spending more can employ unemployed resources, then it can in principle pay for itself.

Let's use aggregate demand and aggregate supply curves to illustrate how fiscal policy works when there are unemployed resources. In Figure 18.1 the economy begins at point a, but suppose that consumers become worried about their future, so they cut back on consumption growth; that is, $\vec{C}$ falls. Because consumers are spending less in order to build up their cash reserves, we can also say equivalently that $\vec{v}$ falls. Figure 18.1 shows the result: The fall in $\vec{C}$ shifts the AD curve to the left and down, moving the economy from a long-run equilibrium at point a to a short-run equilibrium at point b. At point b, the growth rate is negative and the economy is in a recession. The problem at point b is that consumers want to hold more money, and this means that the rate of inflation must decrease. Wages and prices, however, are sticky (see Chapter 13), so when spending growth declines, instead of just a decrease in inflation, we get a decrease in real growth as well.

mru.org/fiscal

Introduction to Fiscal Policy

In the long run, prices and wages will become "unstuck," fear will pass, and $\vec{C}$ will return to its normal growth rate. The economy will thus transition until it returns to point a. But recall John Maynard Keynes's famous statement: "In the long run, we are all dead." Can government do anything to make recovery a reality now? Quite possibly so.

The government has (some) control over government spending, $\vec{G}$, so if $\vec{C}$ falls, why not increase $\vec{G}$ to compensate? In Figure 18.1, we show how an increase in $\vec{G}$ can shift the AD curve to the right and up, thereby putting the economy on a transition path back to point a. In fact, in the best-case scenario, the increase in $\vec{G}$ doesn't even have to be as large as the fall in $\vec{C}$ because of the multiplier effect. When $\vec{G}$ increases and unemployed workers (and other resources) are employed, their spending increases $\vec{C}$. In Figure 18.1 we have drawn the ideal situation—when the net effect of the initial increase in spending plus the multiplier effect ends the recession and returns the economy to point a.

FIGURE 18.1

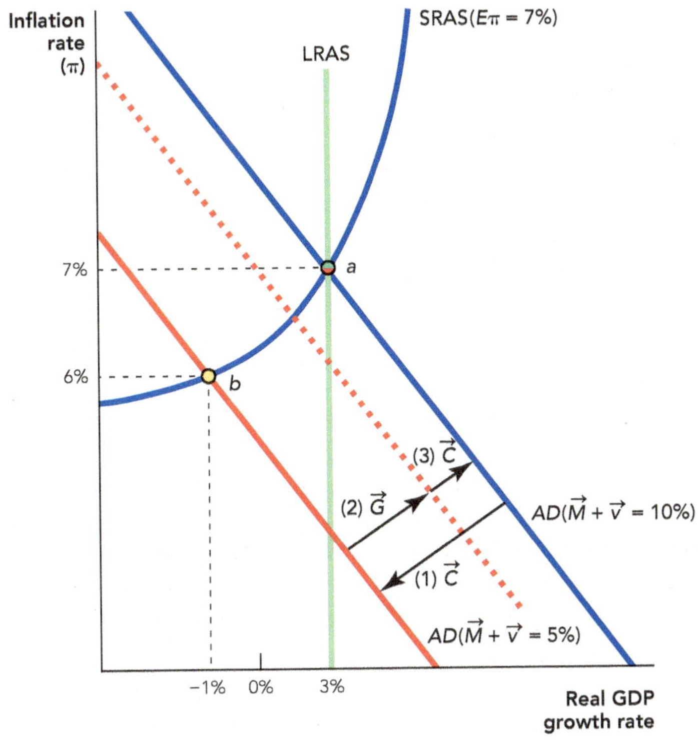

The Multiplier After a decrease in $\vec{C}$ (step 1), an increase in $\vec{G}$ (step 2) stimulates $\vec{C}$ (step 3) so the increase in AD can be larger than the increase in $\vec{G}$ alone.

Great! But, as usual, it's easier to shift lines on a graph than it is to move a multi-trillion-dollar economy. So let's take a look at some of the complications.

What Determines the Size of the Multiplier?

The great debate over fiscal policy is about the balance of two opposing forces: *crowding out* versus the *multiplier effect*. Which is bigger and when? The great debate can be summarized by a single number, the *multiplier*. If government spending increases by $100 billion and all of that additional spending crowds out private sector spending, then the multiplier is zero. If no private sector spending is crowded out, the multiplier is 1. If the increase in government spending causes additional private spending, the multiplier is greater than 1. Figure 18.2 illustrates the two forces.

Fiscal policy is much more likely to be successful when the multiplier is big than when it is small. So what determines the size of the multiplier? We've already indicated one factor: the more unemployed resources, the bigger the multiplier. But the multiplier also depends on how fiscal policy is implemented and on the structure of the economy. If a lot of dam workers are unemployed and the government builds a dam, then that is a well-targeted stimulus and the multiplier is likely to be big. But if a lot of dam workers are unemployed and the government builds an office building, the effect on the multiplier is not so clear—this is a less well targeted stimulus and the multiplier is likely to be smaller. Building dams and office buildings takes a lot more than muscle; each also requires specialized

> ## FIGURE 18.2
>
> ### The Multiplier
>
>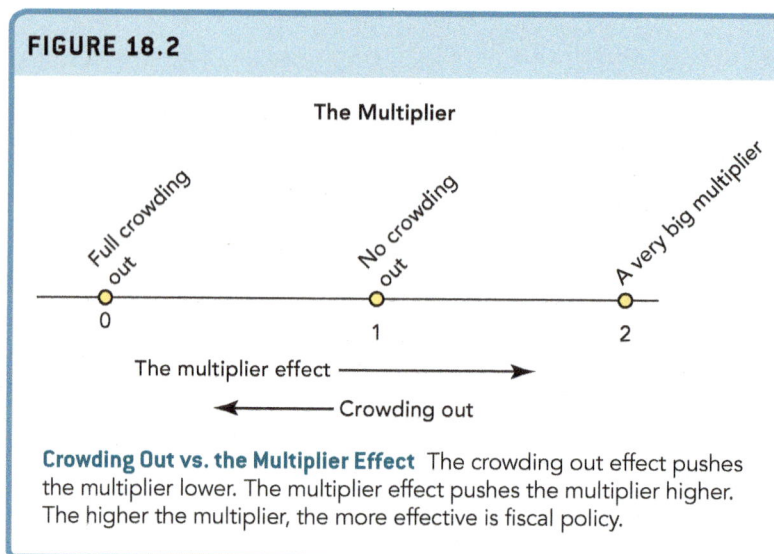
>
> **Crowding Out vs. the Multiplier Effect** The crowding out effect pushes the multiplier lower. The multiplier effect pushes the multiplier higher. The higher the multiplier, the more effective is fiscal policy.

knowledge and skills, even for manual workers. Since unemployed dam workers don't necessarily have the knowledge and skills to easily shift into office building construction, new government construction of office buildings is likely to draw workers from private office building construction rather than from the pool of unemployed dam workers. This will lower the size of the multiplier.

More generally, when politicians talk about fiscal stimulus they often talk about "shovel ready" projects. The modern U.S. economy, however, is dominated by service industries. During the last recession, for example, there were almost as many unemployed workers in the hospitality and leisure industry as there were in the construction industry.

Rather than increasing spending on things, the government can increase spending on people. Unemployment insurance and welfare payments, for example, which automatically increase during recessions, are targeted toward the poor and unemployed, who are more likely to spend the money. For that reason, these types of programs tend to have a relatively big multiplier.

Instead of increasing government spending during a recession, the government can also cut taxes to try to increase private spending. The advantage of a tax cut is that the government doesn't have to pick and choose which economic sectors to stimulate. A tax cut will stimulate anything that the public buys. For the same reason, however, tax cuts are not very targeted. The size of the multiplier will depend, therefore, on how much of the tax cut is spent and on what the spending is on.

If the government cuts taxes on people who want to buy what unemployed workers produce, the multiplier will be big. A tax cut that is targeted to people in regions with high unemployment, for example, could work better than a national tax cut.

For similar reasons, if the government cuts taxes on people who want to spend the entire tax cut immediately, then the multiplier will be big. A tax cut to the poor is likely to have a bigger multiplier than a tax cut to the rich because the poor often have expenses that must be paid immediately while the spending of the rich is subject to greater choice. It's sometimes difficult to cut taxes to the poor, however, because many poor people already don't pay much in taxes, at least not in income taxes (see the previous chapter).

A closely related problem is that many people might choose to save their tax cuts rather than spend them. People might want to save if they fear future unemployment, for example. Saving is not necessarily bad, even in a recession, *if* the saving is quickly turned into investment. In a recession, however, the desired level of savings may exceed the desired level of investment. Instead of flowing into investment, savings may flow into the purchase of government bonds or other unproductive assets— sometimes called the "flight to safety." Recall also from Chapter 9 that one cause of the 2008–2009 recession and the Great Depression was a breakdown in financial intermediation. If financial intermediaries are not channeling funds from savings to investment, then increased savings (i.e., reduced consumption) will not be matched by increased investment. But if consumption falls and investment doesn't increase, total output will fall.

People might also choose to save the money from their tax cuts if they expect that tax cuts today will be matched by tax increases tomorrow. In fact, if we hold government spending constant through time, then a tax cut today *must* be matched by a tax increase in the future. Now imagine that people are patient and very forward-looking. When the government cuts taxes today, these people realize that taxes will be higher in the future. These farsighted people will plan accordingly and save more today. Basically, they are saving more so that the future tax payments don't cause them to give up familiar habits or move into old-age poverty; this "consumption smoothing" was explained in Chapter 9.

But if people save their tax cuts instead of spending them, then the aggregate demand curve does not shift out, the multiplier is zero, and there are no systematic macroeconomic effects. This scenario is sometimes called **Ricardian equivalence**, after the nineteenth-century British economist David Ricardo. Most economists think it is unrealistic to assume that people understand their future tax burden and save accordingly to offset future tax burdens. Tyler knows that he doesn't behave this way (and he's a trained economist), but he does see some signs of this behavior from Alex. So Ricardian equivalence probably describes some people but not most people. In any case, to the extent that Ricardian equivalence reflects how people plan, tax cuts are less effective in the short run than otherwise.

Another factor that influences the size of the multiplier is how the government pays for its spending. The simplest case is when new government spending is financed by an increase in taxes. Higher taxes mean the government spends more money, but of course, higher taxes also mean that private individuals have less money to spend. Thus, the multiplier for tax-financed spending will be bigger when the government can tax those individuals who weren't going to spend immediately, or, more generally, when the government can tax (unproductive) savings rather than consumption. As a long-term proposition, taxing savings may be a bad idea, but during a recession the goal of fiscal policy is to increase spending not saving.

Instead of raising taxes immediately, the government often pays its bills with borrowed money. As we showed in Figure 9.10, when the government borrows more, the interest rate in the market for loanable funds tends to increase. A higher interest rate will encourage people to save more—you might think that is good, but "saving more" is another way of saying "spending less." Thus, when the government pays for its increased spending by borrowing, some of the money comes from reduced private spending. At the same time, a higher

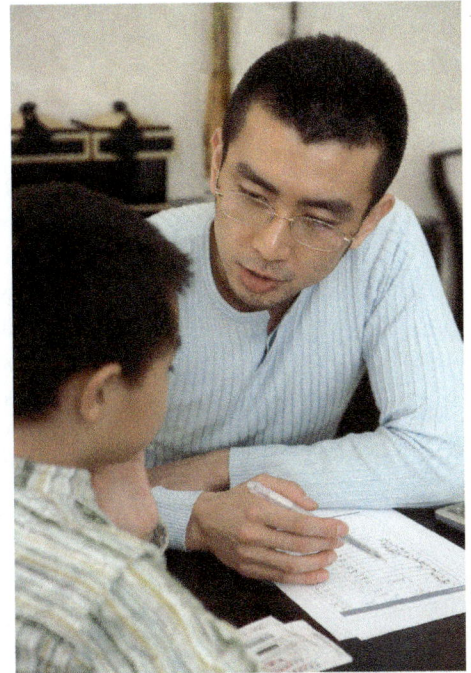

Is the Ricardian equivalence realistic? "I got a tax cut this year, son. But that means that your taxes will be going up in the future so I'm going to save more."

Ricardian equivalence occurs when people see that lower taxes today means higher taxes in the future, so instead of spending their tax cut, they save it to pay future taxes. When Ricardian equivalence holds, a tax cut doesn't increase aggregate demand even in the short run.

interest rate will cause some private borrowers to borrow and invest less. Thus, some of the money the government borrows comes from reduced private investment. So when the government borrows, there is some crowding out due to reduced consumption and some crowding out due to reduced investment, and these forces result in a lower multiplier.

Given the possibilities for crowding out, fiscal policy is most likely to be effective when the private sector is, for some reason, reluctant to spend or invest. This is often the case in a depression or in times of great uncertainty, or when people, for whatever reason, are simply holding onto their cash. In these cases government investments do not displace comparable private investments, as the private investments would not have been forthcoming in any case. In addition, during a recession, investors often want to wait and see how uncertainty is resolved before investing in private projects. In the meantime, investors may be happy to park their money in government bonds, which are seen as safe even if they don't pay a high interest rate—the flight to safety that we mentioned earlier. For both of these reasons, interest rates can fall during a recession and government borrowing may create less crowding out than would occur during a boom.

Summing up, the multiplier is likely to be bigger when there are lots of unemployed resources, when the government can target spending directly on the unemployed, when tax cuts go to people who want to spend immediately, when the government can tax savings, and when government borrowing does not crowd out much private consumption or investment.

So How Big Is the Multiplier?

We've described a number of factors that influence the size of the multiplier. Given those factors, is the multiplier big? Well it's hard to say. Estimating the multiplier in practice is quite difficult, both because the economy is complex and because, as we have just illustrated, there are actually many multipliers, depending on conditions. During the 2008–2009 recession, however, the Congressional Budget Office surveyed a number of different estimates and came up with the following list (Table 18.1).

TABLE 18.1 ESTIMATED FISCAL MULTIPLIERS FOR MAJOR PROVISIONS OF THE AMERICAN RECOVERY AND REINVESTMENT ACT OF 2009

Type of Activity	Estimated Multiplier Low Estimate	High Estimate
Purchase of goods and services by the federal government	0.5	2.5
Transfer payments to state and local governments for infrastructure	0.4	2.2
Transfer payments to state and local governments for other purposes	0.4	1.8
Transfer payments to individuals	0.4	2.1
Two-year tax cuts for lower- and middle-income people	0.3	1.5
One-time payments to retirees	0.2	1.0
One-year tax cut for higher-income people	0.1	0.6

Data from: Congressional Budget Office. 2015. Estimated Impact of the American Recovery and Reinvestment Act on Employment and Economic Output in 2014.

Notice that each item in the list has a low and a high estimate, indicating considerable uncertainty about the size of the multiplier even in a very serious recession. At the bottom of the list is a one-year tax cut for higher income people, where the multiplier is estimated to be between 0.1 and 0.6. As theory suggests, tax cuts to the rich may not go into immediate spending, and one-year tax cuts are especially likely to be saved as people are likely to foresee the future tax increase. One-time payments to retirees and tax cuts to lower- and middle-income people do a little better. Transfer payments to individuals and to state and local governments tend to have much higher multipliers with the high estimates suggesting that one dollar transferred to individuals or state and local governments could increase GDP by $1.8 to $2.1. The difference here is that these transfer payments are likely to be spent quickly. At the top of the list are transfers to state and local governments for infrastructure spending or federal infrastructure spending.

Another important point to note about Table 18.1 is that all of these spending activities were part of the big 2009 fiscal stimulus, the American Recovery and Reinvestment Act (ARRA). Thus, some parts of the act were significantly more effective as fiscal stimulus than other parts. Congress spent funds in some areas that were likely to be less effective than others, in part for political reasons and in part because the most effective areas for fiscal stimulus may be limited. Infrastructure spending tends to work well as fiscal stimulus, for example, but we need only so many roads and dams and we can't always start these projects immediately (the shovel ready problem). Let's take a closer look at size and timing issues.

CHECK YOURSELF

• What are the two types of expansionary fiscal policy?

Limits to Fiscal Policy: Magnitude

Surprisingly, one of the biggest problems with government spending as a boost to aggregate demand is that it is often difficult to spend a lot of money quickly (see the movie *Brewster's Millions*).

In the contemporary United States, changes in fiscal policy, in percentage terms, simply aren't that large in a typical year. Most of the federal budget is determined well in advance and is remarkably stable. As we have seen in the previous chapter, among the largest budget categories are national defense, Social Security, Medicare, and interest on the debt. Those categories alone account for 65% of spending in a typical year and these programs are more or less on automatic pilot, with their yearly levels of spending set by automatic formulas or by previous agreements or commitments. Nonsecurity federal discretionary spending is less than 20% of the federal budget and most of this is not seriously up for grabs in any given year. Government spending, in today's world, simply does not change very much in percentage terms on a year-to-year basis.

The fiscal stimulus plan passed under President Barack Obama in 2009 was the largest fiscal stimulus since military spending rose tremendously during World War II. Even this $800–$900 billion stimulus, however, was spread over 3–4 years so at its peak the stimulus was about 1.6% of annual GDP. These are large numbers relative to previous stimulus plans but, although significant, they are still modest compared to the total size of the economy. For this reason, many Keynesian economists suggested that the stimulus wasn't large enough to succeed, but even if the Keynesians are right in principle, politically speaking, a larger stimulus bill probably was not possible.

In September 2010, after most of the stimulus money was spent, unemployment remained at 9.6%.

Timing

Bad timing provides another reason why fiscal policy is often not very effective, even in the short run. The United States Constitution stipulates that both Congress and the president must approve all expenditures. There are two houses of Congress, and of course legislation must pass through various committees. Sometimes an emergency stimulus occurs quickly, as in 2020, when the United States designed and passed trillions of dollars in emergency relief spending in response to the COVID-19 pandemic in a matter of weeks. But often the proposed fiscal projects are complicated and the budget cycle takes place over many months or sometimes even years; it can take a long time for new bills to be conceived, written, debated, and passed. Specific expenditures often must be coordinated with state and local governments, or the projects must produce environmental impact statements, or they must survive legal challenges. Even once the money is in place, it takes time to spend it; for instance, you can't build a large airport or dam all at once and it doesn't make sense to pay every contractor in advance.

In short, even a single government expenditure can take years to move from dream to reality. Yet fiscal policy is often intended to correct short-term problems in the business cycle. By the time the fiscal policy is in place, macroeconomic conditions often have changed entirely.

The list of relevant lags includes the following:

1. Recognition lag: The problem must be recognized.
2. Legislative lag: Congress must propose and pass a plan.
3. Implementation lag: Bureaucracies must implement the plan.
4. Effectiveness lag: The plan takes time to work.
5. Evaluation and adjustment lag: Did the plan work? Have conditions changed? (Return to lag 1!)

Tax cuts, the other major form of fiscal policy, also involve lags and uncertainties, at least with respect to their role in stimulating aggregate demand.

President George W. Bush cut marginal tax rates in 2001, 2002, and 2003. The latter tax cuts came quite quickly after a recession loomed following 9/11 (in part because the tax cuts were mostly planned in advance for other reasons). But these tax cuts were not very effective as fiscal policy either. Each cut was less than 1% of national income, the economy was already recovering, plus most of the tax cuts went to relatively high-income groups, who tend to save their surplus funds. If we are thinking in terms of fiscal policy alone, tax cuts to the poor would probably result in more spending, except of course, that the poor don't pay that much in taxes.

Monetary policy is also subject to lags, but these are generally shorter than for fiscal policy. Once the Federal Reserve recognizes a problem, it can act very quickly to implement changes to monetary policy. After 9/11, for example, the Federal Reserve stepped in the next *day* with massive infusions of cash to the banking system. The Federal Reserve can also evaluate and adjust its plan quickly as the economy responds or fails to respond. Fiscal policy, in contrast, is

mru.org/fiscal-limits

The Limits to Fiscal Policy

FIGURE 18.3

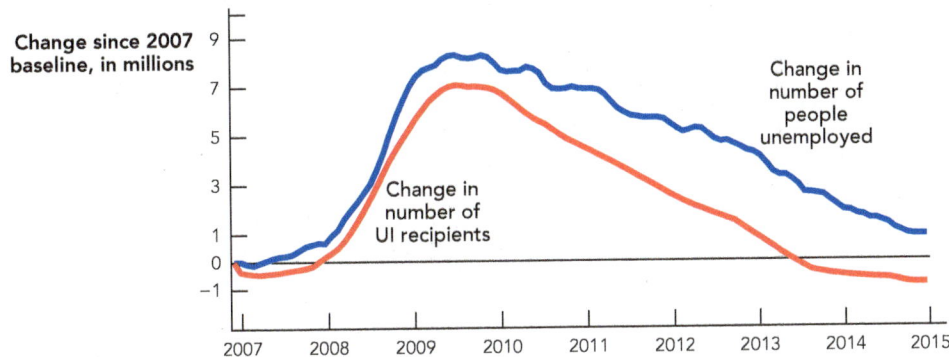

Spending on Unemployment Insurance Increases Automatically with the Number of Unemployed Persons

Data from: Schanzenbach et al. 2016. Nine facts about the great recession and tools for fighting the next downturn. *The Hamilton Project: Economic Facts.* https://www.hamiltonproject.org/assets/files/fiscal_facts.pdf.
Note: Data are smoothed.
Change in number of UI recipients includes emergency programs and extensions.

rarely adjusted in response to changes in economic conditions. The only place where fiscal policy might have an advantage over monetary policy is through the effectiveness lag. As we discussed in Chapters 15 and 16, the effectiveness of changes in monetary policy depends on matters like how willing banks are to lend and businesses are to borrow. A spending program, in contrast, typically has a direct impact on economic conditions, at least once the money is put into the economy. .

Automatic Stabilizers Some kinds of fiscal policy are built right into the tax and transfer system, and they do take effect without significant lags. These are called **automatic stabilizers**. Virtually all economists recognize the virtue of automatic stabilizers in keeping aggregate demand on a steady and regular course.

As unemployment in the United States increased during the financial crisis, for example, so did applications for unemployment insurance (UI), as shown in Figure 18.3.

As a result, spending on unemployment insurance increased automatically without new legislation (although new legislation did extend UI benefits). In addition to UI benefits, Medicaid and Supplemental Nutrition Assistance Program (SNAP, food stamps) are important U.S. automatic stabilizers. Spending on these categories serves a dual purpose: It helps people in tough times and it helps to maintain aggregate demand. Payments to the unemployed and the poor are especially effective at increasing aggregate demand because the unemployed and the poor tend to spend benefits quickly.

Tax policy also creates automatic stabilizers. When the economy is doing poorly, income, capital gains, and corporate profits are all down. As a result, most people and businesses will pay lower taxes and, given that the U.S. tax system is progressive (see the previous chapter), possibly a lower tax rate as well. The lower tax burden makes aggregate demand more robust than it otherwise would be. The lower taxes don't offset the curse of hard times (lowering your

Automatic stabilizers are changes in fiscal policy that stimulate AD in a recession without the need for explicit action by policymakers.

mru.org/duel-fiscal

Econ Duel: Does Fiscal Policy Work?

taxes by lowering your income is not the preferred way to go), but they soften the blow. Pretax incomes are perhaps falling, but posttax incomes are not falling by as much.

The big advantage of automatic stabilizers is that they don't suffer from the recognition, legislation, and implementation lags that we mentioned earlier. President Obama's big stimulus program (the ARRA) was passed quickly but even so, it wasn't passed until more than a year after the start of the recession. At that time, automatic stabilizers had already increased by 2% of GDP.

More automatic stabilizers could be created by setting trigger points in advance. In 2011, for example, the payroll tax was briefly cut by 2% to stimulate the economy. The tax cut was reasonably effective but it might have been more effective if everyone knew that a payroll tax cut would automatically go into effect once say unemployment rose above 6%. Making payroll tax cuts automatic would avoid lags and Republicans and Democrats might be more likely to agree on a trigger point before they knew which party would be in power during a future recession.

It's not just government policy that provides automatic stabilizers. When people save during good times and use their savings to tide them over in bad times (consumption smoothing, as discussed in Chapter 9), it's an automatic stabilizer. Private market innovations, most of all credit, have also contributed to stabilization. Even though the 2008 credit crisis pared back some kinds of borrowing, it is still easier today to take out a second mortgage on one's home than it was 30 years ago. If you need to send your kid to college, you can borrow more rather than cutting your spending ruthlessly. That way you can pay back the money over time, for a smoother adjustment. Credit cards, durable assets, the increased availability of used goods (eBay), and discount outlets all allow the economy to weather hard times more easily.

Government Spending vs. Tax Cuts as Expansionary Fiscal Policy

Before turning to the last limit on fiscal policy, the fact that fiscal policy does not work well with real shocks, let's briefly examine the differences between the two types of fiscal policy we have discussed, government spending and tax cuts. The differences between these types of fiscal policy are political and also economic. Let's discuss the political differences first.

A tax cut or tax rebate puts more spending in the hands of the private sector, while an increase in government spending puts more spending in the hands of the government. People who are skeptical about government spending typically prefer fiscal policy to work through tax rebates and tax cuts rather than through changes in government spending.

On the other hand, people who think that the U.S. government is not spending enough will tend to prefer that fiscal policy work through spending increases. The U.S. highway system is generally regarded as a highly productive investment of capital. If we can find equally productive public investments such as improvements to schools, science funding, and infrastructure, then the case for public investment is strong, and if we can time these spending increases to help offset a recession, so much the better.

Do you recall our opening example? It's a useful illustration of the political differences over fiscal policy. George Bush and Barack Obama both used expansionary fiscal policy to fight a recession but Bush, a Republican,

---

FIGURE 18.4

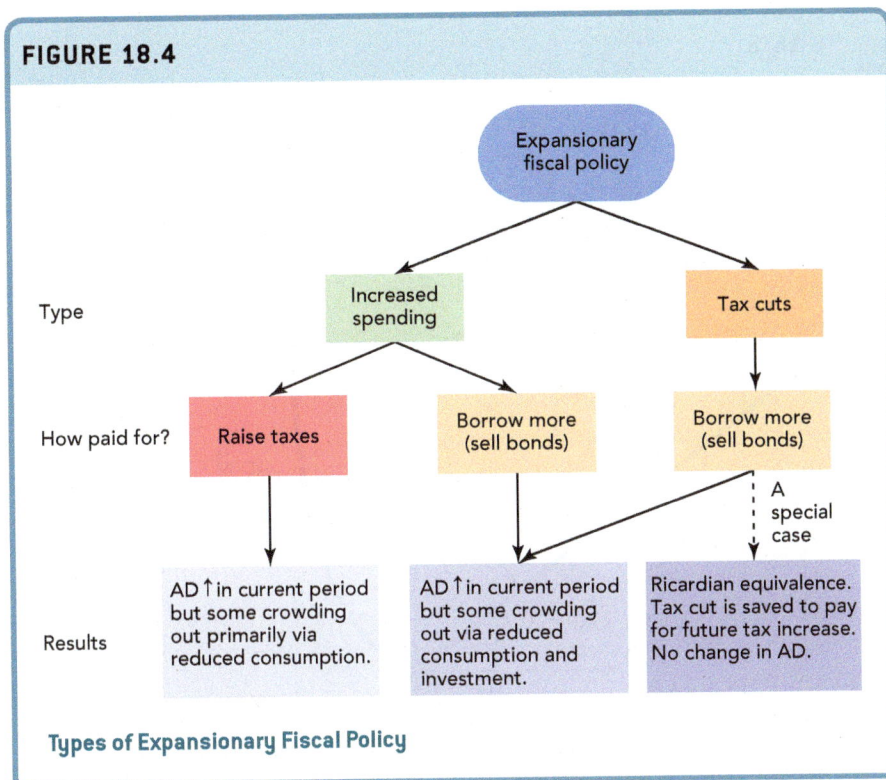

Types of Expansionary Fiscal Policy

---

focused on tax cuts, while Obama, a Democrat, served up a mix of tax cuts and government spending increases.

We summarize the different types of fiscal policy and possible results in Figure 18.4.

Fiscal Policy Does Not Work Well to Combat Real Shocks

We have assumed so far that the problem fiscal policy needs to address is a deficiency in aggregate demand. But imagine, for example, that the recession is caused not by a fall in demand, but by a real shock that reduces the productivity of capital and labor, shifting the long-run aggregate supply curve to the left. In Figure 18.5, for example, a real shock shifts the long-run aggregate supply curve to the left, moving the economy from point a to point b.

As before, the economy is in a recession at point b. Now suppose that government responds by increasing $\overline{G}$. As usual, the aggregate demand curve shifts out, but now the economy is less productive than before, due to the real shock. As a result, an increase in $\overline{G}$ will not move the economy back to point a. Instead, most of the increase in $\overline{G}$ will show up in inflation rather than in real growth, so the economy will shift from point b to point c with a much higher inflation rate and a slightly higher growth rate. As you may recall, this is very similar to the analysis of monetary policy when facing a real shock.

In fact, the situation for fiscal policy is worse than Figure 18.4 indicates because when the problem an economy faces is a real shock, there is no inefficiency. Thus, unlike in Figure 18.1, the increase in $\overline{G}$ is unlikely to create much new growth and most of (perhaps even all of) $\overline{G}$ will *crowd out* other spending. (Another way of seeing this is to remember that the long-run aggregate supply curve shows the real rate of growth when the economy

CHECK YOURSELF
- What happened to make the 2008 Bush tax rebate less powerful than anticipated?
- Explain why a permanent cut in income tax rates can create a larger fiscal stimulus than a temporary cut.
- Keeping your answer to the previous question in mind, why does a permanent investment tax credit create a *smaller* fiscal stimulus than a temporary investment tax credit?

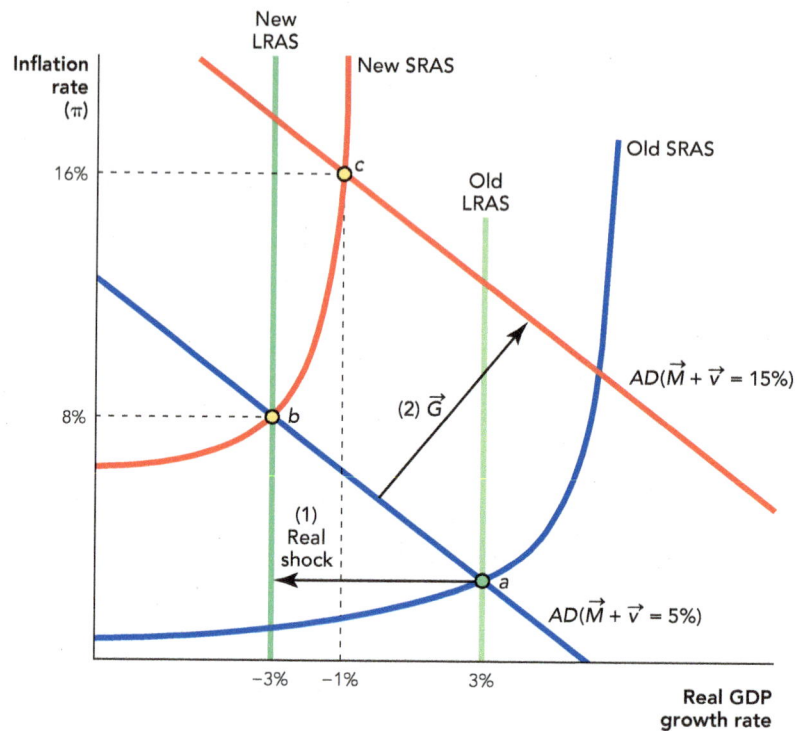

FIGURE 18.5

Fiscal Policy Is Less Effective at Combating a Real Shock A real shock shifts the long-run aggregate supply curve (LRAS) to the left (step 1), moving the economy from point *a* to a recession at point *b*. To combat the recession, the government increases $\vec{G}$ (step 2), but due to the real shock, the economy is now less productive than before, and so the increase in aggregate demand shifts the economy to point *c*, where the growth rate is a little bit higher but the inflation rate is much higher.

is operating at its full potential, and neither fiscal nor monetary policy can increase the growth rate above the rate given by the fundamentals—the Solow rate—for very long.)

The economy is subject to both aggregate demand shocks and real shocks. Since some recessions are driven by real shocks, fiscal policy will not always be an effective method of combating a recession.

"Common Sense" Fiscal Policy

Ideal fiscal policy will increase AD by spending in bad times and reduce AD by taxing and paying off the bill in good times, and in this way make both busts and booms smaller and the economy less volatile, as we show in Figure 18.6. Economists say that the ideal fiscal policy is **counter-cyclical** because when the economy is down the government should spend more, and when the economy is up the government should spend less.

Although counter-cyclical fiscal policy makes sense to economists, it often doesn't make sense to politicians or to voters. The views of economists violate

Counter-cyclical fiscal policy is fiscal policy that runs opposite or counter to the business cycle—spending more when the economy is in a recession and less when the economy is booming.

FIGURE 18.6

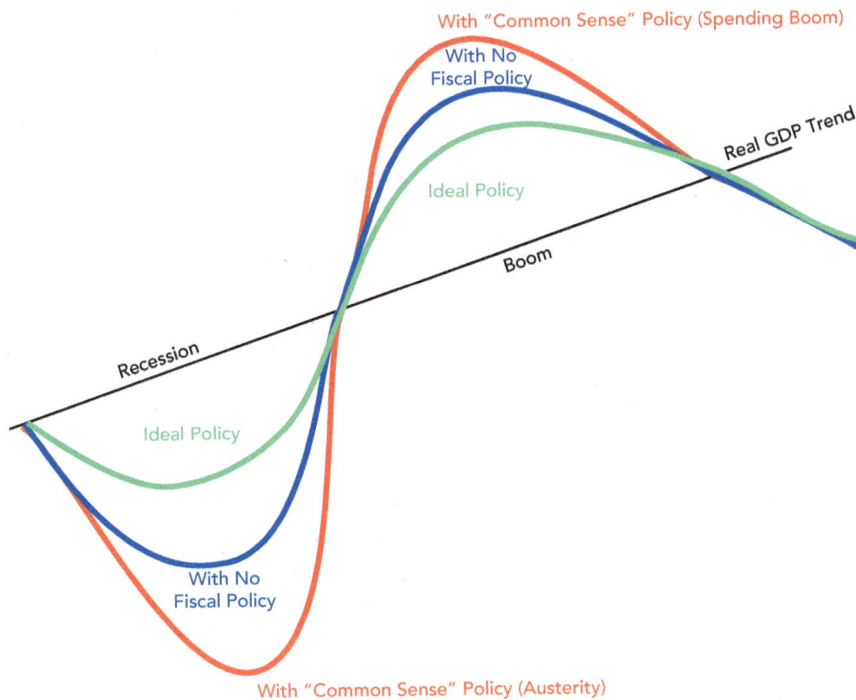

Ideal Fiscal Policy vs. Common Sense Fiscal Policy An ideal stimulus would spend during a recession in order to make the recession less severe and then save during a boom. If the so-called "common sense" policy is followed, however, the government will cut back on spending during a recession and spend more during a boom and in the process make the economy more volatile.

a kind of "common sense" or folk wisdom, which says that in bad times the government should spend less and only in good times should the government spend more. After all, you and I spend less when times are bad and more when times are good, so shouldn't the government behave similarly? If the government follows the "common sense" view, however, it will tend to make recessions deeper and booms larger, thereby making the economy more volatile, again as shown in Figure 18.6.

The common sense view does make sense for you and me because we spend too little to affect the national economy—we only respond to GDP; our decisions do not significantly change GDP. Many governments, however, are big enough that their actions can change GDP, which is why economists suggest that the government act differently than you and I.

The Wisdom of "Common Sense" Fiscal Policy
Common sense fiscal policy can be dangerous when it warns to spend less in a recession and more in a boom. But common sense fiscal policy also warns about having too much debt and that warning can sometimes be wise. Even when governments do spend more in recessions, as economists suggest, they often don't

follow through on the second half of the prescription, which is to spend less during booms. When governments spend more than they tax, even in boom years, then the total debt grows larger, as we discussed in the previous chapter. When the debt is large, governments must spend a large fraction of their budget on interest payments alone. This usually means that there is less room for expansionary fiscal policy when it is needed.

In extreme situations, debt can be such a problem that *expansionary fiscal policy can reduce real growth*. Some countries are so heavily in debt that any more government borrowing runs the risk of total economic collapse. Take, for instance, Argentina, which had a major financial crisis in the 1999–2002 period; in those years, Argentine real GDP fell by rates of −3.4%, −0.8%, −4.4%, and −10.9%, respectively.[1] That's not a good record. In the years leading up to this collapse, the Argentine government spent more and more, and did not pay off its bills. By 2002, Argentine government debt was 150% of GDP, a very high level. (For purposes of contrast, the U.S. federal government has net debt of about 80% of GDP, although that level is rising quickly due to the COVID-19 recession and spending.) The Argentine government could not pay off these debts and the final result was the largest default by a government in the history of the world.

In the years leading up to the collapse, many investors feared that the Argentine currency would lose most of its value and that the economy would fall apart. More government spending led to more anxiety, rather than economic stimulation.

So, in this setting, if the government increases spending, aggregate demand does not go up. Instead, private spending and production fall by so much that real GDP falls (i.e., more than 100% crowding out!). Aggregate demand falls because in times of great uncertainty, people save or hoard their money in anticipation of hard times ahead. In the case of Argentina, people put their wealth into bank accounts in Miami or Switzerland, rather than investing it at home or spending it in the shops of Buenos Aires. Of course, that flight of capital only hastened the economic collapse.

We've mentioned Argentina, but similar scenarios (the details differ) have occurred in many other lesser developed nations, including Thailand, Indonesia, and Mexico. The lesson is this: Too high a debt can drive a nation to ruin by undercutting the credibility of everything a government does and whether that government can meet its commitments. The United States isn't in that position at this time, but if you wish to understand global events, you need to realize that fiscal policy has an immediate negative effect in many economic situations, especially when the credibility of the government is low.

Closer to home, the U.S. states are supposed to maintain "rainy day" funds to help them stabilize spending during a recession—that's common sense fiscal policy—but few states save enough to weather a serious crisis. This is one reason the federal government had to step in during the financial crisis to prop up state and local budgets.

So When Is Fiscal Policy a Good Idea?

The macroeconomic case for government spending is strongest when the government faces some immediate emergency, such as a war, a worsening depression, or a natural disaster. Government spending is best for the macroeconomy when it is worth incurring some long-run costs to get a short-run economic boost.

It is also the case—as with monetary policy—that fiscal policy is most effective when the relevant shock is to aggregate demand and there are many unemployed resources.

Let's consider the stimulus under President Obama. The experiment is still being debated, but so far the consensus seems to be this:

1. Increased spending on automatic stabilizers such as unemployment insurance, Medicaid, and SNAP was well targeted and well timed. The spending was targeted on those who needed it and because they needed it this spending had relatively high multipliers and thus helped to increase aggregate demand.

2. Grants to state and local governments prevented layoffs and helped to maintain spending even as state and local government tax revenue fell. Multipliers were good, and since the spending would have happened anyway or was accelerated (e.g., highway improvements) it was on balance well spent.

3. A lot of the tax cuts were saved or used to pay off debts, rather than spent. This boosted economic security for some people but the multipliers were on the low side; thus, this didn't reemploy a lot of workers. The most effective tax cuts were targeted toward workers (payroll tax cuts) and the poor. Corporate, dividend and capital gain tax cuts were not well targeted for short-run stimulus.

4. The direct expenditures covered a wide range of ground, ranging from medical research to home insulation to high-speed rail—there was even $50 million for the National Cemetery Administration (spending on the dead probably had a low multiplier). Although some of these projects have done the world good, others were perhaps not the best use of funds; the multipliers in this case were mixed.

Takeaway

Fiscal policy is likely to be needed and most effective when:

1. The economy needs a short-run boost, even at the expense of the long run.

2. The problem is a deficiency in aggregate demand rather than a real shock.

3. Many resources are unemployed and the fiscal stimulus, either tax cuts or expenditures, can be targeted to those unemployed resources.

4. Government spending is efficient and productive.

The great debate over fiscal policy is about the balance of two opposing forces: crowding out versus the multiplier effect—or, how big is the multiplier? A multiplier of zero means that fiscal policy is ineffective. A multiplier of 2 means that every dollar spent by government increases GDP by two dollars. Different policies such as government purchases of goods and services, tax cuts, and transfer payments can have different multipliers. Fiscal policy is most effective when it is concentrated on policies with big multipliers. It is not always possible, however, to spend enough at the right time on the right policies to make fiscal policy very effective.

Ideal fiscal policy would be counter-cyclical—spending more in bad times and spending less in good times to offset declines and increases in private spending. Governments, however, often prefer to spend more in bad times and in good times! Automatic stabilizers such as unemployment insurance are counter-cyclical and can help to stabilize aggregate demand.

Some countries, especially some of the world's poorer countries, take fiscal policy too far. They accumulate very large levels of debt. The finances, currencies, and sometimes even the governments of those countries become unstable. Even if good fiscal policy doesn't always do a lot of good, bad fiscal policy can do a great deal of harm.

CHAPTER REVIEW

Go online to practice with more examples of these types of problems, including live links to videos, data sources, and feedback.

▶ Problems with this icon relate to optional MRU videos.

KEY CONCEPTS

fiscal policy, p. 405

crowding out, p. 406

multiplier effect, p. 406

Ricardian equivalence, p. 409

automatic stabilizers, p. 413

counter-cyclical fiscal policy, p. 416

FACTS AND TOOLS

▶ 1. Assume that the economy is growing steadily and hasn't had a recent recession. A new administration increases spending on the military by $200 billion, a significant amount.

   a. What is your estimate of the multiplier in this situation and what do you predict will be the impact on GDP?

   b. How would your answer change if the economy were in recession?

2. What shifts AD to the left: a rise in taxes or a cut in taxes? Does this push $\bar{v}$ up or push it down?

▶ 3. Let's see what the "three difficulties with using fiscal policy" look like in real life. Categorize each of the following three stories as either (1) crowding out, (2) magnitude, or (3) a matter of timing.

   a. During a recession, the State of New York hires 1,000 new trash collectors. The state legislature in Albany takes six months to pass a law to hire the new trash collectors, and because of government rules and paperwork, the government actually hires the workers 18 months after the recession has begun.

   b. During a recession, the State of New York hires 1,000 new trash collectors. Five hundred of the new trash collectors, however, were just people who quit their jobs as restaurant employees in order to take the better paying trash collector jobs.

   c. During a recession, the State of New York hires 1,000 new trash collectors. However, during the course of the recession, 300,000 additional people in New York lose their jobs.

4. When people "buy government bonds," are they borrowing money or saving money?

5. Imagine you live in the land of Ricardia, where every citizen is a Ricardian and thus "Ricardian equivalence" is 100% true. Government spending never changes in Ricardia: It's a fixed amount every year. Thus, when the Ricardian government cuts taxes, it has to pay for the government spending by borrowing more money and raising future taxes to repay the debt.

   a. When Ricardian income taxes are cut, what will Ricardian citizens do with the extra money in their paycheck: Will they spend all of it, save all of it, or spend some and save the rest?

b. Suppose that instead of a tax cut, the Ricardian government just sends citizens "rebate" checks. What will Ricardian citizens do with the extra money from these rebate checks: Will they spend all of it, save all of it, or spend some and save the rest?

6. It's often very difficult to get the timing of fiscal policy right. In this chapter, we listed five relevant lags.

   a. If each of the lags lasts three months, is the total lag longer or shorter than the typical recession since World War II? For data on the length of recessions, go to: https://www.nber.org/cycles.html. Look at the bottom of the column titled "Contraction."

   b. Of the five lags, the last one only involves watching how things turned out. If there are only four important lags, and they last three months each, will the average recession last longer than the average fiscal policy lag?

7. You're flipping through the newspaper, reading about shocks that have hit the U.S. economy and reading what Congress is planning to do about the shocks. (Remember that "shocks" can be either good or bad.) Is Congress even getting the direction of its response right? And if it is getting the basic direction correct, is it fighting against a long-run aggregate supply shock, where a fiscal response may not be very effective? While these policy choices will each have effects on long-run growth and on income distribution, in this chapter you should focus only on the effect on aggregate demand. In each of the following cases, state whether the action taken by Congress is likely to be in the wrong direction, the correct direction for an AD shock, or the correct direction for a long-run aggregate supply shock, but expect a big change in inflation.

   a. Many banks have failed, and the money supply has fallen. In response, Congress decides to raise income taxes to pay down the federal debt. (*Historical note:* This policy response was similar to FDR's campaign platform when he ran for president in 1932.)

   b. Many banks have failed, and the money supply has fallen. In response, Congress decides to cut back on government purchases to save money.

   c. A wave of investor euphoria ("irrational exuberance") about the Internet has increased spending growth. Congress raises income taxes on the richest Americans in response.

   d. Oil prices double over the course of a year, from $3 per gallon to $6 per gallon. In response, Congress sends $300 checks to every American family so that people can better afford to pay for gas.

   e. Oil prices double over the course of a year, from $3 per gallon to $6 per gallon. In response, Congress raises taxes on companies that refine and deliver petroleum products.

   f. The Federal Reserve has followed a slow-money-growth policy, despite the wishes of Congress. In response, Congress cuts taxes and increases government purchases.

8. Which of the following is an "automatic stabilizer" in the U.S. economy? There may be more than one:

   a. Consumers usually spend some of their savings and eat food from the pantry during recessions.

   b. Business owners usually purchase more capital equipment whenever profits fall.

   c. Governments automatically transfer cash to the unemployed when the economy is weak.

   d. When Americans have less demand for U.S. manufactured products, foreigners might pick up some of the slack, buying these unsold U.S.-made goods.

9. Why was the Great Depression an especially appropriate time to use fiscal policy rather than just monetary policy alone?

10. If the U.S. debt-to-GDP ratio were 100% and if the interest rate on the debt were 5% (not far from the truth at present), then what fraction of U.S. GDP would go toward paying interest on the debt? (*Note:* After World War II, U.S. debt was greater than 100% of GDP.)

11. Which kind of aggregate demand shift has fewer lags: changes in monetary policy or changes in fiscal policy?

THINKING AND PROBLEM SOLVING

12. As we showed in Table 18.1, the Congressional Budget Office estimated some fiscal multipliers around the 2009 recession. Let's assume that the average estimated multiplier is 1.5. Now assume that the economy enters into a recession today. Will fiscal policy necessarily be effective?

13. **a.** In the chapter, we wrote that Tyler does not save and plan according to the theory of Ricardian equivalence but Alex is more of a "Ricardian." In light of this, who probably cuts back their spending the most when taxes temporarily rise: someone like Tyler who is not "Ricardian" or someone like Alex who is?

   b. If the U.S. government wants to use fiscal policy to shift AD around easily, which one would the U.S. government prefer to make more copies of: Tyler or Alex?

14. Using the following figure, suppose that a change in fiscal policy shifted AD from AD(1) to AD(2). Which response is most likely to have caused that shift? Choose one of a, b, c, or d.

   a. A rise in taxes AND a rise in government spending

   b. A rise in taxes AND a fall in government spending

   c. A fall in taxes AND a rise in government spending

   d. A fall in taxes AND a fall in government spending

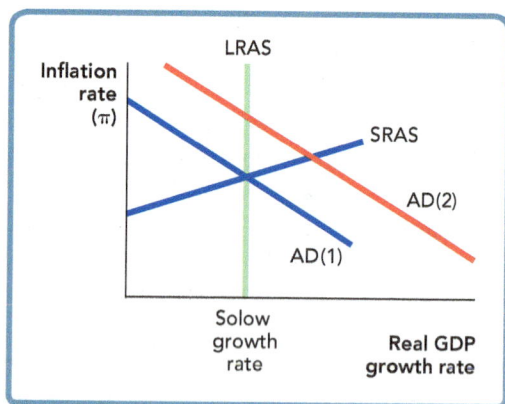

15. Using the figure in Problem 14, suppose that there's a rise in $\vec{v}$ due to business optimism—what Keynes called the "animal spirits" of investors. This pushes us to AD(2). If the government's goal is to keep output close to the long-run aggregate supply growth rate, and if fiscal policy is the tool that the government wants to use, what should it do? Choose one of a, b, c, or d.

   a. A rise in taxes AND a rise in government spending

   b. A rise in taxes AND a fall in government spending

   c. A fall in taxes AND a rise in government spending

   d. A fall in taxes AND a fall in government spending

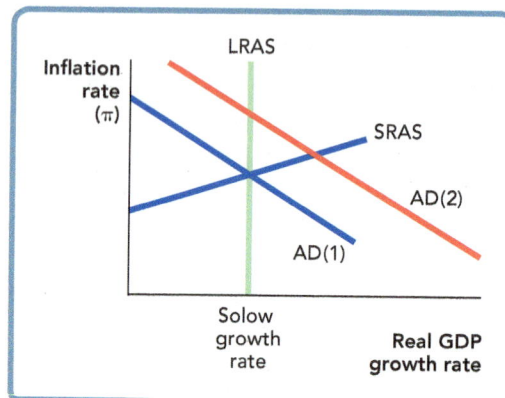

16. Consider the following imaginary newspaper quote, the type that you often read when Congress passes a tax rebate during a recession:

   "Many Americans report that they will put the tax rebate straight into their savings accounts or use it to pay off credit cards that they maxed out during the recent economic boom."

   If Congress is trying to shift AD to the right, are these kinds of quotes good news or bad news from Congress's point of view?

17. Which of the following government policies are "automatic stabilizers" for the economy?

   Unemployment insurance

   Temporary tax cuts that Congress passes when bad economic news hits

   Temporary spending increases that Congress passes when bad economic news hits

18. **a.** Which policy is likely to shift aggregate demand more? In which direction will it shift?

   A tax increase that occurs in the same year as a spending increase

   A tax increase that occurs without a spending increase

   b. Why is this so?

19. Ricardian equivalence is the idea that people might just use the extra money from their tax cuts to buy the very government bonds that pay for the tax cut. Let's think about the opposite situation: If Ricardian equivalence is true, and the government raises taxes (holding spending constant), how does the average person's behavior change? In other words, how do they react to a tax increase?

20. Again, think about the extreme case of crowding out known as "Ricardian equivalence." In real life, few citizens buy or sell government bonds directly; instead, normal people put their money in a bank (or invest it in a mutual fund), and then their bank (or mutual fund) uses that money to buy government bonds.

    a. So does a tax cut mean banks will get more deposits, fewer deposits, or can't you tell with the information given?

    b. How will the average bank's behavior change as a result of this tax cut, taking your response to part a into account?

21. We discussed three situations where fiscal policy is most likely to matter (though fiscal policy is best when *all* three are true):

    1. When the economy needs a short-run boost

    2. When the problem is low AD, not low LRAS

    3. When many machines and workers are unemployed

       Let's fit each of the following news stories into one (or more) of the above categories.

    a. World War II ends, and millions of U.S. soldiers return home. (*Note:* As a matter of history, returning World War II soldiers were overwhelmingly employed by the private sector.)

    b. Consumption spending declines dramatically as people fear a recession.

    c. Foreigners decide they are unwilling to buy U.S.-made airplanes because of rumors they read on the Internet.

22. Fiscal policy cannot cure all ills. Sometimes:

    i. The economy needs a long-run boost.

    ii. The problem isn't low AD, but low LRAS growth.

    iii. Almost all machines and workers are employed; they're just not very productive.

       Sort the following cases into either "fiscal solution possible" or "productivity problem":

    a. American wages have grown slowly for many years.

    b. Peasants in the Middle Ages are using primitive tools to produce food.

    c. Peasants in the Middle Ages suffer from a drought that hurts the season's crops.

    d. American workers get laid off by the hundreds of thousands because of a rapid collapse in investment purchases.

    e. Schools are doing a bad job teaching students, so students become ineffective employees.

    f. High taxes on investment discourage people from saving and building up the capital stock for future workers to use.

    g. High taxes on investment discourage businesses from purchasing investment goods.

CHALLENGES

23. When we discussed unemployment in Chapter 11, we noted that people will search a long time to find a good job. So it might only take you two weeks to find a minimum wage job, but it might take you six months to find a job paying five times the minimum wage.

    Let's investigate how this simple fact might cause expansionary fiscal policy to *increase* the unemployment rate, at least temporarily.

    In the United States, federal contracts to build roads, bridges, or buildings must pay higher-than-average wages. The law requiring this is known as the Davis-Bacon Act, or the "prevailing wage law."

    a. If the unemployment rate is 6% before a rise in government purchases, and if a rise in government purchases induces the typical unemployed person to search 10% longer in the hopes of finding a high-paying government job, what will the unemployment rate be after the rise in government purchases? Only consider the impact of this waiting-for-a-good-job effect.

    b. If the government wanted to get the good aggregate-demand-stimulating effects of fiscal policy, but wanted to eliminate this extra waiting-for-a-good-job unemployment, how could it change current law to do so?

24. Nobel Laureate Amartya Sen has pointed out that one way to prevent starvation during droughts in the poorest countries is to just pay peasants to build roads, sewer lines, and other public goods during these droughts. In the poorest countries, these peasants have no savings accounts, and almost no way to borrow money. In rich countries by contrast, most people have savings accounts and credit cards.

    a. Is the poor-country "multiplier" probably bigger or smaller than the rich-country multiplier, based on these facts?

b. All countries get hit by shocks, but not all countries have the same automatic stabilizers. Based on these facts, which countries probably have smoother GDP growth: poor countries or rich countries? (*Note:* The answer that is true in theory is also true in practice, a point emphasized in a 1995 paper in the *American Economic Review* by Garey and Valerie Ramey, "Cross-Country Evidence on the Link between Volatility and Growth.")

25. If the U.S. government wanted to, it could just say that everyone who is unemployed is "employed in the job search" and receiving a paycheck for this "work," and the government could claim that these government employees are producing "job search services." Recall that in the official definition of GDP, government purchases(*G*), do not include *transfer payments* like unemployment checks and Social Security.

  a. Would this change in the definition of GDP increase GDP? Would it improve well-being?

  b. If the government permanently defined unemployed people as "employed in job search," then over the course of a few decades as the economy fluctuated, would GDP look more volatile or less volatile than it does under the regular definition? (*Hint:* You might find it easier to answer if you consider GDP from the "factor income" perspective.)

26. We usually think about crowding out as a decrease in private consumption or investment in response to an increase in government purchases. But the idea works in reverse as well, an idea we might call "crowding in." Consider the following economy.

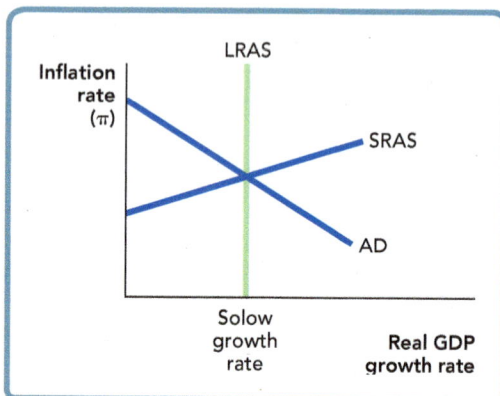

  a. Starting from this initial position, the economy is hit by one shock: a large *decrease* in government purchases, perhaps caused by the end of a war. Holding the growth of *C*, *I*, and *NX*

constant for a moment, illustrate this shock, labeling the change "Fall in growth of *G*."

  b. Now consider a possible side effect of the fall in the growth of *G*: the reversal of crowding out or crowding in. If there is 100% crowding in, what happens to the AD shift you described in part a?

  c. If there were 100% crowding out/in and no multiplier effect, what can we say about the effect of a change in the growth of *G* on aggregate demand?

  d. Consider all of the laid-off government workers in this question: If there were 100% crowding out/in and no multiplier effect, where do these laid-off workers end up?

Discovering DATA :•

27. In this question we will look at one of the automatic stabilizers, unemployment insurance. Using the FRED economic database (https://fred.stlouisfed.org/) search for unemployment insurance. You should find a series like "Personal current transfer receipts: Government social benefits to persons: Unemployment insurance." Graph the annual series.

  a. How much did the government spend on unemployment insurance at the peak of spending around the 2008–2009 recession?

  b. Approximately how much was spent on unemployment insurance in 2007, before the recession began? Compare your answer from part a to your answer from part b.

  The graph shows unemployment insurance spending in billions of dollars. In order to compare this spending to that in previous periods and to evaluate unemployment insurance spending as a fiscal stimulus, we should graph spending as percentage of GDP. Click Edit Graph, and under Customize Data search for Gross Domestic Product. (Do *not* click Real Gross Domestic Product, since we will compare with nominal insurance spending.) Add that data series. Then, under Customize Data, use the formula a/b*100 and click Apply.

  c. As a percentage of GDP how much was spent around the peak of the 2008–2009 recession?

  d. In the historical series, when was the most spent on unemployment, insurance as a percentage of GDP?

28. In February of 2009, Congress passed the American Recovery and Reinvestment Act (ARRA). When this stimulus package was signed into law, White House officials projected that it would create, or at least save, 3.5 million jobs, prevent the unemployment rate from rising above 8%, and have a multiplier effect on GDP of 1.57 after 10 quarters. Prior to the bill's signing, unemployment was at a 25-year high of 7.8%. (It had also reached 7.8% during one month in 1992.) In August of 2011, the Congressional Budget Office (CBO) estimated where the economy was at the end of June that year relative to where it would have been in the absence of the stimulus spending. Some of its findings are given in the table that follows. The low and high estimates under Real GDP define the range of how much greater in percentage terms real GDP was because of the stimulus spending than it would have been without it. The CBO also revised its estimate of the stimulus cost at $825 billion instead of the $787 billion projected at the time of the bill's signing and estimated that about half the impact occurred during 2010 with about 85% of it realized by the end of June 2011.

The 85% of the $825 billion stimulus package spent by the end of the second quarter in 2011, amounting to $701.3 billion, was funded through deficit financing and added to the national debt. For comparison to the real GDP figures, $701.3 billion when adjusted for inflation becomes $677.6 billion.

a. For each year, use the real GDP figures in the table and the low and high percentage estimates of the effect of the stimulus to calculate low and high estimates for the dollar effect of the stimulus.

b. Determine the midpoint of that range for each year and calculate a rough estimate of the total amount of real GDP generated by the stimulus spending for the ten quarters given in the table.

c. Compare the amount you calculated in part b to the inflation-adjusted stimulus expenditures of $677.6 billion for the same period and determine if those expenditures appear to have had a multiplier effect, no effect, or generated some crowding out.

d. How do your findings vary if you use the lower or the upper ends of the range of increased real GDP estimated by the CBO? If multipliers were this simple to generate, which they are not, what do these estimates suggest their sizes might be?

e. Use the chapter material describing the limits to fiscal policy to explain why the size of the impact you found in part c varied from the 1.57 multiplier effect forecasted by the White House at the time of the ARRA legislation.

f. Does the American Recovery and Reinvestment Act of 2009 qualify as one of the times when fiscal policy was a good idea? Defend your answer using economic support from the chapter.

CBO Estimates Aug. 2011	Real GDP Change Attributable to the ARRA (relative to where the economy would be without the ARRA)		Actual Values	
	Low Estimate (% change)	High Estimate (% change)	Real GDP (trillions of chained 2005 $)	Unemployment (%)
2009	0.9	1.9	12.71	9.3
2010	1.5	4.2	13.09	9.6
2011(1st and 2nd Qtr)	0.95	2.85	13.25	9.0

Data from: CBO, Estimated Impact of the American Recovery and Reinvestment Act on Employment and Economic Output from April 2011 Through June 2011, Aug. 2011. Unemployment and GDP data: FRED database of the St. Louis Federal Reserve Bank.

WORK IT OUT

For interactive, step-by-step help in solving this problem, go online.

According to recent estimates by Susan Woodward and Robert Hall, an extra dollar of government purchases raises GDP by one dollar—so there is little evidence for a "multiplier effect" in the short run, but also little evidence for "crowding out" in the short run. (Perhaps both effects are at work, but they just happen to balance out in practice.) Let's use these estimates as a rule of thumb to solve the following economic puzzles:

a. U.S. GDP is about $18 trillion. In a typical recession, GDP is about 2% below the Solow growth rate as given by the LRAS curve. If Congress wants to return growth to the Solow growth rate and thus move the economy back onto the LRAS curve by increasing government purchases, how big a rise in government purchases should it enact? Give your answer in dollars.

b. Suppose Canadian GDP is about $1.2 trillion (U.S. dollars). If Canadian GDP is 3% above its Solow growth rate, and the Canadian Parliament wants to change government purchases to return to the Solow growth rate, what change in government purchases should it enact, measured in U.S. dollars?

c. How do your answers to parts a and b change if there's stronger crowding out, and the multiplier falls to 0.5? (In other words, a rise in G of $1 raises GDP by only $0.50.) Answer in U.S. dollars.

d. How do your answers to parts a and b change if there's a bigger multiplier effect on consumer spending, and the multiplier rises to 2? (In other words, a rise in G of $1 raises GDP by $2.) Answer in U.S. dollars.

▶ MRU VIDEOS

Introduction to Fiscal Policy

mru.org/fiscal

Problems: **1, 9**

Fiscal Policy and the Best Case Scenario

mru.org/fiscal-best

Problems: **1, 13**

The Limits to Fiscal Policy

mru.org/fiscal-limits

Problems: **3, 12**

The Dangers of Fiscal Policy

mru.org/fiscal-avoid

Problem: **12**

Fiscal Policy and Crowding Out

mru.org/fiscal-crowding-out

Problems: **20, 26, 28**

Econ Duel: Does Fiscal Policy Work?

mru.org/duel-fiscal

Problems: **12, 22**

19

International Trade

International trade increased rapidly in the century before World War I. Tariffs and trade barriers fell throughout much of the nineteenth century and it was even possible to move about large parts of the world without a passport. The first era of globalization, however, ended with World War I, which brought passport requirements and numerous tariffs, quotas, and other barriers to international trade. After World War I, not much was done to bring the world back together, and with the coming of the Great Depression and then World War II protectionism grew stronger yet.

After World War II, however, a commitment was made among most of the leading nations of the world to reduce barriers to international trade. In 1947 the second era of globalization began when twenty-three nations signed the General Agreement on Tariffs and Trade (GATT). The goal of the GATT was not only to increase trade but also to bring former enemies together in peaceful cooperation. As one prominent supporter of GATT put it,

> *When goods don't cross borders, armies will.*

In recognition of this goal, Germany and Japan joined the GATT shortly after the initial signatories. Under GATT tariffs fell and trade increased. By the beginning of the twenty-first century, the average level of tariffs among the United States, the European Union, and Japan was under 5%. Despite occasional skirmishes, trade policy was mostly handled through international agreements and the World Trade Organization, and those institutions helped keep tariff and other trade barriers low.

The expansion of world trade was especially beneficial to China and other developing nations, which were able to lift billions of people out of poverty, in part by increasing manufacturing exports to the developed world. Globalization, however, was not without its critics. Low- to medium-skilled jobs in the U.S. manufacturing sector came under pressure, not only from exporting countries such as China, but also from technology, as many American factory jobs were automated. Those pressures became politically influential in the United States with the inauguration of President Donald Trump.

In early 2018, President Trump imposed big new tariffs on washing machines from abroad. By the end of the year, tariffs had increased on over 12,000 products covering $303 billion of U.S. imports, mostly from China but also including Scotch whisky, Irish butter, French wine, and Canadian steel.[1] The Trump tariffs were the largest increase in U.S. tariffs since the 1930 Smoot-Hawley Act and they started a trade war with China, which soon retaliated with tariffs of its own.

In this chapter, we will explain how to analyze tariffs and other forms of protectionism using the tools of supply and demand. We will discuss who wins and who loses from international trade, and we will discuss how the economic consequences of trade can drive the politics of trade. We will then return to the Trump tariffs and look in more detail at what happened in the market for washing machines and then more generally we will look at the consequences of the trade war on the United States and world economy.

Analyzing Trade with Supply and Demand

Let's look at trade—and trade restrictions—using tools that you are already familiar with: demand and supply.

Figure 19.1 shows a domestic demand curve and a domestic supply curve for semiconductors. If there were no international trade, the equilibrium would be, as usual, at $P^{\text{No trade}}$, $Q^{\text{No trade}}$. Suppose, however, that this good can also be bought in the world market at the world price. To simplify our diagram, we will assume that the U.S. market is small relative to the world market, so U.S. demanders can buy as many semiconductors as they want without pushing up the world price. In terms of our diagram, the world supply curve is flat (perfectly elastic) at the world price. Later in the chapter we will discuss the results, which are similar, when this assumption does not hold.

Given that U.S. consumers can buy as many semiconductors as they want at the world price, how many will they buy? As usual, we read the quantity demanded off the domestic demand curve so at the world price, U.S. consumers will demand $Q_d^{\text{Free trade}}$ semiconductors. How many semiconductors will

---

FIGURE 19.1

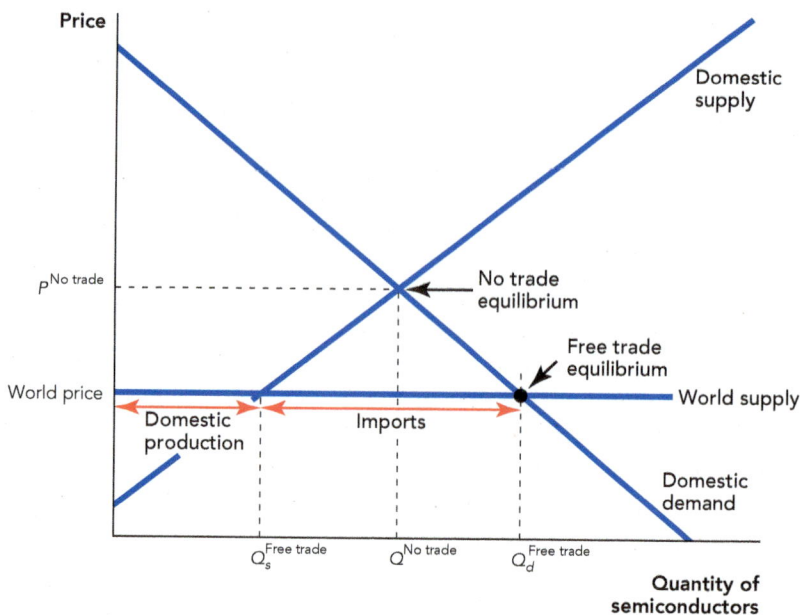

International Trade Using Demand and Supply If there were no international trade, the equilibrium would be found, as usual, at the intersection of the domestic demand and domestic supply curves at $P^{\text{No trade}}$, and $Q^{\text{No trade}}$. With trade, U.S. consumers can buy as many semiconductors as they want at the world price, and at this price U.S. consumers demand $Q_d^{\text{Free trade}}$ units. At the world price, the difference between domestic demand, $Q_d^{\text{Free trade}}$, and domestic supply, $Q_s^{\text{Free trade}}$, is made up by imports.

be supplied by *domestic* suppliers? As usual, we read the quantity supplied off the domestic supply curve so domestic suppliers will supply $Q_s^{\text{Free trade}}$ units. Notice that $Q_d^{\text{Free trade}} > Q_s^{\text{Free trade}}$, so where does the difference come from? From imports. In other words, with international trade, domestic consumption is $Q_d^{\text{Free trade}}$ units; $Q_s^{\text{Free trade}}$ of these units are produced domestically and the remainder, $Q_d^{\text{Free trade}} - Q_s^{\text{Free trade}}$, are imported.

Analyzing Tariffs with Demand and Supply

Many countries, including the United States, restrict international trade with tariffs, quotas, or other regulations that burden foreign producers but not domestic producers—this is called **protectionism.** A **tariff** is simply a tax on imports. A **trade quota** is a restriction on the quantity of foreign goods that can be imported: Imports greater than the quota amount are forbidden or heavily taxed.

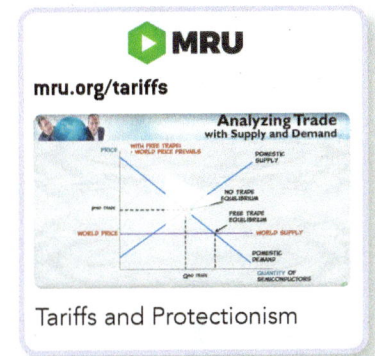

Figure 19.2 shows how to analyze a tariff. The figure looks imposing but it's really the same as Figure 19.1 except that now we analyze domestic consumption, production, and imports before and after the tariff. Before the tariff, the situation is exactly as in Figure 19.1: $Q_d^{\text{Free trade}}$ units are demanded, $Q_s^{\text{Free trade}}$ units are supplied by domestic producers, and imports are $Q_d^{\text{Free trade}} - Q_s^{\text{Free trade}}$.

The tariff is a tax on imports so—just as you learned in Chapter 3—the tariff (tax) shifts the world supply curve up by the amount of the tariff. For example, if the world price of semiconductors is $2 per unit and a new tariff of $1 per semiconductor is imposed, then the world supply curve shifts up to $3 per unit.

At the new, higher price of semiconductors, two things happen. First, there is an increase in the domestic production of semiconductors as domestic suppliers respond to the higher price by increasing production. In the diagram, domestic production increases from $Q_s^{\text{Free trade}}$ to Q_s^{Tariff}. Second, there is a decrease in domestic consumption from $Q_d^{\text{Free trade}}$ to Q_d^{Tariff} as domestic consumers respond to the higher price by buying fewer semiconductors. Since the quantity produced by domestic suppliers rises and the quantity demanded by

Protectionism is the economic policy of restraining trade through quotas, tariffs, or other regulations that burden foreign producers but not domestic producers.

A **tariff** is a tax on imports.

A **trade quota** is a restriction on the quantity of goods that can be imported: Imports greater than the quota amount are forbidden or heavily taxed.

mru.org/tariffs

Tariffs and Protectionism

FIGURE 19.2

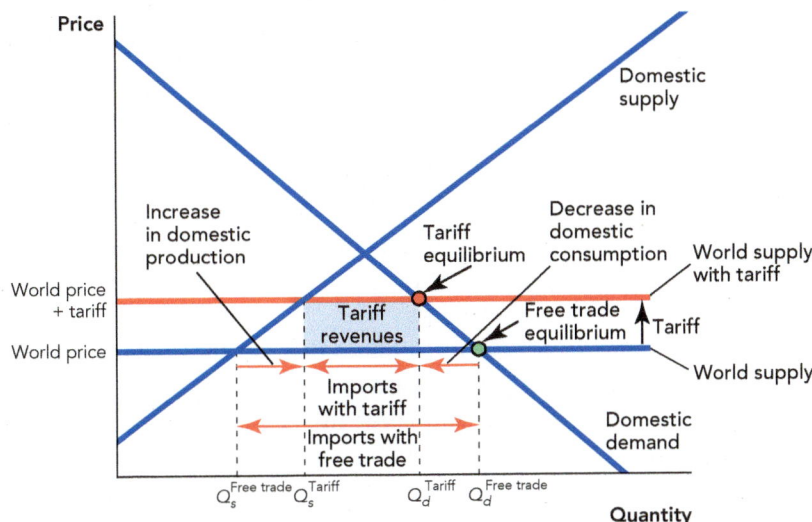

International Trade Using Demand and Supply: Tariffs A tariff shifts the world supply curve up by the amount of the tariff, thus raising the world price. In response to the higher price, consumers reduce their purchases from $Q_d^{\text{Free trade}}$ to Q_d^{Tariff} and domestic suppliers increase their production from $Q_s^{\text{Free trade}}$ to Q_s^{Tariff}. Since domestic consumption decreases and domestic production increases, the quantity of imports falls from $Q_d^{\text{Free trade}} - Q_s^{\text{Free trade}}$ to $Q_d^{\text{Tariff}} - Q_s^{\text{Tariff}}$.

The government collects revenues from the tariff equal to the tariff × the quantity of imports, which is shown as the blue area.

domestic consumers falls, the quantity of imports falls. Specifically, imports fall from $Q_d^{\text{Free trade}} - Q_s^{\text{Free trade}}$ to the smaller amount $Q_d^{\text{Tariff}} - Q_s^{\text{Tariff}}$.

Figure 19.2 illustrates one more important idea. A tariff is a tax on imports so tariffs raise tax revenue for the government. The revenue raised by a tariff is the tariff amount times the quantity of imports (the quantity taxed). Thus, in Figure 19.2 the tariff revenue is given by the blue area.

The Costs of Protectionism

Now that we know that a tariff on an imported good will increase domestic production and decrease domestic consumption, we can analyze in more detail the costs of protectionism. The U.S. government, for example, greatly restricts the amount of sugar that can be imported into the United States. As a result, U.S. consumers typically pay 50% to 100% more for sugar than the world price, depending on the year. So, let's look in more detail at the costs of sugar protectionism.

To simplify our analysis, we make two assumptions. First, we assume that the tariff is so high that it completely eliminates all sugar imports. Although a small amount of sugar is allowed into the United States at a low tariff rate, anything above this small amount is taxed so heavily that no further imports occur. Our assumption that the tariff eliminates all sugar imports is not a bad approximation to what actually happens. Second, we assume that if we had complete free trade, all sugar would be imported. This is also a reasonable assumption because, as we will explain shortly, sugar can be produced elsewhere at much lower cost than in the United States. Making these two assumptions will focus attention on the key ideas. See Challenge question 15 at the end of the chapter for a more detailed analysis.

In Figure 19.3, we show the market for sugar. If there were complete free trade in sugar, U.S. consumers would be able to buy at the world price of 9 cents per pound and they would purchase 24 billion pounds. U.S. producers cannot compete with foreign producers at a price of 9 cents per pound so with free trade all sugar would be imported.

The tariff on sugar imports is so high that with the tariff there are no imports and the U.S. price of sugar—found at the intersection of the domestic demand and domestic supply curve—rises to 20 cents per pound.

Recall that a tariff has two effects: It increases domestic production and reduces domestic consumption. Each of these effects has a cost. First, the increase in domestic production may sound good—and it is good for domestic producers—but domestic producers have higher costs of production than foreign producers. Thus, the tariff means that sugar is no longer supplied by the lowest-cost sellers, and resources that could have been used to produce other goods and services are instead wasted producing sugar. Second, due to higher costs, the price of sugar rises and fewer people buy sugar, reducing the gains from trade. Let's look at each of these costs.

Sugar costs more to grow in the United States than in, say, Brazil, the world's largest producer of sugar, because the climate in the U.S. mainland is not ideal for sugar growing and because land and labor in Florida, where a lot of U.S. sugar is grown, have many alternative uses that are high in value. Sugar farmers in Florida, for example, have to douse their land with expensive fertilizers to increase production—in the process creating environmental damage in the Florida Everglades.[2] The excess resources—the fertilizer, land, and labor—that go into

FIGURE 19.3

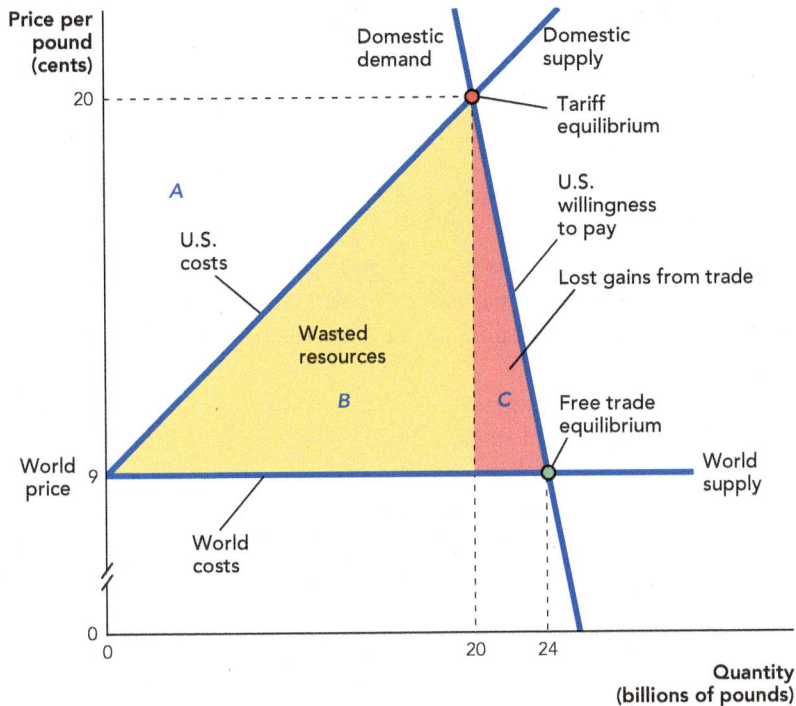

A Restriction on Trade Wastes Resources and Creates Lost Gains from Trade (Dead-weight Loss) With free trade, domestic production of sugar is 0. When imports are restricted, the domestic industry expands to 20 billion pounds, but U.S. costs are above world costs so the expansion of the domestic industry creates wasted resources (area *B*). Together, wasted resources and lost gains from trade (area *C*) represent the deadweight loss from trade restrictions.

producing U.S. sugar could have been used to produce other goods like oranges and theme parks for which the United States and Florida are better suited.

Recall from Chapter 3 that the supply curve tells us the cost of production so at the equilibrium price the cost of producing an additional pound of sugar in the United States is exactly 20 cents. In other words, in the United States it takes 20 cents worth of resources like land and labor to produce one additional pound of sugar. That same pound of sugar could be bought in the world market for just 9 cents so the tariff causes 11 cents worth of resources to be wasted in producing that last pound of sugar.

The total value of wasted resources is shown in Figure 19.3 by the yellow area labeled "Wasted resources"; that area represents the difference between what it costs to produce 20 billion pounds of sugar in the United States and what it would cost to buy the same amount from abroad. We can calculate the total value of wasted resources using our formula for the area of a triangle.

The height of the yellow triangle is 20 − 9 or 11 cents per pound, the base is 20 billion pounds, so the area is 110 billion cents, or $1.1 billion. The sugar tariff wastes $1.1 billion worth of resources.

Notice that if the sugar tariff were eliminated, the price of sugar in the United States would fall to the world price of 9 cents per pound and U.S.

Area of a Triangle

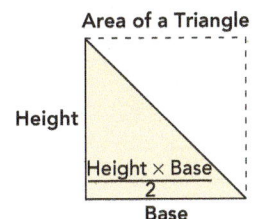

production would drop from 20 billion pounds to 0 pounds. It's important to see that the reduction in U.S. production is a *benefit* of eliminating the tariff because it frees up resources that can be used to produce other goods and services.

There is another cost to the tariff. Remember from Chapter 3 that the demand curve tells us the value of goods to the demanders, so at the equilibrium price demanders are willing to pay up to 20 cents for a pound of sugar. World suppliers, however, are willing to sell sugar at 9 cents per pound. U.S. consumers and world suppliers could make mutually profitable gains from trade, but they are prevented from doing so by the threat of punishment. The value of the lost gains from trade is given by the pink area (area C). Again, we can calculate this area using our formula for the area of a triangle ([20 − 9] cents per pound × 4 billion pounds divided by 2) = 22 billion cents or $0.22 billion.

Thus, the total cost of the sugar tariff to U.S. citizens is $1.1 billion of wasted resources plus $0.22 billion of lost gains from trade for a total loss of $1.32 billion.

Do you remember from Chapter 4, the three conditions that explain why a free market is efficient? Here they are again:

1. The supply of goods is bought by the buyers with the highest willingness to pay.

2. The supply of goods is sold by the sellers with the lowest costs.

3. Between buyers and sellers, there are no unexploited gains from trade or any wasteful trades.

A tariff or quota that restricts consumers from trading with foreign producers means that the market is not free, so we should expect some of the conditions in our list to be violated. In this case, conditions 2 and 3 are violated. A tariff reduces efficiency because the supply of goods is no longer sold by the sellers with the lowest costs, and with a tariff, there are unexploited gains from trade between buyers and sellers.

Winners and Losers from Trade

We can arrive at this same total loss in another revealing way. The sugar tariff raises the price of sugar to U.S. consumers, which reduces consumer surplus. Recall from Chapter 3 that consumer surplus is the area underneath the demand curve and above the price. Thus, consumer surplus with the tariff is the area above the price of 20 cents and below the demand curve (not all of which is shown in Figure 19.3). As the price falls from 20 cents to 9 cents, consumer surplus increases by area *A + B + C*, which has a value (check it!) of $2.42 billion. Or, put differently, the tariff costs consumers $2.42 billion in lost consumer surplus.

The tariff increases price, which increases producer surplus, the area above the supply curve and below the price. Thus, the tariff increases U.S. producer surplus by area *A*, which has a value of $1.10 billion.

Notice that U.S. consumers lose more than twice as much from the tariff as U.S. producers gain. The total loss to U.S. citizens is the $2.42 billion loss to consumers minus the $1.10 billion gain to producers, for a total loss of $1.32 billion a year, *exactly as we found before*.

Our two methods of analyzing the cost of the sugar tariff are equivalent, but they emphasize different things. The first method emphasizes where the loss

How to smuggle sugar The high price of U.S. sugar has encouraged smuggling and attempts to circumvent the tariff. In the 1980s when the U.S. price was four times the world price, Canadian entrepreneurs created super-high-sugar iced tea. The "tea" was shipped into the United States and then sifted for the sugar, which was resold. To combat this entrepreneurship, the U.S. government created even more tariffs for sugar-containing products like iced tea, cake mixes, and cocoa.

comes from: wasted resources and lost gains from trade. The second method focuses on *who* gains and *who* loses. Domestic producers gain but U.S. consumers lose even more.

International Trade and Jobs

Many people believe that protectionism increases the number of U.S. jobs. Economists, however, argue that trade has no major effects on the overall number of jobs in an economy. A tariff on washing machines will create jobs in the domestic washing machine industry, but what the person in the street has difficulty seeing is that tariffs on washing machines will reduce the number of jobs elsewhere in the economy. Let's take a closer look.

A tariff reduces the sales of foreign producers of washing machines. But why were workers and firms in China, for example, making washing machines to sell to the United States? Workers in China want to be paid for their work. Initially, workers in China are paid with U.S. dollars. But dollars are just pieces of paper! We use money to make trade easier, but, ultimately trade is about trading goods and services for other goods and services. People work to consume. Thus, our thought experiment reveals an important principle:

> *We pay for our imports with exports.*

You are undoubtedly familiar with this principle in your own life. If you want to consume more (import), you must produce more (export). That's not quite right because of gifts and other transfers. By borrowing you can also consume more today without producing more today, so long as you produce more tomorrow. These complications also apply to international trade (as we discuss at greater length in Chapter 8). Nevertheless, the principle is an important one and it tells us that if we import more we must eventually export more.

If we import more, we will export more. The reverse is also true. If we import less, we will export less. If we buy less from them, they will buy less from us. As a result, a tariff on our imports means fewer exports and fewer jobs in export industries. The jobs created by a tariff are easy to see. The jobs in our export industries that are destroyed by a tariff are harder to see but no less real.

We pay for our imports with exports but we may import and export very different goods and that has implications for how the benefits and costs of international trade are distributed. Let's go back to the idea of comparative advantage from Chapter 2. Compared to the rest of the world, the United States has a lot of highly educated, skilled workers, so the United States is likely to have a comparative advantage in producing complex goods like aircraft, entertainment, specialized computer chips and research, design and other services. Other countries, such as China, have an abundance of less skilled workers. So China, at least compared to the United States, has a comparative advantage in producing less complex goods such as clothing, footwear, and simpler manufactured goods, and that includes doing the final stages of assembly on more complex manufactured goods, such as iPhones.

Increased trade with a country such as China, therefore, will shift U.S. production towards aircraft production and research and design services and away from producing shoes and washing machines. More generally, increased trade with China will increase the demand for skilled workers, driving up their wages, and it will decrease the demand for unskilled workers driving down their wages.

Between 1996 and 2006, imports from China increased by a factor of six, from about $50 billion per year to $300 billion per year, a large change in a short period of time. The economists Nicholas Bloom, Kyle Handley, André Kurmann, and Philip Luck study this "China shock" and they find that, as theory predicts, there was an increase in demand for high-skilled American workers in complex export industries. Similarly, there was a decrease in demand for low-skilled workers in simple manufacturing industries where Chinese production was very competitive. The increased demand for skilled labor driven by the "China shock" increased the wages for *all* skilled workers, not just skilled workers in export industries. The demand for skilled workers increased first in export industries, but to attract those workers the export industries had to raise wages and pull workers away from other sectors and that pushed up the wages of all skilled workers. Similarly, competition from Chinese imports forced some domestic firms out of business, which initially increased unemployment among low-skilled workers. But, as the newly unemployed workers competed to obtain new jobs in other sectors, the wages of *all* unskilled workers fell. Adjusting took time, but overall just as many jobs were created as were lost and the newly created jobs were in higher-paying industries.

Low- and high-skilled workers, however, tend to live in different parts of the country so the shift in demand had geographic and later political consequences. The decreased demand for low-skill workers hurt the South and the Appalachian region of the United States where college educated workers are in the minority while the increased demand for skilled workers benefitted places such as on the coasts where college educated workers are in the majority.

We will return to the politics of trade a bit later, but you probably already guessed one connection—the areas which were hardest hit by the "China shock" tended to vote for Donald Trump in the 2016 election.[3]

The Washing Machine Tariffs

Now that you know how to analyze international trade using demand and supply, let's see how well the theory holds up by looking at what happened in the market for washing machines after the Trump tariffs were put into place in January of 2018. The tariff came in two parts. The first 1.2 million washing machines were taxed at a rate of 20% and all remaining imports were taxed at a rate of 50%. The tariffs were put in place for three years with slight declines (to 18% and 45% and 16% and 40%) in the 2nd and 3rd year respectively. A 50% tariff on washing machine parts was also included to prevent manufacturers from avoiding the duty by shipping parts to the United States for quick assembly.

Before the tariffs, about 3.8 million washing machines were imported per year. Once the tariffs began, imports declined by 1.2 million units to approximately 2.6 million washing machines per year. Figure 19.4 shows the price index for laundry equipment in the United States. Prices for washer and dryers had been declining since at least 2013, but the moment tariffs were imposed prices jumped dramatically. (Slight declines in prices were also seen in 2019 when the tariff rate decreased modestly.)

Economists estimate that the tariff increased the price of washing machines by about 12%. That's actually a smaller increase in price than one might guess

FIGURE 19.4

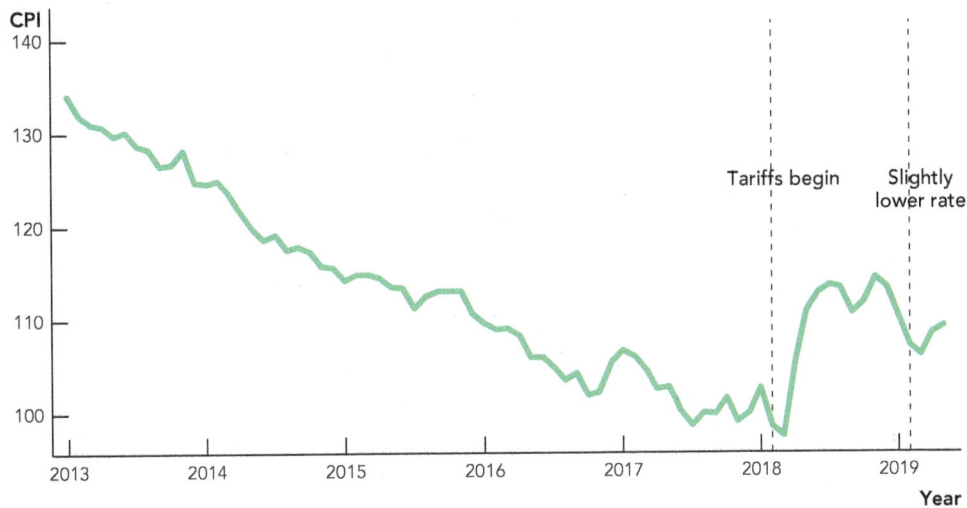

Prices of Laundry Equipment

Data from: Bureau of Labor Statistics.

from the size of the tariff but it turns out that dryer prices also increased by about 12%. Dryers were not subject to the tariff. So why did dryer prices increase? Washers and dryers are typically bought together in a package. Manufacturers, therefore, tend to focus on the package price and they "smoothed" out the washer tariff over both washers and dryers. Looking at thousands of goods, economists estimated that the Trump tariffs were on average entirely passed on to consumers, just as our supply and demand model with a horizontal supply curve predicts (see Figure 19.2).

Another important prediction of the supply and demand model is that the tariff will increase the prices of *all* washing machines, whether produced domestically or imported. When the tariff is first put into place, domestic producers have lower costs than foreign producers and, as a result, they sell more and increase output. As domestic producers increase their output, however, their costs rise until in equilibrium domestic and foreign producers are, once again, selling for the same price. In fact, this is exactly what happened. Domestic producers like Whirlpool raised their prices at least as much as did foreign producers.

The Trump tariffs did have one unexpected consequence. In the model, it's natural to think of domestic producers as being domestically owned firms, but that is not necessarily the case. Whirlpool, a domestic producer of washing machines, did produce more because of the tariffs but something else happened. The foreign producers, Samsung and LG, expanded their U.S. factories! That's good for U.S. workers in the washer and dryer industry. Nevertheless, the expansion of Samsung and LG was probably an unwelcome surprise to Whirlpool, which may have expected that the tariffs would give them more of a competitive advantage in the domestic market than they ended up getting.

The increased in domestic production from both domestically owned and foreign owned firms resulted in about 1800 new jobs in the washer and dryer industry. Remember trade policy does not influence the total number of jobs in an economy. The jobs created in the washer and dryer industry came at the expense of jobs lost in U.S. export industries. The new jobs in the protected industry, however, are visible and they are important politically, because the President can point to them as a benefit of his policies. Thus, it's an interesting question to ask, how much did consumers pay to create these jobs?

The tariffs increased washer and dryer prices by about 12% or $88 each on combined sales of 17.4 million units. The total cost to consumers, therefore, was approximately $1.56 billion per year. The government took in an extra $82.2 million in tariff revenues, which we count as a plus, so the total cost was about $1.48 billion per year. The cost per job created was therefore a whopping $821,000 per job ($1.48 billion/1,800). Instead of creating jobs by paying more for washers and dryers, U.S. consumers would have been much better off paying each new worker in the laundry industry $100,000 to enjoy a nice vacation!

The Economics and Politics of a Trade War

The most important feature of protectionism that is not taken into account by the supply and demand model is the possibility of a trade war. Protectionism is much more costly if other countries respond to U.S. tariffs with tariffs of their own on U.S. exports. The Trump administration increased tariffs on more than 12,000 products imported from China, Canada, Mexico and other countries. These other countries retaliated with tariffs on thousands of U.S. exports. Furthermore, these tariffs are part of a broader pattern of two-way retaliatory interactions, including restrictions on foreign investment, restrictions on foreign market entry (you can't use Facebook in China), restrictions on joint ventures between the firms of the two countries, and new visa restrictions on travel.

Tariffs and other trade restrictions on imports harm U.S. consumers but offer some, less than offsetting, benefits to U.S. producers. Foreign tariffs and other trade restrictions on U.S. exports harm U.S. producers but offer some, less than offsetting, benefits to U.S. consumers. Thus, when U.S. tariffs bring foreign tariffs in retaliation it's likely that U.S. consumers and U.S. producers are both harmed on net. China's retaliatory strike was well targeted to impose economic costs on the United States and also to do maximum political damage to President Trump's political base. Many of China's tariffs and trade restrictions, for example, were placed on goods produced in counties where a majority of voters voted for Republicans in 2016, especially agricultural products.[4] China, for example, abruptly ordered Chinese companies to stop buying American soybeans. U.S. farmers lost sales and billions of pounds of soybeans had to be stored in hopes of finding alternative markets.[5] President Trump authorized over $28 billion in bailouts to compensate farmers for the loss of trade. Thus, instead of Chinese consumers supporting American farmers, American taxpayers ended up supporting American farmers.

China increased its trade restrictions on U.S. soybeans but not on U.S. aircraft. Why the difference? It's much easier to find alternative suppliers of soybeans than aircraft, so China chose to impose trade restrictions that would hurt the United States at least cost to China. Indeed, at the same time as China raised tariffs on U.S. goods, they reduced tariffs on imports from U.S. competitors! China, for example, imposed a tariff of 25% on exports of U.S. lobster and at the same time they reduced the tariff on Canadian exports of lobster. The American lobster industry saw its exports fall by 70%, with most of the loss being made up by increased Canadian exports.

Lobster consumers in China bought more Canadian lobsters to avoid the Chinese tariff on American lobsters. In exactly the same way, American consumers bought more from other countries to avoid American tariffs on Chinese goods. Firms have also been incentivized to move production out of China and into other low-wage countries such as Vietnam and India. Trade networks are costly to set up, so when the trade war ends it is not obvious that either China or the United States will regain the sales they have lost. The worldwide shift in trade networks illustrates how a trade war can increase economic uncertainty and make it harder for businesses to know where to invest. That may stifle investment altogether, which also lowers wages and slows down economic growth.

The lesson is that trade wars are easy to lose.

Nintendo switched production from China to Vietnam to avoid high American tariffs on Chinese imports.

The U.S. Politics of Protectionism

Why does the government sometimes support protectionist tariffs even when U.S. consumers lose more than producers gain? One explanation is that the costs of protectionism are often spread over millions of consumers while the benefits flow to a small number of producers. As a result, the cost to each consumer is small, but the gain to each producer is large. The sugar quota we discussed earlier costs every person in the United States about $8 per year but it benefits a small number of sugar producers by millions of dollars per firm. The small cost per sugar consumer mean that it's not worth knowing about, let alone lobbying against, the sugar quota. Similarly, the washing machine tariff raised the price of a washer/dryer combination by $180, which is substantial. But when the Trump tariffs were announced the stock price of Whirlpool jumped by $20, raising Whirlpool's value by about $1.26 billion.[6] It's not surprising, therefore, that producers are more informed and they lobby harder for trade protectionism than consumers lobby against trade protectionism, even when consumers are harmed more in total.

The sugar quota and washer tariffs are classic examples of spreading the costs of a policy and concentrating the benefits. The Trump tariffs, however, were large and they covered thousands of products making this explanation less applicable. Whirlpool, for example, lobbied hard for the washer tariffs, but just weeks after the washer tariffs were announced the Trump administration imposed new tariffs on steel—and Whirlpool uses steel to make washers and dryers! After the steel tariffs were announced, Whirlpool's sales and their stock price decreased. Taking into account both the washer and steel tariffs, it's not obvious that Whirlpool benefited from U.S. protectionism.

To understand wide-scale support for protectionism, we need to recall that the United States has a comparative advantage in goods and services produced by skilled workers and a comparative disadvantage in goods and services produced by unskilled or less-skilled workers. As a result, increased international trade increases the demand for skilled workers and decreases the demand for unskilled workers. Given these dynamics, it's not surprising that more educated workers and their political representatives tend to support free trade more than do less educated workers and their political representatives. Although it is somewhat unclear whether educated workers support free trade because it is in their *interest*, or because education helps workers to understand the benefits of free trade, or because education makes workers more cosmopolitan and more culturally open to international trade—probably a mix of all these motives.[7]

Less-skilled manufacturing workers have been hit in the last several decades by increased international trade and by technological changes such as automation. It's not surprising, therefore, that regions of the country with more unskilled workers were, all else equal, more supportive of the protectionist policies of Donald Trump. It's less clear, however, that less-skilled workers will end up benefitting from the trade war. In theory, greater U.S. protectionism will increase the demand for unskilled workers and reduce the demand for skilled workers. But that only works for certain if there is no retaliation. Unfortunately, everyone can be made worse off by a trade war. As we mentioned earlier, the Chinese retaliatory tariffs were specifically designed to hit Trump voters. When we combine a trade war with the fact that protectionism reduces world income by pushing countries away from their comparative advantage, it's likely that even many low-skilled U.S. workers will lose from greater protectionism.

If protectionism isn't the answer, how should we respond to rapid changes in the economy that create losers as well as winners? We should first remember that all change generates losers and winners. Thomas Edison destroyed the whale oil industry with his invention of the electric lightbulb in 1879. That was bad for whalers but good for people who like to read at night (and very good for the whales). Compact discs destroyed jobs in the vinyl record industry and then MP3s destroyed jobs in the CD industry. Music lovers, however, gained access to tens of millions of songs on services like Spotify at a price less than the cost of a dozen Beatles CDs in 2001. In each case, however, these changes were ultimately beneficial to most people.

We shouldn't forget the winners but neither, of course, should we ignore the losers. Unemployment insurance, retraining assistance, and a strong education system can help workers respond to economic shocks. If we want the gains from a growing and dynamic economy, it's better to adjust to shocks than to try to prevent change. Over time, the results of adjusting to change have been a tremendous increase in the U.S. standard of living.

Arguments Against International Trade

It would take several books to analyze all the arguments against international trade. We will take a closer look at three of the most common arguments:

- It's wrong to trade with countries that use child labor.
- We need to keep certain industries at home for reasons of national security.
- We can increase U.S. well-being with strategic trade protectionism.

Child Labor

Is child labor a reason to restrict trade? In part, this is a question of ethics on which reasonable people can disagree, but our belief, for which we will give reasons, is that the answer is no.

In 1992, labor activists discovered that Walmart was selling clothing that had been made in Bangladesh by subcontractors who had employed some child workers. Senator Tom Harkin angrily introduced a bill in Congress to prohibit firms from importing any products made by children under the age of 15.

CHECK YOURSELF
- Who benefits from a tariff? Who loses?
- Why does trade protectionism lead to wasted resources?
- If there are winners and losers from trade restrictions, why do we hear more often from the people who gain from trade restrictions than from the people who lose?
- Identify the deadweight loss area in Figure 19.3 and describe in words what is lost.

Harkin's bill didn't pass, but in a panic the garment industry in Bangladesh dismissed 30,000 to 50,000 child workers. A success? Before we decide, we need to think about what happened to the children who were thrown out of work. Where did these children go? To the playground? To school? To a better job? No. Thrown out of the garment factories, the children went to work elsewhere, many at jobs like prostitution with worse conditions and lower pay.[8]

About 11% of all children aged 5–14 around the world work for a significant number of hours each week. The vast majority of these children work in agriculture, often alongside their parents, and not in export industries. Restrictions on trade, therefore, cannot directly reduce the number of child workers, and by making a poor country poorer, trade restrictions may increase the number of child workers. In fact, studies have shown that more openness to trade increases income and reduces child labor.[9]

Child labor is more common in poor countries and it was common in nineteenth-century Great Britain and the United States when people were much poorer than today. Child labor declined in the developed world as people got richer.

The forces that reduced child labor in the developed world are also at work in the developing world. The vertical axis of Figure 19.5 shows the percentage of child laborers against real GDP per capita on the horizontal axis. The sizes of the circles are proportionate to the total number of child laborers, so although the percentage of child laborers is much higher in Peru (22.55%) than in India (1.7%), there are many more child laborers in India. The lesson of Figure 19.5 is that economic growth reduces child labor.

The pin factory Lewis Hine photograph of bowling alley boys in New Haven, CT. Circa 1910.

The Protected Art Archive/Alamy

FIGURE 19.5

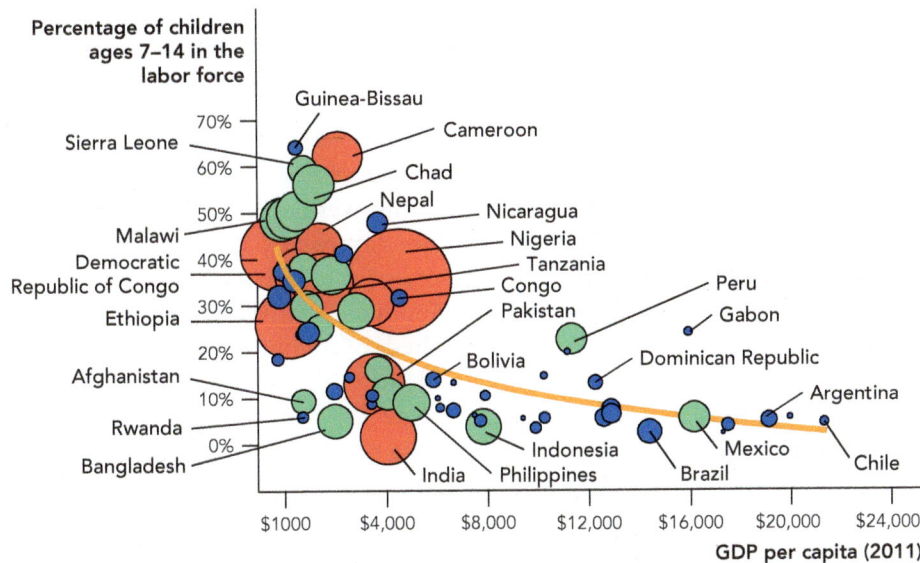

Child Labor Decreases with Increases in GDP Per Capita

Note: Ratio Scale

Data from: https://ourworldindata.org/child-labor

Bans on child labor can also backfire. Bans can help in relatively rich countries where child labor is already low and strong enforcement is possible. But the economists Prashant Bharadwaj, Leah Lakdawala, and Nicholas Li studied India's partial ban on child labor in 1986 and what they found was that instead of reducing child labor, the ban increased child labor.[10] How is this possible? The ban reduced child wages because firms that hired children now faced the possibility of fines. Lower child wages meant that poor families became even poorer. To make up for the decline in their income, poorer families were forced to increase the amount of work done by children. It's a sad story of how well intentioned legislation can sometimes have perverse and unintended consequences.

Rather than pushing them out of work with bans, governments and nonprofits can help by pulling children away from work with opportunity. In Bangladesh, at about the same time that child workers were being thrown out of work by the Harkin bill, the government introduced the Food for Education program. The program provides a free monthly stipend of rice or wheat to poor families who have at least one child attending school that month. The program has been successful at encouraging school attendance. Even more important, increased education of children today means richer parents tomorrow—parents who will have enough wealth to feed their children *and* send them to school.

More generally, it's common for protectionists to lobby under the guise of some other motive. Many people, for example, are concerned about working conditions in developing countries, but does it surprise you that U.S. labor unions are often the biggest lobbyists for bills to restrict trade on behalf of "oppressed foreign workers"? As Youssef Boutros-Ghali, Egypt's former minister for trade, put it, "The question is why all of a sudden, when third world labor has proved to be competitive, why do industrial countries start feeling concerned about our workers? . . . It is suspicious."[11]

Trade and National Security

If a good is vital for national security but domestic producers have higher costs than foreign producers, it can make sense for the government to tax imports or subsidize the production of the domestic industry. It may make sense, for example, to support a domestic vaccine industry. In 1918, more than a quarter of the U.S. population got sick with the flu and more than 500,000 died, sometimes within hours of being infected. The young were especially hard-hit and, as a result, life expectancy in the United States dropped by 10 years. No place in the world was safe, as between 2.5% and 5% of the entire world population died from the flu between 1918 and 1920. Producing flu vaccine requires an elaborate process in which robots inject hundreds of millions of eggs with flu viruses. In an ordinary year, there are few problems with buying vaccine produced in another country, but if something like the 1918 flu swept the world again, it would be wise to have significant vaccine production capacity in the United States.[12] In 2020, the world was struck by the COVID-19 pandemic. We didn't face a shortage of vaccine factories because there wasn't a vaccine, but there was a shortage of masks so the same idea applies. It didn't help that the Trump tariffs had increased the price of medical imports. Fortunately, those tariffs were quickly dropped.

Many people have also argued that the Chinese firm Huawei should not be allowed a critical role in America's communications infrastructure, for fear that the Chinese government could use the company to tap into military and intelligence communications, or the corporate transmission of valuable intellectual property. Restrictions on Huawei became one of the major issues in the U.S.-Chinese trade war.

Don't be surprised, however, if every domestic producer in trouble claims that their product is vital for national security. Everything from beeswax to mohair, not to mention steel and computer chips, has been protected in the name of national security.

Strategic Trade Protectionism

In some cases, it's possible for a country to use tariffs and quotas to grab a larger share of the gains from trade than would be possible with pure free trade. A tariff is a tax but it's a special kind of tax because the demanders live in the United States and the suppliers are foreign firms. Now who bears the burden of a tax? Demanders or suppliers? In Chapter 6, we came up with a simple way to remember: Elasticity = escape, that is the more elastic side of the market can escape (some) of the tax so the more inelastic side of the market bears more of the burden of a tax. See Figure 6.4 for a reminder.

Now let's return to the beginning of this chapter. We assumed that the world supply curve was perfectly elastic. So who bears the burden of a tariff? If the supply curve is perfectly elastic the suppliers escape the tariff/tax so the demanders bear the burden. The assumption that the world supply curve is perfectly elastic makes sense for a small economy in a big world market. A small economy can buy more from the world without pushing up the world price and if it buys less the world price won't fall. Notice from Figure 19.2 that with perfectly elastic supply the price paid by U.S. consumers increases by the full amount of the tariff. The U.S. economy accounts for about 15% of the world economy—pretty big! It's somewhat surprising, therefore, that most empirical studies of tariffs find that tariffs are almost fully passed on to consumers in higher prices. Thus, the small economy assumption is reasonably accurate, even for the United States. Nevertheless, the changes in U.S. demand should be big enough to affect the world price for at least some goods. Figure 19.6 shows what happens in this case.

In Figure 19.6 the foreign supply curve isn't flat but quite inelastic which means that if the foreign suppliers lose the U.S. market they have no other major customers.[13] When the (domestic) demand curve is more elastic than the (foreign) supply curve, a tariff reduces the price received by foreigners much more than it increases the price paid by domestic consumers. Notice that in this case only a fraction of the tariff is passed on to consumers, that is the price paid by U.S. buyers after the tariff is only slightly higher than price under free trade.

The consumers, of course, still don't like the tariff because it raises prices and it also creates a deadweight loss (i.e., lost gains from trade. Can you find this area?). But there is an offsetting factor. The tariff creates revenues that flow to the U.S. government and notice that most of the revenues are paid by the foreign suppliers. Thus, the tariff creates a small deadweight loss for U.S. consumers but a relatively large increase in government revenues that could be used to reduce other taxes. It's quite possible, therefore, that the net effect of these two factors is positive for the United States.

Taxing foreigners may sound like a great idea but it's trickier than it looks. As the tariff increases so does the deadweight loss and if the tariff gets too large

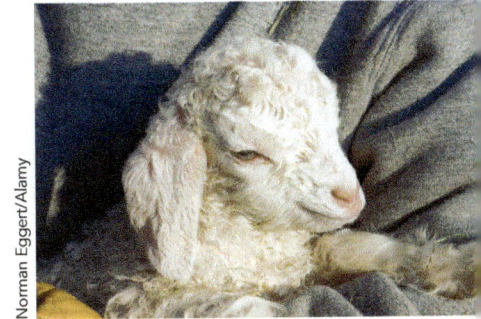

Norman Eggert/Alamy

Vital for national security? In 1954 the U.S. government declared that mohair, the fleece of the Angora goat, was vital for national security (it can be used to make military uniforms). For nearly 40 years mohair producers received millions of dollars in annual payments. Finally, after much ridicule, the program was eliminated in 1993 . . . only to be reestablished in 2002. Hard to believe? Yes, but we aren't kidding.

CHECK YOURSELF

- Over the past 30 years, most U.S. garment manufacturing has moved overseas, to places such as India and China, where wages are lower. The result of this shift has been a sizable drop in the number of garment workers in the United States. While bad for these workers, why has this trend been a net benefit for the United States?

- What would happen if the U.S. government decided that computer chip manufacturing was a strategic national industry and provided monetary grants to Silicon Valley companies? Trace the effects of this policy on Silicon Valley companies, foreign competitors, and the cost and benefit to U.S. taxpayers and consumers.

FIGURE 19.6

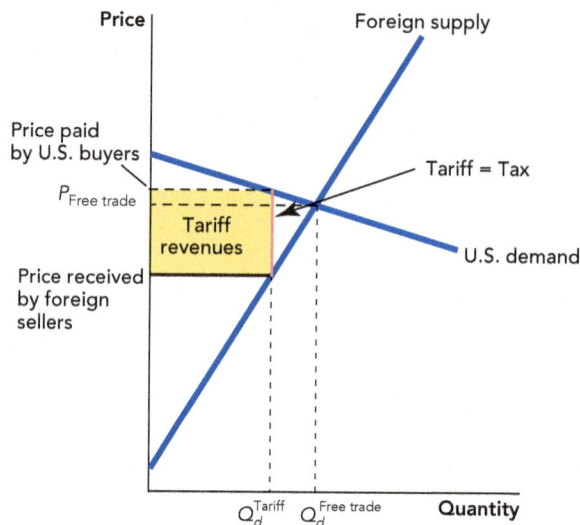

A Tariff Is a Tax When the foreign supply curve is very inelastic relative to the domestic demand curve, most of the burden of the tariff will fall on foreign suppliers. Notice that the price paid by U.S. buyers rises only slightly but the price received by foreign sellers falls a lot. As a result, the tariff revenues that flow to the U.S. government are paid mostly by the foreign sellers, and the net effect of the tariff, even taking into account the deadweight loss on U.S. buyers, could be positive.

revenues will decline. Thus, there is an optimal tariff that balances the increase in deadweight loss with the increase in revenues. Finding such a tariff may be quite difficult. Moreover, how will other nations feel when we try to tax their citizens? Retaliation may be quite likely and the net effect is then likely to be negative.

Takeaway

We have shown in this chapter how to use demand and supply curves to analyze trade and the costs of trade protectionism. As always, make sure you can read and correctly draw the graphs!

Protectionism wastes resources by transferring production from low-cost foreign producers to high-cost domestic producers. Restrictions on trade also prevent domestic consumers from exploiting gains from trade with foreign producers, creating deadweight losses.

International trade creates jobs in some industries and destroys them in other industries raising wages on average. The United States has an abundance of high-skilled labor relative to much of the rest of the world. As a result, the United States will tend to export goods and services produced by high-skilled labor and import goods and services produced by low-skilled labor. Adjusting to changes in demand from trade, technology or other sources of disruption can be costly and traumatic and such adjustment costs may generate demands for protectionism. Small scale protectionism can also persist because the benefits from restrictions are often concentrated on small groups who lobby for protection, while the costs of restrictions are spread over millions of consumers and can be small for each individual.

Protectionism will be especially costly when it leads to retaliation, a trade war. In a trade war, both producers and consumers are likely to lose on net.

We have set out various common arguments for restricting trade. Some of these arguments are valid, but they are usually of limited applicability.

CHAPTER REVIEW

Go online to practice with more examples of these types of problems, including live links to videos, data sources, and feedback.

▶ Problems with this icon relate to optional MRU videos.

KEY CONCEPTS

protectionism, p. 429

tariff, p. 429

trade quota, p. 429

FACTS AND TOOLS

1. The Japanese people currently pay about four times the world price for rice. If Japan removed its trade barriers so that Japanese consumers could buy rice at the world price, who would be better off and who would be worse off: Japanese consumers or Japanese rice farmers? If we added all the gains and losses to the Japanese, would there be a net gain or net loss? Who would make a greater effort lobbying, for or against, this reduction in trade barriers: Japanese consumers or Japanese rice farmers?

2. The supply curve for rice in Japan slopes upward, just like any normal supply curve. If Japan eliminated its trade barriers to rice, what would happen to the number of workers employed in the rice-producing industry in Japan: Would it rise or fall? What would these workers probably do over the next year or so? Will they ever work again?

3. In Figure 19.3, consider triangles *B* and *C*. One of these could be labeled "Workers and machines who could be better used in another sector of the economy," while the other could be labeled "Consumers who have to pay more than necessary for their product." Which is which?

4. In his book *The Choice,* economist Russ Roberts asks how voters would feel about a machine that could convert wheat into automobiles.

   a. Do you think that voters would complain that this machine should be banned, since it would destroy jobs in the auto industry?

   b. Would this machine, *in fact,* destroy jobs in the auto industry? If so, would roughly the same number of jobs eventually be created in other industries?

   c. Here is Roberts's punch line: If voters were told that the wonder machine was in fact just a cargo ship that exported wheat and imported autos from a foreign country, how would voters' attitudes toward this machine change?

5. Spend some time driving in Detroit, Michigan—the Motor City—and you're sure to see bumper stickers with messages like "Buy American" or "Out of a job yet? Keep buying foreign!" or "Hungry? Eat your foreign car!" Explain these bumper stickers in light of what you've learned in this chapter. Who is hurt by imported automobiles? Who benefits?

6. This chapter pointed out that trade restrictions on sugar cause U.S. consumers to pay more than twice the going world price for sugar. However, you are very unlikely to ever encounter bumper stickers that say things like "Out of money yet? Keep taxing foreign sugar!" or "Hungry? It's probably because domestic sugar is so expensive!" Why do you think it is that these bumper stickers are not popular?

7. Of the three conditions that explain why a free market is efficient (from Chapter 4), which condition or conditions cease to hold in the case of a tariff on imported goods? Which condition or conditions continue to hold even in the case of a tariff on imports?

THINKING AND PROBLEM SOLVING

8. a. Just to review: Back in Chapter 5, we illustrated price ceilings with a horizontal line below the equilibrium price. Did price ceilings create surpluses or shortages?

b. The horizontal line in Figure 19.1 is sort of like a price ceiling, but it doesn't cause a surplus or a shortage. What does it represent and why doesn't it cause a surplus or a shortage?

c. Figure 19.1 considers the case of a country that can buy as many semiconductors as it wants at the same world price. Why do people in this country only buy $Q_d^{\text{Free trade}}$ units? Why don't they buy more of this inexpensive product?

9. Figure 19.1 looks at a case in which the world price is below the domestic no-trade price. Let's look at the case in which the world price is *above* the domestic no-trade price. We'll work with the market for airplanes shown in the following figure.

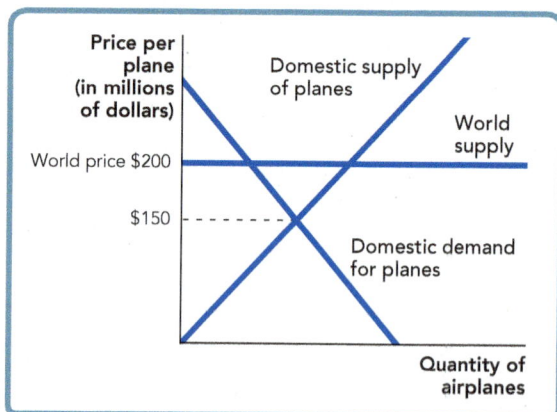

a. In the figure, use the Quantity axis to label $Q_s^{\text{Free trade}}$ and $Q_d^{\text{Free trade}}$. This is somewhat similar to Figure 19.1.

b. What would you call the gap between $Q_s^{\text{Free trade}}$ and $Q_d^{\text{Free trade}}$?

c. Also following Figure 19.1, label "Domestic consumption" and "Domestic production."

d. Will domestic airplane buyers—airlines and delivery companies like FedEx—have to pay a higher or a lower price under free trade compared with the no-trade alternative? Will domestic airplane buyers purchase a higher or a lower quantity of planes if there's free trade in planes?

e. Based on your answer to part d, would you expect domestic airplane demanders to support free trade in planes or oppose it?

10. In the text, we discuss sugar farmers in Florida who use unusually large amounts of fertilizer to produce their crops; they do so because their land isn't all that great for sugar production. If we translate this into the language of the supply curve, would these Florida sugar farms be those on the lower-left part of a supply curve or those along the upper right of the supply curve? Why?

11. Many people will tell you that, whenever possible, you should always buy U.S.-made goods. Some will go further and tell you to spend your money on goods produced in your own state whenever possible. (Just do a simple Google search for "Buy [any state]" and you'll find a Web site encouraging this kind of thinking.) The idea is that if you spend money in your state, you help the economy of *your* state, rather than the economy of some other state. By the same logic, shouldn't one buy only goods produced in one's own city? Or on one's own street? Where does this thinking lead to? And how does it relate to Big Idea Five from Chapter 1?

12. Some people argue for protectionism by pointing out that other countries with whom we trade engage in "unfair trade practices," and that we should retaliate with our own protectionist measures. One such policy is the policy of some countries to subsidize exporting industries. India, for example, subsidizes its steel industry. Obviously, U.S. steel producers are hurt by this policy and would like to restrict imported steel from India. Is this a good reason to place tariffs on Indian steel? Why or why not?

13. In March 2002, then President George W. Bush put a tariff on imported steel as a means of protecting the domestic steel industry. In February, before the tariff went into effect, the United States produced 7.4 million metric tons of crude steel and imported about 2.8 million metric tons of steel products at an average price of $363 per metric ton. Two months later, after the tariff was in effect, U.S. production increased to 7.9 million metric tons. The volume of imported steel fell to about 1.7 million metric tons, but the price of the imported steel rose to about $448 per metric ton. The following supply and demand diagram shows this situation (along with an estimated no-trade domestic equilibrium at a price of $625 per metric ton and a quantity of 8.9 million metric tons).

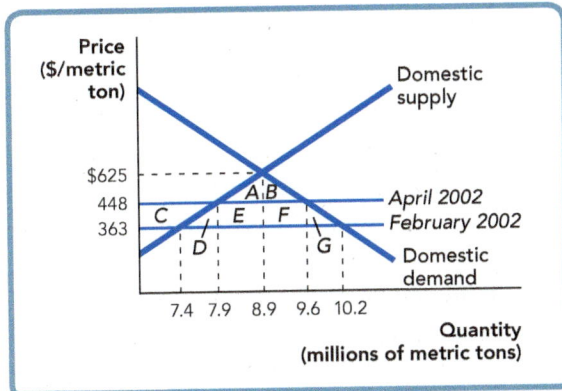

Determine which areas on the graph represent each of the following:

a. The increase in producer surplus gained by U.S. steel producers as a result of the tariff

b. The loss in consumer surplus suffered by U.S. steel consumers as a result of the tariff

c. The revenue earned by the government because of the tariff

d. The wasted resources and lost gains from trade (deadweight loss) created by the tariff

▶ 14. For each of the four parts of question 13, calculate the *values* of these areas in dollars. How much of the deadweight loss is due to the overproduction of steel by higher-cost U.S. steel producers, and how much is due to the underconsumption of steel by U.S. steel consumers?

CHALLENGES

15. In the chapter, we focused on a sugar tariff that eliminated all imports. Let's now take a look at the case where the sugar tariff eliminates some but not all imports. We will also examine the closely related case of a quota on sugar imports. The figure shows a tariff on sugar that raises the U.S. price to 20 cents per pound but at that price some sugar is imported even after the tariff.

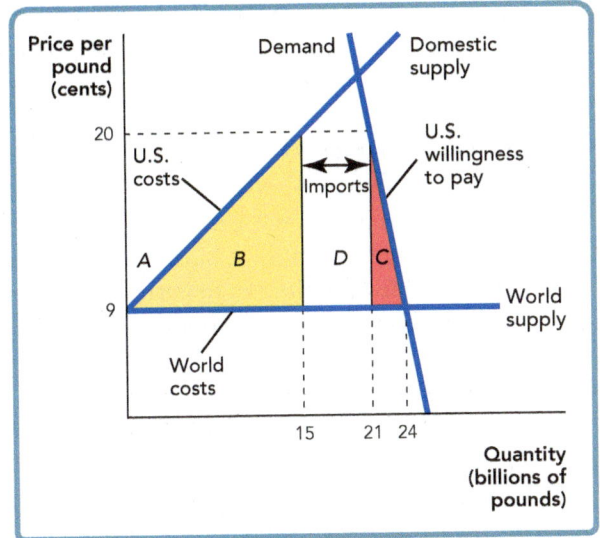

a. Label the free trade equilibrium, the tariff equilibrium, wasted resources, lost gains from trade, and tariff revenues.

b. Now imagine that instead of a tariff, the U.S. government uses a quota that forbids imports of sugar greater than 6 billion pounds. (Equivalently, imagine a tariff that is zero on the first 6 billion pounds of imports but then jumps to a prohibitive level after that quantity of imports—this is closer to how the system works in practice.) Under the quota system what does area *D* represent? Would importers of sugar prefer a tariff or a quota?

c. The sugar quota is allocated to importing countries based on imports from these countries between 1975 and 1981 (with some subsequent adjustments). For example, in 2016 Australia was given the right to export 87 thousand metric tons of sugar to the United States at a very low tariff rate, and Belize was given the right to export 11.5 thousand metric tons of sugar to the United States at a very low tariff rate. How do you think these rights are allocated to firms within the sugar-exporting countries?

d. Discuss how the quota and the way it is allocated could create a misallocation of resources that would further reduce efficiency relative to a tariff that resulted in the same quantity of imports.

16. In a 2005 *Washington Post* article ("The Road to Riches Is Called K Street"), Jeffrey Birnbaum noted that there were 35,000 registered lobbyists in Washington, D.C., people whose primary job

is asking the federal government for something. A lobbyist who comes with long experience as an aide to a powerful politician will earn at least $200,000 per year. Many lobbyists (not all) are attempting to restrict trade to turn consumer surplus into producer surplus.

a. Let's focus just on the lobbyists who are restricting trade. If the United States were to amend the Constitution to permanently ban all tariffs and trade restrictions, these lobbyists would lose their jobs, and they'd have to leave Washington to get "real jobs." Would this job change raise U.S. productivity or lower it?

b. Would most of these lobbyists likely earn more after the amendment was enacted or less?

c. How can you reconcile your answers to parts a and b?

17. One of the assumptions made in the chapter was that the U.S. market for sugar was small relative to the overall world market for sugar, so that when the United States entered the world market for sugar, and U.S. buyers began to buy imported sugar, the price did not change. If we relax this assumption, how do you think that would affect Figure 19.1?

a. Draw the world market for sugar. Show on the graph what happens when the United States enters the market, assuming the United States is large enough to impact market price. What happens to the world price?

b. Show how this changes the U.S. market for sugar, starting with a graph like Figure 19.1, where the world price of sugar is less than the U.S. domestic price. How does this change influence U.S. imports or exports of sugar?

18. The tables that follow show the domestic supply and demand schedules for bushels of flaxseed (used as an edible oil and a nutrition supplement) in the United States and Kazakhstan, with prices measured in U.S. dollars and quantities measured in millions of bushels.

a. In which country is flaxseed cheaper to produce? In which country do the consumers of flaxseed value it more?

b. Complete the blank table that follows by describing each nation's willingness to import or export flaxseed at each price. One row has been done for you as an example.

c. If the United States and Kazakhstan entered into free trade with only one another, what would be the price of flaxseed, and what quantity of flaxseed would be traded?

d. For each of the following four constituent groups, determine whether free trade between the United States and Kazakhstan would help or harm the members of that group relative to the two no-trade domestic equilibriums. Calculate the change in consumer or producer surplus in each country as necessary to support your claim.

i. The buyers of flaxseed in Kazakhstan

ii. The sellers of flaxseed in Kazakhstan

iii. The buyers of flaxseed in the United States

iv. The sellers of flaxseed in the United States

e. Suppose the sellers of flaxseed in the importing country successfully lobby for protection in the form of a $4 tariff per bushel of flaxseed. Describe the impact of this tariff on flaxseed trade and on the consumer and producer surpluses you calculated in part d. How much deadweight loss does this tariff generate?

	Price	$2	$4	$6	$8	$10	$12	$14	$16	$18	$20
U.S.	Q_D	12	11	10	9	8	7	6	5	4	3
	Q_S	0	1	2	3	4	5	6	7	8	9

	Price	$2	$4	$6	$8	$10	$12	$14	$16	$18	$20
Kz	Q_D	5.5	5	4.5	4	3.5	3	2.5	2	1.5	1
	Q_S	1.5	3	4.5	6	7.5	9	10.5	12	13.5	15

At a price of . . .	the United States would be willing to . . .	and Kazakhstan would be willing to . . .
$2	import 12 million bushels	import 4 million bushels
$4		
$6		
$8		
$10		
$12		
$14		
$16		
$18		
$20		

WORK IT OUT

For interactive, step-by-step help in solving this problem, go online.

According to Chinese government statistics, China imported over 1 million cars in 2012. Let's see what would happen to consumer and producer surplus if China were to ban car imports. To keep things simple, let's assume that if car imports were banned, the equilibrium price of cars (holding quality constant!) would rise by $5,000.

a. In the figure, shade the area that represents the total gains when car imports are allowed into China.

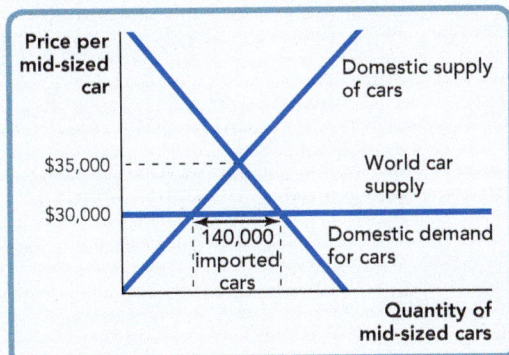

b. Once China bans the import of cars, what is the dollar value of the lost gains from trade? (*Hint:* The chapter provides the formula.)

c. If car imports are banned, Chinese car producers will be better off and Chinese car consumers will be worse off. A polygon in the figure shows the surplus that will shift from consumers to producers. Write the word "Transfer" in this polygon. (*Hint:* It's not the area you calculated in part b.)

d. If quality *weren't* held constant, what would you expect to happen to the additional Chinese cars produced after the import ban? Would they be as good as the ones that used to be imported? (*Hint:* Which types of cars do you think that China imports? Low-quality or high-quality? Why?)

▶ MRU VIDEOS

Tariffs and Protectionism

mru.org/tariffs

Problems: **1–3, 7–10, 13, 14**

Arguments Against International Trade

mru.org/arguments–trade

Problems: **2, 5, 6, 12**

Office Hours: Trade

mru.org/trade

Problem: **14**

20

International Finance

"Why are we spending our dollars in China and Japan rather than in Ohio and Michigan?"

"Why does America have such a large trade deficit?"

"We need to keep our money at home, not send it abroad!"

So run some common questions and complaints about globalization and international finance. The more connected the world economy becomes, the more these kinds of questions arise and increase in importance.

In Chapter 2, we discussed how specialization and trade let us take advantage of the division of knowledge and comparative advantage and thus raise the standard of living. Gains from trade occur when individuals within a nation trade and people in different countries trade.

It's important to keep these deep principles in mind when we discuss trade, but we also want to understand more about the kind of international financial events discussed on a daily basis on the financial blogs and in the newspapers. What does it mean when we are told that the dollar is "strong" or "weak"? What is a trade deficit and is it worse than a trade surplus? And why do zombies protest against the World Bank and the International Monetary Fund? What are these strange institutions?

As we will see, some knowledge of international finance is extremely practical. If you wish to do international business, make international investments, or understand how an exchange rate crisis can wreck an economy, you need to know some basic truths about international finance. Understanding international finance will also help you to pick the best place to take a good vacation. And you will even learn why many James Bond movies have a scene set in Switzerland.

On the surface, international finance is one of the most intimidating fields of economics because the presence of different currencies can be confusing. So let's begin with some of the key principles behind this chapter:

1. Gains from trade occur when people trade across different countries with different currencies, just as gains from trade occur within a single nation with a single currency.

2. The rate of savings is a key variable in understanding international trade and finance.

Protesters claim that IMF policies create walking dead.

449

3. Market equilibrium means that, at the margin, the gains from holding or spending one currency are equal to the gains from holding or spending some other currency. That sounds simple but we'll see that this principle will be a building block for understanding the market value of one currency relative to another.

The U.S. Trade Deficit and Your Trade Deficit

Let's start by looking at the trade deficit in more detail. In 2016, Americans exported (sold) to China $115.8 billion worth of goods, and they imported (bought) from China $462.8 billion in goods. The difference between what Americans exported to China and what they imported from China, −$347.0 billion, is called the U.S. **trade deficit** with China.

*A **trade deficit** occurs when the value of a country's imports exceeds the value of its exports.*

The U.S. trade deficit with China is controversial. In response to the trade deficit, President Trump called for tariffs on imports of Chinese goods. In response, China increased its tariffs on imports of American goods. Many economists worried that a trade war would be bad for Americans and Chinese alike. To understand this debate, it will be useful to begin with some trade deficits closer to home, namely your trade deficit with your local supermarket.

Do you shop at Giant, Safeway, or the Piggly Wiggly? If you do, you run a trade deficit with those stores. That is, you buy more goods from them than they buy from you (unless, of course, you work at one of these stores or sell them goods from your farm). The authors of this book also run a trade deficit with supermarkets. In fact, we have been running a trade deficit with Whole Foods for many years. Is our Whole Foods deficit a problem?

*A **trade surplus** occurs when the value of a country's exports exceeds the value of its imports.*

Our deficit with Whole Foods isn't a problem because it's balanced with a **trade surplus** with someone else. Who? You, the students, whether we teach you or whether you have bought our book. You buy more goods from us than we buy from you. We export education to you, but we do not import your goods and services. In short, we run a trade deficit with Whole Foods but a trade surplus with our students. In fact, it is only because we run a trade surplus with you that we can run a trade deficit with Whole Foods. Thanks!

The lesson is simple. Trade deficits and surpluses are to be found everywhere.

Taken alone, the fact that the United States has a trade deficit with one country is not special cause for worry. Trade across countries is very much like trade across individuals. Not every person or every country can run a trade surplus all the time. Suddenly, a trade deficit does not seem so troublesome, even though the word "deficit" makes it sound like a problem or an economic shortcoming.

What if the United States runs a trade deficit not just with China or Japan or Mexico but with the world as a whole, as indeed it does? Is that a bad thing?

This will require some deeper investigation. So far we have looked at only the flow of goods from the grocery store to you or from China to the United States, but for every flow of goods there is a corresponding and opposite flow of money or financial claims. When China sells us goods, we pay for those goods in dollars. At the present time, China and other countries are not using all of those dollars to buy U.S. goods and thus the United States is running a trade deficit on net. What is China doing with the dollars and is this cause for concern? We need some more tools and a few more terms to answer these questions.

The Balance of Payments

Let's start with the international balance of payments. The **balance of payments** is a yearly summary of all the economic transactions between residents of one country and residents of the rest of the world. The balance of payments records sales of goods and services and also transfers of financial claims including stocks, bonds, loans, and ownership rights. We can also speak of the balance of payments with a specific country such as the balance of payments with China.

That sounds a little forbidding, but let's go back to your trade deficit with the local supermarket. You spend money at the supermarket but earn money through your job. In the simplest case, when there is no borrowing or lending, a person's trade deficits must be matched with other trade surpluses. In other words, if you want to spend, you must earn so your balance of payments does, in fact, balance (nets out to zero).

Now let's make this more realistic by adding borrowing and lending. Suppose you take out a student loan to pay for books, supplies, and housing. You have to pay back the loan someday, but in the meantime you are running a trade deficit. You are spending but you are not earning or "exporting" equivalent goods and services. In this case, your trade deficit is balanced with a loan, which we call a capital inflow or **capital surplus**. When we add up your trade deficit and the capital surplus, the balance of payments once again nets out to zero.

In the long run, unless you default on the loan, your trade deficit must disappear, and indeed it must turn into a trade surplus. That is, someday you will get a job and use your surplus earnings to pay back the bank loan. Paying back the loan limits your future consumption, that is, your ability to buy goods and services, but all things considered, your earlier borrowing was still a good idea, at least if you invested the money well.

We have seen that you can finance a trade deficit with a job or a loan. How else could you finance a trade deficit? If you had assets from previous transactions, you could sell the assets and spend the proceeds. If you owned some land, for example, you could sell the land, creating a capital surplus, which would offset your current deficit. Similarly, if you had reserves of cash from previous periods, you could draw on your reserves to finance a deficit. The more assets or cash that you had from previous transactions, the longer you could live the partying lifestyle by spending more than you were earning in the current period. Notice that when we add up the trade deficit, the capital inflow, and the changes in reserves, the balance of payments still balances.

We can write down these relationships as an identity, an equality that is always true:

$$\text{Earning} - \text{Spending} = \text{Changes in debt} + \text{Changes in ownership}$$
$$\text{of assets} + \text{Changes in your cash reserves}$$

If earnings are less than spending, then you are running a trade deficit. A trade deficit must be balanced by increases in debt (written as a negative number), sales of assets, or reductions in cash reserves. The reverse holds as well: If earnings are greater than spending, then a trade surplus must be balanced by reductions in debt, purchases of assets, or increases in cash reserves.

If you can understand that equation—and indeed you live it every day—you can understand the basic categories of international finance. The terms simply become a little more complicated once we move to the bigger level of a nation.

The **balance of payments** is a yearly summary of all the economic transactions between residents of one country and residents of the rest of the world.

A country runs a **capital surplus** when the inflow of foreign capital is greater than the outflow of domestic capital.

The international balance of payments presents a comparable expression:

$$\text{Current account} = (-)\text{Capital account} + \text{Change in official reserves}$$

Now let's go through each term in detail.

The Current Account

The **current account** is the sum of three items:

1. The balance of trade (exports minus imports of goods and services)

2. Net income on capital held abroad, including interest and dividends

3. Net transfer payments, such as foreign aid

What unites the items in the current account is that they all measure transactions that are fully completed or closed out in a *current* period; they do not require any further transfer of funds in the future. To relate these categories back to the example of a single individual, category (1) is like earnings minus spending; category (2) is like earning money on a savings bond that your grandmother gave you when you were 10 years old ("interest income from abroad"); and category (3) is like getting money from relatives ("foreign aid").

Now let's apply these concepts to the United States. The U.S. current account will be higher and positive to the extent that, for instance, (1) America exports a lot of tractors, (2) American-owned beer factories in Canada pay high dividends to Americans, and (3) America receives foreign aid (this latter example is not usually the case). To consider the alternative, the current account balance will be lower and negative to the extent that, for instance, (1) America buys imported grapes from Chile, (2) German investments in Florida pay high dividends to Germans, and (3) America sends foreign aid to Afghanistan.

Categories 2 and 3 in a country's current account tend to be stable over time. We can simplify by speaking as if the current account was just the balance of trade, exports minus imports. But keep in the back of your mind that terms 2 and 3 can be important for some countries. Foreign aid, for example, is important for smaller and poorer nations, where it can account for 10% or more of GDP. But when it comes to the United States, the balance of trade and the capital account are where we find most of the action.

The Capital Account, Sometimes Called the Financial Account

The **capital account** measures changes in foreign ownership of domestic assets including financial assets likes stocks and bonds as well as physical assets. When the Chinese government buys American government bonds or when Japanese investors buy assets like Rockefeller Center in Manhattan, the capital account of the United States increases. More generally, when there is more investment going into a country than out, that country is running a capital account surplus. When more investment is leaving a country than coming in that is called a capital account deficit; an example is when Zimbabwe residents send their money abroad rather than investing under their corrupt dictatorship. Less dramatically, many banks in New Zealand have been bought by Australian companies and that represents a shift of capital from Australia to New Zealand.

The **current account** is the sum of the balance of trade, net income on capital held abroad, and net transfer payments.

The **capital account** measures changes in foreign ownership of domestic assets including financial assets likes stocks and bonds as well as physical assets.

Notice how the capital account differs from "net income held on foreign assets abroad," component 2 of the current account. When a Belgian buys a U.S. stock, the U.S. *capital account* increases (money flows into the United States). Three months later, when that same Belgian receives a dividend from the company, the U.S. *current account* decreases as "net income held on foreign assets abroad" is suddenly higher for Belgium. The capital account measures transactions, like buying a stock, that may result in future financial flows. The current account measures current financial flows.

The investments in the capital account are divided into the following categories:

Foreign direct investment (FDI)—When foreigners construct new business plants or set up other specific and tangible operations in the United States.

Portfolio investment—When foreigners buy U.S. stocks, bonds, and other asset claims. Unlike FDI, portfolio investment switches the ownership of already existing investments and does not immediately create new investment on net.

Other investment—This usually consists of movements of bank deposits. For instance, a wealthy French citizen might shift their bank account from Paris to New York.

The Official Reserves Account

The third component of the international balance of payments, the official reserves account, measures reserves or currency held by the government. This can include foreign currencies, gold reserves, and also International Monetary Fund (IMF) claims known as special drawing rights (SDRs), but for simplicity we will focus on foreign currencies. (We'll discuss the IMF in greater detail later in this chapter.) Sometimes governments stockpile U.S. dollars or other currencies such as the euro. Right now the Chinese government and central bank have stockpiled more than $1 trillion worth of U.S. dollars and dollar-denominated assets.

How the Pieces Fit Together

To understand the balance of payments in its totality, consider more concretely how this accounting identity stays in balance. Say that Walmart decides to buy more toys from China. Spending money on the toys increases the current account deficit of the United States. Toy makers in China receive the money and must do something with it. If they take the money and use it to buy American tractors, the current account is back in balance. If they take the money and invest it back in the United States, say, by buying stocks, the American capital account surplus goes up by an equivalent amount. If they take the money and send it to a bank in New York, the capital account surplus goes up (this time in the "other investment" category). If they keep the money in a Chinese bank, there has been a change in reserves. No matter what they do with the money, the balance of payments will balance.

Two Sides, One Coin

Usually, the major changes in the balance of payments come through the current account and the capital account, rather than through changes in official reserves. So, a country that is running a current account deficit, such as the

FIGURE 20.1

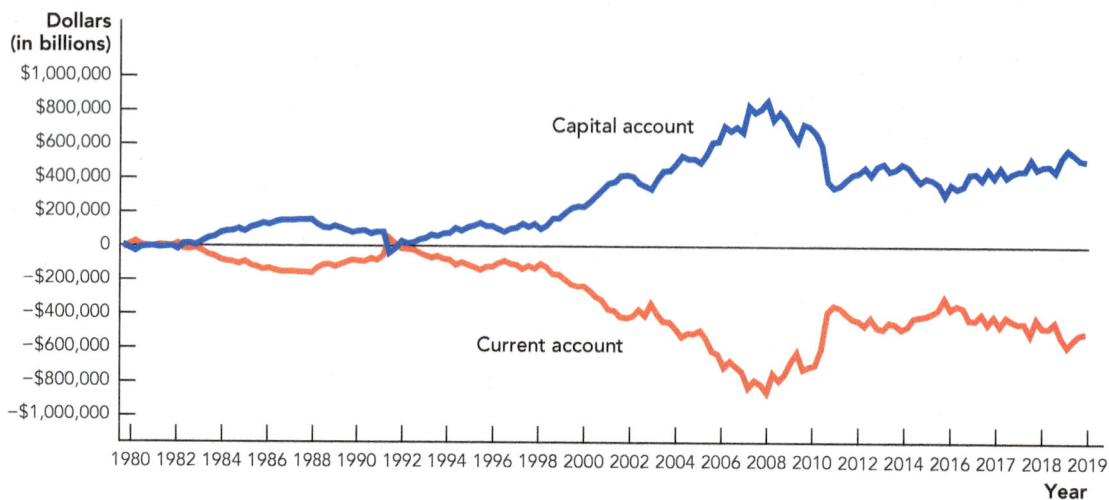

U.S. Balance of Payments, 1980–2019

Data from: FRED Economic Database, Economic Research, Federal Reserve Bank of St. Louis, https://fred.stlouisfed.org /graph/?=qevt.

United States, balances its payments by running a capital account surplus. Similarly, a country, such as China, that is running a current account surplus, is usually also running a capital account deficit.

Figure 20.1 shows the U.S. balance of payments from 1980 to 2019. Notice that the two accounts are close to mirror images—when the current account is in deficit (negative), the capital account is in surplus (positive), and vice versa. (Differences are in fact almost entirely due to statistical discrepancies and the difficulty of identifying all financial transactions.)

The current account and capital account are two sides of the same coin. The media and politicians typically focus on the trade deficit, but it's equally correct to look at the other side of the coin, the capital account surplus.

Now that we know that a trade deficit is typically balanced by a capital account surplus, let's go back to our opening question and ask whether our trade deficit is a problem. First, note that this is the same thing as asking whether our capital account surplus is a problem. A surplus sounds better than a deficit so it is not surprising that many economists who think that trade deficits are not a problem focus on the flip side, the capital account surplus. We call the most optimistic view of those who focus on the capital account the "Great Place to Invest" view. We call the less optimistic view the "Foolishly Saving Too Little" view. Let's start with optimism.

"The United States Is a Great Place to Invest" In this view, the trade deficit is driven by the fact that foreigners want to invest in the United States, the world's wealthiest country and largest single, unified market. Instead of using dollars to buy U.S. cars, foreigners are using dollars to buy bonds and stocks and this inflow of investment is great for the United States. A capital account surplus will necessitate a current account deficit, but this is no problem. The investments in America will create more wealth and allow the United States to pay off future obligations without major problems. From this perspective, the fact that America is borrowing or selling assets is like borrowing money or selling assets to pay for medical school—it isn't a problem because the investment will pay off with a high-wage job. Advocates of this view sometimes speak of the rest of the world as having a "savings glut," namely a lot of savings but no good place to put them, other than in the United States, that is.

"Americans Are Foolishly Saving Too Little" Not all economists who focus on the capital account are optimists, however. It's also possible to look at the inflow of capital and ask, Why are Americans saving so little? In this view, the reason that capital is flowing into the United States is that Americans are consuming too much and not saving enough. Proponents of this view often tie the trade deficit with the government's budget deficit. The U.S. government is spending more than it is taxing and the difference is being made up by borrowing from foreigners, creating a capital account surplus. In this view, a day of reckoning will come. Foreign investments in America represent a claim on American assets and someday Americans will have to pay off those investment claims. This will lower American living standards and bring higher taxes, as well as the pain of significant economic adjustments. American borrowing from this perspective is like borrowing to buy a closet full of Manolo Blahnik shoes—fun while it lasts but not necessarily wise.

The Josefa can be yours for $1,425 a pair, but what happens when the bill comes due?

The Bottom Line on the Trade Deficit

The bottom line is this: Most economists think that the trade deficit per se is not a problem. As discussed in Chapter 2, trade is beneficial for the United States, and as previously shown, there is nothing peculiar about running a trade deficit—we all run trade deficits in some areas (e.g., with Whole Foods) and for some periods of time (e.g., when we finance education with a student loan). Countries, in this respect, are no different than individuals.

The trade deficit, however, might indicate, or *signal*, a problem of low savings. If the United States has a problem with low savings, however, then it's better to address the savings problem directly—in which case, the balance of trade will take care of itself—rather than blaming the Chinese or obsessing over the balance of trade numbers. Quotas, tariffs, and trade wars, for example, are unlikely to solve a savings problem. Indeed, if the United States is saving too little, then Americans are at least fortunate that they can borrow in international markets so that investment remains high even when U.S. savings rates are low.

To the extent that Americans are saving too little, there is a stronger case for reducing the government's budget deficit by a combination of tax hikes and spending cuts. In the "Foolishly Saving Too Little" view, the United States is spending too much and the government could do its share to limit this problem by saving more, which means moving closer to a balanced budget or perhaps even running a surplus. We discussed the government budget deficit at greater length in Chapter 17.

Let us now turn to exchange rates. Working with the concepts in the balance of payments identity, we can see how supplies and demands will determine the relative values of different currencies.

CHECK YOURSELF

- An inhabitant of Lincoln, Nebraska, buys a German sports car for $30,000. What changes does this make to the U.S. current account?
- A German sports car manufacturer opens a new plant in South Carolina. How does this affect the U.S. current account and capital account?
- Is there a link between a current account deficit and a capital account surplus?

TABLE 20.1 MAJOR CURRENCY EXCHANGE RATES

Currency	U.S. $	¥en	Euro	Can $	U.K. £	Swiss Franc
1 U.S. $	1	113.2560	0.9154	1.3692	0.7727	0.9989
1 ¥en	0.0088	1	0.0081	0.0121	0.0068	0.0088
1 Euro	1.0925	123.7265	1	1.4957	0.8442	1.0912
1 Can $	0.7304	82.7199	0.6686	1	0.5644	0.7296
1 U.K. £	1.2941	146.5646	1.1846	1.7718	1	1.2927
1 Swiss Franc	1.0011	113.3807	0.9164	1.3707	0.7736	1

Note: Data collected on May 8, 2017.

What Are Exchange Rates?

The most common means of payment in most (but not all!) foreign countries is a foreign currency and not the U.S. dollar. So, if you travel to a foreign country and you want to buy goods and services in that country, you will usually have to buy foreign currency with U.S. dollars. An **exchange rate** is the price of one currency in terms of another currency.

The *Wall Street Journal* publishes a table like Table 20.1 every day. Table 20.1 gives exchange rates that held on May 8, 2017.

We can read this table in either the vertical or horizontal direction. Read vertically, it tells us that the price of 1 yen is 0.0088 dollar, the price of 1 euro is 1.0925 dollars, the price of 1 Canadian dollar is 0.7304 U.S. dollars, and so forth. Read horizontally, it tells us that the price of 1 dollar is 113.2560 yen, 0.9154 euro, 1.3692 Canadian dollars, and so forth. Notice that there are always two ways of writing the price of a currency. We can say that 1 yen trades for 0.0088 dollar or that 1 dollar trades for 113.2560 yen—this sometimes causes confusion so always make sure you know which rate is being quoted!

Exchange Rate Determination in the Short Run

Exchange rates, like other market prices, are determined by supply and demand. For each currency, there is a price in every other currency. At any given moment, the exchange rate for a currency is determined by the intersection of the supply and demand for that currency. Figure 20.2, for example, shows the supply and demand for yen and the exchange rate in dollars per yen.

Notice that we have written "Dollars per yen" ("$/yen" in many books) on the vertical axis. This is the price of 1 yen in dollars. If this price goes up—that is, we move up along the vertical axis—it means that the Japanese yen is stronger, namely it takes more dollars to buy 1 yen. If this price goes down, the Japanese yen is weaker.

In this chapter when we are analyzing the supply and demand for yen, we will always put the price of yen, "Dollars per yen," on the vertical axis. But if we analyze the supply and demand for dollars, we will put the *price of dollars* in, say, euros per dollar on the vertical axis.*

Let's now look at some factors that can shift the demand and supply curves.

An **exchange rate** is the price of one currency in another currency.

▶▶ **SEARCH ENGINE**

For current information on exchange rates, search for the "Yahoo! currency converter."

---

* Other textbooks or sources, however, might put "yen per dollar" (or "yen/$") instead of "dollars per yen" on the price axis. Either way is correct so long as you remember which one you are working with.

FIGURE 20.2

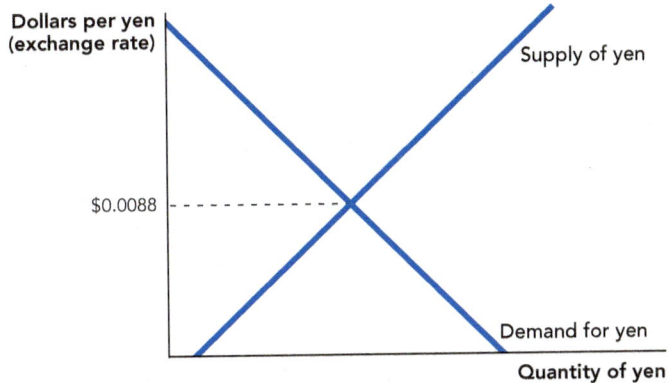

The Exchange Rate Is Determined by the Supply and Demand for Currencies The exchange rate, the number of dollars it takes to buy 1 yen, is determined by the supply and demand for yen. In this case, the equilibrium exchange rate is 0.0088 dollars for 1 yen.

Changes in Demand for a Currency We'll explore three main principles that can influence the demand for a currency. The first principle is simple:

1. *An increase (decrease) in the demand for a country's exports tends to increase (decrease) the value of its currency.*

When Japanese cars become popular around the world, this strengthens the value of the yen. For instance, when U.S. car dealerships order more Toyotas from Japan, they must (ultimately) pay for the cars in yen. An increase in the demand for Japanese goods, therefore, shifts the demand curve for yen up and to the right, illustrated in Figure 20.3.

As usual, an increase in demand increases the price. In this case, the price of one yen increases from 0.0088 dollars to 0.0094 dollars. An increase in the price of a currency is called an **appreciation**.

Increasing exports are not the only way a currency can change in value. We also have a second principle:

2. *The more desirable (undesirable) a country is for foreign investment, the higher (lower) the value of that nation's currency.*

An **appreciation** is an increase in the price of one currency in terms of another currency.

FIGURE 20.3

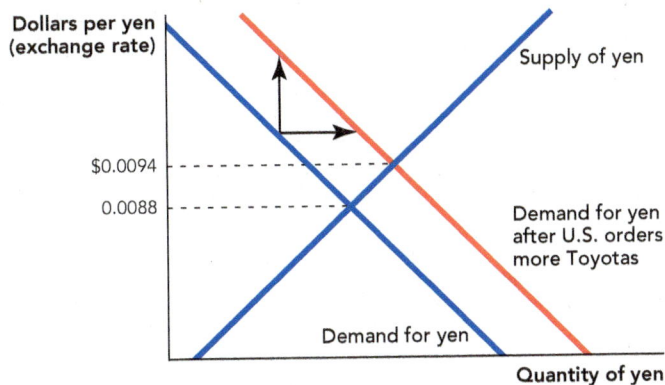

An Increase in the Demand for Yen Increases the Price of Yen An increase in the demand for Toyotas increases the demand for yen, which shifts the demand curve for yen outward (up and to the right). The increase in the demand for yen increases the exchange rate from 0.0088 dollars per yen to 0.0094 dollars per yen.

Ever since the signing of NAFTA (North American Free Trade Agreement) and the evolution of real democracy in Mexico in the mid-1990s, American investors have been keener to invest in that country. To invest in Mexico, an American business must convert dollars into pesos, thereby shifting the demand curve for pesos to the right and raising the value of the peso. In this context, note that a "stronger peso" means a "weaker dollar," or whatever other currency we are considering.

Alternatively, many governments of sub-Saharan Africa have failed to secure the property rights of foreign investors. The demand to invest is correspondingly weak, shifting the demand curve for these countries' currencies to the left and lowering the value of these currencies.

High interest rates, all other factors held equal, is another factor that attracts investment, increasing the demand for and thus the value of a currency. For instance, if New Zealand "Kiwi bonds" are yielding 9%, and U.S. Treasury securities of comparable maturity are yielding 4%, this favors the strength of the New Zealand currency. (The New Zealand currency is also called the dollar; investors sometimes say "the Kiwi dollar" to avoid confusion with the U.S. dollar.) Investors will be more inclined to hold New Zealand securities, and of course to do so, they must use the New Zealand currency, thereby shifting out demand.

There is yet another cause of stronger demand for a currency:

3. *An increase (decrease) in the demand to hold dollar reserves boosts (reduces) the value of the dollar on international markets.*

Many governments and central banks hold U.S. dollars as a "reserve currency." This means simply that U.S. dollars are a preferred means of saving and enjoying liquidity. Of all the currencies held in the world for these official reserves purposes, U.S. dollars comprise two-thirds of the total.

The U.S. dollar is truly a global currency. If a Brazilian company buys a turbine engine from Turkey, it is probably billed in dollars and probably pays in dollars, not the currency of either Turkey or Brazil. If Colombian drug dealers bury some money in their backyard, it is probably dollars. When these demands for dollars rise, the dollar becomes more valuable. Again, the demand curve for dollars will shift to the right. However, if the Colombian government ever succeeds in stopping the drug trade, the demand for U.S. dollars would fall and the demand curve for dollars would shift back to the left.

The Swiss franc, by the way, is another global reserve currency. Even though Switzerland is a small country, it has a long tradition of peace and stability, and to some extent bank secrecy. The Swiss franc is viewed as a "safe haven" currency, even when the rest of the world is experiencing trouble. This is one reason why the Swiss franc tends to be relatively strong. Furthermore, the proverbial "bad guys" used to have secret Swiss bank accounts (since 9/11 and the growth of financial investigations, they're not so secret any more) and to invest some of their money in Swiss francs; that is one reason why so many James Bond movies have scenes set in Switzerland, and of course because the Alps look pretty on the big screen.

Changes in the Supply of a Currency Now let's turn to factors that can shift the supply curve. An increase in the supply of a currency causes the currency to lose some of its value, that is, fall in price. A fall in the price of a currency is also called a **depreciation**. Figure 20.4 shows the effects of an increase in supply, a shift of the supply curve down and to the right.

A **depreciation** is a decrease in the price of a currency in terms of another currency.

If the Federal Reserve increases the supply of U.S. money, this will reduce the value of the dollar relative to other currencies. The not-so-surprising result, as shown in Figure 20.4, is a lower value for the U.S. dollar on world markets.

You may recall from Chapter 12 that the government in Zimbabwe printed trillions of Zimbabwe dollars, causing a large increase in the Zimbabwean inflation rate. At the beginning of 2002, for example, one Zimbabwe dollar was worth about 0.018 of a U.S. dollar or just under 2 cents. With the massive increase in the supply of Zimbabwean dollars, the value of the Zimbabwean dollar fell, so that by 2006 1 Zimbabwe dollar was worth less than 0.00001 of a U.S. dollar or about one-thousandth of a U.S. penny.

A tighter monetary policy, which means a decrease (or slower increase) in the supply of a currency, would shift the supply curve up and to the left and raise the value of the dollar, as we show in Figure 20.5.

FIGURE 20.4

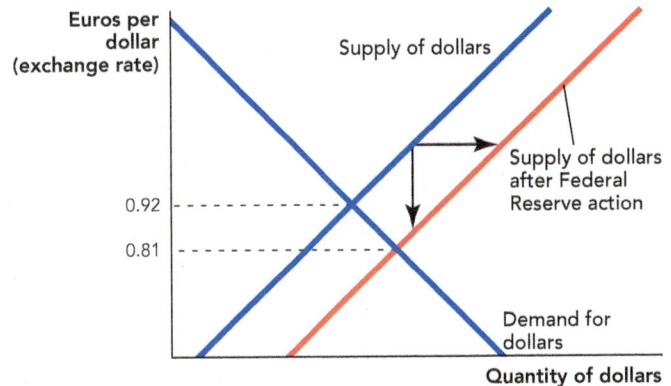

An Increase in the Supply of a Currency Reduces Its Price
An increase in the supply of a currency shifts the supply curve down and to the right, which reduces the exchange rate. In the figure, the Federal Reserve increases the supply of dollars and the price of dollars in euros per dollar decreases from 0.92 euros per dollar to 0.81 euros per dollar.

Exchange Rate Determination in the Long Run

These changes play themselves out in foreign exchange markets every day. But a full explanation outlines why the supply and demand curves lie where they do in the first place, and not just what happens when they shift.

To see the broader picture, consider that the value of a currency is derived, ultimately, from the value of what it can purchase. Money buys or is a potential claim on goods, services, and investments. Given this fact, equilibrium requires that a dollar spent on goods, services, or investment yields the same expected return regardless of whether that dollar (or the equivalent in local currency) is spent in Chicago, Berlin, or Tokyo.

Before we can explain this point fully and use it to give a more exact account of exchange rates, we must first outline the difference between real and nominal exchange rates.

We are already familiar with the distinction between real and nominal variables from earlier chapters. To recap, in a domestic setting how much a dollar is worth depends on the level of prices for goods and services. We now extend this same comparison to Chicago, Berlin, and Tokyo. How much a dollar is worth in Tokyo depends on two things: the exchange rate between the dollar and the Japanese yen, and the level of prices for goods and services in Japan, measured in Japanese yen.

FIGURE 20.5

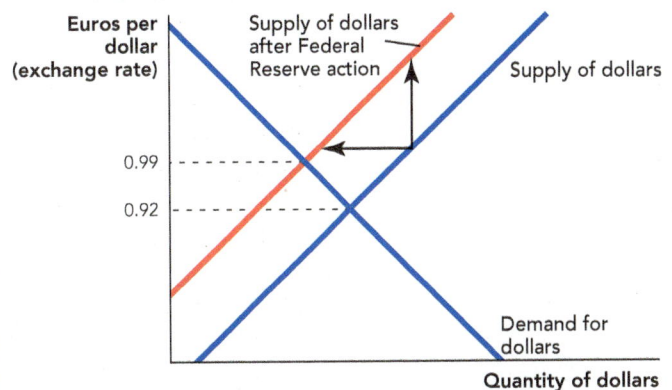

A Decrease in the Supply of a Currency Increases Its Price
A decrease in the supply of a currency shifts the supply curve up and to the left. In the figure, the Federal Reserve decreases the supply of dollars and the price of dollars in euros increases from 0.92 euros per dollar to 0.99 euros per dollar.

On May 8, 2017, 1 dollar would buy 113.2560 yen. At first glance, it might appear that the Japanese yen is a very weak currency. Why should one dollar buy so many yen, if not for the weakness of the yen? But it is wrong to think that the stated rate of exchange reflects the relative weakness of the yen.

If 1 dollar buys 113.2560 yen, we know only the **nominal exchange rate**, which is simply the rate at which you can exchange one currency for another; this is the rate you find quoted in the newspaper or by searching using Google.

The **real exchange rate** is the rate at which you can exchange the goods and services of one country for the goods and services of another. To calculate the real exchange rate between the United States and Japan, for example, you need to know the nominal exchange rate plus the price of a similar basket of goods in both the United States and Japan. Notice that an exchange rate of 1 dollar to 110 yen means very different things, depending on whether an order of sushi costs 1 yen, 1 million yen, or about 330 yen (the true price, roughly). If an order of sushi costs 3 dollars in the United States and 330 yen in Japan, then the real exchange rate is about 1:1.

The Purchasing Power Parity Theorem The **purchasing power parity (PPP) theorem** states:

The real purchasing power of a money should be about the same, whether it is spent at home or converted into another currency and spent abroad.

Put in other words, the quantity of goods and services that can be obtained for a given currency should be about the same everywhere, adjusting for the costs of trading those goods and services. The core idea is that spending your dollars in Chicago, or converting them into yen and spending them in Tokyo (which might include buying Japanese goods and shipping them back home for resale), should yield about the same benefits.

More concretely, the PPP theorem makes two predictions. First, Toyotas in Japan should cost about as much as Toyotas in California; the same should be true for other individual goods. Second, the cost of a general bundle of goods and services should be about the same everywhere.

Purchasing power parity is an application of the **law of one price**, the principle that if trade were free, then identical goods will sell for about the same price throughout the world. If Toyotas were cheaper in Tokyo, it would make sense to buy Toyotas in Japan and ship them to the United States. Conversely, if Toyotas are cheaper in the United States, they will be shipped to Japan. Of course, shipping cars from one country to another is not the only way to gain from a difference in prices. Toyota might set up a new auto plant in Tennessee rather than in Tokyo or Osaka, thereby shifting supply into the North American market.

That example is only for cars but the principle can be extended to a broader set of possible transactions. The return to spending a dollar (or yen, or euro, etc.) at home or abroad must be roughly equal, and exchange rates and prices will adjust to equalize those returns. Those adjustments will determine the real exchange rate between any two currencies.

Recall from Chapter 12 that in the long run, money is neutral. We used that principle to explain why in the long run the money supply does not influence real GDP, real interest rates, or real prices. Exactly the same principle applies here, except that now we apply the principle to two monies! Since money is neutral in the United States and money is neutral in Japan, neither the supply

The **nominal exchange rate** is the rate at which you can exchange one currency for another.

The **real exchange rate** is the rate at which you can exchange the goods and services of one country for the goods and services of another.

The **purchasing power parity (PPP) theorem** says that the real purchasing power of a money should be about the same, whether it is spent at home or converted into another currency and spent abroad.

The **law of one price** says that if trade were free, then identical goods will sell for about the same price throughout the world.

MRU
mru.org/purchasing-power-parity
Purchasing Power Parity

of dollars nor the supply of yen can change the real exchange rate in the long run. In other words, governments or central banks set nominal exchange rates, but market forces set the real exchange rate. As usual, however, this applies only in the long run. In the short run, as we will discuss further later in the chapter, the government can influence the real exchange rate and this will be important for macroeconomic policy.

The Purchasing Power Parity Theorem Is Only Approximately True

Purchasing power parity is limited by the costs of trading, transacting, and shuffling resources. That is one reason why purchasing power parity holds only approximately. At least three constraints on trade prevent prices from being fully equalized across borders:

1. **Transportation costs.** The price of cement might be much higher in Japan than in California, but it still will not be profitable to put cement on a boat and ship it from California to Japan. Cement is very heavy and the shipping would cost a great deal. Purchasing power parity applies only to the extent that goods can be transported easily. Notice also that many personal services—haircuts are the classic example—cannot easily be shipped, although sometimes the labor behind those services can migrate from one country to another. Thus, purchasing power parity is more likely to hold for goods that are cheap to ship, like iPhones, than for cement or haircuts.

2. **Some goods cannot be shipped at all.** Sipping a coffee in Paris is different from going to a Starbucks in suburban Ohio, even if the coffee is the same. The coffee can be transported cheaply but Paris cannot be shipped.

   Similarly, an apartment in London, Canada, costs less than a similar-sized apartment in London, England. Canada cannot easily cut off its land and ship it to England so prices of apartments will not equalize. More generally, the price of land and any good that uses a lot of land in its consumption will not equalize across countries.

3. **Tariffs and quotas.** To the extent that governments tax or otherwise restrict trade, prices will not equalize across countries. Tariffs or quotas will hinder market exchange and thus the arbitrage of differing prices.

These constraints show that purchasing power parity will hold approximately—rather than strictly—for a broad basket of goods and services. In other words, living in London, England, will remain more expensive than living in London, Canada.

Deviations from purchasing power parity are often large and long-lasting for services. Goods are easy to transport and so tend to equalize in price more than services, which are difficult to transport. Services, therefore, are cheaper in poorer countries because immigration laws limit the extent to which labor can move from poor countries to rich countries. Wages on the American side of the border are much higher than wages on the Mexican side of the border. The result is that a haircut is much cheaper in Mexico than in the United States. One of the thriftier authors of this textbook often gets his hair cut during trips to Mexico for this reason! Servants are also much cheaper in poorer countries. Even a middle-class family in Mexico, India, or Thailand will often employ many servants. The services of a physician, even a high-quality Western-trained physician, are also cheaper in poorer countries; that explains why many people are going to India for plastic surgery or hip replacements—plus you can see the Taj Mahal after your surgery is over. Computers, copper, automobiles, and

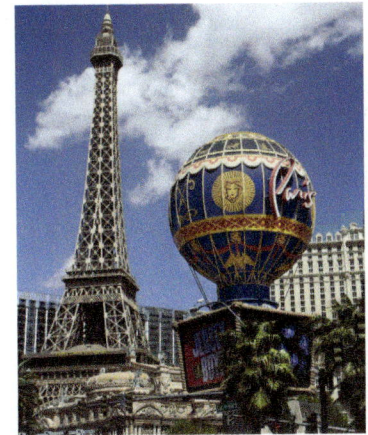

Paris, Las Vegas. There is no parity here.

MRU
https://www.mru.org/india-haircut

Why Should You Get a Haircut in a Poorer Country?

other goods that can be easily shipped are not systematically cheaper in poorer countries.

How close the real world fits purchasing power parity depends on the nations involved and their ease of trading. As trading costs fall, purchasing power parity is more likely to hold closely. As trading costs rise, the bounds become looser. Purchasing power parity holds more exactly true between the United States and Canada—similar and adjacent countries—than between Japan and Mexico. Note that the concept of "tradeable" is a matter of degree, not an absolute, so how much purchasing power parity holds is a matter of degree as well.

Purchasing power parity also holds more tightly in the long run than in the short run. In the short run, trading costs might hinder entrepreneurs from erasing differences in prices. In the long run, it is more likely that entrepreneurs will find a way to bring prices closer together across international borders.

When it comes to the short run, and within the boundaries set by purchasing power parity, economists still debate the causes of daily exchange rate movements. About $4 *trillion* in foreign exchange transactions take place in a typical day. Most of those trades are speculative, done to earn a profit by trying to outguess the market. The short-run froth of daily price movements is set largely by psychology and expectations. Traders are guessing where the market is headed, as shaped by supply and demand, but some of the short-run trading is just guessing at the short-run behavior of other traders. Sometimes the small, short-run movements in exchange rates are called "noise," which is the economist's polite way of saying we don't understand what causes them or what they mean.

How Monetary and Fiscal Policy Affect Exchange Rates and How Exchange Rates Affect Aggregate Demand

Monetary and fiscal policy will alter the exchange rate and trade balance (exports minus imports) of a country. To understand how, keep in mind that an approximate version of purchasing power parity (for tradable goods) holds in the long run, but that deviations from parity are possible in the short run.

Monetary Policy

Imagine that the Federal Reserve increases $\overline{M}$ (growth rate of the money supply) through open market operations, a concept discussed in Chapters 15 and 16. The increase in $\overline{M}$ shifts the supply curve for dollars down and to the right, which will result in a lower exchange rate (a depreciation). In the short run, dollar prices are sticky so as far as the rest of the world is concerned, it's as if U.S. goods went on sale! Let's look at this in more detail.

Imagine that a Caterpillar tractor sells for $50,000 and the exchange rate starts out at 1 euro per dollar, so in Europe a Caterpillar tractor costs €50,000. Now suppose that as a result of Fed actions, the exchange rate depreciates so that a European needs only 0.8 euros to buy a dollar. The dollar price is still $50,000, but because of the change in the exchange rate, the price in euros has fallen from €50,000 to €40,000, which is in essence a

20% discount. Thus, a depreciation will increase U.S. exports. Recall from Chapter 13 that an increase in exports increases AD, which boosts the economy in the short run.

Figure 20.6 shows the process in a diagram. Keep in mind that this is exactly the same analysis of an increase in aggregate demand that we discussed in Chapter 13 and also in Chapters 16 and 18. The only difference is that the *source* of the shift in AD is now a depreciation in the exchange rate; the mechanics are exactly as before.

The economy begins at point *a* in long-run equilibrium. The increase in $\overrightarrow{M}$ causes a depreciation in the exchange rate, which in turn reduces the price of U.S. exports. As a result, exports increase, AD increases, and the growth rate of the economy increases, moving the economy in the short run to point *b*. But what about the long run?

In the long run, money is neutral, which means that domestic prices will rise to match the increase in $\overrightarrow{M}$, so eventually the price of the Caterpillar tractor will increase by 20%. As a result, the nominal exchange rate will be lower but the real exchange rate—in the long run—won't have changed much, if at all. So, in the long run the real depreciation (the sale on U.S. exports) proves to be temporary and so the boost in exports is temporary as well. But if the increase in $\overrightarrow{M}$ is not reversed, the U.S. inflation rate increases. Thus, in the long run, the economy moves from point *b* to point *c* and the boost to real output growth is not permanent.

FIGURE 20.6

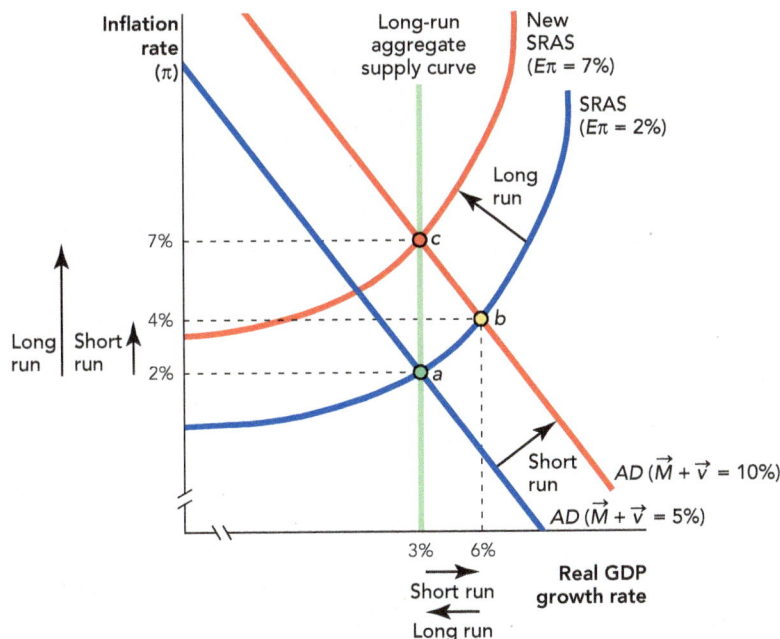

A Depreciation Increases AD in the Short Run An increase in the growth rate of the money supply pushes the exchange rate down (a depreciation). As a result, exports increase, AD increases, and the growth rate increases, moving the economy from point *a* to point *b*. In the long run, the domestic inflation rate increases enough to restore the real exchange rate so there is no longer a boost to exports and the economy moves to a new long-run equilibrium at point *c*.

FIGURE 20.7

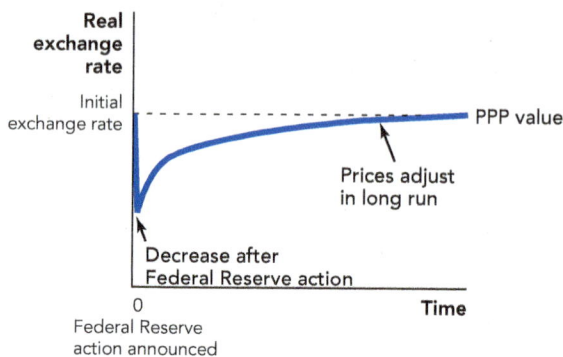

The Dynamics of the Real Exchange Rate An increase in $\overline{M}$ increases the supply of dollars, thus causing a depreciation in the nominal exchange rate. Domestic prices are sticky, so at first the nominal depreciation is also a real depreciation. Over time, however, domestic prices rise, so in the long run the real exchange rate returns to its fundamental value as determined by approximate purchasing power parity.

We can, however, see one additional reason why politicians and central banks sometimes favor increases in the growth rate of money $\overline{M}$. An increase in $\overline{M}$ usually will boost a nation's exports and thus employment. It will appear that the economy is doing better, at least for a little while but, as usual, the boost to the economy is temporary and it raises the possibility of higher inflation rates.

Furthermore, although the depreciation makes exports cheaper, it makes imports more expensive. The diminished ability of the nation to invest abroad at good prices or buy imports at good prices—because of the lower real exchange rate—is a less visible but real cost of the lower real exchange rate. The lower real exchange rate nonetheless represents a political temptation, if only because the economy at least appears stronger when exports increase in the short run.

When it comes to the real exchange rate itself, the path of the market to equilibrium looks like the one portrayed in Figure 20.7. Once a Fed action is announced, the dollar moves on international currency markets within seconds. Prices for most goods and services, even if they are relatively flexible, do not respond with this speed. So, at first the dollar has lower international value in real terms.

For a decrease in $\overline{M}$, the process is the reverse. In the short run, the real exchange rate will appreciate, causing U.S. exports to be more expensive on world markets. In the long run, the real exchange rate will be reestablished at the approximate PPP value. Notice that we can see once again why nations with a high rate of inflation may be reluctant to lower $\overline{M}$ even though they should. In the short run, a reduction in $\overline{M}$ reduces exports, reducing AD and reducing the real growth rate in the short run.

Fiscal Policy

Expansionary fiscal policy, or an increase in the budget deficit, will raise domestic interest rates. As explained in Chapters 9 and 18, when government borrows more money, the demand for loanable funds shifts outward and interest rates go up.

As a result, the higher interest rates will cause the nation—let's say the United States—to run a greater surplus on its capital account. That is, more foreigners will want to invest in the United States to enjoy those high interest rates. The greater demand to invest will cause an appreciation of the U.S. dollar. What does an appreciation of the dollar do to U.S. exports? An appreciation makes U.S. exports more expensive, thus reducing U.S. exports. Thus, a budget deficit can cause a trade deficit. These are sometimes called "the twin deficits."

We now see one more limitation of fiscal policy. The boost to domestic aggregate demand, resulting from the new government spending, will to some extent be offset by the greater difficulty of exporting at the new and higher real exchange rate. Total aggregate demand—domestic plus foreign—might not go up at all. In other words, the argument for fiscal policy discussed in the previous chapter is less justified the more open the economy. This is yet another reason why monetary policy has typically become more important than fiscal policy as a tool of macroeconomic management.

Fixed vs. Floating Exchange Rates

So far we have treated the case of **floating exchange rates** with currency prices determined in open world markets. This is by far the most common scenario in the world today and indeed throughout history.

Still, in other cases the world has seen **fixed,** or **pegged, exchange rates**, where currencies do not fluctuate against one another on a daily basis. Fixed exchange rate systems can take three forms:

1. *Simply adopting the money of another country*

Panama, Ecuador, and El Salvador all use U.S. dollars as their currency; this is called **dollarization**. The central banks of these nations have no active role in managing their money supplies.

The disadvantage of this approach is that Ecuador must buy and save enough dollars to use that currency. The advantage is that, once in place, Ecuador receives the monetary policy of the United States. Once the transition is made, the common currency runs on automatic pilot. Overall, it is plausible that the U.S. Fed does a better job than would an Ecuadorian central bank. Indeed, at the time of dollarization in 2000, the rate of inflation in Ecuador was above 50%. Today, the rate of inflation in Ecuador roughly tracks that of the United States and of course this is much lower.

2. *Setting up a currency union*

Many European countries gave up their currencies and created the euro, a common currency under the supervision of the European Union and (as of 2020) shared by 19 different EU countries. The wealthier European countries, such as Germany and France, saw the euro as a way to unify Europe economically. Some of the poorer countries, such as Greece, saw the euro as a way to obtain a more stable currency. In any case, all of these countries allow the European Central Bank to control their common monetary policy; the euro does not belong to any single country. The euro, however, is unique and no other comparable arrangement exists today. In the early part of 2010, however, the euro started to come under considerable strain. The basic dilemma is simple: Some countries in the eurozone, such as Greece, want a relatively expansionary monetary policy. Since the Greek economy was shrinking during 2010, they wanted monetary policy to stimulate aggregate demand. Other countries in the eurozone, such as Germany, were growing rapidly and did not want an expansionary monetary policy. So far Germany is getting its way, but it remains to be seen whether it makes sense for Greece or other slower growing countries to remain in the eurozone forever.

3. *Backing a currency with high levels of reserves and promising convertibility at a certain rate*

A country could promise to convert its currency into U.S. dollars, or some other currency, at a specified rate. Holding sufficient reserves of the foreign currency to ensure conversion would make this promise more credible. Since 1983, Hong Kong has pledged that 7.80 Hong Kong dollars are equal to 1 U.S. dollar and required Hong Kong banks to have full U.S. dollar backing for any note issued. For many years, Austria pegged its currency to the value of the German mark, prior to adopting the euro.

Option 3 is, of course, a matter of degree. Economists refer to a "peg" to describe a relatively rigid commitment to a specified conversion rate. A **dirty,** or **managed, float** refers to a relatively loose commitment to a floating

A **floating exchange rate** is one determined primarily by market forces.

A **fixed**, or **pegged, exchange rate** means that a government or central bank has promised to convert its currency into another currency at a fixed rate.

Dollarization occurs when a foreign country uses the U.S. dollar as its currency.

A **dirty**, or **managed, float** is a currency whose value is not pegged, but governments will intervene extensively in the market to keep the value within a certain range.

mru.org/optimum-currency

The Theory of Optimum Currency Areas

exchange rate. Under a dirty float, a currency will vary in value daily, although the central bank or treasury will intervene if that currency moves too far outside a band of intended or preannounced values.

The Problem with Pegs

The pegging option has become less popular in recent years. Many nations have attempted currency pegs, but usually they have failed. For instance, Thailand, Indonesia, Brazil, and Argentina, among others, all tried to peg their currencies to the U.S. dollar or to a weighted basket of currencies. In each case, the peg was broken by speculators, largely because these countries did not and could not match the monetary and fiscal policies of the United States. Why hold one Argentine peso—supposedly equal in value to a dollar throughout the late 1990s—when you can hold a U.S. dollar instead?

When Argentina pegged its currency to the U.S. dollar in 1991, it promised that 1 Argentine peso was equal in value to 1 U.S. dollar. For a while, markets believed this promise. The Argentine economy was doing well, foreign investment was flowing in, and the Argentine government instituted many desirable economic reforms.

But over time people began to doubt whether this peg could be maintained. Eventually, the weaknesses of the Argentine economy became revealed more clearly. The government was unable to bring about true fiscal balance. Many foreign investors began to believe that the Argentine peg would break and that the one-to-one rate would go away. This would mean that 1 peso would be worth less than 1 U.S. dollar. Many people who had invested in pesos withdrew their money from the country or tried to convert their peso holdings into dollars before the one-to-one rate disappeared. Argentine citizens panicked as well, and many of them also sought to convert their pesos into U.S. dollars.

The resulting rush to convert pesos into dollars put great strain on the peso. The Argentine government did not have enough U.S. dollars to keep up the value of the peg. The result was that the peso fell from being worth a dollar (January 6, 2002) to being worth about 26 cents (June 28, 2002), across the course of only five and a half months. In other words, the Argentine government had to officially announce a new peg with a much lower value for the Argentine currency.

The rapid reduction in the official exchange rate ruined the economic reputation of Argentina and the withdrawal of money from the country led to a collapse of the banking system. This is sometimes called capital flight. Argentina probably would have been better off had it never pegged its currency in the first place.

Overall, the lesson is simple. Most countries should not attempt exchange rate pegs. An effective peg requires a very serious commitment to a high level of monetary and fiscal stability. If a country doesn't have as sound an economy as that of the United States, in the long run it cannot peg to the U.S. dollar.

What Are the IMF and the World Bank?

To close this chapter, let us look at two very controversial global institutions, the International Monetary Fund and the International Bank for Reconstruction and Development, more commonly known as the World Bank. These institutions have occasioned protests, the throwing of bricks, conspiracy

CHECK YOURSELF

- When the value of a country's currency is determined by the forces of supply and demand, is this a floating exchange rate or a fixed exchange rate?
- Who controls the monetary policy of the European Union?

theories, and political T-shirts. What is up? Are they noxious carriers of evil global forces, benevolent do-gooders, or something else altogether?

For the most part, these agencies are bureaucracies. They do some good, some bad, but they are not as important—for better or worse—as many people think.

International Monetary Fund

Today the International Monetary Fund (IMF) serves as an international lender of last resort. That is, when countries experience financial troubles, the IMF steps in to organize a rescue package, lend money, and monitor the economic situation. Often the loans are tied to a country's willingness to take the IMF's economic advice.

The IMF, created after the end of World War II, is located in Washington, D.C., but it is a "multilateral" institution. It is set up by the world's governments and is independent of any single government. It receives a monetary allocation from each government and also may earn income from its loans. Historically, the director of the IMF is a European. The director reports to a board, and board membership is roughly proportional to how much money a country puts into the institution. The United States, Western Europe, and Japan exercise a dominant influence in this regard, but its staff is drawn from around the world.

The IMF was very active in the Asian currency crises of the 1990s (in Indonesia, Thailand, and South Korea), the Argentine financial crisis starting in 2001, and the recent financial crisis in Greece. Critics of the IMF, such as Nobel Laureate Joseph Stiglitz, charge that it forces borrowing governments to cut government spending, tighten monetary policy, and raise interest rates. In other words, the claim is that the IMF has encouraged contractionary macroeconomic policies when (perhaps) expansionary policies were called for. Defenders of the IMF have argued that the advice is more subtle than is often portrayed, that tough fiscal reforms are sometimes needed, or that borrowing countries do not in fact follow the advice, regardless of whether or not it is good advice.

The World Bank

The World Bank also dates from the immediate aftermath of World War II. It was designed to facilitate the flow of capital to poor countries, especially those parts of the world not being served by private capital markets. Its full-time staff of about 10,000 employees is headquartered in Washington, D.C., right next to the IMF. The Bank is ruled by a board, whose members are drawn from supporting nations, and a president who has historically been an American.

Mostly the World Bank lends money for specific projects in developing countries. This includes loans for water projects, roads, dams, health care, and environmental projects, among other activities. World Bank loans are tied to the use of Bank expertise and the understanding that the borrowing country will work cooperatively with the Bank.

In a typical year, the World Bank lends $25–$30 billion to developing nation governments. Overall, the Bank's largest borrower, by far, is China. Other top borrowers are India, Brazil, Mexico, and Turkey. This has led to debate over the Bank's proper mission. China receives at least $70 billion in foreign investment per year, while it is sitting on more than $1 trillion in foreign currency reserves. So why is the World Bank lending to China? Defenders of the Bank note that much of China remains poor, and the Chinese loans turn a profit and help the Bank carry out its mission in poorer places like Africa. In addition, in 2010, World Bank lending increased to $44 billion in response to the financial crisis when many governments had trouble raising funds from private markets.

The World Bank also gives away money, lends it out at very low rates of interest, or makes loans that it does not expect will be repaid. This is the aid side of the Bank, which is separate from the Bank's loans. To an increasing extent, the Bank's aid is flowing to sub-Saharan Africa.

Critics claim that the Bank does not pay enough attention to results. The commercial incentive is for the Bank to make many loans. The lent funds first go to governments and then they often are used to purchase goods and services from Western companies. For instance, a World Bank loan to Senegal might help finance a contract with a French company for the supply of urban water. This benefits commercial interests in the countries that control the Bank. Accountability is often low, since each year another round of loans will be made in any case. The World Bank makes money off its loans, so perhaps not enough attention is paid to whether those projects deliver their promised benefits. Defenders note that the Bank has responded to criticism in the past, improved its environmental record, and avoided many previous mistakes. Foreign aid is a difficult business to succeed at, and many people believe that the World Bank is overall a force for good.

The IMF and the World Bank attract so much attention because they are seen as icons of global capitalism. Furthermore, both groups hire many technocrats, and neither is subject to direct accountability through democratic rule. They seem to stand above national borders and make decisions, while reporting to no one. They encourage poor countries to borrow money and those debts cannot always be repaid. Such are the charges, but the reality is more prosaic. Both agencies are highly constrained in what they can accomplish, if only because their resources are limited and they deal frequently with contrary governments. At the margin, they make a difference, but they are not the driving forces behind global capitalism.

Takeaway

International currencies are a tricky business, but basic economic principles hold internationally as well as nationally. Contrary to the statements of many politicians, trade deficits are not necessarily a problem, unless a country is investing foolishly or not saving enough. In either case, the trade deficit is not the root of the relevant problem. Instead of complaining about America's current trade deficit with China, it is better to consider how the United States might save more. The trade balance is simply one side of the coin, with the capital account serving as the other side. If a lot of capital is flowing into a country, that country also will be running a trade deficit.

Exchange rates are set in active markets, changing by the second every day, and following the laws of supply and demand. Monetary policy can affect real exchange rates in the short run, but not in the long run. In the long run, exchanges rates are set according to purchasing power parity, so that profits cannot be made buying goods in one country and shipping them to another.

Both monetary and fiscal policies will affect a country's real exchange rate in the short run and these exchange rate effects will influence aggregate demand by affecting some mix of exports, imports, and the flow of capital from one country to another.

Most countries today have floating exchange rates with values determined in international currency markets. Fixed or pegged exchange rates are possible but in most circumstances they are difficult to maintain over the longer run. Thus, a combination of currency unions and floating exchange rates has increasingly become the global norm.

The IMF and the World Bank may inspire protests but for good or ill these institutions are modestly sized bureaucracies in a much larger globalized world.

CHAPTER REVIEW

Go online to practice with more examples of these types of problems, including live links to videos, data sources, and feedback.

▶ Problems with this icon relate to optional MRU videos.

KEY CONCEPTS

trade deficit, p. 450

trade surplus, p. 450

balance of payments, p. 451

capital surplus, p. 451

current account, p. 452

capital account, p. 452

exchange rate, p. 456

appreciation, p. 457

depreciation, p. 458

nominal exchange rate, p. 460

real exchange rate, p. 460

purchasing power parity (PPP) theorem, p. 460

law of one price, p. 460

floating exchange rate, p. 465

fixed, or pegged, exchange rate, p. 465

dollarization, p. 465

dirty, or managed, float, p. 465

FACTS AND TOOLS

Discovering DATA ⁚⁚

1. Let's use the FRED economic database (https://fred.stlouisfed.org/) to examine U.S. exports, imports, and the balance of trade (Exports–Imports, the most widely discussed component of the current account). Search first for U.S. exports by finding the series EXPGS (use this series rather than the series for real exports). Click Edit Graph and Modify Frequency to change to an annual rate (use the average method). Now click Add Line and look for a similar series for imports (IMPGS). Click Modify Frequency to change to an annual rate (using the average method). In 2019, how much did the United States export (in trillions)? How much did the United States import? What was the trade balance?

Discovering DATA ⁚⁚

2. Let's examine the U.S. balance of trade (Exports–Imports) as we did in Problem 1, but this time we will do so as a percent of GDP. Using the FRED economic database (https://fred.stlouisfed.org/), search for U.S. Exports. Again, find the series EXPGS (use this series

rather than the series for real exports). Click Edit Graph and Modify Frequency to change to an annual rate (use the average method). Now, under Customize Data, look for a similar series for imports (IMPGS) and add it. Now, under Customize Data, search for gross domestic product (again, don't use real GDP), and add that.

You now have three series: Exports (a), Imports (b), and Gross Domestic Product (c). Write a formula for the balance of trade as a percentage of GDP using a, b, and c, and enter it in the formula box, clicking Apply.

a. In 2005, before the 2008–2009 recession, what was the trade deficit as a percent of GDP?

b. In 2009, during the recession, what was the trade deficit as a percent of GDP?

c. Was the trade deficit bigger or smaller in 2009 compared to 2005? Why? Using your answers to this Problem and Problem 1, comment on whether a trade deficit is necessarily a bad thing.

3. Practice with the balance of payments:

Current account + Capital account
= Change in official reserves

a. Current account = −$10, Capital account = +$15. What is the change in reserves?

b. Current account = −$10, Change in reserves = −$3. What is the capital account?

c. Your college expenses = $12,000, Income from your barista job = $4,000. What is your current account? If you haven't changed your reserves (i.e., cash savings) at all, what is the capital account (i.e., borrowing from parents or bank)?

4. In the chapter, two stories about the deficit are told: "the great place to invest" story and the "foolishly saving too little" story. In the following examples, which is more like the "great place to invest" story and which is more like the "foolishly saving too little" story?

a. Goofus uses his student loan money to buy a nice flat-screen TV and can't afford most of his textbooks. Gallant uses his student loan money to buy his textbooks and coffee that keeps him awake during study sessions.

b. Carter borrows money from his dad to attend the right parties, make useful industry connections, and build his career. Ernest borrows money from his dad to attend fun parties, meet fun people, and, well, that's about it.

c. America 1 borrows money to invest in her future. America 2 borrows money to pay for a spending binge.

5. a. According to Table 20.1, how many Japanese yen could you get for 1 dollar in May 2017? Use the currency converter on Yahoo! Finance to find out how many yen you could buy for a dollar today.

b. Given your answer to the previous question, did the dollar gain or lose buying power, in terms of Japanese goods, over this period? (Get this one right: It's crucial to understanding exchange rates.)

c. Repeat parts a and b for one other currency in Table 20.1.

6. According to the purchasing power parity theorem, what must be approximately equal across countries: the nominal exchange rate or the real exchange rate?

7. a. According to purchasing power parity theory, a country with massive inflation should also experience a massive fall in the price of its currency in terms of other currencies (a depreciation). Is this what happened in Zimbabwe, or did the opposite occur?

b. Hyperinflation is defined as a rapid rise in the price of goods and services. According to purchasing power parity theory, does hyperinflation also cause a rapid rise in the price of foreign currencies?

8. Which international financial institution focuses on the long-run health of developing countries: the IMF or the World Bank? Which one focuses on short-run financial crises in developing countries?

9. Let's translate between newspaper jargon about exchange rates and the economic reality of exchange rates.

a. Last week, the currency of Frobia was trading one for one with the currency of Bozzum. This week, one unit of Frobian currency buys two units of Bozzumian currency. Which currency "rose"? Which currency became "stronger"? Which currency "appreciated"?

b. The currency in the nation of Malvolio becomes "weaker." Now that it's weaker, can 10 U.S. dollars buy more of the

Malvolian currency than before or less than before?

c. A college student travels from the United States to Germany. Just before he leaves, he changes $400 into euros. He spends only half the money while in Germany, so on his return to the United States, he exchanges his euros back into dollars. However, while he was admiring Munich's historic Marienplatz, the dollar "weakened" considerably. Is this good news or bad news from the college student's point of view?

10. a. When the Japanese government slows the rate of money growth, will that tend to strengthen the yen against the dollar or weaken the yen against the dollar?

b. When the Japanese government slows the rate of money growth, will the dollar tend to appreciate against the yen or will the dollar tend to depreciate against the yen?

c. When Americans increase their demand for Japanese-made cars, will that tend to strengthen the yen against the dollar or weaken the yen against the dollar?

d. When Americans increase their demand for Japanese-made cars, will the dollar tend to appreciate against the yen or will the dollar tend to depreciate against the yen?

THINKING AND PROBLEM SOLVING

11. Practice with the current account: Which of the following tend to raise the value of Country X's current account?

a. Country X sends cash to aid war victims in Country Y.

b. Investors living in Country X receive more dividend payments than usual from businesses operating in Country Y.

c. Investors living in Country Y receive more interest payments than usual from businesses operating in Country X.

d. Immigrants from Country Y who live and work in Country X send massive amounts of currency back to their families in Country Y.

e. The government of Country X imports more jet fighters and missiles from Country Y.

12. Practice with the capital account: Which of the three categories of the capital account does each belong in? Which of the following tend to raise the value of Country X's capital account?

a. A corporation in Country Y pays for a new factory to be built in Country X.

b. A corporation in Country Y sells all of its stock in a corporation located in Country X to a citizen of Country X.

c. A citizen of Country Y purchases 20% of the shares of a corporation in Country X from a citizen of Country X.

d. A business owner in Country X pays for a new factory to be built in Country Y.

13. Let's translate "Americans are foolishly saving too little" into a simple GDP story. Recall that GDP = $C + I + G$ + Net exports. GDP is fixed and equal to 100 throughout the story: After all, it's pinned down by the production function of Chapter 9. Thus, the size of the pie is fixed: The only question is how the pie is sliced into C, I, G, and net exports. To keep it simple, assume that $I + G = 40$ throughout.

a. The "saving too little" story comes in two parts: In part one (now), the United States has high C and low (really, negative) net exports. If $C = 70$, what do net exports equal? Is this a trade deficit or a trade surplus?

b. In part two (later), foreign countries are tired of sending so many goods to the United States, and want to start receiving goods *from* the United States. Net exports now become positive, rising to +5. What does C equal? If citizens value consumption, which period do they prefer: "now" or "later"?

14. Let's translate "The United States is a great place to invest" into a simple GDP story. Recall that GDP = $C + I + G$ + Net exports. In this story, foreigners build up the U.S. capital stock by pushing investment (I) above its normal level. Thus, GDP equals 100 in the "now" period but equals 110 in the "later" period. To keep it simple, assume that $C + G = 80$ throughout.

a. The "great place to invest" story comes in two parts: In part one (now), the United States has high I and low (really, negative) net exports. If $I = 35$, what do net exports equal? Is this a trade deficit or a trade surplus?

b. In part two (later), foreign countries are tired of sending so many machines and pieces of equipment to the United States, and want to start receiving goods from the United States. Net exports now become positive, rising to +5. What does I equal?

15. The market for foreign currencies is a lot like the market for apples or cars or fish, so we can use the same intuition—as long as we keep reminding ourselves which way is "up" and which is "down." Consider the market for something called "euros" (maybe it's a new breakfast cereal) and measure the price in dollars. Discuss the following cases:

   a. The people who make "euros" decide to produce many more of them. Is this a shift in supply or in demand, and in which direction? What does this do to the price of euros?

   b. Consumers and businesses decide that they'd like to own a lot more euros than before. Is this a shift in supply or in demand, and in which direction? What does this do to the price of euros?

   c. There's a slowdown in the production of euros, initiated by the executives in charge of euro production. Is this a shift in supply or in demand, and in which direction? What does this do to the price of euros?

   d. Suppose that the price of apples rises. Using the same language as in parts a and b, would you describe this as a strengthening of the dollar or a weakening of the dollar?

16. Now that we've built up some intuition about exchange rates, let's apply the principles more thoroughly. In this question, we discuss the U.S.–China exchange rate. Officially, the Chinese government fixed this exchange rate for years at a time, but in this question, we treat it as a market rate that can change every day.

   a. In the following figure, shift the appropriate curves to illustrate the effect of the following news story: Chinese factory sells poisonous dog food.

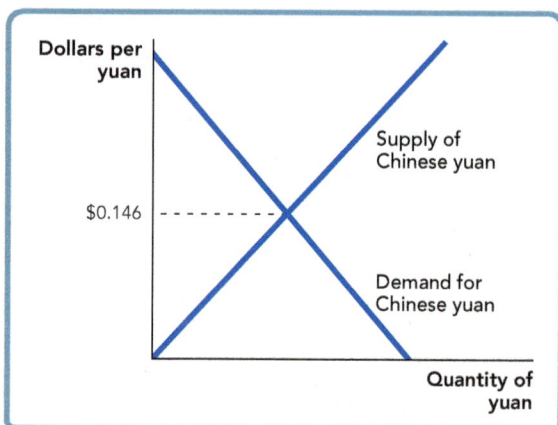

   b. Does this news story raise or lower the price of the yuan? Does this strengthen or weaken the Chinese currency? Does this strengthen or weaken the U.S. dollar?

17. Nobel Laureate Robert Solow once jokingly noted, "I have a chronic [trade] deficit with my barber, who doesn't buy a darned thing from me." Is this a problem? Why or why not? How does this relate to the U.S.–China, U.S.–Mexico, and U.S.–Japan trade deficits?

18. Corey, a young entrepreneur, notices that cigarette lighters sell for only $0.50 each in Utah but they sell for $1.00 each in Nevada.

   a. If Corey wants to make money by buying and selling lighters, where should he buy the lighters and where should he sell them?

   b. If many other people imitate Corey's behavior, what will happen to the supply of lighters in Utah (rise, fall, unchanged)? What will happen to the supply of lighters in Nevada (rise, fall, unchanged)?

   c. What will the behavior in part b do to the price of lighters in Utah? In Nevada?

   d. According to the law of one price, what can we say about the price of cigarette lighters in Nevada after all of this arbitrage? More than one of the following may be true:

   Less than $1.00 each

   More than $1.00 each

   The same as the Utah price

19. At Christmas, five-year-old Gwen runs a massive trade deficit with her parents: She "exports" only a wrapped candy cane to her parents, but she "imports" a massive number of video games, dolls, and pairs of socks.

   a. Is this trade deficit a good thing for Gwen?

   b. When Gwen turns 25, her parents insist on being repaid for all those years of Christmas presents—that is, they require her to run a "trade surplus." Is this "trade surplus" good news for Gwen? Why or why not?

20. a. Suppose that the price level in the United States doubled, while the price level in the U.K. remained unchanged. According to purchasing power parity theory, would the dollar/pound nominal exchange rate double or would it fall in half?

   b. In practice, PPP tends to hold more true in the long run than in the short run, because many prices are sticky. So if the U.S. money supply increased dramatically—a big enough rise for the price level to double in the long run—would this be good news for British tourists headed to the United States or would it be good news for U.S. tourists headed to Britain? Incidentally, would this be good news or bad news (in the short run) for U.S. tourists staying in the United States?

21. Consider two equally wealthy families: One family lives in a relatively poor country while the other family lives in a relatively rich country. Which family is more likely to own a mechanical dishwasher? Why? Remember: The families are equally wealthy.

CHALLENGES

22. In our basic model, a rise in money growth causes currency depreciation: We also know from Chapters 13 and 16 that a rise in money growth normally raises aggregate demand and boosts short-run real growth. But in the 2001 Argentine crisis and the 1997 Asian financial crisis, a currency depreciation seemed to cause a massive *fall* in short-run output.

   a. What type of shock could cause a currency depreciation to be associated with a fall in short-run output?

   b. In both the Argentine and the Asian crises, these countries' banking sectors were hit especially hard: They had made big promises to pay their debts in foreign currencies—often dollars—and the depreciation made it impossible for them to keep those promises. What became more "expensive" as a result of the depreciation: foreign currency (dollars, yen, pounds) or domestic currency?

   c. In these crises, depreciation created bankruptcies: These bankruptcies are what caused the shock discussed in part a. To avoid this outcome in the future, Berkeley economist Barry Eichengreen, an expert on exchange rate policy, recommended that businesses in developing countries encourage foreigners to invest in stock that pays dividends rather than in debt. He believed this would make it easier for countries to endure surprise depreciations. Why would he recommend this?

23. In Panama, a dollarized country, a Big Mac is about 30% cheaper than in the United States. Why?

24. A supply-and-demand model can illustrate the difficulty of keeping a fixed exchange rate: It's much the same as any other price floor. Consider the following fixed exchange rate. Sparta uses a currency called the spartonian, Athenians use the aton; the Spartans have chosen a fixed exchange rate of two atons per spartonian:

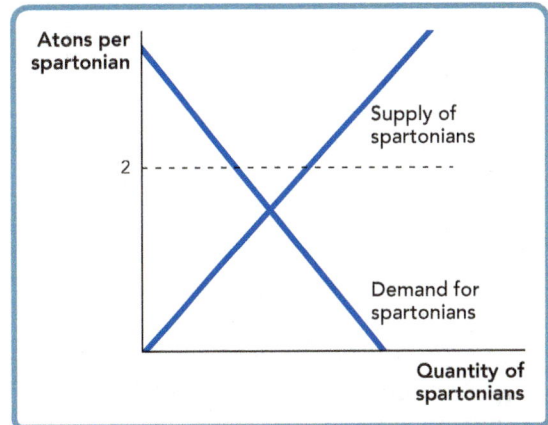

   a. In a typical supply and demand model, what would you call the gap that exists between quantity supplied and quantity demanded at this fixed exchange rate: a surplus or a shortage? Of which currency?

   b. If the Spartan government wants to keep this exchange rate fixed, what will tend to happen to its official reserve account supply of atons: Will it rise, or will it tend to fall? (*Hint:* Remember that the suppliers of spartonians want to buy atons. How does this explain why governments of fixed exchange rate countries hold large amounts of foreign currencies in their accounts?)

   c. If demand for spartonians fell because of a weak Spartan economy, would this make it harder or easier for this government to maintain the exchange rate?

   d. If the Spartan government wanted to bring quantity supplied and quantity demanded closer together, would it want to slow money growth or raise money growth? When real world countries have "overvalued" currencies, do you think they should fix them by slowing money growth or by raising money growth?

25. a. Ecuador is currently dollarized: Bank accounts are denominated in U.S. dollars, for example. If Ecuadoreans believe rumors that the country is going to go off the dollar and convert all bank account deposits into a new unit of money called the "Ecuado" (similar

to what Argentina actually did in 2001), what will this probably do to the Ecuadorean banking system?

   b. "There is no such thing as a fixed exchange rate: Just pegs that haven't been changed . . . yet." Explain how this belief, by itself, can make it difficult for a country to maintain a fixed exchange rate. Does this belief have a direct impact on the demand for a currency or on the supply of a currency?

26. We said that "an effective peg requires a very serious commitment to a high level of monetary and fiscal stability." As in our discussion of monetary policy, people's *beliefs* about what government *might* do in the future put limits on what governments should do *today*. Discuss how "commitment" can keep an exchange rate stable. Compare with how commitment can make it easier to keep inflation low. What can a government do in these situations to convince foreign investors and domestic citizens that it will keep its commitments? (Certainly, there is more than one good way to answer this question: The problem of creating commitment is an active area of research across the social sciences.)

Discovering DATA ⠃

27. Let's look at the U.S. to U.K. foreign exchange rate using the FRED economic database (https://fred.stlouisfed.org/). Search for US/UK Foreign Exchange Rate then change the beginning date to January 1, 2016.

   a. On June 23, 2016, how many dollars did it take to buy one British pound?

   b. On June 27, 2016, how many dollars did it take to buy one British pound?

   c. Over the time period, did the British pound appreciate or depreciate? Does this suggest an increased demand to hold pounds or a decreased demand to hold them?

   d. What political event happened to cause such a change in the exchange rate? Why did this event cause an appreciation/depreciation (as per your answer to c)?

▶ 28. We have said that services are likely to be cheaper in poorer countries, but is this true for all kinds of services? Can you think of some services that are more likely to sell for similar prices everywhere? What kinds of services?

WORK IT OUT

For interactive, step-by-step help in solving this problem, go online.

   a. Consider two headlines: "Money is pouring into the U.S. faster than ever" vs. "Record U.S. trade deficit." How can both be true simultaneously?

   b. Consider two headlines: "Money is fleeing the U.S. faster than ever" vs. "Record U.S. trade surplus." How can both be true simultaneously?

▶ MRU VIDEOS

Purchasing Power Parity

mru.org/purchasing-power-parity

Problems: **6, 20**

Why Should You Get a Haircut in a Poorer Country?

mru.org/india-haircut

Problems: **21, 25, 28**

The Theory of Optimum Currency Areas

mru.org/optimum-currency

Problems: **21, 25, 28**

21

Political Economy and Public Choice

If you have read this far, you may now be asking, "What's wrong with the world?" Economists tend to favor free and competitive markets and to be skeptical about policies like price controls, tariffs, command and control regulation, and high inflation rates. Yet around the world, markets are often suppressed, monopolies are supported, and harmful policies, such as those just listed, are quite common. Why do the arguments of economists fall on deaf ears?

One possible answer is that politicians are right to reject mainstream economics. Some people do argue that mainstream economics ignores important ethical values. Or perhaps mainstream economics is simply wrong about economics. Of course, that is not our view, so you will have to seek other books to judge that question for yourself. A third answer to what's wrong with the world and the one we will explore in this chapter is . . . can you guess? Bad incentives.

A good incentive system aligns self-interest with the social interest. When studying the price system, we explored the conditions under which markets do and do not align self-interest with the social interest. It's now time to turn to government. The critical question is this: When does the self-interest of politicians and voters align with the social interest and when do these interests collide? This question is at the heart of political economy, or **public choice**, which is the study of political behavior using the tools of economics.

We just made an important but implicit assumption that is worth emphasizing. We assumed that self-interest is as important in politics as in economics.[*] Economists call this the assumption of *behavioral symmetry*—we assume that institutions differ but people are the same. Comparative institutional analysis is all about analyzing the incentive issues associated with alternative institutional arrangements.

This is exactly what political economists such as James Madison, Alexander Hamilton, Thomas Jefferson, and George Mason were doing when they

> **CHAPTER OUTLINE**
>
> **Voters and the Incentive to Be Ignorant**
>
> **Special Interests and the Incentive to Be Informed**
>
> **A Formula for Political Success: Diffuse Costs, Concentrate Benefits**
>
> **Voter Myopia and Political Business Cycles**
>
> **Two Cheers for Democracy**
>
> **Takeaway**
>
> ▶ **MRU** Video
>
> • Democracy and Famines

Public choice is the study of political behavior using the tools of economics.

---

[*] Note that we are not assuming that self-interest is the only important motivator only that self-interest is equally important across different institutions.

debated the design of the U.S. Constitution. As James Madison put it famously in Federalist 51:

> *Ambition must be made to counteract ambition . . . In framing a government which is to be administered by men over men, the great difficulty lies in this: you must first enable the government to control the governed; and in the next place oblige it to control itself.*

Federalist 51

Ambition is another word for self-interest, and framing is another word for designing, so Madison was trying to design a constitution that channeled the self-interest of political actors towards the social good.

We will begin this chapter looking at some of the major institutions and incentives that govern the behavior of voters and politicians in a democracy. As we will see, democracies have many problems, including voter ignorance, control of politics by special interests, and political business cycles. Yet, to quote Winston Churchill, "No one pretends that democracy is perfect or all-wise. Indeed, it has been said that democracy is the worst form of government except all those other forms that have been tried from time to time."[1] Thus, in the latter half of the chapter, we look at nondemocracies and some of the reasons why nondemocracies have typically failed to produce either wealth or political or economic liberty for their citizens.

Let's begin with voters and the question: "Do voters have an incentive to be well informed about politics?"

Voters and the Incentive to Be Ignorant

Knowledge is a good thing, but sometimes the price of knowledge is too high. Imagine that your professor changed the grading scheme. Instead of awarding grades based on individual performance, your professor averages test scores and assigns the same grade to everyone. Will you study more or less under this new grading scheme? We think that most people would study less because studying now has a lower payoff. Let's say that before the change an extra few hours of studying would raise your grade by 10 points. What is the payoff to studying under the new system? Imagine that there are 100 people in your class. The same hours of studying will now raise your grade by just 10/100 or 0.1 points.* Studying doesn't pay under the second system because your grade is mostly determined by what other people do, not by what you do.

Now let's apply the same idea to politics. When you choose a politician, does studying their record have a high payoff? No. Studying position papers, examining voting histories, and listening to political speeches is sometimes entertaining, but it doesn't offer much concrete return. Even when studying changes your vote, your vote is very unlikely to change the outcome of the election. Studying politics doesn't pay because the outcome of an election is mostly determined by what other people do, not by what you do.

Economists say that voters are **rationally ignorant** about politics because the incentives to be informed are low.

Rational ignorance occurs when the benefits of being informed are less than the costs of becoming informed.

---

* It's possible that some people could study more under the new system. Under the old system, studying only raises an individual's grade, but under the new system, it raises everyone's grades! Thus, if there are some super-altruistic students, they might study more under the new system. We have not met many such students. Have you?

It's not hard to find evidence that Americans are uninformed about politics. Consider the following questions. Who is the speaker of the U.S. House of Representatives? Who sings "Bad Guy"? Be honest. Which question was it easier for you to answer? And which question is more important? (At the time of writing, Nancy Pelosi is speaker of the House. "Bad Guy" is a Billie Eilish hit.)

Not knowing who the speaker of the House is might not be critical, but Americans are equally uninformed or worse—misinformed—about important political questions. For example, in one survey Americans were asked to name the two largest sources of government spending out of the following six choices.

- Welfare
- Interest on the federal debt
- Defense
- Foreign aid
- Social Security
- Health care

Amazingly, 41% named foreign aid as one of the two biggest programs. But foreign aid is by far the smallest program of the six listed. Do you know the correct answers? The two biggest programs are defense and Social Security. Americans were not even close to the correct answers; for instance, the second most popular choice was welfare, which, though a large program, is still much smaller than defense and Social Security.[2]

Similarly, by their own admission, most Americans know "not much" or "nothing" about important pieces of legislation such as the USA Patriot Act. Most Americans cannot estimate the inflation rate or the unemployment rate to within five percentage points. Hundreds of surveys over many decades have shown that most Americans know little about political matters. Of course, we'd all like to change that—we are glad you are reading this book!—but in the meantime it is simply a fact. And it appears to be a fact that is not easily changed.

Rational ignorance Do you recognize this man?

Why Rational Ignorance Matters

Ignorance about political matters is important for at least three reasons. First, if voters don't know what the USA Patriot Act says or what the unemployment rate is, then it's difficult to make informed choices. Moreover, voters who think that the unemployment rate is much higher than it actually is are likely to make quite different choices than if they knew the true rate. The difficulty is compounded if voters don't know the positions that politicians take on the issues, and it is worse yet if voters don't know much about possible solutions to problems such as unemployment. Voters are supposed to be the drivers in a democracy, but if the drivers don't know where they are or where they want to go or how to get there, they are unlikely to ever arrive at a desirable destination.

Second, voters who are rationally ignorant will often make decisions on the basis of low-quality, unreliable, or potentially biased information. Not everyone has read a good principles of economics textbook and those who haven't are likely to vote in ways that are quite different from someone who is better informed.[*] It's not really surprising, for example, that better-looking politicians get more votes even if good looks have nothing to do with policy. Once again, we should not expect too much in the way of wise government policy when voters are rationally ignorant.

The third reason that rational ignorance matters is that not everyone is rationally ignorant. Let's look at this in more detail.

CHECK YOURSELF

• Would you expect more rational ignorance about national issues among national voters or about local issues among local voters? Make an argument for both possibilities.

Special Interests and the Incentive to Be Informed

Let's return to the sugar quota discussed in Chapter 19. As you may recall, the government restricts how much sugar can be imported into the United States. As a result, the U.S. price of sugar is about double the world price. American consumers of candy, soda, and other sweet goods pay more for these goods than they would if the quota was lifted. Why does the government harm sugar consumers, many of whom are voters?

Although sugar consumers are harmed by the quota, few of them even know of the quota's existence. That's rational because even though the quota costs consumers more than a billion dollars, the costs are diffused over millions of consumers, costing each person about $5 or $6 per year. Even if sugar consumers did know about the quota, they probably wouldn't spend much time or effort to oppose it. Will you? After all, just writing an email to your Congressperson opposing the quota might cost $5 or $6 in time and trouble, and what's the probability that your email will change the policy?

Sugar consumers, therefore, won't do much to oppose the quota but what about U.S. sugar producers? U.S. sugar producers benefit enormously from the quota. As we saw in Chapter 19, if the quota were lifted, most sugar producers in Florida would be outcompeted by producers in Brazil where better weather makes sugar cheaper to produce. But with the quota, U.S. producers are shielded from competition and sugar farming in Florida becomes very profitable. Moreover, although there are millions of sugar consumers, sugar production is concentrated among a handful of producers. Each producer benefits from the quota by millions of dollars.

Sugar producers, unlike sugar consumers, have a lot of money at stake so they have a strong incentive to be *rationally informed*. The sugar producers know when the sugar quota comes up for a vote, they know who is pictured on the previous page, they know who is on the House and Senate agricultural committees that largely decide on the quota, they know which politicians are running for reelection and in need of campaign funds, and they act accordingly. Table 21.1, for example, lists the members of the Senate Agricultural Committee in 2008 and the amount of money from 2006 to 2008 that they received from the American Crystal Sugar Political Action Committee (PAC), an industry lobby group in favor of the sugar quota.

As you can see, 13 of the 21 senators on the Agricultural Committee (perhaps not coincidentally just over a majority!) received money from the American Crystal Sugar PAC. Many senators on the committee *also* received money from the American Sugar Cane League, the Florida Sugar Cane League, the

---

[*] For a superb treatment of this issue, see Caplan, Bryan. 2007. *The Myth of the Rational Voter: Why Democracies Choose Bad Policies.* Princeton, NJ: Princeton University Press.

American Sugarbeet Growers Association, and the U.S. Beet Sugar Association! But that isn't even the end of the story. The owners and executives of the major players in the sugar industry also donate campaign funds as individuals. The "sugar barons" José and Alfonso Fanjul, for example, head Florida Crystals Corporation, which is one of the country's largest sugar cane growers. The Fanjuls donate money to the Florida Sugar Cane League and give money to politicians in their own names. Interestingly, José directs most of his support to Republicans, while his brother Alfonso supports Democrats. Do you think there is a difference of political opinion between the two brothers? Or can you think of another explanation for their pattern of donations? Other Fanjul family members, including brothers, wives, daughters, sons, and even sisters-in-law, are also active political contributors.

A Formula for Political Success: Diffuse Costs, Concentrate Benefits

The politics behind the sugar quota illustrate a formula for political success: Diffuse costs and concentrate benefits. The costs of the sugar quota are diffused over millions of consumers, so no consumer has much of an incentive to oppose the quota. But the benefits of the quota are concentrated on a handful of producers; they have strong incentives to support the quota. So, the sugar quota is a winning policy for politicians. The people who are harmed are rationally ignorant and have little incentive to oppose the policy, while the people who benefit are rationally informed and have strong incentives to support the policy. Thus, we can see one reason why the self-interest of politicians does not always align with the social interest.

The formula for political success works for many types of public policies, not just trade quotas and tariffs. Agricultural subsidies and price supports, for example, fit the diffused costs and concentrated benefits story. It's interesting that the political power of farmers has *increased* as the share of farmers in the population has *decreased*. The reason? When farmers decline in population, the benefits of, for example, a price support become more concentrated (on farmers) and the costs become more diffused (on nonfarmers).

The benefits of many government projects such as roads, bridges, dams, and parks are concentrated on local residents and producers, while the costs of these projects can be diffused over all federal taxpayers. As a result, politicians have an incentive to lobby for these projects even when the benefits are smaller than the costs.

TABLE 21.1 SPECIAL INTERESTS ARE RATIONALLY INFORMED

Senators on the Agriculture Committee, 2008	Donations from the American Crystal Sugar PAC (2006–2008)
Tom Harkin, D-IA	$15,000
Sherrod Brown, D-OH	$15,000
Saxby Chambliss R-GA	$10,000
Mitch McConnell, R-KY	$10,000
Robert Casey, Jr., D-PA	$10,000
E. Benjamin Nelson, D-NE	$8,000
Amy Klobuchar, D-MN	$7,000
Patrick J. Leahy, D-VT	$6,000
Max Baucus, D-MT	$6,000
Pat Roberts, R-KS	$3,000
Kent Conrad, D-ND	$2,000
Ken Salazar, D-CO	$2,000
Debbie Stabenow, D-MI	$1,000
Richard G. Lugar, R-IN	$0
Thad Cochran, R-MS	$0
Blanche Lincoln, D-AR	$0
Lindsey Graham, R-SC	$0
Norm Coleman, R-MN	$0
Mike Crapo, R-ID	$0
John Thune, R-SD	$0
Charles Grassley, R-IA	$0

Data from: Federal Election Commission data compiled by OpenSecrets.org.

▶▶ **SEARCH ENGINE**

Extensive information on campaign contributions can be found at www.OpenSecrets.org.

Consider the infamous "Bridge to Nowhere," a proposed bridge in Alaska that would connect the town of Ketchikan (population 8,900) with its airport on Gravina Island (population 50) at a cost to federal taxpayers of $320 million. At present, a ferry service runs to the island but some people in the town complain that it costs too much ($6 per car). If the town's residents had to pay the $320 million cost of the bridge themselves—that's $35,754 each!—do you think they would want the bridge? Of course not, but the residents will be happy to have the bridge if most of the costs are paid by other taxpayers.

As far as the residents of Ketchikan are concerned, the costs of the bridge are *external costs*. When the costs of a good are paid for by other people—rather than the consumers or producers of the good—we get an inefficiently large quantity of the good. An example is a firm that pollutes—since the firm doesn't pay all the costs of its production, it produces too much. The same thing is true here, except the external cost is created by government. When government makes it possible to push the costs of a good onto other people—to *externalize the cost*—we get too much of the good. In this case, we get too many bridges to nowhere.

The formula for political success works for tax credits and deductions, as well as for spending. The federal tax code, including various regulations and rulings, is more than 60,000 pages long and it grows every year as politicians add special interest provisions. Tax breaks for various manufacturing industries, for example, have long been common, but in 2004, the term "manufacturing" was significantly expanded so that oil and gas drilling as well as mining and timber could be included as manufacturing industries. The new tax breaks were worth some $76 billion to the firms involved. One last-minute provision even defined "coffee roasting" as a form of manufacturing. That provision was worth a lot of *bucks* to one famous corporation.

Every year Congress inserts many thousands of special spending projects, exemptions, regulations, and tax breaks into major bills. A multibillion-dollar lobbying industry works the system on behalf of their clients, and it is not unusual for those lobbies, in essence, to propose and even write up the details of the forthcoming legislation. Many lobbyists are former politicians who find that lobbying their friends can be very profitable.

Many small distortions can tie a giant down.

When benefits are concentrated and costs are diffuse, resources can be wasted on projects with low benefits and high costs. Consider a special interest group representing 1% of society that proposes a simple policy that benefits the special interest by $100 and costs society $100. Thus, the policy benefits the special interest by $100 and it costs the *special interest* just $1 (if you are wondering where that came from, $1 is 1% of the total cost to society). The special interest group will certainly lobby for a policy like this.

But now imagine that the policy benefits the special interest by $100 but costs society twice as much, $200. The policy is very bad for society, but it's still good for the special interest, which gets a benefit of $100 at a cost (to the lobby) of only $2 ($2 is 1% of the total social costs of $200). Indeed, a special interest representing 1% of the population will benefit from any policy that transfers $100 in its favor, even if the costs to society are nearly 100 times as much!

If each policy, taken on its own, wastes a few million or billion dollars' worth of resources, the country will be much poorer. A country with many inefficient policies will have less wealth and slower economic growth. No society can get rich by passing policies with benefits that are less than costs.

In extreme situations, an economy can falter or even collapse when fighting over the division of the pie becomes more profitable than making the pie grow larger. The fall of the Roman Empire, for instance, was caused in part by bad political institutions. As the Roman Empire grew, courting politicians in Rome became a more secure path to riches than starting a new business. Toward the end of the empire, the emperors taxed peasant farmers heavily. Rather than spending the money on roads or valuable infrastructure, the activities that had made Rome powerful and rich, tax revenues were used to pay off privileged insiders and to placate the public in the city of Rome with "bread and circuses." When the empire finally collapsed in 476 CE, the tax collector was a hated figure and the government enjoyed little respect.[3]

Another Formula: Concentrated Costs, Diffuse Benefits We have just seen an example of government failure: policies with concentrated benefits and diffuse costs can win in a democratic process even when the benefits are less than the costs. When *costs* are concentrated and benefits are diffuse another government failure can happen—policies with concentrated costs and diffuse benefits can lose in a democratic system even when the benefits are *more* than the costs. The logic is similar. Concentrated benefits or costs concentrate the mind and lead to lobbying and political action, while diffuse benefits or costs are often too small to motivate awareness or action.

Many cities make it costly and difficult to build new housing. In part, this may be due to preferences held by a majority of voters but it's also a consequence of the decentralized permit and approval process. In a typical process, even when land is zoned for construction, a builder must also get approval from a neighborhood review board which holds hearings. Who shows up and speaks to the neighborhood review board?

The next-door neighbor worried about parking might show up to argue against the project. As might the older resident concerned about new people moving into "their" neighborhood. The costs of the project, whether real or imagined, are concentrated on a small number of people who are likely be vocal about their opposition. The benefits, however, are diffuse.

The developer will benefit and will speak in favor, but what about the future residents of the apartment building? The future residents are probably unknown, even to themselves. As a result, it's not surprising that one careful survey in Massachusetts found that at local review boards opposition to new housing proposals always far exceeded support. The surprise is that at the same time, voters in Massachusetts passed legislation favoring more building. Why the difference? Diffuse beneficiaries are more likely to vote about general rules (a relatively low cost activity) than they are to attend and speak at a review board about a specific proposal (a relatively high cost activity). Thus, the power of local review boards magnifies the power of interest groups with concentrated costs and, as result of this political structure, small groups with concentrated costs can often veto projects with large benefits.[4]

Voter Myopia and Political Business Cycles

We turn now from the microeconomics of political economy to an application in macroeconomics. Rational ignorance and another factor, voter myopia, can encourage politicians to boost the economy before an election to increase their chances of reelection.

Presidential elections appear to be fought on many fronts. Candidates battle over education, war, health care, the environment, and the economy. Pundits scrutinize the daily chronicle of events to divine how the candidates advance and retreat in public opinion. Personalities and "leadership" loom large and are reckoned to swing voters one way or another. When the battle is done, historians mark one personality and set of issues as having won the day and as reflecting the "will of the voters."

But economists and political scientists have been surprised to discover that a simpler logic underlies this apparent chaos of seemingly unique and momentous events. Over the past 100 years, the American voter has voted for the party of the incumbent when the economy is doing well and voted against the incumbent when the economy is doing poorly. Voters are so responsive to economic conditions that the winner of a presidential election can be predicted with considerable accuracy, even if one knows nothing about the personalities, issues, or events that seem, on the surface, to matter so much.

The green line in Figure 21.1 shows, for each presidential election since 1948, the share of the two-party vote won by the party of the incumbent (that is, a share greater than 50% usually means the presidency stayed with the incumbent party and a share less than 50% usually means the presidency switched party). The blue line is the share of the two-party vote predicted by just three variables: growth in personal disposable income (per capita) in the year of the election, the inflation rate in the year of the election, and a simple measure of how long the incumbent party has been in power. Notice that these three variables alone give us great power to predict election results.

More specifically, the incumbent party wins elections when personal disposable income is growing, when the inflation rate in the election year is low, and

---

FIGURE 21.1

Predicted and Actual Vote Share of the Incumbent Party, 1948–2012

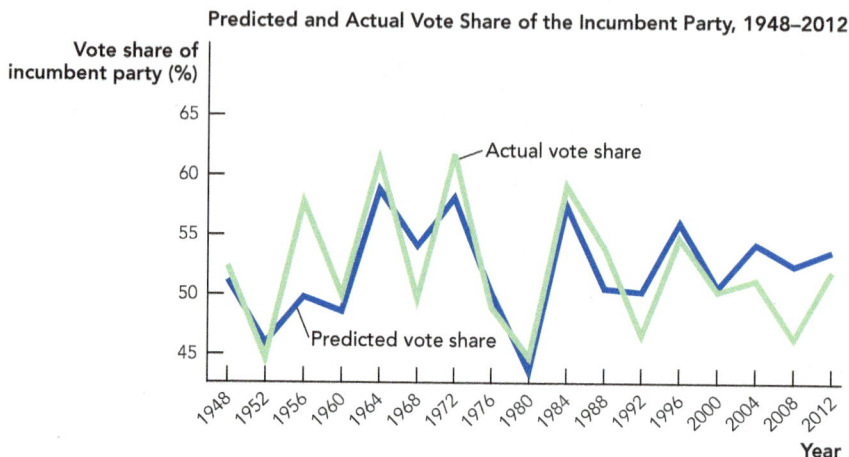

Economic Conditions In an Election Year Predict Presidential Votes

Notes:
Vote share is predicted using growth in disposable income in year of election, inflation in year of election, and a measure of how long the incumbent party has been in office. Actual vote share is the share of the two-party vote captured by the party of the presidential incumbent.

when the incumbent party has not been in power for too many terms in a row. Personal disposable income is the amount of income a person has after taxes. It includes income from wages, dividends, and interest but also income from welfare payments, unemployment insurance, and Social Security payments. The inflation rate is the general increase in prices. The last variable, a measure of how long the incumbent party has been in power, reduces a party's vote share. Voters seem to get tired or disillusioned with a party the longer it has been in power, so there is a natural tendency for the presidency to switch parties even if all else remains the same.

Figure 21.1 tells us that voters are responsive to economic conditions, but more deeply it tells us that voters are surprisingly responsive to economic conditions *in the year of an election*. Voters are myopic—they don't look at economic conditions over a president's entire term. Instead, they focus on what is close at hand, namely economic conditions in the year of an election. Politicians who want to be reelected, therefore, are wise to do whatever they can to increase personal disposable income and reduce inflation in the year of an election even if this means decreases in income and increases in inflation at other times. Is there evidence that politicians behave in this way? Yes.

One of the most brazen examples comes from President Richard Nixon. Just two weeks before the 1972 election, he sent a letter to more than 24 million recipients of Social Security benefits. President Nixon's letter read:

Higher Social Security Payments

Your social security payment has been increased by 20 percent, starting with this month's check, by a new statute enacted by Congress and signed into law by President Richard Nixon on July 1, 1972.

The President also signed into law a provision that will allow your social security benefits to increase automatically if the cost of living goes up. Automatic benefit increases will be added to your check in future years according to the conditions set out in the law.

Of course, higher Social Security payments must be funded with higher taxes, but Nixon timed things so that the increase in payments started in October but the increase in taxes didn't begin until January, that is, not until after the election! Nixon was thus able to shift benefits and costs so that the benefits hit before the election and the costs hit after the election.

To be fair, President Nixon's policies were not unique or even unusual. Government benefits of all kinds typically increase before an election while taxes hardly ever do—taxes increase only after an election!

Using 60 years of U.S. data, Figure 21.2 shows the growth rate in personal disposable income in each quarter of a president's 16-quarter term. Growth is much higher in the year before an election than at any other time in a president's term. In fact, in an election year personal disposable income grows on average by 3.01% compared with 1.79% in a nonelection year. The difference is probably not due to chance.

Inflation also follows a cyclical pattern, but since voters dislike inflation, it tends to decrease in the year of an election and increase after the election. These patterns have been observed in many other countries, not just the United States. We also see political patterns at lower levels of politics. Mayors and governors, for example, try to increase the number of police on the streets in an election year, so that crime will fall and people will feel safer.

FIGURE 21.2

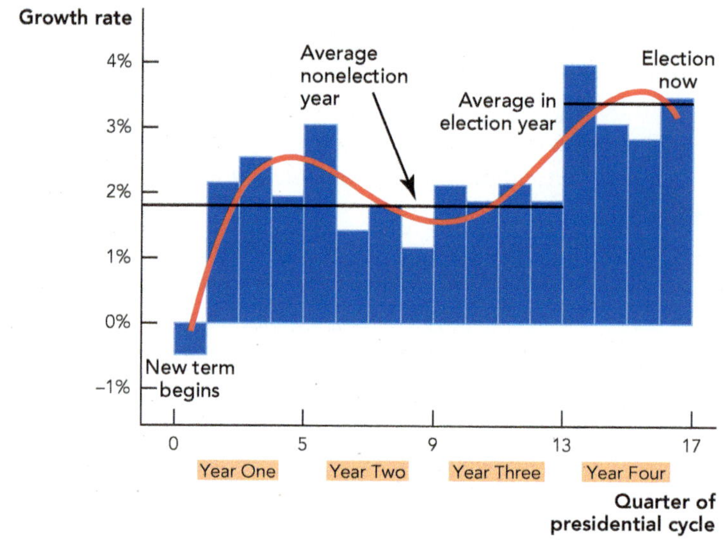

Growth in Disposable Personal Income Peaks in an Election Year, 1947–2007

Data from: Bureau of Economic Analysis.

- If voters are myopic, will politicians prefer a policy with small gains now and big costs later, or a policy with small costs now but big gains later?

There are a limited number of things that a president can do to influence the economy, so presidents do not always succeed in increasing income during an election year. Presidents can influence transfers and taxes much more readily than they can influence pure economic growth. This is one reason why cyclical patterns are more difficult to see in GDP statistics than they are in personal disposable income.

Two Cheers for Democracy

You might be wondering by now: Why isn't everything from the federal government handed out to special interest groups, and why aren't politicians always reelected? Do the voters ever get their way? In fact, voters in a democracy can be very powerful. If you want to think about when voters matter most and when lobbies and special interests matter most, turn to the idea of incentives.

When a policy is specialized in its impact, difficult to understand, and affects a small part of the economy, it is likely that special interests get their way. Let's say the question is whether the depreciation deduction in the investment tax credit should be accelerated or decelerated. This issue is important to many powerful corporations, but you can expect that most voters have never heard of the issue and so it will be settled behind closed doors by a relatively small number of people.

But when a policy is highly visible, appears often in the news and on social media, and has a major effect on the lives of millions of Americans, the voters are likely to have an opinion. The point isn't that voter opinions are always well informed or rational, but that voters do care about some of the biggest issues such as Social Security, Medicare, and taxes and when they do care, politicians have an incentive to serve them. But how exactly does voter opinion translate into policy? After all, opinions are divided, so which voters will get their way in a democracy?

The Median Voter Theorem

To answer this question, we develop a model of voting called the "median voter model." Imagine that there are five voters, each of whom has an opinion about the ideal amount of spending on Social Security. Max wants the least spending, followed by Sofia, Inez, Peter, and finally Alex, who wants the most spending. In Figure 21.3, we plot each voter's ideal policy along a line from least to most spending. We also assume that each voter will vote for the candidate whose policy position is closest to his or her ideal point.

The median voter is defined as the voter such that half of the other voters want more spending and half want less spending. In this case, the median voter is Inez, since compared with Inez, half of the voters (Peter and Alex) want more spending and half the voters (Max and Sofia) want less spending.

The **median voter theorem** says that under these conditions, the median voter rules! Or more formally, the median voter theorem says that when voters vote for the policy that is closest to their ideal point on a line, then the ideal point of the median voter will beat any other policy in a majority rule election.

Let's see why this is true and, as a result, how democracy will tend to push politicians toward the ideal point of the median voter. First, consider any two policies such as those adopted by Candidate D and Candidate R. Which policy will win in a majority rule election? Max and Sofia will vote for Candidate D since D's policy is closer to their ideal point than R's policy. But Inez, Peter, and Alex will vote for Candidate R. By majority rule, Candidate R will win the election. Notice that, of the two policies offered, the policy closest to that of the median voter's ideal policy won the election.

Most politicians don't like to lose. So in the next election Candidate D may shift her position, becoming Candidate D'. By exactly the same reasoning as before, Candidate D' will now win the election. If we repeat this process, the

> The **median voter theorem** says that when voters vote for the policy that is closest to their ideal point on a line, then the ideal point of the median voter will beat any other policy in a majority rule election.

FIGURE 21.3

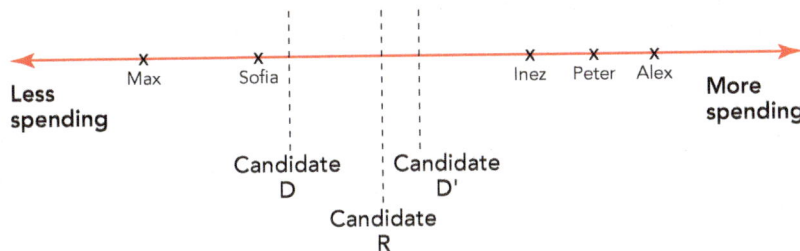

The Median Voter Theorem Each voter has an ideal policy, marked by an x, on the less-to-more spending line. Voters will vote for the candidate whose policy is closest to their ideal. The median voter is the voter such that half of the other voters want more spending and half of the other voters want less spending—Inez is the median voter. Under majority rule, the ideal policy of the median voter will beat any other policy. Consider any two candidate policies, such as those of Candidate D and Candidate R. Candidate D will receive two votes (Max and Sofia) and Candidate R will receive three votes (Inez, Peter, and Alex). But Candidate R's position can be beaten by a policy even closer to the ideal policy of the median voter, such as that of Candidate D'. Over time, competition pushes both candidates toward the ideal policy of the median voter, which is the only policy that cannot be beaten.

only policy that is not a *sure loser* is the ideal point of the median voter (Inez). As Candidates D and R converge on the ideal point of the median voter, there will be little difference between them and each will have a 50% chance of winning the election.*

The median voter theorem can be interpreted quite generally. Instead of thinking about less spending and more spending on Social Security, we can interpret the line as the standard political spectrum of left to right. In this case, the median voter theorem can be interpreted as a theory of democracy in a country such as the United States where there are just two major parties.

The median voter theorem tells us that in a democracy, what counts are noses—the number of voters—and not their positions per se. Imagine, for example, that Max decided he wanted even less spending or that Alex decided he wanted even more spending. Would the political outcome change? No. According to the median voter theorem, the median voter rules, and if the median voter doesn't change, then neither does policy. Thus, under the conditions given by the median voter theorem, democracy does not seek out consensus or compromise or a policy that maximizes voter preferences, on average—it seeks out a policy that cannot be beaten in a majority rule election.

The median voter theorem does not always apply. The most important assumption we made was that voters will vote for the policy that is closest to their ideal point. That's not necessarily true. If no candidate offers a policy close to Max's ideal point, he may refuse to vote for anyone, not even the candidate whose policy is (slightly) closer to his own ideal. In this case, a candidate who moves too far away from the voters on her wing may lose votes even if her position moves closer to that of the median voter. As a result, this type of voter behavior means that candidates do not necessarily converge on the ideal point of the median voter.

We have also assumed that there is just one major dimension over which voting takes place. That's not necessarily true either. Suppose that voters care about two issues, such as taxes and war, and assume that we cannot force both issues into a left-right spectrum (so knowing a person's views about taxes doesn't necessarily predict much about his or her views about war). With two voting dimensions, it's very likely that there is *no* policy that beats every other policy in a majority rule contest, so politics may never converge on a stable policy.

To understand why a winning policy sometimes doesn't exist, consider an analogy from sports. Imagine holding a series of (hypothetical) boxing matches to figure out who is the greatest heavyweight boxer of all time. Suppose that Muhammad Ali beats Lennox Lewis and Lewis beats Mike Tyson but Tyson beats Muhammad Ali. So who is the greatest of all time? The question may have no answer if there is more than one dimension to boxing skill, so Ali has the skills needed to beat Lewis and Lewis has the skills needed to beat Tyson, but Tyson has the skills to beat Ali. In a similar way, when there is more than one dimension to politics, no policy may exist that beats every other policy. In terms of politics, the result may be that every vote or election brings a new winner, or alternatively, constitutions and procedural restrictions may slow down the rate of political change. The U.S. Constitution, for example, requires

---

* In terms of the game theory, the ideal policy of the median voter is the only policy that cannot be beaten by another policy and thus the only Nash equilibrium of a two-candidate game is for both candidates to choose this policy.

that new legislation must pass two houses of Congress and evade the president's veto, which is more difficult than passing a simple majority rule vote.

As a predictive theory of politics, the median voter theorem is applicable in some but not all circumstances. The theorem, however, does remind us that politicians have substantial incentives to listen to voters on issues that the voters care about. This is a powerful feature of democracy, although the quality of the democracy you get will depend on the wisdom of the voters behind it.

Democracy and Nondemocracy

Our picture of democracy so far has been a little disillusioning, at least compared with what you might have learned in high school civics. Yet when we look around the world, democracies tend to be the wealthiest countries, and despite the power of special interests, they also tend to be the countries with the best record of supporting markets, property rights, the rule of law, fair government, and other institutions that support economic growth.

Figure 21.4 graphs an index meant to capture good economic policy, called the economic freedom index (with higher numbers indicating greater economic freedom), on the horizontal axis against a measure of the standard of living on the vertical axis (gross national income per capita in 2007). The figure shows two things. First, there is a strong correlation between economic freedom and a higher standard of living. Second, the countries that are most democratic (full democracies are shown in red) are among the wealthiest counties in the world and the countries with the most economic freedom. The only interesting exceptions to this rule are Singapore and Hong Kong; both score very highly on economic freedom and the standard of living, but are not quite full democracies. (Hong Kong even less so today.)

Notice, however, that in part there is an association between democracy and the standard of living because greater wealth creates a greater demand for democracy. When citizens have satisfied their basic needs for food, shelter, and security, they demand more cerebral goods, such as the right to participate in the political process. This is exactly what happened in South Korea and Taiwan,

FIGURE 21.4

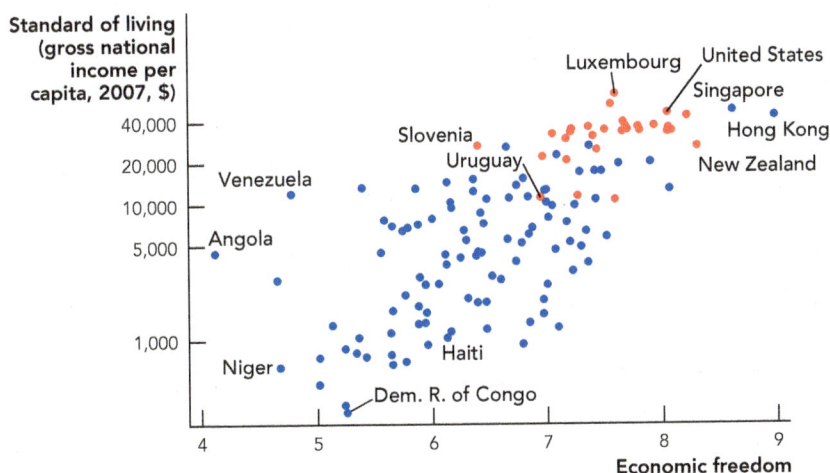

Economic Freedom, Democracy, and Living Standards

Note: GNI per capita on ratio scale.
Note: Full democracies are in red.

Data from: Economic freedom index from Gwartney, J., R. Lawson, and S. Norton. 2008. *Economic Freedom of the World: 2008 Annual Report.* Vancouver, BC: The Fraser Institute. Gross national income per capita (2007) from the World Bank.

two countries that became more democratic as they grew wealthier. Many people predicted that China would become a more democratic country as it grew wealthier; so far that does not seem to be the case. But it's not just that wealth brings democracy. Democracy also seems to bring wealth and favorable institutions. Democracies must be doing something right. We therefore need to examine some of the benefits of democratic decision making.

We've already discussed rational ignorance under democracy, but keep in mind that public ignorance is often worse in nondemocracies.[5] In many quasi democracies and in nondemocracies, the public is not well informed because the media are controlled or censored by the government.

In Africa, for example, most countries have traditionally banned private television stations. In fact as of 2000, 71% of African countries had a state monopoly on television broadcasting. Most African governments also control the largest newspapers in the country. Government ownership and control of the media are also common in most Middle Eastern countries and, of course, the former Communist countries controlled the media extensively.

Control of the media has exactly the effects that we would expect from our study of rational ignorance in democracies—it enables special interests to control the government for their own ends. Greater government ownership of the press, for example, is associated with lower levels of political rights and civil liberties, worse regulation (more policies like price controls that economists think are ineffective and wasteful), higher levels of corruption, and a greater risk of property confiscation. The authors of an important study of media ownership conclude that "government ownership of the press restricts information flows to the public, which reduces the quality of the government."[6]

Citizens in democracies may be "rationally ignorant," but on the whole they are much better informed about their governments than citizens in quasi democracies and nondemocracies. Moreover, in a democracy, citizens can use their knowledge to influence public policy at low cost by voting. In a democracy, knowledge is power. In nondemocracies, knowledge alone is not enough because intimidation and government violence create steep barriers to political participation. Many people just give up or become cynical. Other citizens in nondemocracies fall prey to propaganda and come to accept the regime's portrait of itself as a great friend of the people.

The importance of knowledge and the power to vote for bringing about better outcomes is illustrated by the shocking history of mass starvation.

Democracy and Famine

At first glance, the cause of famine seems obvious—a lack of food. Yet the obvious explanation is wrong or at least drastically incomplete. Mass starvations have occurred during times of plenty, and even when lack of food is a contributing factor, it is rarely the determining factor of whether mass starvation occurs.

Many of the famines in recent world history have been intentional. When Stalin came to power in 1924 in the Soviet Union, for example, he saw the Ukrainians, particularly the relatively wealthy independent farmers known as kulaks, to be a threat. Stalin collectivized the farms and expropriated the land of the kulaks, turning them out of their homes and sending hundreds of thousands to gulag prisons in Siberia.

Agricultural productivity in Ukraine plummeted under forced collectivization and people began to starve. Nevertheless, Stalin continued to ship food out of Ukraine. Peasants who tried to escape starving regions were arrested or turned back at the border by Stalin's secret police. Desperate Ukrainians ate dogs, cats, and even tree bark. Millions died.[7]

The starvation of Ukraine was intentional and it's clear that it would not have happened in a democracy. Stalin did not need the votes of the Ukrainians and thus they had little power to influence policy. Democratically elected politicians will not ignore the votes of millions of people.

Even unintentional mass starvations can be avoided in democracies. The 1974 famine in Bangladesh was not on the scale of that in Ukraine, but still 26,000 to 100,000 people died of mass starvation. It was probably the first televised starvation, and it illustrates some important themes in the relationship between economics and politics.

Floods destroyed much of the rice crop of 1974 at the same time as world rice prices were increasing for other reasons. The flood meant that there was no work for landless rural laborers who in ordinary years would have been employed harvesting the rice.

The lower income from work and the higher rice prices, taken together, led to starvations. Yet in 1974, Bangladesh in the aggregate did not lack for food. In fact, food per capita in 1974 was at an all-time high, as shown in Figure 21.5.

Mass starvation occurred not because of a lack of food per se, but because a poor group of laborers lacked both economic and political power. Lack of economic power meant they could not purchase food. Lack of political power meant that the elites then running Bangladesh were not compelled to avert the famine. Bangladesh continued to pursue bad economic policies; for instance, government regulations made it very difficult to purchase foreign exchange so it wasn't easy for capitalists to import rice from nearby Thailand or India. In fact, rice was even being smuggled out of Bangladesh and into India to avoid price controls and other regulations.

Amartya Sen, the Nobel Prize–winning economist and philosopher, has argued that "no famine has taken place in the history of the world in a functioning democracy." The precise claim can be disputed depending on how one defines "functioning democracy" but the lesson Sen draws is correct:

> Perhaps the most important reform that can contribute to the elimination of famines, in Africa as well as in Asia, is the enhancement of democratic practice, unfettered newspapers and—more generally—adversarial politics.[8]

Economists Timothy Besley and Robin Burgess have tested Sen's theory of democracy, newspapers, and famine relief in India.[9] India is a federal democracy with 16 major states. The states vary considerably in their susceptibility to food crises, newspaper circulation, education, political competition, and other factors.

Besley and Burgess ask whether state governments are more responsive to food crises when there is more political competition and more newspapers. Note that both of these factors are important. Newspapers won't work without political competition and political competition won't work without newspapers. Knowledge and power together make the difference.

FIGURE 21.5

Food availability index

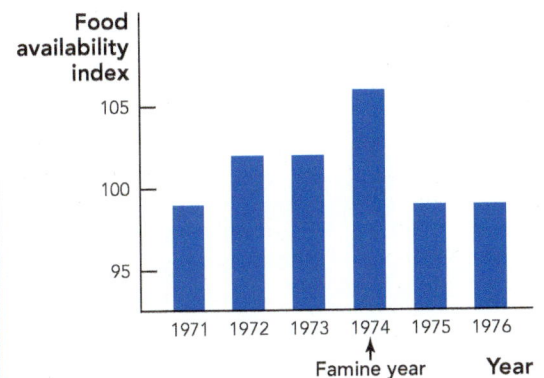

Food Availability per Head in Bangladesh

Data from: Sen, Amartya. 1990. Public Action to Remedy Hunger. Arturo Tanco Memorial Lecture given in London on August 25, 1990.

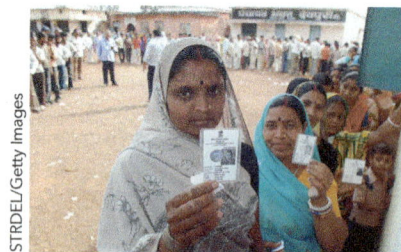 +  =

Democracy, newspapers, and famine relief

Besley and Burgess find that greater political competition is associated with higher levels of public food distribution. Public food distribution is especially responsive in election and preelection years. In addition, as Sen's theory predicts, government is more responsive to a crisis in food availability when newspaper circulation is higher. That is, when food production falls or flood damage occurs, governments increase food distribution and calamity relief more in states where newspaper circulation is higher. Newspapers and free media inform the public and spur politicians to action.

Notice that there is nothing special about democratic politicians. Democratic politicians may also ignore the public. It's only when democratic politicians face the right incentives due to competitive elections and good information that their incentives become more aligned with the social good.

Democracy and Growth

Democracies have a good record of not killing their own citizens or letting them starve to death. Not killing your own citizens or letting them starve may seem like rather a low standard, but many governments have failed to meet this standard so we count this accomplishment as a serious one favoring democracies. Democracies also have a relatively good record of supporting markets, property rights, the rule of law, fair government, and other institutions that promote economic growth, as shown in Figure 21.4.

One reason for the good record of democracies on economic growth may be that the *only* way the public as a whole can become rich is by supporting efficient policies that generate economic growth. In contrast, small (nondemocratic) elites can become rich by dividing the pie in their favor even if it means making the pie smaller.

Recall the special interest group that we discussed earlier that made up 1% of the population. Consider a policy that transfers $100 to the special interest group at a cost of $4,000 to society. Will the group lobby for the policy? Yes, because the group gets $100 in benefits but it bears only $40 of the costs (1% of $4,000).

By definition, oligarchies or quasi democracies are ruled by small groups. Thus, the rulers in these countries don't have much incentive to pay attention to the larger costs of their policies as borne by the broader public. The ruling elites may even have incentives to promote and maintain policies that keep their nations poor. An entrenched, nondemocratic elite, for example, might not want to support mass education. Not only would a more educated populace compete with the elite, but an informed people might decide that they don't need the elite and, of course, the elite know this. As a result, the elites will often want to keep the masses weak and uninformed, neither of which is good for economic growth or, for that matter, preventing starvation.

But now let's think about a special interest group that represents 20% of society. Will this special interest favor a policy that transfers $100 to it at a cost of $4,000 to society? No. The special interest group receives $100 in benefits from the transfer but its share of the costs is now $800 (20% of $4,000), so the policy is a net loser even for the special interest. Thus, the larger the group, the greater the group's incentives to take into account the social costs of inefficient policies.

Large groups are more concerned about the cost to society of their policies simply because they make up a large fraction of society. Thus, large groups tend to favor more efficient policies. In addition, the more numerous the group in charge, the less lucrative transfers are as a way to get rich. A small group has a big incentive to take $1 from 300 million people and transfer it to themselves. But a group of 100 million that takes $1 from each of the remaining 200 million gets only $2 per person. Even if you took 100 times as much, $100, from each of the 200 million people and gave it to the 100 million, that's only $200 each. Pretty small pickings. It's usually better for a large group to focus on policies that increase the total size of the pie.

In other words, the greater the share of the population that is brought into power, the more likely that policies will offer something for virtually everybody, and not just riches for a small elite.

The tendency for larger groups to favor economic growth is no guarantee of perfect or ideal policies, of course. As we have seen, rational ignorance can cause trouble. But on the big questions, a democratic leader simply will not want to let things become too bad. That's a big reason why democracies tend to be pretty good—although not perfect—for economic growth.

CHECK YOURSELF

• The free flow of ideas helps markets to function. How does the free flow of ideas help democracies to function?

Takeaway

Incentives matter, so a good institution aligns self-interest with the social interest. Does democracy align self-interest with the social interest? Sometimes. On the negative side, voters in a democracy have too little incentive to be informed about political matters. Voters are rationally ignorant because the benefits of being informed are small—if you are informed, you are more likely to choose wisely at the polls, but your vote doesn't appreciably increase the probability that society will choose wisely, so why bother to be informed? Being informed creates an external benefit because your informed vote benefits everyone, but goods with external benefits are underprovided.

Rational ignorance means that special interests can dominate parts of the political process. By concentrating benefits and diffusing costs, politicians can often build political support for themselves even when their policies generate more costs than benefits. And special interests can also block good policies when costs are concentrated and benefits diffused.

Incumbent politicians can use their control of the government to increase the probability that they will be reelected. Politicians typically increase spending before an election and increase taxes only after the election. Voters pay attention to current economic conditions even when the prosperity is temporarily and artificially enhanced at the expense of future economic conditions.

Our study of political economy can usefully be considered a study of government failure that complements the theory of market failure due to externalities and monopoly. When markets fail to align self-interest with the social interest, we get market failure. When the institutions of government fail to align self-interest with the social interest, we get government failure. No institutions are perfect and trade-offs are everywhere—this is a key lesson when thinking about markets and government.

A close look at democracy can be disillusioning, but the record of democracies on some of the big issues is quite good. It's hard for politicians in a democracy to ignore the major interests of voters. And if things do go wrong, voters in a democracy can always "throw the bums out" and start again with new ideas. Partially as a result, democracies have a good record on averting mass famines, maintaining civil liberties like free speech, and supporting economic growth. Most of all, democracies tend not to kill their own citizens, who after all are potential voters.

CHAPTER REVIEW

Go online to practice with more examples of these types of problems, including live links to videos, data sources, and feedback.

Problems with this icon relate to optional MRU videos.

KEY CONCEPTS

public choice, p. 475

rational ignorance, p. 476

median voter theorem, p. 485

FACTS AND TOOLS

1. Which of the following is the smallest fraction of the U.S. federal budget? Which are the two largest categories of federal spending?

   Welfare

   Interest on the federal debt

   Defense

   Foreign aid

   Social Security

   Health care

2. **a.** How many famines have occurred in functioning democracies?

   b. What percentage of famines occurred in countries without functioning democracies?

3. Around 138 million voters participated in the 2016 U.S. presidential election. Imagine that you are deciding whether to vote in the next presidential election. What do you think is the probability that your vote will determine the outcome of the election? Is it greater than 1%, between 1% and 0.1%, between 0.1% and 0.01%, or less than 0.01% (i.e., less than 1 in 10,000)?

4. If a particular government policy—like a decision to go to war or to raise taxes—works only when citizens are informed, is that an argument for that policy or against that policy?

5. True or false?

a. During Bangladesh's worst famine, average food per person was much lower than usual.

b. Democracies are less likely to kill their own citizens than other kinds of governments.

c. Surprisingly, newspapers aren't that important for informing voters about hungry citizens.

d. Compared with a dictatorship or oligarchy, democracies have a stronger incentive to make the economic pie bigger.

e. Compared with most other countries, full democracies tend to put a lot of restrictions on markets and property rights.

f. When it comes to disposable income, American presidents seem to prefer "making a good first impression" rather than "going out with a bang."

g. When the government owns most of the TV and radio stations, it's motivated to serve the public interest, so voters tend to get better, less biased information.

6. The median voter theorem is sometimes called the "pivotal voter theorem." This is actually a fairly good way to think of the theorem. Why?

7. Perhaps it was in elementary school that you first realized that if everyone in the world gave you a penny, you'd become fantastically rich. This insight is at the core of modern politics. Sort the following government policies into "concentrated benefits" and "diffuse benefits."

a. Social Security

b. Tax cuts for families

c. Social Security Disability Insurance for the severely disabled

d. National Park Service spending for remote trails

e. National Park Service spending on the National Mall in Washington, D.C.

f. Tax cuts for people making more than $250,000 per year

g. Sugar quotas

THINKING AND PROBLEM SOLVING

8. David Mayhew's classic book *Congress: The Electoral Connection* argued that members of Congress face strong incentives to put most of their efforts into highly visible activities like foreign travel and ribbon-cutting ceremonies, instead of actually running the government. How does the rational ignorance of *voters* explain why *politicians* put so much effort into these highly visible activities?

9. An initiative on Arizona's 2006 ballot would have handed out a $1 million lottery prize every election: The only way to enter the lottery would be to vote in a primary or general election. How do you think a lottery like this would influence voter ignorance?

10. We mentioned that voters are myopic, mostly paying attention to how the economy is doing in the few months before a presidential election. If they want to be rational, what should they do instead? In particular, should they pay attention to all four years of the economy, just the first year, just the last two years, or some other combination?

11. In his book *The Myth of the Rational Voter*, our GMU colleague Bryan Caplan argues that not only can voters be rationally ignorant, they can even be rationally irrational. People in general seem to *enjoy* believing in some types of false ideas. If this is true, then they won't challenge their own beliefs unless the cost of holding these beliefs is high. Instead, they'll enjoy their delusion.

Let's consider two examples:

a. John has watched a lot of Bruce Lee movies and likes to think that he is a champion of the martial arts who can whip any other man in a fight. One night, John is in a bar and he gets into a dispute with another man. Will John act on his beliefs and act aggressively, or do you think he is more likely to rationally calculate the probability of injury and seek to avoid confrontation?

b. John has watched a lot of war movies and likes to think that his country is a champion of the military arts that can whip any other country in a fight. John's country gets into a dispute with another country. John and everyone else in his country go to the polls to vote on war. Will John act on his beliefs and vote for aggression, or do you think he is more likely to rationally calculate the probability of defeat and seek to avoid confrontation?

12. In the television show *Scrubs*, the main character J. D. is a competent and knowledgeable doctor. He also has very little information outside of the field of medicine, admitting he doesn't know the difference between a senator and a representative and believes New Zealand is near "Old Zealand."

a. Suppose J. D. spends some time learning some of these common facts. What benefits would he receive as a result? (Assume there are no benefits for the sake of knowledge itself.)

b. Suppose instead J. D. spends that time learning how to diagnose a rare disease that has a slight possibility of showing up in one of his patients. What benefits would he receive as a result? (Again, assume there are no benefits for the sake of knowledge itself.)

c. Make an *economic* argument that even given your answer to part b, voters have too little incentive to be informed about political matters.

13. Driving along America's interstates, you'll notice that few rest areas have commercial businesses. Vending machines are the only reliable source of food or drink, much to the annoyance of the weary traveler looking for a hot meal. Thank the National Association of Truck Stop Operators (NATSO), who consistently lobby the U.S. government to deny commercialization. They argue:

> Interchange businesses cannot compete with commercialized rest areas, which are conveniently located on the highway right-of-way . . . Rest area commercialization results in an unfair competitive environment for privately-operated interchange businesses and will ultimately destroy a successful economic business model that has proven beneficial for both consumers and businesses.[10]

The sorrow of a land without burgers

a. How does NATSO make travel more expensive for consumers?

b. Do you think most Americans have heard of NATSO and the legislation to commercialize rest stops? How does your answer illustrate rational ignorance? Do you think that the owners of interchange businesses (i.e., restaurants, gas stations, and other businesses located near but not on highways) have heard of NATSO?

c. Why does NATSO often succeed in its lobbying efforts despite your answer to part a? (*Hint:* What is the concentrated benefit in this story? What is the diffused cost?)

14. The following figure shows the political leanings of 101 voters. Voters will vote for the candidate who is closest to them on the spectrum, as in the typical median voter story. Again as usual, politicians compete against each other, entering the "political market" just as freely as firms enter the economic market.

a. Which group of voters will get their exact wish: the group on the left, the center-left, the center-right, or the right?

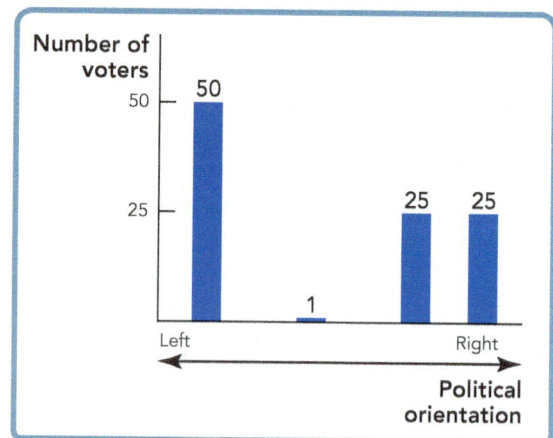

b. Now, four years later, it's time for a new election. Suppose that in the meantime, the two right-leaning groups of voters have merged: The 25 center-right voters move to the far right, forming a far-right coalition. In the new election, whose position will win now?

c. As you've just seen, there's a "pivotal voter" in this model. Who is it?

15. Let's rewrite a sentence from the chapter concerning the Roman Empire: "As the American Empire grew, courting politicians in Washington became a more secure path to riches than starting a new business." Does this seem true today? If it started happening, how would you be able to tell? In your answer, put some emphasis on market signals that could point in favor of or against the "decadent empire" theory. (*Hint:* By some measures, Moscow has the highest real estate prices in the world, and it's probably not due to low housing supply.)

CHALLENGES

16. Is rational ignorance the whole explanation for why voters allow programs like the sugar quota to persist? Perhaps not. In the early 1900s, the government of New York City was controlled by a Democratic Party organization known as Tammany Hall. In a delightful essay entitled "Honest Graft and Dishonest Graft" by George Plunkitt, one of the most successful politicians from the Tammany machine, Plunkitt argued that voters actually approve of these kinds of government-granted favors. (The essay and the entire book, *Plunkitt of Tammany Hall: A Series of Very Plain Talks on Very Practical Politics*, are available for free online.)

For example, Plunkitt said that ordinary voters like it when government workers get paid more than the market wage: "The Wall Street banker thinks it is shameful to raise a [government] clerk's salary from $1,500 to $1,800, but every man who draws a salary himself says, 'That's all right. I wish it was me.' And he feels very much like votin' the Tammany ticket on election day, just out of sympathy."

a. Plunkitt said this in the early 1900s. Do you think this is more true today than it was back then, or less true? Why?

b. If more Americans knew about the sugar quota, do you think they would be outraged? Or would they approve, saying, "That's all right, I wish it was me"? Why?

c. Overall, do you think that real-world voters prefer a party that gives special favors to narrow groups, even if those voters aren't in the favored group? Why?

17. a. When a drought hits a country, and a famine is possible, what probably falls more: the demand for food or the demand for haircuts? Why?

b. Who probably suffers more from a deep drought: people who own farms or people who own barbershops? (*Note:* The answer is on page 164 of economist Amartya Sen's summary of his life's work, *Development as Freedom, 1999.*)

c. Sen emphasizes that "lack of buying power" is more important during a famine than "lack of food." How does Sen's barber story illustrate this?

18. Political scientist Jeffrey Friedman and law professor Ilya Somin say that since voters are largely ignorant, that is an argument for keeping government simple. Government, they say, should stick to a few basic tasks. That way, rationally ignorant voters can keep track of their government by simply catching a few bits of the news between reruns of *Modern Family*.

a. What might such a government look like? In particular, what policies and programs are too complicated for today's voters to easily monitor? Just consider the U.S. federal government in your answer.

b. Which current government programs and policies are fairly easy for modern voters to monitor? What programs do you think that you and your family have a good handle on?

c. Can you think of easy replacements for the too complex programs in part a? For instance, cutting one check per farmer and posting the amount on a Web site might be easier to monitor than the hundreds of farm subsidies and low-interest farm loans that exist today.

19. We mentioned that the median voter theorem doesn't always work, and sometimes a winning policy doesn't exist. This fact has driven economists and political scientists to write thousands of papers and books, both proving that fact and trying to find good workarounds. The most famous theoretical example of how voting doesn't work is the Condorcet paradox. The Marquis de Condorcet, a French nobleman in the 1700s, wondered what would happen if three voters had the preferences like the ones in the following table. Three friends are holding a vote to see which French economist they should read in their study group. Here are their preferences:

	Jean	Marie	Claude
1st choice	Walras	Bastiat	Say
2nd choice	Bastiat	Say	Walras
3rd choice	Say	Walras	Bastiat

a. They vote by majority rule. If the vote is Walras vs. Say, who will win? Say vs. Bastiat? Bastiat vs. Walras?

b. They decide to vote in a single-elimination tournament: Two votes and the winner of the first round proceeds on to the final round. This is the way many sporting events and legislatures work. Now, suppose that Jean is in charge of deciding in which order to hold the votes. He wants to make sure that his favorite, Walras, wins the final vote. How should he stack the order of voting to make sure Walras wins?

c. Now, suppose that Claude is in charge instead: How would Claude stack the votes?

d. And Marie? Comment on the importance of being the agenda setter.

(In case you think these examples are unusual, they're not. Any kind of voting that involves dividing a fixed number of dollars can easily wind up the same way—check for yourself! Condorcet himself experienced another form of democratic failure: He died in prison, a victim of the French Revolution that he supported.)

20. In the previous question, you showed that sometimes there may be no policy that beats every other policy in a majority rule election and, as a result, the agenda can determine the outcome. In the previous question, all of the policy choices on the agenda were as good as any other, but this is not always the case. Imagine that three voters, L, M, and R, are choosing among seven candidates. The preferences of the voters are given in the following table. Voter M, for example, likes Grumpy the best and Doc the least.

Preferences for President of Voters L, M, R

	Voter L	Voter M	Voter R
1st Choice	Happy	Grumpy	Dopey
2nd Choice	Sneezy	Dopey	Happy
3rd Choice	Grumpy	Happy	Sleepy
4th Choice	Dopey	Bashful	Sneezy
5th Choice	Doc	Sleepy	Grumpy
6th Choice	Bashful	Sneezy	Doc
7th Choice	Sleepy	Doc	Bashful

a. Imagine that we vote according to a given agenda starting with Happy vs. Dopey. Who wins? We will help you with this one. Voter L ranks Happy above Dopey, so voter L will vote for Happy. Voter M prefers Dopey to Happy, so voter M will vote for Dopey. Voter R ranks Dopey above Happy so voter R will vote for Dopey. So _____ wins.

b. Now take the winner from part a and match him against Grumpy. Who wins?

c. Now take the winner from part b and match him against Sneezy. Who wins?

d. Now take the winner from part c and match him against Sleepy. Who wins?

e. Now take the winner from part d and match him against Bashful. Who wins?

f. Finally, take the winner from part e and match him against Doc. Who wins?

g. We have now run through the entire agenda so the winner from part f is the final winner. Here is the point. Look carefully at the preferences of the three voters. Compare the preferences of each voter for Happy (or Grumpy or Dopey) with the final winner. Fill in the blank: Majority rule has led to an outcome that _____ voter regards as worse than some other possible outcome. The answer to this question should shock you.

(This question is drawn from the classic and highly recommended introduction to game theory, *Thinking Strategically* by Avinash K. Dixit and Barry J. Nalebuff [New York: Norton, 1993].)

21. In the 1998 Minnesota gubernatorial election, there were three main candidates: Norm Coleman (the Republican), Jesse "The Body" Ventura (an Independent), and Hubert Humphrey III (the Democrat). Although we can't know for certain, the voters probably ranked the candidates in a way similar to that found in the following table. The table tells us, for example, that 35% of the voters ranked Coleman first, Humphrey second, and Ventura third; and 20% of the voters ranked Ventura first, Coleman second, and Humphrey third; and so forth.

Minnesota Gubernatorial Election, 1998

Rank	35%	28%	20%	17%
1	Coleman	Humphrey	Ventura	Ventura
2	Humphrey	Coleman	Coleman	Humphrey
3	Ventura	Ventura	Humphrey	Coleman

a. Suppose the election is by plurality rule, which means that the candidate with the most first-place votes wins the election. Who wins in this case?

b. In Challenges question 19, you were introduced to the Marquis de Condorcet. Today, voting theorists call a candidate a Condorcet *winner* if he or she can beat every other candidate in a series of 1:1 or *"face-off"* elections. Question 19 showed you that in some cases, there is no Condorcet winner. What about in the Minnesota gubernatorial election of 1998?

c. A Condorcet winner beats every other candidate in a face-off. A Condorcet loser loses to every other candidate in a face-off. Was there a Condorcet loser in the 1998 Minnesota gubernatorial election (given the preferences we have estimated)?

Jesse "The Body" Ventura
Who are you calling a loser?

WORK IT OUT

For interactive, step-by-step help in solving this problem, go online.

Let's walk through the median voter theorem in a little more detail. Consider a town with three voters, Enrique, Nandini, and Torsten. The big issue in the upcoming election is how high the sales tax rate should be. As you'll learn in macroeconomics (and in real life), on average, a government that wants to do more spending has to bring in more taxes, so "higher permanent taxes" is the same as "higher government spending." Enrique wants low taxes and small government, Nandini is in the middle, and Torsten wants

the biggest town government of the three. Each one is a stubborn person, and his or her favorite position—what economic theorists call the "ideal point"—never changes in this problem. Their preferences can be summed up like this, with the x denoting each person's favorite tax rate:

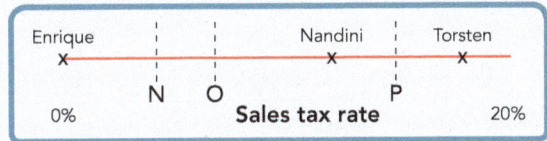

a. Suppose there are two politicians running for office, N and O. Who will vote for N? Who will vote for O? Which candidate will win the election?

b. O drops out of the campaign after the local paper reports that he hasn't paid his sales taxes in years. P enters the race, pushing for higher taxes, so it's N vs. P. Voters prefer the candidate who is closest to them, as in the text. Who will vote for N? Who will vote for P? Who will win? Who will lose?

c. In part b, you decided who was heading for a loss. You get a job as the campaign manager for this candidate just a month before election day. You advise her to retool her campaign and come up with a new position on the sales tax. Of course, in politics as in life, there's more than one way to win, so give your boss a choice: Provide her with two different positions on the sales tax, both of which would beat the would-be winner from part b. She'll make the final pick herself.

d. Are the two options you recommended in part c closer to the median voter's preferred option than the loser's old position, or are they further away? So in this case, is the median voter theorem roughly true or roughly false?

MRU VIDEOS

Democracy and Famines

mru.org/seniii-democracy-and-famines

Problems: **2, 5**

APPENDIX B

Solutions to Check Yourself Questions

Here are suggested answers to the Check Yourself questions found within the chapters.

Chapter 2

Page 21

1. Specialization increases productivity because it increases knowledge.

2. If people can't trade for other goods, they won't specialize in producing just one good. Thus, trade is necessary if people are to benefit from specialization.

3. Usain Bolt has a comparative advantage in running, but Harry has a comparative advantage in mowing Usain's lawn because Harry faces a much lower opportunity cost in mowing lawns than Usain Bolt does.

Chapter 3

Page 35

The operating system for smartphones is a complement to Google's search and advertising business. Free smartphone software, therefore, increases the demand for Google's primary product, advertising.

Page 36

1. A rise in the income of Indian workers will lead to an increase in the demand for automobiles. At first as income rises, workers may demand more charcoal bricks for heating, but charcoal bricks are a dangerous and unpleasant way to heat a home, so as income increases beyond a certain level,

workers will demand fewer charcoal bricks. Thus, a good can be a normal good over some levels of income and an inferior good over other (usually higher) levels of income.

2. As the price of oil rises, some people will substitute mopeds for automobiles so the demand for mopeds will increase.

Page 44

1. Improvements in chip-making technology have driven down the costs of this input so the supply of computers increases, meaning that the supply curve for computers shifts to the right and down.

2. The ethanol subsidy lowers the cost of producing ethanol, therefore increasing the supply of ethanol (the supply curve for ethanol shifts to the right and down).

Chapter 4

Page 53

1. If the demand for large trucks and SUVs falls unexpectedly, auto companies will find that at the current price they have a surplus of trucks and SUVs. The quantity supplied is greater than the quantity demanded, so they will lower prices in order to sell already manufactured trucks and SUVs.

2. Sellers have produced too many clothes if they have them available at outlet malls where price discounts are the norm. Sellers are cutting their prices to reduce the surplus and move the clothes out the door.

Page 56

1. As the price of cars goes up, the least-valued wants will be the first to stop being satisfied. For example, parents may be more reluctant to buy their teenage sons and daughters a new automobile.

2. If telecommunication firms overinvest in fiber-optic cable, for example, they will have to lower the price of using fiber-optic lines. For example, a company such as Verizon will offer fiber-optic Internet and phone connections at discount prices. The ensuing losses from price cutting will dampen future investment in fiber-optic cable. More generally, firms invest in order to make a profit. If firms overinvest, they will take losses, which give them an incentive to invest carefully.

3. Kiran values the good at $50, and in a free market will buy it from store B for $35, earning a total consumer surplus of $15 ($50 − $35). If store B is prevented from selling, say by a regulation or a tax, then Kiran will buy from store A for $45, but total consumer surplus will fall to $5 ($50 − $45).

Page 60

1. If flooding destroys some of the corn and soybean crops, these crops will have a decrease in supply. This decrease in supply will lower the equilibrium quantity and increase the equilibrium price.

2. If resveratrol (from Japanese knotweed) increases life expectancy in fish, people might think it will have the same effect in humans, and so more people will demand it, increasing demand. This will increase the price of Japanese knotweed and lead to an increase in the quantity grown.

3. The demand for hybrid cars will increase as the price of gas increases, that is, the demand curve shifts to the right/up. We show this in Figure 4.7: Think of the New demand as the demand for hybrids when the price of gas is high, and the Old demand as the demand for hybrids when the price of gas is low. The price of hybrids will rise with an increase in demand, especially in the short run.

Page 64

1. The price of oil rose in 1991 primarily because of a supply shock, the Persian Gulf War. (It would also be okay to label this as a demand shock because the demand for oil increased when people expected that the war would reduce the future supply of oil.) Bonus points if you recognized both possibilities.

2. From 1981 to 1986, the price of oil fell steadily. The higher price in the preceding years encouraged exploration, which several years later led to increased supply, especially from non-OPEC sources.

Chapter 5
Page 82

1. Price ceilings set below equilibrium prices cause shortages. Price ceilings set above equilibrium prices have no effects.

2. A price control reduces the incentive to respond to shifts in demand, thus resources become misallocated according to essentially random factors. For example, it costs much more to ship oil from Alaskan oil fields to refineries on the East Coast than to those on the West Coast. Price ceilings did not let that difference become factored in the price, and therefore reduced the incentive to ship oil to where it was most needed, so shortages could be worse in some areas than in others.

Page 85

1. If landlords under rent control have an incentive to do only minimum upkeep, deteriorating buildings inevitably accompany rent control. Only major repairs are made. Tenants with dripping faucets may never get a response from landlords, and have to fix it themselves. At a minimum, they will have to wait, maybe until the drip becomes something larger and so has an effect on the landlord's water bill.

2. Vested interests will fight any attempt at rolling back rent control, and these vested interests become powerful over time. It's especially difficult to eliminate rent controls because tenants (people who already have an apartment) don't care much about the shortage—they do not have to find a new apartment every week. In contrast, buyers of gasoline have to deal with the shortage every time they need a fill-up so it may be easier to get rid of price controls on oil than on apartments.

Page 87

1. Price ceilings cause shortages. Universal price controls cause shortages across the economy, with no obvious pattern. Sometimes one product is in

abundance, at other times there are shortages. A rational response when there are products that face inexplicable shortages is to buy as much as possible when possible: buy as much toilet paper now because who knows when it will come available again? In other words, hoarding is a standard response to universal price controls. Hoarding is wasteful because it implies a misallocation of resources. Some people, for reasons of luck (or influence), may have a lot of toilet paper while others have none. If trade were allowed, people would experience gains from trade and products would gravitate to their highest-value uses.

2. The Soviet Union also faced surpluses of goods as well as shortages because under universal price controls there was no incentive to get products to the places at the times that they had the highest-value uses. As a result, goods would be misallocated and production and consumption would be chaotic. One week a farm might get enough oil to deliver its chickens to the city and in that week the city shops would get a lot of chickens as the farm dumped its accumulated stock. A few weeks later there might be no oil available and chickens would disappear from the shops.

Page 92

1. A price floor set above the equilibrium price leads to surpluses. Because the European Union price floor for butter is above the equilibrium price, the EU has created a surplus of butter, which the government must buy. The surplus has been so large that it has been called a butter mountain.

2. The U.S. price floor for milk, set above the equilibrium price, has led to a surplus of milk. The government has dealt with the surplus by buying the surplus and giving away milk and dairy products produced from milk (such as cheese) to schools. This accounts for the low or zero price you paid for milk at most schools.

Chapter 6
Page 104

GDP is 21.4 trillion. From Figure 26.2 about 68% of GDP is from services so finished goods are $21.4 * (1 − 0.68) = 6.8$ trillion of GDP.

Page 105

1. The purchase of wheat flour used to make bread is the purchase of an intermediate good. Thus, it is not counted in GDP: Only finished goods are counted in GDP.

2. Pokémon cards were counted in GDP when they were first produced. Selling used Pokemon cards on eBay does not contribute to GDP.

3. Because the worker from Colombia earns his money in New York, this is considered part of the GDP of the United States, not Colombia. GDP counts what is produced within a country, whether by its citizens or others.

Page 106

The growth rate is found by subtracting $5,803 billion from $5,995 billion, and then dividing that number by $5,803 billion:

$$(\$5,995 − \$5,803) ÷ \$5,803 = \$192 ÷ \$5,803 = 0.033, \text{ or } 3.3\%$$

Page 108

1. China has a high GDP but a low GDP per capita.

2. Of the top 10 countries ranked by GDP in Table 6.1, the United Kingdom and France have GDP under $2.5 trillion but have considerable GDP per capita.

3. We convert nominal variables into real variables to account for price changes so that we can make comparisons over time.

Page 110

1. Business fluctuations are the short-run movements in real GDP around its long-term trend.

2. It is sometimes difficult to determine if an economy is in a recession because of simple data problems. It takes time to collect data; then the conclusions drawn from the data may be revised once additional data become available after additional time has passed.

Page 114

1. Consumption (C) is the largest component of national expenditure, averaging 63.1%.

2. Consumption expenditures are more stable than investment expenditures. It's usually easier to delay

investment than consumption, so consumption normally varies only slightly, but investment expenditure can vary dramatically, especially in an economic downturn, as businesses hold off on investment. For these reasons, the part of consumption that is most volatile is consumption of durable goods such as cars and major appliances, because the purchase of these goods can usually be easily delayed.

3. The income approach is the flip side of the spending approach: Every dollar that someone earns in income is a dollar of income that someone else has spent.

Page 118

1. GDP measures things for which market values can be obtained. It does not measure things such as illegal activities or clean air because it is difficult to determine their market values.

2. Two countries that have the same level of GDP per capita do not necessarily have the same level of inequality. Let's take Country A and Country B, each of which has only two citizens. Country A's citizens earn $999 and $1, respectively, with GDP per capita of $500. Country B's citizens earn $500 and $500, respectively, with GDP per capita of $500 also. Note that the two countries have the same GDP per capita but they have different levels of inequality.

3. Because they do not account for everything, GDP statistics are not perfect. Nevertheless, they are useful in giving a good sense of how the value of what a nation produces changes over time.

Chapter 7
Page 131

1. According to Figure 7.2, approximately 30% of the world's population lived in China in 2014.

2. Using the rule of 70, if you make 5% on your savings, it will take 70/5 or 12 years for your savings to double. At 8%, it will take 70/8 or a little under 9 years to double.

3. According to Figure 7.4, Japan's real GDP per capita crossed the $10,000 barrier around 1970 and the $20,000 barrier around 1990. Using the rule of 70, we know that it took 20 years to double, or $70/x = 20$. Therefore, the growth rate was approximately 3.5% per year over this time span.

Page 133

1. The United States has much more physical capital—tools, machines, equipment—than China, but China has more than Nigeria.

2. Physical capital, human capital, and technological knowledge are the three primary factors of production.

Page 141

1. Five institutions that promote economic growth are property rights, honest government, political stability, a dependable legal system, and competitive and open markets.

2. Under a system of collective farming where corn production was shared, increased individual effort would bring very little reward to the individual. Because individual incentives were poor, you would expect limited corn production, maybe even starvation.

Chapter 8
Page 159

1. In Figure 8.6, when the capital stock is 400, depreciation is higher than investment.

2. When capital is 400, investment is 6 units.

3. When capital is 400, depreciation is 8 units.

4. When depreciation is greater than investment, the capital stock shrinks.

Page 162

1. As more capital is added, the marginal product of capital declines.

2. Capital depreciates because machines wear out over time and have to be replaced, roads wear out and need to be repaired or replaced, bridges wear out. As the capital stock increases, the total amount of capital depreciation increases.

Page 165

1. At the steady-state level of capital, investment and depreciation are equal.

2. In Figure 8.7, output is 15 units available to be consumed in the old steady state, and 20 units in the new steady state.

3. The farther they are below their steady-state level, the more quickly countries can grow.

4. Countries with higher investment rates have higher GDP per capita.

Page 169

1. High tax rates on imports would reduce trade and thus lower the incentive to produce new ideas.

2. Spillovers occur when ideas benefit other consumers and firms, besides the creator of the idea. If the creator of an idea cannot get the full benefit of the idea, this will reduce the incentive to generate new ideas.

3. The economic reason to support a prize for malaria research rather than cancer research is that the incentive to produce cancer drugs is already high because of a large and wealthy market. Malaria tends to be located in poorer countries where people have a lower ability to pay for drugs and thus the incentive to develop new drugs is lower.

Chapter 9

Page 187

1. Financial institutions build a bridge between savers and borrowers.

2. If people have saved enough for their retirement, they can have a smooth consumption path over their lives. If greater life expectancy means that not enough has been saved for retirement, then consumption during the retirement years will have to be lower than currently planned. Thus, the consumption path throughout their lifetimes will not be smooth.

3. Other than retirement, numerous potential things can generate a demand to save because these things can cause income to be volatile: loss of a job, chronic illness, or accidents that cause some bodily harm. One saves for a rainy day.

Page 189

1. Under the lifecycle theory, individual savings are likely to be at their peak during an individual's prime earning years.

2. If interest rates fall from 7% to 5%, all else being equal, this is a fall in the price of borrowed funds. This fall in price will encourage more people to buy homes (they now may be able to afford something they could not afford before) or start businesses.

Page 192

1. Greater patience will shift the supply of savings curve to the right, leading to an increase in the quantity of savings and a decrease in the equilibrium interest rate.

2. An increase in investment demand shifts the demand curve to the right, leading to an increase in the equilibrium interest rate and an increase in the quantity of funds demanded and supplied.

Page 197

1. The primary role of financial intermediaries is to reduce the costs of moving savings from savers to borrowers and investors.

2. Interest rates and bond prices move in opposite directions. If you own a bond paying 6% in interest and the interest rate falls to 4%, the price of the bond must go up. If interest rates rise to 8%, the price of the 6% bond must fall.

3. An IPO is a first-time sale of a firm's stock to the market, and so usually increases net investment: The firm can take this new capital and use it to expand the business. Buying shares of stock from someone else, in contrast, is buying shares already issued and represents a transfer of ownership, not a net increase to investment: The firm does not get the purchase price of the stock.

Page 205

1. Usury laws are price ceilings. Remember from Chapter 8 that price ceilings cause shortages. If savers can get only the ceiling rate rather than the market rate for their savings, they will save less.

2. Bank failures can hinder financial intermediation in a variety of ways. If savers become reluctant to put their money in banks, for example, the supply of credit will decline and the cost of borrowing will rise. This can lead to a credit crisis as credit dries up.

3. Lending money to political cronies, or pals, lowers the efficiency of the economy because loans do not go to their highest-valued uses.

Chapter 10

Page 221

According to the efficient markets hypothesis, one cannot consistently beat the market. Therefore, past performance is not a good guide to future success.

On average, mutual funds that have performed well in the past are no more likely to perform well in the future than mutual funds that have performed poorly in the past.

Page 227

1. Investing in the stocks of other countries helps to diversify your investments because the economies of other countries do not always rise and fall at the same time as the U.S. economy. If all economies tended to rise and fall together, there would not be any large benefits in diversifying across countries.

2. If many people dream of owning a football or baseball team, it is likely that the rewards to owning one go beyond monetary rewards. Thus, the monetary return on these assets is likely to be relatively low.

Page 229

This question is being hotly debated by many economists. It can be said that identifying and bursting bubbles is more difficult than it looks. How does the Federal Reserve know when there is a bubble? Increases in prices do not necessarily signify a bubble. Even if it can be said to be fairly certain that a bubble is present, how does the Federal Reserve burst the bubble while avoiding widespread collateral damage?

Chapter 11

Page 238

1. Frictional unemployment is caused by the ordinary difficulties of matching employee to employer. A reason for the difficulty of matching employer to employee is scarcity of information.

2. Some frictional unemployment is not bad if it means that prospective employers and prospective employees take the time to determine whether they are a good fit. Being forced to take the first job offered is not a good way to establish a good fit.

Page 245

1. Structural unemployment is persistent, long-term unemployment caused by long-lasting shocks or permanent features of an economy that make it more difficult for some workers to find jobs.

2. In the United States, "employment at-will" fairly accurately describes the employment situation: Employees may quit at any time and employers may fire an employee at any time and for any reason. In contrast, laws in Western European countries hinder the ability of employers to act at will. For example, in Portugal any business must get the government's permission to lay off workers, and even then the business must follow guidelines as to who can be laid off first.

Page 248

1. Cyclical unemployment is determined by the business cycle. It increases during a recession and decreases during a boom.

2. Lower growth is correlated with increasing unemployment; higher growth is correlated with decreasing unemployment.

Page 253

1. Lowering the marginal tax rate for married couples provided an incentive for more women to enter the labor force because they could now keep more of their pay rather than have it taxed away.

2. Raising the age that one can obtain Social Security benefits increases the incentive to stay in the labor force longer, thus increasing the labor force participation rate.

Chapter 12

Page 269

1. Using the formula on page 266, $(125 - 120) \div 120 = 4.16\%$.

2. If the inflation rate goes from 1% to 4% to 7% over a period of two years, the prices of a great majority of goods are likely to go up.

3. Use real prices rather than nominal prices to compare the price of goods over time. Real prices subtract out the effect of inflation and thus give a better measure of whether a particular good is becoming more or less expensive over time compared with most other goods and services.

Page 274

1. In the long run, inflation is always and everywhere a monetary phenomenon: Growth in the money supply causes inflation.

2. The quantity theory of money is $Mv = PY_R$.

Page 280

1. Under unexpected inflation, wealth is redistributed from lenders to borrowers. Under unexpected disinflation, wealth is redistributed from borrowers to lenders.

2. When the expected inflation rate increases, nominal interest rates rise to compensate. We call this the Fisher effect.

3. Unexpected inflation distorts price signals. They become more difficult to interpret. This leads to waste.

Chapter 13

Page 291

1. Because $\overline{M} + \vec{v} = \vec{P} + \vec{Y}_R$ in the AD/AS model, if $\overline{M}$ equals 7% and $\vec{v}$ equals 0%, by definition inflation plus real growth will equal 7%. If in this situation we find that real growth equals 0%, then inflation must be 7%.

2. Increased spending growth shifts the aggregate demand curve outward.

Page 297

1. Putting down phone lines is very expensive, compared with the cost of putting up cell phone towers. Cell phones have improved communications in all countries, but the change has been most dramatic in less developed countries. This has been a positive shock throughout the world.

2. A large and sudden increase in taxes would suppress economic activity, especially in the short run, as consumers and firms reallocated from more energy-intensive sectors of the economy to less energy-intensive sectors. The reallocation would decrease the fundamental capacity of the economy to produce goods and services, which is a shift of the long-run aggregate supply curve to the left.

Page 303

1. The long-run aggregate supply curve is vertical because price and wage stickiness does not affect the fundamental productive capacity of the economy over the long run. However, price and wage stickiness does affect aggregate supply in the short run, and this accounts for the fact that the SRAS curve is *not* vertical.

2. In the short run, inflation expectations may deviate from actual inflation, and spending growth can lead to some GDP growth.

3. In the long run, inflation expectations equal actual inflation.

Page 305

1. In the long run, unexpected inflation always becomes expected inflation.

2. If consumers fear a recession and cut back on their expenditures, the aggregate demand curve will shift inward.

Page 309

1. The U.S. money supply fell in the early 1930s. This initially affected aggregate demand (the AD curve shifted inward—down/left), not the long-run aggregate supply curve. The decrease in aggregate demand resulted in bank failures that decreased the productivity of financial intermediation, which was a real shock, and so affected the long-run aggregate supply curve, shifting it to the left.

2. In an ordinary year, the real shocks of the 1930s might have been shrugged off but the combination of large shocks to AD and real shocks at the same time made the Great Depression great.

Chapter 14

Page 324

The 9/11 attacks brought a high level of uncertainty into the economy. No one knew if more attacks were planned so no one wanted to be on an airplane. Cutting back on air travel hurt the airlines and all associated businesses: airports, airport services such as food vendors, companies that provide transportation to and from airports. When no one flew on airplanes to take business trips, some local business trips were still undertaken (by train or car), but longer trips (such as cross-country travel) came to a standstill. As travel declined, so did the need for hotel rooms and restaurant meals. Hotels were hit hard: Cutting the price of hotel rooms had little effect when uncertainty dried up business travel.

The near-cessation in business travel amplified the economic effects of the attacks nationwide: The attacks in New York City and Washington, D.C., had nationwide repercussions.

Chapter 15
Page 336

1. The monetary base is defined as currency plus reserves held by banks at the Fed.

2. In September 2016, there was approximately $1.5 trillion of currency in the United States compared with approximately $1.9 trillion in checkable deposits. Thus, currency accounts for slightly less than checkable deposits.

Page 338

1. If the reserve ratio is 1/20, then 5% of deposits are kept as reserves.

2. If the reserve ratio is 1/20, then the money multiplier is 20.

3. If the Fed increases bank reserves by $10,000 and the reserve ratio is 1/20, then the change in the money supply is $200,000.

Page 342

1. The Fed wants to lower interest rates. It does so by *buying* bonds in open market operations. By doing this, the Fed *adds* reserves and through the multiplier process, it *increases* the money supply.

2. An increase in the amount paid on reserves will draw money from other sectors of the economy, decreasing aggregate demand.

Page 345

1. The Fed might not let a large bank fail if it fears systemic risk, the possibility that the failure will bring down other banks and financial institutions. In this case, the Fed will use its powers as the lender of last resort to support a bank that is "too big to fail."

2. Moral hazard increases my incentives to double my bet to make up for a large loss. If the Fed always bails out large banks, my actions will never lead to the bank's bankruptcy, so why not take the chance?

Page 347

1. Money is neutral in the long run but has a short-run effect on the economy. This explains the Fed's concerns with the money supply in the short run.

2. If banks are afraid of a recession, they will be more reluctant to lend. This will hamper the Fed's ability to shift aggregate demand in a recession. In this case, the Fed is sometimes said to be "pushing on a string."

Chapter 16
Page 362

Data problems affect the Fed's ability to set monetary policy that is "just right" because the problems make it difficult for the Fed to determine just what is going on with the economy. If the Fed does not know exactly what is going on, it cannot prescribe the correct medicine.

Page 364

1. If the Fed wanted to restore some growth to the economy, it could work to increase aggregate demand. The problem is that increasing growth in this case comes at the expense of adding more inflation. This is the policy dilemma.

2. If the Fed increases AD every time as a response to a series of negative real shocks, the inflation rate will climb. Eventually, the Fed will have to act to reduce inflation, possibly pushing the economy into a recession.

Page 368

1. The Fed can never be certain when asset prices reach the bubble stage. Bubbles are easier to identify with hindsight, but even then identification is a judgment call.

2. Collateral damage to a contraction in the money supply could be reducing the growth rate for GDP for the broader economy as a whole.

Page 369

Milton Friedman argued for a 3% money growth rate because the long-run growth rate for the U.S. economy trends around 3%. When money growth equals long-run growth in the economy, there will be a tendency for price stability.

Chapter 17

Page 387

Individual income taxes plus Social Security and Medicare taxes represent 76% of federal revenues.

Page 394

1. According to Figure 17.4, in 2017, Social Security and Medicare spending accounted for just under 40% of federal spending.

2. GDP gives us an idea of the capacity of the economy to pay debt, so the debt-to-GDP ratio tells us what the debt is relative to the capacity to pay the debt.

Page 397

1. In the next 40 years, Social Security and especially Medicare and Medicaid are likely to increase relative to GDP. This means that the level of overall government spending relative to GDP is likely to increase.

2. If the pace of idea generation quickens, this will lead to a positive shift in the long-run aggregate supply growth curve. In other words, the economy will be able to produce more goods and services. This would lead to a decrease in the debt-to-GDP ratio (all other things equal). This would increase the government's ability to pay for increased benefits for retirees.

Chapter 18

Page 411

The two types of expansionary fiscal policy are when the government spends more money, or when the government cuts taxes and thereby gives people more money to spend.

Page 415

1. The 2008 tax rebate was less powerful than expected because many people saved the rebate and paid down debt, rather than spending the extra money.

2. A permanent cut in income tax rates can generate a larger fiscal stimulus than a temporary cut because people likely will save a large portion of a temporary tax cut, to pay for future taxes. But if the tax cut is permanent, they may choose to spend more. Of course, telling people that a tax cut is permanent is quite different from getting people to *believe* that it is permanent!

3. A permanent investment tax credit produces a smaller fiscal stimulus than a temporary investment tax credit because to get the temporary tax credit, firms must spend money on equipment right away; a permanent investment tax credit, however, gives firms the option of waiting to invest.

Chapter 19

Page 438

1. Domestic producers gain from a tariff and domestic consumers lose.

2. Trade protectionism leads to wasted resources because it shifts production from the lowest-cost producers to higher-cost producers.

3. You hear more often about people who gain from trade restrictions than people who lose because the gains from trade restrictions are concentrated on a few winners, while the losses are diffused over many losers. Even though the total gains are smaller than the total losses, the concentrated benefits mean that the winners have a greater incentive to argue for trade restriction than the losers do to argue against it.

4. In Figure 19.3, area *C* represents the deadweight loss; it results from the lost gains from trades not happening.

Page 441

1. The movement of the garment trade overseas has been a net benefit for the United States because clothing is now much cheaper for U.S. consumers and U.S. workers specialize in the fields in which they are most productive.

2. If the U.S. government subsidized the Silicon Valley computer industry, it would encourage more computer chip manufacturing, but at a higher cost (production would not be as efficient). This would be a waste of resources. Foreign competitors would be pushed out of the industry. Consumers of computer chips would benefit from the subsidy, but they would benefit by less than the cost to U.S. taxpayers.

Chapter 20

Page 455

1. If an inhabitant of Nebraska buys a German sports car for $30,000, this lowers the U.S. current account balance by $30,000.

2. If a German sports car manufacturer opens a new plant in South Carolina, this investment is a capital account surplus for the United States.

3. The current and capital accounts are two sides of the same coin. When the capital account is in surplus, the current account will tend to mirror that in deficit, and vice versa.

Page 462

1. If the U.S. dollar is a safe haven currency, then in times of risk people will demand dollars, increasing their value.

2. If the Fed increases the money supply, this will reduce the value of the dollar compared with the euro.

3. If purchasing power parity holds and the nominal exchange rate is 1 pound for 2 dollars, a Big Mac should cost £2 in London if it costs $4.00 in New York.

4. A tariff will hinder market exchange and thus the arbitrage of differing prices. This limits purchasing power parity.

Page 464

1. In the short run, a Fed increase in the money supply will cause a depreciation in the exchange rate, leading to an increase in U.S. exports. In the long run, the temporary boost to exports will dissipate, and the increase in the money supply will lead to inflation.

2. In an open economy, monetary policy is more effective than fiscal policy. Expansionary monetary policy will tend to reduce interest rates, causing a currency depreciation and increased exports. In contrast, expansionary fiscal policy will tend to increase interest rates, causing an appreciation of the exchange rate and reduced exports.

Page 466

1. A floating exchange rate describes when the value of a country's currency is determined by the forces of supply and demand.

2. The European Central Bank controls the monetary policy of the European Union.

Chapter 21

Page 478

National voters have a smaller chance of influencing the election than do local voters, which suggests that people have a greater incentive to be informed about local issues. On the other hand, local issues are less important than national issues and there is less free information (e.g., from online news sources like BuzzFeed or news satire like *The Daily Show*) about local issues than about national issues, which suggests local voters would be even more rationally ignorant than national voters.

Page 482

1. Because of the benefits that special interests receive from current programs, they would fight against the establishment of a commission to examine federal waste. If the commission was set up, these special interests would then try to "capture" the commission: argue that their specific programs were needed, and exert political pressure to keep these programs. The bearers of the costs of these programs—the taxpayers—are too large and diverse a group to zero in on any particular program. The commission idea might be popular, but the chance of its success is low.

2. The beneficiaries of the local history collection at the library are the users of the collection. Ultimately, the taxpayers of the state pay for it. Benefits are concentrated on a small group, while the costs are spread over a large body of people (the taxpayers). Don't be surprised if the reading room is named after the state senator!

Page 484

If voters are myopic, politicians could prefer a policy with small gains now and big costs later (let's get reelected and maybe someone else will have to deal with the large costs down the road) than a policy with small costs now and large gains later (why jeopardize my chance to get reelected?). For these reasons, dealing with a large potential problem, such as the fiscal sustainability of Medicare, is often put off until the last minute when the solutions are much more difficult and costly.

Page 491

The free flow of ideas helps democracies function by getting alternatives out and on the table. Voters will always be rationally ignorant to some extent, but the more information that is out there and available at low cost, the more voters will be informed, at least about the big issues. Debate and dissent can improve the quality of ideas. The free flow of information reduces the possibility of corruption. New ideas help democracies adapt to changing conditions.

GLOSSARY

absolute advantage the ability to produce the same good using fewer inputs than another producer

active labor market policies policies that focus on getting unemployed workers back to work, such as job-search assistance, job-retraining programs, and work tests

aggregate demand curve curve that shows all the combinations of inflation and real growth that are consistent with a specified rate of spending growth $(\overrightarrow{M} + \overrightarrow{v})$

aggregate demand shock a rapid and unexpected shift in the AD curve (spending)

alternative minimum tax (AMT) a separate income tax code, begun in 1969 to prevent the rich from not paying income taxes; not indexed to inflation and thus now an extra tax burden on many upper middle class families

appreciation an increase in the price of one currency in terms of another currency

arbitrage the practice of taking advantage of price differences for the same good in different markets by buying low in one market and selling high in another market

automatic stabilizers changes in fiscal policy that stimulate AD in a recession without the need for explicit action by policymakers; unemployment insurance is one example of an automatic stabilizer

average tax rate the total tax payment divided by total income

baby boomers people born during the high-birth-rate years of 1946–1964

balance of payments a yearly summary of all the economic transactions between residents of one country and residents of the rest of the world

bond a sophisticated IOU that documents who owes how much and when payment must be made

business fluctuations (or business cycles) the short-run movements in real GDP around its long-term trend

buy and hold the practice of buying stocks and then holding them for the long run, regardless of what prices do in the short run

capital account in the balance of payments, the account that measures changes in foreign ownership of domestic assets, including financial assets like stocks and bonds as well as physical assets

capital surplus (also called *capital inflow*) the excess that exists when the inflow of foreign capital into a country is greater than the outflow of domestic capital

catching-up growth growth due to capital accumulation and adopting already existing ideas

club goods goods that are excludable but nonrival

collateral something of value that helps to secure a loan; if the borrower defaults, ownership of the collateral transfers to the lender

collateral shock a reduction in the value of collateral; collateral shocks make borrowing and lending more difficult

common resources goods that are nonexcludable but rival

comparative advantage the ability to produce a good or service at a lower opportunity cost than another producer

complements two goods for which a decrease in the price of one leads to an increase in the demand for the other, for example hamburgers and hamburger buns

conditional convergence the tendency—among countries with similar steady-state levels of output—for poorer countries to grow faster than richer countries and thus for poor and rich countries to converge in income

consumer surplus the consumer's gain from exchange, or the difference between the maximum price a consumer is willing to pay for a certain quantity and the market price

consumer surplus (total) quantity measured by the area beneath the demand curve and above the price

consumption private spending on finished goods and services

counter-cyclical fiscal policy fiscal policy that runs opposite or counter to the business cycle—spending more when the economy is in a recession and less when the economy is booming

credible monetary policy when it is expected that a central bank will stick with its policy

crowding out the decrease in private consumption and investment that occurs when government borrows more; also, the decrease in private spending that occurs when government increases spending

current account in the balance of payments, the sum of the balance of trade, net income on capital held abroad, and net transfer payments

cutting-edge growth growth due to new ideas

cyclical unemployment unemployment correlated with the business cycle

deficit the annual difference between federal spending and revenues

deficit, trade see trade deficit

deflation a decrease in the average level of prices; that is, a negative inflation rate

demand curve a function that shows the quantity demanded at different prices

depreciation a decrease in the price of a currency in terms of another currency

diminishing marginal utility each additional unit of a good adds less to utility than the previous unit

dirty (or managed) float a currency whose value is not fixed but for which governments will intervene extensively in the market to keep its value within a certain range

discount rate the interest rate banks pay when they borrow directly from the Fed at the discount window

discouraged workers jobless individuals who have given up looking for work but who would still like to find a job

disinflation a reduction in the inflation rate

dollarization a foreign country's use of the U.S. dollar as its currency

economic growth the growth rate of real GDP per capita:

$$g_t = \frac{Y_t - Y_{t-1}}{Y_{t-1}} \times 100$$

where Y_t is real per capita GDP in period t

efficient markets hypothesis the claim that the prices of traded assets reflect all publicly available information

employment at-will doctrine the policy that an employee may quit and an employer may fire an employee at any time and for any reason; the most basic U.S. employment law despite many exceptions to it

equilibrium price the price at which the quantity demanded is equal to the quantity supplied

equilibrium quantity the quantity at which the quantity demanded is equal to the quantity supplied

equity the value of the asset minus the debt, $E = V - D$

exchange rate the price of one currency in terms of another currency

federal funds rate the overnight lending rate from one major bank to another

financial intermediaries institutions such as banks, bond markets, and stock markets that reduce the costs of moving funds from savers to borrowers and investors

fiscal policy federal government policy on taxes, spending, and borrowing that is designed to influence business fluctuations

Fisher effect the tendency of nominal interest rates to rise one to one with expected inflation rates

fixed exchange rate (also known as a pegged exchange rate) an exchange rate based on the promise of a government or central bank to convert its currency into another currency at a fixed (set) rate

flat tax an income tax with the same tax rate on all levels of income (compare with progressive and regressive tax)

floating exchange rate an exchange rate determined primarily by market forces

forced rider someone who pays a share of the costs of a public good but who does not enjoy the benefits

fractional reserve banking a system in which banks hold only a portion of deposits in reserve, lending the rest

frictional unemployment short-term unemployment caused by the ordinary difficulties of matching employee to employer

government purchases spending by all levels of government on finished goods and services not including transfers

gross domestic product (GDP) the market value of all finished goods and services produced within a country in a year

gross domestic product (GDP) per capita GDP divided by population

gross national product (GNP) the market value of all finished goods and services produced by a country's residents, wherever located, in a year

human capital tools of the mind; the productive knowledge and skills that workers acquire through education, training, and experience

illiquid asset an asset that cannot be quickly converted into cash without a large loss in value; note that a bank could be illiquid but not insolvent

illiquid bank a bank whose short-term liabilities are greater than its short-term assets but overall has assets that are greater than its liabilities

incentives rewards and penalties that motivate behavior

inferior good a good for which demand decreases when income increases

inflation an increase in the general or average level of prices.

inflation rate $= \frac{P_2 - P_1}{P_1} \times 100$ the percentage increase in the average level of prices (as measured by a price index) over a period of time

initial public offering (IPO) the first instance of a corporation selling stock to the public in order to raise capital

insolvent bank/institution a bank or institution whose liabilities are greater in value than its assets

institutions the "rules of the game" that structure economic incentives

intertemporal substitution the allocation of consumption, work, and leisure across time to maximize well-being

investment the purchase of new capital goods; private spending on tools, plant, and equipment used to produce future output

investment expenditures private spending on tools, plant, and equipment used to produce future output; that is the purchase of new capital goods

irreversible investments investments that cannot be easily moved, adjusted, or reversed if conditions change

labor adjustment costs the costs of shifting workers from declining sectors of the economy to growing sectors

labor force all workers, employed plus unemployed

labor force participation rate the percentage of adults in the labor force

law of one price the principle that if trade were free, then identical goods will sell for about the same price throughout the world

lender of last resort a lender that loans money to banks and other financial institutions when no one else will, often a central bank or a country's treasury or finance department

leverage ratio the ratio of debt to equity, D/E

liquid asset an asset that can be used for payments or, quickly and without loss of value, be converted into an asset that can be used for payments

liquidity trap situation in which interest rates are close to the zero lower bound, so pushing them lower is not possible or not effective at increasing aggregate demand

long-run aggregate supply curve (LRAS) a vertical line at the Solow growth rate

marginal product of capital the increase in output caused by the addition of one more unit of capital; the marginal product of capital diminishes as more and more capital is added

marginal tax rate the tax rate paid on an additional dollar of income

market confidence one of the Federal Reserve's most powerful tools is its influence over expectations, not its influence over the money supply

market for loanable funds the market where suppliers of loanable funds (savers) trade with demanders of loanable funds (borrowers), thereby determining the equilibrium interest rate

median wage the wage such that one-half of all workers earn wages below that amount and one-half of all workers earn wages above that amount

menu costs the costs of changing prices

monetizing the debt the result of government paying off its debts by printing money

money a widely accepted means of payment

money illusion the false perception that occurs when people mistake changes in nominal prices for changes in real prices

money multiplier (MM) the amount the money supply expands with each dollar increase in reserves; MM = 1/RR where RR is the reserve ratio

multiplier effect the additional increase in spending caused by the initial increase in government spending

national debt held by the public all federal debt held outside the U.S. government

natural unemployment rate the rate of structural plus frictional unemployment

net exports the value of exports minus the value of imports

nominal exchange rate the rate at which you can exchange one currency for another

nominal rate of return the rate of return that does not account for inflation

nominal variables variables, such as nominal GDP, that have not been adjusted for changes in prices

nominal wage confusion situation that occurs when workers respond to their nominal wage instead of to their real wage, that is, when workers respond to the wage number on their paychecks rather than to what their wage can buy in goods and services (the real wage)

nonexcludable when people who don't pay cannot easily be prevented from using the good, the good is nonexcludable

nonrival (or nonrivalrous) goods when one person's consumption of the good does not limit another person's consumption

normal good a good for which demand increases when income increases

open market operations the buying and selling of government bonds by the Fed

opportunity cost the value of possibilities lost when a choice is made

owner's equity *see* equity

physical capital the stock of tools including machines, structures, and equipment

price ceiling a maximum price allowed by law

price floor a minimum price allowed by law

private goods goods that are excludable and rival goods

producer surplus the producer's gain from exchange, or the difference between the market price and the minimum price at which a producer would be willing to sell a particular quantity

producer surplus (total) an amount measured by the area above the supply curve and below the price up to the quantity traded

production possibilities frontier all the combinations of goods that a country can produce given its productivity and supply of inputs

progressive tax an income tax with higher tax rates on people with higher incomes

protectionism the economic policy of restraining trade through quotas, tariffs, or other regulations that burden foreign producers but not domestic producers

purchasing power parity (PPP) theorem the principle that the real purchasing power of money should be about the same, whether it is spent at home or converted into another currency and spent abroad

quantitative easing situation that occurs when the Fed buys longer-term government bonds or other securities

quantitative tightening what occurs when the Fed sells longer-term government bonds or other securities

quantity demanded the quantity that buyers are willing and able to buy at a particular price

quantity supplied the quantity that sellers are willing and able to sell at a particular price

real exchange rate the rate at which you can exchange the goods and services of one country for the goods and services of another

real price a price that has been corrected for inflation; used to compare the prices of goods over time

real rate of return the nominal rate of return minus the inflation rate

real shock (also called a productivity shock) any shock that increases or decreases the potential growth rate

real variables variables such as real GDP, that have been adjusted for changes in prices by using the same set of prices in all time periods

recession a significant, widespread decline in real income and employment

rent control a price ceiling on rental housing

reserve ratio (RR) the ratio of reserves to deposits

Ricardian equivalence the theory according to which people understand that, for a given level of government spending, lower taxes today mean higher taxes in the future and therefore save the money from a tax cut to pay future taxes

risk-return trade-off higher returns come at the price of higher risk

saving income that is not spent on consumption goods

scarce when there isn't enough of a specific resource to satisfy all of our wants

shortage a situation in which the quantity demanded is greater than the quantity supplied

short-run aggregate supply curve (SRAS) curve that shows the positive relationship between the inflation rate and real growth during the period when prices and wages are sticky

Solow growth rate an economy's potential growth rate, the rate of economic growth that would occur given flexible prices and the existing real factors of production

steady state in a model of economic growth, a situation in which the capital stock is neither increasing nor decreasing

stock (or share) is a certificate of ownership in a corporation

structural unemployment persistent, long-term unemployment caused by long-lasting shocks or permanent features of an economy that make it more difficult for some workers to find jobs

substitutes two goods for which a decrease in the price of one leads to a decrease in demand for the other

supply curve a function that shows the quantity supplied at different prices

surplus a situation in which the quantity supplied is greater than the quantity demanded

systemic risk the risk that the failure of one financial institution can bring down other institutions

tariff a tax on imports

technological knowledge knowledge about how the world works that is used to produce goods and services

time bunching the tendency for economic activities to be coordinated at common points in time

time preference the desire to have goods and services sooner rather than later (all else being equal)

total consumer surplus *see* consumer surplus (total)

total producer surplus *see* producer surplus (total)

trade deficit the annual difference that results when the value of a country's imports exceeds the value of its exports

trade quota a restriction on the quantity of goods that can be imported: imports greater than the quota amount are forbidden or heavily taxed

trade surplus the annual difference that results when the value of a country's exports exceeds the value of its imports

tragedy of the commons the tendency of any resource that is unowned, and hence nonexcludable, to be overused and undermaintained

underemployment rate a Bureau of Labor Statistics measure that includes part-time workers who would rather have a full-time position and people who would like to work but have given up looking for a job

unemployed workers adults who do not have a job but who are looking for work

unemployment rate the percentage of the labor force who are unemployed

union an association of workers that bargains collectively with employers over wages, benefits, and working conditions

velocity of money, v the average number of times a dollar is spent on finished goods and services in a year

zero lower bound situation in which the Federal Funds rate is close to zero

REFERENCES

Chapter 1 Notes

1. Quoted in **Christopher, Emma.** 2007. "The slave trade is merciful compared to [this]": Slave traders, convict transportation and the abolitionists. In **Christopher, E., C. Pybus, and M. Rediker** (eds.), *Many Middle Passages*, Chap. 6, pp. 109–128. Berkeley, CA: University of California Press.

2. **Chadwick, Edwin.** 1862. Opening address of the British Association for the Advancement of Science. *Journal of the Statistical Society of London* **25**(4): 502–524.

3. Opening address.

4. On the impact of new drugs, see **Lichtenberg, Frank.** 2007. The impact of new drugs on U.S. longevity and medical expenditure, 1990–2003. *American Economic Review* **97**(2): 438–443.

5. **Celis III, William.** December 28, 1991. Study finds enrollment is up at colleges despite recession. *New York Times.*

Chapter 2 Notes

1. On this point, see **Sowell, Thomas.** 1980. *Knowledge and Decisions.* New York: Basic Books. See also Chapter 4 of **Reisman, George.** 1996. *Capitalism: A Treatise on Economics.* Ottawa, IL: Jameson.

2. **Smith, Adam.** August 2, 2006. *An Inquiry into the Nature and Causes of the Wealth of Nations.* Edited by Edwin Cannan, Book IV, II. 2.11. Indianapolis, IN: Library of Economics and Liberty. http://www.econlib.org/library/Smith/smWN13 .html. Originally published London: Methuen, 1904 [1776].

3. **Boudreaux, Donald J.** 2008. *Globalization.* Westport, CT: Greenwood Press.

Chapter 3 Notes

1. On changing U.S. demographics and their impact on the economy, see **Kotlikoff, Laurence J., and Scott Burns.** 2004. *The Coming Generational Storm.* Cambridge, MA: MIT Press.

2. **Stigler, George J.** 1971. The theory of economic regulation. *Bell Journal of Economics* Spring: 137–146.

3. **Paleontological Research Institution.** http://www .priweb.org/ed/pgws/history/spindletop/lucas_gusher.html.

4. See information available at the **U.S. Energy Information Administration** Web site. http://www.eia.gov/.

5. On the costs of oil production, see **Joint Economic Committee, United States Congress.** *OPEC and the High Price of Oil.* http://www.house.gov/jec/publications /109/11–17–05opec.pdf.

Chapter 4 Notes

1. **Smith, Vernon.** 1991. Experimental economics at Purdue. In **Smith, V.** (ed.), *Papers in Experimental Economics.* Cambridge, UK: Cambridge University Press. Originally appeared in **Horwich, G., and J. P. Quirk** (eds.), *Essays in Contemporary Fields of Economics.* Lafayette, IN: Purdue University Press, 1981.

2. **Conover, Ted.** July 2, 2006. Capitalist roaders. *New York Times Magazine,* pp. 31–37, 50.

Chapter 5 Notes

1. A 2" × 4" refers to the preplaned dimensions, which after planing, are typically $1\frac{3}{4}$" × $3\frac{3}{4}$"; with price controls, the average size fell to $1\frac{5}{8}$" × $3\frac{5}{8}$". See **Hall, Thomas.** 2003. *The Rotten Fruits of Economic Controls and the Rise from the Ashes: 1965–1989.* New York: University Press of America.

2. *Business Week*. February 16, 1974. Page 122. Quoted in **Bradley, Robert Jr.** 1996. *Oil, Gas and Government: The U.S. Experience*, Vol. 2, p. 1635. Lanham, MD: Rowman & Littlefield.

3. Prices were frozen at levels no higher than the May 25, 1970, price or a price at which 10% or more of transactions took place in the 30 days prior to August 14, 1971. Some adjustments for seasonal differences were allowed for some products, such as fashion items, but not for oil. See **Bradley**, Vol. 2, especially pp. 1607–1608.

4. See **Hall, Thomas E.** 2003. *The Rotten Fruits of Economic Controls and the Rise from the Ashes, 1965–1989.* New York: University Press of America.

5. **Bradley, Robert Jr.** 1996. *Oil, Gas and Government: The U.S. Experience.* Vol. 1. Lanham, MD: Rowman & Littlefield.

6. See *The Washington Post*. November 26, 1973. Steps ordered by Nixon to meet energy crisis. Page A12.

7. *Time*. December 10, 1973. The shortage's losers and winners.

8. **Grayson, Jackson C.** February 6, 1974. Let's end controls—completely. *The Wall Street Journal*, p. 14.

Chapter 6 Notes

1. Data on automobiles are from the **Statistical Abstract of the United States.** Prices from http://nada.org/. Statistics on U.S. chicken production can be found at the U.S. Department of Agriculture, http://www.usda.gov/.

2. **Bureau of Economic Analysis.** Table 2.3.3. http://www .bea.gov.

3. **Board of Governors of the Federal Reserve System.** 2013. Financial Accounts of the United States. http://www .federalreserve.gov/releases/z1/current/.

4. For data on business regulations worldwide, see the **World Bank**'s Web site, http://doingbusiness.org/.

5. http://rru.worldbank.org/Discussions/Topics/Topic18.aspx.

6. http://gapminder.org/.

7. **Murphy, K. M., and R. H. Topel.** 2006. The value of health and longevity. *Journal of Political Economy* **114**(5): 871–904.

8. See **Dollar, David, and Aart Kraay.** 2004. Trade, growth, and poverty. *Economic Journal* **114**(493): F22–F49.

Chapter 7 Notes

1. See **United States Department of Agriculture,** Economic Research Service. *Agricultural Productivity in the United States.* http://www.ers.usda.gov/data-products/agricultural-productivity-in-the-us/.

2. This account draws on **McMillan, John.** 2002. *Reinventing the Bazaar.* New York: W. W. Norton; and **Zhou, Kate Xiao.** 1997. *How Farmers Changed China.* Boulder, CO: Westview Press.

3. **Hall, Robert E., and Charles I. Jones.** 1999. Why do some countries produce so much more output per worker than others? *Quarterly Journal of Economics:* 83–116.

4. **Lewis, William W.** 2004. *The Power of Productivity.* Chicago: University of Chicago Press.

5. On the importance of management practices and multinationals, see **Bloom, Nicholas, and John Van Reenen.** 2010. "Why do management practices differ across firms and countries?" *Journal of Economic Perspectives* **24**(1): 203–224. And **Bloom, Nicholas, Raffaella Sadun, and John Van Reenen.** 2012. "Americans do IT better: US multinationals and the productivity miracle." *American Economic Review* **102**(1): 167–201.

Chapter 8 Notes

1. Germany is excluded for lack of data. Turkey is excluded because its history and institutions were quite different from those of the other founding members of the OECD.

2. On innovations that would occur without patents, see **Mansfield, E.** 1986. Patents and innovation: An empirical study. *Management Science* **32**: 173–181. On patents and cumulative innovations, see **Bessen, J., and E. Maskin.** 2009. Sequential innovation, patents, and imitation. *RAND Journal of Economics* **40**: 611–635. Is there a way to reduce the trade-off between dynamic and static efficiency? Some ideas are suggested by **Tabarrok, A.** 2002. Patent theory versus patent law. *Contributions to Economic Analysis & Policy* **1**(1): Article 9. http://www.bepress.com/bejeap/contributions/vol1/iss1/art9. Also **Kremer, M.** 1998. Patent buyouts: A mechanism for encouraging innovation. *Quarterly Journal of Economics* **113**: 1137–1167.

3. "Rare" is defined as a disease at the bottom quarter of incidence in the United States in 1998; "common" is defined as a disease at the top quarter of incidence. See **Lichtenberg, Frank R., and Joel Waldfogel.** June 2003. Does misery love company? Evidence from pharmaceutical markets before and after the Orphan Drug Act. Working paper W9750, National Bureau of Economic Research, Washington, DC. http://www.ssrn.com/sol3/papers.cfm?abstract_id=414248.

4. **Romer, Paul.** 2007. Economic growth. In **David R. Henderson** (ed.), *The Concise Encyclopedia of Economics.* Indianapolis, IN: Liberty Fund.

Chapter 9 Notes

1. **Bloom, David E., David Canning, and Bryan S. Graham.** 2002. Longevity and life cycle savings. Working paper W8808, National Bureau of Economic Research, Washington, DC. http://www.ssrn.com/sol3/papers.cfm?abstract_ed=302569.

2. **Shoda, Y., W. Mischel, and P. Peake.** 1988. Predicting adolescent cognitive and self-regulatory competencies from preschool delay of gratification: Identifying diagnostic conditions. *Developmental Psychology* **26**: 978–986.

3. **Beshears, John, James Choi, David Laibson, and Brigitte Madrian.** *The Importance of Default Options for Retirement Savings Outcomes: Evidence from the United States.* Washington, DC: National Bureau of Economic Research. http://nber.org/aginghealth/summer06/w12009.html.

4. **Levine, Ross, and Sara Zervos.** 1998. Stock markets, banks, and economic growth. *American Economic Review* **88**(3): 537–558.

5. **Blustein, Paul.** 2005. *And the Money Kept Rolling In (and Out): Wall Street, the IMF, and the Bankrupting of Argentina.* New York: Public Affairs. See, in particular, p. 191.

6. See **La Porta, Rafael, Florencio Lopez-De-Silanes, and Andrei Shleifer.** 2002. Government ownership of banks. *Journal of Finance, American Finance Association* **57**(1): 265–301.

7. **Friedman, Milton, and Anna J. Schwartz.** 1963. *A Monetary History of the United States, 1867–1960.* Princeton, NJ: Princeton University Press.

8. **Bernanke, Ben.** 1983. Nonmonetary effects of the financial crisis in the propagation of the Great Depression. *American Economic Review* **73**(3): 257–276.

9. Leverage ratios can be calculated in different ways so no leverage ratio is written in stone but the increase in leverage during the 2000s is well accepted. Figures on Lehman's leverage in 2004 and 2007 come from https://www.lovemoney.com/news/3909/why-lehman-brothers-collapsed.

Chapter 10 Notes

1. **Malkiel, Burton.** 1996. *A Random Walk Down Wall Street.* 6th ed. New York: W. W. Norton. See, in particular, p. 24.

2. For a comprehensive review of efficient markets and the performance of mutual fund managers, see **Hebner, Mark T.** 2007. *Index Funds: The 12 Step Program for Active Investors.* Irvine, CA: IFA.

3. See **Marshall, Ben, Rochester Cahan, and Jared Cahan.** March 2008. Does intraday technical analysis in the U.S. equity market have value? *Journal of Empirical Finance:* 199–210.

4. On the relatively safe nature of Walmart, see, for instance, this analysis: http://www.slate.com/articles/business/moneybox/2008/02/the_walmart_puzzle.html.

5. **Siegel, Jeremy J.** January/February 1992. The equity premium: Stock and bond returns since 1802. *Financial Analysts Journal* **48**(1): 28–38.

6. **Smith, Vernon L., Gerry L. Suchanek, and Arlington W. Williams.** 1988. Bubbles, crashes, and endogenous expectations in experimental spot asset markets. *Econometrica* **56**(5): 1119–1151. And **Hussam, Reshmaan N., David Porter, and Vernon L. Smith.** 2008. Thar she blows: Can bubbles be rekindled with experienced subjects? *American Economic Review* **98**(3): 924–937.

Chapter 11 Notes

1. Data on unemployment and its duration may be found in various issues of the *OECD Employment Outlook* and on the Web: **OECD,** www.oecd.org/els/oecd-employment-outlook-19991266.htm.

2. The Italian system is more difficult to describe than the systems in the other countries and it has changed considerably over time.

3. For minimum wages relative to average wages, see **OECD.** http://stats.oecd.org/Index.aspx. For minimum wages relative to average wages, see **Lothar Funk and Hagen Lesch.** 2005. *Minimum Wages in Europe.* Dublin: European Foundation for the Improvement of Living and Working Conditions, http://eurofound.europa.eu/observatories /eurwork/comparative-information/minimum-wages -in-europe.

4. **Ford, Peter.** 2005. Deep roots of Paris riots. *Christian Science Monitor* (November 4).

5. **Martin, John P.** 2000. What works among active labour market policies: Evidence from OECD countries' experiences. *OECD Economic Studies* **30:** 79–113.

6. **Kotlikoff, Laurence, and Scott Burns.** 2004. *The Coming Generation Storm.* Cambridge, MA: MIT Press.

7. *60 Minutes.* January 3, 2007. Interview with U.S. Comptroller General David Walker, http://www.cbsnews.com /news/us-heading-for-financial-trouble/.

8. The U.S. Equal Employment Opportunity Commission collects statistics on job patterns by industry. See **EEOC.** *Job Patterns for Minorities and Women in Private Industry.* Rept. EEO-1, http://www.eeoc.gov/eeoc/statistics/employment /jobpat-eeo1/.

9. **Goldin, Claudia, and Lawrence F. Katz.** 2002. The power of the pill: Oral contraceptives and women's career and marriage decisions. *Journal of Political Economy* **110**(4): 730–770.

10. **Council of Economic Advisors.** 2016. The long-term decline in prime-age male labor force participation. https://obamawhitehouse.archives.gov/sites/default/files /page/files/20160620_cea_primeage_male_lfp.pdf; and **Binder, Ariel J., and John Bound.** 2019. The declining labor market prospects of less-educated men. *Journal of Economic Perspectives* **33**(2): 163–190, https://doi. org/10.1257/jep.33.2.163.

11. **Aguiar, Mark, Mark Bils, Kerwin Kofi Charles, and Erik Hurst.** 2017. Leisure luxuries and the labor supply of young men. Working Paper 23552. National Bureau of Economic Research, Washington, DC. https://doi.org /10.3386/w23552.

12. **Binder, Ariel J., and John Bound.** 2019. The declining labor market prospects of less-educated men. *Journal of Economic Perspectives* **33**(2): 163–190, https://doi.org /10.1257/jep.33.2.163.

13. *Ibid.*

14. *Ibid.*

15. **Bucknor, Cherrie, and Alan Barber.** 2016. The price we pay: Economic costs of barriers to employment for former prisoners and people convicted of felonies. 2016–07. CEPR Reports and Issue Briefs. Center for Economic and Policy Research (CEPR). https://ideas.repec.org/p/epo/papers /2016-07.html.

16. There are six employed workers and one unemployed worker, so there are seven people in the labor force. Of the seven, one is unemployed, so the unemployment rate is 1/7 = 14.3%. The adult, civilian, noninstitutional population is eight; of these, seven are in the labor force, so the labor force participation rate is 87.5%.

Chapter 12 Notes

1. https://www.caseyresearch.com/zimbabwean-dollar-point -no-return/.

Chapter 13 Notes

1. **Higgs, Robert.** 1997. Regime uncertainty: Why the Great Depression lasted so long and why prosperity resumed after the war. *The Independent Review* **1**(4): 561–590.

2. For a good overview of the tariff and its effects, see **O'Brien, Anthony.** August 15, 2001. Smoot–Hawley tariff. In **Robert Whaples** (ed.), *EH.Net Encyclopedia,* http://eh.net/encyclopedia /smoot-hawley-tariff/.

Chapter 14 Notes

1. This scenario is covered in a famous paper co-authored by Ben Bernanke (former Fed chairman): **Bernanke, Ben, and Mark Gertler.** March 1989. Agency costs, net worth, and business fluctuations. *American Economic Review* **79**(1): 14–31.

2. For one estimate of the value decline from foreclosure, an average of 27%, see **Campbell, John Y., Stefano Giglio, and Parag Pathak.** August 2011. Forced sales and house prices. *American Economic Review* **101**(5). The authors also provide the one in 12 statistic.

Chapter 16 Notes

1. **Bernanke, Ben S., Mark Gertler, and Mark Watson.** 1997. Systematic monetary policy and the effects of oil price shocks. *Brookings Papers on Economic Activity* **1**: 91–157.

Chapter 17 Notes

1. **Fuest, Clemens, Andreas Peichl, and Sebastian Siegloch.** 2018. Do higher corporate taxes reduce wages? Micro evidence from Germany. *American Economic Review* **108**(2): 393–418. https://doi.org/10.1257/aer.20130570; **Suárez Serrato, Juan Carlos, and Owen Zidar.** 2016. Who benefits from state corporate tax cuts? A local labor markets approach with heterogeneous firms. *American Economic Review* **106**(9): 2582–2624. https://doi.org /10.1257/aer.20141702.

2. **Hall, Robert E., and Alvin Rabushka.** 2007. *The Flat Tax—Revised and Expanded.* Stanford, CA: Hoover Institution.

3. Congressional Budget Office. CBO's 2015 Long-Term Projections for Social Security: Additional Information. https://www.cbo.gov/sites/default/files/114th-congress -2015-2016/reports/51047-ssupdate-2.pdf.

4. **Waldfogel, Joel.** 1993. The deadweight loss of Christmas. *The American Economic Review* **83**(5): 1328–1336.

5. **Special Inspector General for Iraq Reconstruction.** 2013. Learning from Iraq, http://cybercemetery.unt.edu /archive/sigir/20131001083907/http://www.sigir.mil /learningfromiraq/index.html.

6. **Buchanan, James M.** 1997. "The balanced budget amendment: Clarifying the arguments." *Public Choice* **90**(1/4): 117–138.

Chapter 18 Notes

1. **Hornbeck, J. F.** 2004. Argentina's sovereign debt restructuring. Congressional Research Service, RL 32637.

Chapter 19 Notes

1. **Fajgelbaum, Pablo D., Pinelopi K. Goldberg, Patrick J. Kennedy, and Amit K. Khandelwal.** 2019. The return to protectionism. Working Paper 25638. National Bureau of Economic Research. https://doi.org/10.3386/w25638.

2. On the environmental cost of sugar production, see **Schwabach, Aaron.** 2002. How protectionism is destroying the Everglades. *National Wetlands Newsletter* **24**(1): 7–14.

3. https://www.vox.com/new-money/2017/3/29/15035498/autor-trump-china-trade-election.

4. **Fajgelbaum et al.** 2019.

5. **Pitt, David.** 2018. U.S. farmers store record soybean crop as china dispute slashes exports. November 27, 2018. https://www.chicagotribune.com/business/ct-biz-soybean-crop-china-trade-war-20181127-story.html.

6. On the $20 increase in Whirlpool's price, see **Tankersley, Jim.** January 25, 2019. How tariffs stained the washing machine market. *New York Times*, https://www.nytimes.com/2019/01/25/business/economy/how-tariffs-stained-the-washing-machine-market.html. At the time, there were about 63.3 million Whirlpool shares outstanding.

7. On the different reasons why more educated workers and their political representatives tend to be more supportive of free trade, see **Galantucci** (2013) and **Hainmueller and Hiscox** (2006).

8. See **Bellamy, Carol.** 1997. *The State of the World's Children—1997.* New York: Oxford University Press and UNICEF. http://unicef.org/sowc97/.

9. See **Edmonds, Eric V., and Nina Pavcnik.** January 2006. International trade and child labor: Cross-country evidence. *Journal of International Economics*: 115–140.

10. **Bharadwaj, Prashant, Leah K. Lakdawala, and Nicholas Li.** 2013. Perverse consequences of well intentioned regulation: Evidence from India's child labor ban. Working Paper 19602. National Bureau of Economic Research. https://doi.org/10.3386/w19602.

11. On the 1918 flu, see **Barry, John M.** 2005. *The Great Influenza: The Epic Story of the Deadliest Plague in History.* New York: Penguin. On policy for a future pandemic, see **Cowen, Tyler.** 2005. Avian flu: What should be done. Working paper, Mercatus Center, George Mason University, Arlington, VA. https://ppe.mercatus.org/system/files/PDF_WP_Avian_Flu_20060726.pdf.

12. Quoted in **Norberg, Johan.** 2003. *In Defense of Global Capitalism.* Washington, DC: Cato Institute.

13. To simplify the diagram we also assume that that there are no domestic suppliers.

Chapter 21 Notes

1. **House of Commons.** November 11, 1947. Official Report, 5th Series, Vol. 444, cc. 206–207.

2. **Kaiser/Harvard Program on the Public and Health/Social Policy Survey.** January 1995.

3. See, for instance, **DeLorme, Charles D., Stacey Isom, and David R. Kamerschen.** April 2005. Rent seeking and taxation in the ancient Roman Empire. *Applied Economics* **37**: 705–711. http://ideas.repec.org/a/taf/applec/v37y2005i6p705-711.html.

4. **Einstein, Katherine Levine, Glick, David M., Palmer., Maxwell B.** 2019. Neighborhood Defenders: Participatory Politics and America's Housing Crisis. New York: Cambridge Univ. Press.

5. **Leeson, Peter T.** 2008. Media freedom, political knowledge, and participation. *Journal of Economic Perspectives* **22**(2): 155–169.

6. **Djankov, S., C. McLiesh, T. Nenova, and A. Shleifer.** 2003. Who owns the media? *Journal of Law and Economics* **46**(2): 341–381.

7. See **Conquest, Robert.** 1987. *Harvest of Sorrow.* New York: Oxford University Press.

8. **Sen, Amartya.** August 2, 1990. *Public Action to Remedy Hunger.* Arturo Tanco Memorial Lecture.

9. **Besley, T., and R. Burgess.** 2002. The political economy of government responsiveness: Theory and evidence from India. *Quarterly Journal of Economics* **117**(4): 1415–1452.

10. https://www.natso.com/en_us.

Appendix A Notes

1. **Clark, Gerald.** 1969. What happens when the police go on strike. *New York Times Magazine*, November 16, Sec. 6, pp. 45, 176–185, 187, 194–195.

2. **Klick, Jonathan, and Alexander Tabarrok.** 2005. Using terror alert levels to estimate the effect of police on crime. *Journal of Law & Economics* **48**(1): 267–280.

INDEX

Note: Page numbers in bold indicate key terms. Page numbers followed by "f" refer to figures, photos, and illustrations. Page numbers followed by "t" refer to tables. Page numbers followed by "n" refer to footnotes.

Current account, **452**, 454, 454f
Customers. *See* Buyers and sellers
Cutting-edge growth, **151**–152, 162–171, 163f, 164f
Czech Republic, government spending in, 397f

D

Daly, Mary, 347f
Danger. *See* Risk
Dark Ages, 21
Deadweight loss
  price ceiling and, 75–76, 75f
  price floor and, 89–90, 89f
  rent controls and, 85
  tariffs and, 431f, 441–442, 442f
Debt. *See also* Debt-to-GDP ratio; National debt held by the public
  in Great Depression, 307
Debt-to-GDP ratio, 393–394, 394f, 396
Deductions from taxation, 383
Default risk, 194
Defense spending. *See* Military spending
Deficit, **394**, 395f
Deflation, **273**, **360**
Demand. *See also* Borrowing, demand for; Demand curve; Demand for labor; Quantity demanded; Supply and demand
  demand shifters, 33–36, 33f, 35f
  vs. quantity demanded, 60–62, 61f
Demand curve, **29**–36, 30f–33f, 35f, 44. *See also* Aggregate demand curve
  consumer surplus and, 32, 32f
  shifts of, 33–36, 33f, 35f, 62
  equilibrium and, 58–60, 60f
  savings and borrowing and, 190–192, 191f, 192f
Demand for labor, 88–89, 88f
  labor force participation rate and, 253–257, 254f
Democracy, 476, 484–478. *See also* Voters and elections
  famine and, 488–490, 489f, 490f
  growth and, 490–491
  median voter theorem and, 485–487, 485f
  vs. nondemocracy, 487–488, 487f
Democratic Republic of Congo, child labor in, 439f

Demographics, and demand, 34, 34f
Deng Xiaoping, 136
Denmark, 244, 397f
Deposit insurance, 343
Deposits, 334–336, 335f
Depreciation
  economic growth and, 155–157, 156f, 157f, 158–159, 159f, 160f, 164, 164f
  in GDP, 113n
Depreciation in currency price, **458**–459, 459f, 463, 463f
Deregulation. *See* Regulation and deregulation
Diarrhea, 125
Diets, 35
Diminishing returns, 153–155, 153f, 161, 170–171
Diocletian (Roman emperor), 97, 97f
Dirty float, **465**–466
Disability insurance, 255
Discouraged workers, **235**–236, 236f
Discrimination, and rent controls, 84
Disinflation, **273**, **360**–361
Dissaving, 185, 185f, 188, 188f
Distorted price signals, 366
Diversification in investing, 221–224
Dollar (U.S.), and exchange rates, 458, 464, 465
Dollarization, **465**
Domestics (nannies, house cleaners, etc.), and GDP, 115
Dominican Republic, child labor in, 439f
Domino's, 168
Dot.com stocks, 228–229, 229f
Dow Jones Industrial Average, 222
Draft (military), 398
Drug lag, 3, 4
Drug loss, 3, 4
Drugs (medicines). *See* Pharmaceuticals industry
Dust Bowl (U.S.), 308–309

E

Earned Income Tax Credit (EITC), 391
eBay, 13–14, 14f
Economic freedom index, 487–488, 487f
Economic growth, 6–7, 125–182, **128**. *See also* Booms; Business fluctuations; Economics of ideas; GDP

per capita; Gross domestic product; Real GDP per capita; Recessions; Solow model of economic growth
  catching-up growth, 151–152
  cutting-edge growth, 151–152, 162–171, 163f, 164f
  demand and, 34
  democracy and, 490–491
  factors of production and, 131–133, 132f, 133f
  future of, 169–171
  institutions and, 132f, 134–141, 164
  research and development in, 165–166, 170
  interest rates and, 278, 279t
  key facts about, 126–130
  in long run, 301–304, 301f, 302f, 304f
  miracles and disasters of, 129–130, 130f
  rates of, 105–106, 107–108, 108f, 271–272
  primer on, 128–129
  ultimate causes of, 139–141
  unemployment and, 233
  after World War II, 154–155, 155t
Economics. *See also* Economics of ideas
  behavioral economics, 186
  big ideas of, 1–10
  as experimental science, 56–58, 57f, 58f
  importance of, 10
  "marginal revolution" in, 5
Economics of ideas, 152, 165–171. *See also* New ideas; Research and development
Economies of scale, **139**
  economic growth and, 139
  trade and, 6
Ecuador, 63n
Edison, Thomas, 438
Education. *See also* Colleges and universities
  as consumption spending, 111
  GDP per capita and, 158, 158f
  impatience and, 186
  politics and, 491
  protectionism and, 437–438
  wages and, 255–257, 256f, 257f
Egypt, 62, 63
Eiger Labs, 166
Eilish, Billie, 477
EITC (Earned Income Tax Credit), 391
Elasticity

corporate income tax and, 385–386
  strategic trade protectionism and, 441, 442f
Elderly. *See also* Medicare; Social Security
  demand and, 34, 34f
Elections. *See* Voters and elections
Employment. *See also* Unemployment; Wages; *entries beginning "Labor..."*
  employment at-will doctrine, 242
  fiscal policy and, 405–406
  after incarceration, 258
  international trade and, 427, 433–434, 436
Employment at-will doctrine, **242**
Energy. *See entries beginning "Oil..."*
England. *See* United Kingdom
Entrepreneurs, and corruption 3, 136–137
Entry or exit of producers, as supply shifter, 42–43, 42f, 43n
Environmental issues and environmentalism, 36
  GDP and, 115–116
Environmental Protection Agency (EPA), 398
Ephron, Nora, 84–85
Equilibrium, 51–65. *See also* Equilibrium price; Equilibrium quantity
  adjustment process and, 51–53, 52f, 53f
  in labor force participation, 253, 254f
  in market for loanable funds, 190–197, 190f–192f, 195f
  terminology for, 60–62, 61f
  trade and, 53–58, 54f, 56f
  supply and demand model for, tests of, 56–60, 57f, 59f, 60f
Equilibrium price, 51, **52**–56, 52f–54f, 56f
Equilibrium quantity, 51, **52**–56, 52f–54f, 56f
Equity, **324**
Estonia, government spending in, 397f
Ethiopia, child labor in, 439f
Euro, 465
Europe. *See also specific countries*
  currency union in, 465
  structural unemployment in, 238–244, 239t, 240t, 243f

Basic Relationships and Magnitudes

Gross Domestic Product, GDP, is the market value of all finished goods and services produced within a country in a year.

GDP per capita is GDP divided by a country's population.

The **national spending identity:**

$$Y = C + I + G + NX$$

Y = nominal GDP, C = spending on consumption goods and services, I = spending on investment goods (also called capital goods), G = government purchases, NX = net exports defined as the market value of exports minus the market value of imports.

Economic growth is the growth rate of real per capita GDP.

In an average year, U.S. GDP grows by about 3.2% and GDP per capita by about 2.1%. In a recession, GDP declines.

The **Rule of 70:** If the annual growth rate of a variable is x percent, then the doubling time is years.

The **labor force** is all workers, employed plus unemployed.

Unemployed workers are adults who do not have a job but who are looking for work.

The **unemployment rate** is the percentage of the labor force without a job.

The **inflation rate** is the percentage change in the average level of prices (as measured by a price index) over a period of time.

The **Consumer Price Index, CPI,** measures the average price of a large basket of goods bought by a typical American consumer.

A **real price** is a price that has been corrected for inflation. Real prices are used to compare the prices of goods over time.

The **quantity theory of money:**

$$M \times v = P \times Y_R$$

M = Money supply $\qquad$ P = Price level
v = velocity of money $\qquad$ Y_R = Real GDP

When v and Y_R are relatively fixed then increases in the money stock, M, must cause increases in the price level, P.

The **quantity theory in growth form:**

$$\vec{M} + \vec{v} = \vec{P} + \vec{Y}_R$$

$$\vec{M} + \vec{v} = \text{Inflation} + \text{Real growth}$$

An arrow indicates the growth rate of the indicated variable. For example, $\vec{P}$ is the growth rate of prices (the inflation rate, π).

If $\vec{v}$ and Real growth are relatively fixed then an increase in the growth rate of the money supply, $\vec{M}$, must increase the Inflation rate.

Growth

Countries with a high GDP per capita have a lot of physical and human capital per worker and that capital is organized using the best technological knowledge to be highly productive.

Good **institutions** such as property rights, honest government, political stability, a dependable legal system, and competitive and open markets create **incentives** to invest in physical and human capital, create new technological knowledge, and organize the factors of production to be highly productive.

GDP can be written in terms of a production function as $Y = F(A, K, e \times L)$ where Y is output or GDP, A is ideas, K is physical capital, e is human capital per worker (education), and L is the number of workers.

Holding e and L constant, and choosing a particular function, we simplify as:

The **iron logic of diminishing returns** says that increases in K increase Y but at a diminishing rate.

Investment is output that is not consumed.

If investment > depreciation, the capital stock and output grow. If investment < depreciation, the capital stock and output fall.

The iron logic of diminishing returns and a linear depreciation rate imply that at some point all of investment must be just enough to balance capital depreciation. When investment = depreciation, neither the capital stock nor output grows. This is known as the **steady state**.

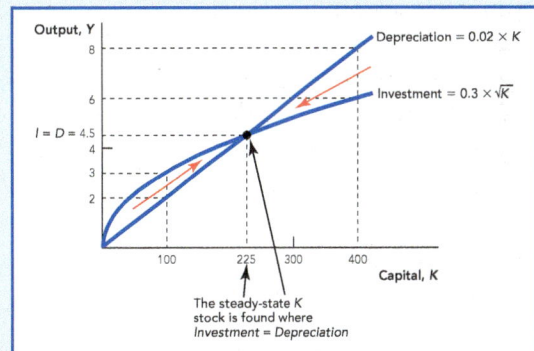

The steady-state K stock is found where Investment = Depreciation

An increase in A, better ideas, means the same capital stock, K, can produce more output.

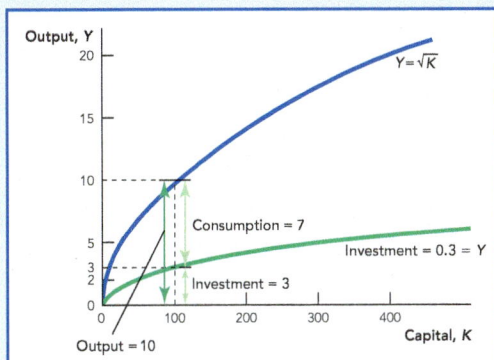

Capital depreciates. It wears out, rusts, and falls apart. Depreciation is a linear function of the capital stock: for example,

$$Depreciation = 0.02 \times K$$

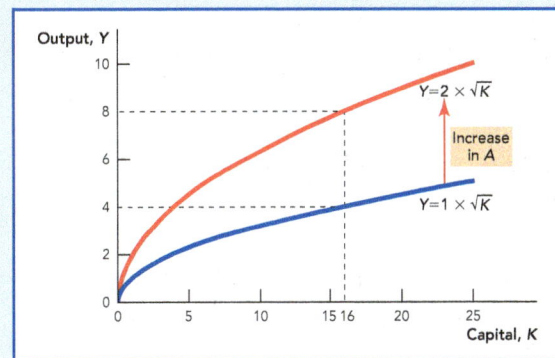

Better ideas are necessary for sustained economic growth.

Aggregate Demand–Aggregate Supply

The **Solow growth rate** is an economy's potential growth rate, the rate of economic growth that would occur given flexible prices and the existing real factors of production.

Rearranging the quantity theory we have an equation for the **aggregate demand curve**.

$$\overrightarrow{M} + \vec{v} = \text{Inflation} + \text{Real Growth}$$

The aggregate demand curve shows all the combinations of inflation and real growth that are consistent with a specified rate of spending growth.

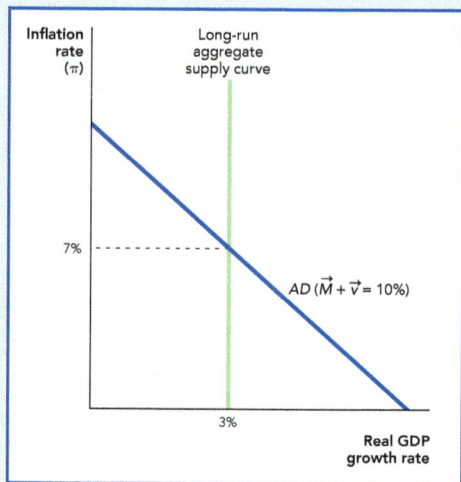

Real shocks and aggregate demand shocks are essential elements of the aggregate demand/aggregate supply model.

The **short-run aggregate supply (SRAS) curve** shows the positive relationship between the inflation rate and real growth during the period when prices and wages are sticky.

Transmission mechanisms transmit and amplify shocks. Intertemporal substitution, uncertainty and irreversible investments, labor adjustment costs, time bunching, and sticky wages and prices are all transmission mechanisms.

Fiscal or monetary policy can be used to increase aggregate demand, reversing a decline in private demand.

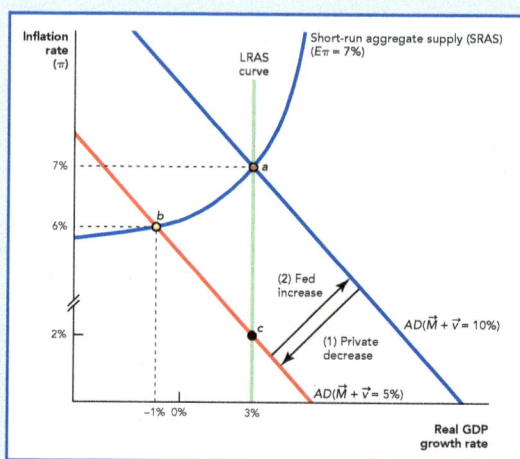

A positive real shock increases the potential growth rate of the economy and shifts the Long-run aggregate supply (LRAS) curve to the right. A **negative real shock** shifts the LRAS curve to the left.

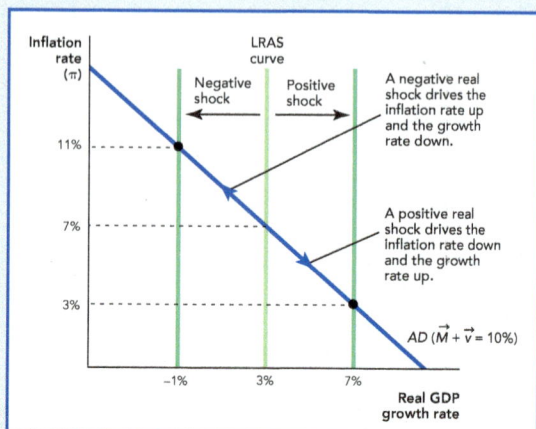

Fiscal and monetary policy are less effective when a recession is caused by a real shock.

A

Reading Graphs and Making Graphs

Economists use graphs to illustrate both ideas and data. In this appendix, we review commonly used graphs, explain how to read them, and give you a few tips on how you can make graphs using Microsoft Excel or similar software.

Graphs Express Ideas

In economics, graphs are used to express ideas. The most common graphs we use throughout this book plot two variables on a coordinate system. One variable is plotted on the vertical or y-axis, while the other variable is plotted on the horizontal or x-axis.

In Figure A.1, for example, we plot a very generic graph of variable Y against variable X. Starting on the vertical axis at $Y = 100$, you read across to the point at which you hit the graph and then down to find $X = 800$. Thus, when $Y = 100$, $X = 800$. In this case, you can also see that when $X = 800$, then $Y = 100$. Similarly, when $Y = 60$, you can read from the graph that $X = 400$, and vice versa. As you may recall, the slope of a straight line is defined as the rise over the run or rise/run. In this case, when Y rises from 60 to 100, a rise of 40, then X runs from 400 to 800, a run of 400, so the slope of the line is $40/400 = 0.1$. The slope is positive, indicating that when Y increases so does X.

Let's now apply the idea of a graph to some economic concepts. In Chapter 3, we show how a demand curve can be constructed from hypothetical data on the price and quantity demanded of oil. We show this here as Figure A.2.

The table on the left of the figure shows that at a price of $55 per barrel buyers are willing and able to buy 5 million barrels of oil a day (MBD), or more simply at a price of $55, the quantity demanded is 5 MBD. You can read this information off the graph in the following way. Starting on the vertical axis, locate the price of $55. Then look to the right for the point where the $55 price hits the demand curve: looking down from this point, you see that the quantity demanded is 5 million barrels of oil per day. How about at a lower price of $20 per day? Start at $20 on the vertical axis and read to the right until the price hits the demand curve, then read down. Can you see that the quantity demanded at this price of $20 per barrel is 25 million barrels of oil per day?

We said that graphs express ideas, so what is the idea being expressed here? The most important fact about a demand curve is that it has a negative slope, that is, it slopes downward. This tells us the important but simple idea that as the price of a good falls, the quantity demanded increases. This is key: as the price of a good such as oil falls, people demand more of it.

FIGURE A.1

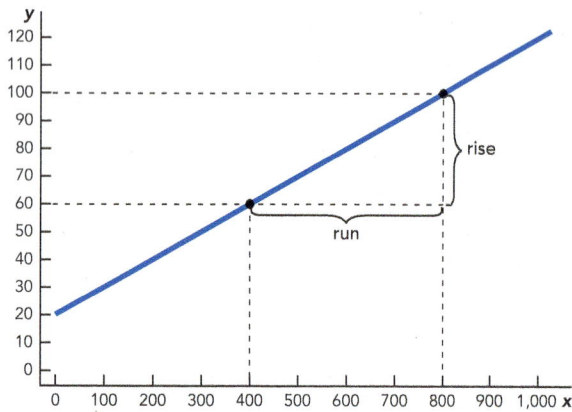

The Slope of a Line

FIGURE A.2

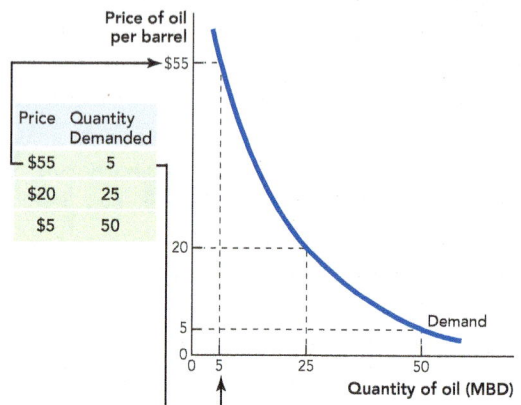

Price	Quantity Demanded
$55	5
$20	25
$5	50

A demand curve is a description of what *would happen* to the quantity demanded as the price of a good changed, *holding fixed all other influences on the quantity of oil demanded.* (In this sense, demand curves are hypothetical and we rarely observe them directly.)

The quantity of oil demanded, for example, depends not just on the price of oil but on many other factors such as income or the price of other goods like automobiles and population, to name just a few of many influences. Today's demand curve for oil, for example, depends on today's income, price of automobiles and population. Imagine, for example, that average income today is $10,000, the price of an average automobile is $25,000 and world population is 7 billion. The blue curve in Figure A.3 shows the demand curve for oil under these conditions. Note that there are also many other influences on the demand for oil that we don't list but that are also being held fixed. Most importantly, if any of these conditions changes then the demand curve for oil will shift.

FIGURE A.3

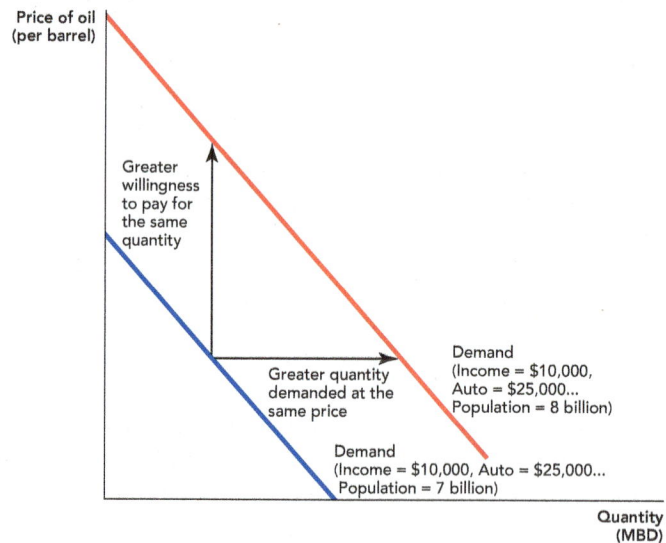

If world population increases to 8 billion, for example, there will be a new demand curve for oil. With a greater population, there will be more barrels of oil demanded at every specific price so the demand curve will shift to the right. Equivalently, as the population increases, there will be a greater willingness to pay for any given quantity of oil, so the demand curve will shift up. Thus, we say that an increase in demand is a shift in the curve up and to the right shown by the red curve in Figure A.3. Chapter 3 explains in greater detail how a demand curve shifts in response to changes in factors other than price.

What is important to emphasize here is that a demand curve is drawn holding fixed every influence on the quantity demanded other than price. Changes in any factor that influences the demand for oil other than price will produce a new demand curve.

One more important feature of two variables graphed in a coordinate system is that these figures can be read in two different ways. For example, as we mention in Chapter 3, demand curves can be read both horizontally and vertically. Read "horizontally," you can see from Figure A.4 that at a price of $20 per barrel demanders are willing and able to buy 25 million barrels of oil per day. Read "vertically," you can see that the maximum price that demanders are willing to pay for 25 million barrels of oil a day is $20 per barrel. Thus, demand curves show the quantity demanded at any price or the maximum willingness to pay (per unit) for any quantity.

FIGURE A.4

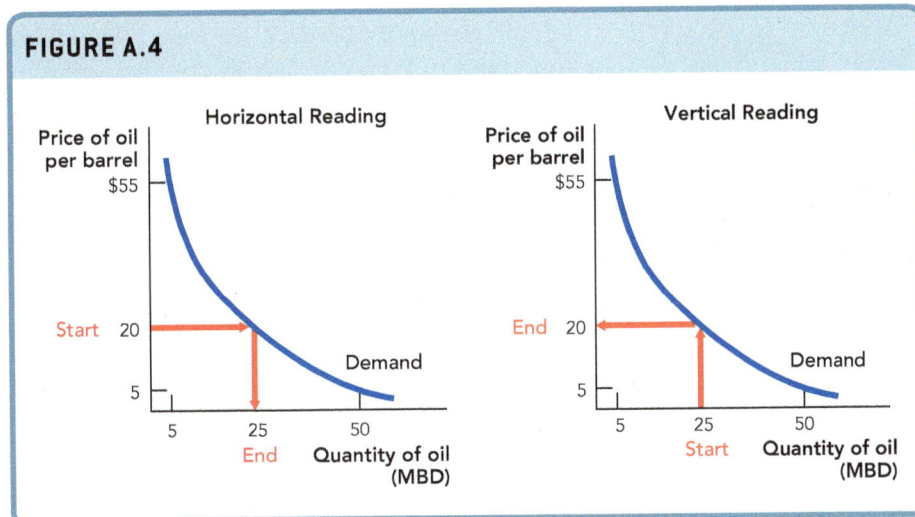

It may seem difficult at first to interpret these graphs, but as you will see, graphs are amazingly useful for thinking about difficult economic problems. It's like learning to drive a car—at first it's not easy and you will make some mistakes but once you learn how to drive, your ability to do things and go places increases enormously. The same thing is true with graphs!

Data Graphs

As well as expressing ideas, graphs can also be used to illustrate data. For example, GDP can be broken down according to the national spending identity into these components: Consumption, Investment, Government Purchases, and Net Exports (Exports minus Imports), that is, $GDP = Y = C + I + G + NX$. U.S. GDP for 2007 is shown in Table A.1.

TABLE A.1 U.S. GDP 2007 (in billions of dollars)

Category	GDP
Consumption	9,710.2
Investment	2,130.4
Government	2,674.8
Net Exports	–707.8
GDP (Total)	13,807.6

Data from: U.S. Bureau of Economic Analysis.

FIGURE A.5

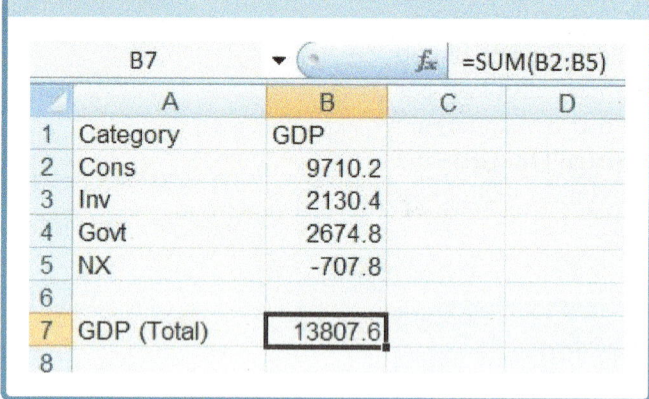

If you type the components into Excel, as shown in Figure A.5, you can use the sum function to check that the components do add up to GDP.

Highlighting the data in columns A and B and clicking Insert > Column > Clustered Column and (with a few modifications to add axis titles and to make the graph look pretty), we have the graph on the left side of Figure A.6.

The graph on the right side of Figure A.6 shows exactly the same data only on the right side we chose Stacked Column (and we switched the rows and columns). Sometimes one visualization of the data is more revealing than another so it's a good idea to experiment a little bit with alternative ways of presenting the same data. But please don't get carried away with adding 3-D effects or other chart junk. Always keep the focus on the data, not on the special effects.

In this book, we explain the economics of stocks, bonds, and other investments. A lot of financial data is available for free on the web. We used Yahoo! Finance, for example, to download data for the value of the S&P 500 Index on the first trading day of the month from 1950 to the end of 2000. The data is graphed in Figure A.7.

To graph the S&P 500 data, we used a line graph. The top graph in Figure A.7 shows the data graphed in the "normal" way, with equal distances on the

FIGURE A.6

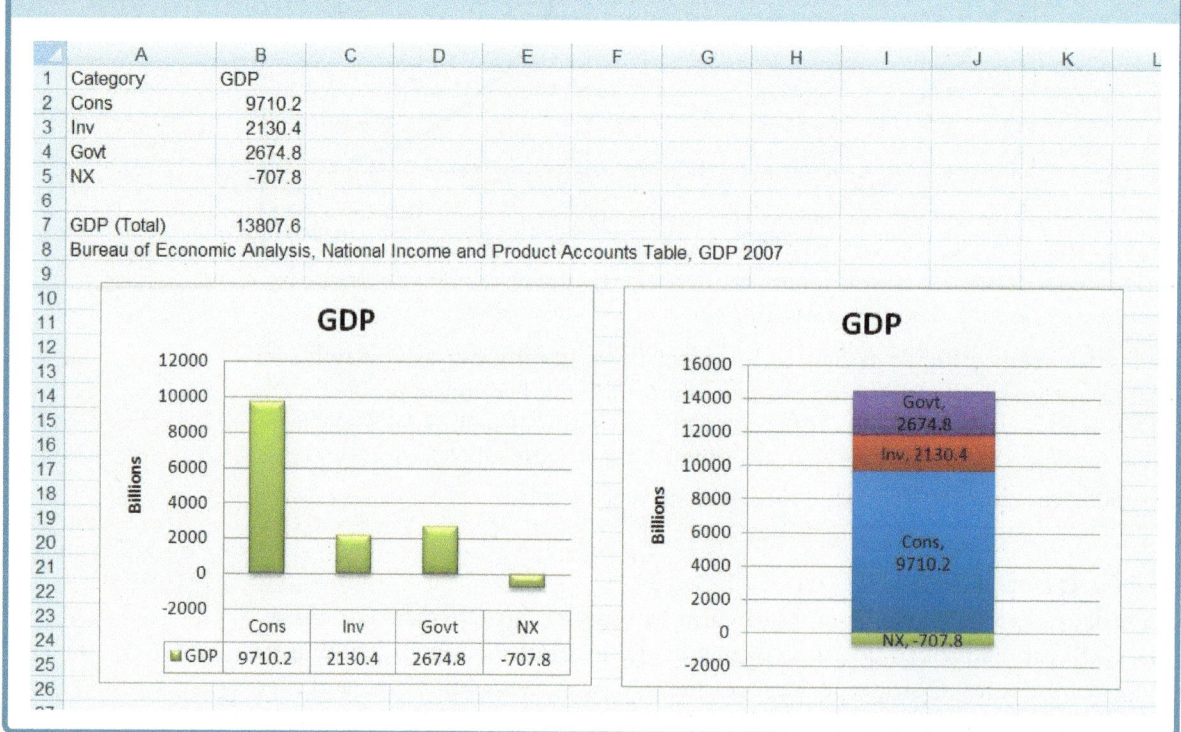

FIGURE A.7

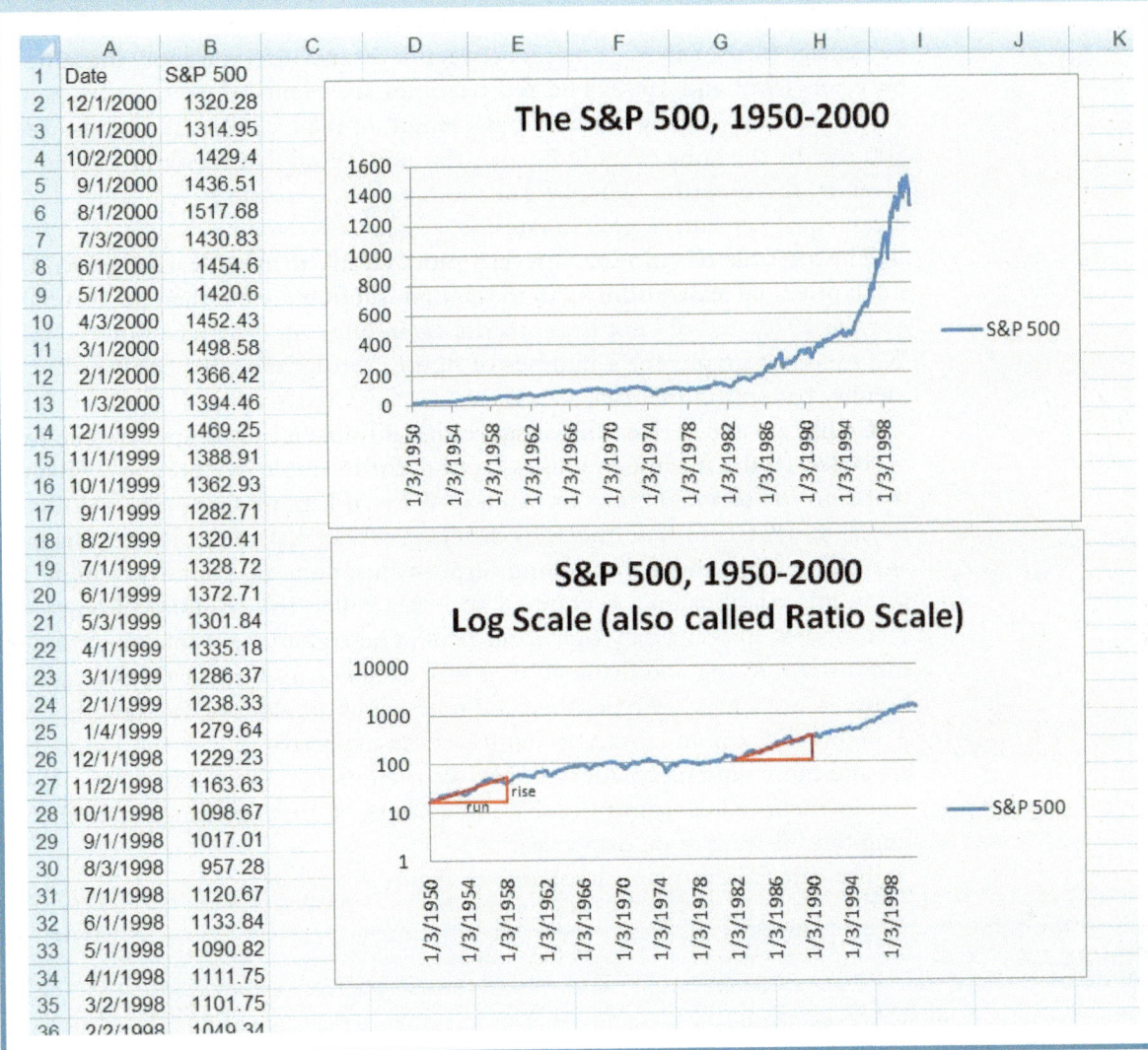

	A	B
1	Date	S&P 500
2	12/1/2000	1320.28
3	11/1/2000	1314.95
4	10/2/2000	1429.4
5	9/1/2000	1436.51
6	8/1/2000	1517.68
7	7/3/2000	1430.83
8	6/1/2000	1454.6
9	5/1/2000	1420.6
10	4/3/2000	1452.43
11	3/1/2000	1498.58
12	2/1/2000	1366.42
13	1/3/2000	1394.46
14	12/1/1999	1469.25
15	11/1/1999	1388.91
16	10/1/1999	1362.93
17	9/1/1999	1282.71
18	8/2/1999	1320.41
19	7/1/1999	1328.72
20	6/1/1999	1372.71
21	5/3/1999	1301.84
22	4/1/1999	1335.18
23	3/1/1999	1286.37
24	2/1/1999	1238.33
25	1/4/1999	1279.64
26	12/1/1998	1229.23
27	11/2/1998	1163.63
28	10/1/1998	1098.67
29	9/1/1998	1017.01
30	8/3/1998	957.28
31	7/1/1998	1120.67
32	6/1/1998	1133.84
33	5/1/1998	1090.82
34	4/1/1998	1111.75
35	3/2/1998	1101.75
36	2/2/1998	1049.34

vertical axis indicating equal changes in the index. That's not necessarily the best way to graph the data, however, because a quick look at the top figure suggests that stock prices were rising faster over time. In other words, the graph looks pretty flat between 1950 and approximately 1980, after which it shoots up. The appearance of faster growth, however, is mostly an illusion. The problem is that when the S&P 500 was at the level of 100, as it was around 1968, a 10% increase moves the index to 110, or an increase of 10 points. But when the index is at the level of 1,000, as it was around 1998, a 10% increase moves the index to 1,100, or an increase of 100 points. Thus, the same percentage increase looks much larger in 1998 than in 1968.

To get a different view of the data, right-click on the vertical axis of the top figure, choose "Format Axis" and click the box labeled "Logarithmic Scale," which produces the graph in the bottom of Figure A.7 (without the red triangles, which we will explain shortly).

Notice on the bottom figure that equal distances on the vertical axis now indicate equal percentage increases or ratios. The ratio 100/10, for example, is the same as the ratio 1,000/100. You can now see at a glance that if stock prices move the same vertical distance over the same length of time (as measured by the horizontal distance) then the percentage increase was the same. For example, we have superimposed two identical red triangles to show that the percentage increase in stock prices between 1950 and 1958 was about the same as between 1982 and 1990. The red triangles are identical, so over the same 8-year period, given by the horizontal length of the triangle, the run, the S&P 500 rose by the same vertical distance, the rise. Recall that the slope of a line is given by the rise/run. Thus, we can also say that on a ratio graph, equal slopes mean equal percentage growth rates.

The log scale or ratio graph reveals more clearly than our earlier graph that stock prices increased from 1950 to the mid-1960s but were then flat throughout the 1970s and did not begin to rise again until after the recession in 1982. We use ratio graphs for a number of figures throughout this book to better identify patterns in the data.

Graphs are also very useful for suggesting possible relationships between two variables. In the macroeconomics section, for example, we present evidence that labor employment laws in much of Western Europe that make it difficult to fire workers also raise the costs of hiring workers. As a result, the percentage of unemployment that is long term in Europe tends to be very high. To show this relationship, we graphed an index called the "rigidity of employment index," produced by the World Bank. The rigidity of employment index summarizes hiring and firing costs as well as how easy it is for firms to adjust hours of work (e.g., whether there are restrictions on night or weekend hours). A higher index number means that it is more expensive to hire and fire workers and more difficult to adjust hours. We then graphed a country's rigidity of employment index against the share of a country's unemployment rate that is long term (lasting more than a year).

The data for this graph are shown in Figure A.8.

FIGURE A.8

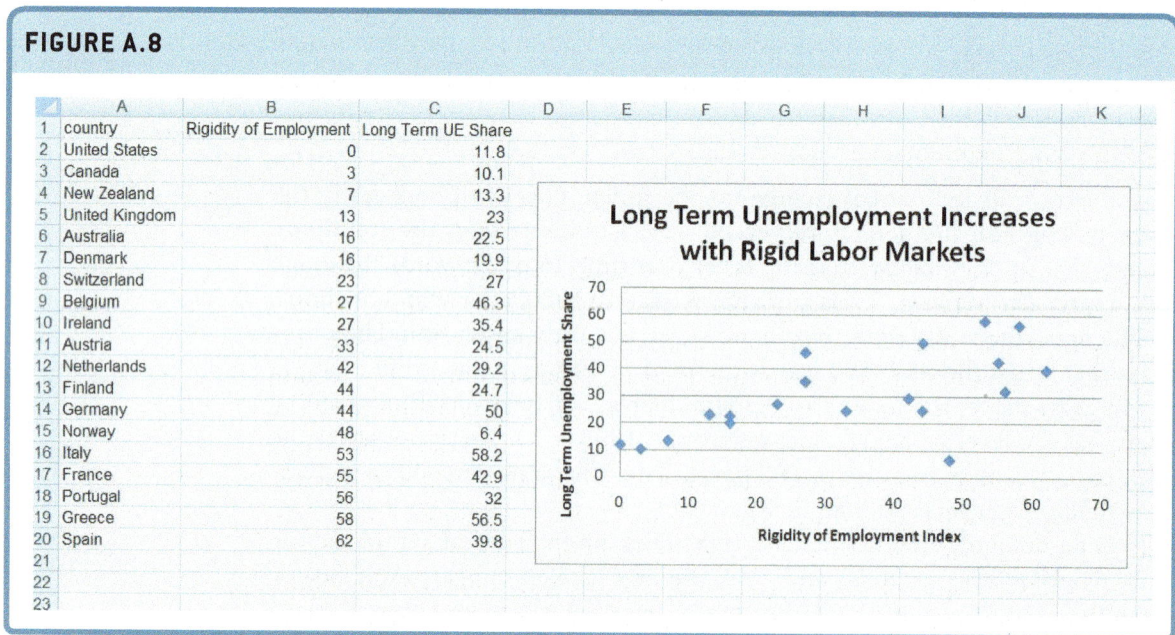

	A	B	C	D	E	F	G	H	I	J	K
1	country	Rigidity of Employment	Long Term UE Share								
2	United States	0	11.8								
3	Canada	3	10.1								
4	New Zealand	7	13.3								
5	United Kingdom	13	23								
6	Australia	16	22.5								
7	Denmark	16	19.9								
8	Switzerland	23	27								
9	Belgium	27	46.3								
10	Ireland	27	35.4								
11	Austria	33	24.5								
12	Netherlands	42	29.2								
13	Finland	44	24.7								
14	Germany	44	50								
15	Norway	48	6.4								
16	Italy	53	58.2								
17	France	55	42.9								
18	Portugal	56	32								
19	Greece	58	56.5								
20	Spain	62	39.8								
21											
22											
23											

We can do something else of interest with this data. If you right-click on any of the data points in the figure, you will get the option to "Add Trendline." Clicking on this and then clicking the two boxes "Linear" and "Display Equation on Chart" produces Figure A.9 (absent the red arrow, which we added for clarity).

FIGURE A.9

	A	B	C	D	E	F	G	H	I	J	K	
1	country	Rigidity of Employment	Long Term UE Share									
2	United States	0	11.8									
3	Canada	3	10.1									
4	New Zealand	7	13.3									
5	United Kingdom	13	23									
6	Australia	16	22.5									
7	Denmark	16	19.9									
8	Switzerland	23	27									
9	Belgium	27	46.3									
10	Ireland	27	35.4									
11	Austria	33	24.5									
12	Netherlands	42	29.2									
13	Finland	44	24.7									
14	Germany	44	50									
15	Norway	48	6.4									
16	Italy	53	58.2									
17	France	55	42.9									
18	Portugal	56	32									
19	Greece	58	56.5									
20	Spain	62	39.8									
21												
22												

Long Term Unemployment Increases with Rigid Labor Markets

(Chart: Long Term Unemployment Share vs. Rigidity of Employment Index, with best-fit line $y = 0.4987x + 13.726$)

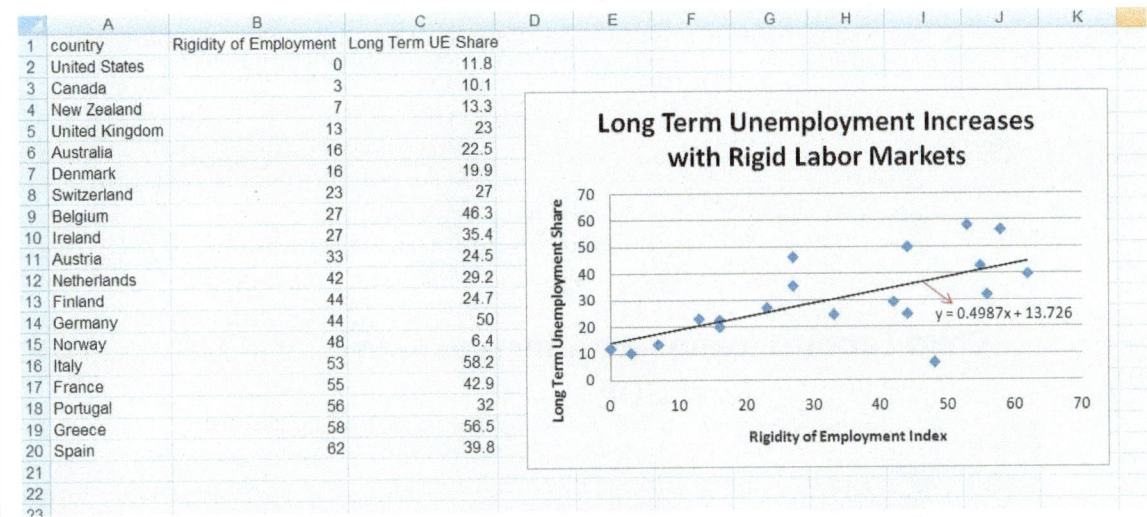

The black line is the linear curve that "best fits" the data. (Best fit in this context is defined statistically; we won't go into the details here but if you take a statistics class you will learn about ordinary least squares.) Excel also produces for us the equation for the best-fit line, $Y = 0.4987 \times X + 13.726$.

Do you remember from high school the formula for a straight line, $Y = m \times X + b$? In this case m, the slope of the line or the rise/run is 0.4987 and b, the intercept, is 13.726. The slope tells us that a 1 unit increase in the rigidity of employment index (a run of 1) increases the share of unemployment that is long term by, on average, 0.4987 percentage points (a rise of 0.4987). Using the equation, you can substitute any value for the index to find a predicted value for the share of long-term unemployment. If the rigidity of employment index is 15, for example, then our prediction for the long-term unemployment share is $21.2065 = 0.4987 \times 15 + 13.726$ If the index is 55, our prediction for the long-term unemployment share is $41.1545 = 0.4987 \times 55 + 13.726$.

Graphing Three Variables

In our international trade chapter, we present evidence that child labor decreases with increases in GDP per capita. Figure A.10 shows a subset of that data. We put our X variable, real GDP per capita, in column B and our Y variable, the percentage of children ages 10–14 in the labor force, in column C. In column D, we have the total number of children in the labor force. In Burundi, a larger fraction (48.5%) of the children are in the labor force than in India (12.1%), but since Burundi is a small country, the total number of children in the labor force is larger in India. To understand the problem of child labor, it's important to understand both types of information so we put both types of information on a graph.

Excel's bubble chart will take data arrayed in three columns and use the third column to set the area of the bubble or data point. In Figure A.10, for example, India has the largest number of children in the labor force and so has the bubble with the largest area. The area of the other bubbles is in relative proportion, so Mexico's bubble is 1/25th the size of India's bubble because there are 1/25th as many children in the labor force in Mexico as in India. (Unfortunately, Excel doesn't label the bubbles automatically so we added these by hand.)

FIGURE A.10

	A	B	C	D	E
1	Country	Real GDP Per Capita	% Children in Work Force	Total Children in Work Force	
2	Burundi	523	48.5	439,623	
3	Ethiopia	635	41.1	3,472,114	
4	Bangladesh	1,684	27.7	4,592,758	
5	Thailand	6,857	12.2	666,602	
6	India	2,479	12.1	13,300,000	
7	Mexico	8,762	4.9	531,132	
8	Argentina	11,006	2.4	80,265	
9					
10					

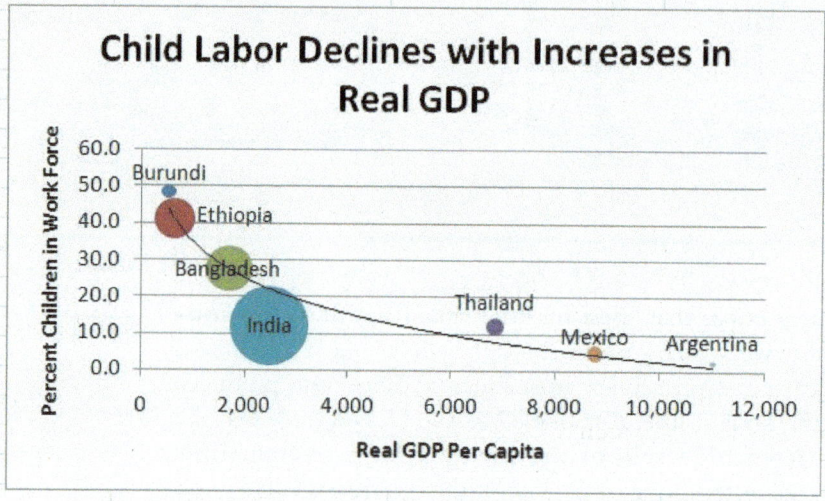

Child Labor Declines with Increases in Real GDP

Cause and Effect

Do police reduce crime? If so, by how much? That's a key question that economists and criminologists are interested in understanding because local governments (and taxpayers) spend billions of dollars on police every year and would like to know whether they are getting their money's worth. Should they spend less on police or more? Unfortunately, it's surprisingly difficult to answer this question. To illustrate why, Figure A.11 shows the relationship between crime per capita and police per capita from across a large number of U.S. cities.

Figure A.11 shows that cities with more police per capita have more crime per capita. Should we conclude that police cause crime? Probably not. More likely is "reverse causality," crime causes police—that is, greater crime rates lead to more hiring of police. We thus have two chains of potential cause and effect, more police reduce crime and more crime increases police. Unfortunately, you can't tell much about either of these two potential cause-and-effect relationships by looking at Figure A.11, which shows the correlation between police and crime but not the causation. But if you want to estimate the value of police, you need to know causation not just correlation. So what should you do?

The best way to estimate how much police reduce crime would be to take say 1,000 roughly similar cities and randomly flip a coin dividing the cities into two groups. In the first group of cities, double the police force and in the second group do nothing. Then compare crime rates over say the next year

FIGURE A.11

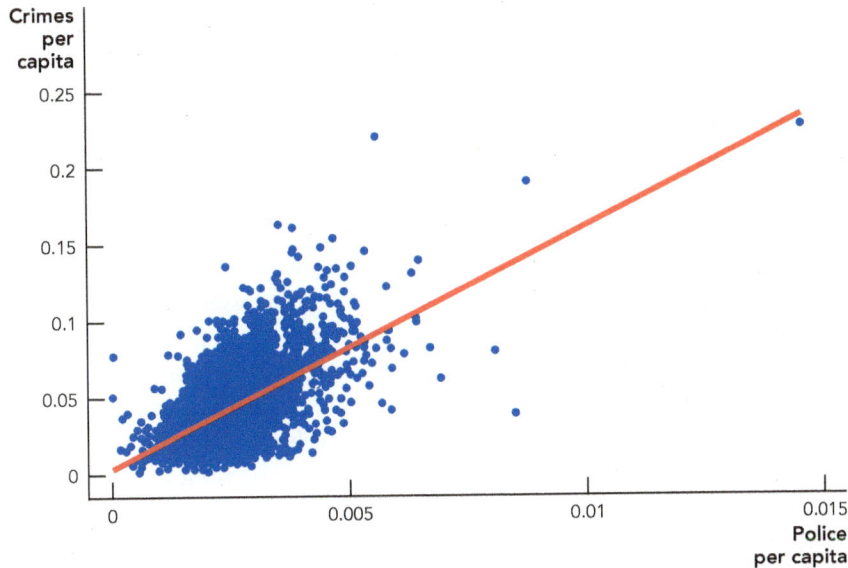

in cities with and without an increase in police. If the cities with an increase in police have lower rates of crime, then you can safely ascribe this differ-ence to the effect of police on crime. What makes the correlation evidence in Figure A.11 difficult to interpret is that increases in crime sometimes cause increases in police. But if you increase the number of police randomly, you eliminate the possibility of this "reverse causality." Thus, if crime falls in the cities that have random increases in police, the cause is most plausibly the increase in police. Similarly, if crime were to increase in cities that have random decreases in police, the cause is most plausibly the decrease in police.

Unfortunately, randomized experiments have at least one big problem—they are very expensive. Occasionally, large randomized experiments are done in criminology and other social sciences but because they are so expensive we must usually look for alternative methods for assessing causality.

If you can't afford a randomized experiment, what else can you do? One possibility is to look for what economists call quasi-experiments or natural experiments. In 1969, for example, police in Montreal, Canada, went on strike and there were 50 times more bank robberies than normal.[1] If you can think of the strike as a random event, not tied in any direct way to increases or decreases in crime, then you can be reasonably certain that the increase in bank robberies was caused by the decrease in police.

The Montreal experiment tells you it's probably not a good idea to eliminate all police, but it doesn't tell you whether governments should increase or decrease police on the street by a more reasonable amount, say 10% to 20%. Jonathan Klick and Alex Tabarrok use another natural experiment to address this question.[2] Since shortly after 9/11, the United States has had a terror alert system run by the Department of Homeland Security. When the terror alert level rises from "elevated" (yellow) to "high" (orange) due to intelligence reports regarding the current threat posed by terrorist organizations, the Washington, D.C. Metropolitan Police Department reacts by increasing the number of hours each officer must work.

Because the change in the terror alert system is not tied to any observed or expected changes in Washington crime patterns, this provides a useful quasi-experiment. In other words, whenever the terror alert system shifts from yellow to orange—a random decision with respect to crime in Washington—the effective police presence in Washington increases. Klick and Tabarrok find that during the high terror alert periods when more police are on the street, the amount of crime falls. Street crime such as stolen automobiles, thefts from automobiles, and burglaries decline especially sharply. Overall, Klick and Tabarrok estimate that a 10% increase in police reduces crime by about 3%. Using these numbers and figures on the cost of crime and of hiring more police, Klick and Tabarrok argue that more police would be very beneficial.

Economists have developed many techniques for assessing causality from data and we have only just brushed the surface. We can't go into details here. We want you to know, however, that in this textbook when we present data that suggests a causal relationship—such as when we argue in the international trade chapter that higher GDP leads to lower levels of child labor—that a significant amount of statistical research has gone into assessing causality, not just correlation. If you are interested in further details, we have provided you with the references to the original papers.

APPENDIX A QUESTIONS

1. We start with a simple idea from algebra: Which of the graphs at the top of the next page have a positive slope and which have a negative slope?

2. When social scientists talk about social and economic facts, they usually talk about a "positive relationship" or a "negative relationship" instead of "positive slope" or "negative slope." Based on your knowledge, which of the following pairs of variables tend to have a "positive relationship" (a positive slope when graphed), and which have a negative relationship? (*Note:* "Negative relationship" and "inverse relationship" mean the same thing. Also, in this question, we're only talking about correlation, not causation.)

   a. A professional baseball player's batting average and his annual salary.

   b. A professional golfer's average score and her average salary.

   c. The number of cigarettes a person smokes and her life expectancy.

   d. The size of the car you drive and your probability of surviving a serious accident.

   e. A country's distance from the equator and how rich its citizens tend to be. (For the answer, see Hall, Robert, and Charles Jones. 1999. Why do some countries produce so much more output per worker than others? *Quarterly Journal of Economics* 114: 83–116.)

3. Let's convert Klick and Tabarrok's research on crime into a simple algebra equation. We reported the result as the effect of a 10% increase in police on the crime rate in Washington, D.C. In the equation below, fill in the effect of a 1% increase in the police on the crime rate:

   The percent change in crime = _____ × The percent change in police officers

4. Let's read the child labor graph (Figure A.10) horizontally and then vertically:

   a. According to the trendline, in a typical country with 10% of the children in the labor force, what's the real GDP per person?

   b. According to the trendline, when a country's GDP per person is $2,000, roughly what percentage of children are in the labor force?

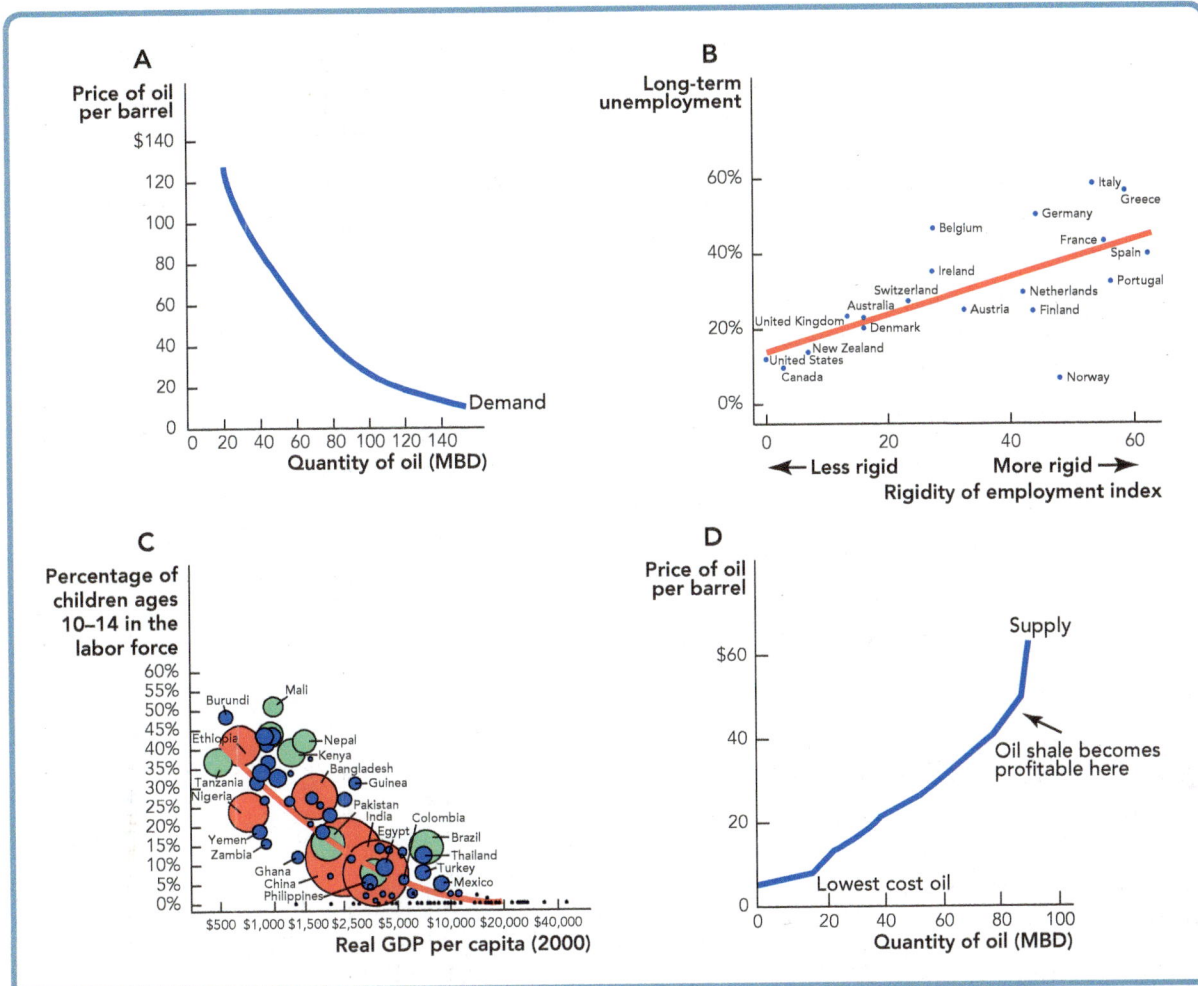

A

Price of oil per barrel — Demand; Quantity of oil (MBD)

B

Long-term unemployment vs. Rigidity of employment index (← Less rigid, More rigid →)

C

Percentage of children ages 10–14 in the labor force vs. Real GDP per capita (2000)

D

Price of oil per barrel — Supply; Oil shale becomes profitable here; Lowest cost oil; Quantity of oil (MBD)

5. Let's take another look at the ratio scale, and compare it to a normal scale.

   a. In Figure A.7, which one is presented in ratio scale and which in normal scale?

   b. In the top graph, every time the S&P 500 crosses a horizontal line, how many points did the S&P rise?

   c. In the bottom graph, every time the S&P 500 crosses a horizontal line, how many *times* higher is the S&P?

6. As a scientist, you have to plot the following data: The number of bacteria you have in a large petri dish, measured every hour over the course of a week. (*Note: E. coli* bacteria populations can double every 20 minutes.) Should this data be plotted on a ratio scale and why?

7. Educated people are supposed to point out (correctly) that "correlation isn't proof of causation." This is an important fact—which explains why economists, medical doctors, and other researchers spend a lot of time trying to look for proof of causation. But sometimes, correlation is good enough. In the following examples, take the correlation as a true fact, and explain why the correlation is, all by itself, useful for the task presented in each question.

   a. Your task is to decide what brand of car to buy. You know that Brand H usually gets higher quality ratings than Brand C. You don't know what causes Brand H to get higher ratings—maybe Brand H hires better workers, maybe Brand H buys better raw materials. All you have is the correlation.

   b. Your task is to hire the job applicant who appears to be the smartest. Applicant M has a degree from MIT, and applicant S has a degree from a typical state university. You don't know what causes MIT graduates to be smarter than typical state university graduates—maybe they start off smarter before they get to MIT, maybe their professors teach them a lot, maybe having smart classmates for four years gives them constant brain exercise.

c. Your task is to decide which city to move to, and you want to move to the city that is probably the safest. For some strange reason, the only fact you have to help you with your decision is the number of police per person.

8. If you haven't practiced in a while, let's calculate some slopes. In each case, we give two points, and you can use the "rise over run" formula to get the right answer.

a. Point 1: $x = 0$, $y = 0$. Point 2: $x = 3$, $y = 6$

b. Point 1: $x = 6$, $y = -9$. Point 2: $x = 3$, $y = 6$

c. Point 1: $x = 4$, $y = 8$. Point 2: $x = 1$, $y = 12$

9. We mentioned that a demand curve is a hypothetical relationship: It answers a "what if" question: "What if today's price of oil rose (or fell), but the average consumer's income, beliefs about future oil prices, and the prices of everything else in the economy stayed the same?" When some of those other features change, then the demand curve isn't fixed any more: It shifts up (and right) or left (and down). In Figure A.3, we showed one shift graphically: Let's make some changes in algebra:

The economy of Perovia has the following demand for oil:

$$Price = B - M \times Quantity$$

When will B tend to be a larger number:

a. When population in Perovia is high or when it is low?

b. When the price of autos in Perovia is high or when it is low?

c. When Perovian income is high or when it is low?

Discovering DATA ⁚⁚

10. Using the FRED economic database (http://fred.stlouisfed.org) search for U.S. Real Gross Domestic Product and graph the seasonally adjusted quarterly series.

a. What was U.S. Real GDP in the first quarter of 1980?

b. Click on Edit Graph and change the Units to Percent Change from Year Ago and Modify Frequency to Annual. By how much did the U.S. economy shrink in 2009?